ARCO

Everything you need to score high on the

MILITARY FLIGHT APTITUDE TESTS

4th Edition

SOLOMON WIENER
COLONEL, *AUS-Ret.*

The views expressed in this book are those of the author and do not reflect the official position of the Army or the U.S. Government.

IDG Books Worldwide, Inc.
An International Data Group Company
Foster City, CA • Chicago, IL • Indianapolis, IN • New York, NY

ACKNOWLEDGMENTS

Special thanks to Major Scott Ostrow of the United States Air Force for his invaluable advice and support of this project.

Solomon Wiener
New York, New York

4th Edition

IDG Books Worldwide, Inc.
An International Data Group Company
919 E. Hillsdale Boulevard
Suite 400
Foster City, CA 94404

Copyright © 2000, 1997, 1994, 1989 by Solomon Wiener.

All rights reserved including the right of reproduction in whole or in part in any form.

An Arco Book

ARCO and colophon is a registered trademark of Macmillan General Reference USA, Inc., a wholly owned subsidiary of IDG Books Worldwide, Inc.

MACMILLAN and colophon is a registered trademark of Macmillan USA.

For general information on IDG Books Worldwide's books in the U.S., please call our Consumer Customer Service department at 800-762-2974. For reseller information, including discounts and premium sales, please call our Reseller Customer Service department at 800-434-3422.

Library of Congress Number: available upon request.

ISBN: 0-02-863544-2

Manufactured in the United States of America

10 9 8 7 6 5 4 3 2 1

CONTENTS

Part 1

Careers in Military Aviation

CAREER OPPORTUNITIES AS MILITARY PILOTS, NAVIGATORS, OR FLIGHT OFFICERS

Military pilots, navigators, and flight officers are commissioned officers of the Armed Forces of the United States. All commissioned officers, regardless of area of specialization or career field, are afforded the same career opportunities.

Career Opportunities as a Commissioned Officer

Commissioned officers in the Military Services of the United States—Air Force, Army, Marines, Navy, and Coast Guard—enjoy a diversified professional career interwoven with adventure and travel plus a variety of assignments geared to challenge and develop individual skills and expertise. In addition, opportunities for promotion are excellent.

Commissioned officers enjoy a combination of privileges, benefits, opportunities, and responsibilities rarely offered elsewhere. Currently, approximately 225,000 men and women are serving as officers both on active duty and in Reserve components of the Armed Forces of the United States.

Among the many advantages of a military career are the following:

- Responsibility and an opportunity to exercise leadership at an early age
- Opportunity for advanced education through tuition assistance programs
- Excellent pay
- Opportunity for travel
- Opportunity to gain personnel and management experience
- Low-cost life insurance of up to $200,000
- Medical and dental care
- Government-paid moving expenses when changing duty stations
- 30 days annual leave with pay
- Shopping privileges at military commissaries and exchanges
- Periodic promotions based on performance
- Membership privileges at officers' clubs
- Outstanding retirement benefits

Some of the major disadvantages include:

- Family relocation
- Separation from family when on certain assignments
- Slightly greater hazard than in some other occupations
- Working hours not always constant
- Desired job assignment or duty station not always available

General Qualification Requirements for a Commission

Each year, approximately 25,000 men and women become commissioned officers in the Armed Forces. The term "commissioned" refers to the certification that officers receive upon meeting all qualification requirements. The certification confers military rank, authority, and obligation. To join the military as a commissioned officer, applicants must generally have a four-year college degree. The general qualification requirements are presented below. Specific requirements vary by service.

General Qualification Requirements for Becoming a Commissioned Officer*

Age	Must be between 19 and 30 years for OCS/OTS; 17 and 21 years for ROTC; 17 and 22 years for the service academies.
Citizenship Status	Must be U.S. citizen.
Physical Condition	Must meet minimum physical standards listed below. Some occupations have additional physical standards.

*Each service sets its own qualification requirements for officers.

	Height— For males: Maximum - 6'8" Minimum - 4'10" For females: Maximum - 6'8" Minimum - 4'10"
	Weight—There are minimum and maximum weights, according to age and height, for males and females.
	Vision—There are minimum vision standards.
	Overall Health—Must be in good health and pass a medical exam. Certain diseases or conditions may exclude persons from enlistment, such as diabetes, severe allergies, epilepsy, alcoholism, and drug addiction.
Education	Must have a four-year college degree from an accredited institution. Some occupations require advanced degrees or four-year degrees in a particular field.
Aptitude	Must achieve the minimum entry score on an officer qualification test. Each service uses its own officer qualification test.
Moral character	Must meet standards designed to screen out persons unlikely to become successful officers. Standards cover court convictions, juvenile delinquency, arrests, and drug use.
Marital Status and Dependents	May be either single or married for ROTC, OCS/OTS, and direct appointment pathways. Must be single to enter and graduate from service academies. Number of allowable dependents varies by branch of service.
Waivers	On a case-by-case basis, exceptions (waivers) are granted by individual services for some of the above qualification requirements.

Pathways to Becoming an Officer

There are four main ways to become a commissioned officer:

- Service Academies
- Officer Candidate School (OCS) and Officer Training School (OTS) depending on branch of service
- Reserve Officers' Training Corps (ROTC)
- Direct Appointment

The figure on page 5 shows the percentage of new officers who become officers through these pathways. A description of each pathway follows.

Service Academies

The four service academies are:

United States Military Academy (Army)
West Point, New York 10996

United States Naval Academy (Navy and Marine Corps)
Annapolis, Maryland 21402

United States Air Force Academy (Air Force)
Colorado Springs, Colorado 80840

United States Coast Guard Academy
(Coast Guard)
New London, Connecticut 06320

The competition for entry into the academies is keen. Of the candidates who meet all the eligibility requirements, the academies offer admission to only the most qualified. To be eligible for admission to any of the academies, a young person must be at least 17 years of age, a citizen of the United States, of good moral character, and academically and physically qualified. In addition, candidates for the Army, Navy, and Air Force Academies must have a nomination to be considered for admission. Nominations are not necessary for admission to the Coast Guard Academy. Most candidates seek nominations from their members of Congress. It is not necessary to know Senators or Representatives personally to be nominated.

Each of the academies offers a four-year program of study leading to a bachelor of science degree in one of many disciplines. Students, called cadets or midshipmen, receive free tuition, room, board, medical and dental care, and a monthly allowance. Graduates receive a commission as a military officer and must serve on active duty for at least five years. Each year, about 13 percent of the military's new officers are graduates of these four academies.

Officer Candidate/Training School

Each service offers a program for college graduates with no prior military training who want to become military officers. These programs are called Officer Candidate School (OCS) or Officer Training School (OTS), depending on the service. Interested candidates should apply through a local recruiter in the fall of their senior year of college. After graduation, young men and women selected for OCS/OTS join the military as enlisted members for the duration of their OCS/OTS training. Depending on the service, OCS/OTS lasts up to 20 weeks. After successful completion, candidates are commissioned as military officers and have a minimum active-duty service obligation of four years. Each year, about 21 percent of the military's new officers are commissioned through OCS/OTS. For more information, contact a recruiter.

Reserve Officers' Training Corps

Undergraduate students in public or private colleges or universities may receive training to become military officers under the Reserve Officers' Training Corps (ROTC). ROTC programs for the Army, Navy, Air Force, and Marine Corps are available in over 1,400 colleges and universities nationwide.

Depending on the service and ROTC option selected, students train for two, three, or four years. Often, they receive scholarships for tuition, books, fees, uniforms, and a monthly allowance. In addition to their military and college course work, ROTC candidates perform drills for several hours each week and participate in military training exercises for several weeks each summer. Graduating ROTC candidates become commissioned as military officers and either go on active duty or become members of Reserve or National Guard units. Each year, about 44 percent of the military's new officers are gained through ROTC programs.

For information on the colleges and universities that offer ROTC programs for a particular service, contact a recruiter from that service.

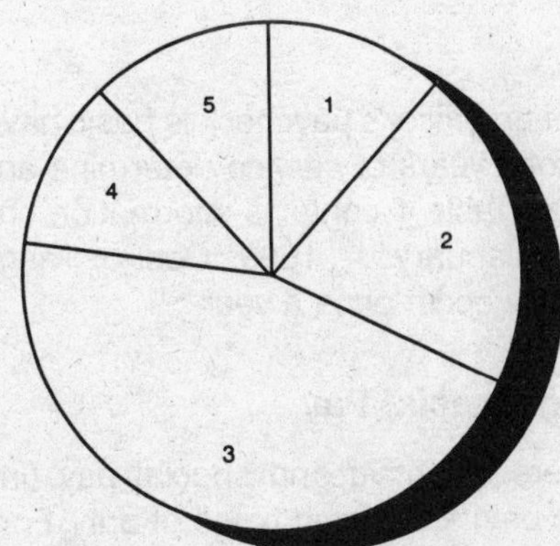

Pathways to Becoming Newly Commissioned Officers

1. Service Acadamies
2. Officer Candidate School (OCS) and Officer Training School (OTS)
3. Reserve Officer's Training Corps (ROTC)
4. Direct Appointment
5. Other

Direct Appointments

Medical, legal, engineering, and religious professionals who are fully qualified in their field may apply to receive direct appointments as military officers. These individuals enter military service and begin practicing their profession with a minimum of military training. The service obligation for officers entering through direct appointment is two years. Each year, direct appointments make up about 11 percent of the military's new officers.

Other

In addition to the four main pathways described above, the services have programs for qualified enlisted personnel to earn commissions as officers. Once selected to an enlisted commissioning program, enlisted personnel must follow one of the four major pathways described above to receive their commissions. These programs are exclusive, as they account for only 10 percent of newly commissioned officers each year.

Basic Officer Training

An important part of every pathway leading to officer commissioning is training in the basic knowledge required to become a military officer. The topics covered in this training include:

- The role and responsibilities of the officer
- Military laws and regulations
- Service traditions
- Military customs and courtesies
- Leadership
- Career development
- Military science
- Administrative procedures

In addition, most commissioning pathways involve physical conditioning consisting of calisthenics, running, and drills.

The duration and timing of officer training may vary with the commissioning pathway followed. For example, ROTC candidates receive basic officer training over the course of their two- to four-year ROTC programs. The same is true for cadets or midshipmen at the service academics. In contrast, OCS/OTS candidates receive their basic officer training in the 12-to-20-week OCS/OTS programs they attend after graduation from college.

Rank, Pay, and Benefits

Ranks and Insignia

The comparable commissioned ranks and insignia for the various military services are tabulated on page 8.

Pay and Benefits

Military officers in all five services are paid according to the same pay scale and receive the same basic benefits. Military pay and benefits are set by Congress, which normally grants a cost-of-living pay increase once each year. In addition to pay, the military provides many of life's necessities, such as food, clothing, and housing. The following sections describe officer pay, allowances, and benefits in more detail.

Officer Pay Grades

Officers can progress through 10 officer pay grades during their careers. Pay grade and length of service determine an officer's pay. Figure 1 contains information on the relationship between pay grade and rank and also illustrates the insignia for the ranks in each service.

Most newly commissioned officers begin at pay grade 0-1. Those who have certain professional qualifications and receive a direct appointment may enter at a higher pay grade. After two years, officers usually move up to 0-2. After an additional two years, the military generally promotes officers to 0-3 if job performance is satisfactory and other requirements are met. Promotions to 0-4 and above are based on job performance, leadership ability, years of service, and time in present pay grade. Each promotion, of course, is accompanied by a substantial pay raise. Because the number of officers at advanced pay grades is limited by Congress, competition for promotion at these levels is intense.

Basic Pay

The major part of an officer's paycheck is basic pay. Pay grade and total years of service determine an officer's basic pay. Table 1 contains information on basic pay as of January 1, 1999. Cost-of-living increases generally occur once a year.

Incentives and Special Pay

The military offers incentive and special pay (in addition to basic pay) for certain types of duty. For

Table 1—1999 Basic Pay for Officers (Annual Figures)

	Years of Service								
Pay grade	**Under 2 yrs**	**2**	**3**	**4**	**6**	**8**	**10**	*******	**26**
0-10	*	*	*	*	*	*	*	***	$137,351
0-9	*	*	*	*	*	*	*	***	$141,072
0-8	*	*	*	*	*	*	*	***	$129,841
0-7	*	*	*	*	*	*	*	***	$117,273
0-6	*	*	*	*	*	*	$76,876	***	$103,846
0-5	*	*	*	*	*	*	$68,249	***	*
0-4	*	*	*	*	*	$60,648	$63,897	***	*
0-3	*	*	$49,377	$53,081	$54,928	$56,391	$58,767	***	*
0-2	$37,037	$39,606	$45,690	$46,813	$47,522	*	*	***	*
0-1	$32,074	$32,975	$38,323	*	*	*	*	***	*

* Military personnel with this many years of service will probably not be in this pay grade. (Pay scale between 10 and 26 years not shown.)

example, incentives are paid for submarine and flight duty. Other types of hazardous duty with monthly incentives include parachute jumping, flight deck duty, and explosives demolition. In addition, the military gives special pay for sea duty, diving duty, duty in some foreign countries, and duty in areas subject to hostile fire. Special pay is also provided for officers in certain occupations, such as doctors, dentists, and veterinarians.

Allowances

Many officers and their families live free of charge in military housing on the base to which they are assigned. Those living off the base receive a quarters (housing) allowance in addition to their basic pay. In 1999, the monthly housing allowance ranges from $385 to $1,081 depending on pay grade and if the officer has dependents. Each officer also receives a subsistence (food) allowance of $157.26 per month. Because allowances are not taxed as income, they provide a significant tax savings in addition to their cash value.

Employment Benefits

Military officers receive substantial benefits in addition to their pay and allowances. While they are in the service, officers' benefits include health care, vacation time, legal assistance, recreational programs, educational assistance, and commissary/exchange (military store) privileges. Families of officers also receive some of these benefits.

Retirement Benefits

The military offers one of the best retirement programs in the country. After 20 years of active duty, officers may retire and receive a monthly payment equal to 40 percent of their average basic pay for their last five years of active duty. Officers who retire with more than 20 years of active service receive higher pay. Other retirement benefits include medical care and commissary/exchange privileges.

Figure 1—Officer Insignia of the United States Armed Forces

SERVICE / PAY GRADE	ARMY	NAVY	AIR FORCE	MARINE CORPS	COAST GUARD
O-10	GENERAL	ADMIRAL	GENERAL	GENERAL	ADMIRAL
O-9	LIEUTENANT GENERAL	VICE ADMIRAL	LIEUTENANT GENERAL	LIEUTENANT GENERAL	VICE ADMIRAL
O-8	MAJOR GENERAL	REAR ADMIRAL (UPPER HALF)	MAJOR GENERAL	MAJOR GENERAL	REAR ADMIRAL (UPPER HALF)
O-7	BRIGADIER GENERAL	REAR ADMIRAL (LOWER HALF)	BRIGADIER GENERAL	BRIGADIER GENERAL	REAR ADMIRAL (LOWER HALF)
O-6	COLONEL	CAPTAIN	COLONEL	COLONEL	CAPTAIN
O-5	LIEUTENANT COLONEL	COMMANDER	LIEUTENANT COLONEL	LIEUTENANT COLONEL	COMMANDER
O-4	MAJOR	LIEUTENANT COMMANDER	MAJOR	MAJOR	LIEUTENANT COMMANDER
O-3	CAPTAIN	LIEUTENANT	CAPTAIN	CAPTAIN	LIEUTENANT
O-2	FIRST LIEUTENANT	LIEUTENANT JUNIOR GRADE	FIRST LIEUTENANT	FIRST LIEUTENANT	LIEUTENANT JUNIOR GRADE
O-1	SECOND LIEUTENANT	ENSIGN	SECOND LIEUTENANT	SECOND LIEUTENANT	ENSIGN

Veterans' Benefits

Veterans of military service are entitled to certain veterans benefits set by Congress and provided by the Department of Veterans Affairs. In most cases, these include guarantees for home loans, hospitalization, survivor benefits, educational benefits, disability benefits, and assistance in finding civilian employment.

Improved Benefits for the Year 2000

In February of 1999, the Senate passed the Soldiers', Sailors', Airmen's, and Marines' Bill of Rights Act of 1999. This bill makes major changes to the way military personnel are compensated. Those changes include:

- **Pay Raise** Provides for a 4.8 percent increase effective January 1, 2000.
- **Pay Table Reform** Realigns pay tables, targeting mid-career personnel for weighted pay raises and could raise pay by as much as 10.3 percent. The change would be effective on July 1, 2000.
- **Retirement Benefits** would give members under the current REDUX retirement plan two options upon reaching the 15 year point.
    1. Choose the old retirement plan (50 percent of base pay at 20 years of service).
    2. Choose to receive a $30,000 bonus and remain in the current retirement plan.
- **Thrift Savings Plan** Would allow a contribution of five percent of base pay (pre-tax).
- **Montgomery GI Bill** Enhanced benefits including elimination of the $1,200 contribution by the service member.

As of this writing, this bill has not yet gone to the House.

Opportunities in the Guard and Reserve

Instead of a career as an active duty officer, you may choose to pursue a career in the Reserve or National Guard.

Generally, the only pathway to a commission through the Guard or Reserve is through Officer Candidate School or Officer Training School. The Air Force also commissions enlisted members through the Deserving Airman Program. Additionally, Merchant Marine Academy graduates are commissioned as ensigns in the Naval reserve.

Reserve and Guard officers generally serve in most career fields as their Active Duty counterparts but on a part-time basis. Reserve officers usually serve one weekend a month and one two-week active duty tour per year.

Reserve officers enjoy some of the same benefits as their Active Duty counterparts including; Commissary and Exchange privileges, membership in officers' clubs, a twenty year retirement plan, and, in some cases, tuition assistance.

Because most Guard and Reserve officers come fully trained from their "sister" Active Duty branches, the competition is keen.

If you want more information on Reserve and National Guard opportunities, contact:

Air Force
www.afreserve.com
(800) 257-1212

Army
www.goarmy.com
(800) 872-2769

Coast Guard
www.uscg.mil/reserve/reshmpg.html
(800) 438-8724

Marines
www.marforres.usmc.mil
(800) 552-8762

Navy
www.navy-reserve-jobs.com
(800) 872-8767

Air National Guard
www.goang.af.mil
(800) 864-6264

Army National Guard
www.1800goguard.com
(800) 464-8273

MILITARY AVIATION

The military operates one of the largest fleets of specialized airplanes in the world. Supersonic fighters and bombers fly combat missions. Large transports carry troops and equipment. Intelligence-gathering airplanes take photographs from high altitudes. Helicopters transport troops and cargo, perform search and rescue missions, and provide close combat support for ground troops.

All five services—Air Force, Army, Navy, Marine Corps, and Coast Guard—have airplanes and helicopters, and continually need airplane pilots and helicopter pilots. Airplane navigators are needed by the Air Force. Flight officers are needed by the Navy and the Marine Corps.

Airplane Pilots

Military airplane pilots fly the thousands of jet and propeller airplanes operated by the services.

What They Do

Airplane pilots in the military perform some or all of the following duties:

- Check weather reports to learn about flying conditions
- Develop flight plans showing air routes and schedules
- Contact air traffic controllers to obtain take-off and landing instructions
- Fly airplanes by controlling engines, rudders, elevators, and other controls
- Monitor gauges and dials located on cockpit control panels
- Perform combat maneuvers, take photographs, transport equipment, and patrol areas to carry out flight missions

Physical Demands

Airplane pilots must pass the most demanding physical test of any job in the military. To be accepted for pilot training, applicants must have 20/20 vision and be in top physical condition. They must have very good eye-hand coordination and have extremely quick reaction times to maneuver at high speeds.

Special Qualifications

A 4-year college degree is normally required to enter this occupation. Although the military has many women pilots, specialties involving duty in combat airplanes once were open only to men. However, this policy has been reevaluated and women are being admitted.

Work Environment

Airplane pilots may be stationed at airbases or aboard aircraft carriers anywhere around the world. They fly in all types of weather conditions. Military pilots take off and land on airport runways and aircraft carrier landing decks.

Training Provided

Pilot training is a 2-year program covering 1 year each in initial and advanced training. Initial training includes time spent in flight simulators, classroom training, officer training, and basic flight training. Course content typically includes:

- Aircraft aerodynamics
- Jet and propeller engine operation
- Operation of aircraft navigation systems
- Foul weather flying
- FAA (Federal Aviation Administration) regulations

This is among the most challenging training given by the services; not everyone who attempts this training can meet the strict requirements for completion. Advanced training begins when pilots successfully complete initial training and are awarded their "wings." Advanced training consists of instruction in flying a particular type of aircraft.

Helpful Attributes

Helpful fields of study include physics, aerospace, and electrical or mechanical engineering. Helpful attributes include:

- Strong desire to fly airplanes
- Self-confidence and ability to remain calm in stressful situations
- Determination to complete a very demanding training program

Civilian Counterparts

Civilian airplane pilots who work for passenger airlines and air cargo businesses are called commercial pilots. Other civilian pilots work as flight instructors at local airports, as cropdusters, or as pilots transporting business executives in company planes.

Opportunities

The services have about 24,500 airplane pilots. On average, they need 400 new pilots each year. After initial and advanced training, most pilots are assigned to flying squadrons to fly the types of aircraft for which they were trained. In time, pilots train for different aircraft and missions. Eventually, they may advance to senior management or command positions.

Helicopter Pilots

Helicopter pilots fly the many helicopters operated by the five services.

What They Do

Helicopter pilots in the military perform some or all of the following duties:

- Prepare flight plans showing air routes and schedules
- Fly helicopters by controlling engines, flight controls, and other systems
- Monitor gauges and dials located on cockpit control panels
- Perform combat maneuvers, spot and observe enemy positions, transport troops and equipment, and evacuate wounded troops.
- Check weather reports to learn about flying conditions

Physical Demands

Helicopter pilots must pass the most demanding physical tests of any job in the military. To be accepted for pilot training, applicants must have excellent vision and be in top physical condition. They must have very good eye-hand-foot coordination and have quick reflexes.

Special Qualifications

A 4-year college degree is normally required to enter this occupation. Some specialties in the Army do not require a 4-year college degree. Although there are women helicopter pilots, some specialties once were open only to men. (The Marine Corps had no women helicopter pilots because all specialties involve duty in combat aircraft.) However, this policy has been reevaluated and women are being admitted.

Helpful Attributes

Helpful fields of study include physics and aerospace, electrical, or mechanical engineering. Helpful attributes include:

- Strong desire to fly aircraft
- Determination to complete a very demanding training program
- Self-confidence and ability to remain calm under stress

Training Provided

Job training consists of 1 to 2 years of academic and flight instruction. Flight training consists of at least 80 hours of flying time. Training length varies depending on specialty. Course content typically includes:

- Principles of helicopter operation
- Principles of helicopter inspection
- Flying techniques and emergency procedures
- Combat skills and tactics

Work Environment

Helicopter pilots are stationed at military bases or aboard aircraft carriers around the world. They fly in all types of weather conditions. Helicopter pilots take off and land from airports, forward landing areas, and ship landing decks.

Civilian Counterparts

Civilian helicopter pilots work for police forces, local commuter services, and private businesses. They also work as crop dusters, fire fighters, traffic spotters, and helicopter flight instructors.

Opportunities

The military has about 6,000 helicopter pilots. On average, the services need 150 new pilots each year. After receiving their pilot ratings, helicopter pilots are assigned to flying units. With experience, they may become group leaders or flight instructors. Helicopter pilots may advance to senior management and command positions.

Airplane Navigators

Navigators keep the aircraft on course. Airplane navigators use radar, radio, and other navigation equipment to determine position, direction of travel, intended course, and other information about military flights.

What They Do

Airplane navigators in the military perform some or all of the following duties:

- Direct aircraft course using radar, sight, and other navigation methods
- Operate radios and other communication equipment to send and receive messages
- Locate other aircraft using radar equipment
- Operate bombardier systems during bombing runs
- Inspect and test navigation and weapons systems before flights
- Guide tankers and other airplanes during in-flight refueling operations
- Provide pilots with instrument readings, fuel usage, and other flight information

Physical Demands

For this physically and mentally demanding job, navigators are required to have excellent vision and must be in top physical shape.

Special Qualifications

A 4-year college degree is required to enter this occupation. Although there are women airplane navigators, some specialties were only open to men. However, this policy has been reevaluated and women are being admitted.

Work Environment

Airplane navigators perform their work in aircraft. They may be stationed at airbases or aboard aircraft carriers anywhere around the world.

Training Provided

Job training consists of between 6 and 12 months of classroom instruction concerning:

- Principles and methods of navigation
- Operation of communication, weapon, and radar systems
- Inspection and testing of navigation equipment and systems
- Combat and bombing navigation procedures and tactics

Practical experience in navigation is gained through training in aircraft simulators and through about 100 hours of actual flying time. Further training occurs on the job and through advanced courses.

Helpful Attributes

Helpful fields of study include cartography, geography, and surveying. Helpful attributes include:

- Ability to read maps and charts
- Interest in work requiring accuracy and attention to detail
- Ability to respond quickly to emergencies
- Strong desire to fly

Civilian Counterparts

Civilian airplane navigators work for passenger and cargo airlines. They perform many of the same duties as those performed by military navigators.

Opportunities

The services have about 10,000 airplane navigators. On average, they need 100 new navigators each year. After job training, airplane navigators are assigned to flying sections for duty. They work as officer crewmembers on bombers, tankers, fighters, or other airplanes. In time, they may advance to senior management or command positions.

Naval Flight Officers

Navy and Marine Corps flight officers receive similar training and perform similar duties to those of Air Force navigators.

Flight officers' primary training is in areas such as meteorology, air navigation, flight planning, and aircraft safety. Their advanced training is in radar intercept, advanced radar navigation, airborne tactical data systems, or advanced navigation.

Navy flight officers may be radar intercept officers, bombardier/navigators, tactical coordinators, or airborne electronic warfare specialists. Marine Corps flight officers may have one of the following military occupational specialties: radar intercept officer, tactical navigator, electronic countermeasure officer, airborne reconnaissance officer, or weapons and sensors officer.

At the present time, there are only a few flight officers in the Coast Guard aviation fleet. Highly trained specialists, when needed, are generally transferred from one of the other military services.

SERVICE INFORMATION ON FLIGHT TRAINING PROGRAMS

Air Force

Pilot Training

As a newly commissioned Air Force officer, you will report to one of the following undergraduate Air Force pilot training bases to begin 52 weeks of intensive training.

Columbus AFB, Columbus, Mississippi
Laughlin AFB, Del Rio, Texas
Vance AFB, Enid, Oklahoma
Sheppard AFB, Texas

During the first several weeks, you will learn the basics of flight, such as aerodynamics and engine operation, as well as body physiology in the aerospace environment.

Flight Screening

As of early 1994, the T-41 flight screening aircraft was gradually replaced, first at Hondo, Texas, and then at the USAF Academy, by the Slingsby Firefly, USAF designation T-3A. The program became the Enhanced Flight Screening Program (EFSP). The course lasts 5 weeks and contains 19 sorties and 21.5 flying hours (3 of which are flown solo). The T-3A is a fully acrobatic aircraft with a much expanded flight envelope compared to that of the T-41. (Generally, if you have received flight training through AFROTC or the Air Force Academy, this flight screening phase is waived.)

T-3A

Specialized Undergraduate Pilot Training (SUPT)

Upon graduation from Officer Training School, AFROTC, or the academy, you will enter undergraduate pilot training in the Cessna T-37 aircraft—the first phase of jet flight training. The T-37 is a light, subsonic jet trainer.

This training lasts 26 weeks (19 days pre-flight academics are included). It contains 62 sorties and 80.9 flying hours (10 solo sorties and 12.1 flying hours). Students gain experience in aerobatics, instrument flying, formation, and navigation.

After completion of the T-37 course, students are selected to complete either the Bomber/Fighter (B/F) track or the Airlift/Tanker (A/T) track. B/F students will then fly the T-38 in a course designed to better prepare them in the specific skills required for bomber and fighter-type aircraft operations. As the track name suggests, B/F students will go on to fly aircraft such as the B-1B, B-52, F-15, and F-16. A/T students will fly the T-1A, a derivative of a twin-engine corporate jet aircraft, in a course designed to better prepare them in the specific skills required in airlift and tanker-type aircraft operations. As the track name suggests, A/T students will go on to fly aircraft such as the C-130, C-5, and KC-135. Under SUPT, students are awarded their wings on completion of the T-38 B/F course or at the end of the T-1A A/T course.

T-37B

T-38

T-1A

1. SUPT (T-37)

Currently lasts 26 weeks (19 days pre-flight academics included). Contains 68 sorties and 89.0 flying hours (8 solo sorties and 9.5 flying hours).

2. SUPT T-38 (B/F TRACK)

Currently lasts 26 weeks. Contains 96 sorties and 119.2 flying hours (approximately 17 solo sorties and 21.0 flying hours).

3. SUPT T-1A (A/T TRACK)

Currently lasts 26 weeks. Contains 73 sorties and 119.0 flying hours (approximately 4 sorties are flown "team," i.e., with another student observing). The T-1A course includes practice airdrop profiles and practice air-to-air refueling rendezvous exercises.

After earning wings, the new aviator is assigned to an operational aircraft. Although pilots are allowed much latitude in selection of the aircraft they will fly, the needs and requirements of the Air Force remain the determining factor. Advanced training usually ranges from three to six months and is designed to acquaint fliers with their assigned aircraft and the characteristics of each.

After completion of advanced training, the pilot joins an assigned operational flying unit made up of the aircraft in which advanced training was received. A normal assignment may continue for three to four years at the conclusion of which the pilot may be considered for transfer to a new aircraft and a new base.

Women Pilots

There are now no restrictions on the types of aircraft that women pilots are allowed to fly in the USAF. All combat restrictions have been removed, and the first women pilots are now entering combat aircraft training.

Helicopter Training

Helicopter pilot training is at present available only to rated (i.e., wings awarded) fixed-wing pilots. A few pilots graduate from pilot training, or are selected from other fixed-wing aircraft types, to attend Rotary Wing Qualification training at the U.S. Army Aviation Center at Fort Rucker, Alabama. This course is approximately 11 weeks long, with 42 flying hours and 24 hours simulator. These pilots then move on to Kirtland AFB, New Mexico, to complete their advanced training on either the UH-IN, MH-60G, MH-53J, or HH-1H. However, the future shape of USAF undergraduate helicopter training is under review, so additional information is not available at this time.

Navigator Training

To the educated eyes of the navigator, the radarscope's blur of light, lines, and shadow becomes a clear indication of coastline, land contour, and position.

Aircraft location is the primary concern of the navigator. The wind, the weather, the speed, the heading, and the altitude must be considered. There is no margin for error. The trained navigator can guide the aircraft safely and surely between points hundreds or thousands of miles apart.

Undergraduate Navigator Training

As a navigator trainee, you will begin with the very basics of air navigation—dead reckoning. You will learn to maintain an accurate record of time, speed, direction, and wind effect, using them to determine the exact position of the aircraft without reference to landmarks. You will study map reading, radar, day and night celestial, inertial, radio, and low-level navigation. There are also courses in weather, aviation physiology, flight instruments, aircraft flight regulations, and integrated navigation systems.

Specialized Undergraduate Navigator Training (SUNT)

SUNT is conducted at Randolph AFB, Texas, and lasts approximately 40 weeks.

As a student navigator, your training will begin in the Core navigation phase (approximately 17 weeks) of SUNT. Studies in this phase include Aerospace Physiology, Basic Procedures, Weather, Flight Regulations, Dead Reckoning, and Integrated Navigation procedures.

Upon completion of the Core phase of SUNT, students are placed in one of three specialized training tracks (approximately 23 weeks): Navigator (NAV), Systems Officer (SO), or Electronic Warfare Officer (EWO).

Some Air Force Aircraft

F-16 Fighting Falcon

KC-135 Stratotanker

F-15 Eagle

C-5 Galaxy

- The Navigator track provides those skills necessary to navigate worldwide in "heavy-type" aircraft (e.g., KC-135 and C-130). Courses include Navigation Procedures, Celestial Navigation, Global Navigation, and Low-Level Navigation.
- The Systems Officer track prepares student navigators for "fighter-type" assignments (e.g., F-15E, F-111, F-4G, and B-1B). Instruction includes courses in Instrument Procedures, Low-Level, Tactical Low-Level, Electronic Warfare, Integrated Tactics, and Advanced Airmanship.
- The Electronic Warfare Officer track provides the student navigator with the skills necessary to detect, identify, and counter an enemy's electronic defenses. The electronic warfare officer functions in several roles, including electronic intelligence, electronic warfare support measures, electronic attack, and C2 warfare.

The flying portion of SUNT is conducted in the T-37, T-38, and T-43 aircraft. These aircraft are specially designed to allow instruction during flight. Additional training includes student navigator missions in the T-25, T-45, and T-50 simulators.

Army

The Aviation Training Brigade at the Army Training Center conducts all initial and advanced flight training at Fort Rucker, Alabama, at various training sites. Flight training quotas are established to meet Army requirements. Because the number of qualified applicants usually exceeds available training quotas, applicants are selected on a best-qualified basis.

Army Regulation 611-110 pertains to the selection and training of Army aviation officers.

Helicopter Pilot Training for Commissioned Officers

Newly commissioned Army officers who wish to earn their "wings" must successfully complete all phases of initial entry flight training. The duration of such training is generally from 36 to 40 weeks.

The five phases of initial entry flight training are:

1st Phase: (2 weeks) Academic instruction is given in aviation health hazards and applicable preventive measures.

2nd Phase: (10 weeks) During this primary flight phase, a student learns the fundamentals of flight, make their first solo flight, learns basic maneuvers, and progresses to more complex maneuvers. The UH-1 Iroquois helicopter is used in this phase.

3rd Phase: (8 weeks) Students are taught basic instrument procedures and then progress to flight on federal airways. Students become instrument qualified upon successful completion of this training phase and will receive helicopter instrument ratings upon graduation. The UH-1 flight simulator and the UH-1 helicopter are used to provide simulated and actual instrument flight conditions.

4th Phase: (14-16 weeks) This phase is combat mission oriented. Student pilots are designated for training in any of the following: UH-1 or UH-60 as a utility helicopter pilot OH-58 observation helicopter as an aeroscout helicopter pilot AH-1 as an attack helicopter pilot

5th Phase: (2 weeks) Basic leadership skills are developed in this professional development phase which prepares graduates for operational unit assignments.

Assignment instructions are issued by the aviation career management branch.

Some Army Aircraft

AH-64 Apache

UH-1B Iroquois (Huey)

AH-1S Cobra

UH-60 Black Hawk

CH-47 Chinook

OV-1C Mohawk

Aircraft found in the operational units include the AH-1 (Cobra)—the world's first attack helicopter—AH-64 (Apache) attack helicopter, CH-47 (Chinook) medium lift helicopter, OH-58 (Kiowa) observation helicopter, UH-1 (Huey) light helicopter, UH-60 (Black Hawk) combat helicopter, and a variety of fixed-wing aircraft, including the OV-1 (Mohawk), U-21 (Ute), and C-12 twin-engine planes.

Advanced flight training may be given to many of the graduates to provide them with additional aviation-related skills, including operation of specialty helicopters and fixed-wing aircraft.

Prerequisites for Flight Training:

- Be a warrant officer, lieutenant, or captain, or be in training for a commission.
- Have less than 48 months of active federal commissioned service at the start of flight training.
- Obtain a minimum score of 90 on the Alternate Flight Aptitude Selection Test (AFAST). Those who fail to score 90 may be retested only once and no sooner than six months later. Applicants may not request a flight duty medical examination until they obtain a passing score on the AFAST. Candidates who score 90 on the AFAST may not retake the test solely to improve their score. Study guides are available for this test and applicants are strongly advised to obtain and use these guides prior to taking the AFAST.
- Undergo a flight duty medical examination, and be found medically qualified.
- Besides meeting prescribed height and weight standards (AR 600-9), all applicants must have anthropometric measurements performed (sitting height, total arm reach, crouch height, and leg length.)
- Vision: Uncorrected—less than 20/50 in each eye; correctable to 20/20 in each eye.
- Be older than 18 years but not more 30 years of age at the start of flight training.

Service Commitment: All Army officers, upon entry into flight training, incur a six-year service obligation. They are obliged to remain on active duty for six years following completion of flight training, or from the date of voluntary termination of training.

Warrant Officer Flight Training Program

The Aviation Warrant Officer program provides excellent opportunities for flight duty. In this program, which produces many rated aviators each year, both commissioned officers and warrant officers attend the same course of flight instruction and meet the same standards.

The Warrant Officer Flight Training Program consists of two phases—Phase I is attendance at the Warrant Officer Candidate School (WOCS) and Phase II is attendance at the Initial Entry Rotary Wing (IERW) Qualification Course and Warrant Officer Basic Course. Both phases are conducted at the U.S. Army Aviation Center, Fort Rucker, Alabama.

Active-duty enlisted service members from the Army, Air Force, Navy, Marine Corps, Coast Guard, U.S. Army Reserve, and Army National Guard are eligible to apply for this flight training program. Civilians are also accepted for the program through direct recruitment.

Prerequisites for eligibility are that the applicant:

- Be at least 18 but not have reached their 29th birthday at time of board selection. U.S. Army Reserve and Army National Guard applicants must not have reached their 27th birthday at time of board selection.
- Have a diploma from an accredited high school or a GED diploma. Preferably, applicants should have two years of college.
- Score 90 or higher on the Alternate FAST (AFAST).
- Score 110 or higher on the general technical (GT) aptitude area of the ASVAB.*
- Meet Class I medical standards prescribed for flight duty and prescribed weight standards.
- Receive a favorable recommendation from an interview conducted by an aviator.
- Be able to score at least 180 points out of a possible 300 points on the Army Physical Fitness Test at the time of entry into WOCS. Candidates must score a minimum of 60 points in each of three events—sit-ups, push-ups, and 2-mile run.

*Test 2 (Arithmetic Reasoning), Test 3 (Word Knowledge), and Test 4 (Paragraph Comprehension) of ASVAB are used to construct the general technical (GT) aptitude area.

- Agree to accept appointment as warrant officer and serve as an aviator for no less than six years.
- Be a United States citizen.
- Must never have been eliminated from an undergraduate military flight course for disciplinary or flight deficiency reasons.

Warrant Officer Candidate School is the Army course for all warrant officer candidates—both aviation and non-aviation. It provides standardized training and evaluation of leadership, ethics, communicative arts, military history, structure of the Army, land navigation, support functions, and other common military subjects. Upon successful completion of WOCS, all warrant officer candidates are appointed to the rank of Warrant Officer 1 (WO-1).

Newly appointed warrant officers who wish to earn their "wings" must successfully complete the following three phases of initial entry flight training:

1st Phase:	(12 weeks) Primary Students receive academic and flight instruction in the basic rotary wing maneuvers, make their first solo flight, and progress to more complex maneuvers. The UH-1 (Huey) helicopter is used in this phase.
2nd Phase:	(8 weeks) Instruments Students learn to fly in almost any type of weather, or even total darkness, relying solely on aircraft instrument readings. The UH-1 flight simulator and the UH-1 helicopter are used to provide simulated and actual instrument flight conditions.
3rd Phase:	(14 weeks) Advanced Advanced flight training is in one of two aircraft systems (tracks)—UH-1 utility or OH-58 scout—and is known as the combat skills phase. It consists of aircraft qualification, basic combat skills, night flight, night vision goggles, and professional development.

Warrant officers, upon completion of flight training and the follow-on Warrant Officer Basic Course, are awarded Army Aviation Wings and are designated Army Aviators.

For further information and application procedures for the U.S. Army Warrant Officer Flight Training Program:

- Applicants not in the military should contact their nearest local Army recruiter.
- Active-duty Army enlisted applicants should contact their battalion Personnel Actions Center.
- U.S. Army Reserve and Army National Guard enlisted applicants should contact their unit commander or the state Army Aviation Officer.
- Enlisted members from other armed services should write to the U.S. Army Recruiting Command at the following address:

Headquarters
U.S. Army Recruiting Command
ATTN: RCRO-SM-A
Fort Knox, KY 40121-5000
1-800-USA-ARMY
www.goarmy.com

Navy

Pilot Training

Preliminary Training

The transition from civilian life to aviation officer takes place during 13 weeks of intensive physical training, strict military discipline, and advanced academics at the Combined Officer Candidate School, Naval Air Station (NAS), Pensacola, Florida, where aviation and non-aviation candidates train together. Students are also taught survival techniques and to become proficient swimmers. Upon successful completion of preliminary training, future Navy pilots are commissioned ensigns in the United States Naval Reserve and are ready to move on to the next phase, primary pilot training.

Non-aviation commissioned officers who wish to enter the naval aviation program begin their preliminary training with a six-week preflight indoctrination course to prepare for primary flight training. This course is conducted at the Naval Aviation Schools Command, Naval Air Station (NAS), Pensacola, Florida, and is designed to provide these officers with the basic knowledge and skills needed for primary training for pilots. The aviation indoctrination includes, in addition, rigorous physical fitness, swimming, and water survival training.

Primary Training

Primary flight training for prospective Navy pilots lasts about 22 weeks at Whiting Field, Milton, Florida, near Pensacola, or at NAS Corpus Christi, Texas.

Before actually flying, pilots go through a familiarization course in the cockpit of a mock-up T-34C trainer aircraft, learning the position of the throttle, rudder pedals, landing gear handle, fuel gauge, and other instruments vital to an aircraft in flight.

The student pilots then take to the air in a T-34C Mentor, an aerobatic turbo prop. After 13 flights with their instructors and many hours of briefings they're ready for their first major hurdle—flying solo. They complete a total of 41 flights (four solo) in primary training.

During training, students study meteorology, aerodynamics, aircraft engines, instruments and navigation, and take other related flight courses.

Intermediate and Advanced Training

Following primary training, and depending upon preference, overall class rank, grade average in training, and the needs of the Navy, students are assigned to one of four training pipelines. These are:

Jets (Strike)
E2/C2
Multiengines (Maritime)
Helicopters (Rotary)

Every effort is made to give student pilots their choice.

1. Intermediate and Advanced Jets (Strike)

Student jet pilots take intermediate training for 22 weeks in a T-2C Buckeye jet trainer at either NAS Meridian, Mississippi or NAS Kingsville, Texas. They concentrate on formation flying, air-to-air gunnery, and more instrument work. They also make about a half-dozen carrier arrested landings aboard a fleet aircraft carrier.

During advanced training at the same location, students fly a TA-4J Skyhawk, a two-seat, light attack trainer. They learn strike tactics, weapons delivery, and air combat maneuvering. In addition, they make several arrested landings.

Strike training, from the start of Aviation Preflight Indoctrination until students earn their wings, lasts about 75 weeks and includes about 260 hours of flight training and 140 hours of simulator training.

2. Intermediate and Advanced E2/C2

Student E2/C2 pilots take about 13 weeks of intermediate training in a T-44 King Air at NAS Corpus Christi, Texas, during which they are expected to develop the knowledge and skills needed to fly multiengine aircraft with heavy airlift capability and to qualify in carrier landing.

Advanced training for 23 weeks in a T-2C Buckeye jet aircraft takes place at NAS Pensacola, Florida. Similar to the intermediate strike training, this phase is designed to develop knowledge and skills needed to perform flight maneuvers to control jet aircraft used to provide early warning services and command and control facilities. Students must also qualify in carrier landing. E2/C2 training, from the start of Aviation Preflight Indoctrination until students earn their wings, lasts about 64 weeks and includes about 198 hours of flight training and 110 hours of simulator training.

3. Intermediate and Advanced Maritime

Student maritime (multiengine) pilots take five weeks of intermediate training in a T-34C Mentor turboprop trainer at NAS Corpus Christi, Texas. Advanced maritime training takes place at the same location. During advanced training, maritime students use the T-44 Pegasus (King Air) aircraft and concentrate on improving more complicated

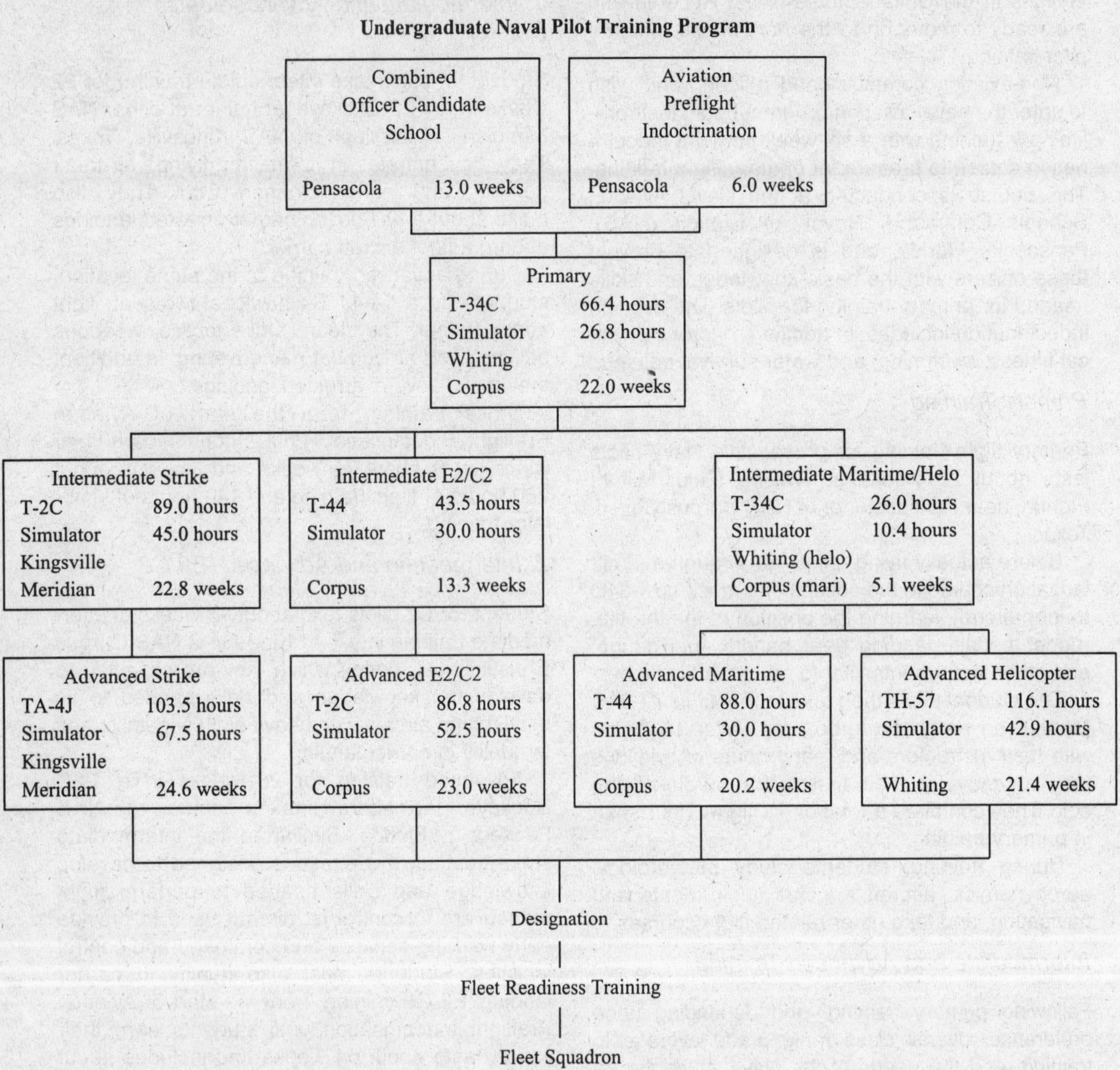

flying skills, such as instrument capability and single-engine approaches in simulated weather conditions, and perform many mock missions with training aircraft.

Maritime training, from the start of Aviation Preflight Indoctrination until students earn their wings, lasts 54 weeks and includes about 180 hours of flight training and 67 hours of simulator training.

4. Intermediate and Advanced Helicopter

Student helicopter pilots take five weeks of intermediate training in a T-34C Mentor turboprop trainer at NAS Whiting Field, Milton, Florida. The emphasis is on additional instrument navigation. Advanced helicopter training takes place at the same location for about 21 weeks. During advanced training, students use the TH-57 Sea Ranger; advanced training includes learning the unique characteristics of rotary-winged aviation, more instruments, reading charts, low-level contour flying, formations, tactical approaches, external loads, and confined-area landings.

The duration of helicopter training from the start of Aviation Preflight Training until students earn their wings is about 55 weeks and includes about 208 hours of flight training and 80 hours of simulator training.

Designation

Upon successful completion of advanced training, students are designated naval aviators and earn their wings of gold. They are now ready for fleet readiness training and assignment to the fleet.

Fleet Readiness Training

Fleet readiness training lasts about 26 weeks. It consists of flying and ground training in advanced survival techniques, air traffic control procedures, and aircraft and weapons systems associated with the type of aircraft flown by the new aviator's operational squadron.

The readiness training phase provides full preparation for operational flying in first-line fleet aircraft during the pilot's first tour of duty.

However, that first operational tour is not all flying. The primary duties are as manager, supervisor, and/or administrator. Throughout the first tour, new aviation team members can expect to be periodically rotated through a variety of officer positions that broaden and enhance their managerial and administrative skills and experience.

Duties may include those of a branch or division officer in aircraft maintenance, or positions in personnel, administration, operations, or training.

Flight time depends on the type of squadron to which the pilot is assigned, and whether it is deployed or in home port. Possible assignments include squadrons which embark aboard aircraft carriers during deployment, long-range patrol squadrons operating from land-based sites both at home and overseas, or helicopter squadrons which may operate from aircraft carriers or various types of surface ships.

Most "at home" flight time consists of training flights to sharpen mission-required skills and obtain or renew flight qualifications.

The first operational tour of duty with a squadron usually lasts about three years, including two or three deployments at sea or overseas lasting anywhere from five to nine months each.

Prerequisites for Navy Pilot Training:

- Must have an accredited bachelor's degree. Degrees in engineering, mathematics, physics, or management are preferred.
- Be at least 19 but less than 27 years of age at time of commissioning. There are no age waivers for pilot applicants.
- Be physically qualified and aeronautically adapted according to Navy standards. Must have 20/20 uncorrected vision with normal color and depth perception.
- Standard height requirements for all Navy pilots are 5'2"–6'8" for men and 4'10"–6'8" for women. Weight must be proportional to height and within the standards for age.
- Must meet anthropometric standards. Candidate's arms, legs, and other parts of the body are measured to determine whether he or she can safely fit into the cockpit of an aircraft.
- Applicants for pilot training must achieve a qualifying score on Pilot Flight Aptitude Rating and the Pilot Biographical Interest in the U.S. Navy and Marine Corps Aviation Test Selection Battery.

Service Commitment: Active duty obligation is six years from date of designation as naval aviator.

Flight Officer Training

Preliminary Training

The transition from civilian life to aviation officer takes place during 13 weeks of intensive physical training, strict military discipline, and advanced academics at the Combined Officer Candidate School, Naval Air Station (NAS) Pensacola, Florida, where aviation and non-aviation candidates train together. Students are also taught survival techniques and become proficient swimmers. Upon successful completion of preliminary training, future naval flight officers are commissioned ensigns in the United States Naval Reserve and are ready to move on to the next phase, primary naval flight officer training.

Non-aviation commissioned officers who wish to enter the naval aviation program begin their preliminary training with a six-week aviation preflight indoctrination course to prepare for primary naval flight officer training. This course is conducted at the Naval Aviation School Command, NAS Pensacola, Florida, and is designed to prepare these officers with the basic knowledge and skills needed for primary training for naval flight officers. The aviation indoctrination includes, in addition, rigorous physical fitness, swimming, and water survival training.

Primary Training

Primary training for prospective NFOs takes place with Training Squadron 10 (VT-10) at Sherman Field in Pensacola, Florida.

The 22 weeks with VT-10 consist of three phases: academics, about 27 hours of simulator training, and about 22 hours of flight time. Cockpit awareness and crew coordination are emphasized. The T-34C is the training aircraft used.

Ground school academic courses include visual and instrument navigation, meteorology, UHF and VHF communication procedures, computer systems, and radar fundamentals.

During simulator training, NFO students learn how to navigate and operate various aircraft systems while conducting necessary in-flight duties. While training in flight, they are responsible for the safe navigation and basic tactical deployment of the aircraft.

Undergraduate Naval Flight Officer Training Program

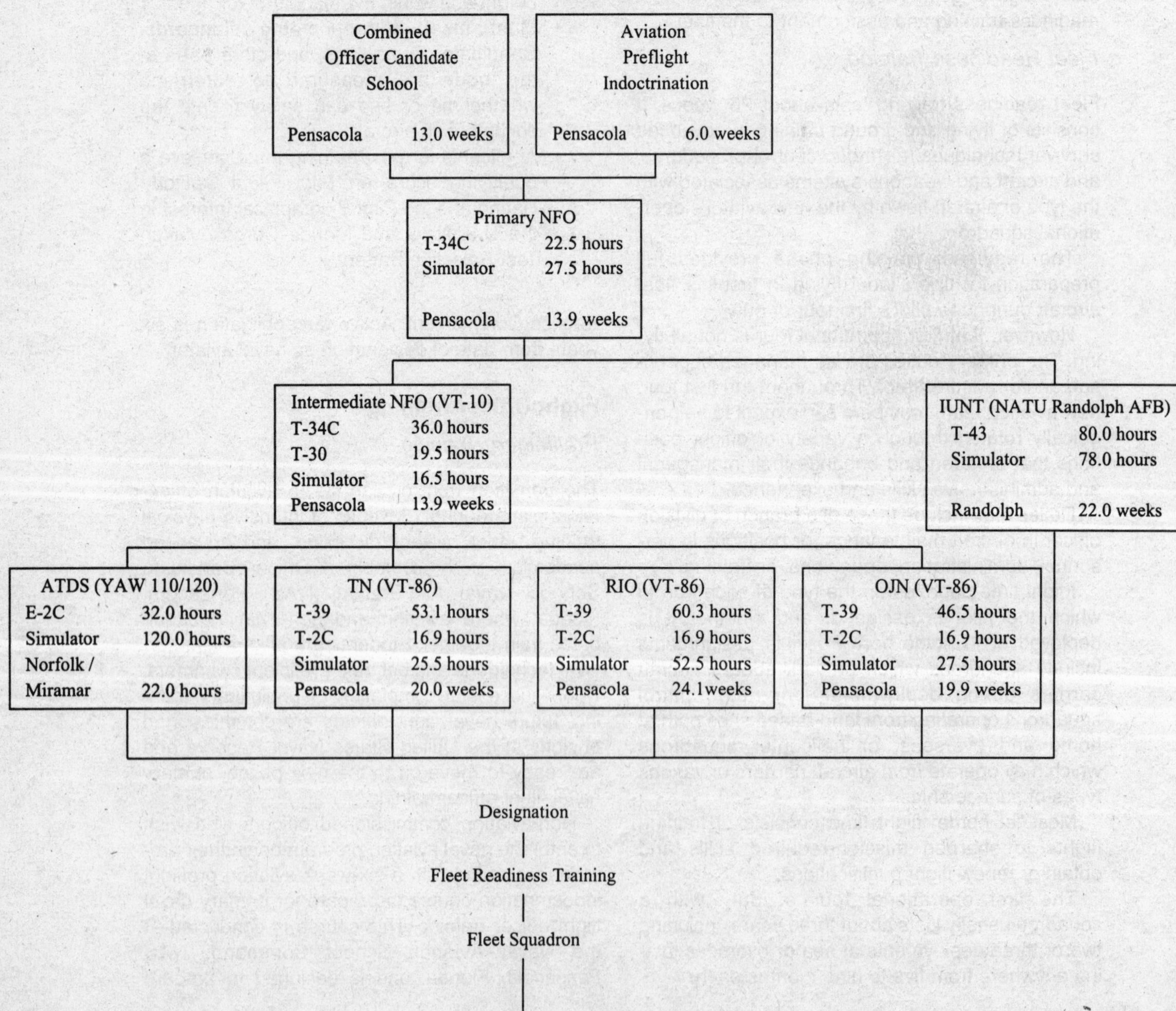

Some Navy Aircraft

Training Aircraft

T-34C (Primary Trainer) Mentor

TA-4J (Advanced Jet) Skyhawk

T-44A (Multiengine) King Air

T-2C (Basic Jet) Buckeye

TH-57 (Primary Helo) Sea Ranger

T-45 Goshawk

Land-Based and Sea-Based Aircraft

P-3C (Patrol) Orion

SH-3 (Anti-submarine) Sea King

C-2 Greyhound

F/A-18 (Fighter-Attack) Hornet

EA-6B (Electronic Warfare) Prowler

E-2C (Electronic Warfare) Hawkeye

S-3 Viking

F-14 Tomcat

Intermediate and Advanced Training

Following primary training, and depending upon preference, class rank, and needs of the Navy, students proceed to intermediate training in jets or training in maritime aircraft. Helicopter crews do not have NFOs.

Students selected for jet training take the intermediate phase with VT-10 for about 14 weeks. This training includes 13 more hours of in-flight training and 30 more hours of academic training. The training aircraft used are the T-2C Buckeye and the T-39, a militarized Saberliner.

Students selected for navigator training are sent to Randolph AFB, San Antonio, Texas, for training with their Air Force counterparts.

1. Airborne Tactical Data Systems (ATDS)

ATDS training is given at NAS Miramar, San Diego, California, and at NAS Norfolk, Virginia. This 22-week course trains students in the airborne early-warning E-2C Hawkeye aircraft. Academics include air-intercept control, anti-air warfare, electronic warfare, radar systems, and related areas.

ATDS training, from the start of Aviation Preflight Indoctrination until students earn their wings, lasts about 55 weeks and includes about 110 hours of flight training and 120 hours of simulator training.

2. Tactical Navigation (TN)

TN training is given at NAS Pensacola, Florida. This 20-week course trains NFO students in air-to-ground radar and strengthens their skills in navigation, communication, and aircraft systems management. Training aircraft include the T-2C Buckeye and the T-39 aircraft.

TN training, from the start of Aviation Preflight Indoctrination until students earn their wings, is about 54 weeks and includes 150 hours of flight training and 70 hours of simulator training.

3. Radar Intercept Officer (RIO)

RIO training is given at NAS Pensacola, Florida. This 24-week course trains NFO students in air-to-air radar. They study advanced tactical maneuvering, aircraft electrical systems, airways navigation, electronics, radar interception, and related areas. Training aircraft include the T-2C Buckeye and the T-39 aircraft.

RIO training, from the start of Aviation Preflight Indoctrination until students earn their wings, lasts about 58 weeks and includes 155 hours of flight training and 96 hours of simulator training.

4. Overwater Jet Navigation (OJN)

OJN training is given at NAS Pensacola, Florida. This 24-week course trains students to operate anti-submarine systems. They study airways navigation, low-level navigation, radar systems, surface and subsurface surveillance coordination, tactical maneuvering, and related areas.

OJN training, from the start of Aviation Preflight Indoctrination until students earn their wings, lasts about 54 weeks and includes 142 hours of flight training and 72 hours of simulator training.

5. Interservice Navigator

Navigator training for NFOs is given at Interservice Undergraduate Navigator Training (IUNT), Naval Aviation Training Unit (NATU), at Randolph AFB, San Antonio, Texas. The training aircraft is the T-43 (Boeing 737).

During 22 weeks of navigator training they spend 80 hours of flying time in the T-43 training plane and also receive 78 hours of intensive simulator training. Academic ground courses include basic navigation, day and night celestial navigation, maritime navigation, and emergency procedures.

Designation

Upon successful completion of advanced training, students are designated naval flight officers and are awarded their wings of gold prior to fleet readiness training.

Readiness Training

This consists of about 26 weeks of flying and ground training in advanced survival techniques, air traffic control procedures, and aircraft and weapons systems associated with the type of aircraft flown by the new NFO's operational squadron.

Naval flight officers complete their training phase fully ready for their first operational tour flying with the fleet.

As mentioned in the pilot training section, that first operational tour is not all flying. The NFO's primary duties on the first tour are also as manager, supervisor, and/or administrator with flight time depending on the type of squadron to which assigned and whether it is deployed or in home port.

Prerequisites for Flight Officer Training:

- Must have an accredited bachelor's degree.
- Be at least 19 but less than 27 years of age at time of commissioning. Applicants for

naval flight officer may be granted waivers up to three years for prior military service.

- Be physically qualified and aeronautically adapted according to Navy standards. Any degree of vision within refractive standards correctable to 20/20 is acceptable. Must have normal color and depth perception.
- Standard height requirements for all naval flight officers are 5'2"–6'8" for men and 4'10"–6'8" for women. Weight must be proportional to height and within the standards for age.
- Must meet anthropometric standards. Candidate's arms, legs, and other parts of the body are measured to determine that he or she can safely fit into the cockpit of an aircraft.
- Applicants for naval flight officer training must attain a qualifying score on the Flight Officer Flight Aptitude Rating (FOFAR) and the Flight Officer Biographical Interest (FOBI) in the U.S. Navy and Marine Corps Aviation Test Selection Battery.

Service Commitment: Active duty obligation is six years from date of designation as a naval flight officer.

Training Aircraft

Some of the Navy aircraft used in training prospective Navy pilots and naval flight officers are shown on page 25.

Marine Corps

Pilot Training

Preliminary Training

Marine student naval aviators report directly from the Basic School to Naval Air Station Pensacola, Florida. They check in with Marine Aviation Training Support Group (MATSG), the major Marine Command responsible for all administrative requirements. Six weeks of Aviation Indoctrination follow.

During this period, students must pass a number of physical tests including:

- The obstacle course
- The cross-country course
- A strength test (push-ups, sit-ups, and $1\frac{1}{2}$-mile run)
- Swim test (four basic strokes—crawl, back, breast, and side—treading water, underwater swim, and one-mile endurance swim with full flight gear)

The study areas are:

- Aerodynamics (basic principles of flight)
- Aviation physiology (effects of flight on the human body)
- Engines (reciprocating and jet engines)
- Navigation (basic principles)
- Sea and land survival (survival equipment, release mechanisms, survival techniques, food procurement, map reading, shelter building)

Primary Training

Upon completion of Aviation Indoctrination, student naval aviators report to NAS Whiting Field, Florida, or NAS Corpus Christi, Texas, for 22 weeks of primary flight training.

Before actual flying, student pilots go through a familiarization course in the cockpit of a mock-up T-34C trainer aircraft, learning the position of the throttle, rudder pedals, landing gear handle, fuel gauge, and other instruments vital to an aircraft in flight.

The student pilots then take to the air in the T-34C Mentor, an aerobatic turbo prop. After 13 flights with their instructors and many hours of briefings, they are ready to fly solo. They complete a total of 41 flights (four solo) in primary training.

During training, students study meteorology, aerodynamics, aircraft engines, instruments and navigation, and take other related flight courses.

Upon completion of primary flight training, the student aviators are channeled into the jet, multiengine, or helicopter pipeline. The selection is based upon the student's preference and grades, as well as the needs of the service.

Intermediate and Advanced Training

Following primary training, and depending upon preference, overall class rank, grade average in training, and the needs of the Marine Corps, students are assigned to one of three training pipelines. These are:

Jet (Strike)
Multiengine (Prop)
Helicopter (Rotary)

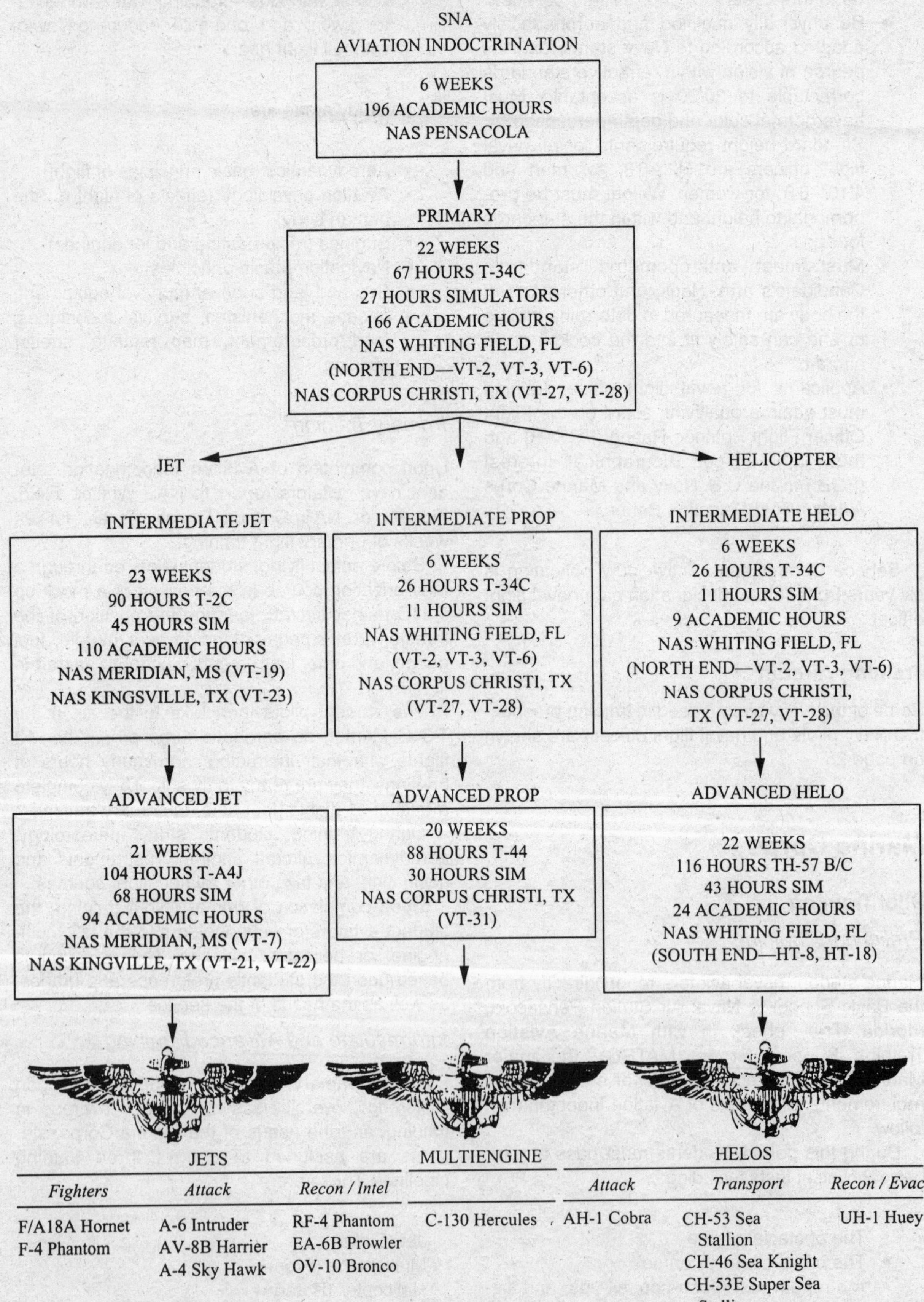
Undergraduate Training Program for Marine Naval Aviators
SNA
AVIATION INDOCTRINATION
6 WEEKS
196 ACADEMIC HOURS
NAS PENSACOLA
PRIMARY
22 WEEKS
67 HOURS T-34C
27 HOURS SIMULATORS
166 ACADEMIC HOURS
NAS WHITING FIELD, FL
(NORTH END—VT-2, VT-3, VT-6)
NAS CORPUS CHRISTI, TX (VT-27, VT-28)
JET
HELICOPTER
INTERMEDIATE JET
23 WEEKS
90 HOURS T-2C
45 HOURS SIM
110 ACADEMIC HOURS
NAS MERIDIAN, MS (VT-19)
NAS KINGSVILLE, TX (VT-23)
INTERMEDIATE PROP
6 WEEKS
26 HOURS T-34C
11 HOURS SIM
NAS WHITING FIELD, FL
(VT-2, VT-3, VT-6)
NAS CORPUS CHRISTI, TX
(VT-27, VT-28)
INTERMEDIATE HELO
6 WEEKS
26 HOURS T-34C
11 HOURS SIM
9 ACADEMIC HOURS
NAS WHITING FIELD, FL
(NORTH END—VT-2, VT-3, VT-6)
NAS CORPUS CHRISTI,
TX (VT-27, VT-28)
ADVANCED JET
21 WEEKS
104 HOURS T-A4J
68 HOURS SIM
94 ACADEMIC HOURS
NAS MERIDIAN, MS (VT-7)
NAS KINGVILLE, TX (VT-21, VT-22)
ADVANCED PROP
20 WEEKS
88 HOURS T-44
30 HOURS SIM
NAS CORPUS CHRISTI, TX
(VT-31)
ADVANCED HELO
22 WEEKS
116 HOURS TH-57 B/C
43 HOURS SIM
24 ACADEMIC HOURS
NAS WHITING FIELD, FL
(SOUTH END—HT-8, HT-18)
JETS
MULTIENGINE
HELOS
Fighters
Attack
Recon / Intel
Attack
Transport
Recon / Evac
F/A18A Hornet
F-4 Phantom
A-6 Intruder
AV-8B Harrier
A-4 Sky Hawk
RF-4 Phantom
EA-6B Prowler
OV-10 Bronco
C-130 Hercules
AH-1 Cobra
CH-53 Sea Stallion
CH-46 Sea Knight
CH-53E Super Sea Stallion
UH-1 Huey

1. Intermediate and Advanced Jets (Strike)

Student jet pilots take intermediate training for 22 weeks in a T-2C Buckeye jet trainer at either NAS Meridian, Mississippi, or NAS Kingsville, Texas. They concentrate on formation flying, air-to-air gunnery, and more instrument work. They also make about a half-dozen carrier arrested landings aboard a fleet aircraft carrier.

During advanced training at the same location, students fly a TA-4J Skyhawk, a two-seat, light attack trainer. They learn strike tactics, weapons delivery, and air combat maneuvering. In addition, they make several arrested landings.

Strike training, from the start of Aviation Preflight Indoctrination until students earn their wings, lasts about 75 weeks and includes about 260 hours of flight training and 140 hours of simulator training.

2. Intermediate and Advanced Maritime

Student maritime (multiengine) pilots take five weeks of intermediate training in a T-34C Mentor turboprop trainer at NAS Whiting Field, Milton, Florida, or NAS Corpus Christi, Texas. Advanced maritime training takes place at NAS Corpus Christi, Texas. During advanced training, maritime students use the T-44 Pegasus (King Air) aircraft and concentrate on improving more complicated flying skills, such as instrument capability and single-engine approaches in simulated weather conditions, and perform many mock missions with training aircraft.

Maritime training, from the start of Aviation Preflight Indoctrination until students earn their wings, lasts 54 weeks and includes about 180 hours of flight training and 67 hours of simulator training.

3. Intermediate and Advanced Helicopter

Student helicopter pilots take five weeks of intermediate training in a T-34C Mentor turboprop trainer at NAS Whiting Field, Milton, Florida, or NAS Corpus Christi, Texas. The emphasis is on additional instrument navigation. Advanced helicopter training takes place at NAS Whiting Field, Milton, Florida, for about 21 weeks. During advanced training, students use the TH-57 Sea Ranger; advanced training includes learning the unique characteristics of rotary-winged aviation, more instruments, reading charts, low-level contour flying, formations, tactical approaches, external loads, and confined-area landings.

Helicopter training, from the start of Aviation Preflight Training until students earn their wings, lasts about 55 weeks and includes about 208 hours of flight training and 80 hours of simulator training.

Designation

Upon successful completion of advanced training, students are designated naval aviators and earn their wings of gold. They are now ready for squadron training and assignment.

Squadron Assignment and Training

Upon completion of flight training, an officer can expect assignment to either the 2nd or 3rd Marine Aircraft Wing. There are also a limited number of billets available with the 1st Marine Brigade in Hawaii. Newly designated Naval Aviators are not normally assigned directly to the 1st Marine Aircraft Wing.

The officer reporting to a squadron from the training command will usually be placed in the type aircraft in which he qualified during advanced training. His MOS will be that of a basic pilot for fixed wing or for helicopters. Upon completion of a squadron training syllabus, he will be recommended for an MOS compatible with the type aircraft he is flying.

A training flow chart for Marine Naval Aviators for jets, multi-engine props, and helicopters is shown on page 28.

Photos of some of the Marine Corps aircraft are shown on pages 30 and 31.

Flight Officer Training

Preliminary Training

Marine student naval flight officers report directly from the Basic School to Naval Air Station Pensacola, Florida. They check in with marine Aviation Training Support Group (MATSG), the major Marine Command responsible for all administrative requirements. Six weeks of Aviation Indoctrination follows. The training is similar to that for Marine student naval aviators.

Primary Training

Primary naval flight officer training for prospective Marine Corps flight officers at NAS Pensacola is similar to the training given to the other student naval flight officers. They receive their first flight instruction in the T-34C cockpit. Cockpit awareness and crew coordination are emphasized.

Some Marine Corps Aircraft

F/A 18A Hornet

CH-53E Super Stallion

AV-8 Harrier

CH-46 Sea Knight

CH-53 Sea Stallion

AH-1J Cobra

UH-1 Huey

Intermediate Training

Following 14 weeks of basic NFO training, and depending upon preference, class rank, and the needs of the Marine Corps, student flight officers proceed to 14 weeks of intermediate training that is similar to that given to the other student naval flight officers.

There are several Marine Corps military occupational specialties available for naval flight officers. These include:

Radar Intercept Officer
Weapons and Sensors Officer
Tactical Navigator

Other career paths are also available.

For Radar Intercept Officer, student flight officers must attend an Airborne Radar Intercept Operator course (24 weeks) at NAS Pensacola and then check out in the specific aircraft to be flown at a Marine Corps Combat Readiness Training Group (MCCRTG-10).

For Weapons and Sensors Officer, student flight officers must attend a Weapons and Sensors Officer Course (26 weeks) at NAS Pensacola for training in both air-to-air and air-to-ground radar systems before going on to the F/A-18D Hornet.

For Tactical Navigator, student flight officers must attend a 20-week Tactical Navigator course at MCCRTG2A following basic jet navigation training at NAS Pensacola. Approximately one year of flight training is required from the start of aviation preflight indoctrination to designation as a naval flight officer. Successful completion of such training indicates that they have truly earned their wings of gold.

Upon completion of flight training, officers are assigned to either the second or third Marine aircraft wing. Those reporting to a squadron from the training command are usually placed in the type aircraft in which they qualified during advanced training.

Coast Guard

Coast Guard aviators are obtained from three principal sources. These are:

1. Commissioned officers who graduated from the Coast Guard Academy
2. Commissioned officers who graduated from the Coast Guard Officer Candidate School
3. Selectees of the Coast Guard's Direct Commission Aviation Program

Pilot training for each of these categories is considered in the following section.

Pilot Training

Commissioned Coast Guard officers selected for flight training are sent to the Naval Air Training Command located in Pensacola, Florida. Coast Guard student naval aviators commence their flight training with six weeks of Aviation Indoctrination.

Upon completion of Aviation Preflight Indoctrination, student naval aviators report to NAS Whiting Field for 22 weeks of primary flight training. They are assigned to one of the three training squadrons (VT-2, VT-3, or VT-6). The T-34C is the airplane used in this phase of training.

Upon completion of primary flight training, the student aviators are channeled into the fixed wing patrol (fixed wing, multiengine turboprops) or helicopters. The selection is based upon the student's preference and grades, as well as the needs of the Coast Guard.

Maritime Patrol

Prospective maritime patrol pilots take five weeks of intermediate training in a T-34C turboprop trainer at Whiting Field. Their advanced training is at Corpus Christi, Texas.

In advanced training, student aviators concentrate on improving more complicated flying skills, such as instrument capability, and perform mock missions in a training aircraft.

Upon successful completion of advanced training, students are designated naval aviators and earn their wings. About one year of training time is required before being designated a naval aviator. The next step is transitional training and subsequent assignment to the aviation fleet.

Transitional training for those who will fly the HC-130 Hercules is given at the USAFB, Little Rock, Arkansas. Transitional training for those who will fly the HU-25A Guardian produced by the Falcon Jet Corporation is given at the Coast Guard Training Center, Mobile, Alabama.

Helicopters

Prospective helicopter pilots take five weeks of intermediate training in a T-34C turboprop trainer at Whiting Field.

Some Coast Guard Aircraft

HU-25 Guardian

HH-65A Dolphin

HH-60J Jayhawk

C-130 Hercules

Advanced helicopter training, also at Whiting Field, includes basic landing pattern work, instrument flying, reading charts, low-level contour flying, formations, tactical approaches, external loads, and confined-area landings.

Upon successful completion of advanced training, helicopter-designated students earn their wings and become naval aviators. About one year of training time is required to become a naval aviator. Transitional training and subsequent assignment to the aviation fleet follows.

Transitional training for those who will fly the HH-65A Dolphin or the HH-60J Jayhawk helicopters is given at the Coast Guard Training Center, Mobile, Alabama.

Eligibility Requirements:

- Be less than 30 years of age.
- Be physically qualified and aeronautically adapted according to Coast Guard standards; must meet anthropometric standards.
- Have 20/20 vision, normal color and depth perception. Waivers are routinely granted to applicants who have 20/50 or better vision correctable to 20/20.
- Must achieve a qualifying score on the Pilot Flight Aptitude Rating (PFAR) and the Pilot Biographical Interest (PBI) in the Navy and Marine Corps Aviation Test Selection Battery.

Coast Guard Academy graduates must serve for at least one year at their first duty station before being considered by a Selection Board for flight training. Service evaluations are used by the Selection Board in making its final selections. Officer Candidate School (OCS) graduates may go directly into flight training upon being commissioned in the Coast Guard Reserve.

Service Commitment: Active duty obligation is five years from date of designation as naval aviator.

Direct Commission Aviation Program

The Coast Guard commissions a limited number of prior service aviators. A selection board is convened when the needs of the service dictate. Those selected spend four weeks at the Coast Guard Academy in New London, Connecticut, for Coast Guard orientation and then undergo any necessary transitional training (usually minimal) prior to reporting to their first duty station.

Eligibility Requirements:

- Be a U.S. citizen at least 21 years of age but under 32 as of convening of orientation course.
- Be a graduate of a U.S. military flight training program.
- Must not be on active duty with another service unless application includes an approved release or resignation.
- Must have served on active duty as a commissioned or warrant officer, and as a pilot for a minimum of two years, but not more than 10 years.
- Must have a minimum of 500 hours military flight time. Does not include training hours.
- Must have had full-time military or civilian pilot experience within two years of published application deadline.
- Must pass a Class 1, Service Group 1, flight physical as specified in Chapter 3 of the Coast Guard Medical Manual.
- Must have a baccalaureate degree, or
- Have attained 25th-percentile scores on all parts of the DANTES General Examinations of the College-Level Examination Program, or
- Must have completed one year of study (30 semester hours or 45 quarter hours) at an accredited degree-granting college or university, and

1. Have satisfactorily completed one college-level course in mathematics, or
2. Have passed the DANTES General Mathematics Examination of the College-Level Examination Program.

Service Commitment: Prior service aviators who were commissioned officers in the other services receive a commission as Lieutenant (junior grade, 0-2), or ensign, (0-1) in the Coast Guard Reserve.

All must serve four years of active duty. As the tour nears completion they have the same opportunity as other reserve officers to either request integration into the regular Coast Guard or be extended on active duty. These requests are granted on the basis of individual performance and the current needs of the service.

Date of rank will coincide with the date of appointment to commissioned status in the Coast Guard. Prior service time is creditable for base pay and retirement benefits, but not for promotion.

Undergraduate Training Program for Coast Guard Naval Aviators

SNA

AVIATION INDOCTRINATION

6 WEEKS
196 ACADEMIC HOURS
NAS PENSACOLA

PRIMARY

22 WEEKS
67 HOURS T-34C
27 HOURS SIMULATORS
166 ACADEMIC HOURS
NAS WHITING FIELD, FL
(NORTH END–VT-2, VT-3, VT-6)

HELICOPTER

INTERMEDIATE

6 WEEKS
26 HOURS T-34C
11 HOURS SIM
9 ACADEMIC HOURS
NAS WHITING FIELD, FL
(NORTH END–VT-2, VT-3, VT-6)

ADVANCED

22 WEEKS
116 HOURS TH-57 B/C
24 HOURS SIM
24 ACADEMIC HOURS
NAS WHITING FIELD, FL
(SOUTH END–HT-8, HT-18)

TRANSITIONAL TRAINING
at
CGATC, MOBILE, AL
(HH-65A; HH-3F)

FIXED WING

INTERMEDIATE

6 WEEKS
26 HOURS T-34C
11 HOURS SIM
9 ACADEMIC HOURS
NAS WHITING FIELD, FL
(NORTH END–VT-2, VT-3, VT-6)

ADVANCED

20 WEEKS
88 HOURS T-44
20 HOURS SIM
182 ACADEMIC HOURS
NAS CORPUS CHRISTI, TX

TRANSITIONAL TRAINING
at
USAFB, LITTLE ROCK, AR
(HC-130)
or
CGATC, MOBILE, AL
(HU-25A)

AVIATION FLEET

As a Coast Guard pilot, you could:

- be part of a search and rescue team, evacuating flood victims, rescuing boaters in a storm, or delivering pumps to a burning ship on the high seas
- give aerial assistance in the patrol and enforcement of the 200-mile fishing conservation zone
- be assigned to the International Ice Patrol, pinpointing the position and assessing the movement of icebergs in international waters
- be part of a pollution patrol monitoring oil spillage in lakes, rivers, and coastal waters
- fly drug interdiction and anti-smuggling missions

Aircraft flown by Coast Guard pilots include the HC-130 Hercules and the HU-25A Guardian fixed-wing aircraft, and the HH-60J Jayhawk and the HH-65A Dolphin helicopters. Photos of some of these aircraft appear on page 33. A Pilot Training flow chart is shown on page 35.

Part 2

Military Flight Aptitude Tests

MILITARY FLIGHT APTITUDE TESTS

General Information

Multiple-choice tests are the basic measuring instruments used in military personnel selection. The versatility of these tests, the ease of scoring, the development of sophisticated test scoring machines and ancillary equipment, the reliability of the scoring, and the adaptability of the test results for statistical analysis and for research and development have made this test format the one most widely accepted and used in military testing.

All military flight aptitude tests in current use are multiple-choice tests. Most multiple-choice questions in the military flight aptitude tests have either four or five options. However, two- or three-option test items may be found.

An understanding of the form and structure of multiple-choice test items is essential for anyone interested in testing. It has special importance to the hundreds of thousands who take military tests to enter the Armed Forces or to advance in its many different career fields.

The parts of the multiple-choice test item are illustrated below:

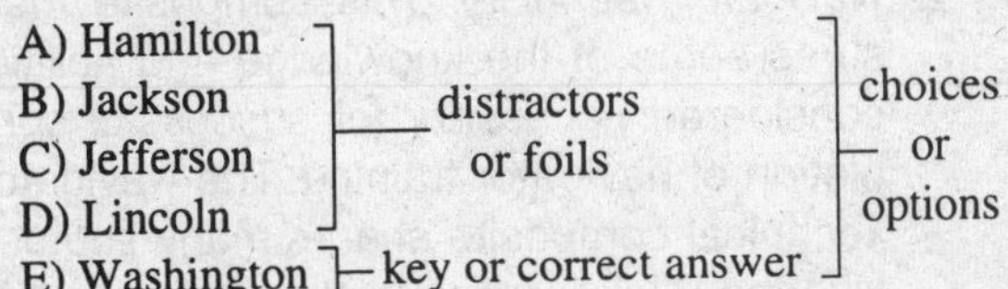

The stem either asks the question or presents the problem with which the test item is concerned. The stem may be written as an incomplete statement that may be completed by any one of the choices or options that follow, as a direct question, or as a command.

Which American president's portrait is found on a $1 bill? (interrogative)

Name the American president whose portrait is on a $1 bill. (imperative)

Options consist of a key or correct answer and foils or distracters that are absolutely incorrect although they may seem to be plausible to those unfamiliar with the right answer.

More than two million individuals are tested annually by the military using machine-scored answer sheets. Answer sheets now in use by the military have response positions indicated by ovals, circles, brackets, and rectangles. These answer sheets contain for each four- or five-option test item four or five response positions, which are lettered (A), (B), (C), (D), and so on. The sets of response positions are numbered consecutively to correspond to the number of the questions in the test booklet. Similarly, the ovals, circles, brackets, or rectangles are labeled to correspond to the designation given to the options in the test items.

Examples of some of the more common line arrangements and labeling are shown below:

Five-Option Items

A B C D E

Four-Option Items

A B C D

Each military flight aptitude test has its own special answer sheets that are printed for the exclusive use of testing organizations that require a particular type of test format or a special type of answer sheet layout.

The heading of the answer sheet provides space for identifying the test, identifying the test-taker, recording the test site and date, recording the test-taker's status, social security number, date of birth, sex, racial/ethnic group, and other pertinent information.

The body of the answer sheet is the actual testing section and is used to record the answers to the test questions. A No. 2 pencil must be used to record the answers by blackening the space in the marking position with the same letter as the option selected as the best answer. The mark should be dark and cover the entire area of the marking position.

A No. 2 pencil makes marks that are sufficiently dark and can also be readily erased. A No. 3 pencil does not sufficiently darken the marked position unless additional pressure is exerted. Marks that are too light may not be picked and credited by the test-scoring machine. A No. 1 pencil should not be used, as marks made with such pencil are difficult to erase. Incomplete erasures or smudges may be read as marks by the test-scoring machine.

For example:

The test-taker should make a pencil mark in the response position on the answer sheet that corresponds to the answer selected as being correct. Space E on a bracketed answer sheet is marked like this:

Remember:

NOT

NOT

NOT

NOT

NOT

NOT

NOT

BUT

The same principle applies if the response positions are indicated by ovals, circles, rectangles, or any other design.

To change an answer, first erase it completely and then blacken the space in the response position with the same designation as the new answer.

Avoid making stray marks on your answer sheet. Such marks may be read by the test-scoring machine as a second answer to a question, and your answer, even if correct, may not be credited.

With the general information about multiple-choice tests just presented, we can now discuss in detail the three flight aptitude tests currently in use. These are as follows:

Air Force Officer Qualifying Test (AFOQT)

Army Alternate Flight Aptitude Selection Test (AFAST)

Navy and Marine Corps Aviation Selection Test Battery

Air Force Officer Qualifying Test (AFOQT)

The AFOQT was designed to measure aptitudes essential for various commissioned officer training programs in the Air Force. It is based on analyses of tasks required for student pilots, navigators, and officers.

The first AFOQT was published in 1953. This test has been revised every few years to minimize obsolescence and the possibility of compromise. However, successive forms of the AFOQT are similar in many respects. The current forms of the AFOQT were made operational in 1988.

The AFOQT consists of 16 subtests. The various subtests are combined to generate one or more of five composite scores used to help predict success in certain types of Air Force training programs.

The five AFOQT composites, and the kinds of knowledge and abilities they measure, are described below.

1. *Pilot.* This composite measures some of the knowledge and abilities considered necessary for successful completion of pilot training. The Pilot composite includes subtests which measure verbal ability, knowledge of aviation and mechanical systems, the ability to determine aircraft attitude from instruments, knowledge of aeronautical concepts, the ability to read scales and interpret tables, and certain spatial abilities.
2. *Navigator-Technical.* This composite measures some of the knowledge and abilities considered necessary for successful completion of navigator training. The Navigator-Technical composite shares many subtests with the Pilot composite, with the exception that measures verbal ability, ability to determine aircraft attitude, and knowledge of aeronautical concepts not included. However, subtests are added measuring quantitative aptitudes, some spatial or visual abilities, and science knowledge.
3. *Academic Aptitude.* This composite measures verbal and quantitative knowledge and abilities. The Academic Aptitude composite combines all subtests used to score the Verbal and Quantitative composites.
4. *Verbal.* This composite measures various types of verbal knowledge and abilities. The Verbal composite includes subtests which measure the ability to reason and recognize relationships among words, the ability to read and understand diverse paragraphs, and the ability to understand synonyms.
5. *Quantitative.* This composite measures various types of quantitative knowledge and abilities. The Quantitative composite shares subtests with the Navigator-Technical composite discussed above and includes

subtests which measure the ability to understand and reason with arithmetic relationships, interpret data from graphs and charts, and to use mathematical terms, formulas, and relationships.

The pilot and the navigator-technical composite scores are used to select candidates for these two types of training. The academic aptitude composite is used to select individuals for Officer Training School (OTS). The verbal composite and the quantitative composites are used for counseling in order to help officer candidates find appropriate military occupations.

The AFOQT, published in several booklets, contains 380 test items and requires a total of $4\frac{1}{2}$ hours of administrative and testing time. The test is administered on a monthly basis. Thousands of applicants for flight training or officer training are tested each year.

AFOQT subtests, the number of items in each subtest, and aptitude composites are shown in the table below.

The table on page 42 gives the testing schedule for the AFOQT. On most of the subtests, you will have more than enough time to answer all the questions. On several subtests, however, you may not finish. Don't worry if this happens since many people do not finish these subtests. Just work as quickly and accurately as you can. If you are not sure of the answer to a question, make a selection anyway, even if you have to guess. Your score on the AFOQT will be based on the number of correct answers you select. You will not lose points or be penalized for guessing.

When you arrive for test administration, you will be given complete and specific instructions on how to take the test. The number of questions in each of the sixteen subtests and the time you will be given to complete each one will vary from subtest to subtest.

You will be instructed not to make any marks in your actual test booklet. You will record all of your answers on a separate answer sheet with a pencil that allows the answer sheet to be scored by machine. Scratch paper will be provided for you to use for any figuring or calculations.

Before you take some of the subtests, you will have the opportunity to answer some practice questions to be sure that you understand what you are to do on the test. If you are not sure what you are supposed to be doing, ask your test administrator or proctor to explain before you start answering the actual test questions. However, test

Construction of AFOQT Composites

Subtest	# of Items	Pilot	Nav-Tech	Acad. Apt.	Verbal	Quant.
Verbal Analogies	25	X		X	X	
Arithmetic Reasoning	25		X	X		X
Reading Comprehension	25			X	X	
Data Interpretation	25		X	X		X
Word Knowledge	25			X	X	
Math Knowledge	25		X	X		X
Mechanical Comprehension	20	X	X			
Electrical Maze	20	X	X			
Scale Reading	40	X	X			
Instrument Comprehension	20	X				
Block Counting	20	X	X			
Table Reading	40	X	X			
Aviation Information	20	X				
Rotated Blocks	15		X			
General Science	20		X			
Hidden Figures	15		X			

AFOQT TESTING SCHEDULE

	Administration Time (In minutes)	Testing Time (In minutes)	Total Time (In minutes)
Pretest Activities	24		24
Verbal Analogies	1	8	9
Arithmetic Reasoning	1	29	30
Reading Comprehension	1	18	19
Data Interpretation	1	24	25
Word Knowledge	1	5	6
Math Knowledge	1	22	23
Break	10		10
Mechanical Comprehension	1	22	23
Electrical Maze	3	10	13
Scale Reading	3	15	18
Instrument Comprehension	3	6	9
Block Counting	2	3	5
Table Reading	2	7	9
Aviation Information	1	8	9
Rotated Blocks	2	13	15
General Science	1	10	11
Hidden Figures	2	8	10
Collection of Materials	2		2
TOTAL TIME REQUIRED	1 hr 2 min	3 hrs 28 min	4 hrs 30 min

administrators or proctors can only assist you in understanding the directions. They cannot give you guidance concerning test questions and answers or test-taking strategy.

It is recommended that you get a good night's rest before taking the test. You will be asked before you take the test if you are physically able to take the AFOQT. If you do not feel that you are able to take the test at this time, inform the test administrator and you will be scheduled to take the AFOQT at a later date. Be relaxed, follow instructions, read each question carefully, and do the best you can.

Alternate Flight Aptitude Selection Test (AFAST)

The AFAST was designed to measure those special aptitudes and personality/background characteristics that are predictive of success in Army helicopter flight training.

AFAST has been found to be highly effective in screening applicants to ensure that only those persons with the capabilities to succeed in flight school are accepted for training. People who score higher on the test stand a better chance of being selected to attend flight training than those who pass but score low. It is to your advantage to score as high as you can on this test. Your application for flight training will be given further consideration only if your AFAST score is equal to or higher than the established cut score. A minimum score of 90 is currently required.

AFAST has a total of 200 questions broken down into seven subtests. Each subtest has separate directions and testing time limits.

The following table shows the subtests, number of items in each subtest and the testing time allowed.

When you go in to take the test, you will be given a test booklet, a separate answer sheet and two soft lead pencils. You will receive complete instructions for each test section and be told how to mark your answers.

In some subtests, it is to your advantage to answer every question. In other subtests, a portion of the wrong answers are counted against the right answers. Even in the latter case you should make the best choice you can unless your answer would be a pure guess. For this reason it is important that you listen closely to the test administration instructions and that you read the instructions for each test section to yourself as the test examiner reads the instructions aloud.

The answer sheet heading has space for your name, social security number, and other identifying information. This must be carefully completed.

Following the identification part are the subtest sections, with a different answer block for each question. The questions are numbered from 1 to 200. Be sure you are always marking the same answer on the answer sheet that matches the question number in the test booklet.

Below is an example of how to properly mark an answer.

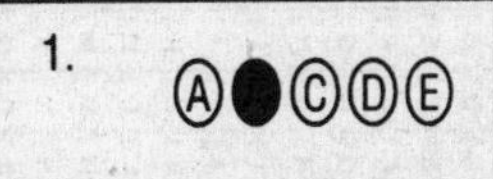

If this were Question No. 1 on the test, and you decide that answer 'B' is the best choice, you would carefully darken in the circle marked 'B' in block number 1 on your answer sheet. Remember to mark the circle heavily, completely filling in the circle. If your mark is too small or too light, the machine that scores the test may not read the mark. If you decide to change an answer you must *completely erase* the answer you wish to change, then mark your new answer. Also, never have more than one answer marked for each question. If you do, you will not receive credit for the answer.

AFAST Subtests

Subtest Number	Subtest	# of Items	Testing Time (In Minutes)
1.	Background Information Form	25	10
2.	Instrument Comprehension	15	5
3.	Complex Movements	30	5
4.	Helicopter Knowledge	20	10
5.	Cyclic Orientation	15	5
6.	Mechanical Functions	20	10
7.	Self-Description Form	75	25
		200	70

Sample AFAST Answer Sheet

B. YOUR NAME

C. EXAMINEE STATUS: Civilian, Officer, ROTC, Enlisted

D. YOUR SOCIAL SECURITY ACCOUNT NUMBER

E. DATE OF BIRTH: DAY, MO., YR.

F. Station Code

LEAVE BLANK

A. AFAST IDENTIFICATION BLANK

1. SIGNATURE ____________________

2. Sex: Male ○ Female ○

3. GRADE or RANK ____________________

4. DATE ____________________ (Day) (Month) (Year)

5. RACIAL/ETHNIC GROUP: American Indian ○ Black ○ White ○ Asian American ○ Spanish Heritage ○ Other ○

6. MILITARY ORGANIZATION ____________________

7. INSTALLATION OR PLACE OF TESTING ____________________

Testing Schedule and Construction of Composites

	No. of items	Testing Time (in minutes)	AQR	PFAR	FOFAR	PBI	FOBI	OA
Math/Verbal (MVT)	37	35	X	X	X			X
Mechanical Comprehension (MCT)	30	15	X	X				X
Spatial Apperception (SAT)	35	10	X	X	X			
Aviation/Nautical Information (ANT)	30	15	X	X	X			
Biographical Information (BI)	76	20				X	X	
	208	95						

Navy and Marine Corps Aviation Selection Test Battery

This test battery is used by the Navy, the Marine Corps, and the Coast Guard for selecting officer candidates for both their pilot and flight officer training programs. The battery is also used by the Navy and the Coast Guard for screening officer candidates for their OCS programs. The battery consists of the following tests:

1. Math/Verbal Test (MVT)
2. Mechanical Comprehension Test (MCT)
3. Spatial Apperception Test (SAT)*
4. Aviation/Nautical Information Test (ANT)*
5. Biographical Inventory (BI)*

The Math/Verbal Test measures quantitative aptitude (arithmetic reasoning, general mathematics, algebra, and plane geometry) and verbal aptitude (sentence comprehension).

The Mechanical Comprehension Test measures mechanical aptitude (understanding of the principles involved in the operation of mechanical devices, basic physics, and so on).

The Spatial Apperception Test is designed to measure ability to recognize simple changes in the position or attitude of an airplane by viewing the ground and horizon from the cockpit.

The Aviation/Nautical Information Test measures knowledge of basic aviation and nautical terminology, principles, and practices.

The Biographical Inventory is designed to obtain essential biographical data, including general background, education, employment experience, skills, values and opinions, and other personal attributes essential for successful performance in pilot and flight officer training.

The table below shows the number of items in each test, testing time, and how the various tests are combined to produce the six composite scores.

The Academic Qualification Rating (AQR) is a composite derived from a weighted combination of the Math/Verbal (MVT), Mechanical Comprehension (MCT), Spatial Apperception (SAT), and Aviation/Nautical Information (ANT) tests. It predicts academic performance in both the pilot and flight officer training programs.

The Pilot Flight Aptitude Rating (PFAR) is a composite derived from a weighted combination of the same four tests (MVT, MCT, SAT, and ANT). It predicts flight performance in primary in the pilot training program.

The Flight Officer Flight Aptitude Rating (FOFAR) is a composite derived from a weighted combination of the following three tests: Math/Verbal (MVT), Spatial Apperception (SAT), and Aviation/Nautical Information (ANT). It predicts flight performance in basic in the flight officer training program.

The Pilot Biographical Interest (PBI) is the score received on the Biographical Inventory (BI). It predicts attrition through primary in the pilot training program.

The Flight Officer Biographical Interest (FOBI) is the score received in the Biographical Inventory (BI). It predicts attrition through basic in the flight officer training program.

The Officer Aptitude Rating (OAR) is a composite derived from a weighted combination of the Math/Verbal (MVT) and the Mechanical Comprehension (MCT). The OAR is used by the Navy and the Coast Guard to screen applicants for their Officer Candidate Schools.

Each aviation applicant obtains six scores. Except for the OAR, all obtained scores are on the 1–9 (stanine) scale. The OAR score is a standard score.

The typical aviation applicant scores are:

AGR	7
PFAR	6
FOFAR	5
PBI	8
FOBI	9
OAR	56

For all scores, except the OAR, applicants must obtain at least a 3 to be considered for further processing. Applicants have only two chances to take this test battery. At least 180 days must elapse before a retake.

General directions and special instructions are provided in the test booklets.

The answer sheet heading has space for your name, social security number, educational status, test date, date of birth, racial/ethnic group data, and other identifying information. This section must be carefully completed.

Following the identification section on the answer sheet are the response positions for each of the questions in each of the five tests. Both

*Given only to aviation applicants.

sides of the answer sheet must be completed by those taking all five tests of the battery.

All of the tests have multiple-choice questions. If you are not sure of an answer to a question, make a selection anyway, even if you have to guess. Your scores will be based on the number of correct answers you select. You will not lose points or be penalized for guessing.

Composite Scoring

If any Air Force Officer Qualifying Test composite or any composite of the Navy and Marine Corps Aviation Selection Test Battery is administered to a large number of examinees for whom it is appropriate, the raw score most frequently encountered will be near the mean of the group, and the least frequently encountered raw scores will be at the extremes. If raw scores are shown on the horizontal axis and frequencies on the vertical axis, a figure is generated which closely approximates Figure 2. Figure 2 is the normal probability curve. Many sets of psychological and biological data assume the form of this curve.

In a normal distribution, the mean score is located so that half the cases lie above it. Hence it can also be taken as the median score. The partition of the distribution at this point is shown in Figure 2. Other partitions are shown at one, two, three, and four standard deviations above and below the mean, and the percentages of the total area under the curve and between the partitions are indicated. These percentages also represent the proportions of the total number of cases in the distribution lying within these areas.

There are definite mathematical relationships between these properties of the normal probability curve and the stanine scale used for the Navy and Marine Corps Aviation Selection Test Battery, the percentile scale used for the Air Force Officer Qualifying Test, and the College Entrance Examination Board (CEEB) scale used for the Scholastic Assessment Test (SAT). The relationships that exist in a normal distribution among these three common types of scoring are shown below the curve in Figure 2.

The raw composite scores in the Navy and Marine Corps Aviation Selection Test Battery, except for the OAR, are converted to normalized standard scores on the stanine scale. The stanine scale, developed by the Air Force during World War II, has scores that run from 1 to 9. Limiting the scores to single-digit numbers simplified certain computations as each score required only a single column on computer punched cards. The term "stanine" is actually a contraction of *standard nine.*

On the stanine scale, the median and the mean are 5 and the standard deviation is about 2. To convert to the single-digit system of stanine scores, the lowest 4 percent would be given a value of 1; the next 7 percent, 2; the next 12 percent, 3; the

Figure 2—Relationship among Common Types of Test Scores in a Normal Distribution

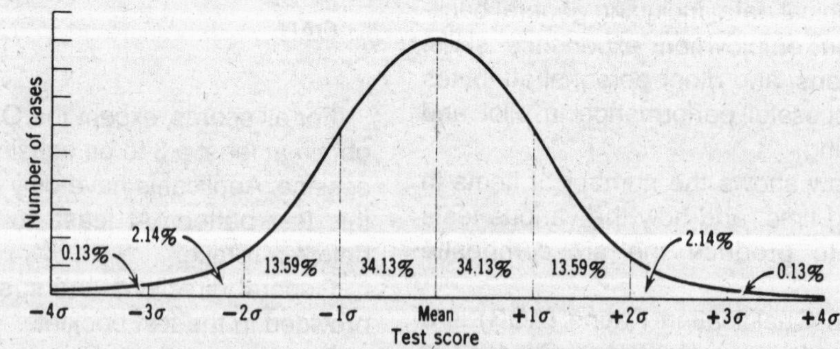

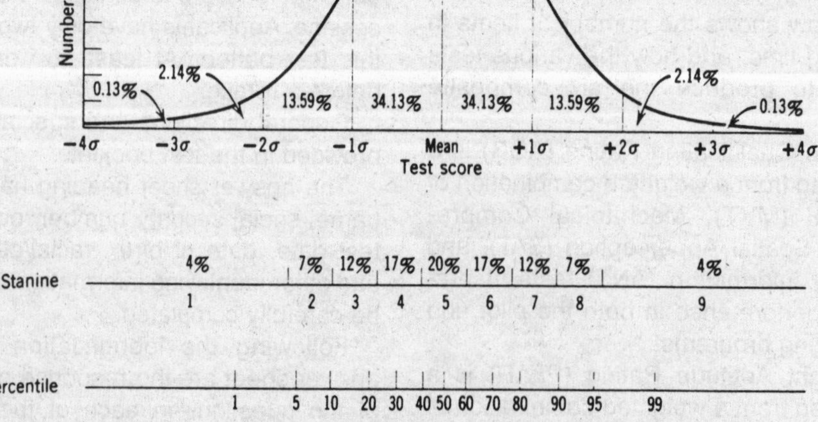

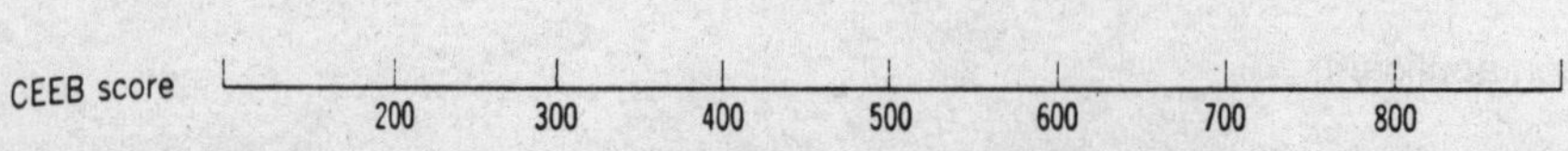

next 17 percent, 4; the next 20 percent, 5; the next 17 percent, 6; the next 12 percent, 7; the next 7 percent, 8; and the highest 4 percent, 9.

Air Force Officer Qualifying Test composite scores, formerly expressed in stanines, are now reported in percentiles. Percentiles serve, as do stanines, to permit meaningful interpretation of test performance.

A percentile score is the rank expressed in percentage terms and indicates what proportion of the group received lower composite raw scores. A person at the 50th percentile would be the "typical" individual. The 50th percentile is known as the median and indicates a score exactly in the middle of the test group. The higher the percentile, the better the individual's standing; the lower the percentile, the poorer the individual's standing. Percentiles above 50 indicate above-average performance; percentiles below 50 indicate below-average performance.

If a score at the 25th percentile or better is required for a certain aviation program, the lowest quarter of the distribution is cut off. If a score at the 75th percentile or better is required, the lowest three-quarters of the distribution are cut off and only those in the top quarter are accepted.

The scores on the Scholastic Assessment Test (SAT) of the College Entrance Examination Board, reported on a scale of 200 to 800, are standard scores adjusted to a mean of 500 and a standard deviation of 100.

STRATEGIES FOR PREPARING FOR AND TAKING MILITARY FLIGHT APTITUDE TESTS

Preparing for the Test

Whether it be studying subject matter, reviewing sample questions in practice exercises, or getting into condition for a strenuous physical test, the "test-wise" individual will *immediately* begin preparing for the tests ahead.

Become familiar with the format of multiple-choice test items. These items are used exclusively in written tests given by the military in the selection process for flight training programs.

Become familiar with the layout of machine-scored answer sheets. Know the proper way to record your answers in the spaces provided, whether they be brackets, rectangles, squares, ovals, or circles. These standard answer sheets are not complicated if you understand the layout and have practiced blackening the answer space in the correct manner.

Once you determine the military flight aptitude test or tests in which you are interested, ascertain what the test or tests will cover. This book, as well as the officer in charge of aviation officer recruiting or a recruiting representative, is an excellent source for invaluable suggestions and guidance.

Review subject matter covered in the test or tests in which you are interested. Books and other study material may be borrowed from libraries or purchased in bookstores.

Review carefully the next section of this book that covers the various types of questions used by the military in the flight aptitude tests.

Take the specimen test as if it were the real one—under actual test conditions. Record your answers on the specimen answer sheet. Keep within the allotted time limits. Work quickly but carefully.

Check your answers with the key answers and rationale that follow each specimen test. For those questions that you answered incorrectly, determine why your original answers are incorrect. Make certain that you understand the rationale for arriving at the correct answer. This is essential to broaden your background, increase your test sophistication, and prepare you for the real test.

Set aside definite hours each day for concentrated study. Adhere closely to this schedule. Don't fritter away your time with excessive breaks. A cup of coffee, a piece of fruit, a look out of the window are fine—but not too often.

Study with a friend or a group. The exchange of ideas that this arrangement affords may be beneficial. It is also more pleasant to get together in study sessions than it is to study alone.

Eliminate distractions. Study efforts will prove more fruitful when there is little or no diversion of attention. Disturbances caused by family and neighbor activities (telephone calls, chitchat, TV programs, etc.) will work to your disadvantage. Study in a quiet, private room.

Use the library. Most colleges and universities have excellent library facilities. Take full advantage of them. The library is free from those distractions that may inhibit your home study.

To reemphasize, take each practice specimen test as though you were taking the real test. With this attitude, you will derive greater benefits. Put yourself under strict test conditions. Tolerate no interruptions while you are "taking the test." Work steadily. Do not spend too much time on any one question. If a question seems too difficult, go to the next one. Go back to the omitted questions only after you complete the initial pass through the entire subtest or section.

Be sure to acquire a basic understanding of aviation, including types of aircraft, components, and operations involving aircraft. To accomplish this you may:

- Read books or periodicals on aviation.
- Visit your local airfield and observe the arrival and departure of aircraft.
- Arrange to fly in a light, fixed-wing plane and in a helicopter.
- If possible, sit next to or in front of the pilot.
- Observe the instrument panels and controls.
- Observe the pilot using the controls.
- Study the terrain in front of you.
- Notice how the natural landscape and man-made structures change in configuration and shape as you view them from different heights and angles.
- Observe the terrain and the horizon as the aircraft climbs, banks to the left, banks to the right, and descends.

- Observe the runway both at takeoff and when landing.
- Arrange to soar aloft in a glider.
- Observe how the towline is released. (You may be permitted to release the bowline towline and even get the "feel" of the controls.)
- Notice how the natural landscape and man-made structures change in configuration and shape as you view them from different heights and angles.
- Observe the terrain and the horizon as the glider ascends, banks to the left, banks to the right, and descends.
- Observe the landing area both at takeoff and when landing.

Keep physically fit. You cannot study effectively when you are uncomfortable, have a headache, or are tense. Physical health promotes mental efficiency. Guarding your health takes into account such factors as:

- Sufficient sleep
- Daily exercise and recreation
- A balanced diet
- Avoidance of eyestrain

If possible, avoid taking the test under adverse conditions, such as when you are fatigued, ill, injured, emotionally upset, or dispirited; have your mind on other problems; are experiencing an "off day"; or any other condition that may handicap you physically, mentally, or emotionally.

Go to bed early the night before the test and get a good night's sleep.

Eat a light meal before taking the test. Consuming a heavy meal just before the test can make you somewhat lethargic and may reduce your effectiveness as a test-taker.

Bring along all supplies you will need for the test—a pen, several No. 2 pencils, an eraser, a ruler, and so on. Be certain to bring eyeglasses if you need them for reading.

Bring a watch to help you allocate your time. Be certain that you know the amount of time you have for the test and for each timed test section or subtest. With military tests, you are frequently not permitted to go back and check your answers on test sections or subtests that have already been completed.

Arrive at the test site well before the scheduled time for the test.

Last-minute review is inadvisable. Relax before the start of the test.

Refrain from drinking excessive amounts of liquids before the test. Going to the restroom during the test wastes valuable testing time. Use the restroom before or after the test, not during the test.

Guessing

When unsure of an answer to a multiple-choice test item, should you guess? Emphatically, *yes,* if it is to your advantage! If there is no penalty for incorrect answers (the test score is based solely on the number of correct responses), be certain that all questions are answered before handing in your answer sheet to the proctor. If there is a penalty for wrong answers (the test score is determined by subtracting from the number of right answers the number of wrong answers or some fraction of the number of wrong answers), guess only if the odds are in your favor.

In both the Air Force Officer Qualifying Test and the Navy and Marine Corps Aviation Test Selection Battery, the test scores are based solely on the number of correct responses. There is no penalty for incorrect answers.

In the Flight Aptitude Selection Test (FAST), it is to your advantage to answer every question on some subtests. On other subtests a portion of the wrong answers are counted against the right answers. Even in the latter case, you should make the best choice you can unless the answer would be a pure guess.

To obtain the maximum score possible by guessing, you should understand what is meant by *guessing "blindly," "educated" guessing,* and *probability.*

To guess "blindly" is to select at random the correct answer to the question from all the options given. To make an "educated" guess is first to eliminate those options that you know to be definitely incorrect and then to make your selection from among the remaining options.

Probability is the likelihood or chance of some event or series of events occurring. When tossing a coin, what is the probability that a head will appear? The probability is one out of two. Similarly, the probability of obtaining a tail is also one out of two. Head and tail are equally likely. Such probability is expressed as $\frac{1}{2}$ or .50.

Probability ranges between *one* and *zero.* At *one*, the event will occur every time. At *zero*, the event will never occur. The probability of occurring plus the probability of not occurring always equals one.

Assume that there are three marbles in a jar and only one marble is red. What is the probability of picking the red marble strictly by chance? The probability is one out of three, expressed as $\frac{1}{3}$ or .33. Similarly, if there are four marbles in a jar and only one is red, the probability of picking the red marble strictly by chance is one out of four, expressed as $\frac{1}{4}$ or .25. If there are five marbles in a jar and only one is red, the probability of picking the red marble strictly by chance is one out of five, expressed as $\frac{1}{5}$ or .20.

With a true-false or two-option item, the probability of guessing the correct answer when the test-taker knows nothing about the item is one out of two ($\frac{1}{2}$). For a three-option multiple-choice item, the probability of guessing the correct answer strictly by chance is one out of three ($\frac{1}{3}$). For a four-option multiple-choice item, the probability of guessing the correct answer strictly by chance is one out of four ($\frac{1}{4}$). For a five-option multiple-choice item, the probability of guessing the correct answer strictly by chance is one out of five ($\frac{1}{5}$). Obviously, the probability of selecting the correct answer increases with every incorrect option eliminated before making that "educated" guess.

By guessing "blindly" or picking strictly by chance, the test-taker will probably answer correctly 50 percent of the test items in a true-false or two-option test, 33 percent of the test items in a three-option multiple-choice test, 25 percent of the test items in a four-option test, and 20 percent of the test items in a five-option test.

Is probability important for the test-taker? Definitely! Understanding and applying the principles of probability will increase the test score by several to many points. It can make the difference between passing or failing a test, and it may make the difference between being reached for appointment or not being reached.

The following two examples illustrate how the principles of probability may influence test scores. In the first example we will assume that no deduction is made for incorrect answers and that only the number of correct answers determines the test score. In the second example we will assume that deductions are made for incorrect answers and that the number of correct answers minus some fraction of one for each incorrect answer determines the test score.

Example 1: Correct Answers Only

Assume that you are taking a 100-item, five-option, multiple-choice test and that test scores are based solely on the number of correct answers. Assume further that there are twenty answers of which you are uncertain. If you do not answer these twenty items, you will receive no credit for them. If you guess "blindly" by picking any option at random, you will probably answer four out of the twenty items correctly and earn four extra points.

If you are able to eliminate one option that you know is incorrect on each of the twenty items and then pick at random from the remaining four options, you will probably answer five of the twenty items correctly and earn five extra points.

If you are able to eliminate two options that you know are incorrect on each of the twenty items and then pick at random from the remaining three options, you will probably answer seven of the twenty items correctly and earn seven extra points.

If you are able to eliminate three options that you know are incorrect on each of the twenty items and then pick at random from the remaining two options, you will probably answer ten of the twenty items correctly and earn ten extra points.

ANSWER ALL ITEMS.

FOR THOSE ITEMS WHERE YOU ARE UNSURE OF THE CORRECT ANSWER, FIRST ELIMINATE OPTIONS THAT YOU KNOW ARE INCORRECT AND THEN PICK AT RANDOM FROM THE REMAINING OPTIONS.

Example 2: Penalty Scoring

Assume that you are taking a 100-item, five-option, multiple-choice test and that the test score is based on the number of correct answers minus $\frac{1}{4}$ point for each incorrect answer. Assume further that there are twenty answers of which you are uncertain.

A penalty of $\frac{1}{4}$ point for each incorrect answer may be used on a five-option multiple-choice test to compensate for guessing "blindly" by picking an option strictly at random. Similarly, for a four-option multiple-choice test, a penalty of $\frac{1}{3}$ point for each incorrect answer may be used. In a true-false test, the formula items right minus items wrong may be used to compensate for guessing "blindly."

If you do not answer the twenty items, you will receive no extra points and incur no penalty. If you guess "blindly" by picking any option at random, you will probably answer four of the twenty items correctly and sixteen of the items incorrectly. You will receive four extra points for the four correct answers and will be penalized four points ($\frac{1}{4}$ of 16) for the sixteen incorrect answers. With this penalty formula, there is no advantage in answering the twenty items by picking options strictly at random or not answering these twenty items.

However, if you are able to eliminate an option that you know is incorrect on each of the twenty items and then select at random from the remaining four options, you will probably select five correct answers and fifteen incorrect answers. You will receive five extra points for the five correct answers and will be penalized $3\frac{3}{4}$ points ($\frac{1}{4}$ of 15) for the fifteen incorrect answers, and you will earn an extra $1\frac{1}{4}$ points ($5 - 3\frac{3}{4}$).

If you are able to eliminate two options that you know are incorrect on each of the twenty items and then select at random from the remaining three options, you will probably select seven correct and thirteen incorrect answers. You will receive seven extra points for the seven correct answers and will be penalized $3\frac{1}{4}$ points ($\frac{1}{4}$ of 13) for the thirteen incorrect answers. You will earn an extra $3\frac{3}{4}$ points ($7 - \frac{31}{4}$).

If you are able to eliminate three options that you know are incorrect on each of the twenty items and then select at random from the remaining two options, you will probably select ten correct and ten incorrect answers. You will receive ten extra points for the ten correct answers and will be penalized $2\frac{1}{2}$ points ($\frac{1}{4}$ of 10) for the ten incorrect answers. You will earn an extra $7\frac{1}{2}$ points ($10 - 2\frac{1}{2}$).

ANSWER ONLY THOSE ITEMS WHERE THE PROBABILITY OF GAIN IS GREATER THAN THE PROBABILITY OF LOSS.

FOR THOSE ITEMS WHERE THE ODDS ARE IN YOUR FAVOR, FIRST ELIMINATE OPTIONS THAT YOU KNOW ARE INCORRECT AND THEN PICK AT RANDOM FROM THE REMAINING OPTIONS.

AN "EDUCATED" GUESS IS BETTER THAN GUESSING "BLINDLY."

Taking the Test

Arrive early at the test location.

If you have a choice, choose a comfortable seat with good lighting and away from possible distractions such as friends, the proctor's desk, the door, open windows, etc.

If you are left-handed or have any special physical needs, inform the proctor of your special needs and ask if some arrangements can be made to enable you to compete equally with the other candidates.

If the examination room is too cold, too warm, or not well ventilated, call these conditions to the attention of the person in charge.

Be confident and calm. A certain amount of anxiety is not only normal but is highly desirable. Test-takers will not be at their best when they are completely relaxed. If you have prepared faithfully, you will attain your true score based on your ability, your degree of preparation for the test, and your test sophistication.

Use your watch and apportion your time intelligently.

Give the test your complete attention. Blot out all other thoughts, pleasant or otherwise, and concentrate solely on the task before you.

Listen carefully to all oral instructions. Read carefully the directions for taking the test and marking the answer sheet. If you don't understand the instructions or directions, raise your hand and ask the proctor for clarification. Failure to follow instructions or misreading directions can only result in a loss of points.

When the signal is given to begin the test, start with the first question. Don't jump to conclusions. Carefully read the stem of the question and all the options before selecting the answer.

Answer the question as it is presented in the test booklet and not what you believe should be the question.

Work steadily and quickly but not carelessly. Do not spend too much time on any one question. If you can't figure out the answer in a few seconds, go on to the next question. If you skip a question, be sure to skip the answer space for that question on the answer sheet.

Make certain that the number of the question you are working on in the test booklet corresponds to the number of the question you are answering on the answer sheet.

Go back to the more difficult questions you skipped and attempt to answer them. If still unsure of the correct answer, eliminate those options that you know are incorrect, and make an "educated" guess as to which one of the remaining options is correct. If there is a penalty for wrong answers, make that "educated" guess only when the odds are in your favor.

If time permits, recheck your answers for errors. If you find that your initial response is incorrect, erase it completely and blacken your new choice.

Keep working until you have rechecked all your answers and made all corrections. If necessary, be a "bitter ender" and remain working until the signal is given to stop.

Part 3

Types of Questions Used in Military Flight Aptitude Tests

Answer Sheet for Practice Questions

Synonyms

1. Ⓐ Ⓑ Ⓒ Ⓓ Ⓔ 2. Ⓐ Ⓑ Ⓒ Ⓓ Ⓔ 3. Ⓐ Ⓑ Ⓒ Ⓓ Ⓔ 4. Ⓐ Ⓑ Ⓒ Ⓓ Ⓔ 5. Ⓐ Ⓑ Ⓒ Ⓓ Ⓔ 6. Ⓐ Ⓑ Ⓒ Ⓓ Ⓔ 7. Ⓐ Ⓑ Ⓒ Ⓓ Ⓔ 8. Ⓐ Ⓑ Ⓒ Ⓓ Ⓔ 9. Ⓐ Ⓑ Ⓒ Ⓓ Ⓔ 10. Ⓐ Ⓑ Ⓒ Ⓓ Ⓔ

Verbal Analogies

1. Ⓐ Ⓑ Ⓒ Ⓓ Ⓔ 2. Ⓐ Ⓑ Ⓒ Ⓓ Ⓔ 3. Ⓐ Ⓑ Ⓒ Ⓓ Ⓔ 4. Ⓐ Ⓑ Ⓒ Ⓓ Ⓔ 5. Ⓐ Ⓑ Ⓒ Ⓓ Ⓔ

Reading Comprehension

1. Ⓐ Ⓑ Ⓒ Ⓓ Ⓔ 2. Ⓐ Ⓑ Ⓒ Ⓓ Ⓔ 3. Ⓐ Ⓑ Ⓒ Ⓓ Ⓔ 4. Ⓐ Ⓑ Ⓒ Ⓓ Ⓔ 5. Ⓐ Ⓑ Ⓒ Ⓓ Ⓔ 6. Ⓐ Ⓑ Ⓒ Ⓓ 7. Ⓐ Ⓑ Ⓒ Ⓓ 8. Ⓐ Ⓑ Ⓒ Ⓓ 9. Ⓐ Ⓑ Ⓒ Ⓓ 10. Ⓐ Ⓑ Ⓒ Ⓓ 11. Ⓐ Ⓑ Ⓒ Ⓓ 12. Ⓐ Ⓑ Ⓒ Ⓓ 13. Ⓐ Ⓑ Ⓒ Ⓓ 14. Ⓐ Ⓑ Ⓒ Ⓓ 15. Ⓐ Ⓑ Ⓒ Ⓓ 16. Ⓐ Ⓑ Ⓒ Ⓓ 17. Ⓐ Ⓑ Ⓒ Ⓓ 18 Ⓐ Ⓑ Ⓒ Ⓓ 19. Ⓐ Ⓑ Ⓒ Ⓓ 20. Ⓐ Ⓑ Ⓒ Ⓓ

Arithmetic Reasoning

1. Ⓐ Ⓑ Ⓒ Ⓓ Ⓔ 2. Ⓐ Ⓑ Ⓒ Ⓓ Ⓔ 3. Ⓐ Ⓑ Ⓒ Ⓓ Ⓔ 4. Ⓐ Ⓑ Ⓒ Ⓓ Ⓔ 5. Ⓐ Ⓑ Ⓒ Ⓓ Ⓔ

Math Knowledge

1. Ⓐ Ⓑ Ⓒ Ⓓ Ⓔ 2. Ⓐ Ⓑ Ⓒ Ⓓ Ⓔ 3. Ⓐ Ⓑ Ⓒ Ⓓ Ⓔ 4. Ⓐ Ⓑ Ⓒ Ⓓ Ⓔ 5. Ⓐ Ⓑ Ⓒ Ⓓ Ⓔ

Data Interpretation

1. Ⓐ Ⓑ Ⓒ Ⓓ Ⓔ 2. Ⓐ Ⓑ Ⓒ Ⓓ Ⓔ 3. Ⓐ Ⓑ Ⓒ Ⓓ Ⓔ 4. Ⓐ Ⓑ Ⓒ Ⓓ Ⓔ 5. Ⓐ Ⓑ Ⓒ Ⓓ Ⓔ

Mechanical Comprehension

1. Ⓐ Ⓑ Ⓒ Ⓓ Ⓔ 2. Ⓐ Ⓑ Ⓒ Ⓓ Ⓔ 3. Ⓐ Ⓑ Ⓒ Ⓓ Ⓔ 4. Ⓐ Ⓑ Ⓒ Ⓓ Ⓔ 5. Ⓐ Ⓑ Ⓒ Ⓓ Ⓔ 6. Ⓐ Ⓑ Ⓒ 7. Ⓐ Ⓑ Ⓒ 8. Ⓐ Ⓑ Ⓒ 9. Ⓐ Ⓑ Ⓒ 10. Ⓐ Ⓑ Ⓒ

Electrical Maze

1. Ⓐ Ⓑ Ⓒ Ⓓ Ⓔ 2. Ⓐ Ⓑ Ⓒ Ⓓ Ⓔ 3. Ⓐ Ⓑ Ⓒ Ⓓ Ⓔ 4. Ⓐ Ⓑ Ⓒ Ⓓ Ⓔ 5. Ⓐ Ⓑ Ⓒ Ⓓ Ⓔ

Scale Reading

1. Ⓐ Ⓑ Ⓒ Ⓓ Ⓔ 2. Ⓐ Ⓑ Ⓒ Ⓓ Ⓔ 3. Ⓐ Ⓑ Ⓒ Ⓓ Ⓔ 4. Ⓐ Ⓑ Ⓒ Ⓓ Ⓔ 5. Ⓐ Ⓑ Ⓒ Ⓓ Ⓔ

Instrument Comprehension

1. Ⓐ Ⓑ Ⓒ Ⓓ 2. Ⓐ Ⓑ Ⓒ Ⓓ 3. Ⓐ Ⓑ Ⓒ Ⓓ 4. Ⓐ Ⓑ Ⓒ Ⓓ 5. Ⓐ Ⓑ Ⓒ Ⓓ 6. Ⓐ Ⓑ Ⓒ Ⓓ Ⓔ 7. Ⓐ Ⓑ Ⓒ Ⓓ Ⓔ 8. Ⓐ Ⓑ Ⓒ Ⓓ Ⓔ 9. Ⓐ Ⓑ Ⓒ Ⓓ Ⓔ 10. Ⓐ Ⓑ Ⓒ Ⓓ Ⓔ

Block Counting

1. Ⓐ Ⓑ Ⓒ Ⓓ Ⓔ 2. Ⓐ Ⓑ Ⓒ Ⓓ Ⓔ 3. Ⓐ Ⓑ Ⓒ Ⓓ Ⓔ 4. Ⓐ Ⓑ Ⓒ Ⓓ Ⓔ 5. Ⓐ Ⓑ Ⓒ Ⓓ Ⓔ 6. Ⓐ Ⓑ Ⓒ Ⓓ Ⓔ 7. Ⓐ Ⓑ Ⓒ Ⓓ Ⓔ 8. Ⓐ Ⓑ Ⓒ Ⓓ Ⓔ 9. Ⓐ Ⓑ Ⓒ Ⓓ Ⓔ 10. Ⓐ Ⓑ Ⓒ Ⓓ Ⓔ

Table Reading

1. Ⓐ Ⓑ Ⓒ Ⓓ Ⓔ 2. Ⓐ Ⓑ Ⓒ Ⓓ Ⓔ 3. Ⓐ Ⓑ Ⓒ Ⓓ Ⓔ 4. Ⓐ Ⓑ Ⓒ Ⓓ Ⓔ 5. Ⓐ Ⓑ Ⓒ Ⓓ Ⓔ

Aviation Information

1. Ⓐ Ⓑ Ⓒ Ⓓ Ⓔ	6. Ⓐ Ⓑ Ⓒ Ⓓ Ⓔ	11. Ⓐ Ⓑ Ⓒ Ⓓ Ⓔ	16. Ⓐ Ⓑ Ⓒ Ⓓ Ⓔ	21. Ⓐ Ⓑ Ⓒ Ⓓ Ⓔ
2. Ⓐ Ⓑ Ⓒ Ⓓ Ⓔ	7. Ⓐ Ⓑ Ⓒ Ⓓ Ⓔ	12. Ⓐ Ⓑ Ⓒ Ⓓ Ⓔ	17. Ⓐ Ⓑ Ⓒ Ⓓ Ⓔ	22. Ⓐ Ⓑ Ⓒ Ⓓ Ⓔ
3. Ⓐ Ⓑ Ⓒ Ⓓ Ⓔ	8. Ⓐ Ⓑ Ⓒ Ⓓ Ⓔ	13. Ⓐ Ⓑ Ⓒ Ⓓ Ⓔ	18. Ⓐ Ⓑ Ⓒ Ⓓ Ⓔ	23. Ⓐ Ⓑ Ⓒ Ⓓ Ⓔ
4. Ⓐ Ⓑ Ⓒ Ⓓ Ⓔ	9. Ⓐ Ⓑ Ⓒ Ⓓ Ⓔ	14. Ⓐ Ⓑ Ⓒ Ⓓ Ⓔ	19. Ⓐ Ⓑ Ⓒ Ⓓ Ⓔ	24. Ⓐ Ⓑ Ⓒ Ⓓ Ⓔ
5. Ⓐ Ⓑ Ⓒ Ⓓ Ⓔ	10. Ⓐ Ⓑ Ⓒ Ⓓ Ⓔ	15. Ⓐ Ⓑ Ⓒ Ⓓ Ⓔ	20. Ⓐ Ⓑ Ⓒ Ⓓ Ⓔ	25. Ⓐ Ⓑ Ⓒ Ⓓ Ⓔ

Nautical Information

1. Ⓐ Ⓑ Ⓒ Ⓓ Ⓔ	7. Ⓐ Ⓑ Ⓒ Ⓓ Ⓔ	13. Ⓐ Ⓑ Ⓒ Ⓓ Ⓔ	19. Ⓐ Ⓑ Ⓒ Ⓓ Ⓔ	25. Ⓐ Ⓑ Ⓒ Ⓓ Ⓔ
2. Ⓐ Ⓑ Ⓒ Ⓓ Ⓔ	8. Ⓐ Ⓑ Ⓒ Ⓓ Ⓔ	14. Ⓐ Ⓑ Ⓒ Ⓓ Ⓔ	20. Ⓐ Ⓑ Ⓒ Ⓓ Ⓔ	26. Ⓐ Ⓑ Ⓒ
3. Ⓐ Ⓑ Ⓒ Ⓓ Ⓔ	9. Ⓐ Ⓑ Ⓒ Ⓓ Ⓔ	15. Ⓐ Ⓑ Ⓒ Ⓓ Ⓔ	21. Ⓐ Ⓑ Ⓒ Ⓓ Ⓔ	27. Ⓐ Ⓑ Ⓒ
4. Ⓐ Ⓑ Ⓒ Ⓓ Ⓔ	10. Ⓐ Ⓑ Ⓒ Ⓓ Ⓔ	16. Ⓐ Ⓑ Ⓒ Ⓓ Ⓔ	22. Ⓐ Ⓑ Ⓒ Ⓓ Ⓔ	28. Ⓐ Ⓑ Ⓒ
5. Ⓐ Ⓑ Ⓒ Ⓓ Ⓔ	11. Ⓐ Ⓑ Ⓒ Ⓓ Ⓔ	17. Ⓐ Ⓑ Ⓒ Ⓓ Ⓔ	23. Ⓐ Ⓑ Ⓒ Ⓓ Ⓔ	29. Ⓐ Ⓑ Ⓒ
6. Ⓐ Ⓑ Ⓒ Ⓓ Ⓔ	12. Ⓐ Ⓑ Ⓒ Ⓓ Ⓔ	18. Ⓐ Ⓑ Ⓒ Ⓓ Ⓔ	24. Ⓐ Ⓑ Ⓒ Ⓓ Ⓔ	30. Ⓐ Ⓑ Ⓒ

Rotated Blocks

1. Ⓐ Ⓑ Ⓒ Ⓓ Ⓔ 2. Ⓐ Ⓑ Ⓒ Ⓓ Ⓔ 3. Ⓐ Ⓑ Ⓒ Ⓓ Ⓔ 4. Ⓐ Ⓑ Ⓒ Ⓓ Ⓔ 5. Ⓐ Ⓑ Ⓒ Ⓓ Ⓔ

General Science

1. Ⓐ Ⓑ Ⓒ Ⓓ Ⓔ 2. Ⓐ Ⓑ Ⓒ Ⓓ Ⓔ 3. Ⓐ Ⓑ Ⓒ Ⓓ Ⓔ 4. Ⓐ Ⓑ Ⓒ Ⓓ Ⓔ 5. Ⓐ Ⓑ Ⓒ Ⓓ Ⓔ

Hidden Figures

1. Ⓐ Ⓑ Ⓒ Ⓓ Ⓔ 2. Ⓐ Ⓑ Ⓒ Ⓓ Ⓔ 3. Ⓐ Ⓑ Ⓒ Ⓓ Ⓔ 4. Ⓐ Ⓑ Ⓒ Ⓓ Ⓔ 5. Ⓐ Ⓑ Ⓒ Ⓓ Ⓔ

Complex Movements

1. Ⓐ Ⓑ Ⓒ Ⓓ Ⓔ 2. Ⓐ Ⓑ Ⓒ Ⓓ Ⓔ 3. Ⓐ Ⓑ Ⓒ Ⓓ Ⓔ 4. Ⓐ Ⓑ Ⓒ Ⓓ Ⓔ 5. Ⓐ Ⓑ Ⓒ Ⓓ Ⓔ

Cyclic Orientation

1. 2. 3. 4. 5.

Spatial Apperception

1. Ⓐ Ⓑ Ⓒ Ⓓ Ⓔ 2. Ⓐ Ⓑ Ⓒ Ⓓ Ⓔ 3. Ⓐ Ⓑ Ⓒ Ⓓ Ⓔ 4. Ⓐ Ⓑ Ⓒ Ⓓ Ⓔ 5. Ⓐ Ⓑ Ⓒ Ⓓ Ⓔ

THE KINDS OF QUESTIONS YOU'LL BE ASKED

Verbal ability is an important communication skill. Testing for such ability is one of the best measures for predicting academic and vocational success, particularly for positions of leadership. Tests of verbal ability generally consist of synonym and/or antonym questions to measure word knowledge, verbal analogies to measure verbal reasoning, and skill and reading comprehension to measure ability to understand written communication.

Synonyms

Synonym questions appear in Subtest 5, Word Knowledge, of the Air Force Officer Qualifying Test; however, this subtest is not used in constructing the pilot or the navigator-technical composite. Synonym questions are also found in one of the ASVAB tests (Word Knowledge) that make up the general technical (GT) score used in screening active-duty enlisted service members of any branch of the Armed Forces who wish to enter the Army Warrant Officer Flight Training Program.

Synonyms are commonly used to measure breadth of vocabulary. For each word given (usually capitalized, underlined, or in italics), you are required to select from among the five options the one that is the same or most nearly the same in meaning. The usual dictionary definition is required when only the word is given. If the word appears in a sentence, the meaning of the word as used in the sentence is necessary.

Consider all options before answering the question. Although several options may have some connection with the key word, the correct answer is the one that is closest in meaning to the key word.

Sample Items:

SUCCUMB means most nearly to

(A) aid
(B) be discouraged
(C) check
(D) oppose
(E) yield

To *succumb* means "to cease to resist before a superior strength or overpowering desire or force." Option (D) indicates the stage prior to succumbing. Options (A) and (C) are unrelated in meaning. Option (B) is only remotely related in the sense that one who succumbs may be discouraged. Option (E) is the only one that means almost the same as *succumb.*

SUBSUME means most nearly to

(A) belong
(B) cover
(C) include
(D) obliterate
(E) understate

To *subsume* is "to include within a larger class or category." Options (A), (B), and (D) are somewhat related since an element included within a larger class or category may be said to belong to it, to be covered by it, or to be obliterated by it. Option (E) is completely unrelated in meaning.

Of all the options given, (C) is closest in meaning to *subsume.*

Practice items *1* to *5* follow. For each question, select the best answer and then, in the space on the Answer Sheet on page 55 numbered the same as the question, blacken the circle with the same letter as your answer.

Use a soft (No. 2) pencil to mark your answers. If you wish to change an answer, erase it thoroughly and then mark the new answer.

Use the correct answers and rationale that appear on page 126 to help you determine your score, as well as to enable you to review those questions you did not answer correctly or of which you are uncertain.

Practice Items

Each of the following five questions consists of a word in capital letters followed by five suggested meanings of the word. For each question, select the word or phrase that means most nearly the same as the word in capital letters.

1. ANOMALOUS

(A) disgraceful
(B) formless
(C) irregular
(D) threatening
(E) unknown

2. CREDENCE

(A) belief
(B) claim
(C) payment
(D) surprise
(E) understanding

3. FORTUITOUS

(A) accidental
(B) conclusive
(C) courageous
(D) prosperous
(E) severe

4. MALIGN

(A) disturb
(B) mislead
(C) praise
(D) provoke
(E) slander

5. PERMEABLE

(A) flexible
(B) penetrable
(C) soluble
(D) variable
(E) volatile

Each of the following five questions has an underlined word. You are to decide which one of the five choices most nearly means the same as the underlined word.

6. The packages were kept in a <u>secure</u> place.

(A) distant
(B) safe
(C) convenient
(D) secret
(E) obscure

7. The benefits of the plan are likely to be <u>transitory</u>.

(A) significant
(B) obvious
(C) temporary
(D) cumulative
(E) encouraging

8. It is my <u>conviction</u> that you are wrong.

(A) guilt
(B) imagination
(C) firm belief
(D) fault
(E) vague recollection

9. The hikers found several <u>crevices</u> in the rocks

(A) plants
(B) minerals
(C) uneven spots
(D) puddles
(E) cracks

10. The parent <u>consoled</u> the child.

(A) found
(B) scolded
(C) carried home
(D) comforted
(E) bathed

Verbal Analogies

Verbal analogy questions appear in Subtest 1, Verbal Analogies, of the Air Force Officer Qualifying Test. This subtest is used in constructing the pilot composite.

Verbal analogy questions test not only your knowledge of word meanings and your vocabulary level, but also your ability to reason—that is, to see the relationships between words and the ideas they represent. To determine such relationships, you must know the meaning of each word of the first given pair. Then, you must figure out the precise relationship between these two words. Finally, you must complete the analogy by selecting the pair of words that best expresses a relationship similar to that expressed by the first two paired words.

There are two forms of verbal analogy questions in general use. These are:

1. The first pair of words and the first word of the second pair are given in the stem of the question. This is followed by options, only one of which best expresses a relationship similar to that expressed by the first two paired words.

MAN is to BOY as WOMAN is to

(A) baby
(B) bride
(C) child
(D) girl
(E) lad

2. Only the first pair of words appears in the stem of the question. It is followed by options, each consisting of a pair of words.

MAN is to BOY as

(A) adult is to girl
(B) bride is to groom
(C) lass is to child
(D) woman is to youth
(E) woman is to girl

Let us analyze the first analogy form.

What is the relationship of the first two paired words?

MAN—member of the human race, male, mature
BOY—member of the human race, male, young

Both are male members of the human race. MAN is mature; BOY is young.

What is the meaning of the word WOMAN and each of the words appearing in the options?

WOMAN—member of the human race, female, mature
"baby"—member of the human race, either male or female, very young
"bride"—member of the human race, female, about to be married or newly married
"child"—member of the human race, either male or female, young
"girl"—member of the human race, female, young
"lad"—member of the human race, male, young

To complete the analogy with WOMAN as the first word, we need a term denoting a young, female member of the human race.

Option (A) is incorrect, as "baby" may be male or female and is very young. Option (B) is incorrect, as "bride" is a special kind of female—one about to be married or newly married. If GROOM had been substituted for BOY in the first half of the analogy, then "bride" would have been the proper choice. Option (C) is incorrect, as "child" may be male or female. Option (E) is incorrect, as "lad" is a male.

Option (D) is the correct choice, as "girl" denotes a young, female member of the human race.

The most common analogy relationships are listed below.

Relationship	Example
synonyms	plot : conspire
antonyms	victory : defeat
homonyms	hale : hail
measurement (time, distance, weight, volume, etc.)	distance : mile
location (in, at, near)	Boston : Massachusetts
numerical	ten : dime
cause : effect	burn : blister
whole : part	ship : keel
object : purpose or function	pencil : write
object : user	saw : carpenter
creator : creation	composer : opera
raw material : final product	cotton : dress
female : male	goose : gander
general : specific	fruit : apple
larger : smaller	river : stream
more : less (degree)	hot : warm
early stage : later stage	larva : pupa

Grammatical Relationships

NOUN	
singular : plural	child : children
PRONOUN	
singular : plural	she : they
nominative : objective	he : him
first person : third person	we : they

VERB	
tense	fly : flown
ADJECTIVE	
comparative	bad : worse
superlative	little : least
DIFFERENT PARTS OF SPEECH	
noun : adjective	dog : canine
adjective : adverb	good : well

Be careful! The order of the two words in the second pair must be in the same sequence as the order of words in the first pair. As in mathematical proportions, reversing the sequence of the members of the second pair breaks the relationship and destroys the analogy.

2 is to 5 as 4 is to 10 (correct)
2 is to 5 as 10 is to 4 (incorrect)
MAN is to BOY as WOMAN is to GIRL (correct)
MAN is to BOY as GIRL is to WOMAN (incorrect)

Practice items 1 to 5 follow. For each question, choose the answer that best completes the analogy and then, in the correspondingly numbered space on the answer sheet, blacken the circle with the same letter as your answer.

Use a soft (No. 2) pencil to mark your answers. If you wish to change an answer, erase it thoroughly and then mark the new answer.

Use the correct answers and rationale that appear on page 126 to help you determine your score, as well as to enable you to review those questions which you did not answer correctly or of which you are unsure.

Practice Items

Each of the following five questions consists of an incomplete analogy. Select the answer that best completes the analogy developed by the first two words of each question.

1. BOTANY is to PLANTS as ENTOMOLOGY is to

   (A) animals
   (B) climate
   (C) diseases
   (D) languages
   (E) insects

2. EPILOGUE is to PROLOGUE as

   (A) appendix is to index
   (B) appendix is to preface
   (C) preface is to footnote
   (D) preface is to table of contents
   (E) table of contents is to index

3. OCTAGON is to SQUARE as HEXAGON is to

   (A) cube
   (B) military
   (C) pyramid
   (D) rectangle
   (E) triangle

4. GLOW is to BLAZE as

   (A) compact is to sprawling
   (B) eager is to reluctant
   (C) glance is to stare
   (D) hint is to clue
   (E) wicked is to naughty

5. WATER is to THIRST as FOOD is to

   (A) famine
   (B) grief
   (C) hunger
   (D) indigestion
   (E) scarcity

Reading Comprehension

Reading comprehension questions appear as five-option items in Subtest 3, Reading Comprehension, of the Air Force Officer Qualifying Test; however, this subtest is not used in constructing the pilot or the navigator-technical composite. Reading comprehension questions are also found as four-option items in one of the ASVAB tests (Paragraph Comprehension) that make up the general technical (GT) score used in screening active-duty enlisted service members of all branches of the Armed Forces who wish to enter the Army Warrant Officer Flight Training Program.

Reading comprehension questions (Sentence Comprehension) also appear as four-option items in the Math/Verbal Test of the Navy and Marine Corps Aviation Selection Test Battery.

The ability to read and understand written or printed material is an important verbal skill. Reading comprehension tests present reading passages that vary in length from one sentence to several paragraphs, followed by one or more questions about each passage. The reading selections are usually samples of the type of material that you would be required to read, whether at school or on the job.

Following are some of the common types of reading comprehension items:

1. Finding specific information or directly stated detail in the reading passage.

Although this type is commonly found in elementary-level tests, it is also found in intermediate-level tests such as the Armed Services Vocational Aptitude Battery and in advanced-level tests such as the Air Force Officer Qualifying Test. At the intermediate and advanced levels, the vocabulary is more difficult, the reading passages are of greater complexity, and the questions posed are much more complicated.

Samples:

Helping to prevent accidents is the responsibility of ____.
The principal reason for issuing traffic summonses is to ____.
The reason for maintaining ongoing safety education is that ____.

2. *Recognizing the central theme, the main idea, or concept expressed in the passage.*

Although questions of this type may be phrased in different ways, they generally require that you summarize or otherwise ascertain the principal purpose or idea expressed in the reading passage. In addition to reading and understanding, ability to analyze and interpret written material is necessary. Some questions require the ability to combine separate ideas or concepts found in the reading passage to reach the correct answer. Other questions merely require drawing a conclusion that is equivalent to a restatement of the main idea or concept expressed in the passage.

Samples:

The most appropriate title for the above passage is _____.
The best title for this paragraph would be _____.
This paragraph is mainly about _____.
The passage best supports the statement that _____.
The passage means most nearly that _____.

3. *Determining the meaning of certain words as used in context.*

The particular meaning of a word as actually used in the passage requires an understanding of the central or main theme of the reading passage, as well as the thought being conveyed by the sentence containing the word in question.

Samples:

The word "......" as used in this passage means _____.
The expression "......" as used in the passage means _____.

4. *Finding implications or drawing inferences from a stated idea.*

This type of item requires the ability to understand the stated idea and then to reason by logical thinking to the implied or inferred idea. *Implied* means not exactly stated but merely suggested; *inferred* means derived by reasoning. Although the terms are somewhat similar in meaning, *inferred* implies being further removed from the stated idea. Much greater reasoning ability is required to arrive at the proper inference. Accordingly, inference items are used principally at the advanced level.

Samples:

Which of the following is implied by the above passage?
Of the following, the most valid implication of the above paragraph is _____.
The author probably believes that _____.
It can be inferred from the above passage that _____.
The best of the following inferences which can be made is that _____.

5. *Sentence-completion items.*

Sentence-completion items are considered to be both vocabulary items and reading comprehension items. They are considered to be vocabulary items because they test for the ability to understand and use words. However, they also measure an important phase of reading comprehension—the ability to understand the implications of a sentence or a paragraph.

Sentence-completion items consist of a sentence or paragraph in which one or two words are missing. The omissions are indicated by a blank underlined space (_____). You must read and understand the sentence or paragraph as given and then select the option that best completes the thought in the reading passage. Your choice must also be consistent in style and logic with other elements in the sentence.

Sample:

Select the lettered option that best completes the thought expressed in the sentence.

6. *Word-substitution items.*

Word-substitution items are very similar to sentence-completion items and are also considered to be both vocabulary and reading comprehension items. These items consist of a sentence or paragraph in which a key word has been changed. The changed word is incorrect and it is not in keeping with the meaning that the sentence is intended to convey. You must determine which word is incorrectly used and then select from the options given the word which when substituted for the incorrectly used word helps best to convey the meaning the sentence or paragraph is intended to convey.

General Suggestions for Answering Reading Comprehension Questions

1. Scan the passage to get the general intent of the reading selection.
2. Read the passage carefully to understand the main idea and any related ideas. If necessary for comprehension, reread the passage.
3. Read each question carefully and base your answer on the material given in the reading passage. Be careful to base your answer on what is stated, implied, or inferred. Do not be influenced by your opinions, personal feelings, or any information not expressed or implied in the reading passage.
4. Options that are partly true and partly false are incorrect.
5. Be very observant for such words as *least, greatest, first, not*, and so on, appearing in the preamble of the question.
6. Be suspicious of options containing words such as *all, always, every, forever, never, none, wholly*, and so on.
7. Be sure to consider all choices given for the question before selecting your answer.
8. Speed is an important consideration in answering reading comprehension questions. Try to proceed as rapidly as you can without sacrificing careful thinking or reasoning.

Paragraph Comprehension

Sample Items (5 options):

For each of the following sample five-option questions, select the option that best completes the statement or answers the question.

1. The rates of vibration perceived by the ears as musical tones lie between fairly well-defined limits. In the ear, as in the eye, there are individual variations. However, variations are more marked in the ear, since its range of perception is greater.

   The paragraph best supports the statement that the ear

   (A) is limited by the nature of its variations
   (B) is the most sensitive of the auditory organs
   (C) differs from the eye in its broader range of perception
   (D) is sensitive to a great range of musical tones
   (E) depends for its sense on the rate of vibration of a limited range of sound waves

The passage makes the point that individual differences in auditory range are greater than individual differences in visual range because the total range of auditory perception is greater. Although the statements made by options (D) and (E) are both correct, neither expresses the main point of the reading passage. Option (C) is the correct answer.

2. The propaganda of a nation at war is designed to stimulate the energy of its citizens and their will to win, and to imbue them with an overwhelming sense of the justice of their cause.

Directed abroad, its purpose is to create precisely contrary effects among citizens of enemy nations and to assure to nationals of allied or subjugated countries full and unwavering assistance.

The title below that best expresses the ideas of this passage is

(A) Propaganda's Failure
(B) Designs for Waging War
(C) Influencing Opinion in Wartime
(D) The Propaganda of Other Nations
(E) Citizens of Enemy Nations and Their Allies

The theme of this passage is influencing opinion in wartime, both at home and abroad. Option (C) is the correct answer.

Answer the following two sample questions on the basis of the information contained in the passage below.

I have heard it suggested that the "upper class" English accent has been of value in maintaining the British Empire and Commonwealth. The argument runs that all manner of folk in distant places, understanding the English language, will catch in this accent the notes of tradition, pride, and authority and so will be suitably impressed. This might have been the case some nine or ten decades ago but it is certainly not true now. The accent is more likely to be a liability than an asset.

3. The title below that best expresses the ideas of this passage is

(A) Changed Effects of a "British Accent"
(B) Prevention of the Spread of Cockney
(C) The Affected Language of Royalty
(D) The Decline of the British Empire
(E) The "King's English"

4. According to the author, the "upper class" English accent

(A) has been imitated all over the world
(B) has been inspired by British royalty
(C) has brought about the destruction of the British Commonwealth
(D) may have caused arguments among the folk in distant corners of the Empire
(E) may have helped to perpetuate the British Empire before 1900

In sample question 3, the last two sentences of the reading passage indicate that the folk in distant places might have been suitably impressed decades ago, but they're not now. Option (A) is the correct answer.

In sample question 4, the "upper class" English accent might have been of value in maintaining the British Empire nine or ten decades ago (or before 1900). Option (E) is the correct answer.

Sample Items (4 options):

For each of the following sample four-option questions, select the option that best completes the statement or answers the question.

5. The view is widely held that butter is more digestible and better absorbed than other fats because of its low melting point. There is little scientific authority for such a view. As margarine is made today, its melting point is close to that of butter, and tests show only the slightest degree of difference in digestibility of fats of equally low melting points.

The paragraph best supports the statement that

(A) butter is more easily digested than margarine
(B) the concept that butter has a lower melting point than other fats is a common misconception, disproved by scientists
(C) there is not much difference in the digestibility of butter and margarine
(D) most people prefer butter to margarine

The passage states that the melting points of butter and margarine are similar and that therefore they are about equally digestible. Option (C) is the correct answer.

Answer the following two sample questions on the basis of the information contained in the passage below.

Science made its first great contribution to war with gunpowder. But since gunpowder can be used effectively only in suitable firearms, science also had to develop the iron and steel that were required to manufacture muskets and cannon on a huge scale. To this day metallurgy receives much inspiration from war. Bessemer steel was the direct outcome of the deficiencies of artillery as they were revealed by the Crimean War. Concern with the expansion and pressure of gases in guns and combustibility of powder aroused interest in the laws of gases and other matters which seemingly have no relation whatever to war.

6. The title below that best expresses the ideas of this passage is

   (A) Gunpowder, the First Great Invention
   (B) How War Stimulates Science
   (C) Improvement of Artillery
   (D) The Crimean War and Science

7. An outcome of the Crimean War was the

   (A) invention of gunpowder
   (B) origin of metallurgy
   (C) study of the laws of gases
   (D) use of muskets and cannon

In sample question 6, the basic theme of the reading passage is that science contributes to the war effort and that war stimulates science research. Option (B) is the correct answer.

In sample question 7, the last sentence in the reading passage indicates that interest in the laws of gases arose as a direct outcome of artillery deficiencies revealed by the Crimean War. Option (C) is the correct answer.

8. We find many instances in early science of "a priori" scientific reasoning. Scientists thought it proper to carry generalizations from one field to another. It was assumed that the planets revolved in circles because of the geometrical simplicity of the circle. Even Newton assumed that there must be seven primary colors corresponding to the seven tones of the musical scale.

   The paragraph best supports the statement that

   (A) Newton sometimes used the "a priori" method of investigation
   (B) scientists no longer consider it proper to uncritically carry over generalizations from one field to another
   (C) the planets revolve about the earth in ellipses rather than in circles
   (D) even great men like Newton sometimes make mistakes

The tone of the passage and the choice of illustrations showing the fallacy of "a priori" reasoning make it evident that scientists no longer carry generalizations automatically from one field to another. Options (A) and (D) are true statements, but they are only illustrative points. Option (B) carries the real message of the passage and is the correct answer.

Sentence Comprehension

Sample Items (5 options):

Sample question 9 consists of a sentence with a blank space indicating that a word has been omitted. Beneath the sentence are five lettered options. Select the option which, when inserted in the sentence, best fits in with the meaning of the sentence as a whole.

9. If the weather report forecasts fog and smoke, we can anticipate having _____.

   (A) rain
   (B) sleet
   (C) smog
   (D) snow
   (E) thunder

A mixture of fog and smoke is called smog. Option (C) is the correct answer.

Sample question 10 consists of a sentence with two blank spaces, each blank indicating that a word has been omitted. Beneath the sentence are five lettered sets of words. Choose the set of words which, when inserted in the sentence, best fits in with the meaning of the sentence as a whole.

10. Although the publicity has been _____ the film itself is intelligent, well-acted, handsomely produced, and altogether _____.

   (A) extensive . . arbitrary
   (B) tasteless . . respectable
   (C) sophisticated . . amateurish
   (D) risquè . . crude
   (E) perfect . . spectacular

The correct answer should involve two words that are more or less opposite in meaning, as the word *although* suggests that the publicity misrepresented the film. Another clue to the correct answer is that the second word should fit in context with the words "intelligent, well-acted, handsomely produced." Choices (A), (D), and (E) are not opposites. Choice (C) cannot be the correct answer even though the words in it are nearly opposites, because if the film is intelligent, well-acted, and handsomely produced, it is not amateurish. Also, only choice (B), when inserted in the sentence, produces a logical statement. Choice (B) is the correct answer.

Sample question 11 consists of a quotation that contains one word that is incorrectly used; it is not in keeping with the meaning that the quotation is intended to convey. Determine which word is incorrectly used. Then select from the lettered options the word which, when substituted for the incorrectly used word, would best help to convey the intended meaning of the quotation.

11. "College placement officials have frequently noted the contradiction which exists between the public statements of the company president who questions the value of a liberal arts background in the business world and the practice of his recruiters who seek specialized training for particular jobs."

    (A) admissions
    (B) praises
    (C) reject
    (D) science
    (E) technical

A careful reading of the passage shows no inconsistency until the word *questions* is reached. If a contradiction exists and the recruiters seek specialized training, the company president would accept, endorse, or praise rather than question the value of a liberal arts background. Option (B) appears to be the proper substitute which would best convey the intended meaning of the quotation. *Contradiction* is used properly, as none of the options can be substituted for it. Although *reject* may appear to be an appropriate substitution for *seek*, it does not help convey the intended meaning of the quotation. Option (B) is the only correct answer.

Sample question 12 consists of a sentence in which one word is omitted. Select the lettered option which best completes the thought expressed in the sentence.

12. Although her argument was logical, her conclusion was _____.

    (A) illegible
    (B) natural
    (C) positive
    (D) unreasonable

When a subordinate clause begins with *although*, the thought expressed in the main clause will not be consistent with that contained in the subordinate clause. If the argument was *logical*, the conclusion would be illogical. Of the options given, *unreasonable* is the only opposite to logical. Option (D) is therefore the correct answer.

Sample question 13 consists of a sentence with two blank spaces, each blank indicating that a word or figure has been omitted. Select one of the lettered options which, when inserted in the sentence, best completes the thought expressed in the sentence as a whole.

13. The desire for peace should not be equated with _____, for _____ peace can be maintained only by brave people.

    (A) intelligence . . ignoble
    (B) bravery . . stable
    (C) cowardice . . lasting
    (D) neutrality . . apathetic

The word *not* indicates a shift in a meaning between the two parts of the sentence: If peace can be maintained only by the brave, the desire for peace cannot be equated with *cowardice*. Option (C) is the correct answer.

Sample question 14 consists of a quotation which contains one word that is incorrectly used, because it is not in keeping with the meaning that the quotation is intended to convey. Determine which word is incorrectly used. Then select from the lettered options the word which, when substituted for the incorrectly used word, would best help to convey the intended meaning of the quotation.

14. "In manufacturing a fabric-measuring device, it is advisable to use a type of cloth whose length is highly susceptible to changes of temperature, tension, etc."

    (A) decreases
    (B) increases
    (C) instrument
    (D) not

A careful reading of the passage shows no inconsistency until the word *highly* is reached. To give a true measure, the device's length should not change with temperature or tension but should be constant. Option (D) is the only correct answer.

For sample question 15, select the option that best completes the statement or answers the question.

15. "Look before you leap."

    The passage means most nearly that you should

    (A) always be alert
    (B) always be cautious
    (C) move quickly but carefully
    (D) proceed rapidly when directed

This proverb does not state or imply that you should always be alert or cautious, or that you should proceed quickly when directed It directs that you should proceed rapidly but cautiously. Option (C) is the correct answer.

Practice Items

Questions *1* to *5* are five-option items. For each question, select the option that best completes the statement or answers the question. Answers are on page 126.

1. The mental attitude of the employee toward safety is exceedingly important in preventing accidents. All efforts designed to keep safety on the employee's mind and to keep accident prevention a live subject in the office will help substantially in a safety program. Although it may seem strange, it is common for people to be careless. Therefore, safety education is a continuous process.

   The reason given in the above passage for maintaining ongoing safety education is that

   (A) employees must be told to stay alert at all times
   (B) office tasks are often dangerous
   (C) people are often careless
   (D) safety rules change frequently
   (E) safety rules change infrequently

2. One goal of law enforcement is the reduction of stress between one population group and another. When no stress exists between population groups, law enforcement can deal with other tensions or simply perform traditional police functions. However, when stress between population groups does exist, law enforcement, in its efforts to prevent disruptive behavior, becomes committed to reduce that stress.

   According to the above passage, during times of stress between population groups in the community, it is necessary for law enforcement to attempt to

   (A) continue traditional police functions
   (B) eliminate tension resulting from social change
   (C) punish disruptive behavior
   (D) reduce intergroup stress
   (E) warn disruptive individuals

Answer questions *3* through *5* on the basis of the information contained in the following passage.

Microwave ovens use a principle of heating different from that employed by ordinary ovens. The key part of a microwave oven is its magnetron, which generates the microwaves that then go into the oven. Some of these energy waves hit the food directly, while others bounce around the oven until they find their way into the food. Sometimes the microwaves intersect, strengthening their effect. Sometimes they cancel each other out. Parts of the food may be heavily saturated with energy, while other parts may receive very little. In conventional cooking, you select the oven temperature. In microwave cooking, you select the power level. The walls of the microwave oven are made of metal, which helps the microwaves bounce off them. However, this turns to a disadvantage for the cook who uses metal cookware.

3. Based on the information contained in this passage, it is easy to see some advantages and disadvantages of microwave ovens. The greatest disadvantage would probably be

   (A) overcooked food
   (B) radioactive food
   (C) unevenly cooked food
   (D) the high cost of preparing food
   (E) cold food

4. In a conventional oven, the temperature selection would be based upon degrees. In a microwave oven, the power selection would probably be based upon

   (A) wattage
   (B) voltage
   (C) lumens
   (D) solar units
   (E) ohms

5. The source of the microwaves in the oven is

   (A) reflected energy
   (B) convection currents
   (C) the magnetron
   (D) short waves and bursts of energy
   (E) the food itself

Questions *6* to *10* are four-option items. Read the paragraph(s) and select one of the lettered choices that best completes the statement or answers the question.

6. Few drivers realize that steel is used to keep the road surface flat in spite of the weight of buses and trucks. Steel bars, deeply embedded in the concrete, are sinews to take the stresses so that the stresses cannot crack the slab or make it wavy.

   The passage best supports the statement that a concrete road

   (A) is expensive to build
   (B) usually cracks under heavy weights
   (C) looks like any other road
   (D) is reinforced with other material

7. Blood pressure, the force that the blood exerts against the walls of the vessels through which it flows, is commonly meant to be the pressure in the arteries. The pressure in the arteries varies with contraction (work period) and the relaxation (rest period) of the heart. When the heart contracts, the blood in the arteries is at its greatest, or systolic, pressure. When the heart relaxes, the blood in the arteries is at its lowest, or diastolic, pressure. The difference between the two pressures is called the pulse pressure.

   According to the passage, which one of the following statements is most accurate?

   (A) The blood in the arteries is at its greatest pressure during contraction.
   (B) Systolic pressure measures the blood in the arteries when the heart is relaxed.
   (C) The difference between systolic and diastolic pressure determines the blood pressure.
   (D) Pulse pressure is the same as blood pressure.

Questions *8* to *10* are based on the passage below.

Arsonists are persons who set fires deliberately. They don't look like criminals, but they cost the nation millions of dollars in property loss and sometimes loss of life. Arsonists set fires for many different reasons. Sometimes a shopkeeper sees no way out of losing his business and sets fire to it to collect the insurance. Another type of arsonist wants revenge and sets fire to the home or shop of someone he feels has treated him unfairly. Some arsonists just like the excitement of seeing the fire burn and watching the firefighters at work; arsonists of this type have been known to help fight the fire.

8. According to the passage above, an arsonist is a person who

   (A) intentionally sets a fire
   (B) enjoys watching fires
   (C) wants revenge
   (D) needs money

9. Arsonists have been known to help fight fires because they

   (A) felt guilty
   (B) enjoyed the excitement
   (C) wanted to earn money
   (D) didn't want anyone hurt

10. According to the passage above, we may conclude that arsonists

    (A) would make good firefighters
    (B) are not criminals
    (C) are mentally ill
    (D) are not all alike

Questions *11* to *20* are four-option items.

Each of questions *11* to *14* consists of a sentence in which one word is omitted. Select the lettered option which best completes the thought expressed in each sentence.

11. The explanation by the teacher was so _____ that the students solved the problem with ease.

    (A) complicated
    (B) explicit
    (C) protracted
    (D) vague

12. A(n) _____ listener can distinguish fact from fiction.

    (A) astute
    (B) ingenuous
    (C) prejudiced
    (D) reluctant

13. Since corn is _____ to the region, it is not expensive.

    (A) alien
    (B) exotic
    (C) indigenous
    (D) indigent

14. Our colleague was so _____ that we could not convince him that he was wrong.

    (A) capitulating
    (B) complaisant
    (C) light-hearted
    (D) obdurate

Each of questions 15 to 17 consists of a sentence with two blank spaces, each blank indicating that a word or figure has been omitted. Select one of the lettered options which, when inserted in the sentence, best completes the thought expressed in the sentence as a whole.

15. He is rather _____ and, therefore, easily _____.

    (A) caustic . . hurt
    (B) dangerous . . noticed
    (C) immature . . deceived
    (D) worldly . . misunderstood

16. _____ education was instituted for the purpose of preventing _____ of young children, and guaranteeing them a minimum of education.

    (A) Compulsory . . exploitation
    (B) Free . . abuse
    (C) Kindergarten . . ignorance
    (D) Secondary . . delinquency

17. Any person who is in _____ while awaiting trial is considered _____ until he or she has been declared guilty.

    (A) custody . . innocent
    (B) jail . . suspect
    (C) jeopardy . . suspicious
    (D) prison . . rehabilitated

Each of questions 18 to 20 consists of a quotation which contains one word that is incorrectly used, because it is not in keeping with the meaning that the quotation is evidently intended to convey. Determine which word is incorrectly used. Then select from the lettered options the word which, when substituted for the incorrectly used word, would best help to convey the intended meaning of the quotation.

18. "Under a good personnel policy, the number of employee complaints and grievances will tend to be a number which is sufficiently great to keep the supervisory force on its toes and yet large enough to leave time for other phases of supervision."

    (A) complete
    (B) definite
    (C) limit
    (D) small

19. "One of the important assets of a democracy is an active, energetic local government, meeting local needs and giving an immediate opportunity to legislators to participate in their own public affairs."

    (A) citizens
    (B) convenient
    (C) local
    (D) officials

20. "The cost of wholesale food distribution in large urban centers is related to the cost of food to ultimate consumers, because they cannot pay for any added distribution costs."

    (A) eventually
    (B) sales
    (C) some
    (D) unrelated

Arithmetic Reasoning

Arithmetic reasoning questions appear in Subtest 2, Arithmetic Reasoning, of the Air Force Officer Qualifying Test. This subtest is used in constructing the navigator-technical composite. Arithmetic reasoning questions also appear in the Math/Verbal Test of the Navy and Marine Corps Aviation Selection Test Battery.

Arithmetic reasoning questions are also found in one of the ASVAB tests (Arithmetic Reasoning) that make up the general technical (GT) score used in screening active-duty enlisted service members of all branches of the Armed Forces interested in entering the Army Warrant Officer Flight Training Program.

Sample Items:

1. An airplane flying a distance of 875 miles used 70 gallons of gasoline. Under the same conditions, how many gallons will this plane need to travel 3000 miles?

   (A) 108
   (B) 120
   (C) 144
   (D) 188
   (E) 240

$\frac{875}{70} = \frac{3000}{x}$; $875x = 210{,}000$; $x = 240$ gallons.
Option (E) is the correct answer.

2. A mechanic repairs 16 cars per 8-hour day. Another mechanic in the same shop repairs $1\frac{1}{2}$ times this number in the same period of time. Theoretically, how long will it take these mechanics, working together, to repair 12 cars in the shop?

   (A) 2 hours
   (B) $2\frac{2}{5}$ hours
   (C) $2\frac{4}{5}$ hours
   (D) $3\frac{1}{5}$ hours
   (E) $3\frac{3}{5}$ hours

The second mechanic repairs $1\frac{1}{2} \times 16$ or 24 cars per 8-hour day. On an hourly rate, the first mechanic repairs 2 cars/hour; the second mechanic repairs 3 cars/hour. Adding both outputs, they repair 5 cars/hour. To determine the time required to repair 12 cars, divide the 12 cars by the 5 cars/hour. The answer is $2\frac{2}{5}$ hours, or option (B).

3. On a scaled drawing of a warehouse, one inch represents 10 feet of actual floor dimension. A floor which is actually 15 yards long and 10 yards wide would have which of the following dimensions on the scaled drawing?

   (A) $1\frac{1}{2}$ inches long and 1 inch wide
   (B) 3 inches long and 2 inches wide
   (C) $4\frac{1}{2}$ inches long and 3 inches wide
   (D) 6 inches long and 4 inches wide
   (E) none of these

First convert actual floor dimensions to feet: 15 yards = 45 feet; 10 yards = 30 feet.

If one inch represents 10 feet, $4\frac{1}{2}$ inches represents 45 feet (length).

If one inch represents 10 feet, 3 inches represents 30 feet (width).

Option (C) is the correct answer.

4. An empty can weighs 10 pounds. When filled with water, it weighs 85 pounds. If one gallon of water weighs 8.32 pounds, the capacity of the can is approximately

   (A) 8 gallons
   (B) $8\frac{1}{2}$ gallons
   (C) 9 gallons
   (D) $9\frac{1}{2}$ gallons
   (E) 10 gallons

The weight of the filled can (85 pounds) minus the weight of the empty can (10 pounds) equals the weight of the water that can fill the can (85 –10 = 75 pounds). The number of gallons that will fill the can equals $\frac{75}{8.32}$ equals 9.01, or option (C).

5. If there are red, green, and yellow marbles in a jar and 60% of these marbles are either red or green, what are the chances of blindly picking a yellow marble out of the jar?

   (A) 2 out of 3
   (B) 3 out of 4
   (C) 2 out of 5
   (D) 3 out of 5
   (E) 4 out of 5

If 60% of the marbles are either red or green, 40% of the marbles are yellow. With 40% of the marbles being yellow, the probability of selecting a yellow marble is 4 out of 10 or 2 out of 5. Option (C) is the correct answer.

Practice items *1* to *5* follow. For each question, select the best answer and then, in the correspondingly numbered space on the answer sheet, blacken the circle with the same letter as your answer.

Use a soft (No. 2) pencil to mark your answers. If you wish to change an answer, erase it thoroughly and then mark the new answer.

Use the correct answers and rationale that appear on page 127 to help you determine your score, as well as to enable you to review those questions which you did not answer correctly or of which you are uncertain.

Practice Items

Each of the following five questions consists of an arithmetic problem. Solve each problem and indicate which of the five options is the answer.

1. A rectangular bin 4 feet long, 2 feet wide and $1\frac{1}{2}$ feet high is solidly packed with bricks whose dimensions are 8 inches, 4 inches, and 2 inches. The number of bricks in the bin is

   (A) 162
   (B) 243
   (C) 324
   (D) 486
   (E) 648

2. On a house plan on which 2 inches represents 5 feet, the length of a room measures 7 inches. The actual length of the room is

   (A) $14\frac{1}{2}$ feet
   (B) $15\frac{1}{2}$ feet
   (C) $16\frac{1}{2}$ feet
   (D) $17\frac{1}{2}$ feet
   (E) $18\frac{1}{2}$ feet

3. A person travels 24 miles at 6 mph, 20 miles at 10 mph, and 20 miles at 5 mph. What is the person's average rate for the complete distance?

   (A) 6.4 mph
   (B) 6.9 mph
   (C) 7.4 mph
   (D) 7.9 mph
   (E) 8.4 mph

4. A typewriter was listed at $240 and was bought at $192. What was the rate of discount?

   (A) 18%
   (B) 20%
   (C) 22%
   (D) 24%
   (E) 25%

5. If shipping charges to a certain point are 82 cents for the first 5 ounces and 9 cents for each additional ounce, the weight of the package for which the charges are $2.35 is

   (A) 1 pound, 1 ounce
   (B) 1 pound, 2 ounces
   (C) 1 pound, 3 ounces
   (D) 1 pound, 5 ounces
   (E) 1 pound, 6 ounces

Math Knowledge

Questions on math knowledge appear in Subtest 6, Math Knowledge, of the Air Force Officer Qualifying Test. This subtest is used in constructing the navigator-technical composite. Math knowledge questions also appear in the Math Verbal Test of the Navy and Marine Corps Aviation Selection Test Battery.

Math knowledge—the ability to use basic mathematical relationships learned in basic courses in mathematics—is one of the important abilities tested for by the military. Most of these concepts are included in elementary courses in algebra, geometry, and trigonometry.

Sample Items:

1. The reciprocal of 2 is

   (A) .02
   (B) .25
   (C) .50
   (D) .80
   (E) 1.20

If the product of two numbers is 1, either number is called the reciprocal of the other. For example, since $2 \times \frac{1}{2} = 1$, 2 is the reciprocal of $\frac{1}{2}$; and $\frac{1}{2}$ is the reciprocal of 2. As $\frac{1}{2}$ is equivalent to .50, option (C) is the correct answer.

2. If a pole 12 feet high casts a shadow 5 feet long, how long a shadow will be cast by a 6-foot person standing next to the pole?

   (A) $1\frac{1}{2}$ feet
   (B) 2 feet
   (C) $2\frac{1}{2}$ feet
   (D) 3 feet
   (E) $3\frac{1}{2}$ feet

Let x = length of shadow cast by 6-foot person. Use a simple proportion: $12 : 5 = 6 : x$; $12x = 30$; $x = \frac{30}{12} = 2\frac{1}{2}$. Option (C) is the correct answer.

3. The numerical value of 4! is

   (A) 8
   (B) 12
   (C) 16
   (D) 20
   (E) 24

The factorial of a natural number is the product of that number and all the natural numbers less than it. $4! = 4 \times 3 \times 2 \times 1 = 24$. Option (E) is the correct answer.

4. In the following series of numbers arranged in a logical order, ascertain the pattern or rule for the arrangement and then select the appropriate option to complete the series.

   2 3 5 8 12 __

   (A) 14
   (B) 15
   (C) 16
   (D) 17
   (E) 18

A study of the series of numbers shows a pattern of +l, +2, +3, +4, etc. Inserting 17 in the blank space will conform with this pattern. Option (D) is the correct answer.

5. The square root of 998.56 is

   (A) 30.4
   (B) 30.6
   (C) 31.4
   (D) 31.6
   (E) 32.4

Starting from the decimal point, separate the number in groups of two going in both directions and then solve with a modified form of long division as shown in the calculation below.

```
        3   1. 6
      √9  98.56
       9
  61 )0  98
         61
 626 )37 56
      37 56
      00 00
```

The correct answer is 31.6 or option (D).

Practice items *1* to *5* follow. For each question, select the correct answer and then, in the correspondingly numbered space on the answer sheet, blacken the circle with the same letter as your answer.

Use a soft (No. 2) pencil to mark your answers. If you wish to change an answer, erase it thoroughly and then mark the new answer.

Use the correct answers and rationale that appear on page 127 to help you determine your score, as well as to enable you to review those questions which you did not answer correctly or of which you are unsure.

Practice Items

Each of the following five questions is a mathematical problem. Solve each problem and indicate which of the five options is the correct answer.

1. $\frac{2}{3} \times \frac{3}{4} \times \frac{4}{5} \times \frac{5}{6} \times \frac{6}{7} \times \frac{7}{8} =$

   (A) $\frac{1}{16}$
   (B) $\frac{1}{8}$
   (C) $\frac{1}{4}$
   (D) $\frac{1}{2}$
   (E) none of these

2. Of the following, the pair that is not a set of equivalents is

   (A) .15% .0015
   (B) $\frac{1}{4}$% .0025
   (C) 1.5% $\frac{3}{200}$
   (D) 15% $\frac{15}{100}$
   (E) 115% .115

3. $10^4 \times 10^3 \times 10^2 =$

   (A) 10^9
   (B) 10^{12}
   (C) 10^{15}
   (D) 10^{24}
   (E) none of these

4. The hypotenuse of a right triangle whose legs are 3 feet and 4 feet is

   (A) $3\frac{1}{2}$ feet
   (B) 5 feet
   (C) $5\frac{1}{2}$ feet
   (D) 6 feet
   (E) 7 feet

5. If $a = 4b$, then $\frac{3}{4}a =$

   (A) $\frac{3}{3}b$
   (B) $\frac{4}{3}b$
   (C) $3b$
   (D) $\frac{b}{3}$
   (E) $\frac{b}{4}$

Data Interpretation

Questions on data interpretation appear in Subtest 4, Data Interpretation, of the Air Force Officer Qualifying Test. This subtest is used in constructing the navigator-technical composite.

Data interpretation is actually an adaptation of arithmetic reasoning based on information or data given in either tabular or graphic form. This type of question is used to measure ability to read and understand tables and graphs, and to reason with the data or figures presented.

Sample questions to illustrate some of the types of questions that appear in the data interpretation subtest follow. Each table and graph is followed by two, three, or four questions pertaining to the table or graph only. Solutions to these sample questions are given to show how the correct answers are obtained. Practice items follow the sample questions.

Sample Items:

Answer sample questions *1* and *2* on the basis of the information in the following table:

Immigration to the United States by Country of Origin 1971–1990

Country	1971–1980	1981–1990
France	25,069	23,124
Greece	92,369	29,130
Italy	129,368	32,894
Portugal	101,710	40,020
Spain	39,141	15,698
Switzerland	8,235	7,076

1. What country had the greatest decrease in the total number of immigrants to the United States between the 1971–1980 period and the 1981–1990 period?

   (A) France
   (B) Greece
   (C) Italy
   (D) Spain
   (E) Switzerland

2. Which country had the greatest percentage decrease in the number of immigrants to the United States between the 1971–1980 period and the 1981–1990 period?

   (A) Greece
   (B) Italy
   (C) Portugal
   (D) Spain
   (E) Switzerland

For question 1, note that all six countries had a decrease during these periods. Italy had a decrease of 96,474; Greece had a decrease of 63,239; Portugal had a decrease of 61,690. Actually, this question could be answered quickly by estimating by approximation. Option (C) is the correct answer.

For question 2, the percentage decreases are as follows:

Greece	63,239/92,369 = 68.5%
Italy	96,474/129,368 = 74.5%
Portugal	61,690/101,710 = 60.6%
Spain	23,443/39,141 = 59.0%
Switzerland	1,159/8,235 = 14.0%

Option (B) is the correct answer.

Answer sample questions *3* to *5* on the basis of the information given in the graph below which shows the number of citations issued, at 5-year intervals, for various offenses from the year 1970 to the year 1990.

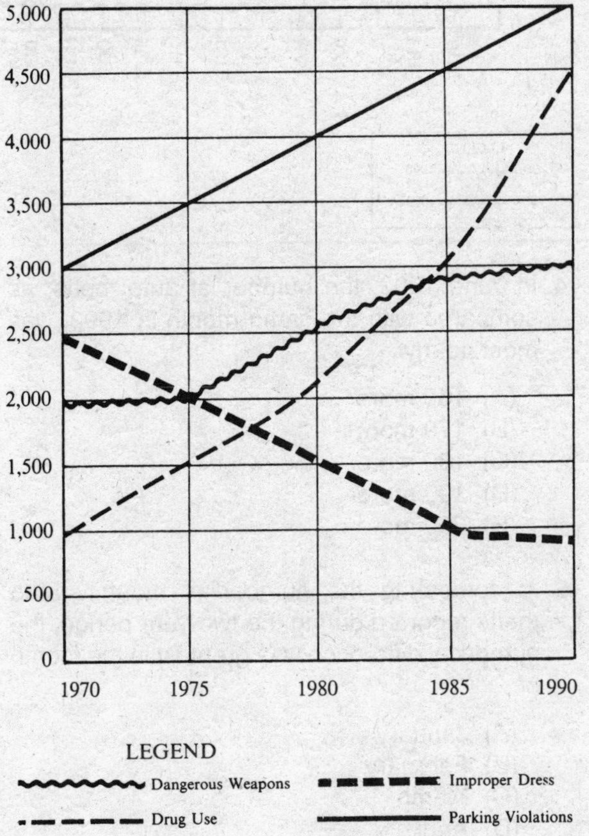

3. Which offense showed a constant rate of increase or decrease over the 20-year period?
   (A) dangerous weapons
   (B) drug use
   (C) improper dress
   (D) parking violations
   (E) none of the foregoing

4. Which offense showed an average rate of change (increase or decrease) of 150 citations per year over the 20-year period?
   (A) dangerous weapons
   (B) drug use
   (C) improper dress
   (D) parking violations
   (E) none of the foregoing

5. The percentage increase in total citations issued from 1975 to 1980 was most nearly
   (A) 7%
   (B) 11%
   (C) 21%
   (D) 31%
   (E) 41%

For question 3, a descending straight line would show a constant rate of decrease, whereas an ascending line would show a constant rate of increase. The continuous line designating parking violations is an ascending straight line showing a constant rate of increase of 100 parking violations each year from 1970 to 1990. Option (D) is the correct answer.

For question 4, an average rate of change of 150 citations per year over a 20-year period would mean a change (increase or decrease) of 3,000 citations from 1970 to 1990. Therefore, option (E) is the correct answer.

For question 5, the total number of citations issued in 1975 is 9,000; the total in 1980 is 10,000. The difference, 1,000, is 11% of the number of citations issued in 1975. Option (B) is correct.

Practice items *1* to *5* follow. For each question, select the correct answer and then, in the correspondingly numbered space on the answer sheet, blacken the circle with the same letter as your answer.

Use a soft (No. 2) pencil to mark your answers. If you wish to change an answer, erase it thoroughly and then mark the new answer.

Use the correct answers and rationale that appear on page 127 to help you determine your score, as well as to enable you to review those questions which you did not answer correctly or of which you are uncertain.

Practice Items

Answer the following three questions numbered 1 to 3 on the basis of the following tabulation showing the number of errors made by four office workers during a half-year period. All four office workers are assigned to the same section.

Month	Butler	Carter	Durkin	Ernest
July	10	9	2	15
Aug	17	7	19	16
Sept	15	16	15	10
Oct	6	9	8	6
Nov	5	8	9	11
Dec	9	4	14	7

1. Of the total number of errors made by the four office workers during the 6-month period, the percentage made in August was most nearly
   (A) 20%
   (B) 21%
   (C) 22%
   (D) 23%
   (E) 24%

2. The average number of errors made per month per office worker was most nearly
   (A) 10
   (B) 11
   (C) 12
   (D) 13
   (E) 14

3. If the total number of errors made by Butler during the 6-month period represents one-sixth of the total errors made by the section during the entire year, what was the total number of errors made by the section during the entire year?
   (A) 360
   (B) 372
   (C) 392
   (D) 720
   (E) 744

Answer questions 4 and 5 on the basis of the data given in the graph below.

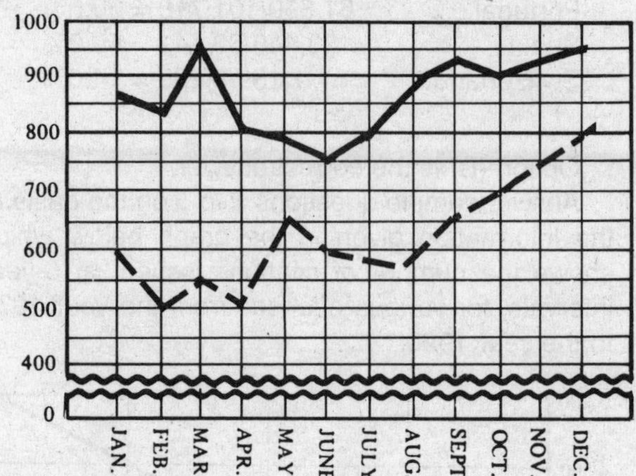

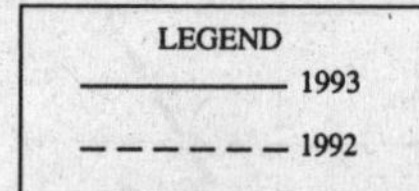

4. In June 1993, the number of auto thefts, as compared with the same month in 1992, was most nearly
   (A) 160 more
   (B) 170 more
   (C) 180 more
   (D) 190 more
   (E) 200 more

5. In comparing the number of monthly auto thefts reported during the two-year period, the numerical difference was greatest in the month of
   (A) January
   (B) February
   (C) March
   (D) April
   (E) September

Mechanical Comprehension

Questions on mechanical comprehension are widely used by the military. They appear in Subtest 7, Mechanical Comprehension, of the Air Force

Tests	Test Time (minutes)	Number of Questions	Options/Questions
Air Force Officer Qualifying Test	22	20	5
Alternate Flight Aptitude Selection Test	10	20	2
Navy and Marine Corps Aviation Selection Test Battery	15	3	3

Officer Qualifying Test and are used in constructing both the pilot and the navigator-technical composites. Similar questions appear in Subtest 6, Mechanical Functions, of the Alternate Flight Aptitude Selection Test (AFAST). They also appear in the Mechanical Comprehension Test of the Navy and Marine Corps Aviation Selection Test Battery and are used in constructing the Pilot Flight Aptitude Rating (PFAR) and the Flight Officer Flight Aptitude Rating (FOFAR).

Mechanical comprehension items utilizing drawings and diagrams about which brief questions are to be answered require an understanding of mechanical principles that comes from observing the physical world, working with or operating mechanical devices, or reading and studying.

It has been found that mechanical comprehension items are among the best predictors for pilot success. It is probable that the mechanical information and the spatial visualization required to answer these questions are responsible for the high correlation.

Test time, number of mechanical comprehension questions, and the number of options for each question in each of the military flight aptitude tests are indicated in the chart below.

Sample Items:

Study each diagram carefully and select the choice that best answers the question or completes the statement.

1. Which of the other gears is moving in the same direction as gear 2?

   (A) gear 1
   (B) gear 3
   (C) neither of the gears
   (D) both of the gears
   (E) it cannot be determined

Gear 2 is moving clockwise and is causing both gear 1 and gear 3 to move counterclockwise. Option (C) is the correct answer.

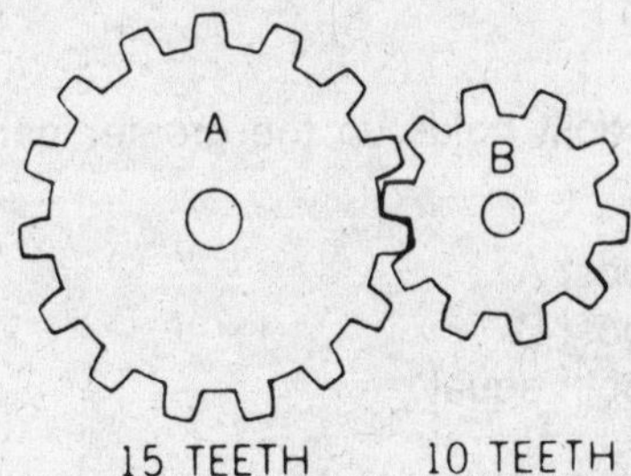

2. In the illustration on the previous page, if gear A makes 30 revolutions, gear B will make

(A) 20 revolutions
(B) 30 revolutions
(C) 35 revolutions
(D) 40 revolutions
(E) 45 revolutions

For every revolution made by gear A, gear B will make $1\frac{1}{2}$ times as many. If gear A makes 30 revolutions, gear B will make 45. Option (E) is the correct answer.

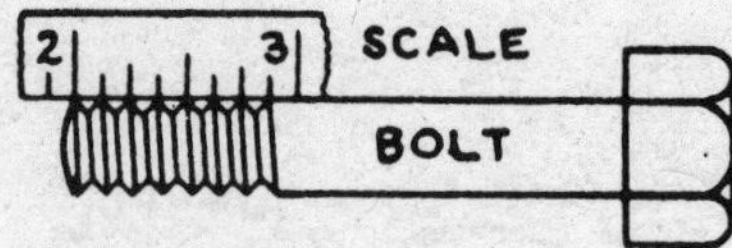

3. The number of threads per inch on the bolt is

(A) 7
(B) 8
(C) 10
(D) 14
(E) 16

The bolt thread makes one revolution per eighth of an inch. Accordingly, it has 8 threads in one inch. Option (B) is the correct answer.

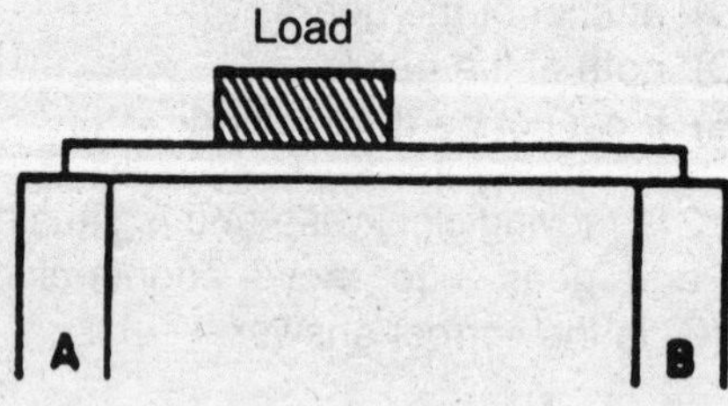

4. Which post holds up the greater part of the load?

(A) post A
(B) post B
(C) both equal

The weight of the load is not centered but is closer to A. The distance from the center of the load to A is less than the distance from the center of the load to B. Therefore, post A would support the greater part of the load. Option (A) is the correct answer.

5. The convenience outlet that is known as a polarized outlet is number

(A) 1
(B) 2
(C) 3

The plug can go into the outlet in only one way in a polarized outlet. In the other outlets, the plug can be reversed. Option (A) is the correct answer.

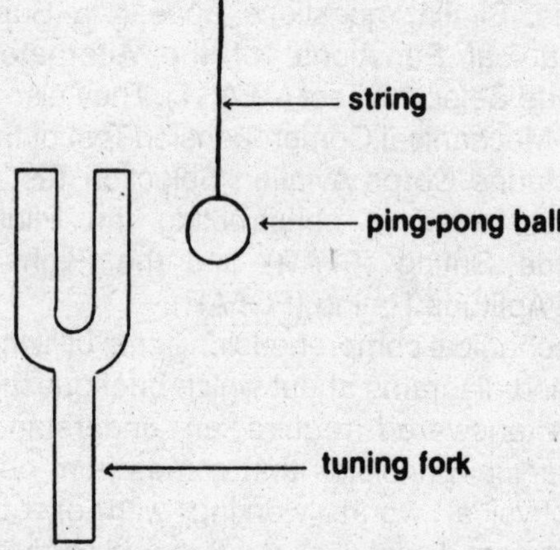

6. When the tuning fork is struck, the Ping-Pong ball will

(A) remain stationary
(B) bounce up and down
(C) swing away from the tuning fork

When a tuning fork vibrates, it moves currents of air. This vibrating air would cause the Ping-Pong ball to be pushed away. Option (C) is the correct answer.

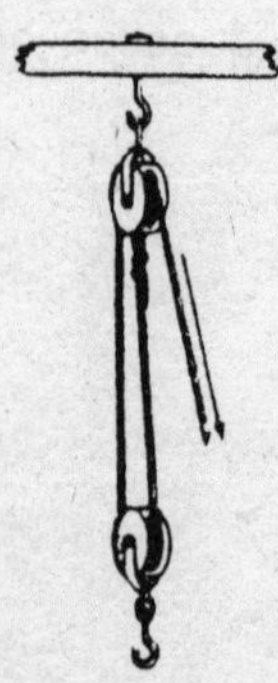

7. In the figure shown on the previous page, the pulley system consists of a fixed block and a movable block. The theoretical mechanical advantage is

   (A) 2
   (B) 3

The number of parts of the rope going to and from the movable block indicates the mechanical advantage. In this case, it is 2. Option (A) is the correct answer.

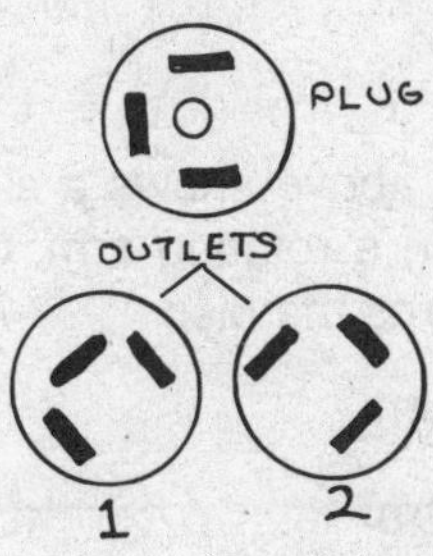

8. The outlet that will accept the plug is

   (A) 1
   (B) 2

Note that the openings in outlet 2 and the prongs of the plug match exactly. The two parallel openings in outlet 1 are too close to the third opening to accept the prongs of the plug. Option (B) is the correct answer.

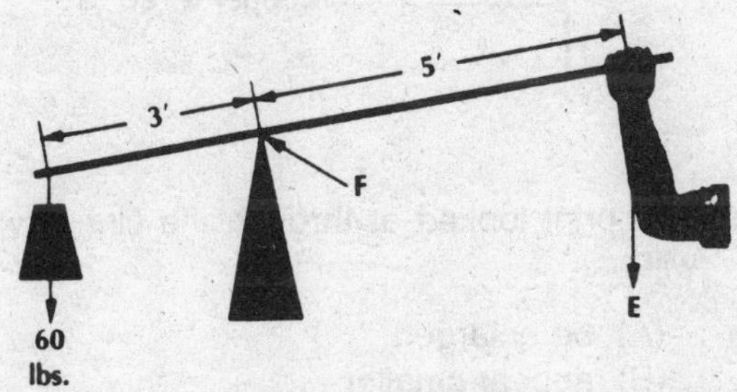

9. What effort must be exerted to lift a 60-pound weight in the figure of a first-class lever shown above (disregard weight of lever)?

   (A) 36 pounds
   (B) 45 pounds

Let x = effort that must be exerted.
$60 \bullet 3 = x \bullet 5;$
$5x = 180$
$x = \frac{180}{5} = 36.$
Option (A) is the correct answer.

Practice items *1* to *10* follow. For each question, select the correct answer and then, in the correspondingly numbered space on the answer sheet, blacken the circle with the same letter as your answer.

Use a soft (No. 2) pencil to mark your answers. If you wish to change an answer, erase it thoroughly and then mark the new answer.

Use the correct answers and rationale that appear on pages 127–128 to help you determine your score, as well as to enable you to review those questions which you did not answer correctly or of which you are uncertain.

Practice Items

Each of the following ten questions contains a diagram followed by a question or an incomplete statement. Study the diagram carefully and select the choice that best answers the question or completes the statement.

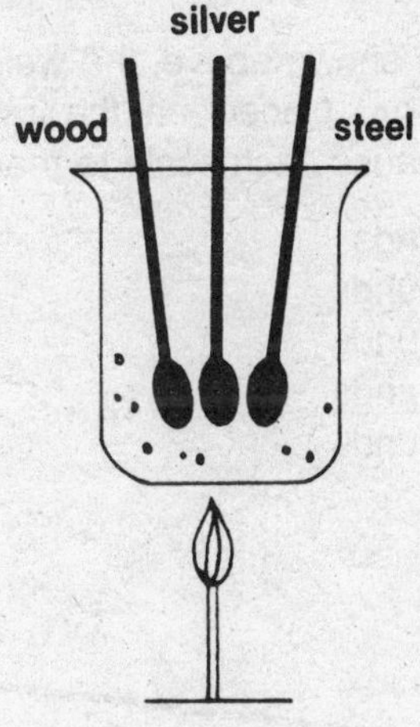

1. Which spoon is hottest?

   (A) wood
   (B) silver
   (C) steel
   (D) silver and steel are equally hot
   (E) wood, silver, and steel are all equally hot

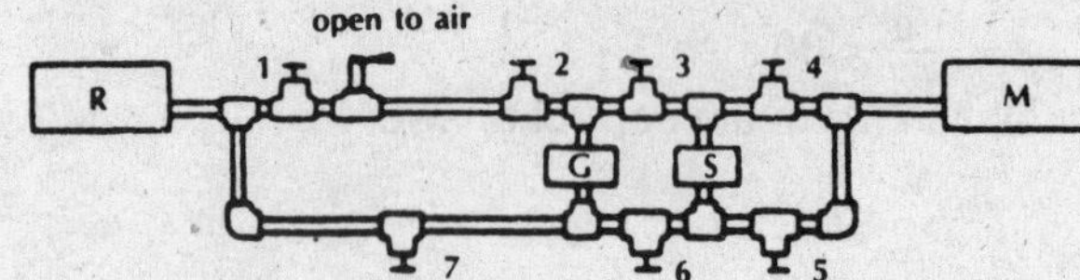

2. In the figure shown above, assume that all valves are closed. For air flow from R through G and then through S to M, open

   (A) valves 7, 6, and 5
   (B) valves 7, 3, and 4
   (C) valves 7, 6, and 4
   (D) valves 7, 3, and 5
   (E) valves 7, 4, and 5

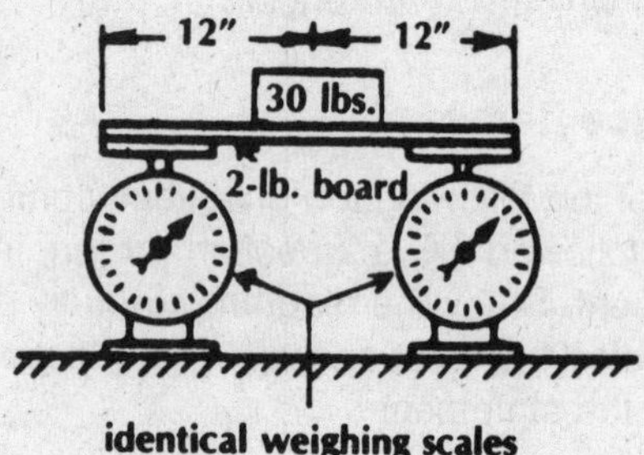

3. In the figure shown above, the weight held by the board and placed on the two identical scales will cause each scale to read

   (A) 8 pounds
   (B) 15 pounds
   (C) 16 pounds
   (D) 30 pounds
   (E) 32 pounds

4. If the block on which the lever is resting is moved closer to the brick,

   (A) the brick will be easier to lift and will be lifted higher
   (B) the brick will be harder to lift and will be lifted higher
   (C) the brick will be easier to lift but will not be lifted as high
   (D) the brick will be harder to lift and will not be lifted as high
   (E) the same effort will be required to lift the brick to the same height

5. The figure above shows a slotted disc turned by a pin on a rotating arm. One revolution of the arm turns the disc

   (A) $\frac{1}{8}$ turn
   (B) $\frac{1}{4}$ turn
   (C) $\frac{1}{2}$ turn
   (D) $\frac{3}{4}$ turn
   (E) one complete turn

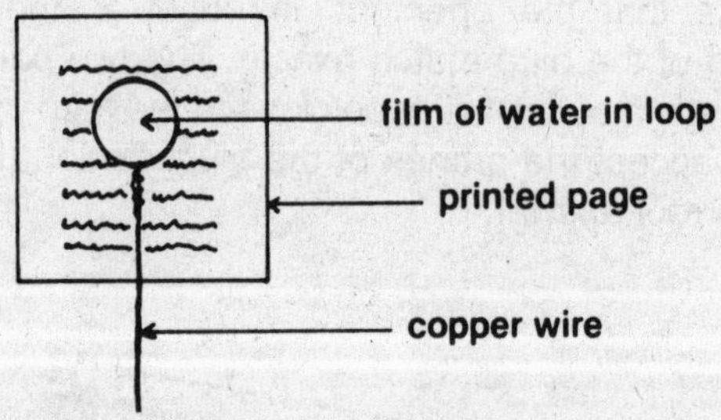

6. The print looked at through the film of water will

   (A) be enlarged
   (B) appear smaller
   (C) look the same as the surrounding print

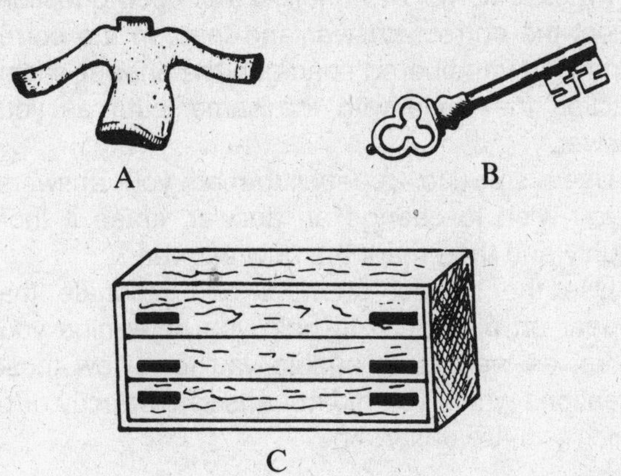

7. If all of these are at the same temperature, which one will feel the coldest?
   (A) A
   (B) B
   (C) C

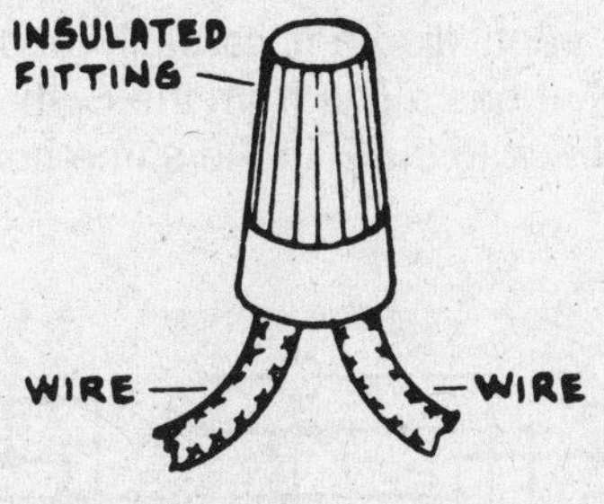

8. Wires are often spliced by the use of a fitting like the one shown above. The use of this fitting does away with the need for
   (A) skinning
   (B) soldering
   (C) twisting

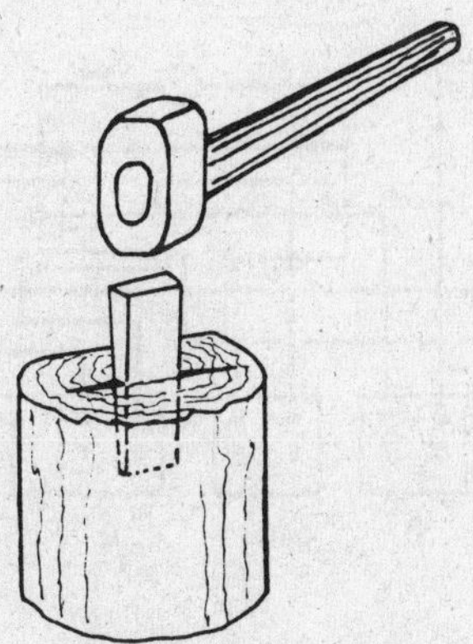

9. The simple machine pictured below in the previous column is a form of
   (A) inclined plane
   (B) torque

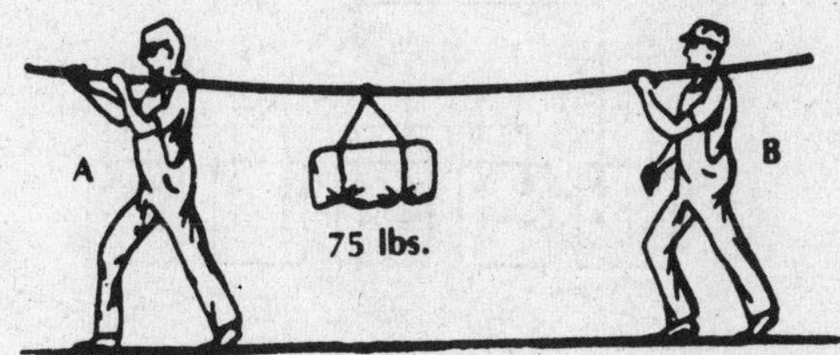

10. The weight is being carried entirely on the shoulders of the two persons shown above. Which person bears the most weight on the shoulders?
   (A) A
   (B) B

Electrical Maze

Electrical maze questions appear in Subtest 8, Electrical Maze, of the Air Force Officer Qualifying Test and are used in constructing both the pilot and the navigator-technical composites. They are designed to test your ability to choose the correct path from among different wiring circuits.

In the diagram below is a box with dots marked S and F. S is the starting point, and F is the finishing point. You must follow the line from S, through the circle at the top of the diagram, and back to F.

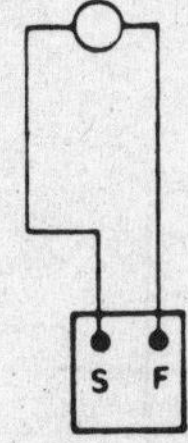

In the problems in this test, there will be five such boxes. Only *one* box will have a line from the S, through the circle, and back to the F in the same box. Dots on the lines show the *only* places where turns or direction changes can be made between lines. If lines meet or cross where there is *no dot*, turns or direction changes *cannot be made*. Now try sample problem 1.

Sample Items:

1.

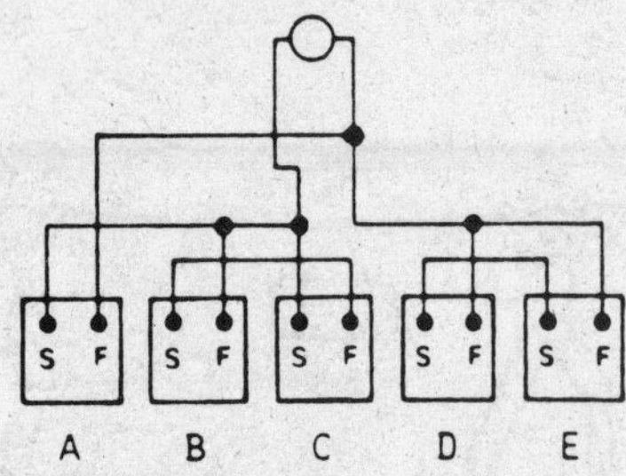

The first box is the one which has the line from S, through the circle, and back to F. Therefore, A is the right answer.

Each diagram in the test has only one box which has a line through the circle and back to F. Some lines are wrong because they lead to a dead end. Some lines are wrong because they come back to the box without going through the circle. Some lines are wrong because they lead to other boxes. Some are wrong because they retrace the same line.

Now try sample problems 2 and 3.

2.

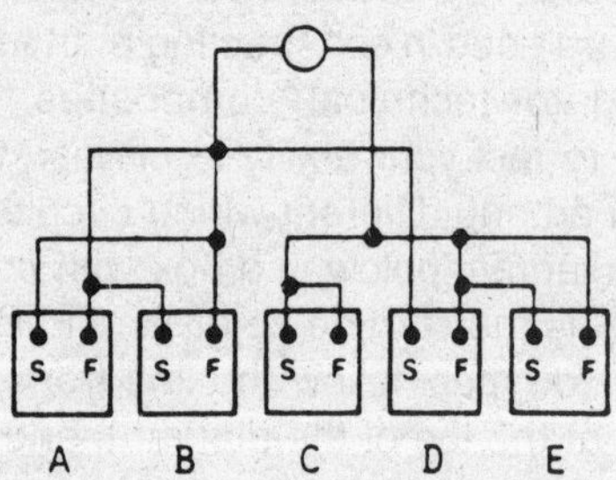

For sample problem 2, the correct answer is D.

3.

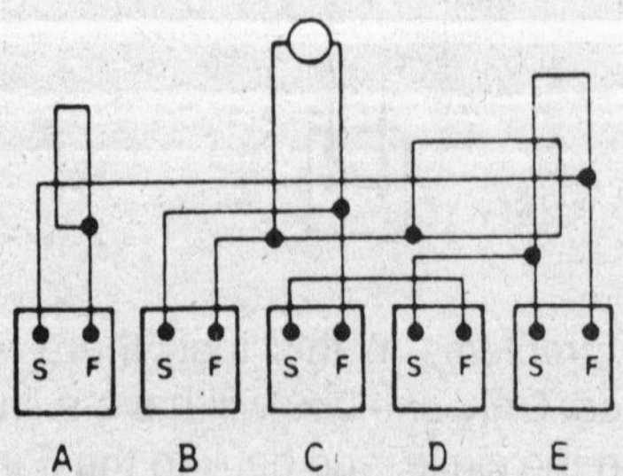

For sample problem 3, the correct answer is B.

Practice items *1* to *5* follow. For each question, select the correct answer and then, in the correspondingly numbered space on the answer sheet, blacken the circle with the same letter as your answer.

Use a soft (No. 2) pencil to mark your answers. If you wish to change an answer, erase it thoroughly and then mark the new answer.

Use the correct answers and rationale that appear on page 128 to help you determine your score, as well as to enable you to review those questions which you did not answer correctly or of which you are uncertain.

Practice Items

Each of the following five questions contains a wiring diagram with five labeled boxes. Only one box will have a line from the S, through the circle, and back to the F in the same box. Dots on the lines show the *only* points where turns or direction changes can be made between lines. If lines meet or cross where there is *no dot*, turns or direction changes *cannot* be made.

Study each diagram carefully and then select the box that has a line from the S, through the circle, and back to the F in the same box.

1.

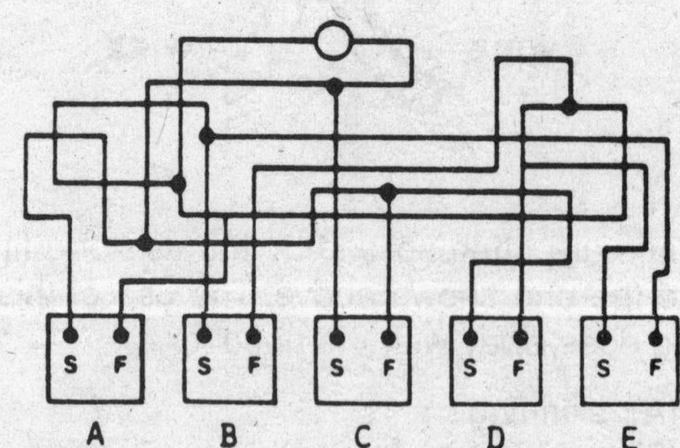

2.

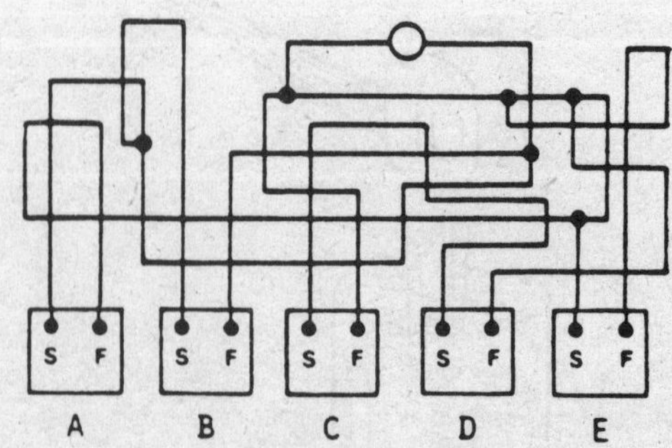

3.

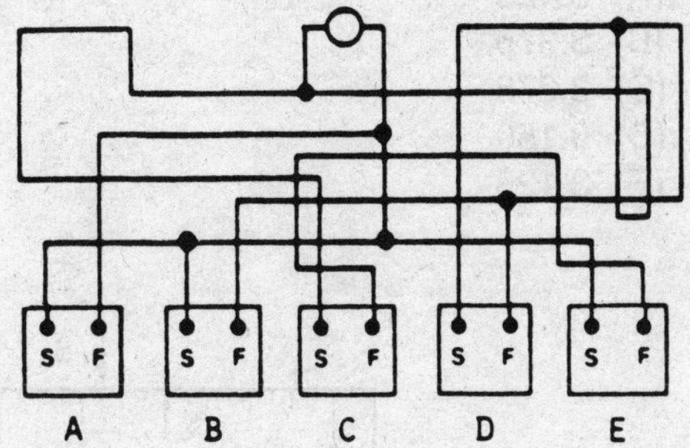

4.

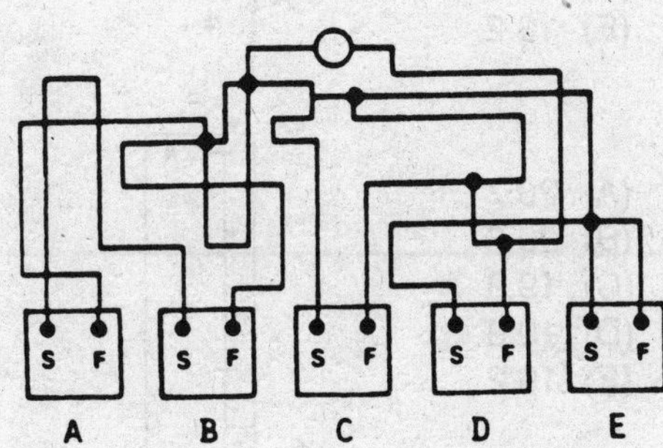

5.

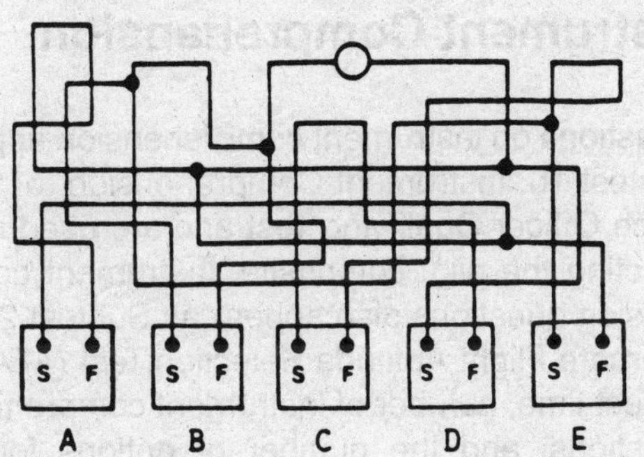

Scale Reading

Questions on reading scales appear in Subtest 9, Scale Reading, of the Air Force Officer Qualifying Test and are used in constructing both the pilot and the navigator-technical composites. They are designed to test your ability to read scales, dials, and meters.

A variety of scales are given with various points indicated on them by numbered arrows. You will be required to estimate the numerical value indicated by each arrow. Some of the items require fine discrimination on nonlinear scales.

Now look at the following sample items.

1.
(A) 6.00
(B) 5.00
(C) 4.25
(D) 2.25
(E) 1.25

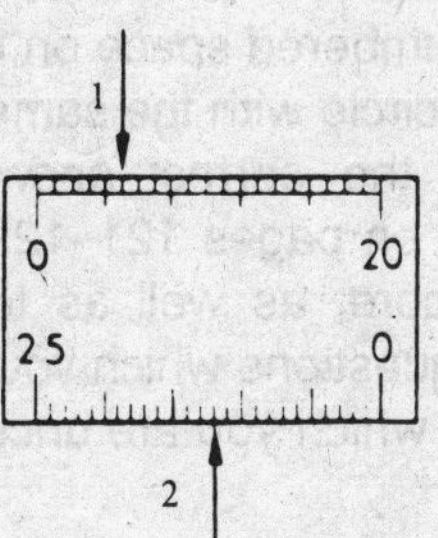

2.
(A) 13.0
(B) 12.0
(C) 10.2
(D) 1.3
(E) 1.2

3.
(A) 81.75
(B) 79.5
(C) 78.75
(D) 77.60
(E) 67.50

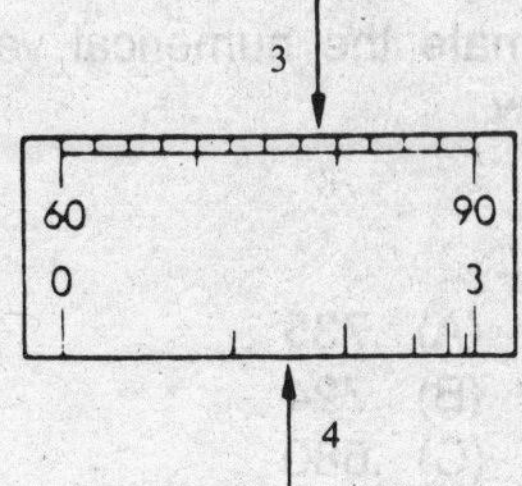

4.
(A) 1.75
(B) 1.65
(C) 1.50
(D) .75
(E) .65

In sample item 1 there are five subdivisions of four steps each between 0 and 20. The arrow points between the long subdivision markers representing 4 and 8. Since it points to the marker that is one step to the right of subdivision marker 4, it points to 5.00. This is choice (B) in sample item 1.

In sample item 2 the scale runs from right to left. There are five subdivisions of five steps each, so each step represents .1, and the arrow points to the marker representing 1.2. This is choice (E) in sample item 2.

In sample item 3 the arrow points between two markers. You must estimate the fractional part of the step as accurately as possible. Since the arrow points halfway between the markers representing 77.5 and 80.0, it points to 78.75. This is choice (C) in sample item 3.

In sample item 4 each step represents .5, but the steps are of unequal width with each step being two-thirds as wide as the preceding one.

Therefore, the scale is compressed as the values increase. The arrow is pointing to a position halfway between the marker representing .5 and 1.0, but because of the compression of the scale the value of this point must be less than .75. Actually, it is .65, which is choice (E) in sample item 4.

Practice items *1* to *5* follow. For each question, select the correct answer then, in the correspondingly numbered space on the answer sheet, blacken the circle with the same letter as your answer.

Use the correct answers and rationale that appear on pages 121–122 to help you determine your score, as well as to enable you to review those questions which you did not answer correctly or of which you are uncertain.

Practice Items

Estimate the numerical value indicated by each arrow.

1.

(A) .735
(B) .724
(C) .680
(D) .660
(E) .570

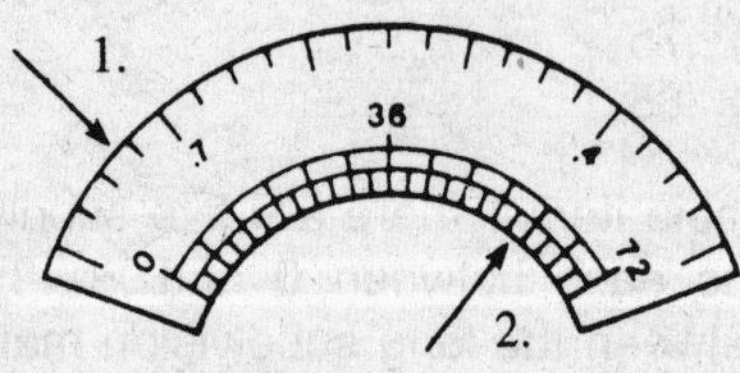

2.

(A) 86
(B) 81
(C) 64
(D) 60
(E) 58

3.

(A) 3.425
(B) 3.375
(C) 3.275
(D) 3.150
(E) 3.125

4.

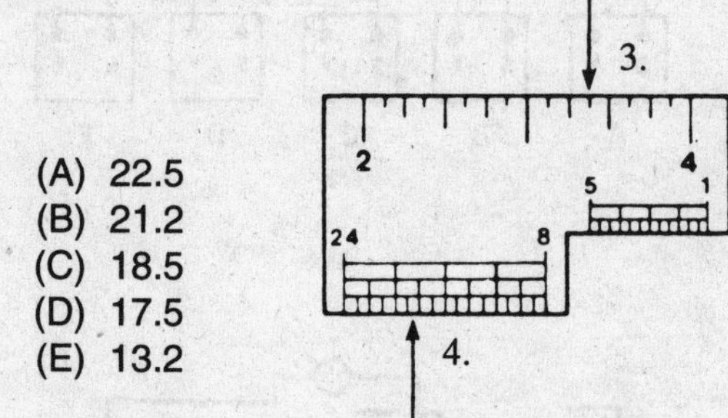

(A) 22.5
(B) 21.2
(C) 18.5
(D) 17.5
(E) 13.2

5.

(A) 20.7
(B) 20.3
(C) 19.9
(D) 19.3
(E) 19.2

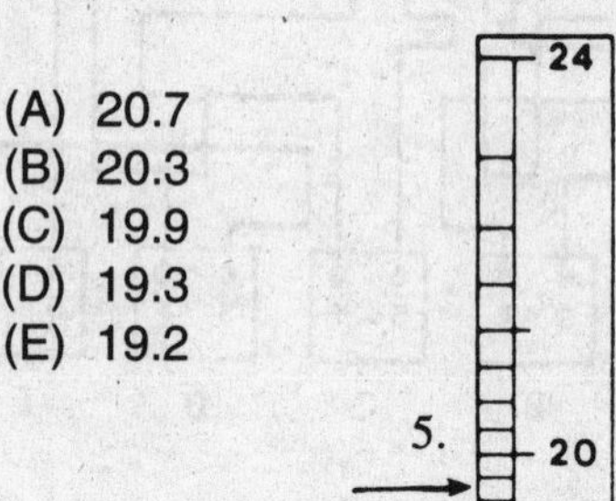

Instrument Comprehension

Questions on instrument comprehension appear in Subtest 10, Instrument Comprehension, of the Air Force Officer Qualifying Test and are used in constructing the pilot composite. Instrument comprehension questions also appear as Subtest 2 in the Alternate Flight Aptitude Selection Test (AFAST).

Test time, number of instrument comprehension questions, and the number of options for each question in each of these tests are indicated in the table below.

These questions measure your ability to determine the position of an airplane in flight from reading instruments showing its compass heading, its

Test	Test Time (minutes)	Number of Questions	Options/Questions
Air Force Officer Qualifying Test	6	20	4
Alternate Flight Aptitude Selection	5	15	5

amount of climb or dive, and its degree of bank to right or left.

In each question, the left-hand dial is labeled ARTIFICIAL HORIZON. On the face of this dial the small aircraft silhouette remains stationary, while the positions of the heavy black line and the black pointer vary with changes in the position of the airplane in which the instrument is located.

The heavy black line represents the HORIZON LINE, and the black pointer shows the degree of BANK to right or left. If the airplane has no bank, the black pointer is at zero. It should be noted that each 3 to the left and right of zero is equivalent to 30° of bank and that each 6 to the left and right of zero is equivalent to 60° of bank. The small marks on either side of the centerline are equivalent to 10° of bank.

Page 84 illustrates how to read the artificial horizon dial.

If the airplane is neither climbing nor diving, the horizon line is directly on the silhouette's fuselage, as in dials 1, 2, and 3.

If the airplane is climbing, the fuselage silhouette is seen between the horizon line and the pointer, as in dials 4, 5, and 6. The greater the amount of climb, the greater the distance between the horizon line and the fuselage silhouette.

If the airplane is diving, the horizon line is seen between the fuselage silhouette and the pointer, as in dials 7, 8, and 9. The greater the amount of dive, the greater the distance between the horizon line and the fuselage silhouette.

The HORIZON LINE tilts as the aircraft is banked and is always at right angles to the pointer. Refer to the illustration on page 84.

Dial 1 shows an airplane neither climbing nor diving, but banked 90° to the pilot's left.
Dial 2 shows an airplane neither climbing nor diving, with no bank.
Dial 3 shows an airplane neither climbing nor diving, but banked 60° to the pilot's right.
Dial 4 shows an airplane climbing and banking 30° to the pilot's left.
Dial 5 shows an airplane climbing, with no bank.
Dial 6 shows an airplane climbing and banking 45° to the pilot's right.
Dial 7 shows an airplane diving and banking 45° to the pilot's left.
Dial 8 shows an airplane diving, with no bank.
Dial 9 shows an airplane diving and banking 30° to the pilot's right.

Dial 1
If the airplane is banked to the pilot's left, the pointer is seen to the right of zero, as in dial 1, above.

Dial 2
If the airplane has no bank, the black pointer is seen to point to zero, as in dial 2, above.

Dial 3
If the airplane is banked to the pilot's right, the pointer is seen to the left of zero, as in dial 3 above.

Dial 4
If the airplane is banked to the pilot's left, the pointer is seen to the right of zero, as in dial 4, above.

Dial 5
If the airplane has no bank, the black pointer is seen at zero, as in dial 5, above.

Dial 6
If the airplane is banked to the pilot's right, the pointer is seen to the left of zero, as in dial 6, above.

Dial 7
If the airplane is banked to the pilot's left, the pointer is seen to the right of zero, as in dial 7, above.

Dial 8
If the airplane has no bank, the black pointer is seen at zero, as in dial 8, above.

Dial 9
If the airplane is banked to the pilot's right, the pointer is seen to the left of zero, as in dial 9, above.

In each question, the right-hand dial is labeled COMPASS. On this dial, the arrow shows the compass direction in which the airplane is headed at the moment.

Compasses are graduated in degrees clockwise from north. The cardinal points are:

North 0° or 360°
East 90°
South 180°
West 270°

The intercardinal points are:

Northeast 45°
Southeast 135°
Southwest 225°
Northwest 315°

The compass card below shows degrees, cardinal points and intercardinal points.

The combination points midway between the cardinal and intercardinal points are:

NNE 22 $\frac{1}{2}$°

ENE 67 $\frac{1}{2}$°

ESE 112 $\frac{1}{2}$°

SSE 157 $\frac{1}{2}$°

SSW 202 $\frac{1}{2}$°

WSW 247 $\frac{1}{2}$°

WNW 292 $\frac{1}{2}$°

NNW 337 $\frac{1}{2}$°

Examples of the compass dial are shown below:

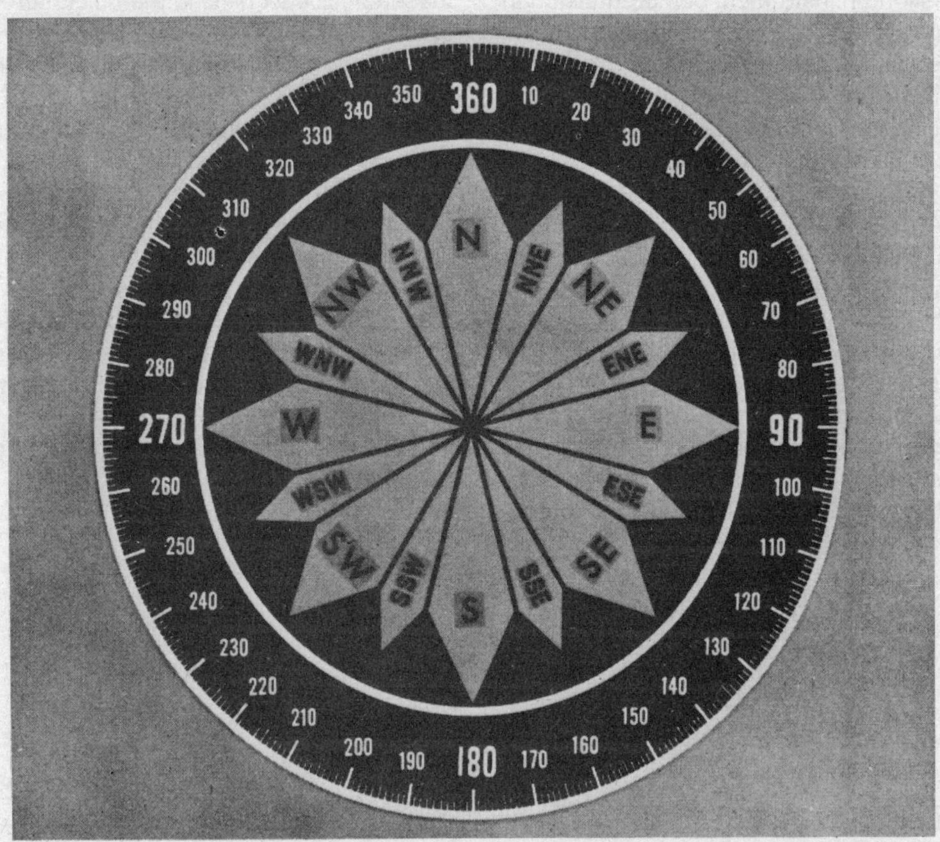

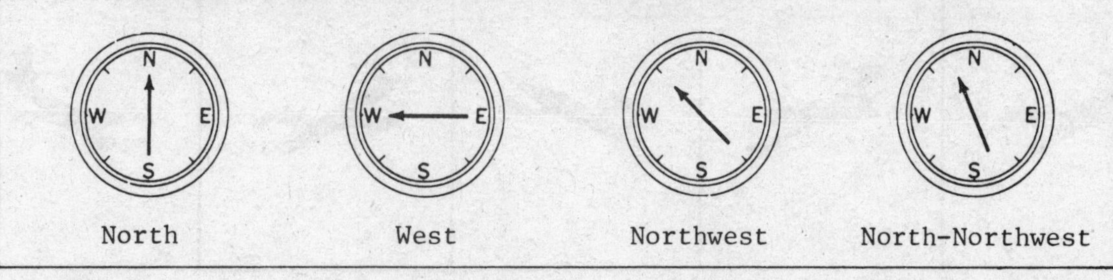

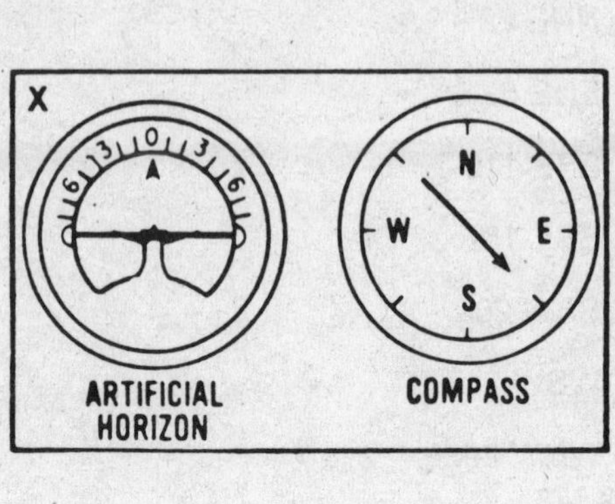

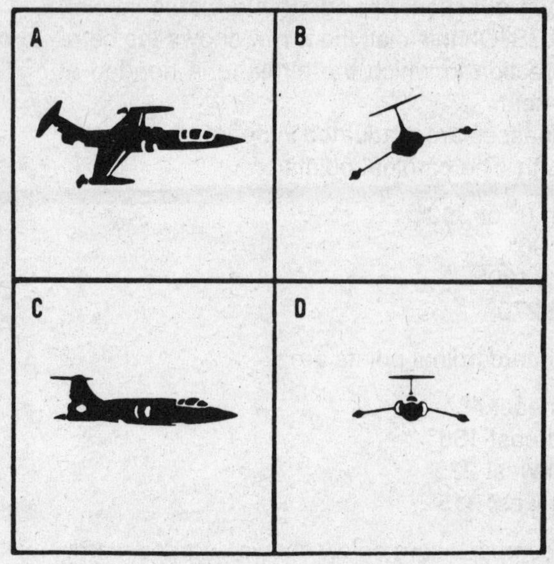

Each question on instrument comprehension in these tests consists of two dials and either four (in the Air Force Officer Qualifying Test) or five (in the Alternate Flight Aptitude Selection Test) silhouettes of airplanes in flight. Your task is to determine which one of the four or five airplanes is MOST NEARLY in the position indicated by the two dials. YOU ARE ALWAYS LOOKING NORTH AT THE SAME ALTITUDE AS EACH OF THE PLANES. EAST IS ALWAYS TO YOUR RIGHT AS YOU LOOK AT THE PAGE.

Item X is a sample from the Air Force Officer Qualifying Test. In item X, the dial labeled ARTIFICIAL HORIZON shows that the airplane is NOT banked, and is neither climbing nor diving. The COMPASS shows that it is headed southeast. The only one of the four airplane silhouettes that meets these specifications is in the box lettered C, so the answer to X is C. Note that B is a rear view, while D is a front view. Note also that A is banked to the right and that B is banked to the left.

Item Y is a sample from the Alternate Flight Aptitude Selection Test. In item Y, the dial labeled ARTIFICIAL HORIZON shows that the airplane is NOT banked, and is climbing to a slight extent. The COMPASS shows that it is headed southeast. The only one of the five airplane silhouettes that meets these specifications is in the box labeled C, so the answer to Y is C. Note that A is diving and is headed southeast; B is neither diving nor climbing, and is banking to the pilot's left; D is in a slight dive, headed southeast; and E is in a slight dive, headed southwest.

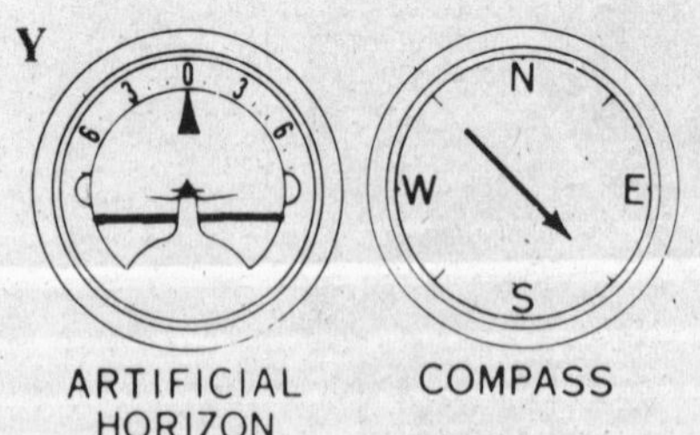

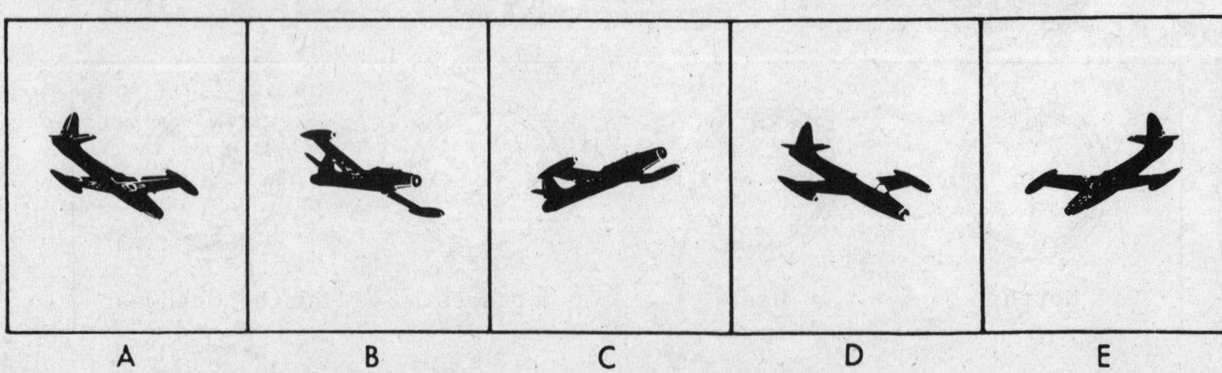

The airplane silhouettes appearing in the Air Force Qualifying Test and those shown in this book are those of the F-104 Starfighter.

The Starfighter, built by Lockheed Aircraft Corporation, served as a tactical fighter with the Air Force Tactical Air Command, and as a day-night interceptor with the Air Defense Command. It had a long, sleek body with short, stubby, razor-sharp wings.

Span 21'11"
Length: 54'9"
Height: 13'6"
Speed: 1400 mph
Ceiling: Above 58,000'
Range: Beyond 1450 miles
Armament: "Sidewinder" missiles and M-61 20 mm cannon

F-104 Starfighters had many revisions. These were lettered A–G. The F-104C featured a removable boom for aerial refueling on the left side of the fuselage, extending the plane's range to intercontinental distances.

The airplane silhouettes appearing in the Alternate Flight Aptitude Selection Test (AFAST) booklets and those shown in this book are those of the F-84 Thunderjet.

The Thunderjet, built by Republic Aviation Corp., was a low-mid-wing monoplane powered by a single turbo-jet engine mounted in a round fuselage with the air intake in the nose. The jet outlet in the tail extended slightly beyond the rudder's trailing edge.

Removable 230-gallon aluminum fuel tanks were fitted to the wing tips.

Span: 36'5"
Length: 37'2"
Speed: 521 knots/sea level
Range: 1360 nautical miles

F-84 Thunderjets had many revisions. These were lettered A–G. All were designed with wings that had tapered leading and trailing edges, except for the F-84F which had sweptback wings.

The silhouettes appearing in this book are those of the F-84G.

Practice items *1* to *10* follow. Questions *1* to *5* are four-option items similar to those in the Air Force Officer Qualifying Test. Questions *6* to *10* are five-option items similar to those in the Alternate Flight Aptitude Selection Test. For each question, select the correct answer and then, in the correspondingly numbered space on the answer sheet, blacken the circle with the same letter as your answer.

Use a soft (No. 2) pencil to mark your answers. If you wish to change an answer, erase it thoroughly and then mark the new answer.

Use the correct answers and rationale that appear on page 129 to help you determine your score, as well as to enable you to review those questions which you did not answer correctly or of which you are uncertain.

Practice Items

Each of the following five questions numbered *1* to *5* consists of two dials and four silhouettes of airplanes in flight. Determine which one of the four airplanes is MOST NEARLY in the position indicated by the two dials. YOU ARE ALWAYS LOOKING NORTH AT THE SAME ALTITUDE AS EACH OF THE PLANES. EAST IS ALWAYS TO YOUR RIGHT AS YOU LOOK AT THE PAGE.

Questions *6* to *10* are five-option items similar to those in the Alternate Flight Aptitude Selection Test. Each question consists of two dials and five silhouettes of airplanes in flight. Determine which one of the five airplanes is MOST NEARLY in the position indicated by the two dials. YOU ARE ALWAYS LOOKING NORTH AT THE SAME ALTITUDE AS EACH OF THE PLANES. EAST IS ALWAYS TO YOUR RIGHT AS YOU LOOK AT THE PAGE.

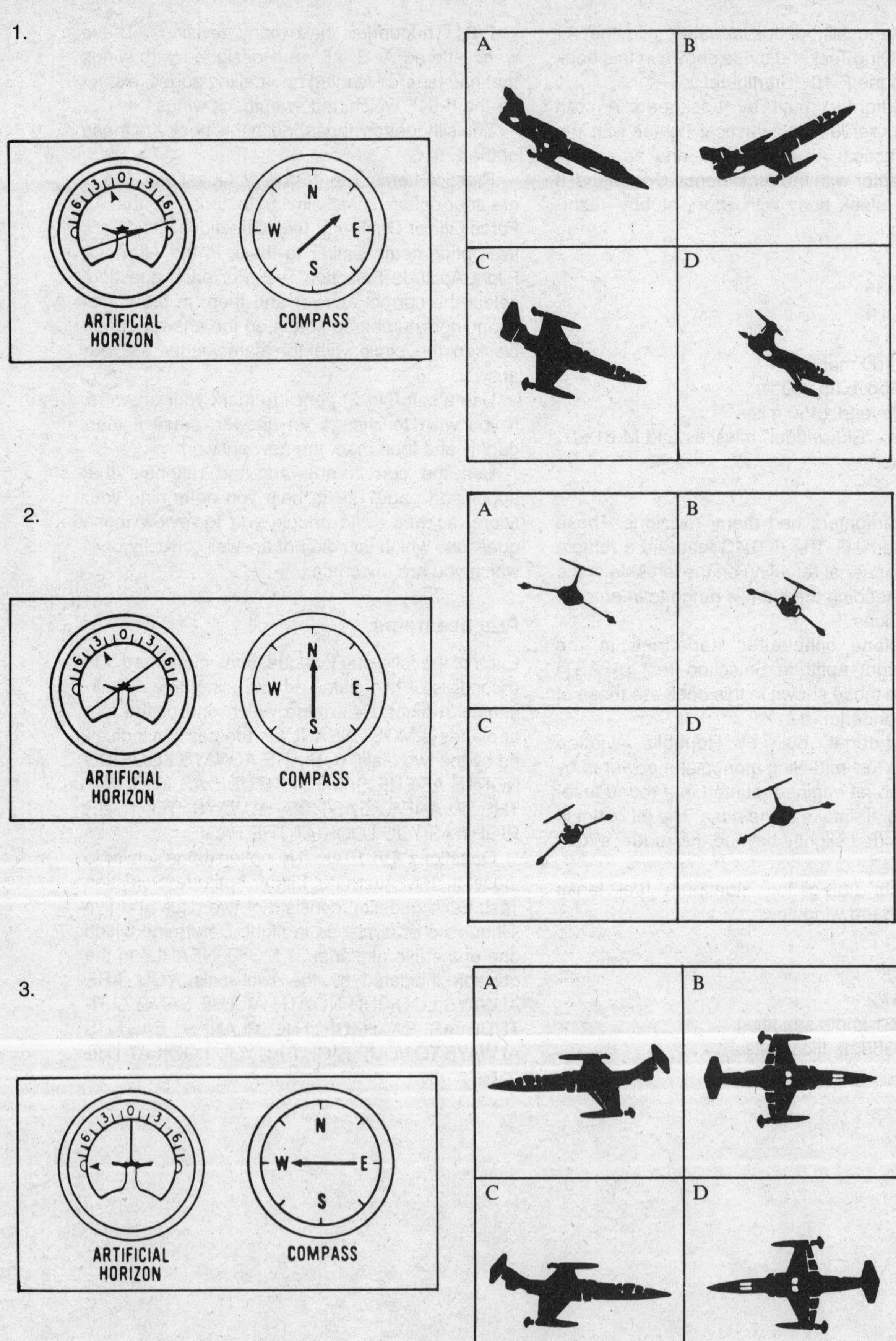
1.
ARTIFICIAL HORIZON
COMPASS
A
B
C
D
2.
ARTIFICIAL HORIZON
COMPASS
A
B
C
D
3.
ARTIFICIAL HORIZON
COMPASS
A
B
C
D

4.

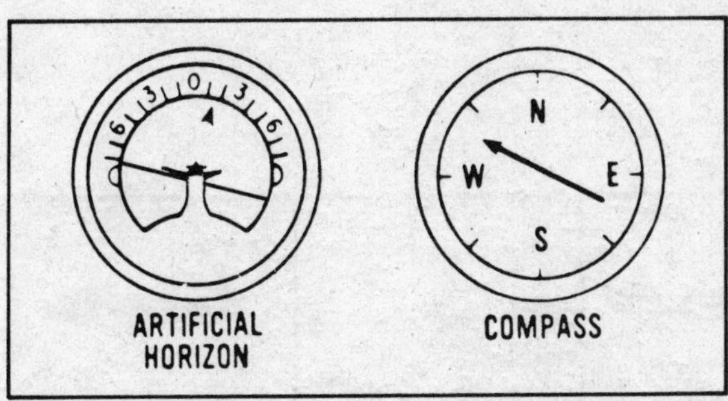
ARTIFICIAL HORIZON
COMPASS
N
W
E
S

A
B
C
D

5.

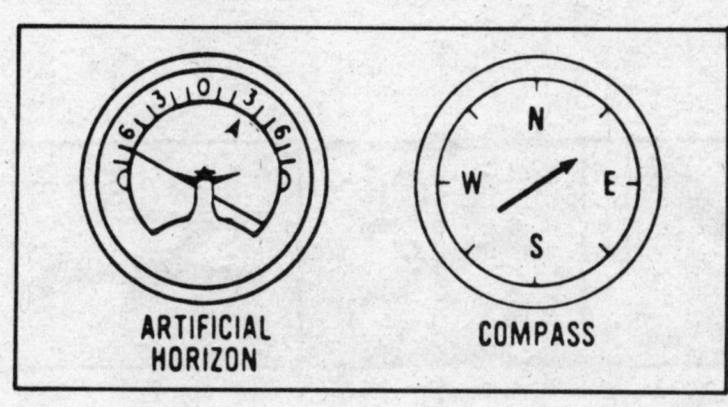
ARTIFICIAL HORIZON
COMPASS
N
W
E
S

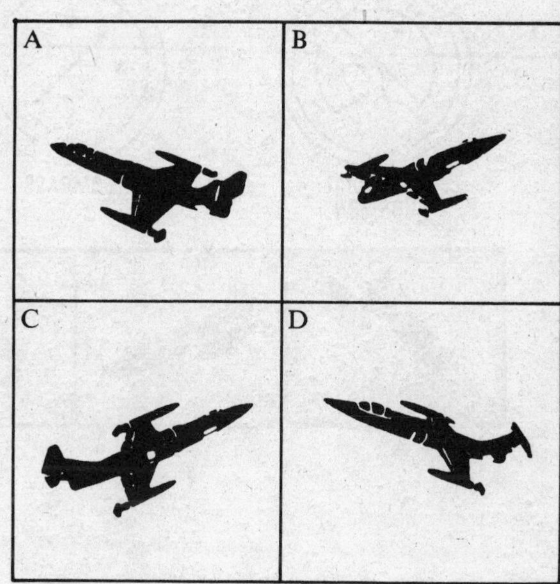
A
B
C
D

6.

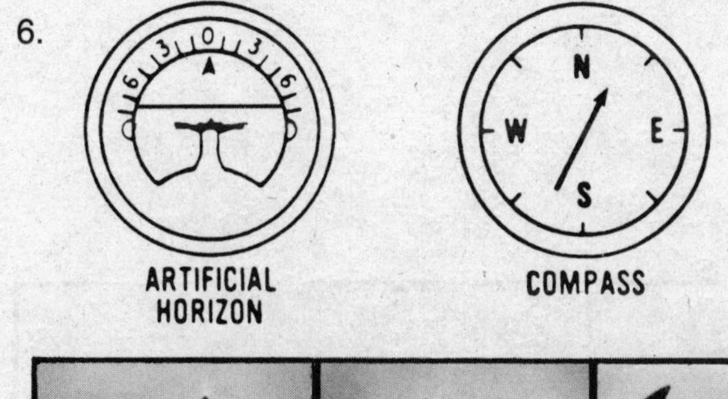
ARTIFICIAL HORIZON
COMPASS
N
W
E
S

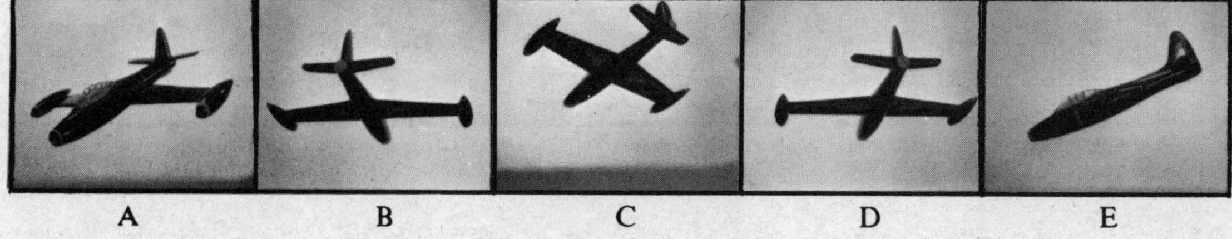

A B C D E

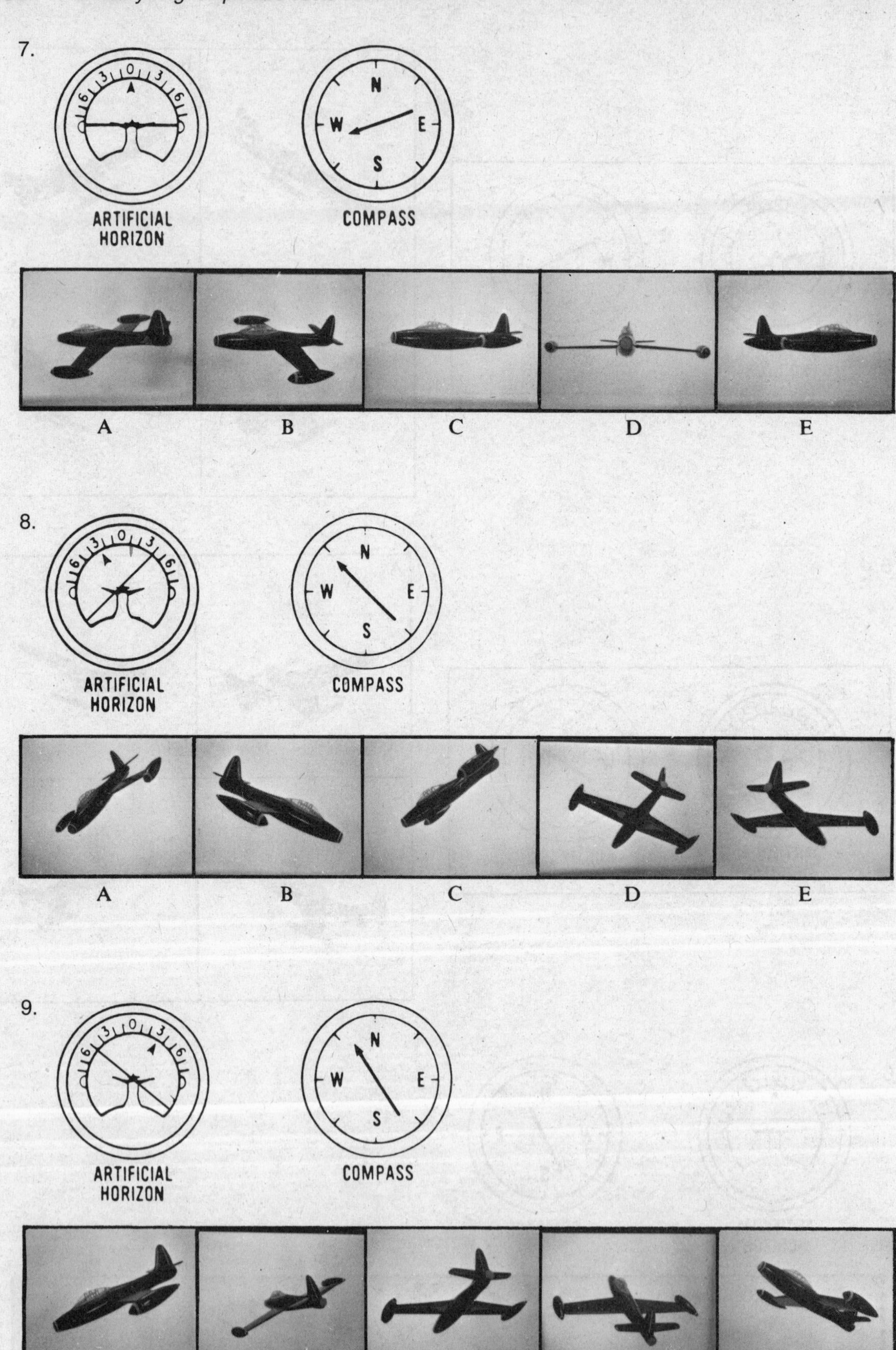
7.
ARTIFICIAL HORIZON
COMPASS
N
E
S
W
A
B
C
D
E
8.
ARTIFICIAL HORIZON
COMPASS
N
E
S
W
A
B
C
D
E
9.
ARTIFICIAL HORIZON
COMPASS
N
E
S
W
A
B
C
D
E

10.

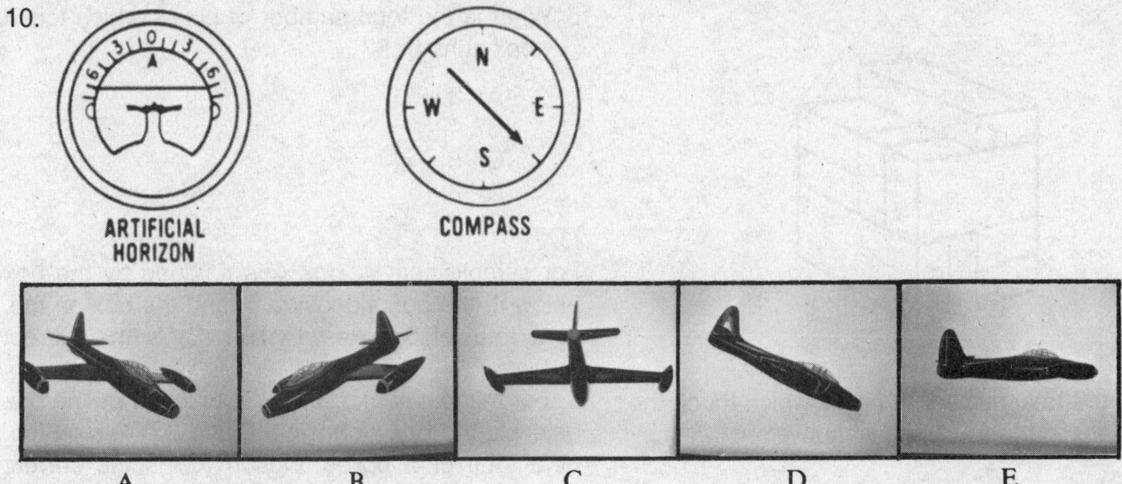

Block Counting

Questions on block counting appear in Subtest 11—Block Counting of the Air Force Officer Qualifying Test and are used in constructing both the pilot and navigator-technical composites. They are designed to test your ability to "see into" a three-dimensional pile of blocks. Such questions ascertain space perception or discern spatial relations. Questions of this type are commonly used in examining for many vocational fields, such as computer technology, design, drafting, engineering, architecture, and many military occupational specialties.

Sample items to illustrate some of the types of block counting questions generally found in such tests follow. All of the blocks in each pile are the same size and shape.

1.

How many boxes are in the preceding diagram?

23
24
25
26
27

There are 12 boxes in the front row and 13 in the back row, or a total of 25 boxes. Option (C) is the correct answer.

2.

How many cubes are in the diagram shown above?

12
13
14
15
16

There are 9 cubes in the bottom tier, 5 in the middle tier and 2 in the top tier, or a total of 16 cubes. Option (E) is the correct answer.

3.

What is the total number of boxes which touch the top box in the stack shown above?

(A) 2
(B) 3
(C) 4
(D) 5
(E) 6

The boxes in the stack that are touching the top box are shaded. A total of three boxes touch the top box. Option (B) is the correct answer.

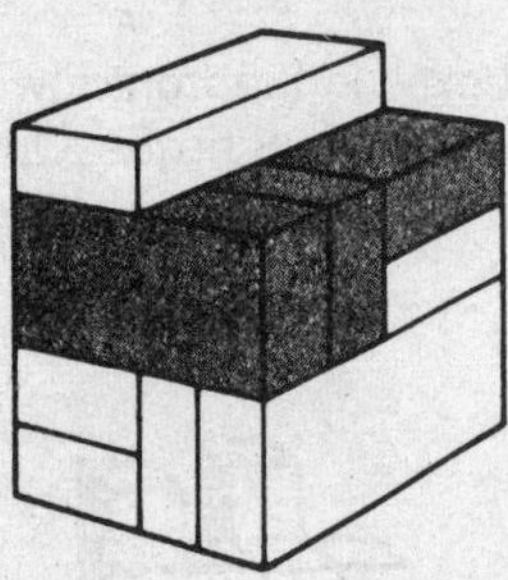

Answer sample items *4* and *5* on the basis of the pile of boxes shown below.

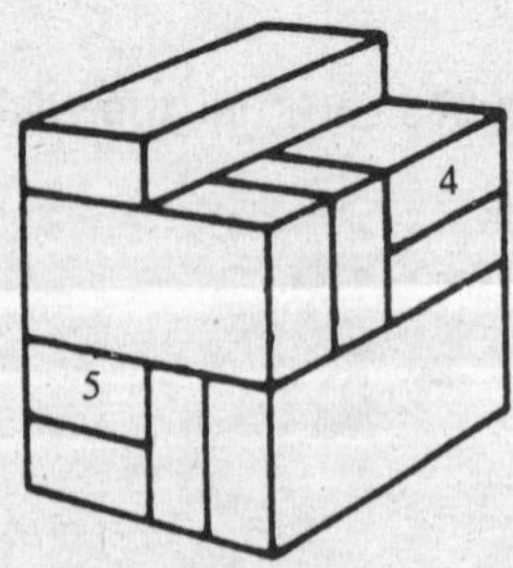

4. What is the total number of boxes which touch box number 4?

(A) 2
(B) 3
(C) 4
(D) 5
(E) 6

5. What is the total number of boxes which touch box number 5?

(A) 3
(B) 4
(C) 5
(D) 6
(E) 7

For sample item 4, box 4 is touched by the box below it, the box alongside it, and the box on top, or a total of 3 boxes. Option (B) is the correct answer.

For sample item 5, box 5 is touched by the box below it, the box alongside it, and 3 boxes on top, or a total of 5 boxes. Option (C) is the correct answer.

Practice items *1* to *10* follow. For each question, select the correct answer and then, in the correspondingly numbered space on the answer sheet, blacken the circle with the same letter as your answer.

Use a soft (No. 2) pencil to mark your answers. If you wish to change an answer, erase it thoroughly and then mark the new answer.

Use the correct answers and rationale that appear on page 122 to help you determine your score, as well as to enable you to review those questions which you did not answer correctly or are uncertain of.

Practice Items

Each of the following five questions numbered *1* to *5* contains a diagram of a three-dimensional pile of blocks. You are to ascertain the number of blocks in each pile. All of the blocks in each pile are the same size and shape.

1.

What is the total number of blocks in the pile shown above?

(A) 11
(B) 12
(C) 13
(D) 14
(E) 15

2.

How many blocks are in the above diagram?

(A) 23
(B) 24
(C) 25
(D) 26
(E) 27

3.

How many blocks are in the diagram shown above?

(A) 40
(B) 41
(C) 42
(D) 43
(E) 44

4.

What is the total number of blocks in the above diagram?

(A) 54
(B) 56
(C) 58
(D) 60
(E) 62

5.

What is the number of blocks in the pile shown above?

(A) 34
(B) 35
(C) 36
(D) 37
(E) 38

Each of the following five questions numbered *6* to *10* are based on the three-dimensional pile of blocks shown below. Determine how many pieces are touched by each numbered block. All of the blocks in the pile are the same size and shape.

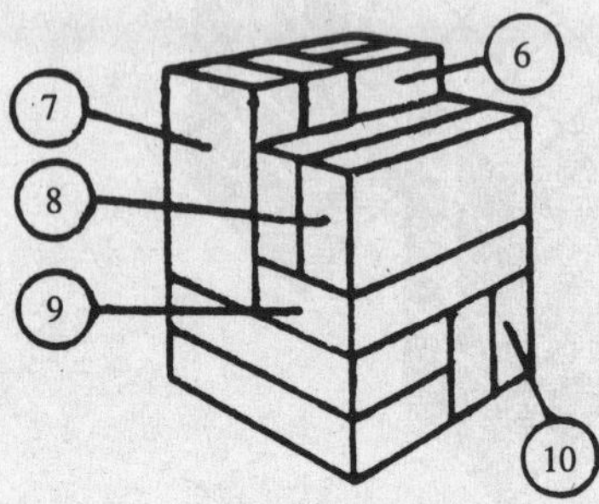

Block	Options				
	A	B	C	D	E
6	3	4	5	6	7
7	4	5	6	7	8
8	1	2	3	4	5
9	4	5	6	7	8
10	4	5	6	7	8

Table Reading

Table reading questions appear in Subtest 12—Table Reading of the Air Force Officer Qualifying Test. They are used in constructing both the pilot and the navigator-technical composites. They are designed to measure your ability to read tabular material quickly and accurately.

Now look at the following sample items.

Answer sample items *1* to *3* on the basis of the table given on page 95.

1. The only employee who was not absent because of illness is:

   (A) Hart
   (B) Lopez
   (C) Page
   (D) Quinn
   (E) Vetter

2. The employee with the lowest salary was absent on vacation for

   (A) 17 days
   (B) 18 days
   (C) 19 days
   (D) 20 days
   (E) 21 days

3. Which one of the following was absent on vacation for more than 20 days?

   (A) Carty
   (B) Ingersoll
   (C) Lopez
   (D) Quinn
   (E) Vetter

In sample item *1*, look down the sick leave column and note that only Quinn had not used any sick leave. Option (D) is the correct answer.

In sample item *2*, look down the yearly salary column and note that the lowest salary is $17,380. This is the salary received by Quinn who was absent on vacation for 19 days. Option (C) is correct.

In sample item *3*, note that there are three employees who were absent on vacation for more than 20 days. However, the only one of the three such employees listed in the options is Vetter. Option (E) is the correct answer.

Record of Employees

Name of Employee	*Where Assigned*	*Number of Days Absent Vacation*	*Sick Leave*	*Yearly Salary*
Carty	Laundry	18	4	$19,300
Hart	Laboratory	24	8	17,860
Intersoll	Buildings	20	17	18,580
King	Supply	12	10	17,860
Lopez	Laboratory	17	8	17,500
Martin	Buildings	13	12	17,500
Page	Buildings	5	7	17,500
Quinn	Supply	19	0	17,380
Sage	Buildings	23	10	18,940
Vetter	Laundry	21	2	18,300

Practice items *1* to *5* follow. For each question, select the best answer and then, in the correspondingly numbered space on the answer sheet, blacken the circle with the same letter as your answer.

Use a soft (No. 2) pencil to mark your answers. If you wish to change an answer, erase it thoroughly and then mark the new answer.

Use the correct answers and rationale that appear on page 122 to help you determine your score, as well as to enable you to review those questions which you did not answer correctly or are uncertain of.

Practice Items

Answer practice items *1* to *5* on the basis of the table shown on the right. Notice that the X values are shown at the top of the table and the Y values are shown on the left of the table. Find the entry that occurs at the intersection of the row and column corresponding to the values given.

X VALUE

Y VALUE	–3	–2	–1	0	+1	+2	+3
+3	22	23	25	27	28	29	30
+2	23	25	27	29	30	31	32
+1	24	26	28	30	32	33	34
0	26	27	29	31	33	34	35
–1	27	29	30	32	34	35	37
–2	28	30	31	33	35	36	38
–3	29	31	32	34	36	37	39

	X	**Y**	**A**	**B**	**C**	**D**	**E**
1.	–1	0	29	33	32	35	34
2.	–2	–2	22	29	23	31	30
3.	+2	–1	25	31	35	30	27
4.	0	+3	22	24	25	27	29
5.	+1	–2	36	33	39	35	32

Aviation information

Questions on aviation information appear in Subtest 13—Aviation Information of the Air Force Officer Qualifying Test—and are used in constructing the pilot composite. Aviation information questions also appear in the Aviation/Nautical Information Test (ANT) of the Navy and Marine Corps Aviation Selection Test Battery. This Aviation/Nautical Information Test (ANT) is used in constructing the pilot flight aptitude rating and the flight officer flight aptitude rating.

General understanding of the principles of helicopter flight is the test area for Subtest 4—Helicopter Knowledge of the Alternate Flight Aptitude Selection Test.

There are many basic books on aviation available at libraries and bookstores. Some of the government manuals available at the government printing offices may also prove to be helpful.

Now look at the following sample items.

Questions *1* to *8* are based on the following diagram of an airplane.

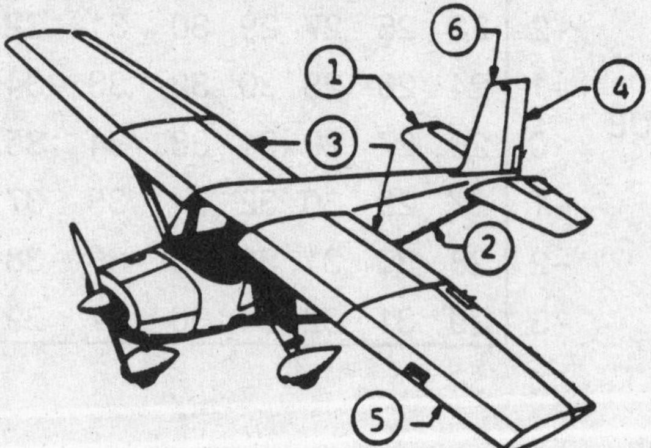

1. The part of the airplane numbered 1 is the
   (A) horizontal stabilizer
   (B) left aileron
   (C) left wing
   (D) right aileron
   (E) right wing

2. The part of the airplane numbered 2 is the
   (A) empennage
   (B) flight control and control surfaces
   (C) fuselage
   (D) landing gear
   (E) wing assembly

3. The parts of the airplane numbered 3 are the
   (A) ailerons
   (B) horizontal stabilizers
   (C) landing flaps
   (D) landing wheels
   (E) trim tabs

4. The part of the airplane numbered 4 is the
   (A) elevator
   (B) fuselage
   (C) landing flap
   (D) rudder
   (E) vertical fin

5. The part of the airplane numbered 5 is the
   (A) horizontal stabilizer
   (B) leading edge, left wing
   (C) leading edge, right wing
   (D) trailing edge, left wing
   (E) trailing edge, right wing

6. The part of the airplane numbered 6 is part of the
   (A) vertical fin
   (B) flight control and control surfaces
   (C) fuselage
   (D) landing gear
   (E) wings

The basic parts of the airplane are shown below for questions 1–6.

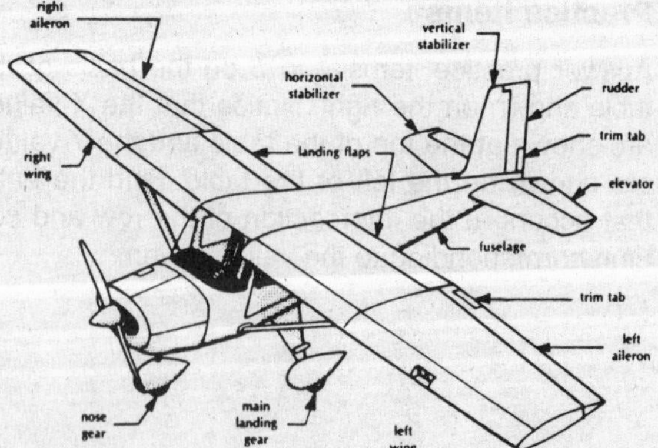

1. (A)
2. (C)
3. (C)
4. (D)
5. (B)
6. (A)

7. The airplane in the diagram above may best be described as

   (A) high wing—externally braced; conventional type landing gear
   (B) high wing—externally braced; tricycle type landing gear
   (C) high wing—full cantilever; conventional type landing gear
   (D) high wing—full cantilever; tricycle type landing gear
   (E) mid wing—semi cantilever; tricycle type landing gear

8. The landing gear on the airplane in the diagram above has a

   (A) nose skid
   (B) nose wheel
   (C) tail skid
   (D) tail wheel
   (E) set of parallel skids

For question 7, note the high wings and external braces, as well as the two main wheels and a steerable nose wheel—the tricycle type. Option (B) is the correct answer.

For question 8, note the nose wheel. There are no skids. Option (B) is the correct answer.

9. The small hinged section on the elevator of most airplanes is called the

   (A) flap
   (B) aileron
   (C) stringer
   (D) trim tab
   (E) vertical fin

The small hinged section on the elevator is called the trim tab. It helps prevent pilot fatigue by relieving control pressure at any desired flight altitude. Option (D) is the correct answer.

10. The wing shape shown below is best described as

   (A) double tapered
   (B) straight leading and trailing edges
   (C) straight leading edge, tapered trailing edge
   (D) tapered leading and trailing edges
   (E) tapered leading edge, straight trailing edge

Note the tapered leading or forward edge of the wing and the straight trailing or rear edge of the wing. Option (E) is the correct answer.

11. Movement about the longitudinal axis of the aircraft is termed

   (A) bank
   (B) pitch
   (C) skid
   (D) slip
   (E) yaw

In aviation terminology, to *bank* is to roll about the longitudinal axis of the aircraft. Option (A) is the correct answer.

12. Which one of the following does *not* affect density altitude?

   (A) Altitude
   (B) Atmospheric pressure
   (C) Moisture content of air
   (D) Temperature
   (E) Wind velocity

Density altitude pertains to a theoretical air density which exists under standard conditions at a given altitude. The four factors which affect density altitude are altitude, atmospheric pressure, temperature, and moisture content of the air. Option (E) is the correct answer.

13. The lifting power for dirigibles is now provided by

   (A) helium
   (B) hot air
   (C) hydrogen
   (D) nitrogen
   (E) oxygen

The dirigible, or zeppelin, is lifted by helium. Hydrogen is highly flammable and is no longer used for lifting. Hot air is used to lift balloons. Option (A) is the correct answer.

14. The name Sikorsky is generally associated with the development of

   (A) lighter-than-air aircraft
   (B) rotary wing aircraft
   (C) supersonic aircraft
   (D) turbojets
   (E) turboprops

Igor Sikorsky designed and produced the first practical helicopter. Versatile rotary wing aircraft are now produced in various military and civilian versions. Option (B) is the correct answer.

15. The maneuver in which the helicopter is maintained in nearly motionless flight over a reference point at a constant altitude and a constant heading is termed

 (A) autorotation
 (B) feathering action
 (C) hovering
 (D) free wheeling
 (E) torque

Hovering is the term applied when a helicopter maintains a constant position at a selected point, usually several feet above the ground. Option (C) is the correct answer.

Practice items *1* to *25* follow. For each question, select the best answer and then, in the correspondingly numbered space on the answer sheet, blacken the circle with the same letter as your answer.

Use a soft (No. 2) pencil to mark your answers. If you wish to change an answer, erase it thoroughly and then mark the new answer.

Use the correct answers and rationale that appear on page 123 to help you determine your score, as well as to enable you to review those questions which you did not answer correctly or are uncertain of.

Practice Items

Each of the questions or incomplete statements is followed by five choices. Decide which one of the choices best answers the question or completes the statement.

1. Most airplanes are designed so that the outer tips of the wing are higher than the wing roots attached to the fuselage in order to

 (A) increase the maximum permissible payload
 (B) provide lateral stability
 (C) provide longitudinal stability
 (D) reduce fuel consumption
 (E) streamline the fuselage

2. If an airfoil moves forward and upward, the relative wind moves

 (A) backward and downward
 (B) backward and upward
 (C) forward and downward
 (D) forward and upward
 (E) forward horizontally

3. Many factors influence lift and drag. If the wing area is doubled

 (A) the lift will be doubled but the drag will be halved
 (B) the lift will be halved but the drag will be doubled
 (C) the lift and drag will be doubled
 (D) the lift and drag will be halved
 (E) there is no effect on lift or drag

4. Tetraethyl lead (TEL) is used principally as an additive that

 (A) absorbs moisture in gasoline
 (B) decreases viscosity of gasoline
 (C) has a low antiknock quality
 (D) increases gasoline antiknock quality
 (E) increases volatility of gasoline

5. Standard weights have been established for numerous items used in weight and balance computations. The standard weight for gasoline used in an airplane is

 (A) 6 lbs./U.S. gal.
 (B) 7.5 lbs./U.S. gal.
 (C) 8.35 lbs./U.S. gal.
 (D) 10 lbs./U.S. gal.
 (E) 15 lbs./U.S. gal.

6. The internal pressure of a fluid decreases at points where the speed of the fluid increases. This statement which partially explains how an airplane wing produces lift is called

 (A) Archimedes' Principle
 (B) Bernocilli's Principle
 (C) Kepler's Law
 (D) Newton's Law
 (E) Pascal's Principle

7. The rearward force acting on an airplane during flight is termed

 (A) drag
 (B) gravity
 (C) lift
 (D) thrust
 (E) weight

8. The acute angle between the chord line of the wing and the direction of the relative wind is the

   (A) angle of attack
   (B) angle of incidence
   (C) axis of rotation
   (D) lift vector
   (E) pitch angle

9. Which of the following statements is true regarding lift and drag?

   (A) As the air density increases, lift and drag decrease.
   (B) As the air density increases, lift increases but drag decreases.
   (C) As the air density increases, lift decreases but drag increases.
   (D) As the air density increases, lift and drag increase.
   (E) Lift varies inversely with the density of air.

10. The aft end of the airfoil where the airflow over the upper surface meets the airflow from the lower surface is called the

   (A) camber
   (B) chord
   (C) leading edge
   (D) relative wind
   (E) trailing edge

11. The empennage of an airplane is the

   (A) fuselage
   (B) landing gear
   (C) power plant
   (D) tail section
   (E) wing assembly

12. The primary use of the ailerons is to

   (A) bank the airplane
   (B) control the direction of yaw
   (C) control the pitch attitude
   (D) permit a lower landing speed
   (E) provide a steeper climb path

13. The pitot is an important component in measuring

   (A) airspeed
   (B) altitude
   (C) direction
   (D) fuel pressure
   (E) oil pressure

14. Applying forward pressure on the control causes the elevator surfaces to move downward. This

   (A) pushes the airplane's tail downward and the nose downward
   (B) pushes the airplane's tail downward and the nose upward
   (C) pushes the airplane's tail upward and the nose downward
   (D) pushes the airplane's tail upward and the nose upward
   (E) yaws the nose in the desired direction

15. Runways are assigned numbers which are determined by the magnetic direction of the runway. The runway's magnetic direction is rounded off to the closest ten degrees and the last zero is omitted. If a runway is numbered 3 at one end of the runway strip, what would it be numbered at the other end?

   (A) 3
   (B) 12
   (C) 15
   (D) 21
   (E) 33

16. At a controlled airport, the light signal used by the tower to warn an aircraft in flight that the airport is unsafe and not to land is a(n)

   (A) alternating red and green
   (B) flashing green
   (C) flashing red
   (D) steady green
   (E) steady red

17. Airport runway lights used to illuminate the runway are

   (A) blue
   (B) green
   (C) red
   (D) white
   (E) yellow

18. The illustration shown below is a ground view of a weathervane, looking up from the street below. The wind is coming from the

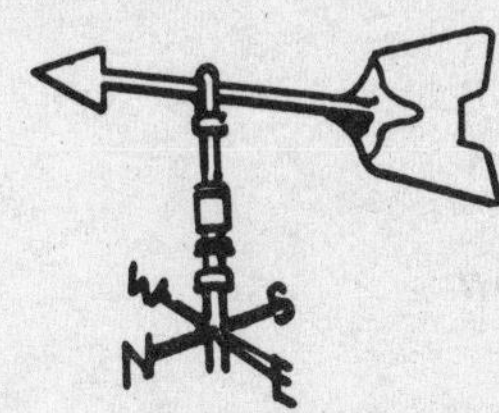

(A) NE
(B) SE
(C) SW
(D) NW
(E) SSE

19. The time 2:00 p.m. is expressed in the 24-hour system as

(A) zero two zero zero
(B) zero four zero zero
(C) one four
(D) one four zero zero
(E) two zero zero

20. In the figure below, the pilot has banked the airplane

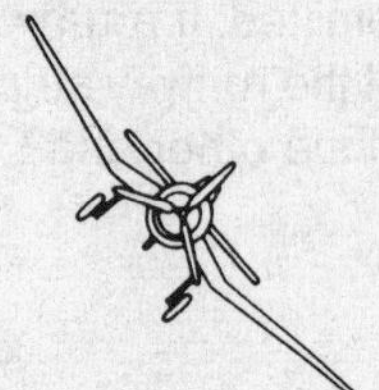

(A) 30° to the right
(B) 45° to the right
(C) 60° to the right
(D) 45° to the left
(E) 30° to the left

Items *21* to *25* pertain to helicopter operations.

21. Which of the following is used by the helicopter pilot to increase or decrease tail-rotor thrust, as needed, to counteract torque effect?

(A) clutch
(B) collective
(C) throttle control
(D) pedals
(E) free wheeling unit

22. Limiting airspeeds are shown on an airspeed indicator by a color coding. The radial line placed on the airspeed indicator to show the airspeed limit beyond which operation is dangerous is colored

(A) blue
(B) brown
(C) green
(D) red
(E) yellow

23. If engine failure is experienced while hovering below 10 feet, the pilot should cushion the landing by applying the

(A) clutch
(B) collective
(C) cyclic
(D) pedals
(E) throttle

24. Weight and balance limitations must be met before takeoff. Which of the following is *not* part of the useful load (payload)?

(A) baggage
(B) oil
(C) passengers
(D) pilot
(E) usable fuel

25. A basic principle of helicopter performance states that for any given gross weight,

(A) the higher the density altitude, the less the rate of climb
(B) the higher the density altitude, the greater the rate of climb
(C) the lower the density altitude, the less the rate of climb
(D) the density altitude and rate of climb are directly proportional
(E) there is no relationship between density altitude and rate of climb

Nautical Information

Questions on nautical information appear in the Aviation/Nautical Information Test of the Navy and Marine Corps Aviation Selection Test Battery. The Aviation/Nautical Information Test is one of the tests used in constructing the pilot flight aptitude rating and the flight officer flight aptitude rating. Now look at the following sample items.

Sample Items:

1. To go in the direction of the ship's bow is to go

(A) aft
(B) below
(C) forward
(D) outboard
(E) topside

The bow is the forward part of a ship. To go in that direction is to go forward. Option (C) is the correct answer.

2. In marine navigation, speed is measured in

(A) knots
(B) miles
(C) nautical miles
(D) range
(E) standard miles

Speed is measured in knots, a term meaning nautical miles per hour. Option (A) is the correct answer.

3. The ratio of the international nautical mile to the statute mile is most nearly

(A) $\frac{3}{4}$

(B) $\frac{7}{8}$

(C) $\frac{1}{1}$

(D) $\frac{8}{7}$

(E) $\frac{4}{3}$

The international nautical mile is most nearly 6078 feet; the statute mile is 5280 feet. The ratio is approximately $\frac{8}{7}$. Option (D) is the correct answer.

4. The compass is used to determine direction. East is indicated at a reading of

(A) 000 degrees
(B) 090 degrees
(C) 180 degrees
(D) 270 degrees
(E) 360 degrees

All directions are measured from north on a 360° system. East is 090 degrees; south is 180 degrees; west is 270 degrees; north is 000 or 360°. Option (B) is the correct answer.

5. Compass north is generally not the same as magnetic north because of

(A) diurnal change
(B) gyrocompass error
(C) parallax
(D) the influence of local magnetic forces
(E) vessel speed, heading and latitude

The influence of local magnetic forces, such as iron, near the compass causes deviation from magnetic north. Option (D) is the correct answer.

6. Using the 24-hour basis in navigation, 8:45 a.m. would be written as

(A) 845
(B) 0845
(C) 08.45
(D) 2045
(E) 20.45

The 24-hour clock uses four digits. Hours and minutes less than 10 are preceded by a zero. Option (B) is the correct answer.

7. Delicate, feather-like, white clouds occurring at very high altitude are termed

(A) altostratus clouds
(B) cirrocumulus clouds
(C) cirrus clouds
(D) cumulus clouds
(E) nimbostratus clouds

Cirrus clouds are high-altitude delicate white clouds with little shading. Option (C) is the correct answer.

8. The formation of fog may be predicted by determining the

(A) atmospheric pressure
(B) changes in atmospheric pressure
(C) color of the sky
(D) difference between the wet- and dry-bulb temperatures
(E) wind speed

The formation of fog may be predicted by using the wet-and-dry bulb. Fog usually forms when the wet-bulb depression is less than 4°. Option (D) is the correct answer.

9. Icebreakers are operated by the

(A) U.S. Army
(B) U.S. Coast Guard
(C) U.S. Department of Commerce
(D) U.S. Department of the Interior
(E) U.S. Navy

The U.S. Coast Guard is responsible for national icebreaking missions. Option (B) is the correct answer.

10. A ship, at a latitude of 35°N and a longitude of 30°E, is in the

(A) Bering Sea
(B) Caribbean Sea
(C) Mediterranean Sea
(D) North Sea
(E) Sea of Japan

The coordinates given indicate a position in the Mediterranean Sea. Option (C) is the correct answer.

Practice items *1* to *30* follow. For each question, select the best answer and then, in the correspondingly numbered space on the answer sheet, blacken the circle with the same letter as your answer.

Use a soft (No. 2) pencil to mark your answers. If you wish to change an answer, erase it thoroughly and then mark the new answer.

Use the correct answers and rationale that appear on pages 130–131 to help you determine your score, as well as to enable you to review those questions which you did not answer correctly or are uncertain of.

Practice Items

Each of the following 25 questions or incomplete statements is followed by five choices. Decide which one of the choices best answers the question or completes the statement.

1. "Zulu Time" used in ship communication is

(A) Daylight Savings Time
(B) Local Mean Time
(C) Greenwich Mean Time
(D) Standard Time
(E) Zone Time

2. Which of the following is a common type of visual communication used shipboard?

(A) Facsimile
(B) Foghorn
(C) Radiotelegraph
(D) Satellite
(E) Semiphore

3. The plane perpendicular to the earth's axis and midway between the two poles divides the earth into the

(A) eastern and western hemispheres
(B) north and south poles
(C) northern and southern hemispheres
(D) parallels and meridians
(E) upper meridian and lower meridian

4. Which of the following types of rope is strongest?

(A) cotton
(B) hemp
(C) manila
(D) nylon
(E) sisal

5. Greenwich, at prime meridian, is at a latitude of approximately 50°N. Which of the following cities is closest to Greenwich?

(A) Amsterdam—52°22'N 4°53'E
(B) Athens—37°58'N 23°43'E
(C) Copenhagen—55°40'N 12°54'E
(D) Oslo—50°57'N 10°42'E
(E) Stockholm—59°17'N 18°3'E

6. A latitude of 21°N and longitude of 159°W is in the vicinity of

(A) Cuba
(B) Falkland Islands
(C) Hawaii
(D) Philippines
(E) Samoa

7. An unlighted buoy, used to mark the left side of a channel when facing inland, is called a

(A) bell buoy
(B) can buoy
(C) nun buoy
(D) spar buoy
(E) whistle buoy

8. If the clock shows the time to be 1400 aboard a ship sailing in time zone +3, what would be the time in the Greenwich zone?

(A) 0800
(B) 1100
(C) 1400
(D) 1700
(E) 2000

9. The navigation light associated with "port" is colored

(A) green
(B) red
(C) white
(D) yellow
(E) none of the above

10. To go in the direction of the ship's stern is to go

(A) aft
(B) below
(C) forward
(D) inboard
(E) topside

11. The vertical distance from the waterline to the lowest part of the ship's bottom is the

(A) draft
(B) freeboard
(C) list
(D) sounding
(E) trim

12. The forward part of the main deck of a ship is generally called the

(A) fantail
(B) forecastle
(C) quarterdeck
(D) superstructure
(E) topside

13. The international Date Line is located at the

(A) 0 meridian
(B) 180th meridian
(C) celestial meridian
(D) Greenwich, England
(E) prime meridian

14. Compass error in a magnetic compass caused by change in the magnetic field of the earth from place to place is termed

(A) bearing
(B) deviation
(C) reckoning
(D) sighting
(E) variation

15. The lubber's line used in ascertaining the ship's heading indicates

(A) compass error
(B) the direction of the ship's bow
(C) the ship's heading
(D) magnetic north
(E) true north

16. A tide falling after high tide is

(A) breaking
(B) bulging
(C) ebbing
(D) flooding
(E) slacking

17. Low even clouds that form just above the earth and give the sky a hazy appearance are termed

(A) altocumulus clouds
(B) altostratus clouds
(C) cirrocumulus clouds
(D) cirrus clouds
(E) stratus clouds

18. The Beaufort scale is generally used at sea in estimating

(A) wind direction
(B) wind speed
(C) atmospheric pressure
(D) relative humidity
(E) water depth

19. The instrument used in celestial navigation to measure angles in degrees, minutes, and seconds is called a(n)

(A) azimuth
(B) compass
(C) protractor
(D) sextant
(E) transit

20. When a person is reported overboard, the action to take first is to

(A) bring the ship to a halt
(B) track the person with a pair of binoculars
(C) throw life buoys over at once
(D) turn the ship around 180°
(E) reduce the ship's speed

21. A fathometer is generally used to

(A) determine direction
(B) determine Greenwich mean time
(C) make deep-sea soundings
(D) make shallow water soundings
(E) measure distance in nautical miles

22. 6:00 p.m. is written in the 24-hour system as

(A) 0600
(B) 0900
(C) 1200
(D) 1500
(E) 1800

23. In marine navigation, which of the following is *not* a method of determining position?
    (A) Celestial navigation
    (B) Dead reckoning
    (C) Electronic navigation
    (D) Piloting
    (E) Ranging

24. The intersection of the ship's main deck with the side plating is termed the
    (A) bilge
    (B) fantail
    (C) gunwale
    (D) platform
    (E) stanchion

25. The docking structure built at right angles to the shore is called a(n)
    (A) abutment
    (B) mooring
    (C) pier
    (D) slip
    (E) wharf

Questions *26* to *30* deal with boat rudder operations on a single-screw boat with a right-hand propeller. These questions are three-option items.

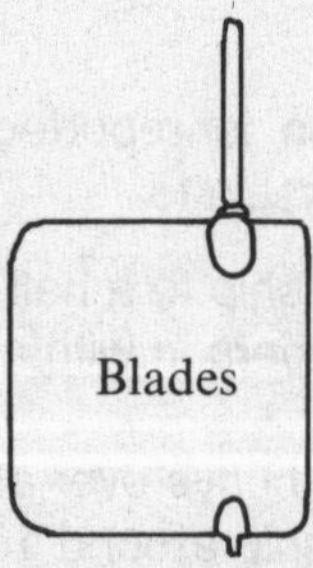

26. A balanced rudder (shown above) has about $\frac{1}{5}$ of the total rudder area projecting ahead of the rudder stock. An unbalanced rudder has the rudder stock attached to the edge of the blade. Which one of the following statements is characteristic of the balanced rudder but not of the unbalanced rudder?
    (A) It makes steering easier.
    (B) It makes steering more difficult.
    (C) It exerts considerable effect in increasing the strain on the steering gear.

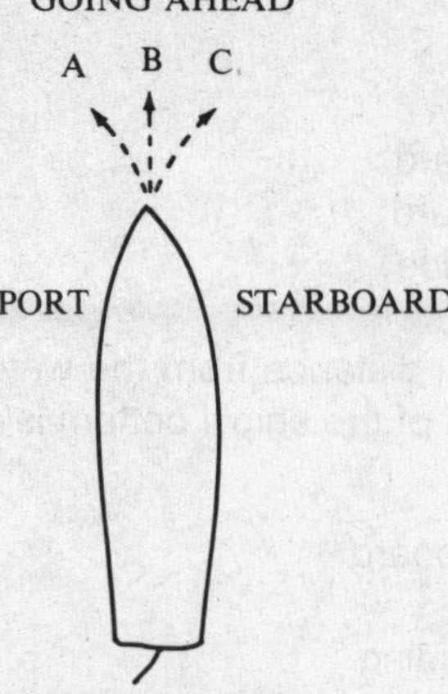

27. The figure above shows a boat that has left rudder and is going ahead. The bow of the boat would proceed in direction
    (A) A
    (B) B
    (C) C

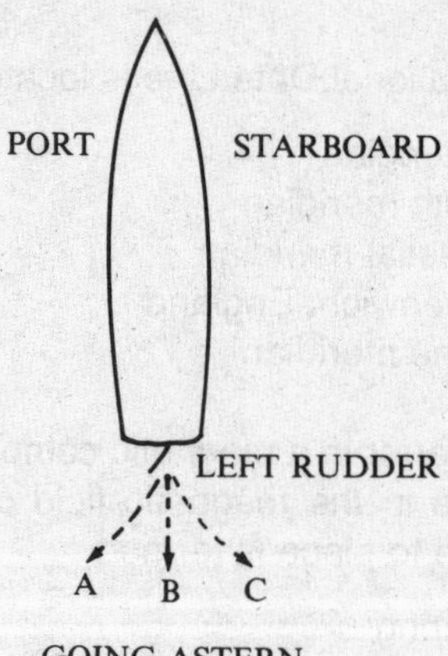

28. The figure above shows a boat that has left rudder and is going astern. The stem of the boat would proceed in direction
    (A) A
    (B) B
    (C) C

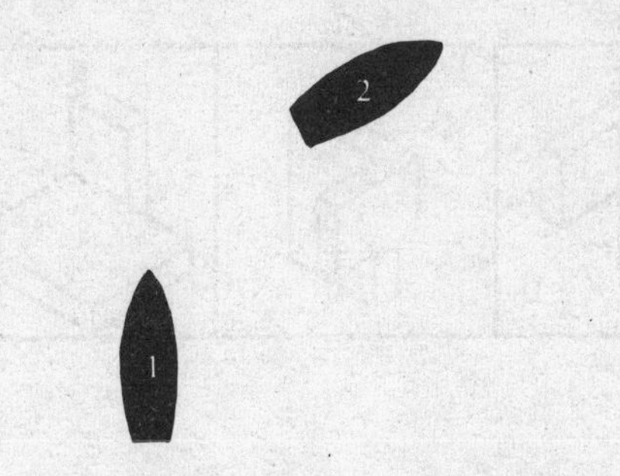

29. In the figure above, for boat to swing from position 1 to position 2, she should proceed with
    (A) left rudder
    (B) right rudder
    (C) rudder amidship

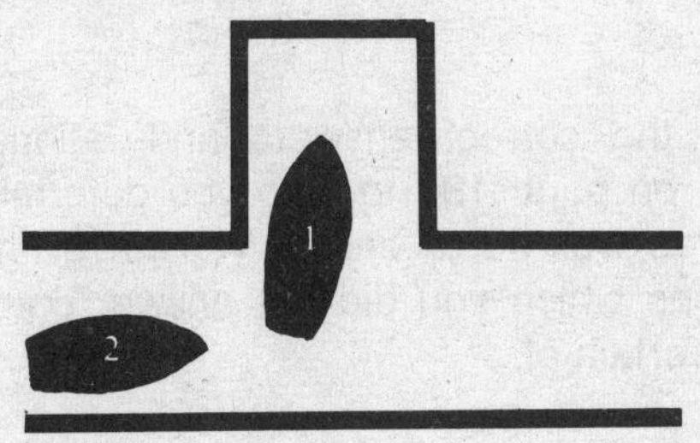

30. In the figure above, for boat to back out from position 1 in a slip to position 2 into the channel, she should back out with
    (A) left rudder
    (B) right rudder
    (C) rudder amidship

Rotated Blocks

Questions on rotated blocks appear in Subtest 14—Rotated Blocks of the Air Force Officer Qualifying Test—and are used in constructing the navigator-technical composite. This subtest is designed to test your ability to visualize and manipulate objects in space.

In each question, you are shown a picture of a block. To the right of the pictured block are five options, each showing a different block. You are required to select the option containing a block which is just like the pictured block at the left although turned in a different position. In order to arrive at the correct answer, you may have to mentally turn blocks over, turn them around, or turn them both over and around.

Look at the two blocks below. Although viewed from different angles, the blocks are just alike.

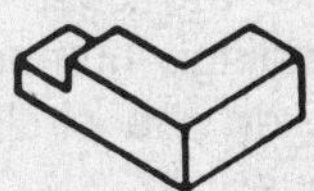

Look at the two blocks below. They are not alike. They can never be turned so that they will be alike.

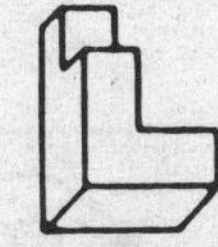

Now look at the sample item below. Which of the five choices is just like the first block?

Sample Items:

1	A	B	C	D	E
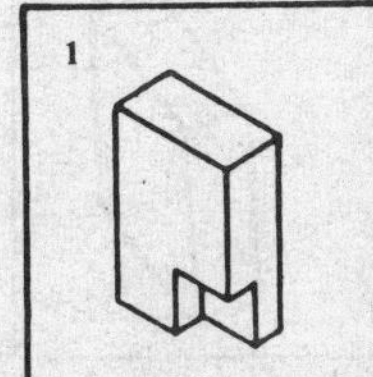	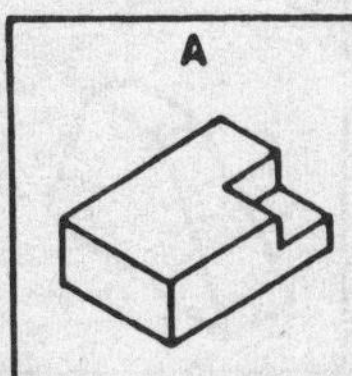		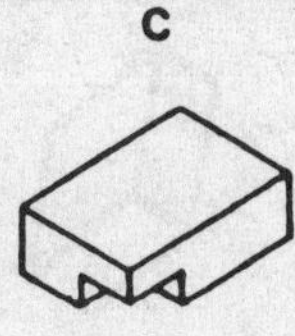	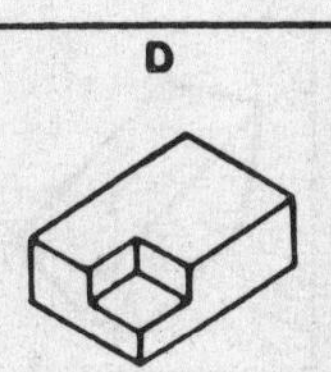	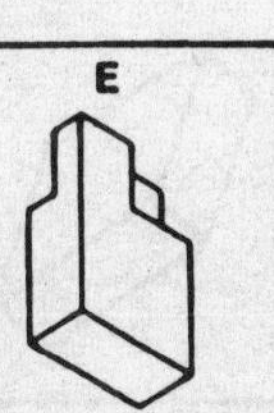

The correct answer for 1 is D.

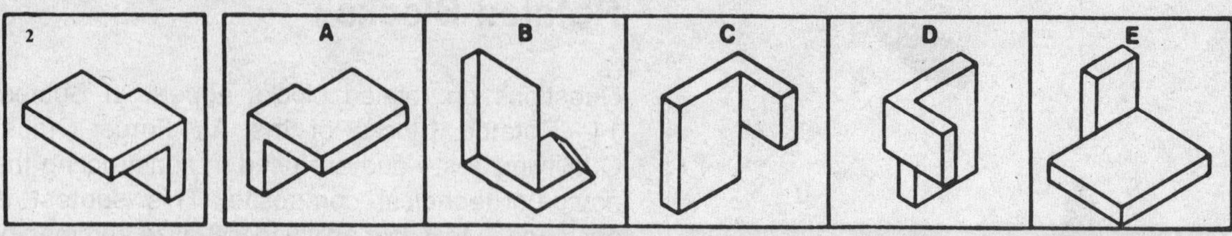

The right answer for 2 is C.

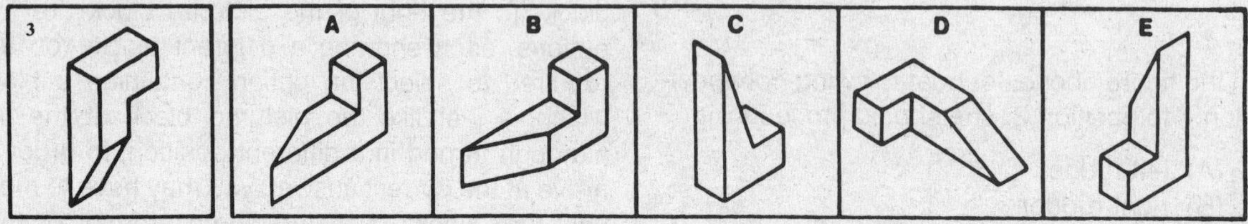

The right answer for 3 is A.

Practice items *1* to *5* follow. For each question, select the best answer and then, in the correspondingly numbered space on the answer sheet, blacken the circle with the same letter as your answer.

Use a soft (No. 2) pencil to mark your answers. If you wish to change an answer, erase it thoroughly and then mark your new answer.

Use the correct answers and rationale that appear on page 131 to help you determine your score, as well as to enable you to review those questions which you did not answer correctly or are uncertain of.

Practice Items

1.

2.

3.

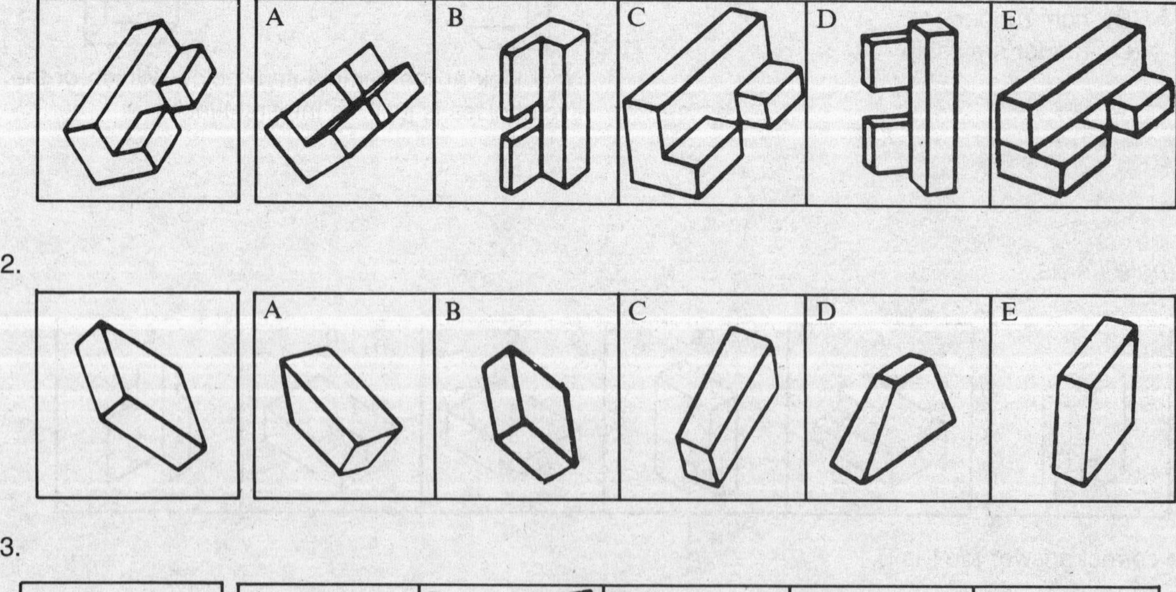

4.

5.

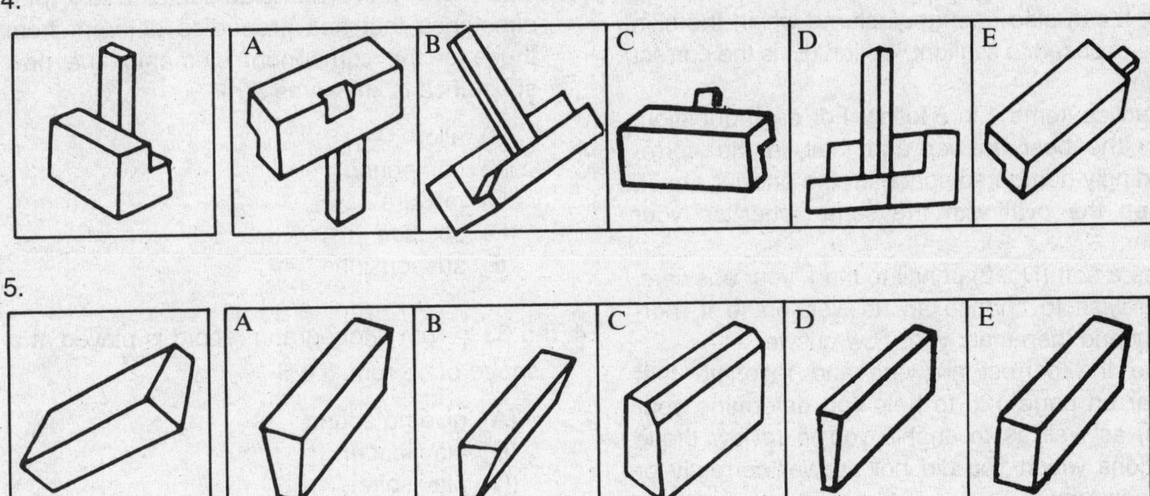

General Science

General science questions appear in Subtest 15—General Science of the Air Force Officer Qualifying Test—and are used in constructing the navigator-technical composite. The 20 questions on this subtest deal with life science, physical science, and earth science.

The life science items pertain to basic biology, human nutrition, and health. The physical science items deal with elementary chemistry and physics. Fundamentals of geology, meteorology, and astronomy may be included in the earth science area.

Now look at the sample items below.

1. What temperature is shown on a Fahrenheit thermometer when the centigrade thermometer reads 0°?

   (A) –40°
   (B) –32°
   (C) 0°
   (D) +32°
   (E) +40°

Water freezes at 0° on the centigrade or Celsius thermometer. Water freezes at 32° Fahrenheit. Option (D) is the correct answer.

2. Saliva contains an enzyme which acts on

   (A) carbohydrates
   (B) fats
   (C) minerals
   (D) proteins
   (E) vitamins

The salivary glands secrete the enzyme ptyalin which acts on carbohydrates. Option (A) is the correct answer.

3. In four hours, the earth rotates

   (A) 20°
   (B) 30°
   (C) 40°
   (D) 60°
   (E) 90°

The earth rotates 360° in 24 hours. Four hours is $\frac{1}{6}$ of 24 hours; $\frac{1}{6}$ of 360° is 60°. Option (D) is the correct answer.

4. The moon is a

   (A) meteor
   (B) planet
   (C) planetoid
   (D) satellite
   (E) star

The moon is a satellite of the earth. Option (D) is the correct answer.

5. The vitamin manufactured by the skin with the help of the sun is

   (A) A
   (B) B^6
   (C) B^{12}
   (D) C
   (E) D

Vitamin D can be found in fish liver oils and egg yolks. It can also be manufactured within the skin that is exposed to sunlight. Option (E) is the correct answer.

Practice items *1* to *5* follow. For each question, select the best answer and then in the correspondingly numbered space on the answer sheet, blacken the oval with the same letter as your answer.

Use a soft (No. 2) pencil to mark your answers. If you wish to change an answer, erase it thoroughly and then mark your new answer.

Use the correct answers and rationale that appear on page 125 to help you determine your score, as well as to enable you to review those questions which you did not answer correctly or are uncertain of.

Practice Items

1. "Shooting stars" are

   (A) exploding stars
   (B) cosmic rays
   (C) meteors
   (D) planetoids
   (E) X rays

2. Organisms that sustain their life cycles by feeding off other living organisms are known as

   (A) bacteria
   (B) molds
   (C) parasites
   (D) saprophytes
   (E) viruses

3. When two or more elements combine to form a substance that has properties different from those of the component elements, the new substance is known as a(n)

   (A) alloy
   (B) compound
   (C) mixture
   (D) solution
   (E) suspension

4. If a $33\frac{1}{3}$ rpm phonograph record is played at a speed of 45 rpm, it will

   (A) give no sound
   (B) play louder
   (C) play softer
   (D) sound higher-pitched
   (E) sound lower-pitched

5. Which one of the following gases is necessary for burning?

   (A) argon
   (B) carbon dioxide
   (C) hydrogen
   (D) nitrogen
   (E) oxygen

Hidden Figures

Questions on hidden figures appear in Subtest 16—Hidden Figures of the Air Force Officer Qualifying Test and are used in constructing the navigator-technical composite. They are designed to measure your ability to see simple figures in complex drawings. Although these figures are fairly well camouflaged, proper visualization should enable you to discern them without too much difficulty.

At the top of each section of this subtest are five figures lettered A, B, C, D, and E. Below these on each page are several numbered drawings. You must determine which lettered figure is contained in each of the numbered drawings.

The lettered figures are shown below:

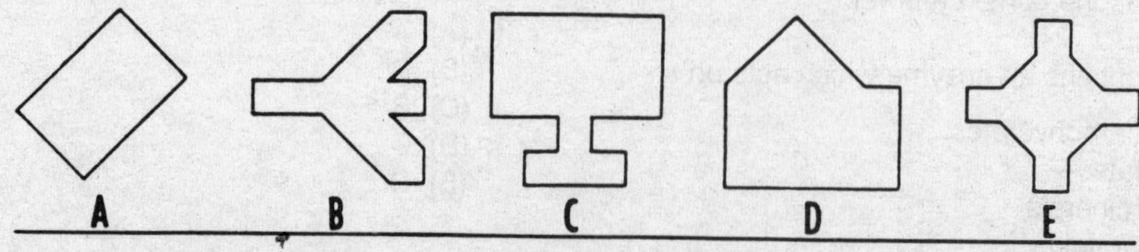

As an example, look at drawing X below.

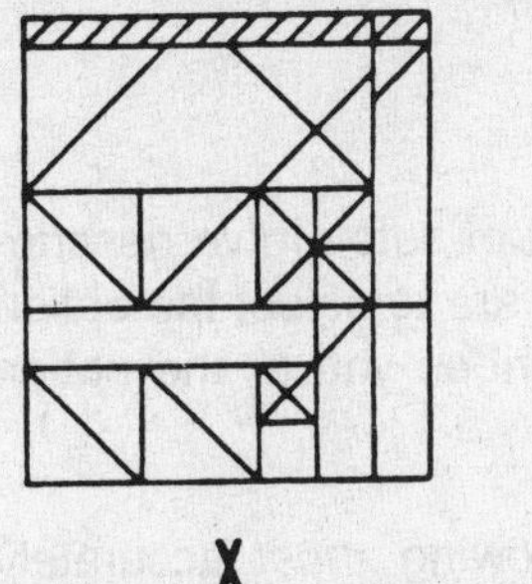

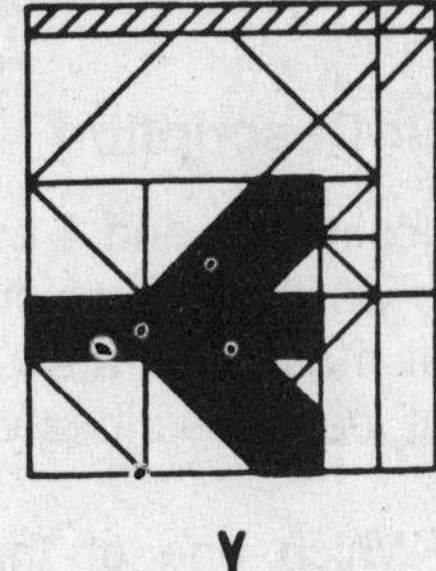

Which one of the five figures is contained in drawing X? Now look at drawing Y, which is exactly like drawing X except that the outline of figure B has been shaded to show where to look for it. Thus, B is the answer to sample item X.

Each numbered drawing contains only *one* of the lettered figures. The correct figure in each drawing will always be of the same size and in the same position as it appears at the top of the page. Therefore, do not rotate the page in order to find it. Look at each numbered drawing and decide which one of the five lettered figures is contained in it.

Practice items *1* to *5* follow. For each question, select the best answer and then, in the correspondingly numbered space on the answer sheet, blacken the circle with the same letter as your answer.

Use a soft (No. 2) pencil to mark your answers. If you wish to change an answer, erase it thoroughly and then mark your new answer.

Use the correct answers and rationale that appear on page 131 to help you determine your score, as well as to enable you to review those questions which you did not answer correctly or are uncertain of.

Practice Items

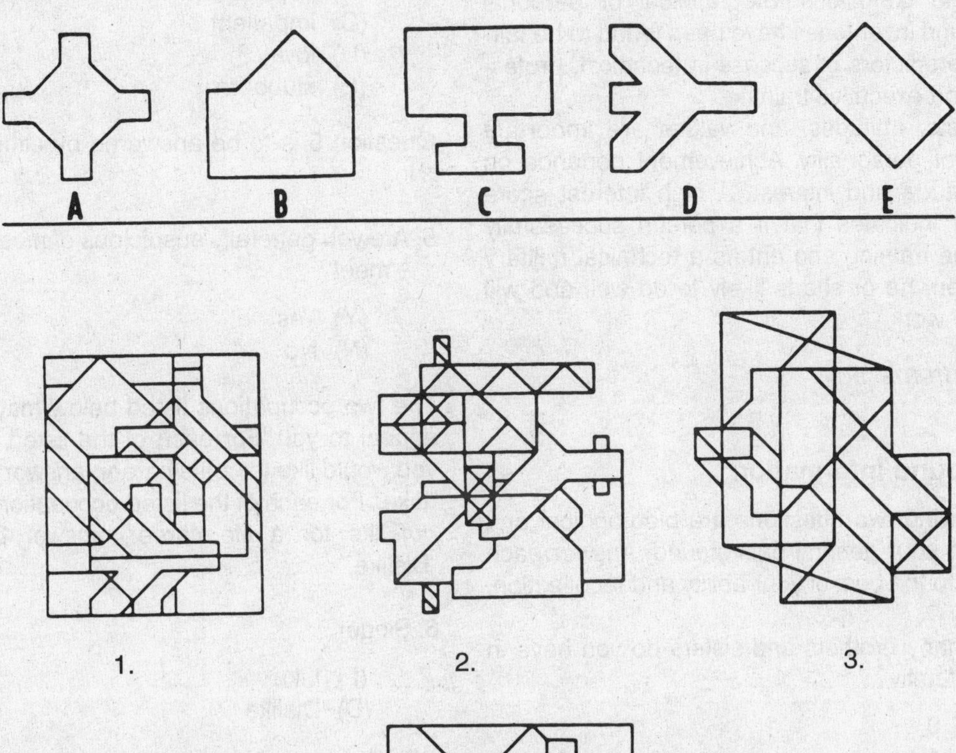

4.

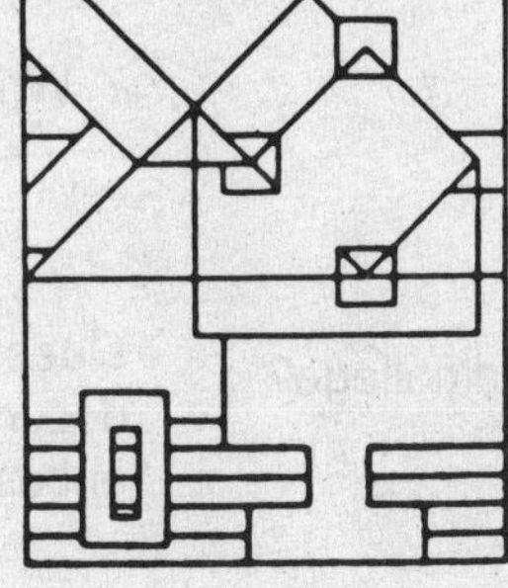

5.

Background Information—Self-Description—Biographical Inventory

Background Information, one of the subtests of the Alternate Flight Aptitude Selection Test (AFAST), consists of 25 questions dealing with your personal background. The Self-Description subtest of the Alternate Flight Aptitude Selection Test consists of 75 questions dealing with your interests, likes, dislikes, opinions, and attitudes. In the Navy and Marine Corps Aviation Selection Test Battery, the Biographical Inventory test consists of 76 items designed to obtain general background information, as well as information regarding personal characteristics and interests.

Personal background or biographical questions deal with such areas as educational and work experiences, special skills, social activities, recreational activities, athletic background, hobbies, and home conditions. Biographical or personal background inventories have been found to be fairly good predictors of success in technical, professional, and executive training.

Interests, attitudes, and values are important aspects of personality. Achievement depends on both aptitude and interest. A high interest score generally indicates that if a person successfully completes training and enters a technical military occupation, he or she is likely to do well and will enjoy the work.

Sample Items:

Background Information

The following two questions are biographical and pertain to your general background. Answer each question to the best of your ability and recollection.

1. How many brothers and sisters do you have in your family?

   (A) 0
   (B) 1
   (C) 2
   (D) 3
   (E) 4 or more

2. How old were you when you entered college?

   (A) 16 years or less
   (B) 17 years
   (C) 18 years
   (D) 19 years
   (E) 20 years or more

Self-Description

Questions 3 and 4 consist of sets of five descriptive words from which you are to select the option that *most* accurately describes you or the option that *least* describes you.

3. Which one of the following *most* accurately describes you?

   (A) argumentative
   (B) dependable
   (C) impatient
   (D) loyal
   (E) stubborn

4. Which one of the following *least* describes you?

   (A) argumentative
   (B) dependable
   (C) impatient
   (D) loyal
   (E) stubborn

Question 5 is to be answered by either a "Yes" or "No."

5. Are you generally suspicious of most people you meet?

   (Y) Yes
   (N) No

The two occupations listed below may or may not appeal to you. For each of the listed occupations you would like for a life career, answer by selecting "Like." For each of the listed occupations you would *not* like for a life career, answer by selecting "Dislike."

6. Singer

   (L) Like
   (D) Dislike

7. Writer

   (L) Like
   (D) Dislike

Question 8 consists of a pair of statements describing personal characteristics and preferences.

8. Select the statement which describes you better.
   - (A) I often feel tense on the job.
   - (B) I enjoy socializing on the job.

Question 9 consists of a statement that may be considered to be somewhat controversial. You must select one of the following options that best describes the extent to which you agree or disagree with the statement.

9. The United States should reduce its military involvement in Europe.
   - (A) Strongly agree
   - (B) Tend to agree
   - (C) Tend to disagree
   - (D) Strongly disagree

Practice items for these test areas are not provided as there are no "correct" answers to these questions. These questions should be answered truthfully and to the best of your ability and recollection.

Complex Movements

Questions on complex movements appear in Subtest 3—Complex Movements of the Alternate Flight Aptitude Selection Test. They are designed to measure your ability to judge distance and visualize motion.

You are required to move a dot from outside a circle into the center of the circle, using a direction key and a distance key. Basically, you must first determine the horizontal (right or left) direction, then the vertical direction (up or down), and finally the distance of movement, using the direction key and the distance key.

For example:

Let us take the following situation.

The dot to be moved may be in any of the 48 positions surrounding the circled dot. The dot must be moved first horizontally and then vertically a certain number of spaces to reach the center of the circle.

We will number several of the dots and see specifically how the dots are to be moved.

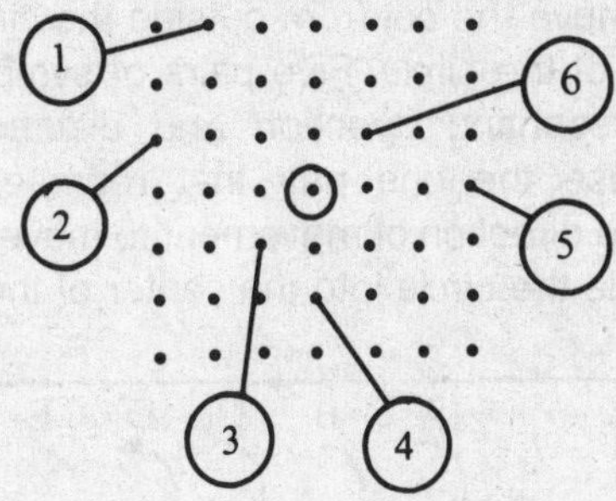

Dot 1 should be moved 2 spaces to the right and 3 spaces down.

Dot 2 should be moved 3 spaces to the right and 1 space down.

Dot 3 should be moved 1 space to the right and 1 space up.

Dot 4 is directly under the circled dot and need not be moved horizontally but should be moved up 2 spaces.

Dot 5 should be moved to the left 3 spaces but need not be moved vertically as it is in direct line with the circled dot.

Dot 6 should be moved 1 space to the left and 1 space down.

Using the same practice grid, let us try with just one outside dot and the circled dot.

It should be moved 2 spaces to the right and 2 spaces down.

It should be moved 3 spaces to the left and 3 spaces down.

It should be moved 3 spaces to the left.

It should be moved 1 space to the right and 1 space up.

After this preliminary practice session, we are now ready for the "real" instructions using the "real" direction and distance keys. For each question, you must move the dot from outside the circle into the center of the circle. Five pairs of symbols are given representing direction and distance. You must choose the one pair that represents the amount and direction of movement to move the dot from outside the circle into the center of the circle.

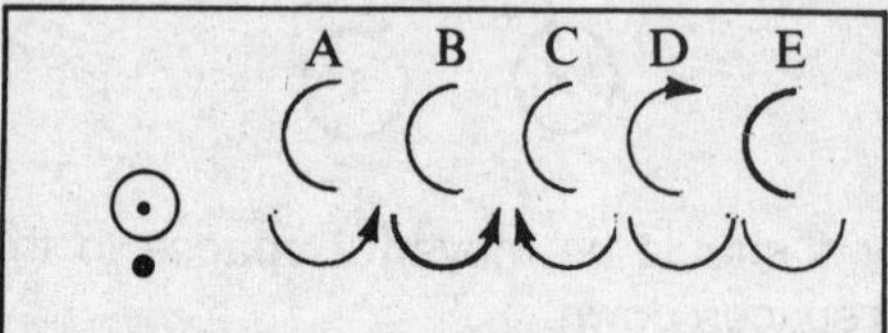

In the example above, look at the heavy dark dot below the circle. Your task is to move this dot to the center of the circle. You will have to decide which *direction* or *directions* (right or left and up or down) the dot has to be moved and the *distance* in each direction moved to reach the center of the circle.

Look at the KEYS below. These show the meaning of the symbols in the test. There is a *Direction Key* which shows the meaning of the *top row of symbols* for movement *right* or *left* (horizontal movement) and the *bottom row of symbols* for movement *up* or *down* (vertical movement). Notice in each there is a symbol for no movement. The *Distance Key* shows the three line widths in which the arrows can be drawn. The thinnest line width represents movement of approximately $\frac{1}{8}$ inch. The medium width line represents approximately $\frac{2}{8}$ inch and the thickest line represents approximately $\frac{3}{8}$ inch.

Now decide which answer is correct by looking at the arrows in the top row and the arrows in the bottom row *and* the width of the line in which the arrows are drawn. Only one pair of symbols is correct.

As no horizontal movement is needed but it must be moved up one width, option A is the correct answer.

Practice items *1* to *5* follow. For each question, select the best answer and then blacken the corresponding circle on your answer sheet.

Use the correct answers and rationale that appear on pages 132 to help you determine your score, as well as to enable you to review those questions which you did not answer correctly or are uncertain of.

Practice Items

1.

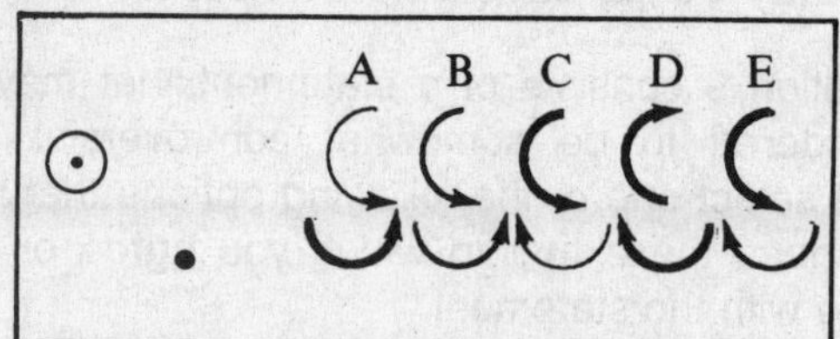

2.

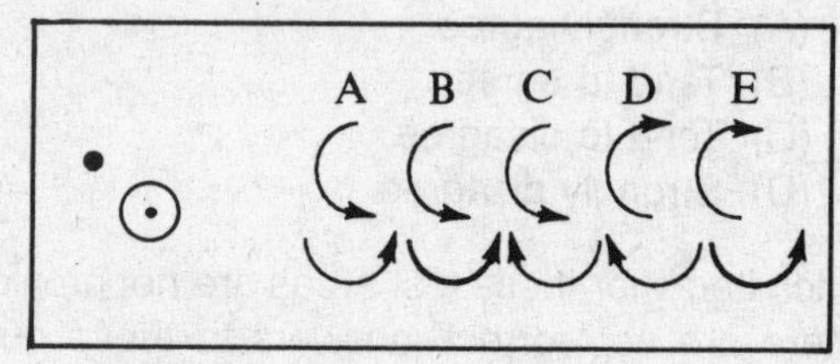

3.

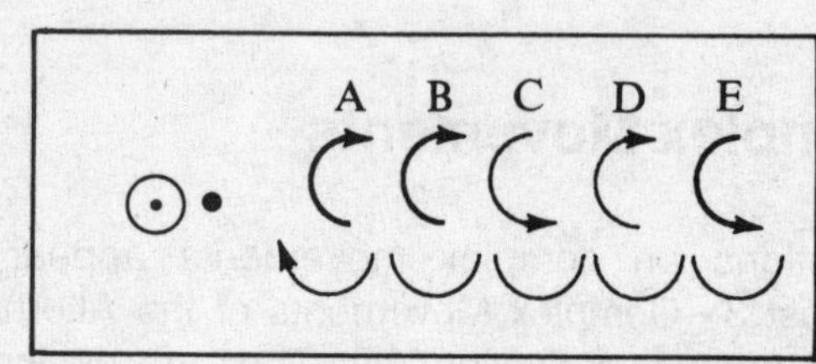

4.

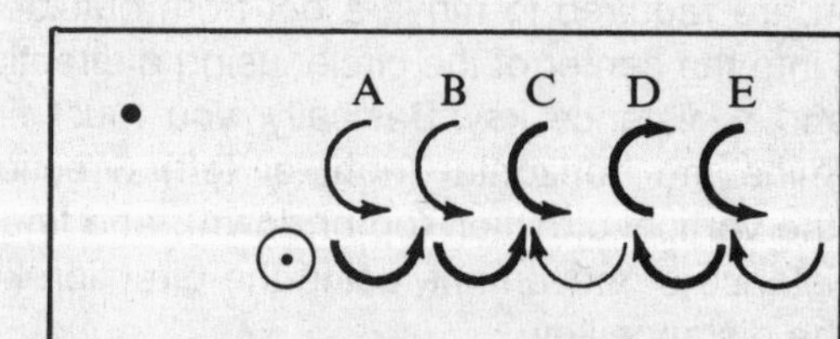

5.

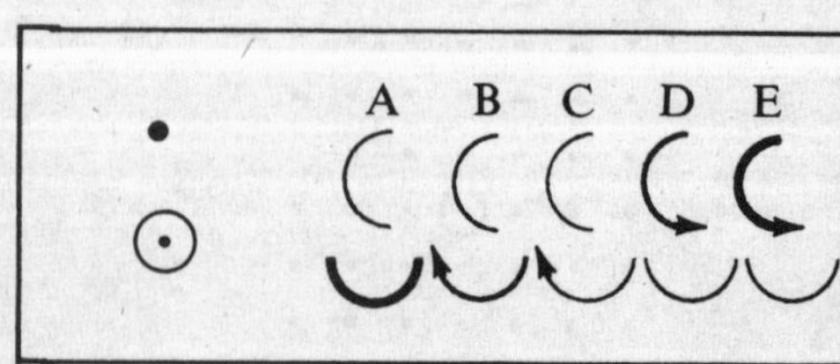

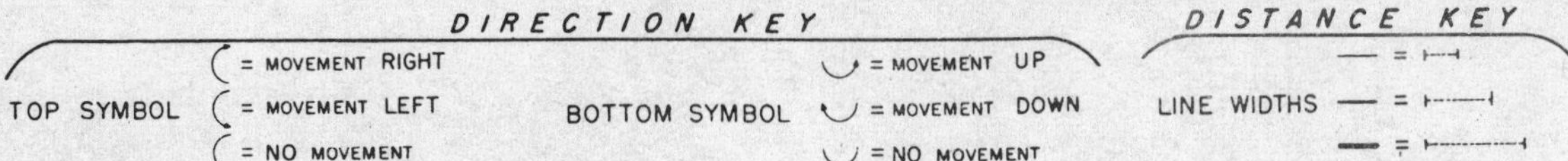

Cyclic Orientation

Cyclic orientation questions appear in Subtest 5—Cyclic Orientation of the Alternate Flight Aptitude Selection Test. They are designed to measure your ability to recognize simple changes in helicopter position and to indicate the corresponding cyclic (stick) movement.

For each question, you are shown a series of three sequential pictures that represent the pilot's view out of a helicopter windshield. The three pictures change from top to bottom showing the view from an aircraft in a climb, dive, bank to the left or right, or a combination of these maneuvers. You must determine which position the cyclic would be in to perform the maneuver indicated by the pictures.

For items in this test, the cyclic is moved as follows: *For banks*: To bank left, move the cyclic stick to left. To bank right, move the cyclic to right. *For climbs and dives*: To dive, push the cyclic forward. To climb, pull the cyclic back.

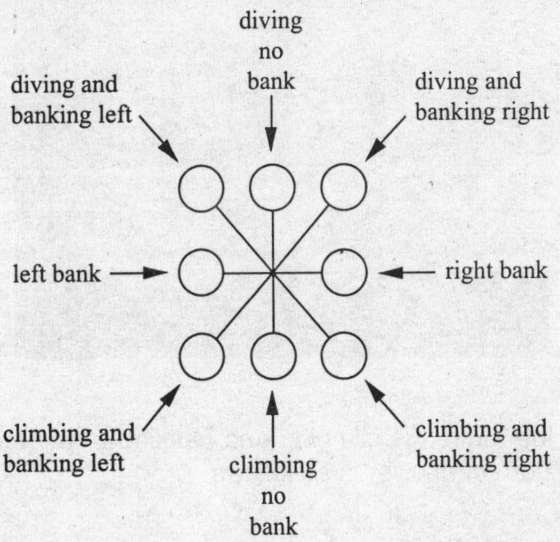

It is strongly recommended that you visit your local airfield and arrange to fly in a light, fixed-wing plane or in a helicopter. If possible, sit next to the pilot. Be certain to:

- Observe the instrument panels and controls
- Observe the pilot using the controls
- Study the terrain in front of you
- Notice how the natural landscape and man-made structures change as you view them from different heights and angles

Such flight orientation will sharpen your ability to recognize simple changes in aircraft position and the control movement required to achieve such changes.

Now let us look at two sample items.

Assume that you are the pilot of a helicopter with a constant power setting going through a maneuver as shown in the pictures below. The helicopter can be climbing, diving, banking (turning) to the right or left, or in a climbing or diving bank. Look at the pictures from *top* to *bottom* and decide what maneuver is being performed. Next, decide which position the cyclic (stick) would be in to perform the maneuver.

1.

As the aircraft is climbing but not banking, the correct answer is as follows:

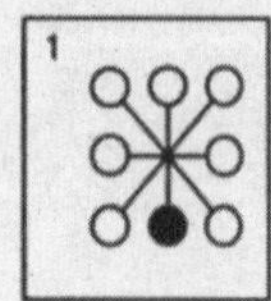

2.

As the aircraft is climbing and banking to the left, the correct answer is as follows:

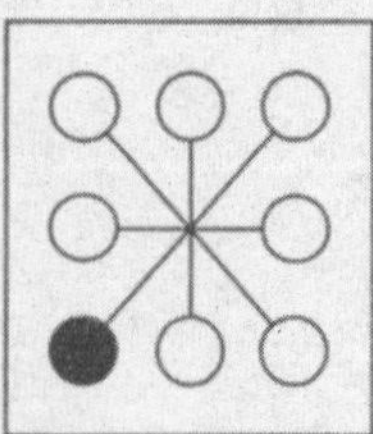

Practice items *1* to *5* follow. For each question, select the best answer and then blacken the appropriate cyclic circle on the answer sheet.

Use the correct answers and rationale that appear on page 132 to help you determine your score, as well as to enable you to review those questions which you did not answer correctly or are uncertain of.

1.

2.

3.

4.

5.

Spatial Apperception

Questions on spatial apperception appear in the Spatial Apperception test of the Navy and Marine Corps Aviation Selection Test Battery and are used in constructing the Pilot Flight Aptitude Rating (PFAR) and the Flight Officer Flight Aptitude Rating (FOFAR).

These questions measure your ability to determine the position or attitude of an airplane in flight by viewing through the windshield of the cockpit the natural horizon and terrain. You must determine whether the airplane is flying straight and level, or climbing, diving, banking to the right or left, or any combination of these maneuvers. You must also determine the general direction of flight of the plane.

Sketches of the view of the horizon and terrain from an airplane in various attitudes are shown on page 121. Note that when the airplane is flying straight and level, the horizon is horizontal and is in the middle of the pictured view. When in a level flight but banking to the left, the horizon is seen tilted to the right with the center point of the horizon still at the middle of the pictured view. When in a level flight but banking to the right, the horizon is seen tilted to the left with the center point of the horizon still at the middle of the pictured view.

When the airplane is nose-down (diving) but not banking either left or right, the horizon is horizontal and is in the upper half of the pictured view. When nose-down and banking to the left, the horizon is seen tilted to the right with the center point of the horizon in the upper half of the pictured view. When nose-down and banking to the right, the horizon is seen tilted to the left with the center point of the horizon in the upper half of the pictured view.

When the airplane is nose-up (climbing) but banking neither left nor right, the horizon is horizontal and is in the lower half of the pictured view. When nose-up and banking to the left, the horizon is seen tilted to the right with the center point of the horizon in the lower half of the pictured view. When nose-up and banking to the right, the horizon is seen tilted to the left with the center point of the horizon in the lower half of the pictured view. Note too that when the horizon is tilted, the coastline also appears to be tilted.

Sketches of airplanes in various attitudes are shown on page 122. Note that when the airplane is banked either left or right, it is either to the left or right of the pilot seated in the cockpit and looking directly forward and not as viewed from outside the airplane.

Notice that the view is out to sea. The land is darkened, the coastline separates the land from the sea, and the horizon is shown where the sea meets the sky. The direction of flight can be determined by looking at the coastline. In all views shown on page 121, the planes are shown flying out to sea.

In each question, the picture at the upper left represents the view as the pilot looks straight ahead through the windshield of the cockpit. Below are five pictures labeled A, B, C, D, and E. Each picture shows a plane in a different position or attitude or in a different direction of flight. Determine from which plane the aerial view shown would have been seen.

Now let's look at several sample items on the following pages.

Sample Items

1.

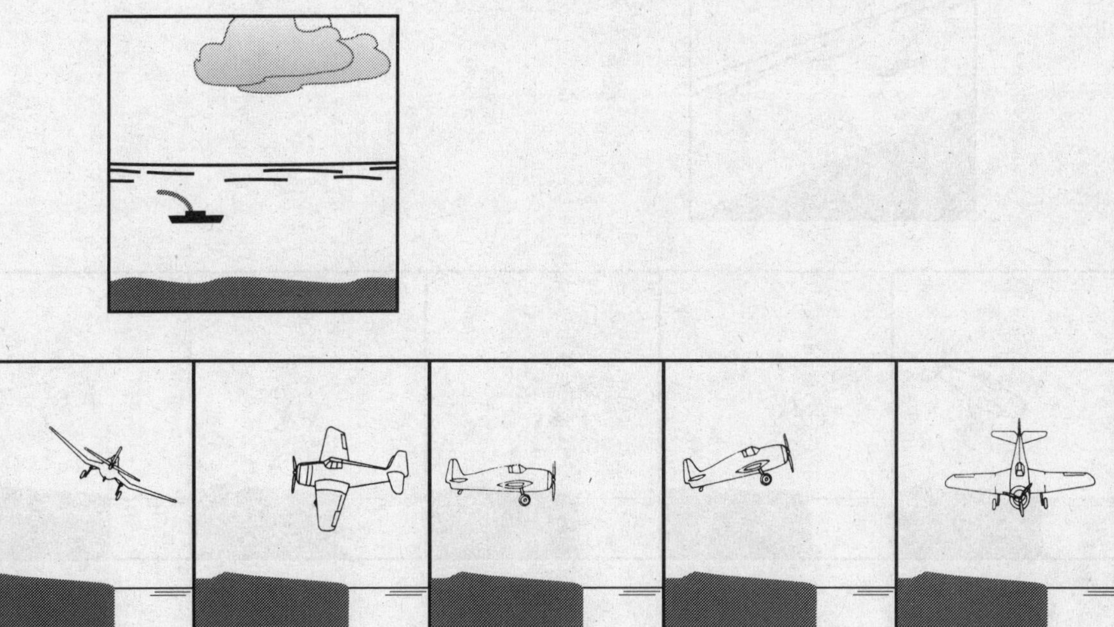

(A) (B) (C) (D) (E)

2.

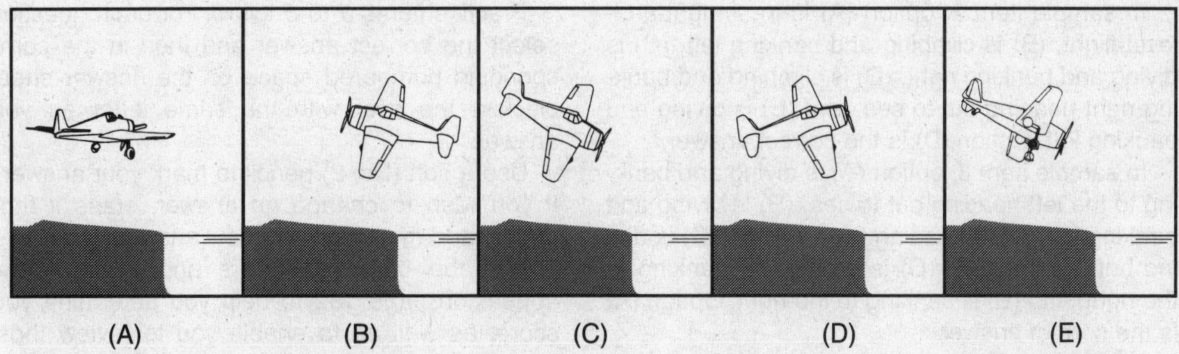

(A) (B) (C) (D) (E)

3.

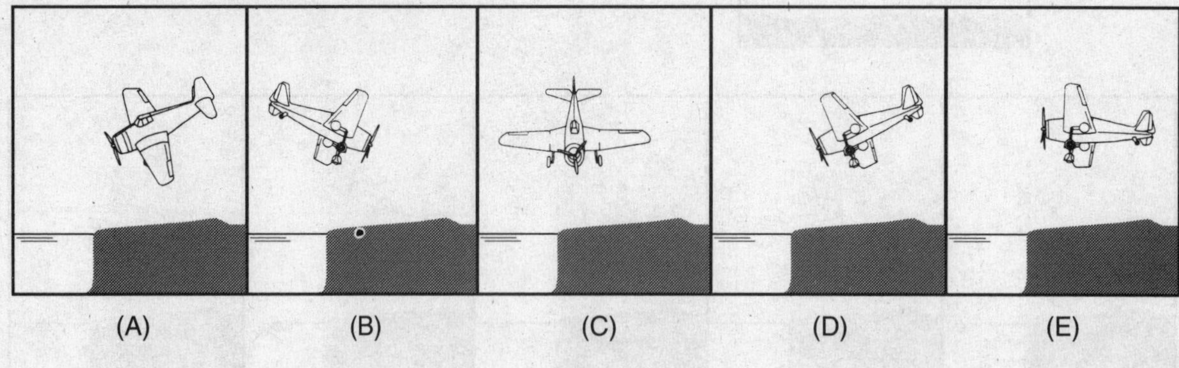

In sample item 1, option (A) is banking to the right, (B) is banking to the left, (C) is in straight-and-level flight heading out to sea, (D) is climbing, and (E) is diving. Option (C) is the correct answer.

In sample item 2, option (A) is in straight-and-level flight, (B) is climbing and banking left, (C) is diving and banking right, (D) is climbing and banking right heading out to sea, and (E) is diving and banking left. Option (D) is the correct answer.

In sample item 3, option (A) is diving and banking to the left heading out to sea, (B) is diving and banking to the left heading toward land, (C) is diving but not banking, (D) is diving and banking to the right, and (E) is banking to the right. Option (A) is the correct answer.

Note that in the five-lettered options in sample items 1 and 2, the sea is to the right of the coastline. In sample item 3, the sea is to the left of the coastline. The sea may be above or below the coastline or be in any other position, depending upon how the coastline is drawn.

Practice items *1* to *5* follow. For each question, select the correct answer and then in the corresponding numbered space on the answer sheet, blacken the oval with the same letter as your answer.

Use a soft (No. 2) pencil to mark your answers. If you wish to change an answer, erase it thoroughly and then mark the new answer.

Use the correct answers and rationale that appear on page 132 to help you determine your score, as well as to enable you to review those questions which you did not answer correctly or are uncertain of.

View of Horizon and Terrain from Airplanes in Various Attitudes

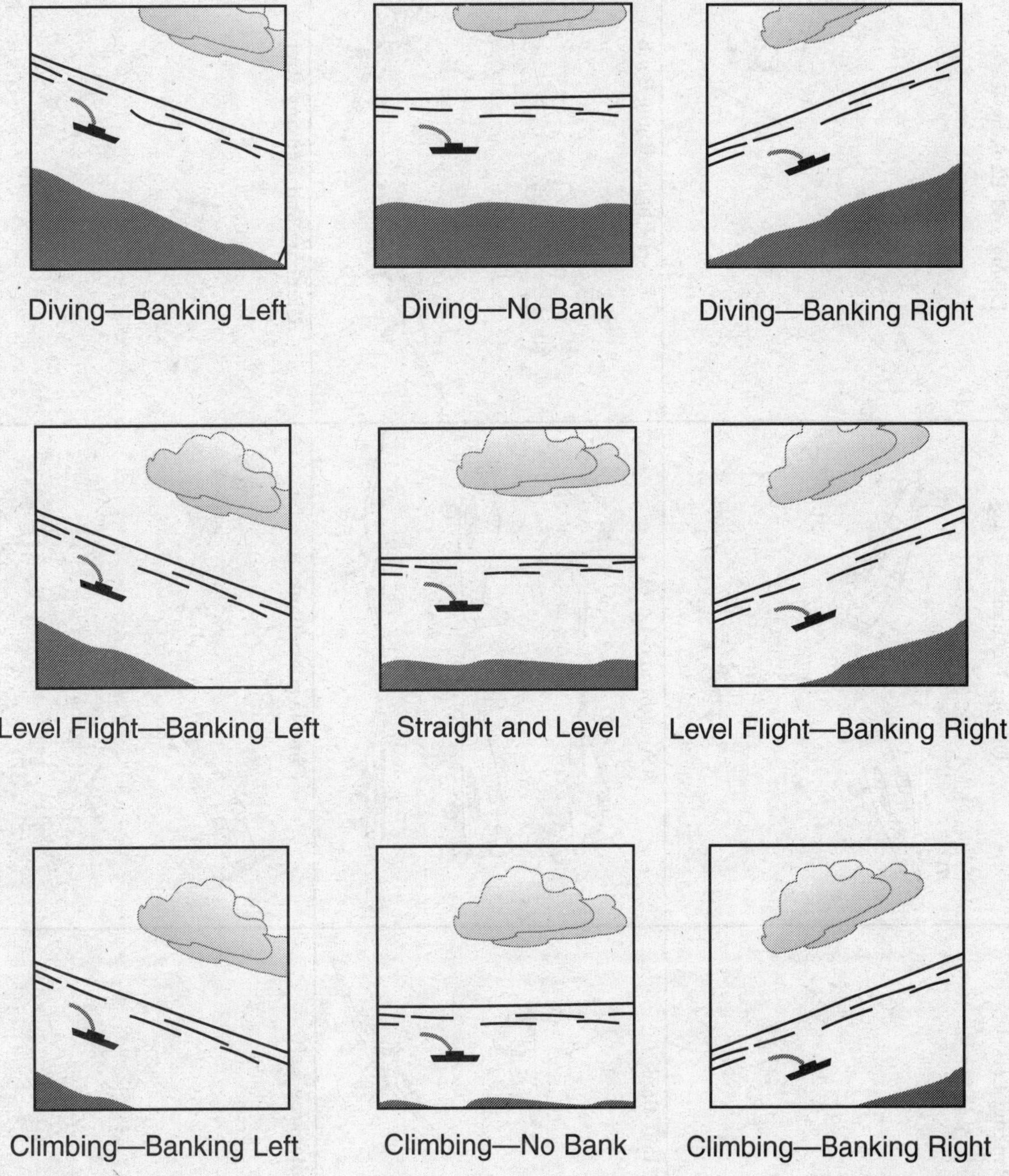

Sketches of Airplanes in Various Attitudes

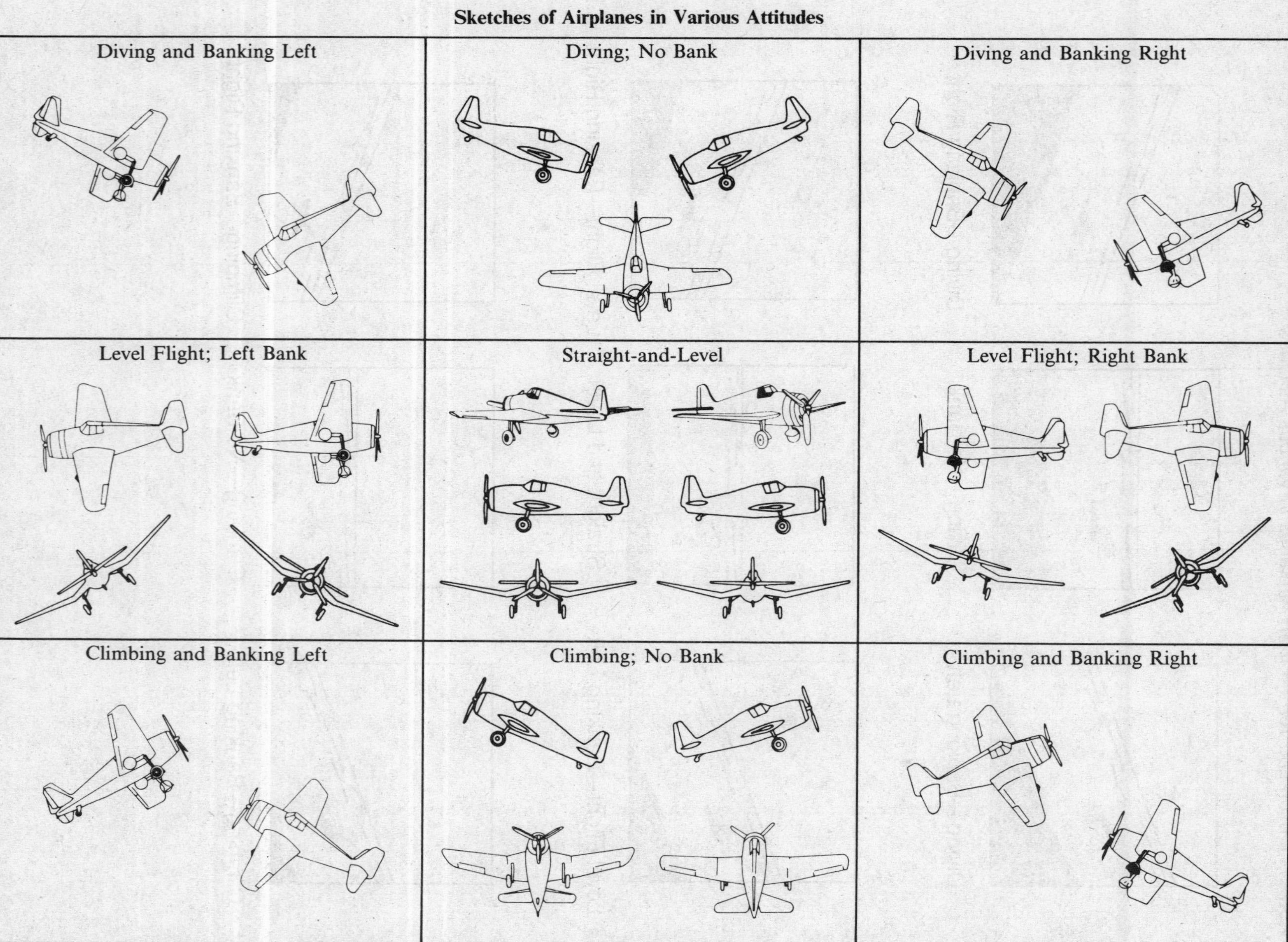

Practice Items

In each question, the view at the upper left represents what the pilot sees looking straight ahead through the windshield of the cockpit. Below are five sketches labeled A, B, C, D, and E. Each lettered sketch shows a plane in a different position or attitude and in a different direction of flight. From the aerial view shown, determine which of the five lettered sketches most nearly represents the position or attitude of the plane and the direction of flight from which the view would have been seen.

1.

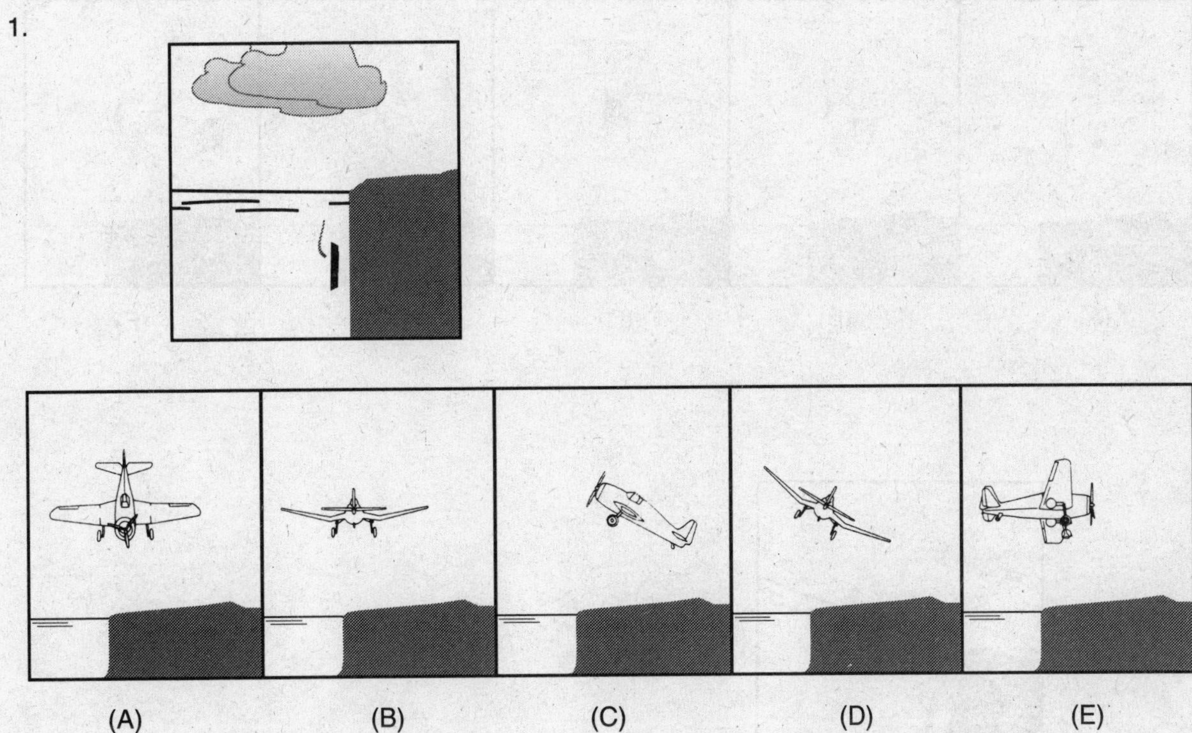

(A) (B) (C) (D) (E)

2.

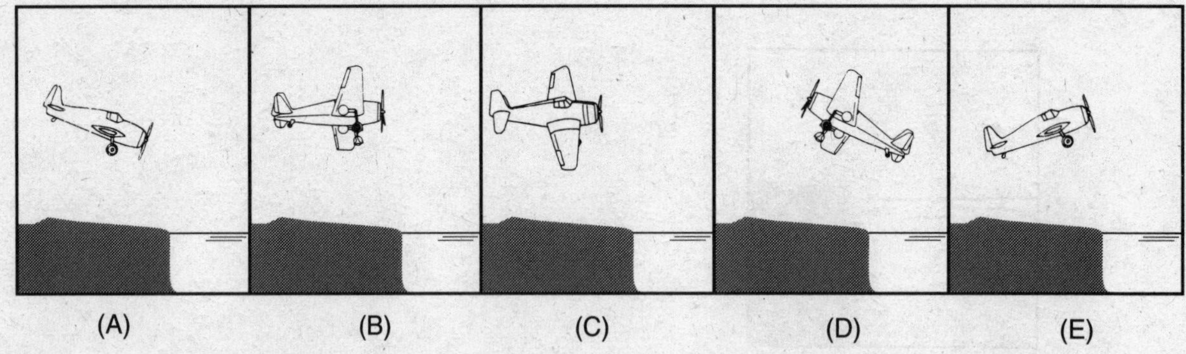

(A) (B) (C) (D) (E)

3.

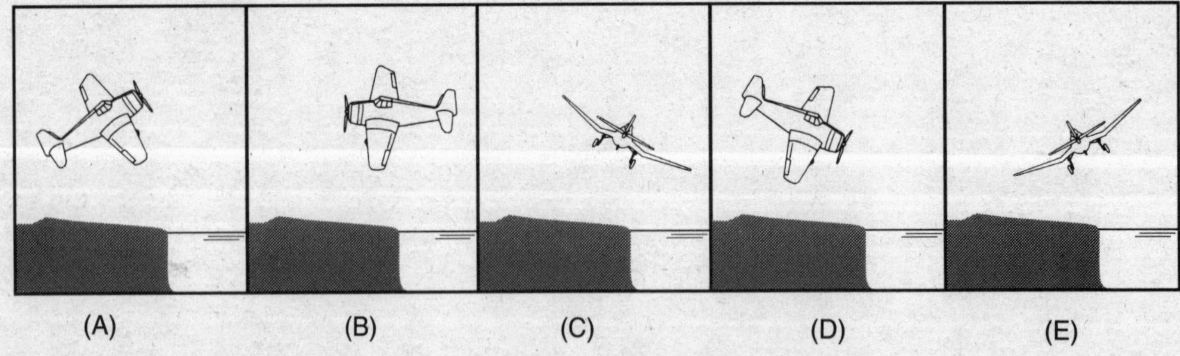

(A) (B) (C) (D) (E)

4.

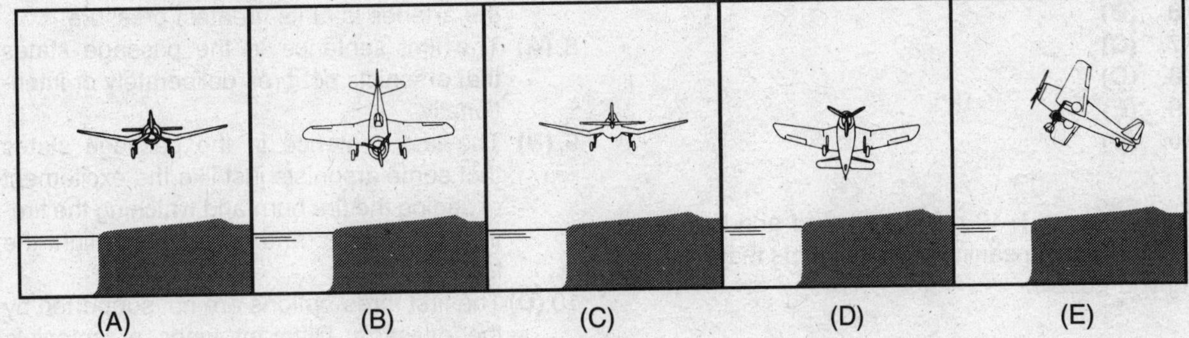

5.

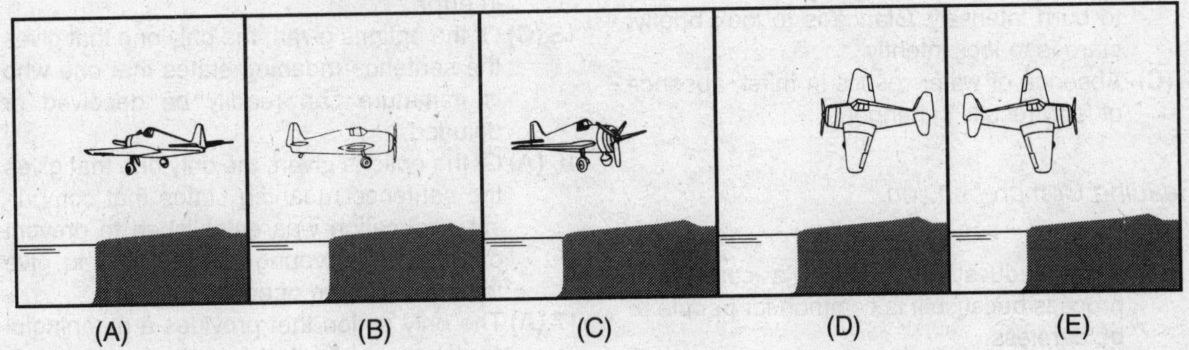

Correct Answers and Rationale for Practice Items

Synonyms

1. **(C)**
2. **(A)**
3. **(A)**
4. **(E)**
5. **(B)**
6. **(B)**
7. **(C)**
8. **(C)**
9. **(E)**
10. **(D)**

For questions 1–10 refer to a good abridged dictionary for the meaning of those words that are giving you trouble.

Verbal Analogies

1. **(E)** Botany is the study of plants; entomology is the study of insects.
2. **(B)** Epilogue is a speech after the conclusion of a play; prologue is an introductory speech to a play. Appendix is material added after the end of the book; preface is an introductory part of a book.
3. **(E)** Octagon is an eight-sided figure; square is a four-sided figure (one-half of eight). Hexagon is a six-sided figure; triangle is a three-sided figure (one-half of six).
4. **(C)** Glow is to burn without any flame; blaze is to burn intensely. Glance is to look briefly; stare is to look intently.
5. **(C)** Absence of water results in thirst; absence of food results in hunger.

Reading Comprehension

1. **(C)** Safety education must be a continuous process because it is common for people to be careless.
2. **(D)** During times of stress, law enforcement becomes committed to reducing that stress between population groups.
3. **(C)** The uneven saturation of energy would result in unevenly cooked food.
4. **(A)** The watt is a measure of electrical energy. Electrical power in the home is measured in watts or kilowatts.
5. **(C)** The magnetron within the microwave oven generates the energy.
6. **(D)** The first three options are not supported by the passage. The second sentence in the passage states that steel bars, deeply embedded in the concrete, are sinews to take the stresses.
7. **(A)** The third sentence in the passage states that when the heart contracts, the blood in the arteries is at its greatest pressure.
8. **(A)** The first sentence in the passage states that arsonists set fires deliberately or intentionally.
9. **(B)** The last sentence in the passage states that some arsonists just like the excitement of seeing the fire burn and watching the firefighters at work, and even helping fight the fire.
10. **(D)** The first three options are not supported by the passage. Different types of arsonists given in the passage lead to the conclusion that arsonists are not all alike.
11. **(B)** For the students to solve the problem with ease, the teacher's explanation must have been clearly expressed or explicit.
12. **(A)** To differentiate between fact and fiction requires that the listeners have keen discernment or be shrewd.
13. **(C)** If corn is native or indigenous to the region, it is readily available and is generally inexpensive as transportation costs are reduced or eliminated.
14. **(D)** It is difficult to change the mind of a stubborn or obdurate individual even when he is in error.
15. **(C)** Of the options given, the only one that gives the sentence meaning states that one who is immature can readily be deceived or deluded.
16. **(A)** Of the options given, the only one that gives the sentence meaning states that compulsory education was established to prevent exploitation of young children and to give them a minimum of education.
17. **(A)** The only option that provides a meaningful sentence states that a person in custody awaiting trial is considered innocent until found to be guilty.
18. **(D)** The word *large* appears to be inconsistent. Substituting *small* for large restores the intended meaning of the quotation.

19. **(A)** The word *legislators* appears to be inconsistent. Substituting *citizens* for *legislators* helps convey the meaning intended.
20. **(A)** The word *cannot* appears to be the cause for confusion. By substituting *eventually* for *cannot*, the intended meaning of the sentence is restored.

Arithmetic Reasoning

1. **(C)** Calculate in inches.
$48 \times 24 \times 18 = 20{,}736$ in^3
(Vol. of bin)
$8 \times 4 \times 2 = 64$ in^3
(Vol. of each brick)
$20{,}736 \div 64 = 324$ bricks
2. **(D)** Let x = actual length of room.
$2:5 = 7:x$; $2x = 35$; $x = 17\frac{1}{2}$ feet
3. **(A)** 4 hours at 6 mph = 24 miles
2 hours at 10mph = 20 miles
4 hours at 5 mph = 20 miles
Total = 10 hours for 64 miles = 6.4 mph
4. **(B)** $240 – $192 = $48 discount
$\frac{48}{240} = \frac{1}{5} = 20\%$
5. **(E)** 2.35 – .82 = 1.53, cost of weight above 5 ounces
$\frac{1.53}{.09} = 20\%$
5 ounces + 17 ounces = 22 ounces = 1 pound, 6 ounces

Math Knowledge

1. **(C)** The 3s, 4s, 5s, 6s, and 7s cancel out leaving
$\frac{2}{8} = \frac{1}{4}$
2. **(E)** All except option (E) are equivalent. 115% = 1.15
3. **(A)** When logarithms with the same base are multiplied, the exponents are added. $10^4 \times 10^3 \times 10^2 = 10^{(4+3+2)} = 10^9$
4. **(B)** The Pythagorean theorem states that for any right triangle, the sum of the squares of the legs is equal to the square of the length of the hypotenuse.
$3^2 + 4^2 = h^2$; $9 + 16 = h^2$; $h^2 = 25$; $h = \sqrt{25}$
5. **(C)** $a = 4b$; $\frac{3}{4}a = \frac{3}{4}(4b) = \frac{12b}{4} = 31$

Data Interpretation

1. **(E)** Errors made in

July	36
Aug	59
Sept	56
Oct	29
Nov	33
Dec	34
Total	247

Errors made in August is 59.
$\frac{59}{247} = .239$ or $.24$
2. **(A)** If 247 errors were made during the 6 month period by 4 office workers, the number made per month per office worker = $\frac{247}{6 \times 4} = \frac{247}{24} = 10.3$
3. **(B)** Let x = errors made by section during the entire year. Total errors made by Butler during 6-month period is $62\frac{1}{6}$ $x = 62$; $x = 62 \times 6 = 372$
4. **(B)** In June 1993, number of auto thefts was 750. In June 1992, number of auto thefts was 580.
750 – 580 = 170
5. **(C)** In March 1993, the number was 960. In March 1992, the number was 540. 960 – 540 = 420. In no other month was the numerical difference equal or greater.

Mechanical Comprehension

1. **(B)** Wood is an insulator. Silver is a better conductor than steel.
2. **(D)** Option A does not permit air flow through G and S; option B does not permit air flow through S; option C does not permit air flow through G; option D is correct; option E does not permit air flow through G and S.
3. **(C)** The total weight of 32 pounds is balanced equally between the two scales. Each records one half of the total weight or 16 pounds.
4. **(C)** If the block is moved toward the brick, the moment for a given force exerted will increase (being further from the force) making it easier to lift; the height will be made smaller, hardly raising the brick when moved to the limit (directly underneath it).

5. **(B)** Each time the rotating arm makes a complete revolution, it moves the slotted disc $\frac{1}{4}$ of a turn.
6. **(A)** The film of water inside the loop would form a lens which would enlarge the printing on the page. If you looked through a water-filled globe, objects will also appear larger.
7. **(B)** The metal key has the highest conductivity. Metals are the best conductors of heat. The other choices can be used as insulators.
8. **(B)** This is a mechanical or solderless connector. It does away with need to solder wires and is found in house wiring.
9. **(A)** An inclined plane is a sloping, triangular shape, used here as a wedge to force open an axe-cut made in the wood.
10. **(A)** The weight is not centered but is closer to A. The distance from the center of the load to A is less than the distance from the center of the load to B. Therefore, A would support the greater part of the load.

Electrical Maze

1. **(D)**

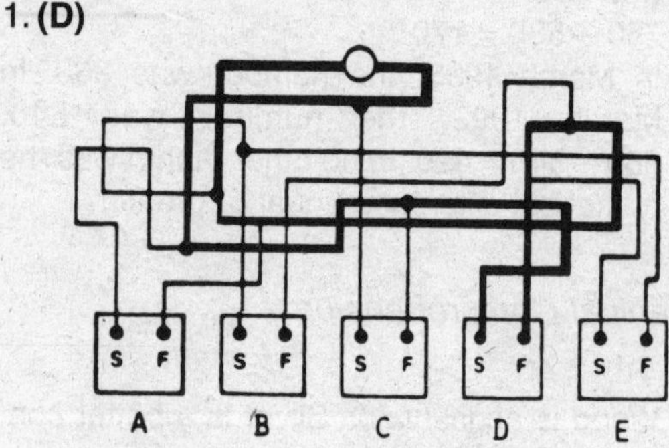

2. **(A)**

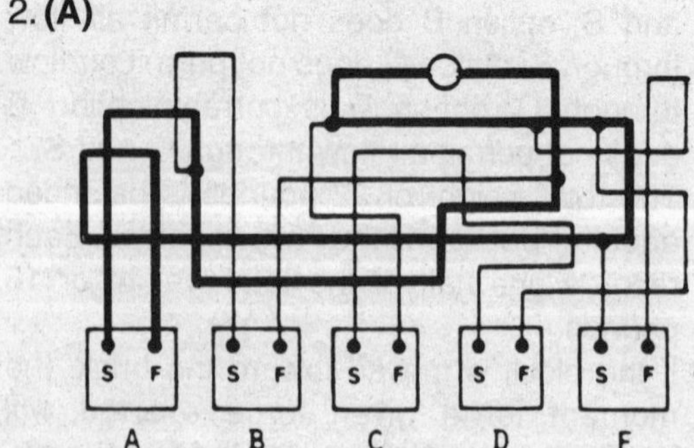

3. **(B)**

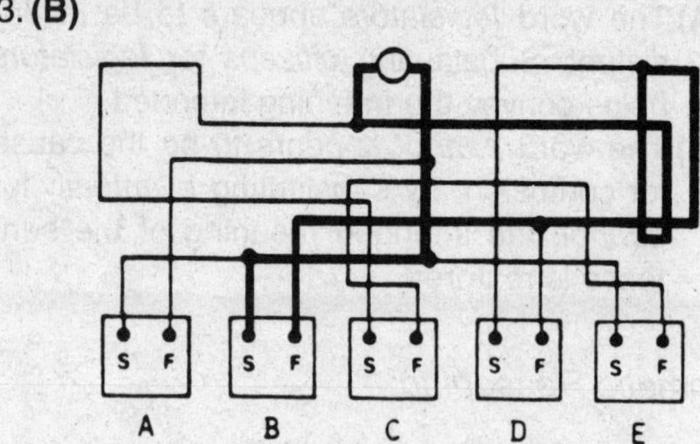

4. **(C)**

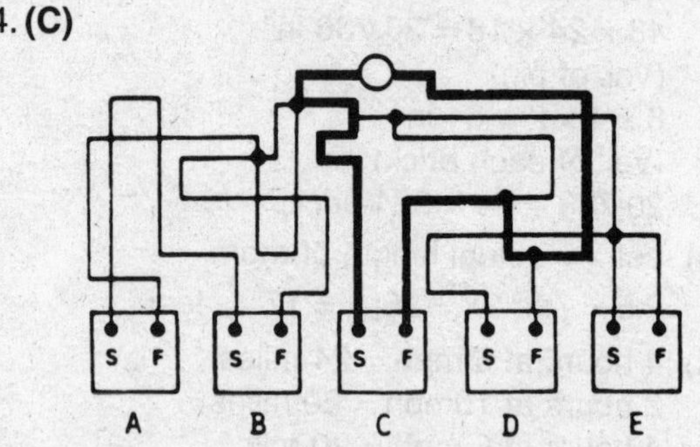

5. **(E)**

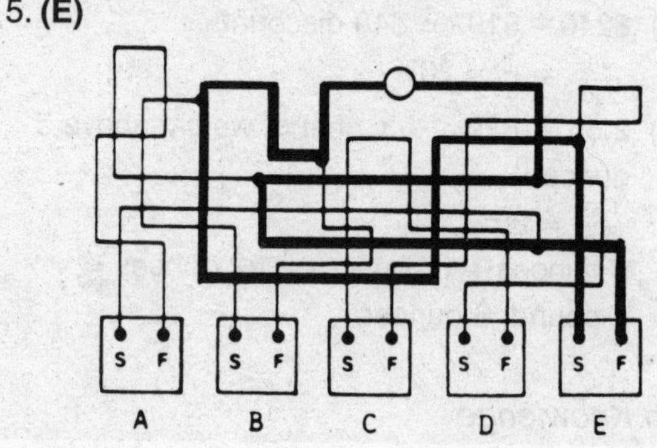

Scale Reading

1. **(A)** The scale runs from right to left. There are three subdivisions of four steps each between .4 and .7, so each step represents .025. The arrow points almost midway between markers .725 and .750. An appropriate estimate is .735.
2. **(E)** There are six subdivisions of two steps each between 36 and 72, so each step represents 3. The arrow points slightly past the marker representing 57. An appropriate estimate would be 58.
3. **(B)** Each step represents an eighth. The arrow points to the marker representing $3\frac{3}{8}$ or 3.375.
4. **(C)** The scale runs from right to left. Each step represents 1. The arrow points midway

between markers representing 18 and 19, or 18.5.

5. **(D)** The scale runs from the bottom to the top. Each step represents .5 but the steps are of unequal width with each step being two-thirds as deep as the one above. Therefore, the scale is compressed as the values decrease, or expanded as the values increase. The arrow is pointing to a position halfway between the markers representing 19.0 and 19.5, but because of the downward compression of the scale, the value of the point must be more than 19.25.

Instrument Comprehension

1. **(B)** Climbing; 15° right; heading 60°.
2. **(A)** Not climbing nor diving; 30° right bank; heading 360° (north).
3. **(D)** Not climbing nor diving; 90° right bank; heading 360° (west).
4. **(B)** Climbing; 15° left bank; heading 300°.
5. **(C)** Climbing; 30° left bank; heading 60°.
6. **(B)** Diving; no bank; heading $22\frac{1}{2}$ ° (NNE).
7. **(C)** Not climbing nor diving; no bank; heading 240°.
8. **(D)** Diving; 30° right bank; heading 315° (northwest).
9. **(B)** Not climbing nor diving; 30° left bank; heading 300°.
10. **(A)** Diving; no bank; heading 150°.

Block Counting

1. **(E)** There are 9 blocks on the bottom tier, 5 on the middle tier, and 1 on the top tier. 9 + 5 + 1 = 15
2. **(B)** There are 14 blocks on the lower tier and 10 blocks on the upper tier. 14 + 10 = 24
3. **(E)** There are 16 blocks on the bottom tier, 16 on the middle tier, and 12 on the top tier. 16 + 16 + 12 = 44
4. **(B)** There are 24 blocks from top to bottom on the left column, 24 blocks from top to bottom on the right column, and 8 blocks in the center. 24 + 24 + 8 = 56
5. **(E)** There are 15 blocks on the bottom tier, 14 on the middle tier, and 9 on the top tier. 15 + 14 + 9 = 38
6. **(D)** There are 4 alongside and 2 below. 4 + 2 = 6
7. **(A)** There are 3 alongside and 1 below. 3 + 1 = 4
8. **(B)** There is 1 alongside and 1 below. 1 + 1 = 2
9. **(E)** There are 2 above, 3 alongside, and 3 below. 2 + 3 + 3 = 8
10. **(A)** There are 3 above and 1 alongside. 3 + 1 = 4

Table Reading

1. **(A)** The entry that occurs at the intersection of an *X* value of –1 and a *Y* value of 0 is 29.
2. **(E)** The entry that occurs at the intersection of an *X* value of –2 and a *Y* value of –2 is 30.
3. **(C)** The entry that occurs at the intersection of an *X* value of +2 and a *Y* value of –1 is 35.
4. **(D)** The entry that occurs at the intersection of an *X* value of 0 and a *Y* value of +3 is 27.
5. **(D)** The entry that occurs at the intersection of an *X* value of +1 and a *Y* value of –2 is 35.

Aviation Information

1. **(B)** The upward angle formed by the wings, called *dihedral*, counteracts any balance upset caused by a gust of wind and returns the airplane to a wing-level attitude.
2. **(A)** The flight path and relative wind are parallel but travel in opposite directions. If an airfoil moves forward and upward, the relative wind moves backward and downward.
3. **(C)** The lift and drag acting on a wing are proportional to the wing area. If the wing area is doubled and the other variables remain the same, the lift and drag created by the wing will be doubled.
4. **(D)** Tetraethyl lead is the best available knock inhibitor. It is added to improve the antiknock quality of a fuel.
5. **(A)** The standard weight for gasoline is 6 lbs./U.S. gal., that for oil is 7.5 lbs./U.S. gal., and that for water is 8.35 lbs./U.S. gal.
6. **(B)** Bernocilli's principle and Newton's third law of motion are the basis for explaining how an airplane wing produces lift.
7. **(A)** The rearward or retarding force acting on an airplane during flight is called drag.
8. **(A)** The angle of attack is the angle between the chord line of the airfoil and the direction of the relative wind.
9. **(D)** Lift varies directly with the density of air. As the density of air increases, lift and drag increase.

10.**(E)** The trailing edge of the airfoil or wing is the aft end of the airfoil, where the airflow over the upper surface meets the airflow from the lower surface.

11.**(D)** The empennage is the tail section and generally consists of a vertical stabilizer, a horizontal stabilizer, a movable rudder and a movable elevator.

12.**(A)** The ailerons, located on the rear edge of the wings near the outer tips, are used to bank or roll the airplane around its longitudinal axis.

13.**(A)** The pitot is used to ascertain the impact pressure of the air as the airplane moves forward.

14.**(C)** Applying forward pressure on the control causes the elevator surfaces to move downward. The flow of air striking the deflected surfaces exerts an upward force, pushing the airplane's tail upward and the nose downward.

15.**(D)** Runway numbers are different at each end of the runway strip because the magnetic directions are 180° apart. The approximate magnetic direction for runway numbered 3 is 30°. The other end would be numbered 21 as it has a magnetic direction of 210°.

16.**(C)** The tower operator uses a flashing red signal to instruct pilots not to land because the airport is unsafe.

17.**(D)** White lights are used to illuminate airport runways.

18.**(D)** The arrow of the weathervane points into the wind midway between North and West, or Northwest.

19.**(D)** The 24-hour system consists of a four-digit number with 0000 as midnight to 2400 the following midnight. The time 2:00 p.m. would be expressed as 1400 hours in the 24-hour system.

20.**(D)** Note the tail assembly on the airplane. The pilot has banked the airplane 45° to the left.

21.**(D)** Foot pedals in the cockpit permit the helicopter to increase or decrease tail-rotor thrust, as needed, to neutralize torque effect.

22.**(D)** A red radial line is placed on the airspeed indicator to show the airspeed limit beyond which operation is dangerous.

23.**(B)** In the event of engine failure while hovering or on takeoff below 10 feet, apply collective pitch as necessary to cushion the landing.

24.**(B)** The useful load (payload) is the weight of the pilot, passengers, baggage, removable ballast and usable fuel. Oil is considered to be part of the empty weight.

25.**(A)** For any given gross weight, the higher the density altitude, the less the rate of climb for any helicopter.

Nautical Information

1. **(C)** Zulu time or Greenwich mean time is used in communications between ships in different time zones.

2. **(E)** The foghorn is a type of sound communication; facsimile, radiotelegraph, and satellite are types of electronic communication; semiphore is a type of visual communication using hand flags.

3. **(C)** The plane intersects the earth's surface at the equator and divides the earth into the northern and southern hemispheres.

4. **(D)** Nylon is a synthetic fiber of great strength and is much stronger than manila rope.

5. **(A)** Amsterdam with coordinates of 52°22'N and 4°53'E is closest to Greenwich.

6. **(C)** Hawaii is located at a latitude of 21°N and longitude of 159°W.

7. **(B)** If unlighted, a green channel marker is can-shaped.

8. **(D)** It would be 1400 + 3 or 1700 Greenwich mean time.

9. **(B)** Red is for port; green is starboard. White navigation lights inform an observer in which direction a vessel is going. Yellow is for special circumstances.

10.**(A)** The stern is the after part of the ship. To go in that direction is to go aft.

11.**(A)** Draft is the vertical distance from the waterline to the lowest part of the ship's bottom. Freeboard is the vertical distance from the waterline to the edge of the lowest outside deck.

12.**(B)** The forward part of the main deck is generally the forecastle. The after part is the fantail.

13.**(B)** The 180th meridian is also known as the International Date Line. Greenwich, England, is located at 0 meridian or prime meridian.

14.**(E)** The magnetic north pole and true north are not at the same location. The magnetic compass does not usually point directly north in most places. This compass error is termed *variation*.

15.**(B)** The lubber's line indicates the fore-and-aft line of the ship.

16.**(C)** When the tide is falling after high tide, it is called ebb tide.

17.**(E)** Stratus clouds are gray clouds found at low altitude and consist of a uniform layer of water droplets.

18. **(B)** The Beaufort scale of wind force is useful in estimating wind speed.
19. **(D)** The sextant is a precision instrument used in celestial navigation to measure angles.
20. **(C)** Life buoys should be thrown over immediately.
21. **(C)** A fathometer is an electronic device used in making deep-sea soundings.
22. **(E)** 12:00 noon would be written as 1200; 6:00 p.m. would be written as 1800.
23. **(E)** In marine navigation, the four methods of determining position are piloting, dead reckoning, celestial navigation, and electronic navigation.
24. **(C)** The gunwale is the deck edge, the intersection of the main deck with the shell or side plating.
25. **(C)** A pier is built at right angle to the shore; a wharf is parallel. The space between adjacent piers is called a slip.
26. **(A)** A balanced rudder with part of the area of the blade surface projected ahead of the rudder stock exerts considerable effect in reducing the strain on the steering gear and in making steering easier.
27. **(A)** With left rudder (to port), water flowing past the hull hits the rudder at the port side forcing the stern to starboard and the boat's bow swings to port.
28. **(A)** With left rudder (to port) and going astern, the stern swings to port.
29. **(B)** With right rudder (to starboard), water flowing past the hull hits the rudder at the starboard side forcing the stern to port and the boat's bow swings to starboard.
30. **(A)** With left rudder (to port), and going astern, the stem swings to port.

Rotated Blocks

1. **(C)**
2. **(E)**
3. **(B)**
4. **(D)**
5. **(A)**

If you examine each set of blocks carefully, you will find that only one of the five options is just like the pictured block at the left although turned in a different position. You may have to mentally turn blocks over, turn them around, or turn the both over and around.

General Science

1. **(C)** Meteors or "shooting stars" come into the earth's atmosphere from outer space with high velocity. The resistance offered by the earth's atmosphere makes these meteors incandescent in flight.
2. **(C)** Organisms that live on or in the body of other living organisms from which food is obtained are called parasites.
3. **(B)** Substances are classified as elements or compounds. A compound is a substance composed of the atoms of two or more different elements.
4. **(D)** The greater the number of vibrations per second produced by the sounding object, the higher will be the pitch produced. Playing a $33\frac{1}{3}$ rpm phonograph record at a faster speed (45 rpm) will produce a higher-pitched sound.
5. **(E)** Combustion cannot occur in the absence of oxygen.

Hidden Figures

1. **(A)**

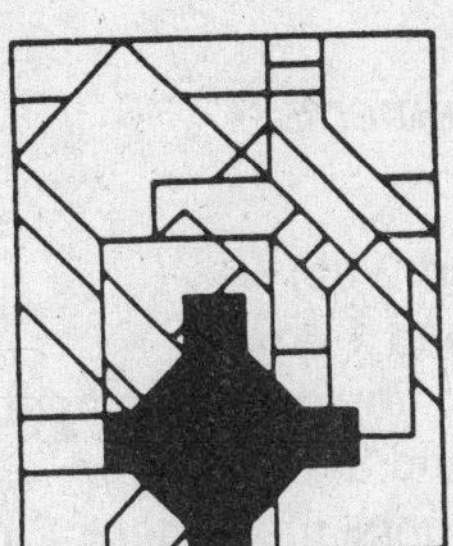

2. **(E)**

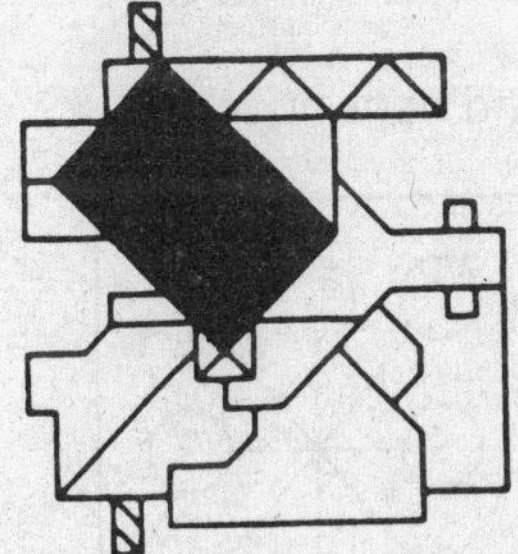

3. **(E)**

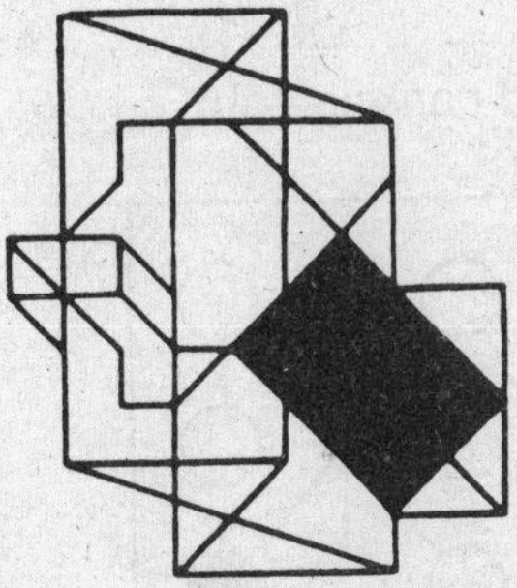

4. **(C)**

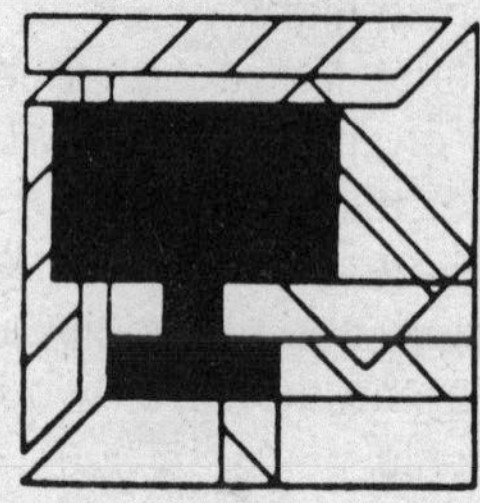

5. **(B)**

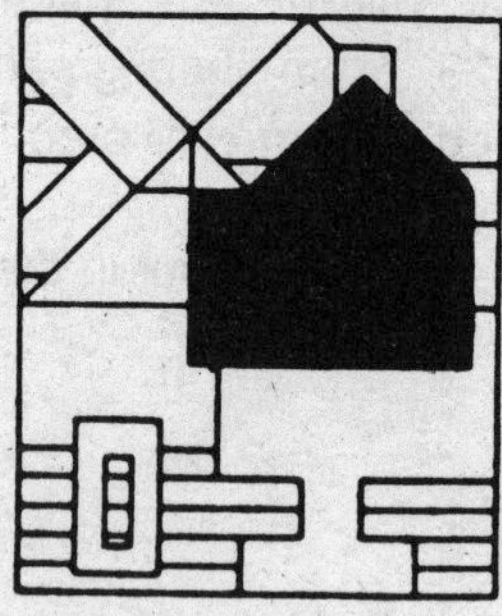

Complex Movements

1. **(B)** (2 left and 2 up)
2. **(D)** (1 right and 1 down)
3. **(C)** (1 left, no vertical movement)
4. **(D)** (3 right and 3 down)
5. **(B)** (no horizontal movement, 2 down)

Cyclic Orientation

1. Climbing and banking left

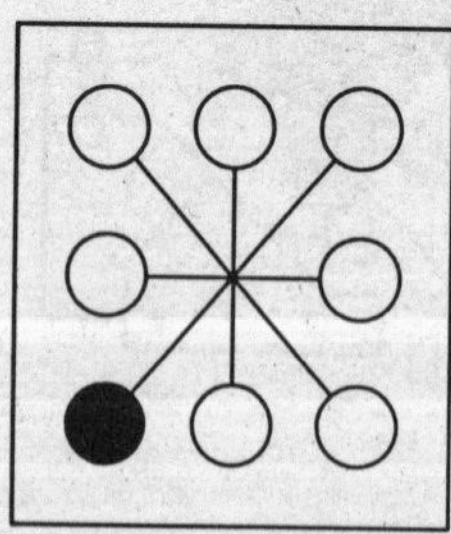

2. Climbing and banking right

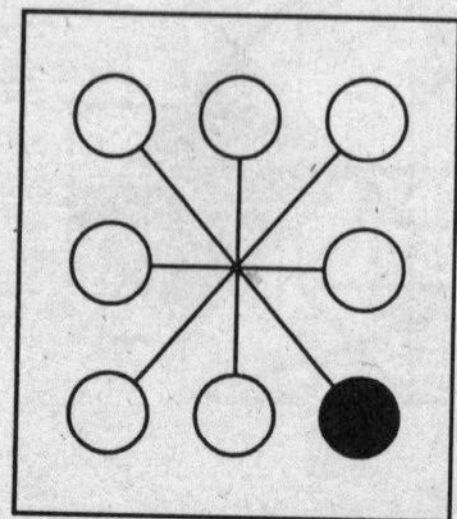

3. Diving; no bank

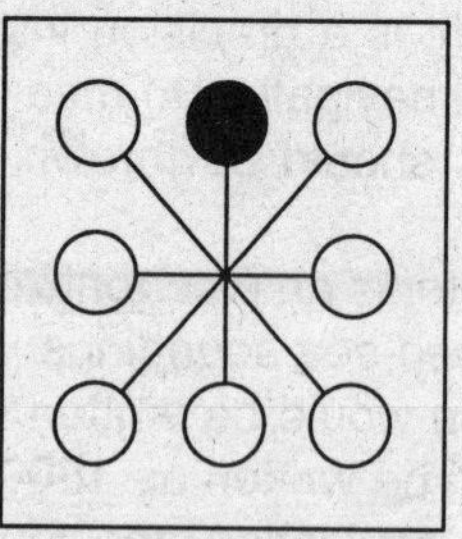

4. Climbing and banking right

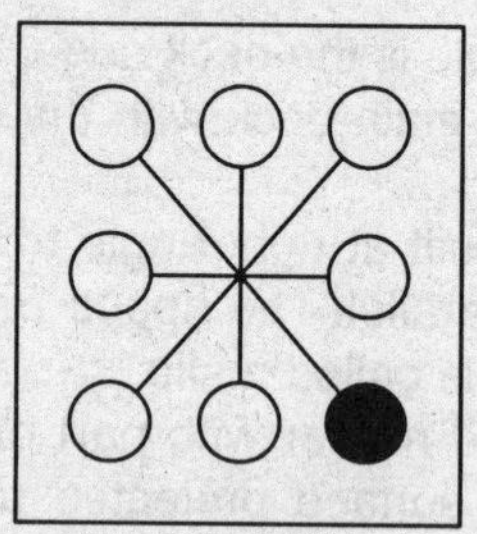

5. Climbing and banking left

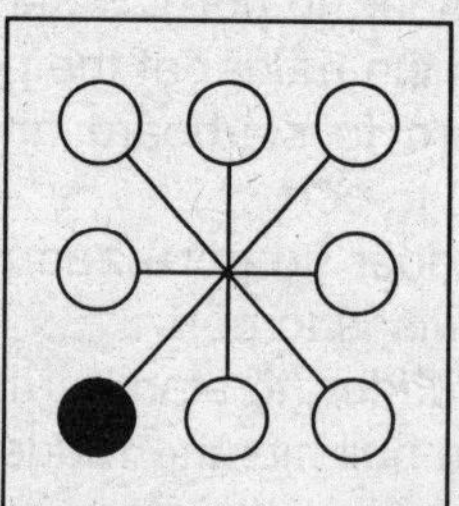

Spatial Apperception

1. **(B)** Straight-and-level flight along the coastline
2. **(E)** Climbing; no bank; flying out to sea
3. **(C)** Level flight; right bank; flying up the coastline
4. **(D)** Climbing, no bank; flying down the coastline. (Note that the sea is left of the coastline in the lettered options but right of the coastline in the aerial view.)
5. **(A)** Straight-and-level flight heading 45° left of coastline

Part 4

Sample Air Force Officer Qualifying Test

SAMPLE AIR FORCE OFFICER QUALIFYING TEST

This part contains specimen answer sheets for use in answering the questions on each subtest, a specimen Air Force Officer Qualifying Test, key answers for determining your scores on these subtests, and the rationale or explanation for each key answer.

Remove (cut out) the specimen answer sheets on the following pages for use in recording your answers to the test questions. The specimen Air Force Officer Qualifying Test is similar in format and content to the actual Air Force Officer Qualifying Test. Take this test under "real" test conditions. Time each subtest carefully.

Use the key answers to obtain your subtest scores and to evaluate your performance on each subtest. Record the number of items you answered correctly, as well as the number of each item you answered incorrectly or wish to review, in the space provided below the key answers for each subtest.

Be certain to review carefully and understand the explanations for the answers to all questions you answered incorrectly and for each of the questions which you answered correctly but are unsure of. This is absolutely essential in order to acquire the knowledge and expertise necessary to obtain the maximum scores possible on the subtests of the real Air Force Officer Qualifying Test.

Format of the Specimen AFOQT

Subtest	Minutes	Questions
Verbal Analogies	8	25
Arithmetic Reasoning	29	25
Reading Comprehension	18	25
Data Interpretation	24	25
Word Knowledge	5	25
Math Knowledge	22	25
Mechanical Comprehension	22	20
Electrical Maze	10	20
Scale Reading	10	40
Instrument Comprehension	6	20
Block Counting	3	20
Table Reading	7	40
Aviation Information	8	20
Rotating Blocks	13	15
General Science	10	20
Hidden Figures	8	15

ANSWER SHEET
AIR FORCE
OFFICER QUALIFYING TEST

SCHEMATIC SAMPLE

MI

FIRST

LAST

PART 1 VERBAL ANALOGIES

1 A B C D E	5 A B C D E	9 A B C D E	13 A B C D E	17 A B C D E	21 A B C D E	25 A B C D E
2 A B C D E	6 A B C D E	10 A B C D E	14 A B C D E	18 A B C D E	22 A B C D E	
3 A B C D E	7 A B C D E	11 A B C D E	15 A B C D E	19 A B C D E	23 A B C D E	
4 A B C D E	8 A B C D E	12 A B C D E	16 A B C D E	20 A B C D E	24 A B C D E	

PART 2 ARITHMETIC REASONING

1 A B C D E	5 A B C D E	9 A B C D E	13 A B C D E	17 A B C D E	21 A B C D E	25 A B C D E
2 A B C D E	6 A B C D E	10 A B C D E	14 A B C D E	18 A B C D E	22 A B C D E	
3 A B C D E	7 A B C D E	11 A B C D E	15 A B C D E	19 A B C D E	23 A B C D E	
4 A B C D E	8 A B C D E	12 A B C D E	16 A B C D E	20 A B C D E	24 A B C D E	

PART 3 READING COMPREHENSION

1 A B C D E	5 A B C D E	9 A B C D E	13 A B C D E	17 A B C D E	21 A B C D E	25 A B C D E
2 A B C D E	6 A B C D E	10 A B C D E	14 A B C D E	18 A B C D E	22 A B C D E	
3 A B C D E	7 A B C D E	11 A B C D E	15 A B C D E	19 A B C D E	23 A B C D E	
4 A B C D E	8 A B C D E	12 A B C D E	16 A B C D E	20 A B C D E	24 A B C D E	

PART 4 DATA INTERPRETATION

1 A B C D E	5 A B C D E	9 A B C D E	13 A B C D E	17 A B C D E	21 A B C D E	25 A B C D E
2 A B C D E	6 A B C D E	10 A B C D E	14 A B C D E	18 A B C D E	22 A B C D E	
3 A B C D E	7 A B C D E	11 A B C D E	15 A B C D E	19 A B C D E	23 A B C D E	
4 A B C D E	8 A B C D E	12 A B C D E	16 A B C D E	20 A B C D E	24 A B C D E	

PART 5 WORD KNOWLEDGE

1 A B C D E	5 A B C D E	9 A B C D E	13 A B C D E	17 A B C D E	21 A B C D E	25 A B C D E
2 A B C D E	6 A B C D E	10 A B C D E	14 A B C D E	18 A B C D E	22 A B C D E	
3 A B C D E	7 A B C D E	11 A B C D E	15 A B C D E	19 A B C D E	23 A B C D E	
4 A B C D E	8 A B C D E	12 A B C D E	16 A B C D E	20 A B C D E	24 A B C D E	

PART 6 MATH KNOWLEDGE

1 A B C D E	5 A B C D E	9 A B C D E	13 A B C D E	17 A B C D E	21 A B C D E	25 A B C D E
2 A B C D E	6 A B C D E	10 A B C D E	14 A B C D E	18 A B C D E	22 A B C D E	
3 A B C D E	7 A B C D E	11 A B C D E	15 A B C D E	19 A B C D E	23 A B C D E	
4 A B C D E	8 A B C D E	12 A B C D E	16 A B C D E	20 A B C D E	24 A B C D E	

ANSWER SHEET
AIR FORCE
OFFICER QUALIFYING TEST

SCHEMATIC SAMPLE

LAST FIRST MI

PART 7 MECHANICAL COMPREHENSION

1 A B C D E	5 A B C D E	9 A B C D E	13 A B C D E	17 A B C D E
2 A B C D E	6 A B C D E	10 A B C D E	14 A B C D E	18 A B C D E
3 A B C D E	7 A B C D E	11 A B C D E	15 A B C D E	19 A B C D E
4 A B C D E	8 A B C D E	12 A B C D E	16 A B C D E	20 A B C D E

PART 8 ELECTRICAL MAZE

1 A B C D E	5 A B C D E	9 A B C D E	13 A B C D E	17 A B C D E
2 A B C D E	6 A B C D E	10 A B C D E	14 A B C D E	18 A B C D E
3 A B C D E	7 A B C D E	11 A B C D E	15 A B C D E	19 A B C D E
4 A B C D E	8 A B C D E	12 A B C D E	16 A B C D E	20 A B C D E

PART 9 SCALE READING

1 A B C D E	9 A B C D E	17 A B C D E	25 A B C D E	33 A B C D E
2 A B C D E	10 A B C D E	18 A B C D E	26 A B C D E	34 A B C D E
3 A B C D E	11 A B C D E	19 A B C D E	27 A B C D E	35 A B C D E
4 A B C D E	12 A B C D E	20 A B C D E	28 A B C D E	36 A B C D E
5 A B C D E	13 A B C D E	21 A B C D E	29 A B C D E	37 A B C D E
6 A B C D E	14 A B C D E	22 A B C D E	30 A B C D E	38 A B C D E
7 A B C D E	15 A B C D E	23 A B C D E	31 A B C D E	39 A B C D E
8 A B C D E	16 A B C D E	24 A B C D E	32 A B C D E	40 A B C D E

PART 10 INSTRUMENT COMPREHENSION

1 A B C D	5 A B C D	9 A B C D	13 A B C D	17 A B C D
2 A B C D	6 A B C D	10 A B C D	14 A B C D	18 A B C D
3 A B C D	7 A B C D	11 A B C D	15 A B C D	19 A B C D
4 A B C D	8 A B C D	12 A B C D	16 A B C D	20 A B C D

PART 11 BLOCK COUNTING

1 A B C D E	5 A B C D E	9 A B C D E	13 A B C D E	17 A B C D E
2 A B C D E	6 A B C D E	10 A B C D E	14 A B C D E	18 A B C D E
3 A B C D E	7 A B C D E	11 A B C D E	15 A B C D E	19 A B C D E
4 A B C D E	8 A B C D E	12 A B C D E	16 A B C D E	20 A B C D E

ANSWER SHEET
AIR FORCE
OFFICER QUALIFYING TEST

SCHEMATIC SAMPLE

LAST FIRST MI

PART 12 TABLE READING

1 A B C D E	9 A B C D E	17 A B C D E	25 A B C D E	33 A B C D E
2 A B C D E	10 A B C D E	18 A B C D E	26 A B C D E	34 A B C D E
3 A B C D E	11 A B C D E	19 A B C D E	27 A B C D E	35 A B C D E
4 A B C D E	12 A B C D E	20 A B C D E	28 A B C D E	36 A B C D E
5 A B C D E	13 A B C D E	21 A B C D E	29 A B C D E	37 A B C D E
6 A B C D E	14 A B C D E	22 A B C D E	30 A B C D E	38 A B C D E
7 A B C D E	15 A B C D E	23 A B C D E	31 A B C D E	39 A B C D E
8 A B C D E	16 A B C D E	24 A B C D E	32 A B C D E	40 A B C D E

PART 13 AVIATION INFORMATION

1 A B C D E	5 A B C D E	9 A B C D E	13 A B C D E	17 A B C D E
2 A B C D E	6 A B C D E	10 A B C D E	14 A B C D E	18 A B C D E
3 A B C D E	7 A B C D E	11 A B C D E	15 A B C D E	19 A B C D E
4 A B C D E	8 A B C D E	12 A B C D E	16 A B C D E	20 A B C D E

PART 14 ROTATING BLOCKS

1 A B C D E	4 A B C D E	7 A B C D E	10 A B C D E	13 A B C D E
2 A B C D E	5 A B C D E	8 A B C D E	11 A B C D E	14 A B C D E
3 A B C D E	6 A B C D E	9 A B C D E	12 A B C D E	15 A B C D E

PART 15 GENERAL SCIENCE

1 A B C D E	5 A B C D E	9 A B C D E	13 A B C D E	17 A B C D E
2 A B C D E	6 A B C D E	10 A B C D E	14 A B C D E	18 A B C D E
3 A B C D E	7 A B C D E	11 A B C D E	15 A B C D E	19 A B C D E
4 A B C D E	8 A B C D E	12 A B C D E	16 A B C D E	20 A B C D E

PART 16 HIDDEN FIGURES

1 A B C D E	4 A B C D E	7 A B C D E	10 A B C D E	13 A B C D E
2 A B C D E	5 A B C D E	8 A B C D E	11 A B C D E	14 A B C D E
3 A B C D E	6 A B C D E	9 A B C D E	12 A B C D E	15 A B C D E

PART 1

VERBAL ANALOGIES

1

Directions

This part of the test has 25 questions designed to measure your ability to reason and see relationships between words. Each question begins with a pair of capitalized words. You are to choose the option that best completes the analogy developed at the beginning of each question. That is, select the option that shows a relationship similar to the one shown by the original pair of capitalized words. Then mark the space on your answer form which has the same number and letter as your choice.

Now look at the two sample questions below.

1. FINGER is to HAND as TOOTH is to

   (A) tongue
   (B) lips
   (C) nose
   (D) mouth
   (E) molar

A finger is part of the hand; a tooth is part of the mouth. Choice (D) is the correct answer.

2. RACQUET is to COURT as

   (A) tractor is to field
   (B) blossom is to bloom
   (C) stalk is to prey
   (D) plan is to strategy
   (E) moon is to planet

A racquet is used (by a tennis player) on the court; a tractor is used (by a farmer) on the field. Choice (A) is the correct answer.

Your score on this test will be based on the number of questions you answer correctly. You should try to answer every question. You will not lose points or be penalized for guessing. Do not spend too much time on any one question.

When you begin, be sure to start with question number 1 of Part 1 of your test booklet and number 1 of Part 1 on your answer form.

DO NOT TURN THIS PAGE UNTIL TOLD TO DO SO.

PART 1

VERBAL ANALOGIES

TIME: 8 Minutes—25 Questions

1. BOOK is to CHAPTER as BUILDING is to

(A) elevator
(B) lobby
(C) roof
(D) story
(E) wing

2. ALPHA is to OMEGA as

(A) appendix is to preface
(B) beginning is to end
(C) head is to body
(D) intermission is to finale
(E) prelude is to intermission

3. CARROT is to VEGETABLE as

(A) dogwood is to oak
(B) foot is to paw
(C) pepper is to spice
(D) sheep is to lamb
(E) veal is to beef

4. MICROMETER is to MACHINIST as TROWEL is to

(A) blacksmith
(B) electrician
(C) mason
(D) pressman
(E) welder

5. CONCAVE is to CONVEX as

(A) cavity is to mound
(B) hill is to hole
(C) oval is to oblong
(D) round is to pointed
(E) square is to round

6. DOZEN is to SCORE as

(A) VII is to XII
(B) IIX is to XX
(C) IIX is to XL
(D) XII is to XX
(E) XII is to XL

7. GOWN is to GARMENT as GASOLINE is to

(A) coolant
(B) fuel
(C) grease
(D) lubricant
(E) oil

8. EMERALD is to GREEN as

(A) canary is to yellow
(B) cocoa is to brown
(C) navy is to blue
(D) royal is to purple
(E) ruby is to red

9. HYPER- is to HYPO- as

(A) actual is to theoretical
(B) diastolic is to systolic
(C) over is to under
(D) small is to large
(E) stale is to fresh

10. HORIZONTAL is to VERTICAL as WARP is to

(A) count
(B) pile
(C) selvage
(D) weave
(E) woof

11. IMMIGRATION is to EMIGRATION as

(A) arrival is to departure
(B) flight is to voyage
(C) legal is to illegal
(D) migration is to travel
(E) passport is to visa

12. KILOMETER is to METER as

(A) century is to decade
(B) century is to year
(C) decade is to month
(D) millennium is to century
(E) millennium is to year

13. OCTAGON is to SQUARE as HEXAGON is to

(A) cube
(B) polygon
(C) pyramid
(D) rectangle
(E) triangle

14. ORDINATION is to PRIEST as

(A) election is to official
(B) inauguration is to president
(C) matriculation is to student
(D) nomination is to officer
(E) retirement is to minister

15. PERJURE is to STATE as

(A) abandon is to desert
(B) concentrate is to focus
(C) marvel is to wonder
(D) rob is to steal
(E) trespass is to enter

16. ORDINANCE is to REGULATION as ORDNANCE is to

(A) law
(B) military
(C) munition
(D) numerical
(E) statute

17. TELL is to TOLD as

(A) ride is to rode
(B) slay is to slew
(C) sink is to sank
(D) weave is to wove
(E) weep is to wept

18. UNIT is to DOZEN as

(A) day is to week
(B) hour is to day
(C) minute is to hour
(D) month is to year
(E) week is to month

19. SHEEP is to LAMB as HORSE is to

(A) colt
(B) doe
(C) fawn
(D) mare
(E) ram

20. ZENITH is to NADIR as

(A) best is to worst
(B) heaviest is to lightest
(C) highest is to lowest
(D) most is to least
(E) widest is to narrowest

21. IGNORE is to OVERLOOK as

(A) agree is to consent
(B) attach is to separate
(C) climb is to walk
(D) dull is to sharpen
(E) learn is to remember

22. SQUARE is to CIRCLE as PERIMETER is to

(A) arc
(B) circumference
(C) diameter
(D) radius
(E) sector

23. FREQUENTLY is to SELDOM as

(A) always is to never
(B) everybody is to everyone
(C) generally is to usually
(D) occasionally is to constantly
(E) sorrow is to sympathy

24. VEHICLE is to BUS as

(A) football is to handball
(B) game is to baseball
(C) hunting is to fishing
(D) play is to sport
(E) sport is to recreation

25. TRICKLE is to GUSH as TEPID is to

(A) cold
(B) cool
(C) frozen
(D) hot
(E) warm

STOP! DO NOT GO ON UNTIL TIME IS UP.

PART 2

2

ARITHMETIC REASONING

Directions

This part of the test measures mathematical reasoning or your ability to arrive at solutions to problems. Each problem is followed by five possible answers. Decide which one of the five options is most nearly correct. Then mark the space on your answer form which has the same number and letter as your choice. Use the scratch paper that has been given to you to do any figuring that you wish.

Now look at the two sample problems below.

1. A field with an area of 420 square yards is twice as large in area as a second field. If the second field is 15 yards long, how wide is it?

   (A) 7 yards
   (B) 14 yards
   (C) 28 yards
   (D) 56 yards
   (E) 90 yards

The second field has an area of 210 square yards. If one side is 15 yards, the other side must be 14 yards ($15 \times 14 = 210$). Option (B) is the correct answer.

2. An applicant took three typing tests. The average typing speed on these three tests was 48 words per minute. If the applicant's speed on two of these tests was 52 words per minute, what was the applicant's speed on the third test?

   (A) 46 words per minute
   (B) 44 words per minute
   (C) 42 words per minute
   (D) 40 words per minute
   (E) 38 words per minute

The formula for finding an average is
average = sum of terms/numbers of terms

In this case the problem provides the average (48), two of the terms (52 + 52) and the number of terms (3). Substitute this information into the formula for average and then solve for x (the missing term).

$$48 = \frac{52 + 52 + x}{3}$$

$$48 \times 3 = 104 + x$$

$$144 = 104 + x$$

$$40 = x$$

Option (D) is correct.

Your score on this test will be based on the number of questions you answer correctly. You should try to answer every question. You will not lose points or be penalized for guessing. Do not spend too much time on any one question.

When you begin, be sure to start with question number 1 of Part 2 of your test booklet and number 1 of Part 2 on your answer sheet.

DO NOT TURN THIS PAGE UNTIL TOLD TO DO SO.

PART 2

ARITHMETIC REASONING

TIME: 29 Minutes—25 Questions

1. An athlete jogs 15 laps around a circular track. If the total distance jogged is 3 kilometers, what is the distance around the track?
   (A) 0.2 meters
   (B) 2 meters
   (C) 20 meters
   (D) 200 meters
   (E) 2000 meters

2. The floor area in an Air Force warehouse measures 200 feet by 200 feet. What is the maximum safe floor load if the maximum weight the floor area can hold is 4000 tons?
   (A) 100 pounds per square foot
   (B) 120 pounds per square foot
   (C) 140 pounds per square foot
   (D) 160 pounds per square foot
   (E) 200 pounds per square foot

3. A crate containing a tool weighs 12 pounds. If the tool weighs 9 pounds, 9 ounces, how much does the crate weigh?
   (A) 2 pounds, 7 ounces
   (B) 2 pounds, 9 ounces
   (C) 3 pounds, 3 ounces
   (D) 3 pounds, 7 ounces
   (E) 3 pounds, 9 ounces

4. Assume that the United States Mint produces one million nickels a month. The total value of the nickels produced during a year is
   (A) $50,000
   (B) $60,000
   (C) $250,000
   (D) $500,000
   (E) $600,000

5. In order to check on a shipment of 500 articles, a sampling of 50 articles was carefully inspected. Of the sample, 4 articles were found to be defective. On this basis, what is the probable percentage of defective articles in the original shipment?
   (A) 8%
   (B) 4%
   (C) .8%
   (D) .4%
   (E) .04%

6. There are 20 cigarettes in one pack and 10 packs of cigarettes in a carton. A certain brand of cigarette contains 12 mg of tar per cigarette. How many grams of tar are contained in one carton of these cigarettes? (1 gram = 1000 milligrams)
   (A) .024 grams
   (B) .24 grams
   (C) 2.4 grams
   (D) 24 grams
   (E) 240 grams

7. Assume that it takes an average of 3 man-hours to stack 1 ton of a particular item. In order to stack 36 tons in 6 hours, the number of persons required is
   (A) 9
   (B) 12
   (C) 15
   (D) 18
   (E) 21

8. Two office workers have been assigned to address 750 envelopes. One addresses twice as many envelopes per hour as the other. If it takes five hours for them to complete the job, what was the rate of the slower worker?
   (A) 50 envelopes per hour
   (B) 75 envelopes per hour
   (C) 100 envelopes per hour
   (D) 125 envelopes per hour
   (E) 150 envelopes per hour

9. A room measuring 15 feet wide, 25 feet long, and 12 feet high is scheduled to be painted shortly. If there are two windows in the room, each 7 feet by 5 feet, and a glass door, 6 feet by 4 feet, then the area of wall space to be painted measures

(A) 842 square feet
(B) 866 square feet
(C) 901 square feet
(D) 925 square feet
(E) 4,406 square feet

10. A pound of margarine contains four equal sticks of margarine. The wrapper of each stick has markings which indicate how to divide the stick into eight sections, each section measuring one tablespoon. If a recipe calls for four tablespoons of margarine, the amount to use is

(A) $\frac{1}{16}$ lb.

(B) $\frac{1}{8}$ lb.

(C) $\frac{1}{4}$ lb.

(D) $\frac{1}{2}$ lb.

(E) $\frac{3}{4}$ lb.

11. The price of a one-hundred-dollar item after successive discounts of 10% and 15% is

(A) $75.00
(B) $75.50
(C) $76.00
(D) $76.50
(E) $77.00

12. A certain governmental agency had a budget last year of $1,100,500. Its budget this year was 7% higher than that of last year. The budget for next year is 8% higher than this year's budget. Which one of the following is the agency's budget for next year?

(A) $1,117,600
(B) $1,161,600
(C) $1,261,700
(D) $1,265,600
(E) $1,271,700

13. The length of a rectangle is 4 times the width. If the area of the rectangle is 324 square feet, the dimensions of the rectangle are

(A) 8' × 32'
(B) 8' × 42'
(C) 9' × 36'
(D) 9' × 40'
(E) 9' × 46'

14. On a scaled drawing of an office building floor, 1/2 inch represents three feet of actual floor dimension. A floor which is actually 75 feet wide and 132 feet long would have which of the following dimensions on the scaled drawing?

(A) 12.5 inches wide and 22 inches long
(B) 17 inches wide and 32 inches long
(C) 25 inches wide and 44 inches long
(D) 29.5 inches wide and 52 inches long
(E) none of these

15. If the weight of water is 62.4 pounds per cubic foot, the weight of the water that fills a rectangular container 6 inches by 6 inches by 1 foot is:

(A) 3.9 pounds
(B) 7.8 pounds
(C) 15.6 pounds
(D) 31.2 pounds
(E) 62.4 pounds

16. If there are red, green, and yellow marbles in a jar and 20% of these marbles are either red or green, what are the chances of blindly picking a yellow marble out of the jar?

(A) 1 out of 3
(B) 1 out of 5
(C) 2 out of 3
(D) 2 out of 5
(E) 4 out of 5

17. An Air Force recruiting station enlisted 560 people. Of these, 25% were under 20 years old and 35% were 20 to 22 years old. How many of the recruits were over 22 years old?

(A) 196
(B) 224
(C) 244
(D) 280
(E) 336

18. A passenger plane can carry two tons of cargo. A freight plane can carry six tons of cargo. If an equal number of both kinds of planes are used to ship 160 tons of cargo and each plane carries its maximum cargo load, how many tons of cargo are shipped on the passenger planes?

    (A) 40 tons
    (B) 60 tons
    (C) 80 tons
    (D) 100 tons
    (E) 120 tons

19. The area of a square is 36 square inches. If the side of this square is doubled, the area of the new square will be:

    (A) 72 square inches
    (B) 108 square inches
    (C) 216 square inches
    (D) 244 square inches
    (E) none of these

20. When 550 gallons of oil are added to an oil tank that is $\frac{1}{8}$ full, the tank becomes $\frac{1}{2}$ full. The capacity of the oil tank is most nearly

    (A) 1,350 gals.
    (B) 1,390 gals.
    (C) 1,430 gals.
    (D) 1,470 gals.
    (E) 1,510 gals.

21. If an aircraft is traveling at 630 miles per hour, how many miles does it cover in 1200 seconds?

    (A) 180 miles
    (B) 210 miles
    (C) 240 miles
    (D) 280 miles
    (E) 310 miles

22. If your watch gains 20 minutes per day and you set it to the correct time at 7:00 a.m., the correct time when the watch indicates 1:00 p.m. is

    (A) 12:45 p.m.
    (B) 12:50 p.m.
    (C) 12:55 p.m.
    (D) 1:05 p.m.
    (E) 1:10 p.m.

23. It takes a runner 9 seconds to run a distance of 132 feet. What is the runner's speed in miles per hour? (5280 ft = 1 mile)

    (A) 5
    (B) 10
    (C) 12
    (D) 15
    (E) 16

24. The arithmetic mean of the salaries paid five employees earning $18,400, $19,300, $18,450, $18,550 and $17,600 respectively is

    (A) $18,450
    (B) $18,460
    (C) $18,470
    (D) $18,475
    (E) $18,500

25. How many meters will a point on the rim of a wheel travel if the wheel makes 35 rotations and its radius is one meter?

    (A) 110
    (B) 120
    (C) 210
    (D) 220
    (E) 240

STOP! DO NOT GO ON UNTIL TIME IS UP.

PART 3

READING COMPREHENSION

3

Directions

This part of the test has 25 questions designed to measure your ability to read and understand paragraphs. For each question, you are to select the answer that best completes the statement or answers the question based on the information contained in the passage. Then mark the space on your answer form which has the same number and letter as your choice.

Here are two sample questions.

1. Because of our short life span of seventy-odd years, it is easy for human beings to think of earth as a planet which never changes. Yet we live on a dynamic planet with many factors contributing to change. We know that wind and rain erode and shape our planet. Many other forces are also at work, such as volcanic activity, temperature fluctuations, and even extraterrestrial interaction such as meteors and gravitational forces. The earth, in actuality, is a large rock

    (A) in a state of inertia
    (B) which is quickly eroding
    (C) which is evolving
    (D) which is subject to temperature fluctuations caused by interplanetary interaction
    (E) which is subject to winds caused by meteor activity

Of the choices given, only option (C) can be implied from the passage. Accordingly, option (C) is the correct answer.

2. One theory that explains the similarities between Mayan art and ancient Chinese art is called "diffusion." This theory evolves from the belief that invention is so unique that it happens only once, then is "diffused" to other cultures through travel, trade, and war. This theory might explain why

    (A) the airplane and birds both have wings
    (B) certain artifacts in Central America resemble those found in Southeast Asia
    (C) most great art comes from Europe, where there is much travel between countries
    (D) rivers in South America and Africa have some similar features
    (E) England, being so remote in the Middle Ages, is the only country to have castles

Of the choices given, option (B) is the only one that the theory might explain. Accordingly, option (B) is the correct answer.

Your score on this test will be based on the number of questions you answer correctly. You should try to answer every question. You will not lose points or be penalized for guessing. Do not spend too much time on any one question.

When you begin, be sure to start with question number 1 of Part 3 of your test booklet and number 1 of Part 3 on your answer form.

DO NOT TURN THIS PAGE UNTIL TOLD TO DO SO.

PART 3

READING COMPREHENSION

TIME: 18 Minutes—25 Questions

1. If they are to function effectively, organizations, like other systems, must achieve a natural harmony or coherence among their component parts. The structural and situational elements of an effective organization form themselves into a tightly knit, highly cohesive package. An organization whose parts are mismatched, however, cannot carry out its missions.

   According to the passage, if managers are to design effective organizations, they need to

   (A) simplify organizational structures
   (B) encourage greater specialization of labor
   (C) emphasize the fit of organizational parts
   (D) introduce more technological innovations
   (E) reduce the span of control in the organization

2. First, *Clostridium botulinum*, the bacterium that produces the poison, must be present. These bacteria are widespread in the environment and are considered by some to be everywhere. Second, the bacterium that produces the deadly toxin must be treated to an atmosphere that's free of oxygen and to temperatures that are just warm enough but not too warm. Those conditions have to be held long enough for the toxin to develop. Acid will prevent the growth of the organism and the production of toxin.

   Which of the following conditions is necessary for botulism to develop?

   (A) presence of oxygen
   (B) a brief period of time
   (C) presence of acid
   (D) warm temperatures
   (E) exposure to rare bacteria

3. The English language is particularly rich in synonyms, and there is scarcely a language spoken among people that has not some representative in English speech. The spirit of the English-speaking peoples has subjugated these various elements to one idiom, making not a patchwork, but a composite language. It can be truly stated that the English language

   (A) has absorbed words from other languages
   (B) has few idiomatic expressions
   (C) has provided words for other languages
   (D) is difficult to translate
   (E) is universally used

4. *Mustela nigripes*, the rarely seen black-footed ferret, is often confused with *Mustela putorius*, the common European polecat. It is true that these two mammals resemble each other in some ways. However, they are two distinct and separate species with differences in color, body form, and other attributes. Indeed it is possible that many sightings of the black-footed ferret

   (A) were the result of seeing the European polecat running loose
   (B) were of species other than the common European polecat
   (C) were made of a related species of the same form and color
   (D) were instead sightings of the *Mustela nigripes*
   (E) were due to the European polecat destroying their habitat.

5. Honest people in one nation find it difficult to understand the viewpoints of honest people in another. Foreign ministries and their ministers exist for the purpose of explaining the viewpoints of one nation in terms understood by the ministries of another. Some of their most important work lies in this direction.

   On the basis of this information, it may be stated that

(A) it is unusual for many people to share similar ideas
(B) people of different nations may not consider matters in the same light
(C) suspicion prevents understanding between nations
(D) the chief work of foreign ministries is to guide relations between nations united by a common cause
(E) the people of one nation must sympathize with the viewpoints of the people of other nations

6. In the metric system, the unit of length is the meter, which is one ten-millionth of the distance from the Equator to the North Pole. One kilometer (1,000 meters) is equal to $\frac{5}{8}$ of a mile. The meter is divided into smaller units, such as the centimeter ($\frac{1}{100}$ of a meter) or the millimeter ($\frac{1}{1000}$ of a meter). The meter is actually equal to

(A) the distance from the Equator to the North Pole
(B) $\frac{1}{1,000,000}$ of the distance from the Equator to the North Pole
(C) $\frac{1}{10,000,000}$ of the distance from the Equator to the North Pole
(D) $\frac{1}{100,000,000}$ of the distance from the Equator to the North Pole
(E) $\frac{1}{1,000,000,000}$ of the distance from the Equator to the North Pole

7. The two systems of weights and measures are the English system and the metric system. The metric system was first adopted in France in 1795 and is now used in most countries of the world. The British recently changed their system of weights and measures to the metric system. However, in the United States, there has been much opposition to this change. It would cost billions of dollars to change all our weights and measures to the metric system. The metric system is actually used

(A) in all of Europe except Great Britain
(B) in almost all countries of the world
(C) in only a few countries
(D) mostly in Europe
(E) only in Europe

8. One key person in a computer installation is a programmer, the man or woman who puts business and scientific problems into special symbolic languages that can be read by the computer. Jobs done by the computer range all the way from payroll operations to chemical process control, but most computer applications are directed toward management data. About half of the programmers employed by business come to their positions with college degrees; the remaining half are promoted to their positions from within the organization on the basis of demonstrated ability without regard to education.

Of the following, the most valid implication of the above passage is that the programmers in industry

(A) do not need a college degree to do programming work
(B) must be graduates of a college or university
(C) need professional training to advance
(D) should be obtained only from outside the organization
(E) should be promoted only from within the organization

9. The recipient gains an impression of a typewritten letter before beginning to read the message. Factors which provide for a good first impression include margins and spacing that are visually pleasing, formal parts of the letter that are correctly placed according to the style of the letter, copy that is free of obvious erasures and over-strikes, and transcript that is even and clear. The problem for the secretary is how to produce that first, positive impression.

According to the above passage, the addressee very quickly judges the quality of the typed letter by

(A) counting the number of erasures and over-strikes
(B) looking at the spacing and cleanliness of the transcript
(C) measuring the margins to ascertain whether they are proper
(D) reading the date line and address for errors
(E) scanning the body of the letter for meaning

10. It is important for every office to have proper lighting. Inadequate lighting is a common cause of fatigue and tends to create a dreary atmosphere in the office. Appropriate light intensity is essential for proper lighting. It is generally recommended that for "casual seeing" tasks such as in reception rooms or inactive file rooms, the amount of light be 30 foot-candles. For "ordinary seeing" tasks such as reading or for work in active file rooms and mail rooms, the recommended lighting is 100 foot-candles. For "very difficult seeing" tasks such as transcribing, accounting, and business machine use, the recommended lighting is 150 foot-candles.

    For copying figures onto a payroll, the recommended lighting is

    (A) less than 30 foot-candles
    (B) 30 foot-candles
    (C) 100 foot-candles
    (D) 150 foot-candles
    (E) more than 150 foot-candles

11. Many factors must be considered when a police officer is deciding whether or not to make an arrest. If an arrest is not considered legal, it could mean that some evidence will not be allowed in court. An arrest made too early may tip off a suspect before evidence can be found. On the other hand, an officer must also realize that if an arrest is delayed too long, the suspect may run away or the evidence may be destroyed. In all cases, an arrest takes away from a person the very important right to liberty.

    On the basis of the above passage, a judge may refuse to accept evidence of a crime if

    (A) it interfered with the suspect's right of liberty
    (B) it was collected during an illegal arrest
    (C) it was found before the suspect was tipped off
    (D) it was found after the suspect was tipped off
    (E) the suspect was able to get away

12. The candidate's personal appearance is one factor that an interviewer may unconsciously over-value. Of course, personal appearance may be relevant if the job is one involving numerous contacts with the public or with other people, but in most positions it is a matter of distinctly secondary importance. Other qualities that have no bearing on the job to be filled should also be discounted.

    According to this passage

    (A) a candidate should not be concerned about his or her appearance unless it is relevant to the job
    (B) there are many factors which should be considered during an interview even though they have no direct bearing on the job to be filled
    (C) in positions involving contact with the public, the personal appearance of the applicant is the most important factor to be considered
    (D) the personal appearance of the candidate should never be considered
    (E) the personal appearance of a candidate should not be considered of primary importance when interviewing persons for most positions

13. Absenteeism is a symptom of difficult working or living conditions or of individual maladjustment. It can be controlled by eliminating or mitigating as many of its causes as possible and by increasing job satisfaction. Spot surveys and interviews with returning absentees will reveal some of the causes, while constant effort and ingenuity are necessary to find workable solutions since remedies are not universally applicable.

    The above passage best supports the statement that

    (A) spot surveys and interviews are the proper cures for absenteeism
    (B) individual maladjustment is the cause of lack of job satisfaction
    (C) absenteeism will end as soon as all causes have been discovered
    (D) absenteeism can be eliminated by increasing job satisfaction
    (E) absenteeism cures are not equally effective in all cases

14. The protection of life and property against antisocial individuals within the country and enemies from without is generally recognized to be the most fundamental activity of government.

GO ON TO THE NEXT PAGE.

Of the following, the one which is *not* an aspect of the fundamental function of government as described above is

(A) sending a delegation to a foreign country to participate in a disarmament conference
(B) prosecuting a drug peddler who has been selling dope to schoolchildren
(C) fining a motorist who failed to stop at a traffic light
(D) providing fire protection
(E) providing postal service

15. No matter how carefully planned or how painstakingly executed a sales letter or other mailing piece may be, unless it is sent to people selected from a good mailing list, it will be useless. A good mailing list is one consisting of the correct names and present addresses of *bona fide* prospects or customers.

The passage best supports the statement that

(A) a good mailing list is more important than the sales letter
(B) a sales letter should not be sent to anyone who is not already a customer
(C) carefully planned letters may be wasted on poor mailing lists
(D) good sales letters do not depend on a good mailing list to be successful
(E) sales letters are more effective when sent to customers rather than *bona fide* prospects

16. In one form or another, data processing has been carried on throughout the entire history of civilization. In its most general sense, data processing means organizing data so that it can be used for a specific purpose—a procedure commonly known simply as "record-keeping" or "paperwork." With the development of modern office equipment, and particularly with the introduction of computers, the techniques of data processing have become highly elaborate and sophisticated, but the basic purpose remains the same—turning raw data into useful information.

According to the above passage, the use of computers has

(A) greatly simplified the clerical operations of an office
(B) had no effect on data processing
(C) led to more complicated systems for data handling
(D) made other modern office machines obsolete
(E) reduced the cost of office procedures

17. How do we evaluate the overall efficiency of an office, the efficiency of each section or unit, and that of the individual worker? Work measurement is essential for effective office management. We can have measurement without work standards, but we cannot have work standards without measurement. Usually, from two-thirds to three-fourths of all work can be measured. However, less than two-thirds of all work is actually measured, because measurement difficulties are encountered when office work is nonrepetitive or when it is primarily mental rather than manual. These obstacles are used as excuses for nonmeasurement far more frequently than is justified.

The type of office work most difficult to measure would be

(A) answering letters of inquiry
(B) answering telephone calls
(C) checking requisitions
(D) developing a new procedure for issuing supplies
(E) recording personnel changes made in the organization

18. In general, business forms are a reflection of work methods, operating procedures, and management know-how. If a company's forms constitute a simple, orderly plan showing clear and related purposes, there is reason to believe that its personnel know what they are doing and why, and may be giving fairly efficient service. If, on the other hand, its forms constitute an unintelligible tangle of red tape, it is pretty safe to assume that its methods and procedures are in much the same shape.

The passage best supports the statement that

(A) an efficient system of business forms will result in an efficient business organization
(B) business forms used by a company should be continuously simplified and revised
(C) the best method for determining whether a company is successful is to study its business forms
(D) the business forms used by a company are a good indication of the efficiency of the company's operations

(E) well-organized companies redesign their business forms to make a more favorable impression

19. In any fire, destruction is present in varying degrees. In addition to the destruction caused directly by the fire, there is also destruction caused in fighting the fire. If the sum of destruction to a building by fire and firefighters is greater for one method of combating the fire than another, the method causing the lowest level of destruction should be employed.

According to the above passage

(A) fire fighting methods rather than fire itself are responsible for the major destruction in most cases
(B) fire rather than the method of fire fighting is responsible for the major destruction in most cases
(C) the aim of the choice of method is the least amount of total damage
(D) unavoidable damage by firefighters should be ignored when choosing a fire fighting method
(E) ways of fighting fires should be chosen which are not dangerous to firefighters

20. The function of business is to increase the wealth of the country and the value and happiness of life. It does this by supplying the material needs of men and women. When the nation's business is successfully carried on, it renders public service of the highest value.

The passage best supports the statement that

(A) all businesses that render public service are successful
(B) business is the only field of endeavor which increases happiness
(C) human happiness is enhanced only by increasing material wants
(D) only by increasing wealth is the value of life increased
(E) the material needs of men and women are supplied by well-conducted businesses

21. Radio plays an important part in the routine operation of toll roads. Personnel responsible for toll collection, patrol services, traffic and safety, and overall supervision are able to get in touch with their employees in the field and may themselves be reached in their radio-equipped cars when they are traveling on the road.

According to the above passage, what is the important part that radio plays in the routine operation of toll roads?

(A) It enables supervisors and subordinates to communicate with each other.
(B) It enables the toll road's police force to communicate with motorists.
(C) It makes it possible for safety personnel to advise motorists directly of approaching danger.
(D) It reduces the number of accidents on toll roads.
(E) It reduces the number of problems involved in the collection of tolls.

22. Inherent in all organized endeavors is the need to resolve the individual differences involved in conflict. Conflict may be either a positive or negative factor, since it may lead to creativity, innovation, and progress, on the one hand, or it may result, on the other hand, in a deterioration or even destruction of the organization. Thus, some forms of conflict are desirable, whereas others are undesirable and ethically wrong.

The word *conflict* as used in the above passage means most nearly

(A) aggression
(B) combat
(C) competition
(D) confusion
(E) cooperation

23. A summons is an official statement ordering a person to appear in court. In traffic violation situations, summonses are used when arrests need not be made. The main reason for traffic summonses is to deter motorists from repeating the same traffic violation. Occasionally motorists may make unintentional driving errors and sometimes they are unaware of correct driving regulations. In cases such as these, the policy should be to have the officer verbally inform the motorist of the violation and warn him or her against repeating it. The purpose of this practice is not to limit the number of summonses, but rather to prevent the issuing of summonses when the violation is not due to deliberate intent or to inexcusable negligence.

GO ON TO THE NEXT PAGE.

Using the distinctions given in the above passage, the one of the following motorists to whom it would be most desirable to issue a summons is the one who exceeded the speed limit because he or she

(A) did not know the speed limit
(B) had a speedometer that was not working properly
(C) speeded to avoid being hit by another car
(D) was driving a sick person to the hospital
(E) was late for an important business appointment

24. There are several general rules which can be followed in order to prepare a properly spaced letter on a sheet of letterhead. Ordinarily, the width of a letter should not be less than four inches nor more than six inches. The side margins should also have a desirable relation to the bottom margin and to the space between the letterhead and the body of the letter. Usually the most appealing arrangement is when the side margins are even and the bottom margin is slightly wider than the side margins. In some offices, however, standard line length is used for all business letters, and the spacing between the date line and the inside address is varied according to the length of the letter.

The side margins of a typewritten letter are most pleasing when they

(A) are even and somewhat larger than the bottom margin
(B) are even and somewhat smaller than the bottom margin
(C) are even and vary with the length of the letter
(D) are uneven and vary with the length of the letter
(E) are uneven and do not vary with the length of the letter

25. The courts and the police consider an "offense" as any conduct that is punishable by a fine or imprisonment. State law classifies offenses according to the penalties that are provided for them. Minor offenses are called "violations." A violation is punishable by a fine of not more than $250 or imprisonment of not more than 15 days, or both. More serious offenses are classified as "crimes." Crimes are classified by the kind of penalty that is provided. A "misdemeanor" is a crime that is punishable by a fine of not more than $1,000 or by imprisonment of not more than 1 year, or both. A "felony" is a criminal offense punishable by imprisonment of more than 1 year.

According to the above passage, which of the following is classified as a crime?

(A) minor offense
(B) misdemeanor
(C) offense punishable by a 15-day imprisonment
(D) offense punishable by a $250 fine
(E) violation

STOP! DO NOT GO ON UNTIL TIME IS UP.

PART 4

DATA INTERPRETATION

4

Directions

This part of the test has 25 questions designed to measure your ability to interpret data from tables and graphs. Each question is followed by four or five possible answers. Decide which answer is correct, then mark the space on your answer form which has the same number and letter as your choice.

Study the two sample questions below before you begin the Data Interpretation Test.

Your score on this test will be based on the number of questions you answer correctly. You should try to answer every question. You will not lose points or be penalized for guessing. Do not spend too much time on any one question.

When you begin, be sure to start with question number 1 of Part 4 of your test booklet and number 1 of Part 4 on your answer form.

Number of days absent per employee (sickness)	1	2	3	4	5	6	7	8 or more
Number of employees	76	23	6	3	1	0	1	0

Total Number of Employees: 400

Period Covered: January 1, 1993–December 31, 1993

1. Based on the data shown above, the total number of man-days lost due to sickness in 1993 was:

   (A) 110
   (B) 137
   (C) 144
   (D) 158
   (E) 164

Multiplying the number of employees by the number of days absent per employee (sickness) and then adding the products, we arrive at:

76 + 46 + 18 + 12 + 5 + 0 + 7 + 0 = 164.
Option (E) is the correct answer.

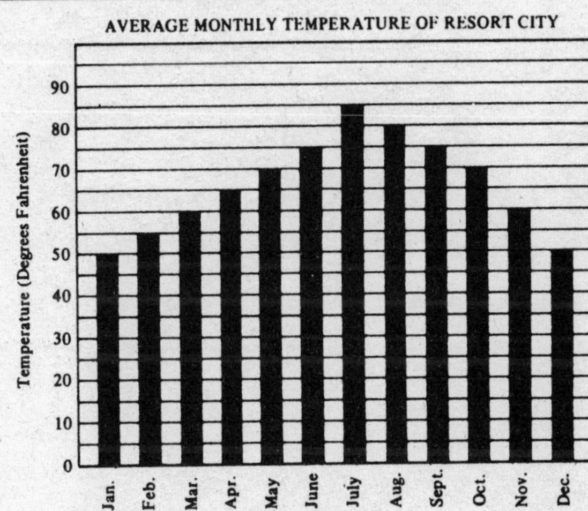

2. Based on the information in the graph above, the average monthly temperature in November is the same as in

   (A) January
   (B) February
   (C) March
   (D) April
   (E) May

The average temperature in November is 60°F. The only other month in which the average temperature is 60°F is March. Option (C) is the correct answer.

DO NOT TURN THIS PAGE UNTIL TOLD TO DO SO.

PART 4

DATA INTERPRETATION

TIME: 24 Minutes—25 Questions

Questions *1* and *2* are to be answered on the basis of the following table.

	Northbound Vehicles	Southbound Vehicles	Eastbound Vehicles	Westbound Vehicles	Total Vehicles
Monday	235	245	175	65	720
Tuesday	160	100	505	280	1045
Wednesday	125	75	100	40	340
Thursday	290	250	350	95	985
Friday	195	325	220	135	875
Totals	1005	995	1350	615	

1. The one day in which the volume of east-west traffic exceeded the volume of north-south traffic is
   (A) Monday
   (B) Tuesday
   (C) Wednesday
   (D) Thursday
   (E) Friday

2. Of the total vehicles recorded on Wednesday, the southbound vehicles comprised approximately
   (A) 22%
   (B) 25%
   (C) 35%
   (D) 75%
   (E) 78%

Answer questions *3* to *5* on the basis of the table on the right and the accompanying notes.

Ration A	Ration B	Ration C	Ration D
4.5	2.8	3.5	6.2
6.5	3.6	7.6	4.6
3.3	4.9	5.3	5.2
4.9	7.1	5.5	6.1
5.8	3.7	4.1	7.0
2.5	5.1	6.7	3.9
4.2	6.0	4.5	5.9
4.7	4.7	6.5	7.1
3.8	6.1	5.7	5.9
5.3	5.0	5.9	8.1
45.5	49.0	55.3	60.0

Four groups of ten rabbits were each fed a complete commercial ration from birth until 5 months of age. Each animal was weighed at birth and at five months. The weight of the animal at birth was subtracted from its weight at five months. These differences, in pounds, are shown above for each rabbit.

3. The average difference in weight gain between the group of rabbits who gained the most and the group who gained the least was

(A) 0.35 lbs.
(B) 0.45 lbs.
(C) 0.47 lbs.
(D) 1.10 lbs
(E) 1.45 lbs.

4. The individual rabbit showing the least gain was fed

(A) Ration A
(B) Ration B
(C) Ration C
(D) Ration D

5. The individual rabbit that gained the most weight gained

(A) 6.0 lbs.
(B) 6.5 lbs.
(C) 7.1 lbs.
(D) 7.6 lbs.
(E) 8.1 lbs.

Answer questions *6* to *9* on the basis of the information given in the table below.

U.S. PRESIDENTS 1921–1997

President	Date of Birth	Term of Office	Age When First Sworn Into Office	Political Party	Date of Death
Warren Harding	11/2/1865	3/1921–8/1923	55	Republican	8/2/1923
Calvin Coolidge	7/4/1872	8/1923–3/1929	51	Republican	1/5/1933
Herbert Hoover	8/10/1874	3/1929–3/1933	54	Republican	10/20/1964
Franklin Roosevelt	1/30/1882	3/1933–4/1945	51	Democrat	4/12/1945
Harry Truman	5/8/1884	4/1945–1/1953	60	Democrat	12/26/1972
Dwight Eisenhower	10/14/1890	1/1953–1/1961	62	Republican	3/28/1969
John Kennedy	5/29/1917	1/1961–11/1963	43	Democrat	11/22/1963
Lyndon Johnson	8/27/1908	11/1963–1/1969	55	Democrat	1/22/1973
Richard Nixon	1/9/1913	1/1969–8/1974	55	Republican	4/22/1994
Gerald Ford	7/14/1913	8/1974–1/1977	61	Republican	—
Jimmy Carter	10/1/1924	1/1977–1/1981	52	Democrat	—
Ronald Reagan	2-6-1911	1/1981–1/1989	69	Republican	—
George Bush	6/12/1924	1/1989–1/1993	64	Republican	—
William Clinton	8/19/1946	1/1993–*	46	Democrat	—

6. Of the presidents listed above who served prior to 1993, the two who served the shortest terms of office are

    (A) Ford and Carter
    (B) Harding and Ford
    (C) Harding and Kennedy
    (D) Kennedy and Carter
    (E) Kennedy and Ford

7. The president who was 70 years old when he completed his term of office is

    (A) Bush
    (B) Eisenhower
    (C) Johnson
    (D) Reagan
    (E) Truman

8. The total number of years the Democratic presidents were in office during the 3/1921–1/1993 period is most nearly

    (A) 30
    (B) 32
    (C) 34
    (D) 36
    (E) 38

9. The average age when first sworn into office of the presidents who served during the 3/1921–l/1997 period is most nearly

    (A) 50
    (B) 52
    (C) 54
    (D) 56
    (E) 58

Answer questions *10* to *13* on the basis of the tabulation given below.

AGE COMPOSITION IN THE LABOR FORCE IN INDUSTRIAL CITY (1980–1990)

Sex	*Age Group*	*1980*	*1985*	*1990*
Men	14–24	840	1,090	1,435
	25–44	2,220	2,235	2,605
	45 & over	1,755	1,980	2,195
Women	14–24	445	690	770
	25–44	910	1,005	1,155
	45 & over	730	945	1,318

*Commenced 2nd term in January 1997.

10. The 14–24 age group of men in the Industrial City labor force increased from 1980 to 1990 by approximately

    (A) 25%
    (B) 40%
    (C) 55%
    (D) 70%
    (E) 85%

11. Between 1980 and 1985, the greatest increase in the number of people in the Industrial City labor force occurred among

    (A) men between the ages of 14 and 24
    (B) women between the ages of 14 and 24
    (C) men age 45 and over
    (D) women age 45 and over
    (E) men between the ages of 25 and 44

12. The total increase in the number of women in the Industrial City labor force from 1980 to 1985 differs from the total increase of men in the labor force from 1980 to 1985 by being

    (A) 65 less than that for men
    (B) 65 more than that for men
    (C) 75 less than that for men
    (D) 75 more than that for men
    (E) 85 less than that for men

13. If the total number of women of all ages in the Industrial City labor force increased from 1990 to 1995 by the same number as it did from 1985 to 1990, the total number of women of all ages in the Industrial City labor force in 1995 would be

    (A) 2,744
    (B) 2,967
    (C) 3,753
    (D) 3,846
    (E) 3,922

GO ON TO THE NEXT PAGE.

Answer questions *14* and *15* on the basis of the information contained in the following chart.

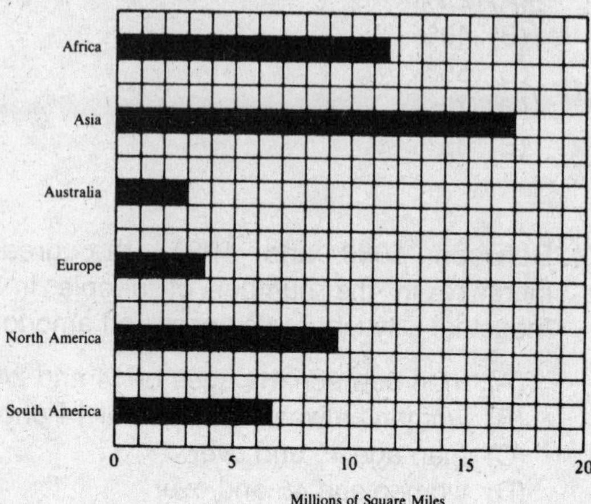

14. The combined area of Europe and South America is approximately the same as the area of
    (A) Africa
    (B) Asia
    (C) Australia
    (D) North America
    (E) Europe + North America

15. How many times larger is the area of Africa compared to that of Australia?
    (A) 2.8 times
    (B) 3.3 times
    (C) 3.8 times
    (D) 4.3 times
    (E) 4.8 times

Answer questions *16* to *18* based on the information given in the graph shown in the next column.

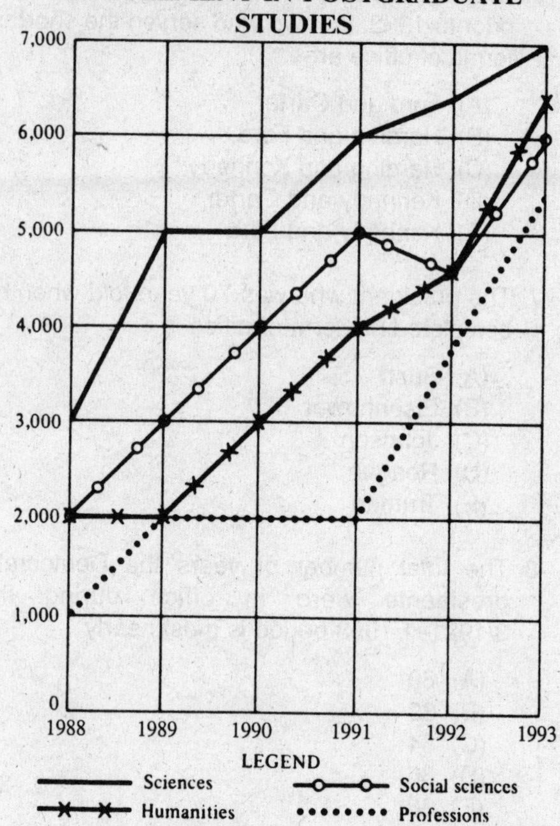

16. A comparison of the enrollment of students in the various postgraduate studies shows that in every year from 1988 through 1993 there were more students enrolled in the
    (A) humanities than in the professions
    (B) humanities than in the sciences
    (C) professions than in the sciences
    (D) social sciences than in the humanities
    (E) social sciences than in the professions

17. The number of students enrolled in the humanities was greater than the number of students enrolled in the professions by the same amount in
    (A) one of the years
    (B) two of the years
    (C) three of the years
    (D) four of the years
    (E) five of the years

18. If enrollment in the professions increased at the same rate from 1993 to 1994 as from 1992 to 1993, the enrollment in the professions in 1994 would be most nearly

    (A) 5,000
    (B) 6,000
    (C) 7,000
    (D) 8,000
    (E) 9,000

Answer questions *19* to *21* on the basis of the information given in the following pie chart.

HOW A FAMILY SPENDS ITS YEARLY EARNINGS OF $45,000 A YEAR

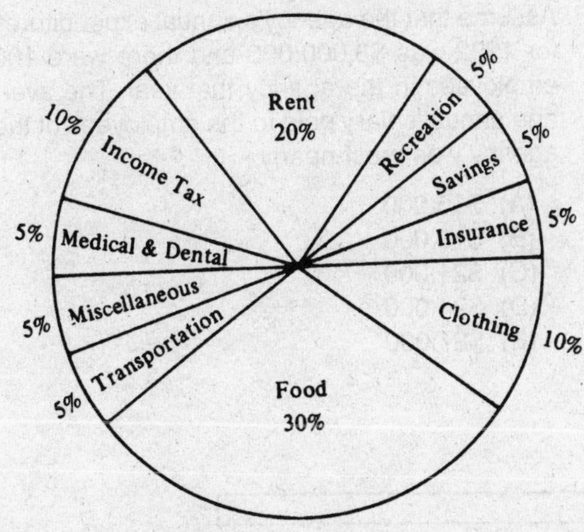

19. How much does the family budget for rent?

    (A) $9,000
    (B) $8,500
    (C) $8,000
    (D) $7,500
    (E) $7,000

20. The amount of money spent for food compared to the amount paid for income tax is

    (A) $2\frac{1}{2}$ times as much
    (B) 3 times as much
    (C) $3\frac{1}{2}$ times as much
    (D) 4 times as much
    (E) $4\frac{1}{2}$ times as much

21. The amount paid for food is the same as the total amount paid for

    (A) clothing, rent, and savings
    (B) clothing, medical and dental, and transportation
    (C) clothing, miscellaneous, and rent
    (D) income tax, rent, and savings
    (E) recreation, rent, and transportation

GO ON TO THE NEXT PAGE.

Answer questions *22* to *25* on the basis of the information contained in the chart at the bottom of this page showing the percentage of an agency's expenditures spent on equipment, supplies and salaries for each of the years 1989–1993.

22. In what year was the amount spent on salaries twice that spent on supplies?

    (A) 1989
    (B) 1990
    (C) 1991
    (D) 1992
    (E) 1993

23. In what year was the amount spent on salaries equal to that spent for both equipment and supplies?

    (A) 1989
    (B) 1990
    (C) 1991
    (D) 1992
    (E) 1993

24. If the percentage of expenditures for salaries in one year is added to the percentage of expenditures for equipment for that year, a total of the two percentages for that year is obtained. The two years for which this total is the same are

    (A) 1989 and 1990
    (B) 1990 and 1991
    (C) 1992 and 1993
    (D) 1989 and 1991
    (E) 1991 and 1993

25. Assume that the agency's annual expenditures for 1992 was $3,000,000 and there were 100 employees in the agency that year. The average annual salary paid to the employees of the agency was most nearly

    (A) $15,000
    (B) $18,000
    (C) $21,000
    (D) $24,000
    (E) $27,000

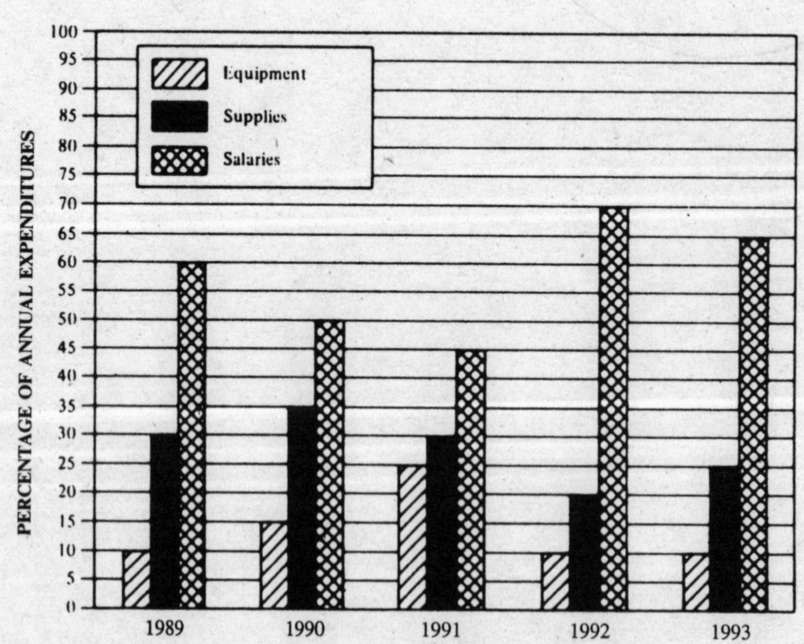

STOP! DO NOT GO ON UNTIL TIME IS UP.

PART 5

5

WORD KNOWLEDGE

Directions

This part of the test is designed to measure verbal comprehension involving your ability to understand written language. For each question, you are to select the option that means the same or most nearly the same as the capitalized word. Then mark the space on your answer form which has the same number and letter as your choice.

Here are two sample questions.

1. CRIMSON

(A) bluish
(B) colorful
(C) crisp
(D) lively
(E) reddish

Crimson means "a deep purple red." Option (E) has almost the same meaning. None of the other options has the same or a similar meaning. Option (E) is the only correct answer of the options given.

2. CEASE

(A) continue
(B) fold
(C) start
(D) stop
(E) transform

Cease means "to stop." Option (D) is the only option with the same meaning and is, therefore, the correct answer.

Your score on this test will be based on the number of questions you answer correctly. You should try to answer every question. You will not lose points or be penalized for guessing. Do not spend too much time on any one question.

When you begin, be sure to start with question number 1 of Part 5 of your test booklet and number 1 of Part 5 on your answer form.

DO NOT TURN THIS PAGE UNTIL TOLD TO DO SO.

PART 5

WORD KNOWLEDGE

TIME: 5 Minutes—25 Questions

1. ADADAMANT

(A) belligerent
(B) cowardly
(C) inflexible
(D) justified
(E) petty

2. ALTERCATION

(A) controversy
(B) defeat
(C) irritation
(D) substitution
(E) vexation

3. ASSENT

(A) acquire
(B) climb
(C) consent
(D) emphasize
(E) participate

4. ATTRITION

(A) act of expanding
(B) act of giving up
(C) act of purifying
(D) act of solving
(E) act of wearing down

5. AUTHENTIC

(A) detailed
(B) genuine
(C) literary
(D) practical
(E) precious

6. CONDUCIVE

(A) confusing
(B) cooperative
(C) energetic
(D) helpful
(E) respectful

7. COUNTERACT

(A) criticize
(B) conserve
(C) erode
(D) neutralize
(E) retreat

8. DELETERIOUS

(A) delightful
(B) frail
(C) harmful
(D) late
(E) tasteful

9. DILATED

(A) cleared
(B) clouded
(C) decreased
(D) enlarged
(E) tightened

10. FLEXIBLE

(A) flammable
(B) fragile
(C) pliable
(D) rigid
(E) separable

11. FORTNIGHT

(A) two days
(B) one week
(C) two weeks
(D) one month
(E) two months

12. IMPARTIAL

(A) complete
(B) fair
(C) incomplete
(D) sincere
(E) watchful

13. INCIDENTAL
    (A) casual
    (B) eventful
    (C) infrequent
    (D) unexpected
    (E) unnecessary

14. INDOLENT
    (A) hopeless
    (B) lazy
    (C) lenient
    (D) rude
    (E) selfish

15. NOTORIOUS
    (A) annoying
    (B) condemned
    (C) ill-mannered
    (D) official
    (E) well-known

16. REBUFF
    (A) forget
    (B) ignore
    (C) recover
    (D) polish
    (E) snub

17. SPURIOUS
    (A) false
    (B) maddening
    (C) obvious
    (D) odd
    (E) stimulating

18. SUCCINCT
    (A) concise
    (B) helpful
    (C) important
    (D) misleading
    (E) sweet

19. SULLEN
    (A) angrily silent
    (B) grayish yellow
    (C) mildly nauseated
    (D) soaking wet
    (E) very dirty

20. SYMPTOM
    (A) cure
    (B) disease
    (C) mistake
    (D) sign
    (E) test

21. TEDIOUS
    (A) demanding
    (B) dull
    (C) hard
    (D) simple
    (E) surprising

22. TERSE
    (A) faulty
    (B) lengthy
    (C) oral
    (D) pointed
    (E) written

23. TRIVIAL
    (A) distressing
    (B) enjoyable
    (C) exciting
    (D) important
    (E) petty

24. VERIFY
    (A) alarm
    (B) confirm
    (C) explain
    (D) guarantee
    (E) question

25. VIGILANT
    (A) cross
    (B) patient
    (C) suspicious
    (D) understanding
    (E) watchful

STOP! DO NOT GO ON UNTIL TIME IS UP.

PART 6

MATH KNOWLEDGE

6

Directions

This part of the test has 25 questions designed to measure your ability to use learned mathematical relationships. Each problem is followed by five possible answers. Decide which one of the five options is most nearly correct. Then mark the space on your answer form which has the same number and letter as your choice. Use scratch paper to do any figuring that you wish.

Here are three sample questions.

1. The reciprocal of 5 is

(A) 0.1
(B) 0.2
(C) 0.5
(D) 1.0
(E) 2.0

The reciprocal of 5 is $\frac{1}{5}$ or 0.2. Option (B) is the correct answer.

2. The expression "3 factorial" equals

(A) $\frac{1}{9}$
(B) $\frac{1}{6}$
(C) 6
(D) 9
(E) 27

"3 factorial" or 3! equals $3 \times 2 \times 1 = 6$. Option (C) is the correct answer.

3. The logarithm to the base 10 of 1,000 is

(A) 1
(B) 1.6
(C) 2
(D) 2.7
(E) 3

$10 \times 10 \times 10 = 1{,}000$. The logarithm of 1,000 is the exponent 3 to which the base 10 must be raised. Option (E) is the correct answer.

Your score on this test will be based on the number of questions you answer correctly. You should try to answer every question. You will not lose points or be penalized for guessing. Do not spend too much time on any one question.

When you begin, be sure to start with question number 1 of Part 6 of your test booklet and number 1 of Part 6 on your answer form.

DO NOT TURN THIS PAGE UNTIL TOLD TO DO SO.

PART 6

MATH KNOWLEDGE

TIME: 22 Minutes—25 Questions

1. Which of the following integers is *not* a prime number?

   (A) 3
   (B) 5
   (C) 7
   (D) 9
   (E) 11

2. The distance in miles around a circular course with a radius of 35 miles is (use pi = $\frac{22}{7}$)

   (A) 110 miles
   (B) 156 miles
   (C) 220 miles
   (D) 440 miles
   (E) 880 miles

3. If $5x + 3y = 29$ and $x - y = 1$, then $x =$

   (A) 1
   (B) 2
   (C) 3
   (D) 4
   (E) 5

4. Solve for *x*: $\frac{2x}{7} = 2x^2$

   (A) $\frac{1}{7}$
   (B) $\frac{2}{7}$
   (C) 2
   (D) 7
   (E) 14

5. If *x* is an odd integer, which one of the following is an even integer?

   (A) $2x + 1$
   (B) $2x - 1$
   (C) $x^2 - x$
   (D) $x^2 + x - 1$
   (E) none of these

6. $\frac{x-2}{x^2 - 6x + 8}$ can be reduced to

   (A) $\frac{1}{x-4}$
   (B) $\frac{1}{x-2}$
   (C) $\frac{x-2}{x+2}$
   (D) $\frac{1}{x+2}$
   (E) $\frac{1}{x+4}$

7. 10^x divided by 10^y equals

   (A) $10^{x/y}$
   (B) 10^{xy}
   (C) 10^{x+y}
   (D) 10^{x-y}
   (E) none of these

8. $(-3)^3$

   (A) 9
   (B) –9
   (C) 27
   (D) –27
   (E) none of these

9. One million may be represented as

   (A) 10^4
   (B) 10^5
   (C) 10^6
   (D) 10^7
   (E) 10^8

10. $\left(\frac{2}{5}\right)^2$ equals

(A) $\frac{4}{5}$

(B) $\frac{2}{10}$

(C) $\frac{4}{10}$

(D) $\frac{2}{25}$

(E) $\frac{4}{25}$

11. If $3^n = 9$, what is the value of $4^n + 1$?

(A) 24
(B) 48
(C) 64
(D) 108
(E) none of these

12. 10^{-2} is equal to

(A) 0.001
(B) 0.01
(C) 0.1
(D) 1.0
(E) 100.0

13. The expression $\sqrt{28} - \sqrt{7}$ reduces to

(A) $\sqrt{4}$

(B) $\sqrt{7}$

(C) $3\sqrt{7}$

(D) $\sqrt{21}$

(E) $-\sqrt{35}$

14. The hypotenuse of a right triangle whose legs are 5" and 12" is

(A) 7"
(B) 13"
(C) 14"
(D) 17"
(E) none of these

15. The sum of the angle measures of a pentagon is

(A) 360°
(B) 540°
(C) 720°
(D) 900°
(E) 1180°

16. If the ratio of $3x$ to $5y$ is 1:2, what is the ratio of x to y?

(A) $\frac{1}{2}$

(B) $\frac{2}{3}$

(C) $\frac{3}{4}$

(D) $\frac{4}{5}$

(E) $\frac{5}{6}$

17. A scale of $\frac{1}{24,000}$ is the same as a scale of

(A) $\frac{1}{32}$ inch ≅ 1 yard

(B) 1 inch ≅ 2,000 feet

(C) 1 foot ≅ $\frac{1}{2}$ mile

(D) 1 yard ≅ 2 miles

(E) none of these

18. The distance between two points on a graph whose rectangular coordinates are (2,4) and (5,8) is most nearly

(A) 4.7
(B) 4.8
(C) 4.9
(D) 5.0
(E) 5.1

19. The volume of a cylinder with a radius of r and a height of h is

(A) πrh
(B) $2\pi rh$
(C) $2\pi r^2h$
(D) $4\pi r^2h$
(E) none of these

20. Which of the following lengths of a side of an equilateral triangle has a perimeter divisible by both 3 and 5?

    (A) 3
    (B) 4
    (C) 5
    (D) 6
    (E) 7

21. The numerical value of $\frac{4!}{3!}$ is

    (A) .75
    (B) 1
    (C) 1.25
    (D) 1.33
    (E) 4

22. The cube root of 729 is equal to the square of

    (A) 11
    (B) 9
    (C) 7
    (D) 5
    (E) 3

23. If the log of x is 2.5464, the number of digits in x to the left of the decimal point is

    (A) 0
    (B) 1
    (C) 2
    (D) 3
    (E) 4

24. What is the appropriate number which would follow the last number in the following series of numbers arranged in a logical order?

    2 4 12 48 __

    (A) 96
    (B) 144
    (C) 192
    (D) 204
    (E) 240

25. What is the appropriate option for the next two letters in the following series of letters which follow some definite pattern?

    A R C S E T G __ __

    (A) UH
    (B) HI
    (C) UI
    (D) IU
    (E) IH

STOP! DO NOT GO ON UNTIL TIME IS UP.

PART 7

MECHANICAL COMPREHENSION

7

Directions

This part of the test has 20 questions designed to measure your ability to learn and reason with mechanical terms. Included in this part of the test are diagrams of mechanical devices. Preceding the diagrams are questions or incomplete statements. Study each diagram carefully and select the choice that best answers the question or completes the statement. Then mark the space on your answer form which has the same number and letter as your choice.

Here are two sample questions.

1. In the figure shown, the weight held by the board and placed on the two identical scales will cause *each* scale to read

(A) 8 lbs.
(B) 15 lbs.
(C) 16 lbs.
(D) 30 lbs.
(E) 32 lbs.

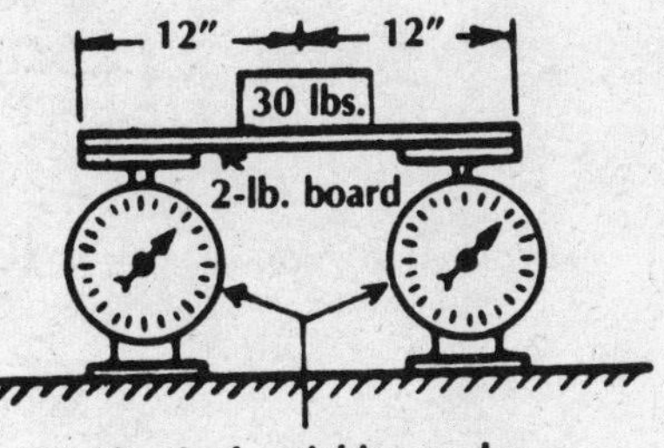

30 lbs. + 2 lbs. = 32 lbs., the total weight equally supported by two scales. $\frac{32}{2} = 16$ lbs., the reading on each scale. Option (C) is correct.

2. In the figure shown, the pulley system consists of a fixed block and a movable block. The theoretical mechanical advantage is

(A) 1
(B) 2
(C) 3
(D) 4
(E) 5

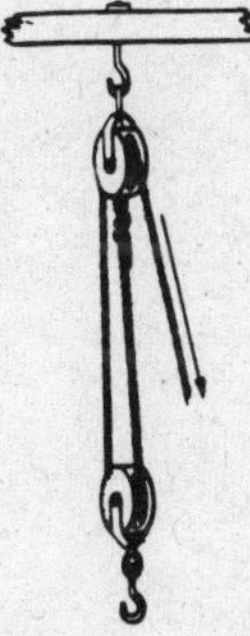

The number of parts of the rope going to and from the movable block indicates the mechanical advantage. In this case it is 2. Option (B) is correct.

Your score on this test will be based on the number of questions you answer correctly. You should try to answer every question. You will not lose points or be penalized for guessing. Do not spend too much time on any one question.

When you begin, be sure to start with question number 1 of Part 7 of your test booklet and number 1 of Part 7 on your answer form.

DO NOT TURN THIS PAGE UNTIL TOLD TO DO SO.

PART 7

MECHANICAL COMPREHENSION

TIME: 22 Minutes—20 Questions

1. If gear R is the driver, at the moment shown, gear S is

   (A) not moving
   (B) jammed
   (C) moving at its highest speed
   (D) moving in the same direction as gear R
   (E) moving in the opposite direction as gear R

2. Which water wheel will turn for the longer time?

   (A) R
   (B) S
   (C) Both wheels will turn for an equal amount of time.
   (D) Neither wheel will turn at all.
   (E) This can't be determined from the drawing.

3. As shaft S makes one complete turn from the position shown, C moves

   (A) left and then right
   (B) right and then left
   (C) up only
   (D) down only
   (E) up and down

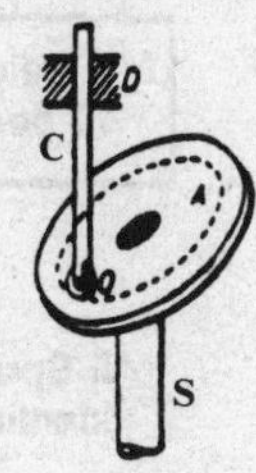

4. If weight B is to slide to the right, what change must be made in the diagram?

   (A) The slope of the inclined plane under A must be increased.
   (B) The slope of the inclined plane under B must be increased.
   (C) The radius of the inner pulley must be decreased.
   (D) The radius of the inner pulley must be increased to a size nearer than that of the outer pulley.
   (E) The radius of the outer pulley must be twice that of the inner pulley.

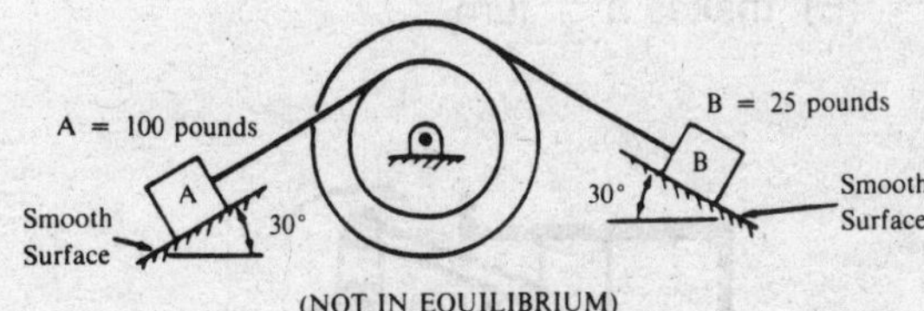

5. Ten-pound weights are each suspended from a ceiling by three identical springs. In A, the extension of each spring is

(A) nine times greater than in B

(B) three times greater than in B

(C) the same as in B

(D) $\frac{1}{3}$ less than in B

(E) $\frac{1}{9}$ less than in B

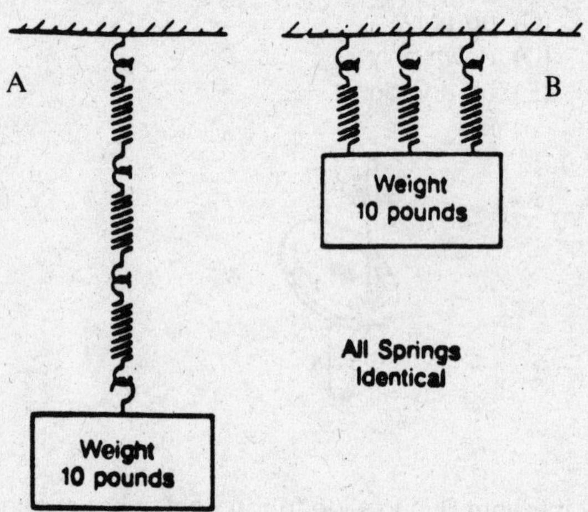

6. The figure below shows a crank and piston. The piston moves from mid-position to the extreme right if the crank

(A) makes 1 $\frac{1}{2}$ turns

(B) makes 1 $\frac{1}{4}$ turns

(C) makes one turn

(D) makes a $\frac{3}{4}$ turn

(E) makes a $\frac{1}{2}$ turn

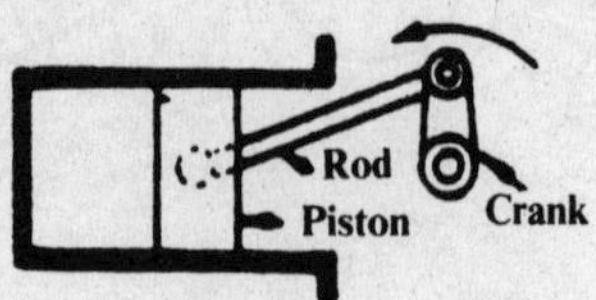

7. If gear A makes 14 revolutions, gear B will make

(A) 9 revolutions
(B) 14 revolutions
(C) 17 revolutions
(D) 21 revolutions
(E) 25 revolutions

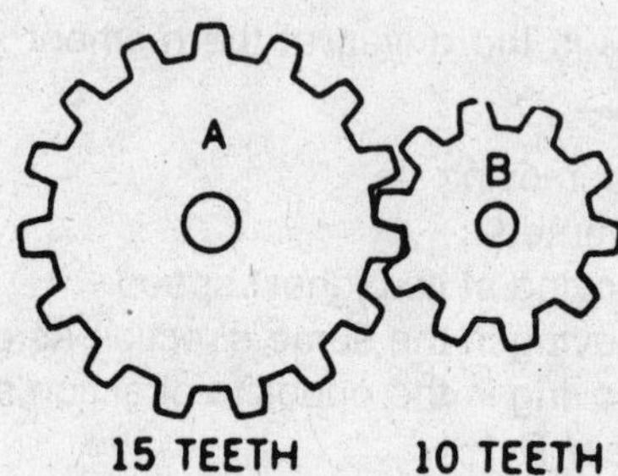

8. What is the function of A and B in the crankshaft shown in the drawing below?

(A) They strengthen the crankshaft by increasing its weight.
(B) They make it easier to remove the crankshaft for repairs.
(C) They are necessary to maintain the proper balance of the crankshaft.
(D) They hold grease for continuous lubrication of the crankshaft.
(E) They reduce the viscosity of the oil.

9. As cam A makes one complete turn, the setscrew will hit the contact point

(A) once
(B) twice
(C) three times
(D) four times
(E) not at all

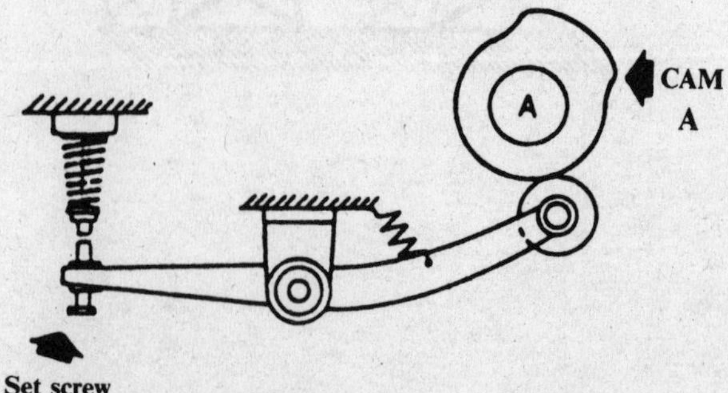

10. In the diagram below, crank arm C revolves at a constant speed of 400 RPM and drives the lever AB. When lever AB is moving the fastest, arm C will be in position

    (A) 3
    (B) 4
    (C) 5
    (D) 6
    (E) 7

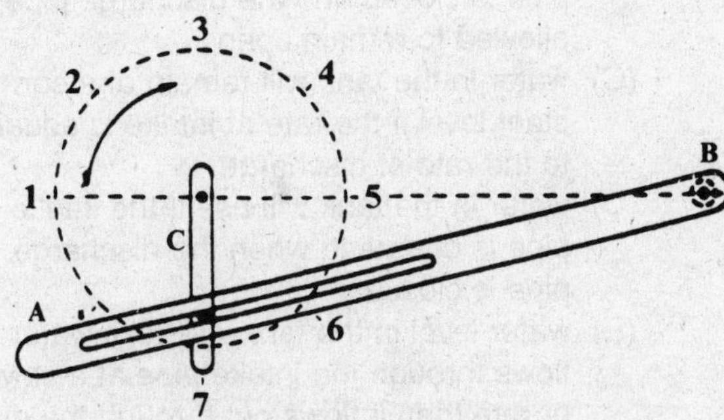

11. The force F needed to balance the lever is, in lbs., most nearly

    (A) 20
    (B) 17.5
    (C) 15
    (D) 12.5
    (E) 10

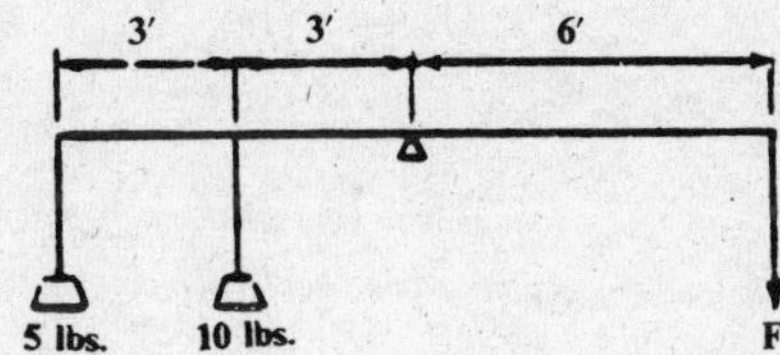

12. A 150-pound man jumps off a 600-pound raft to a point in the water 12 feet away. Theoretically, the raft would move

    (A) 12 feet in the opposite direction
    (B) 9 feet in the opposite direction
    (C) 6 feet in the opposite direction
    (D) 3 feet in the opposite direction
    (E) 1 foot in the opposite direction

13. The figure below shows a governor on a rotating shaft. As the shaft speeds up, the governor balls will

    (A) move down
    (B) move down and outward
    (C) move inward
    (D) move upward and inward
    (E) move upward

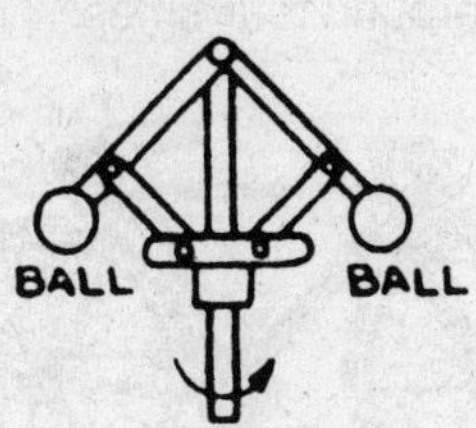

14. If water is flowing into the tank at the rate of 120 gallons per hour and flowing out of the tank at a constant rate of one gallon per minute, the water level in the tank will

    (A) fall 1 gallon per minute
    (B) fall 2 gallons per minute
    (C) remain the same
    (D) rise 2 gallons per minute
    (E) rise 1 gallon per minute

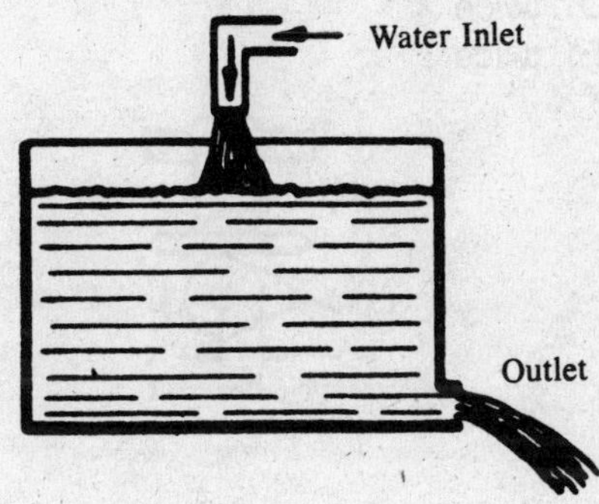

GO ON TO THE NEXT PAGE.

15. There are twenty teeth on the front sprocket and ten teeth on the rear sprocket on the bicycle below. Each time the pedals go around, the rear wheel will

    (A) go one-fourth way around
    (B) go half way around
    (C) go around once
    (D) go around twice
    (E) go around four times

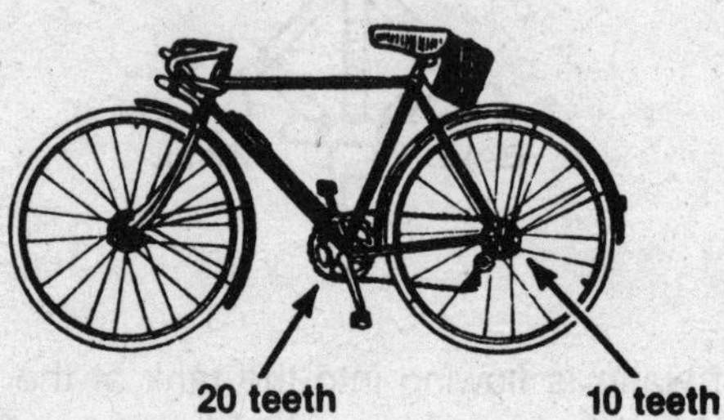

16. The figure below shows a cam and valve. For each cam revolution, the vertical valve rise equals distance

    (A) *X*
    (B) *Y*
    (C) *X* plus *Y*
    (D) twice *X*
    (E) twice *Y*

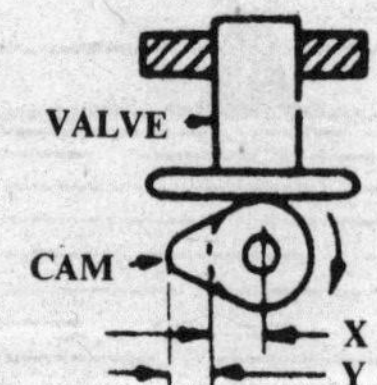

17. The figure below represents a water tank containing water. The number 1 indicates an intake pipe and 2 indicates a discharge pipe. Of the following, the statement which is *least* accurate is that the

    (A) tank will eventually overflow if water flows through the intake pipe at a faster rate than it flows out through the discharge pipe
    (B) tank will empty completely if the intake pipe is closed and the discharge pipe is allowed to remain open
    (C) water in the tank will remain at a constant level if the rate of intake is equal to the rate of discharge
    (D) water in the tank will rise if the intake pipe is operating when the discharge pipe is closed
    (E) water level in the tank will fall if water flows through the intake pipe at a slower rate than it flows out through the discharge pipe

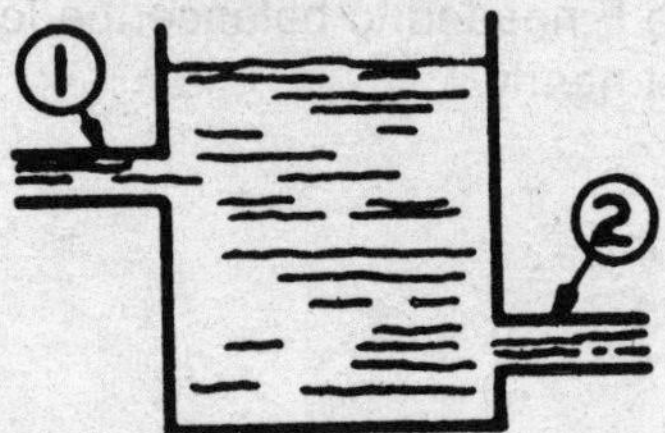

18. The figure below represents a pulley, with practically no friction, from which two ten-pound weights are suspended as indicated. If a downward force is applied to weight 1, it is most likely that weight 1 will

    (A) come to rest at the present level of weight 2
    (B) move downward until it is level with weight 2
    (C) move downward until it reaches the floor
    (D) pass weight 2 in its downward motion and then return to its present position
    (E) move downward to a position midway between the present levels of both weights

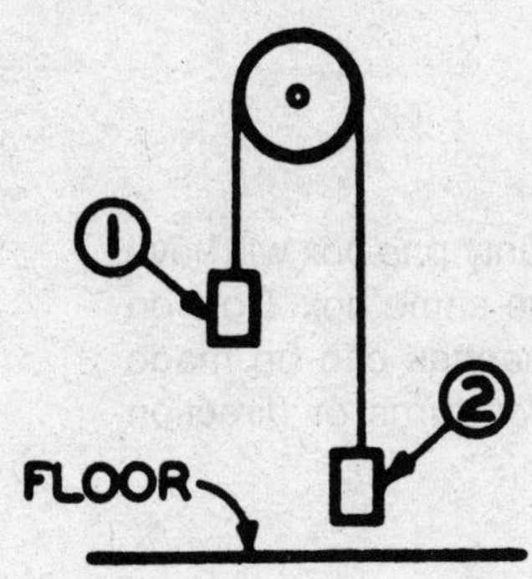

19. If pulley A is the driver and turns in direction 1, which pulley turns fastest?

    (A) A
    (B) B
    (C) C
    (D) D
    (E) both C and D

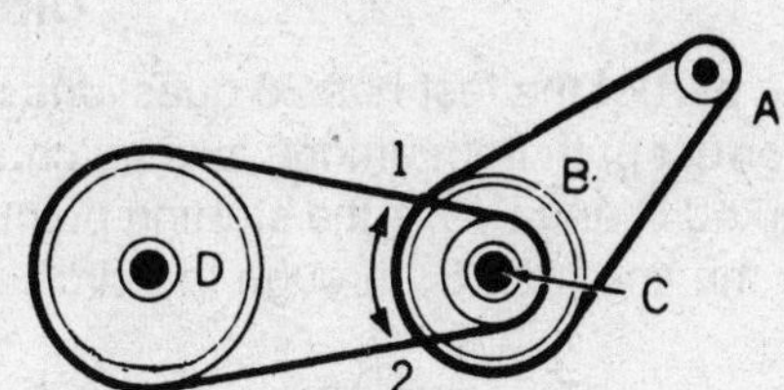

20. In order to open the valve in the figure below once every second, the wheel must rotate at

    (A) 6 rpm
    (B) 10 rpm
    (C) 20 rpm
    (D) 30 rpm
    (E) 60 rpm

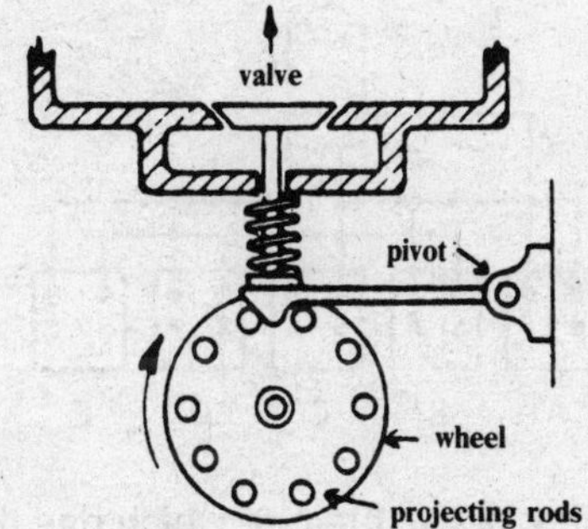

STOP! DO NOT GO ON UNTIL TIME IS UP.

8

PART 8

ELECTRICAL MAZE

Directions

This part of the test has 20 questions designed to measure your ability to choose a correct path from among several choices. In the picture below is a box with dots marked S and F. S is the starting point, and F is the finishing point. You are to follow the line from S, through the circle at the top of the picture, and back to F.

In the problems in this test, there will be five such boxes. Only *one* box will have a line from the S, through the circle, and back to the F in the same box. Dots on the lines show the *only* places where turns or direction changes can be made between lines. If lines meet or cross where there is *no dot,* turns or direction changes *cannot be made.* Now try sample problem 1.

1.

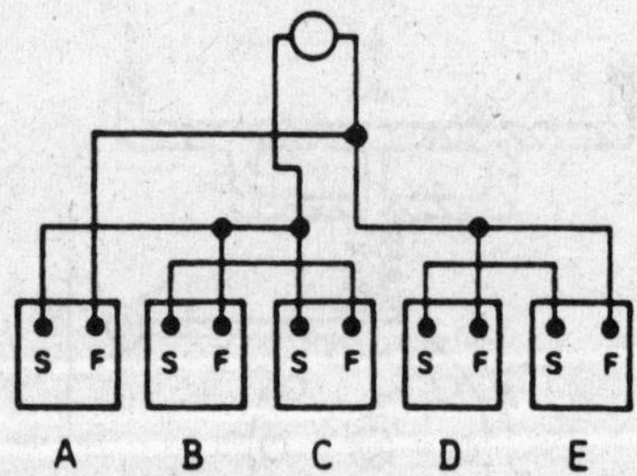

The first box is the one which has the line from S, through the circle, and back to F. Therefore, (A) is the right answer.

Each diagram in the test has only one box which has a line through the circle and back to F. Some lines are wrong because they lead to a dead end. Some lines are wrong because they come back to the box without going through the circle. Some lines are wrong because they lead to other boxes. Some are wrong because they retrace the same line.

Now try sample problems 2 and 3.

2.

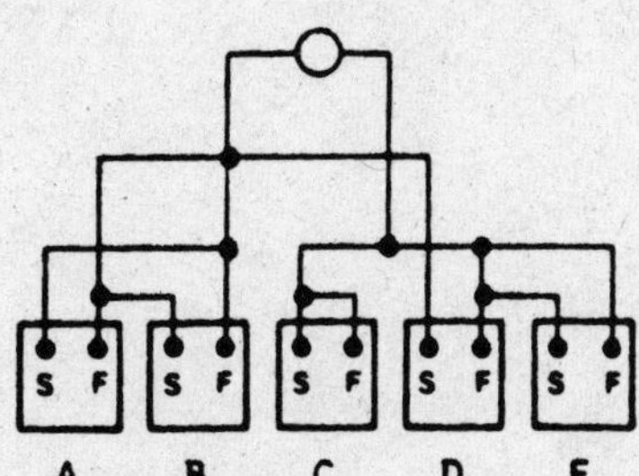

3.

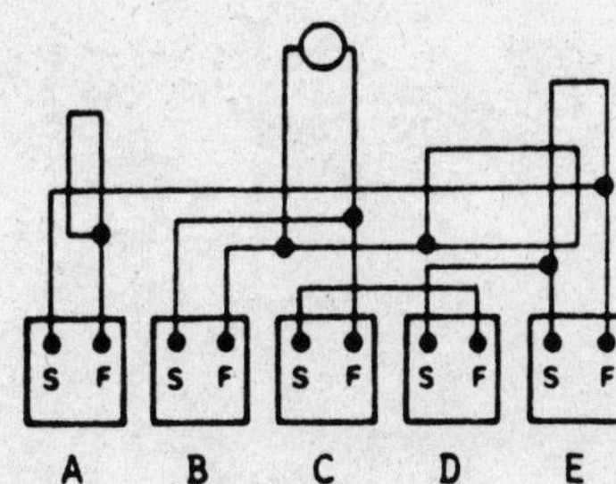

For sample problem 2, the correct answer is (D). For sample problem 3, the correct answer is (B).

Your score on this test will be based on the number of questions you answer correctly. You should try to answer every question. You will not lose points or be penalized for guessing. Do not spend too much time on any one question.

When you begin, be sure to start with question number 1 of Part 8 of your test booklet and number 1 of Part 8 on your answer form.

DO NOT TURN THIS PAGE UNTIL TOLD TO DO SO.

PART 8

ELECTRICAL MAZE

TIME: 10 Minutes—20 Questions

1.

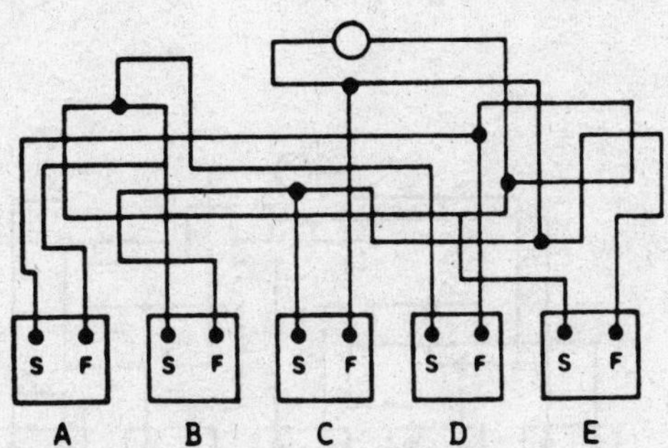

2.

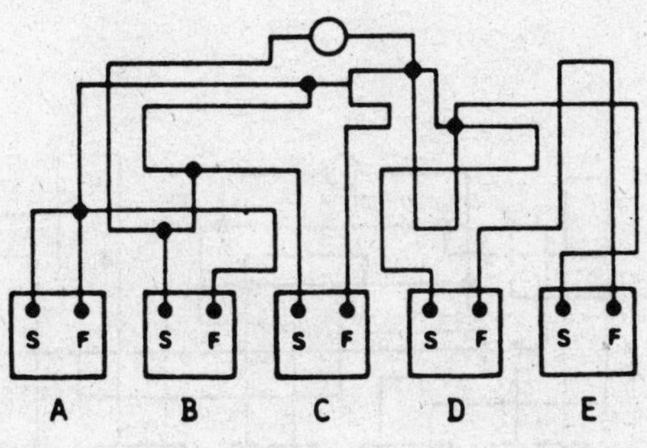

3.

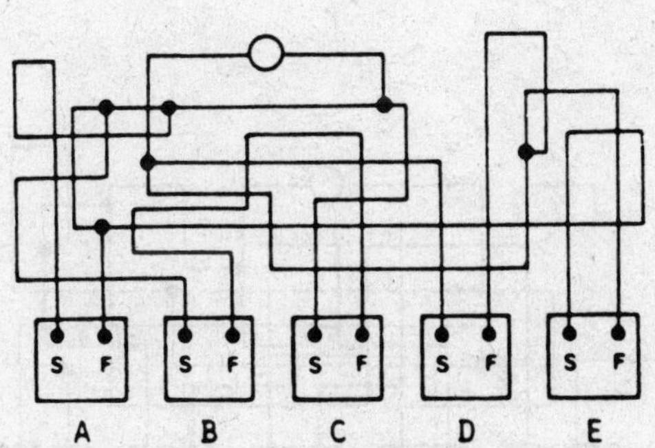

4.

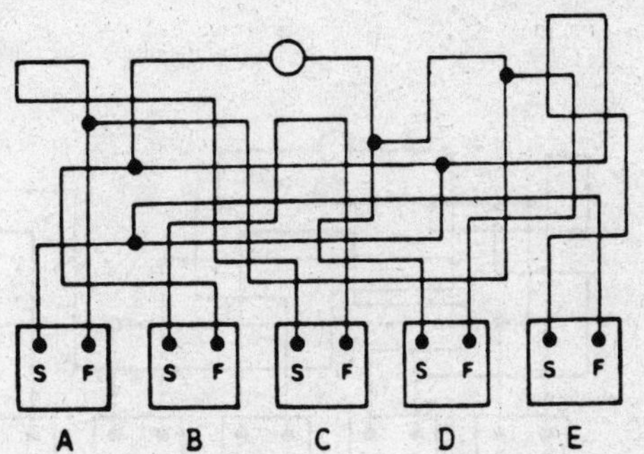

5.

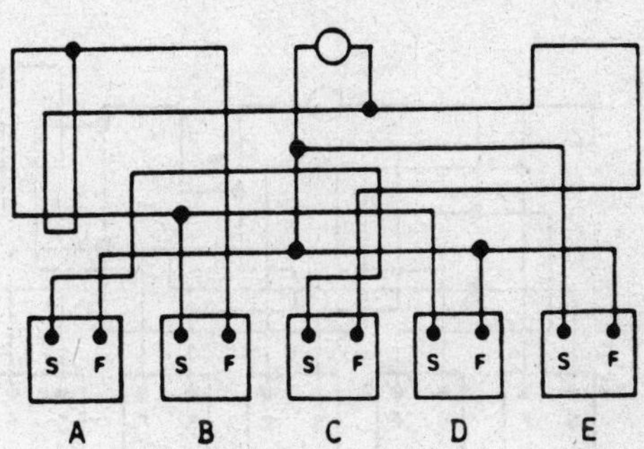

6.

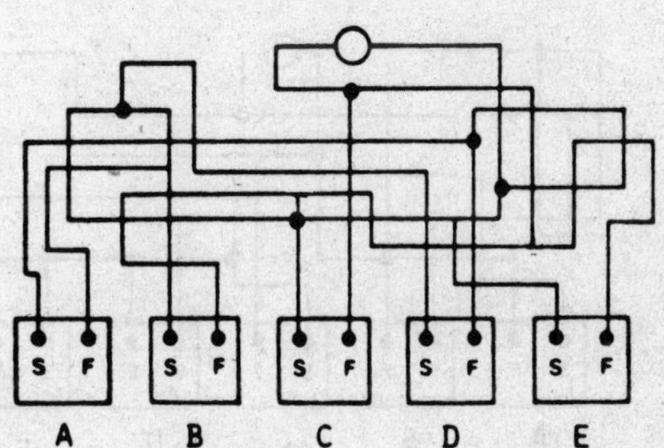

7.

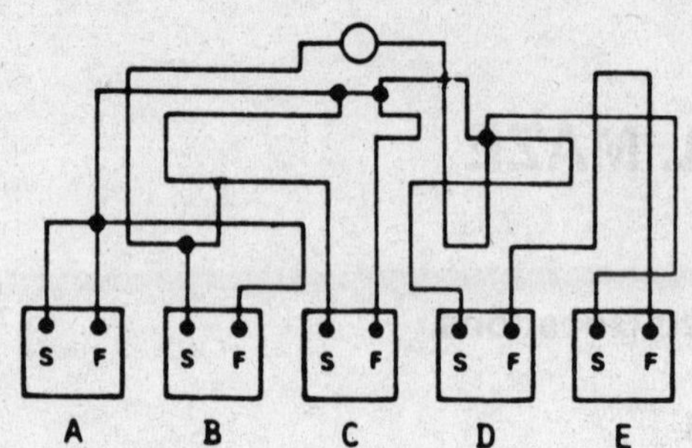

8.

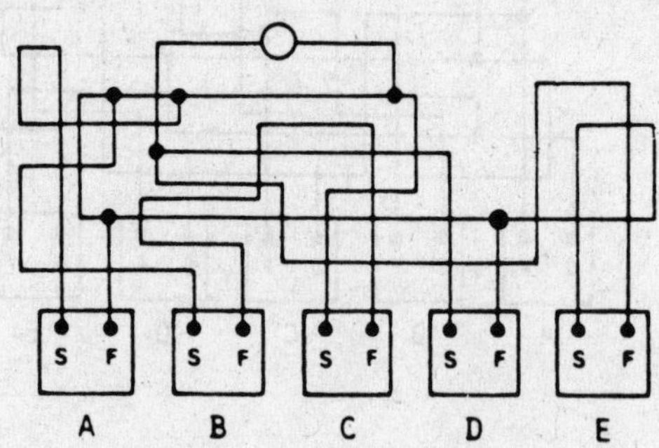

9.

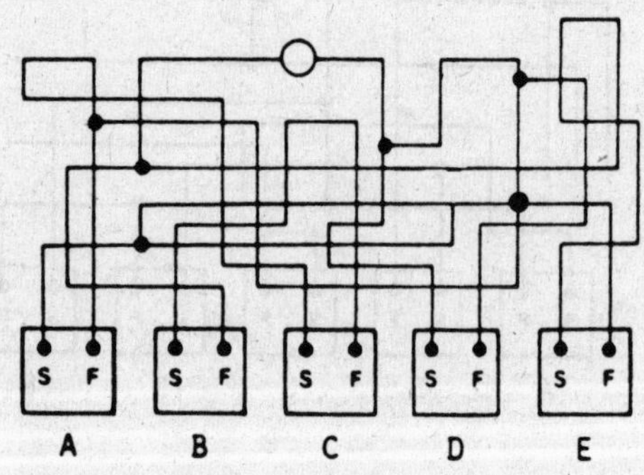

10.

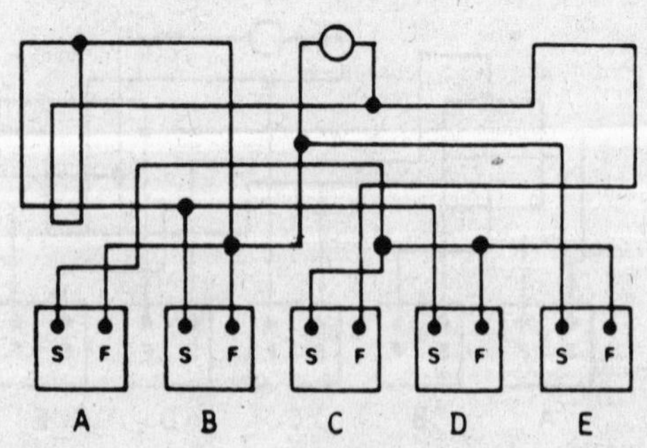

11.

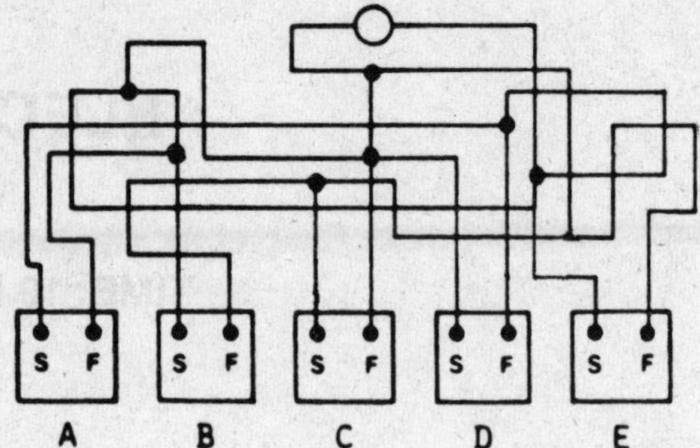

12.

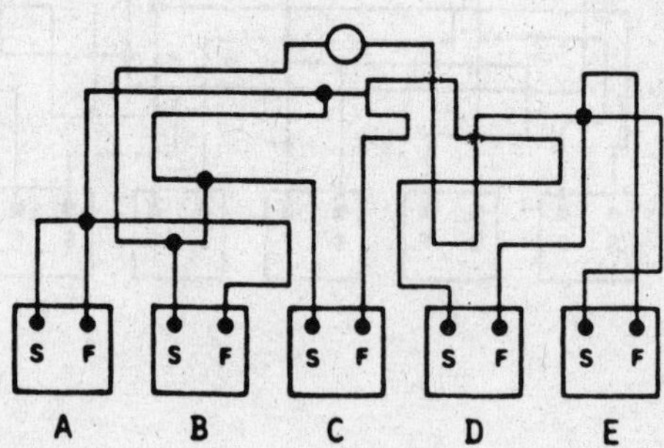

13.

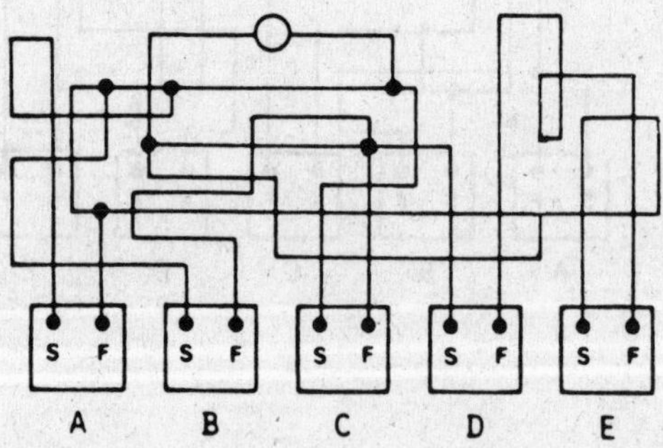

14.

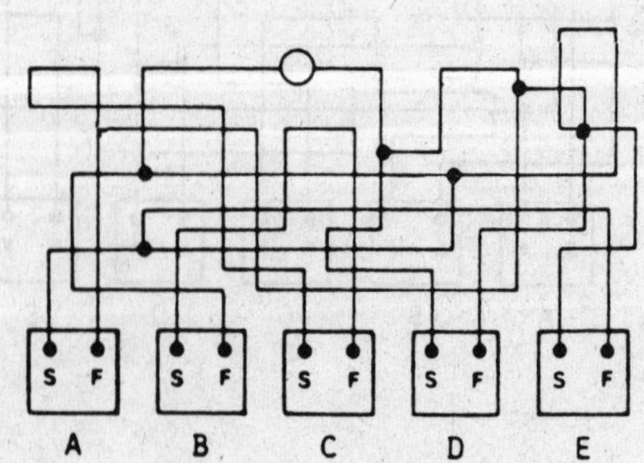

15.

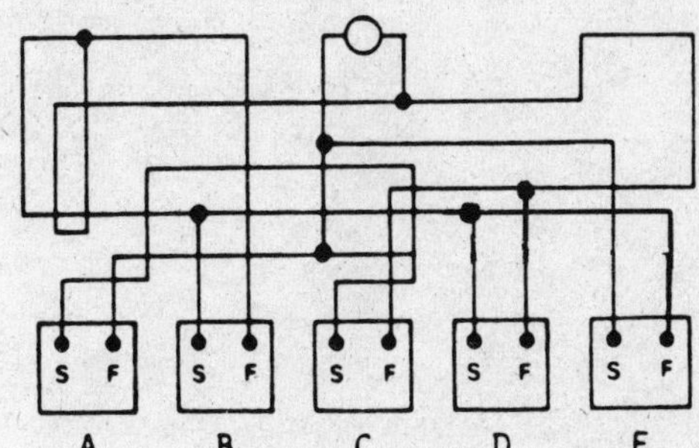

16.

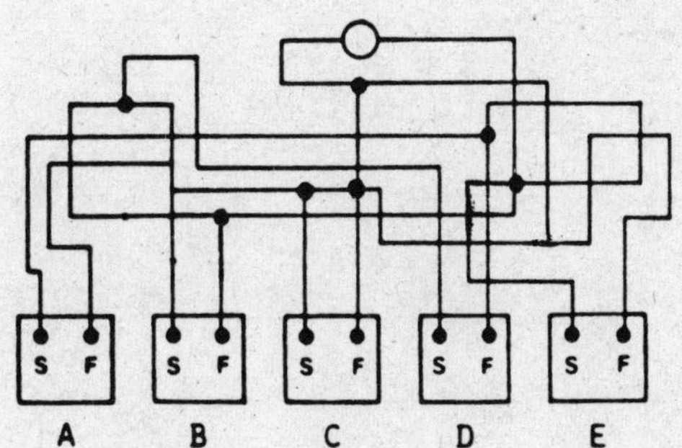

17.

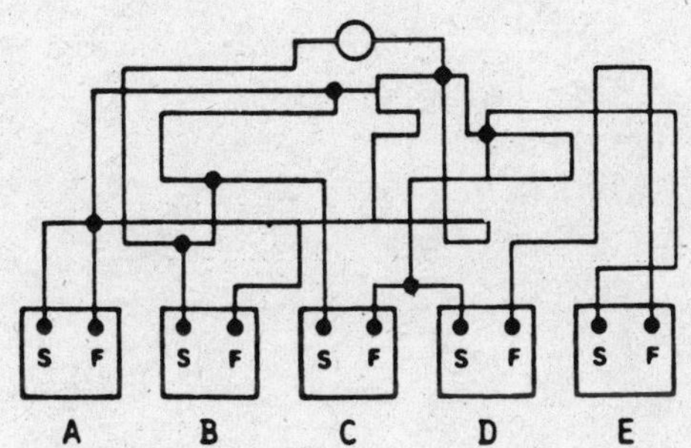

18.

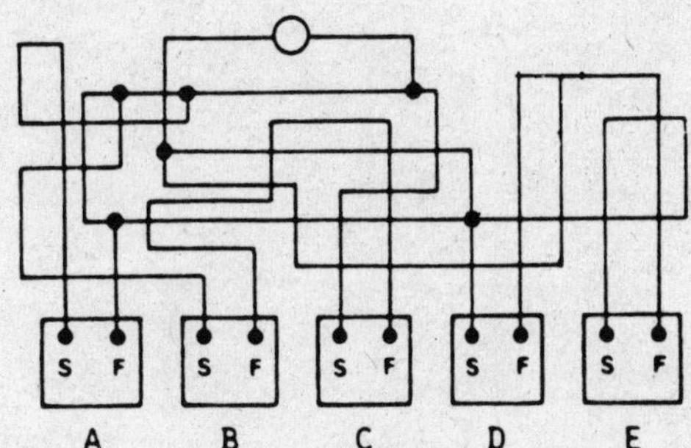

19.

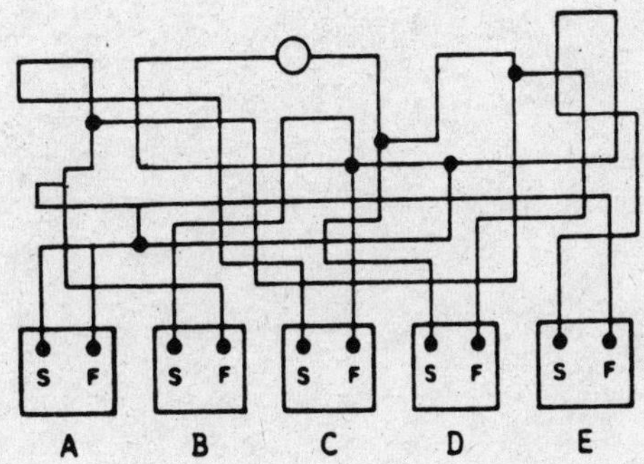

20.

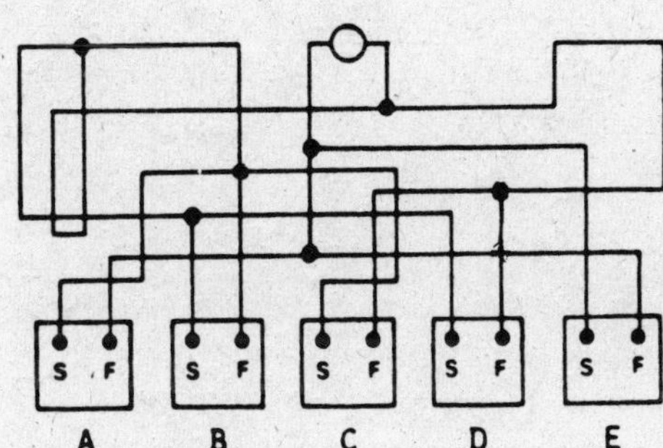

STOP! DO NOT GO ON UNTIL TIME IS UP.

PART 9

SCALE READING

9

Directions

This part of the test has 40 questions designed to measure your ability to read scales, dials, and meters. You will be given a variety of scales on which various points are indicated by numbered arrows. You are to estimate the numerical value indicated by each arrow, find the choice closest to this value in the item having the same numbers as the arrow, and then mark your answer on the answer sheet. Now look at the sample items below.

1.

(A) 6.00
(B) 5.00
(C) 4.25
(D) 2.25
(E) 1.25

2.

(A) 13.0
(B) 12.0
(C) 10.2
(D) 1.3
(E) 1.2

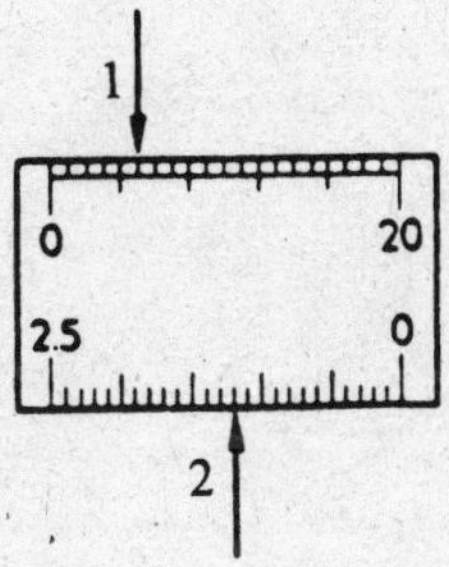

3.

(A) 81.75
(B) 79.5
(C) 78.75
(D) 77.60
(E) 67.50

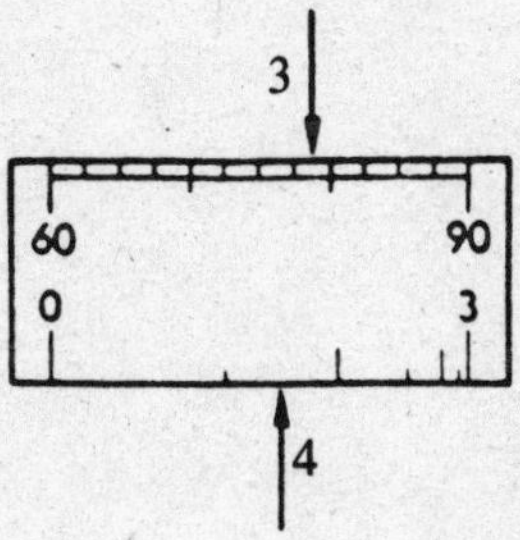

4.

(A) 1.75
(B) 1.65
(C) 1.50
(D) .75
(E) .65

In sample item 1 there are five subdivisions of four steps each between 0 and 20. The arrow points between the long subdivision markers representing 4 and 8. Since it points to the marker that is one step to the right of subdivision marker 4, it points to 5.00. This is choice (B) in sample item 1.

In sample item 2 the scale runs from right to left. There are five subdivisions of five steps each, so each step represents .1, and the arrow points to the marker representing 1.2. This is the choice E in sample item 2.

In sample item 3 the arrow points between two markers. You must estimate the fractional part of the step as accurately as possible. Since the arrow points halfway between the markers representing 77.5 and 80.0, it points to 78.75. This is choice (C) in sample item 3.

In sample item 4 each step represents .5, but the steps are of unequal width, with each step being two-thirds as wide as the preceding one. Therefore, the scale is compressed as the values increase. The arrow is pointing to a position halfway between the marker representing .5 and 1.0, but because of the compression of the scale the value of this point must be less than .75. Actually, it is .65, which is choice (E) in sample item 4.

Your score on this test will be based on the number of questions you answer correctly. You should try to answer every question. You will not lose points or be penalized for guessing. Do not spend too much time on any one question.

When you begin, be sure to start with question number 1 of Part 9 of your test booklet and number 1 of Part 9 on your answer form.

DO NOT TURN THIS PAGE UNTIL TOLD TO DO SO.

PART 9

SCALE READING

TIME: 10 Minutes—40 Questions

1.

(A) .735
(B) .725
(C) .680
(D) .660
(E) .570

2.

(A) 86
(B) 81
(C) 64
(D) 60
(E) 58

3.

(A) 3.425
(B) 3.375
(C) 3.275
(D) 3.150
(E) 3.125

4.

(A) 22.6
(B) 21.2
(C) 18.5
(D) 17.5
(E) 13.2

5.

(A) 23.75
(B) 23.50
(C) 23.25
(D) 23.00
(E) 22.75

6.

(A) 20.7
(B) 20.3
(C) 19.9
(D) 19.3
(E) 19.2

7.

(A) 1.4
(B) 1.5
(C) 1.6
(D) 1.7
(E) 1.8

8.

(A) 3.3
(B) 3.4
(C) 3.5
(D) 3.6
(E) 3.7

9.

(A) 6.5
(B) 6.7
(C) 6.8
(D) 6.9
(E) 7.0

10.

(A) 9.4
(B) 9.45
(C) 9.7
(D) 9.9
(E) 10.0

11.

(A) .05
(B) .06
(C) .4
(D) .5
(E) .6

12.

(A) .24
(B) .245
(C) .25
(D) .255
(E) .29

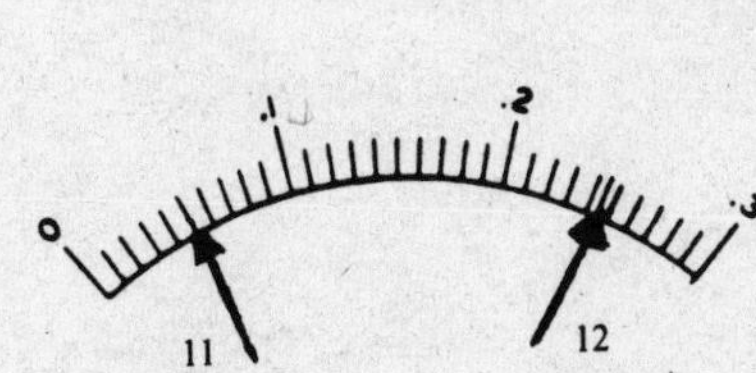

13.

(A) 49
(B) 45
(C) 40
(D) 35
(E) 30

14.

(A) 2.2
(B) 2.5
(C) 2.8
(D) 3.0
(E) 3.5

15.

(A) .2
(B) .25
(C) .3
(D) .35
(E) .4

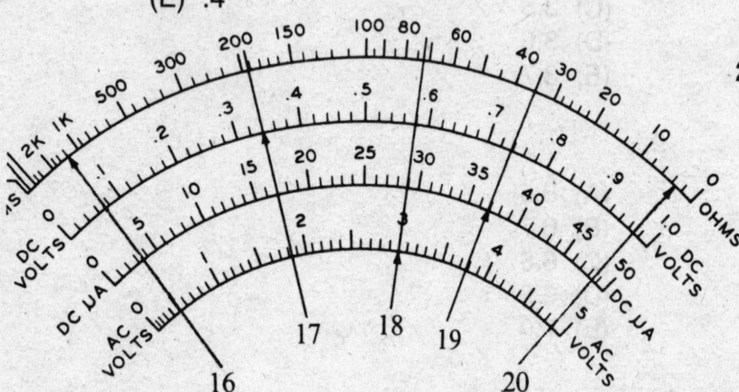

16.

(A) 1000 ohms
(B) 1125 ohms
(C) 1250 ohms
(D) 1375 ohms
(E) 1500 ohms

17.

(A) .34 DC volts
(B) 1.7 DC volts
(C) 3.4 DC volts
(D) 17 volts
(E) 34 volts

18.

(A) 2.8 AC volts
(B) 3.0 AC volts
(C) 5.8 AC volts
(D) 29.0 AC volts
(E) 75.0 AC volts

19.

(A) 36.1 microamperes
(B) 36.5 microamperes
(C) 36.9 microamperes
(D) 37.1 microamperes
(E) 37.5 microamperes

20.

(A) 1.0 ohms
(B) 1.5 ohms
(C) 2.0 ohms
(D) 2.5 ohms
(E) 3.0 ohms

21. The reading of the kilowatt-hour meter shown is

(A) 6862
(B) 6872
(C) 6882
(D) 6962
(E) 6972

22. The reading of the kilowatt-hour meter shown is

(A) 7169
(B) 7179
(C) 7189
(D) 7269
(E) 7279

Answer questions *23–26* on the basis of the graphic scales given below. The extension scales to the left of the primary scales may be used to aid in obtaining more accurate readings.

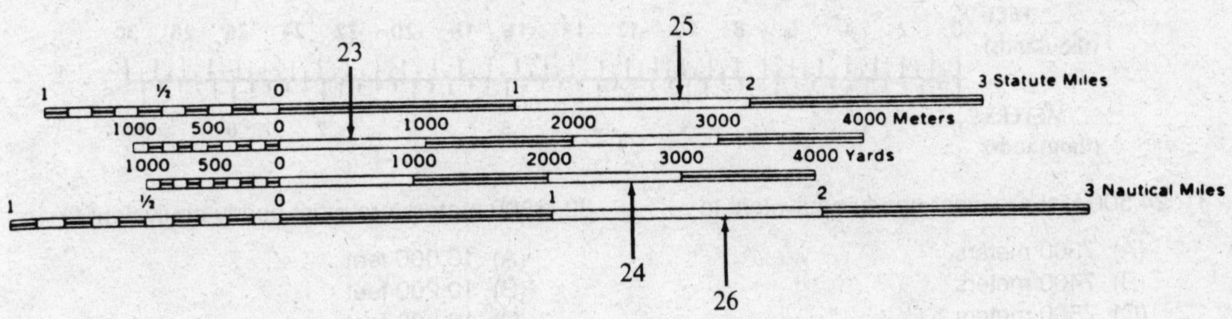

23.

(A) 300 meters
(B) 400 meters
(C) 500 meters
(D) 600 meters
(E) 700 meters

24.

(A) 2300 yards
(B) 2400 yards
(C) 2500 yards
(D) 2600 yards
(E) 2700 yards

25.

(A) 1.4 statute miles
(B) 1.5 statute miles
(C) 1.6 statute miles
(D) 1.7 statute miles
(E) 1.8 statute miles

26.

(A) 1.50 nautical miles
(B) 1.55 nautical miles
(C) 1.60 nautical miles
(D) 1.65 nautical miles
(E) 1.70 nautical miles

Answer questions *27–30* using the graphic scales shown below. The extension scales to the left of the primary scales may be used to aid in obtaining more accurate results.

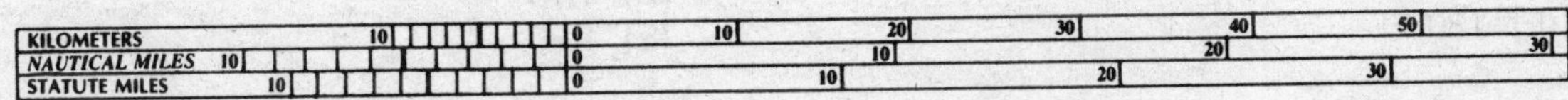

27. Ten kilometers are most nearly equivalent to

(A) 4.0 nautical miles
(B) 4.5 nautical miles
(C) 5.0 nautical miles
(D) 5.5 nautical miles
(E) 6.0 nautical miles

28. Fifteen nautical miles are most nearly equivalent to

(A) 27 kilometers
(B) 28 kilometers
(C) 29 kilometers
(D) 30 kilometers
(E) 31 kilometers

29. Twenty-five nautical miles are most nearly equivalent to

(A) 28.0 statute miles
(B) 28.5 statute miles
(C) 29.0 statute miles
(D) 29.5 statute miles
(E) 30 statute miles

30. Ten statute miles are most nearly equivalent to

(A) 7.75 nautical miles
(B) 8.25 nautical miles
(C) 8.75 nautical miles
(D) 9.25 nautical miles
(E) 9.75 nautical miles

GO ON TO THE NEXT PAGE.

Answer questions *31* and *32* using the Conversion of Elevations scale below.

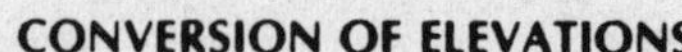

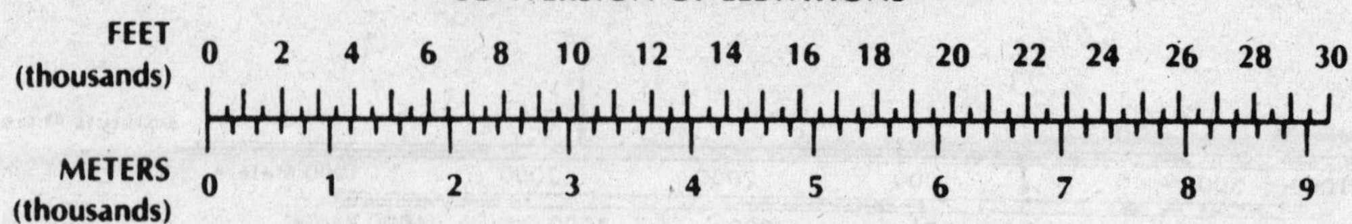

31. 24,500 feet are most nearly equivalent to

(A) 7300 meters
(B) 7400 meters
(C) 7500 meters
(D) 7600 meters
(E) 7700 meters

32. 3300 meters are most nearly equivalent to

(A) 10,000 feet
(B) 10,200 feet
(C) 10,500 feet
(D) 10,800 feet
(E) 11,000 feet

Answer questions 33–35 on the basis of the Temperature Conversion scale given below.

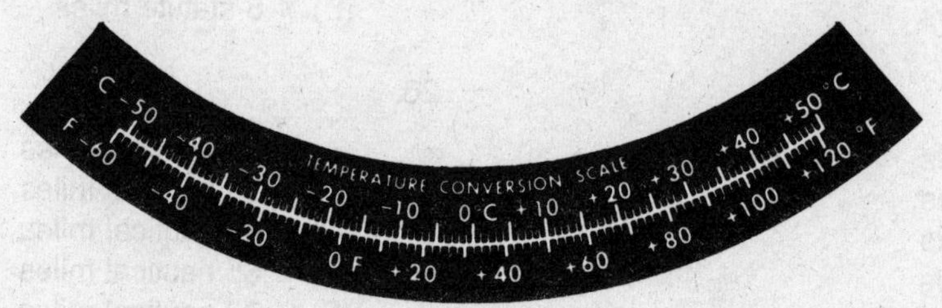

33. 49°C is most nearly equivalent to

(A) –59°F
(B) –57°F
(C) 110°F
(D) 118°F
(E) 120°F

34. 0°F is most nearly equivalent to

(A) –22°C
(B) –18°C
(C) –15°C
(D) 0°C
(E) 32°C

35. At what temperature is the Fahrenheit reading and the Celsius or centigrade reading the same?

(A) –40°
(B) –10°
(C) 10°
(D) 40°
(E) none of the foregoing

36.

(A) 1.60
(B) 1.65
(C) 1.70
(D) 1.75
(E) 1.80

1 2 36

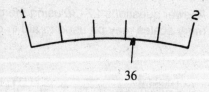

37.

(A) 23.00
(B) 23.25
(C) 23.50
(D) 23.75
(E) 24.00

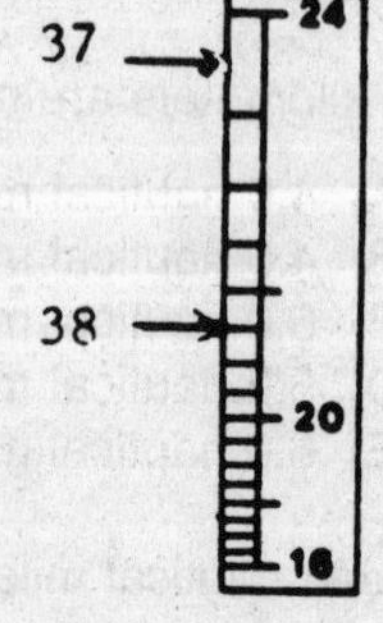

38.

(A) 20.75
(B) 21.00
(C) 21.25
(D) 21.50
(E) 21.75

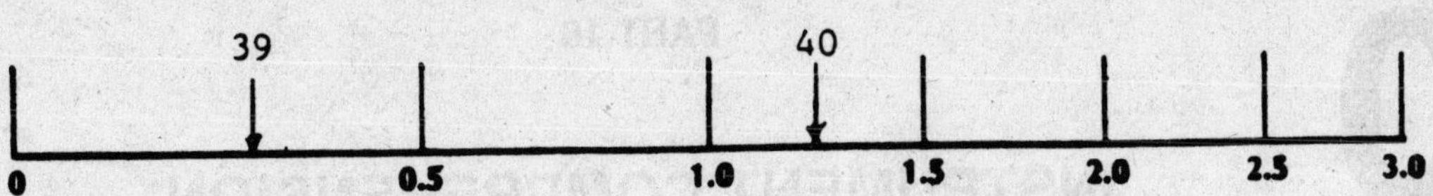

39.

(A) 0.15
(B) 0.25
(C) 0.3
(D) 0.35
(E) 0.4

40.

(A) 1.2
(B) 1.25
(C) 1.3
(D) 1.35
(E) 1.4

STOP! DO NOT GO ON UNTIL TIME IS UP.

10

PART 10

INSTRUMENT COMPREHENSION

Directions

This part of the test has 20 questions designed to measure your ability to determine the position of an airplane in flight from reading instruments showing its compass heading, its amount of climb or dive, and its degree of bank to right or left. In each item the left-hand dial is labeled ARTIFICIAL HORIZON. On the face of this dial the small aircraft silhouette remains stationary, while the positions of the heavy black line and the black pointer vary with changes in the position of the airplane in which the instrument is located.

How To Read The Artificial Horizon Dial

The heavy black line represents the HORIZON LINE. The black pointer shows the degree of BANK to right or left. The HORIZON LINE tilts as the aircraft is banked and is always at a right angle to the pointer.

Dial 1 shows an airplane neither climbing nor diving, with no bank.	Dial 2 shows an airplane climbing and banking 45 degrees to the pilot's right.	Dial 3 shows an airplane diving and banked 45 degrees to the pilot's left.

Dial 1 If the airplane is neither climbing nor diving, the horizon line is directly on the silhouette's fuselage. If the airplane has no bank, the black pointer is seen to point to zero.	Dial 2 If the airplane is climbing, the fuselage silhouette is seen between the horizon line and the pointer. The greater the amount of climb, the greater the distance between the horizon line and the fuselage silhouette. If the airplane is banked to the pilot's right, the pointer is seen to the left of zero.	Dial 3 If the airplane is diving, the horizon line is seen between the fuselage silhouette and the pointer. The greater the amount of dive, the greater the distance between the horizon line and the fuselage silhouette. If the airplane is banked to the pilot's left, the pointer is seen to the right of zero.

Dial 4

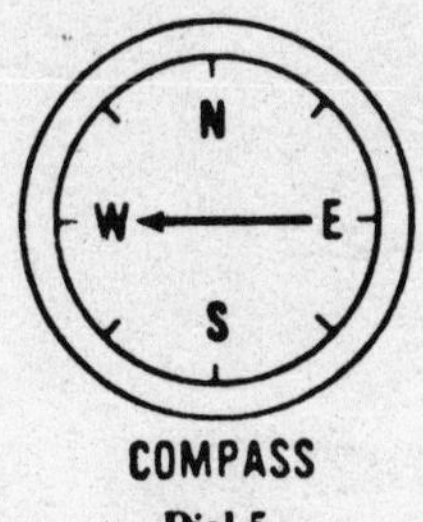

Dial 5

Dial 6

On each item the right-hand dial is labeled COMPASS. On this dial, the arrow shows the compass direction in which the airplane is headed at the moment. Dial 4 shows it headed north; dial 5 shows it headed west; and dial 6 shows it headed northwest.

A Sample Question Explained

Each item in this test consists of two dials and four silhouettes of airplanes in flight. Your task is to determine which one of the four airplanes is MOST NEARLY in the position indicated by the two dials. YOU ARE ALWAYS LOOKING NORTH AT THE SAME ALTITUDE AS EACH OF THE PLANES. EAST IS ALWAYS TO YOUR RIGHT AS YOU LOOK AT THE PAGE. Item X is a sample. In item X the dial labeled ARTIFICIAL HORIZON shows that the airplane is NOT banked, and is neither climbing nor diving. The COMPASS shows that it is headed southeast. The only one of the four airplane silhouettes that meets these specifications is in the box lettered (C), so the answer to X is (C). Note that (B) is a rear view, while (D) is a front view. Note also that (A) is banked to the right and that (B) is banked to the left.

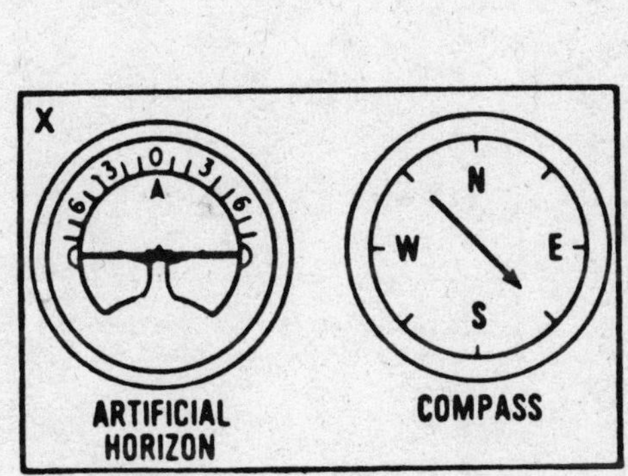

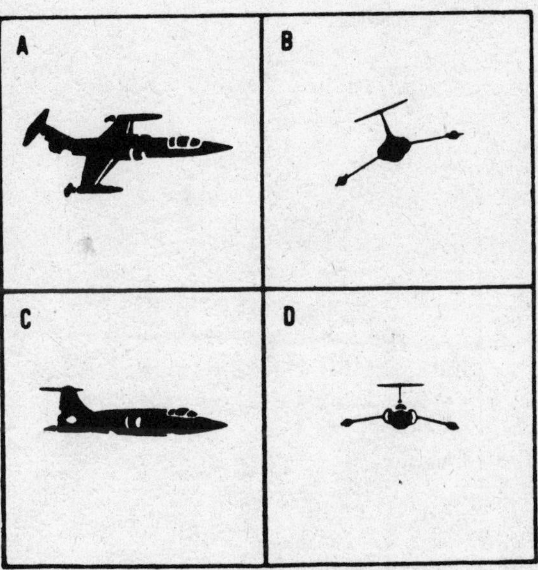

DO NOT TURN THIS PAGE UNTIL TOLD TO DO SO.

PART 10

INSTRUMENT COMPREHENSION

TIME: 6 Minutes—20 Questions

1.

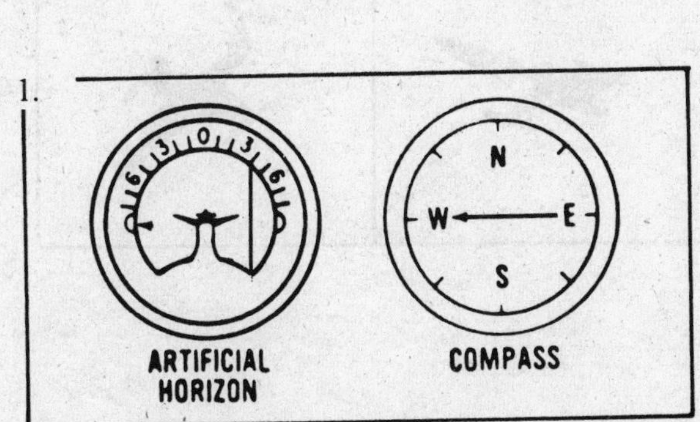

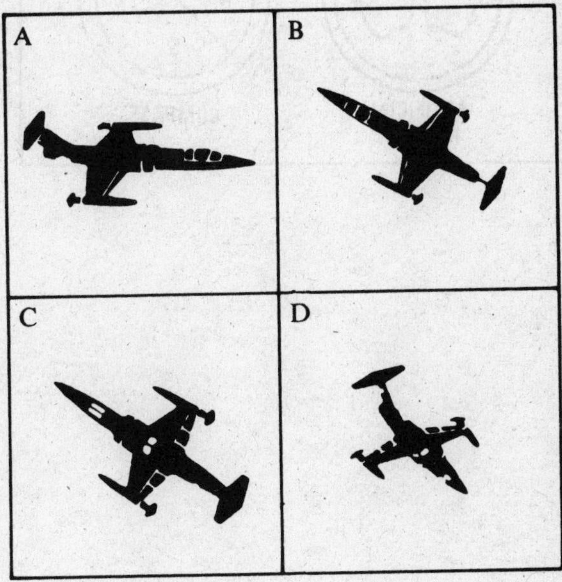

2.

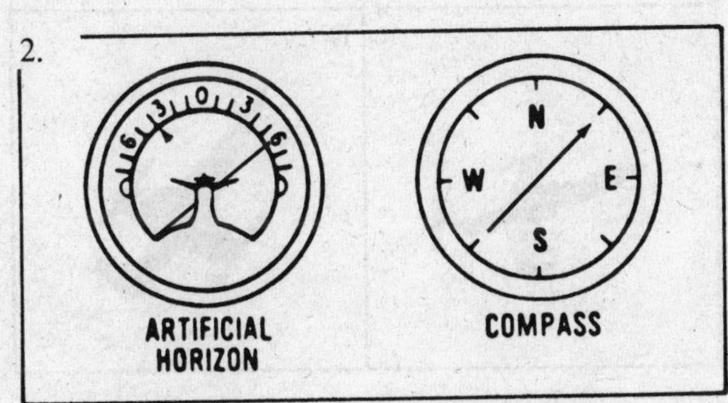

3.

ARTIFICIAL HORIZON
COMPASS
N
W
E
S

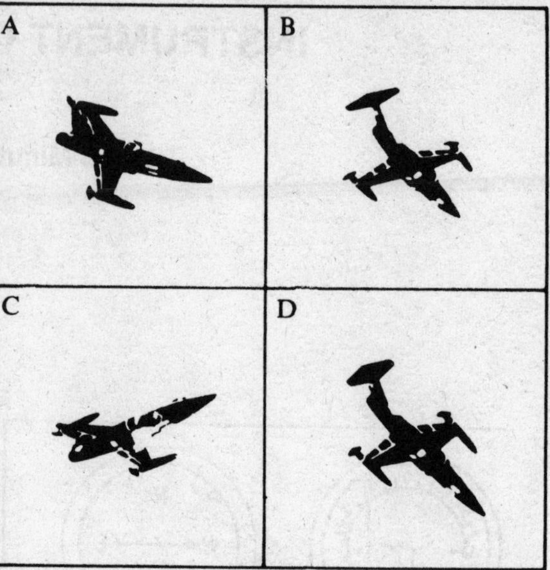
A
B
C
D

4.

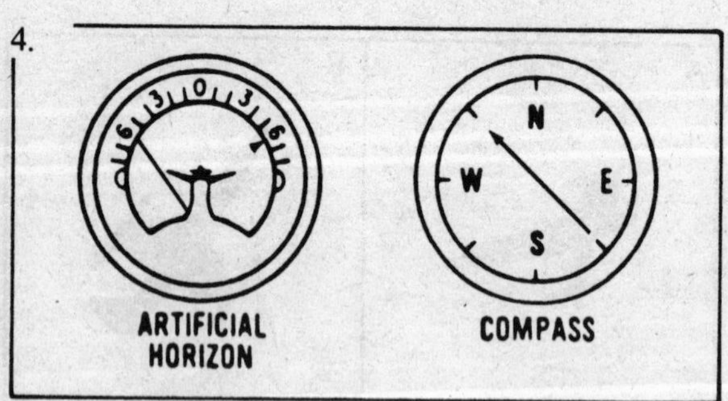
ARTIFICIAL HORIZON
COMPASS
N
W
E
S

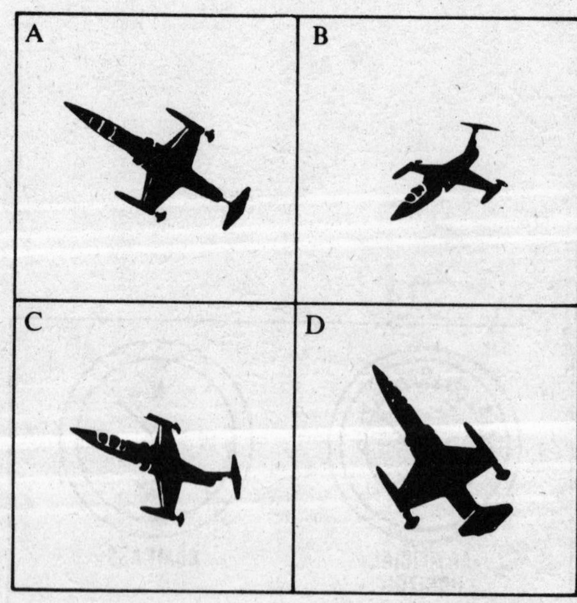
A
B
C
D

5.

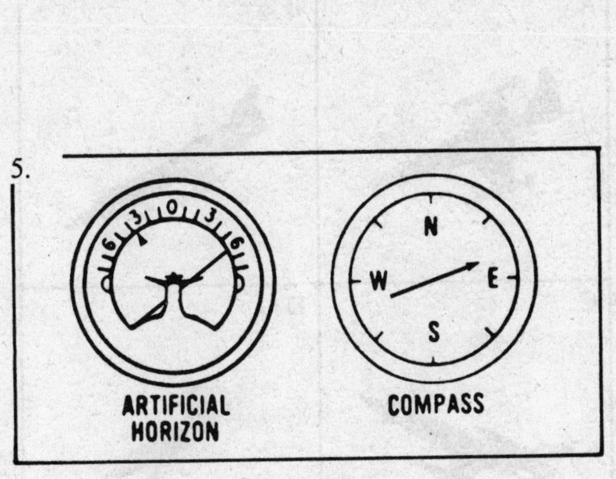

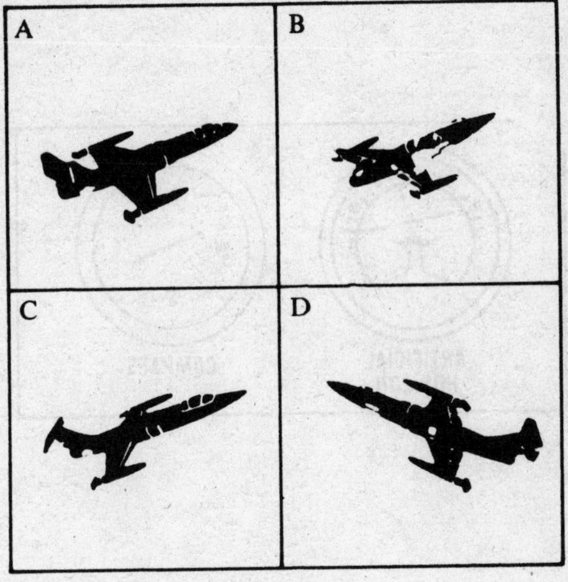

6.

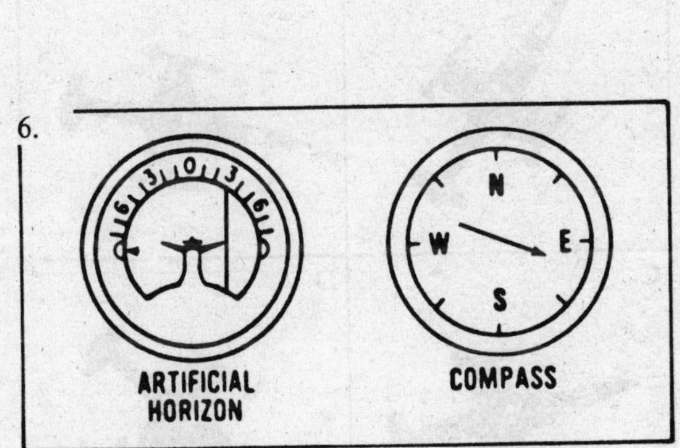

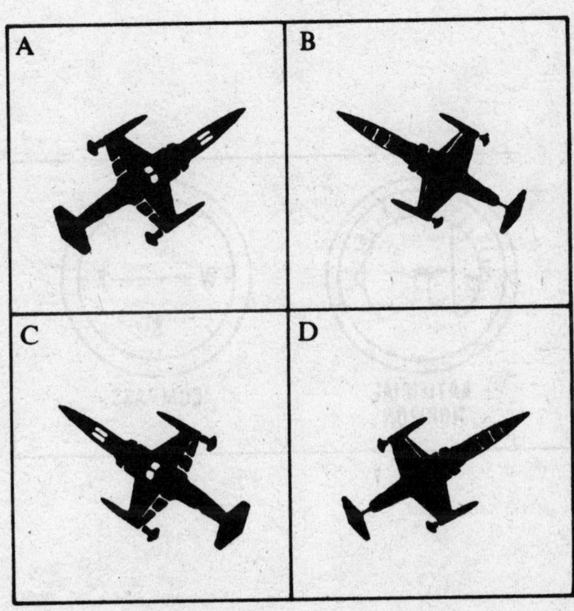

GO ON TO THE NEXT PAGE.

7.

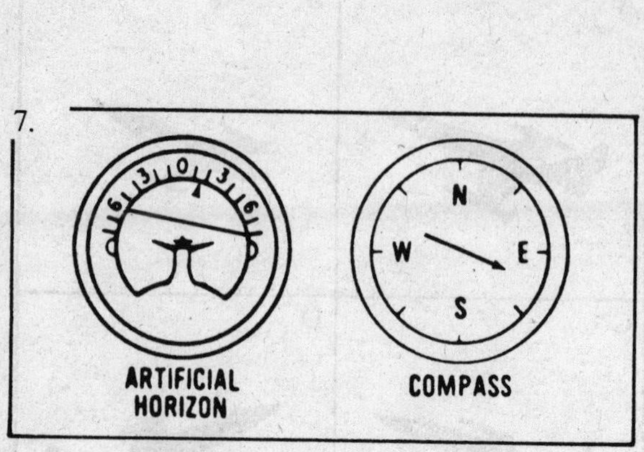
6
3
0
3
6
N
W
E
S
ARTIFICIAL HORIZON
COMPASS

A
B
C
D

8.

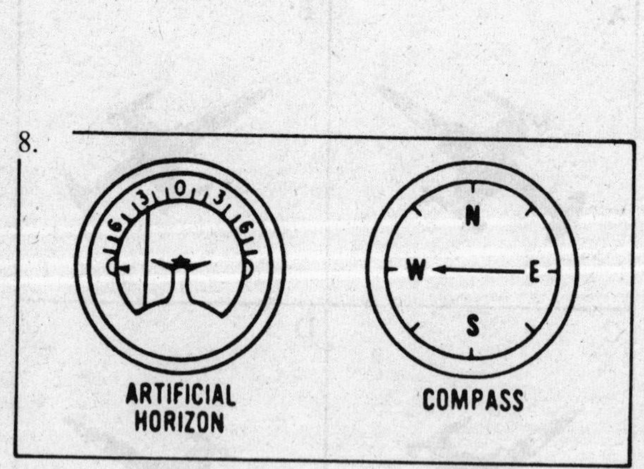
6
3
0
3
6
N
W
E
S
ARTIFICIAL HORIZON
COMPASS

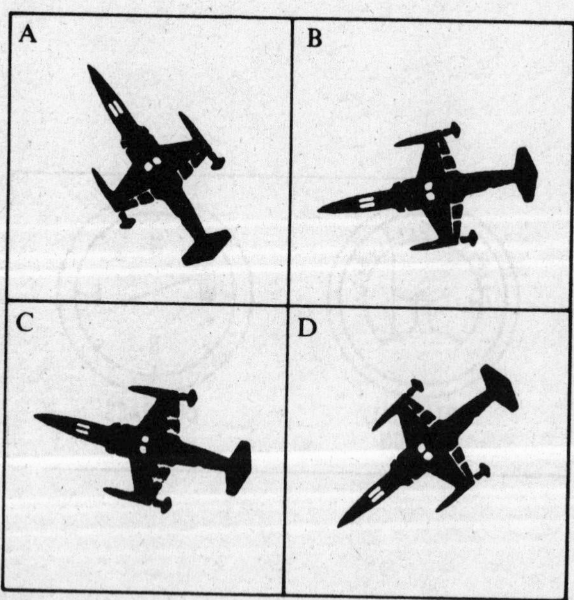
A
B
C
D

9.

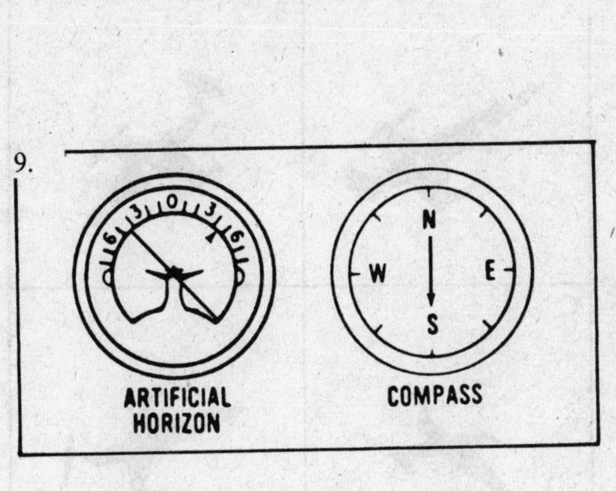

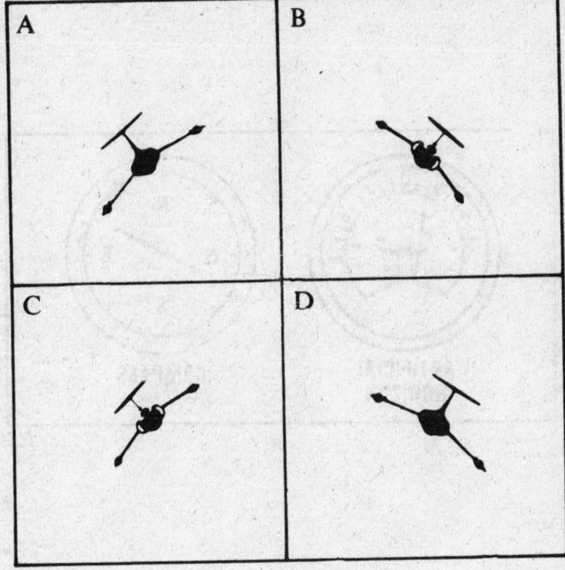

10.

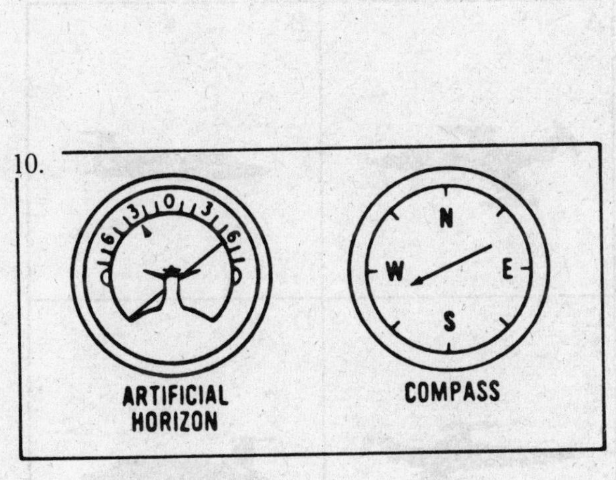

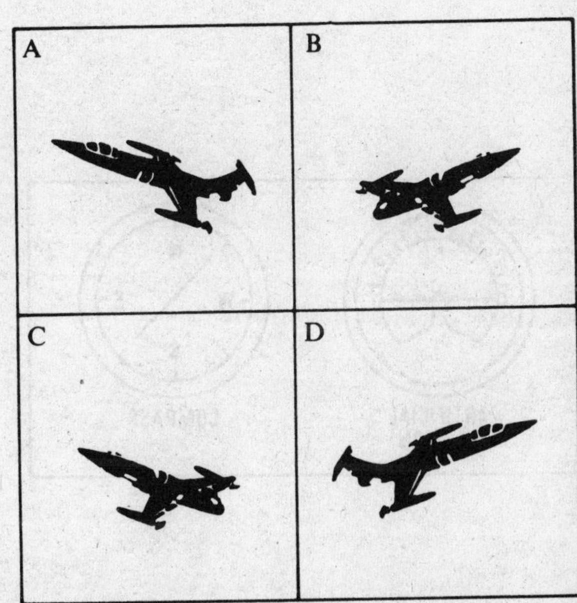

GO ON TO THE NEXT PAGE.

11.

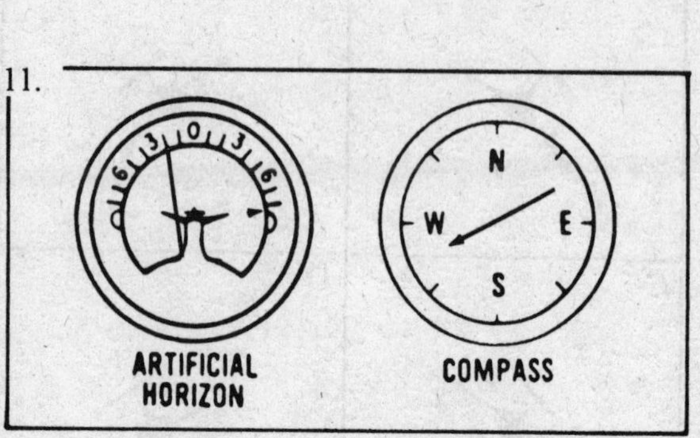
3
0
3
6
6
N
W
E
S
ARTIFICIAL
HORIZON
COMPASS

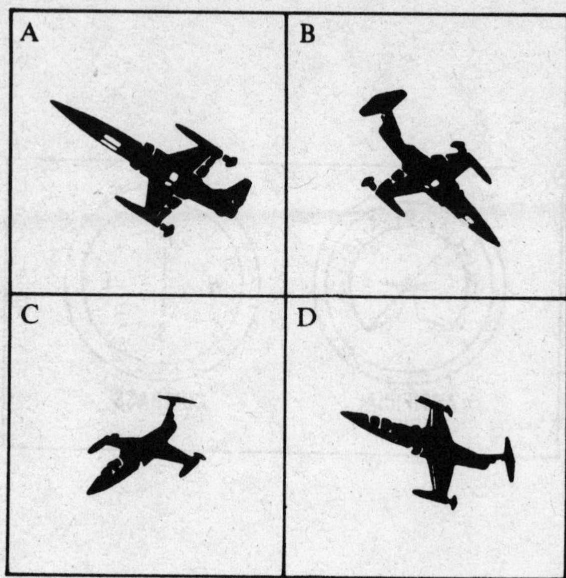
A
B
C
D

12.

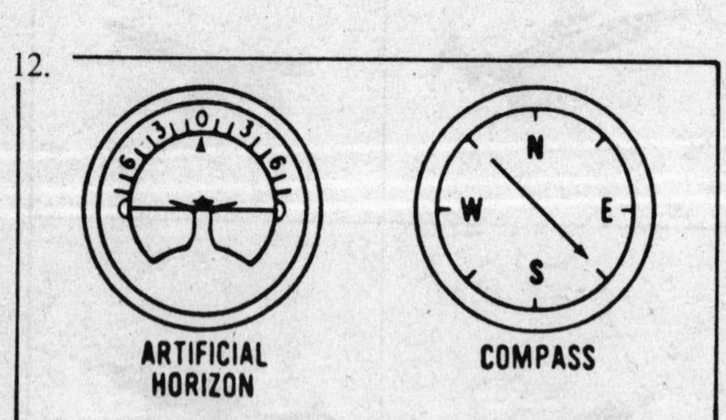
6
3
0
3
6
N
W
E
S
ARTIFICIAL
HORIZON
COMPASS

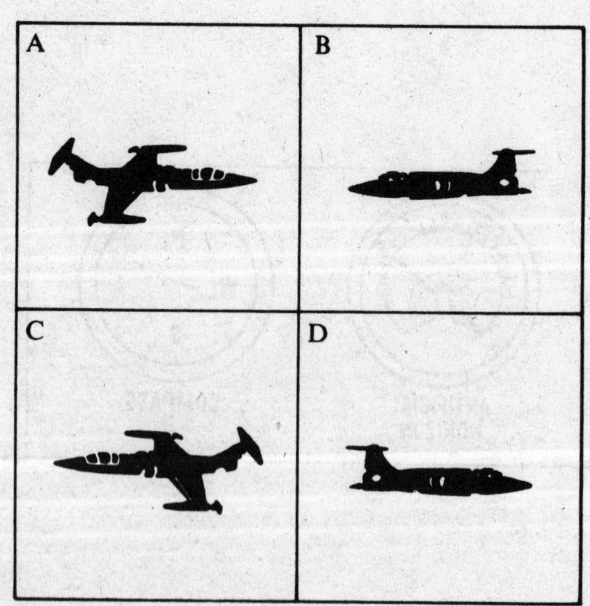
A
B
C
D

13.

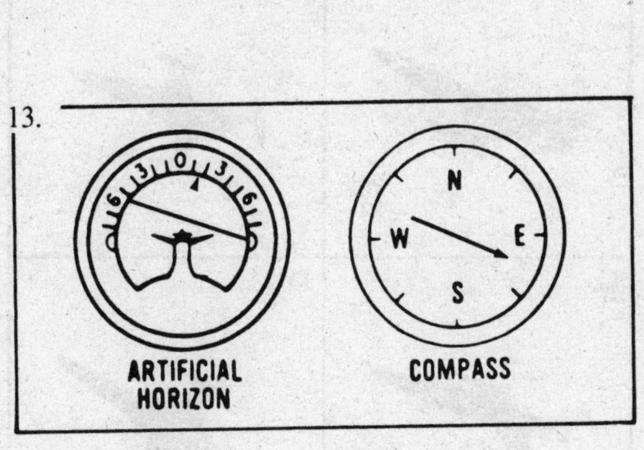

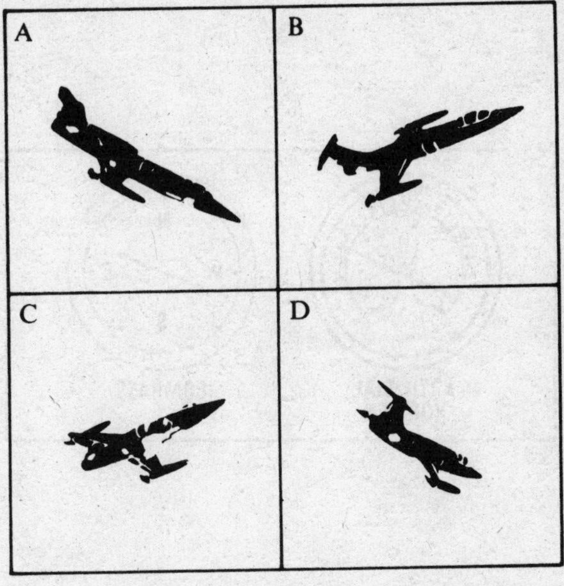

14.

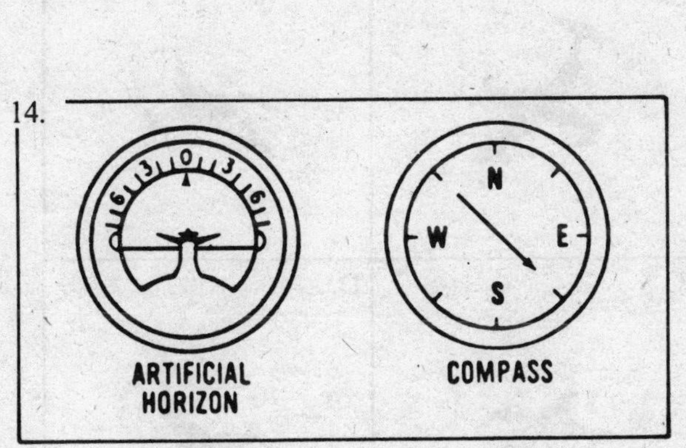

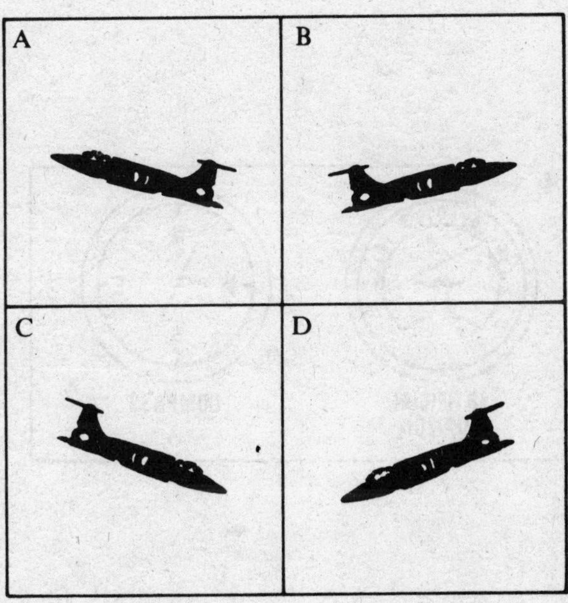

GO ON TO THE NEXT PAGE.

15.

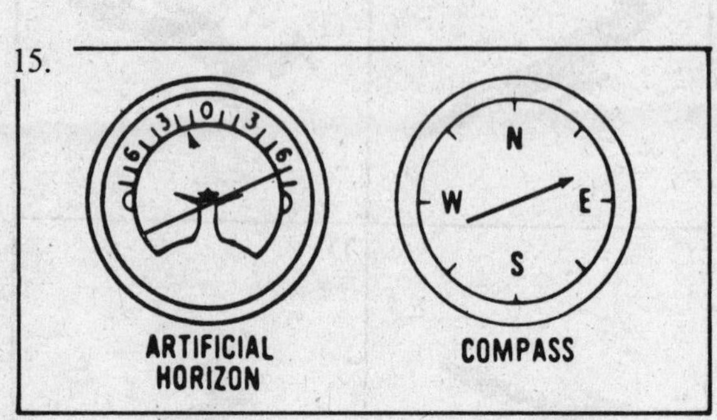
ARTIFICIAL
HORIZON
N
W
E
S
COMPASS

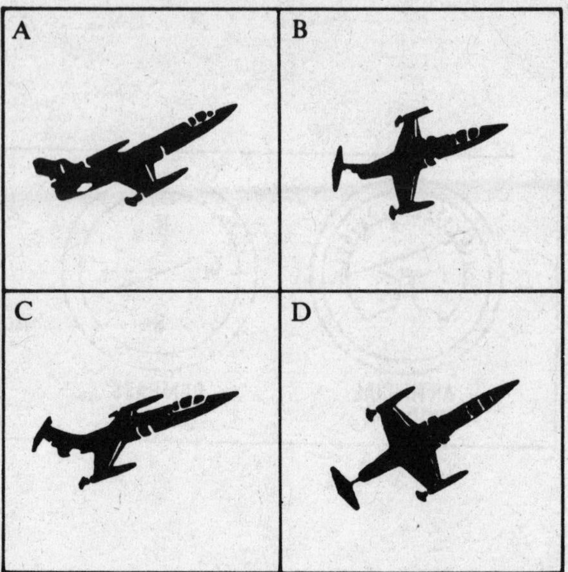
A
B
C
D

16.

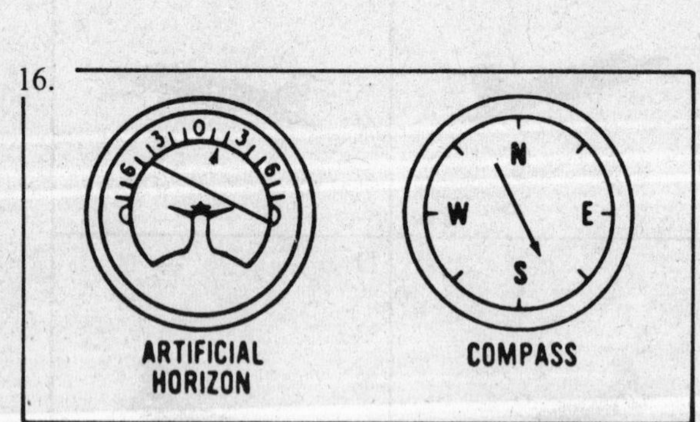
ARTIFICIAL
HORIZON
N
W
E
S
COMPASS

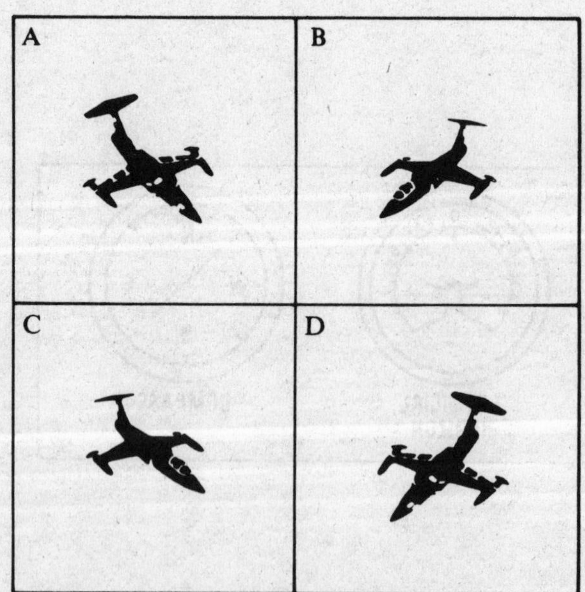
A
B
C
D

17.

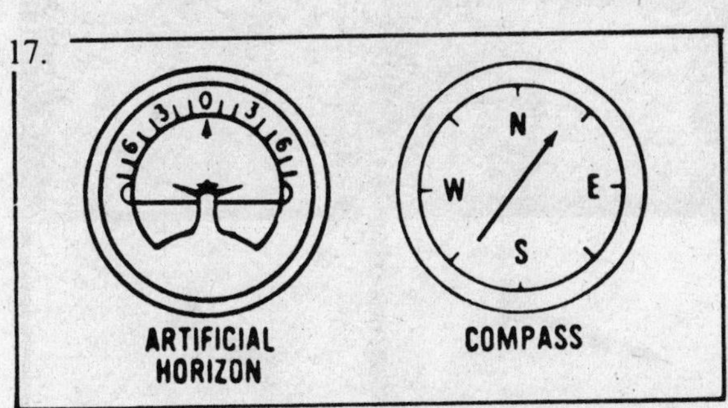

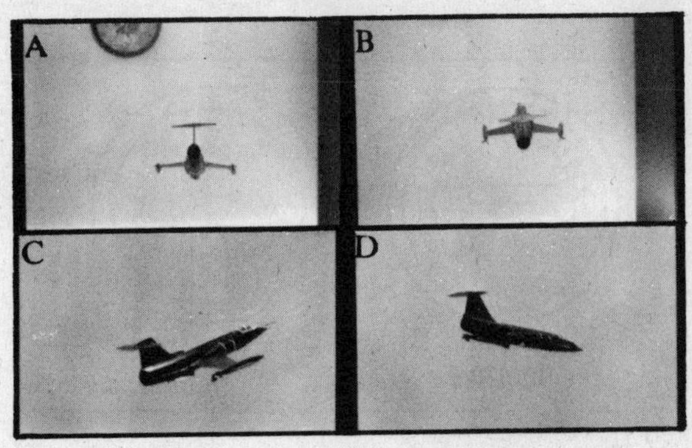

18.

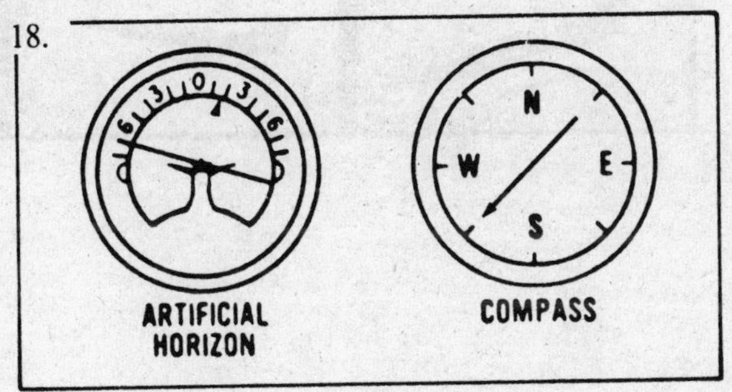

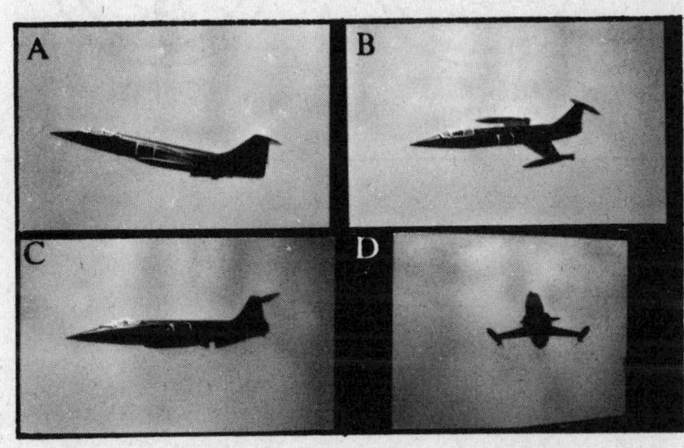

GO ON TO THE NEXT PAGE.

19.

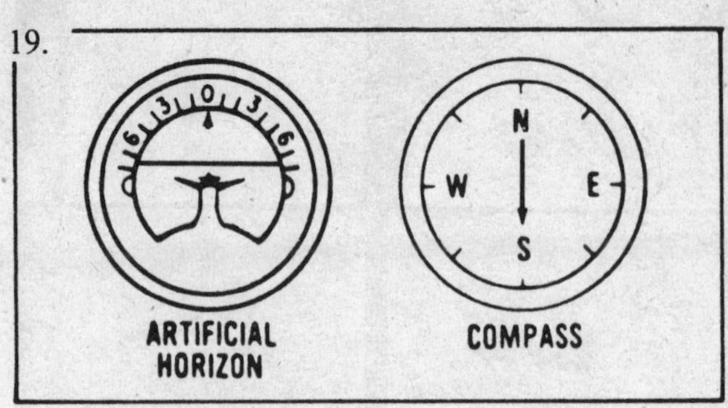

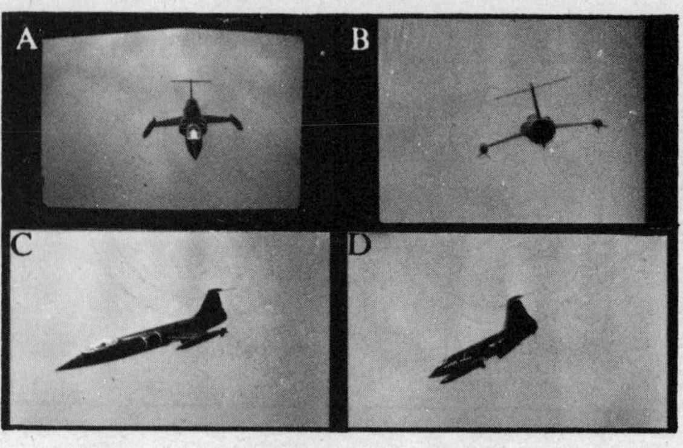

20.

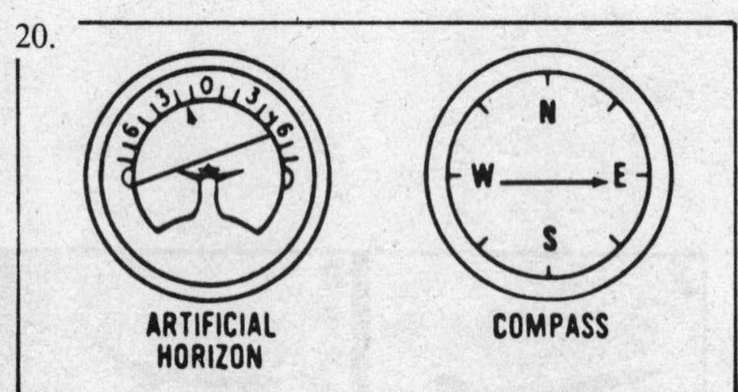

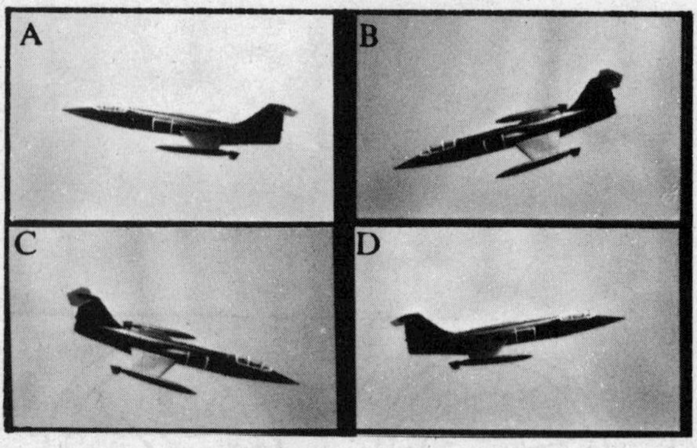

STOP! DO NOT GO ON UNTIL TIME IS UP.

PART 11

BLOCK COUNTING

11

Directions

This part of the test has 20 questions designed to measure your ability to "see into" a three-dimensional pile of blocks and determine how many pieces are touched by certain numbered blocks. *All of the blocks in each pile are the same size and shape.* Look at the sample below.

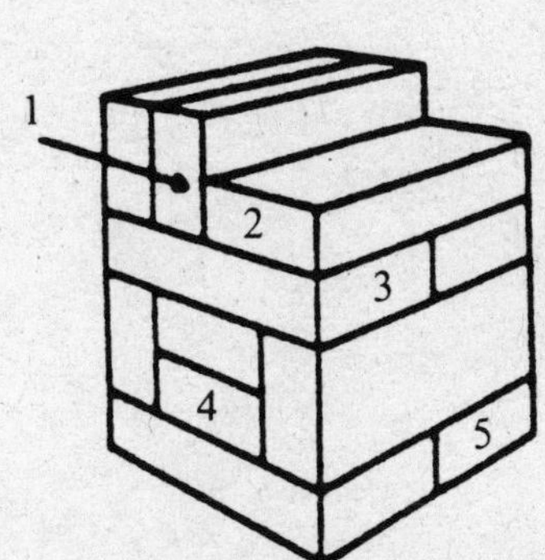

KEY					
Block	*A*	*B*	*C*	*D*	*E*
1	1	2	3	4	5
2	3	4	5	6	7
3	5	6	7	8	9
4	2	3	4	5	6
5	2	3	4	5	6

Block 1 touches the other 2 top blocks and the 2 blocks directly below it. The total number of blocks touched by 1 is, therefore, 4. For sample problem 1, 4 is choice (D) in the key to the right.

Block 2 touches blocks 1 and 3 and the unnumbered block to the right of block 3. Since block 2 touches 3 other blocks, the answer is 3. According to the key, 3 is choice (A) for sample problem 2. Now look at sample problem 3. It touches 3 blocks above, 3 blocks below, and one block on the right. Therefore, the correct answer is 7, so (C) is the correct answer to sample problem 3.

Now count the blocks touching blocks 4 and 5. For block 4, the correct answer is 5, so (D) would be the correct answer. For block 5, the correct answer is 4, so (C) would be the correct answer.

Your score on this test will be based on the number of questions you answer correctly. You should try to answer every question. You will not lose points or be penalized for guessing. Do not spend too much time on any one question.

When you begin, be sure to start with question number 1 of Part 11 of your test booklet and number 1 of Part 11 on your answer form.

DO NOT TURN THIS PAGE UNTIL TOLD TO DO SO.

PART 11

BLOCK COUNTING

TIME: 3 Minutes—20 Questions

KEY					
Block	*A*	*B*	*C*	*D*	*E*
1	3	4	5	6	7
2	5	6	7	8	9
3	5	6	7	8	9
4	4	5	6	7	8
5	4	5	6	7	8

KEY					
Block	*A*	*B*	*C*	*D*	*E*
6	1	2	3	4	5
7	2	3	4	5	6
8	5	6	7	8	9
9	3	4	5	6	7
10	2	3	4	5	6

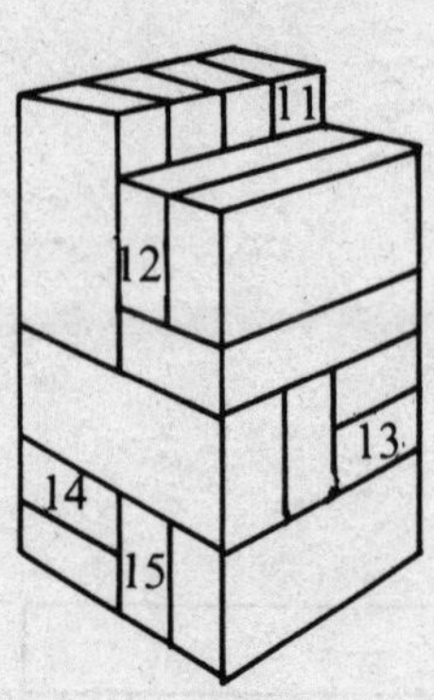

KEY					
Block	*A*	*B*	*C*	*D*	*E*
11	3	4	5	6	7
12	4	5	6	7	8
13	5	6	7	8	9
14	4	5	6	7	8
15	2	3	4	5	6

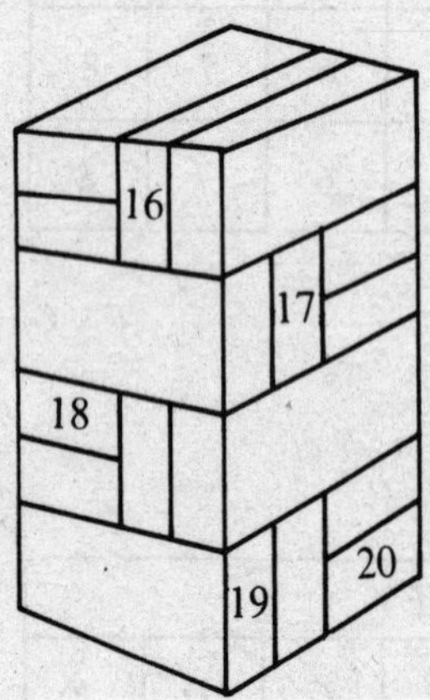

KEY					
Block	*A*	*B*	*C*	*D*	*E*
16	3	4	5	6	7
17	5	6	7	8	9
18	3	4	5	6	7
19	2	3	4	5	6
20	1	2	3	4	5

STOP! DO NOT GO UNTIL TIME IS UP.

PART 12

TABLE READING

12

Directions

This part of the test has 40 questions designed to test your ability to read tables quickly and accurately.

Now look at the following sample items based on the tabulation of turnstile readings shown below.

TABULATION OF TURNSTILE READINGS

	Turnstile Readings At					
Turnstile Number	5:30 A.M.	6:00 A.M.	7:00 A.M.	8:00 A.M.	9:00 A.M.	9:30 A.M.
1	79078	79090	79225	79590	79860	79914
2	24915	24930	25010	25441	25996	26055
3	39509	39530	39736	40533	41448	41515
4	58270	58291	58396	58958	59729	59807
5	43371	43378	43516	43888	44151	44217

For each question determine the turnstile reading for the turnstile number and time given. Choose as your answer the letter of the column in which the correct reading is found.

	Turnstile Number	Time	A	B	C	D	E
1.	1	8:00 A.M.	25441	25996	79225	79590	79860
2.	2	6:00 A.M.	24915	24930	25010	39530	79090
3.	4	9:30 A.M.	41515	44217	44151	59729	59807
4.	5	7:00 A.M.	39530	39736	43516	58291	58396
5.	3	5:30 A.M.	39509	39530	39736	58270	58291

The correct answers are 1. (D); 2. (B); 3. (E); 4. (C); 5. (A).

Your score on this test will be based on the number of questions you answer correctly. You should try to answer every question. You will not lose points or be penalized for guessing. Do not spend too much time on any one question.

When you begin, be sure to start with question number 1 of Part 12 of your test booklet and number 1 of Part 12 on your answer form.

DO NOT TURN THIS PAGE UNTIL TOLD TO DO SO.

PART 12

TABLE READING

TIME: 7 Minutes—40 Questions

Questions *1* to *5* are based on the table below. Note that the X values are shown at the top of the table and the Y values are shown on the left of the table. Find the entry that occurs at the intersection of the row and the column corresponding to the values given.

X VALUE

		−3	*−2*	*−1*	*0*	*+1*	*+2*	*+3*
	+3	22	23	25	27	28	29	30
	+2	23	25	27	29	30	31	32
	+1	24	26	28	30	32	33	34
Y VALUE	**0**	**26**	**27**	**29**	**31**	**33**	**34**	**35**
	−1	27	29	30	32	34	35	37
	−2	28	30	31	33	35	36	38
	−3	29	31	32	34	36	37	39

	X	**Y**	**A**	**B**	**C**	**D**	**E**
1.	0	−1	29	33	32	35	34
2.	−3	−3	22	29	23	31	28
3.	−1	+2	25	31	29	30	27
4.	+3	0	30	34	35	37	39
5.	−2	+1	26	23	29	25	22

Questions *6* to *10* are based on the following table showing height-weight standards used by the Air Force in its commissioning program.

COMMISSION HEIGHT-WEIGHT STANDARDS

MEN			WOMEN		
HEIGHT	WEIGHT		HEIGHT	WEIGHT	
Inches	Minimum	Maximum	Inches	Minimum	Maximum
60	100	153	60	92	130
61	102	155	61	95	132
62	103	158	62	97	134
63	105	164	63	100	136
64	105	169	64	103	139
65	106	169	65	106	144
66	107	174	66	108	148
67	111	179	67	111	152
68	115	184	68	114	156
69	119	189	69	117	161
70	123	194	70	119	165
71	127	199	71	122	169
72	131	205	72	125	174
73	135	211	73	128	179
74	139	218	74	130	185
75	143	224	75	133	190
76	147	230	76	136	196
77	151	236	77	139	201
78	153	242	78	141	206
79	157	248	79	144	211
80	161	254	80	147	216

	A	B	C	D	E
6. The maximum weight for 66" women is	152	148	169	144	174
7. The minimum weight for 72" men is	128	125	127	23	131
8. The maximum weight for 68" men is	189	156	179	184	161
9. The minimum weight for 62" women is	100	97	95	92	103
10. The maximum weight for 75" men is	224	190	236	196	230

Questions *11* to *15* are based on the table below showing the blood alcohol content in relation to body weight and the number of drinks consumed during a 2-hour period. For each question, ascertain the blood alcohol content-percent.

BLOOD ALCOHOL CONTENT (BAC)-PERCENT

Number of Drinks* (2-Hour Period)	Body Weight (in pounds) 100	120	140	160	180	200	220	240
12	.33	.25	.21	.19	.17	.16	.15	.14
11	.29	.23	.19	.18	.16	.15	.14	.14
10	.26	.21	.18	.17	.15	.14	.13	.13
9	.23	.19	.16	.15	.14	.13	.12	.12
8	.20	.17	.15	.14	.13	.12	.11	.11
7	.17	.15	.14	.13	.12	.11	.10	.10
6	.15	.13	.12	.11	.11	.10	.09	.08
5	.13	.11	.10	.10	.09	.08	.08	.07
4	.10	.09	.08	.08	.07	.06	.06	.06
3	.08	.07	.06	.05	.05	.04	.04	.04
2	.05	.04	.04	.03	.03	.03	.02	.02
1	.03	.02	.02	.02	.01	.01	.01	.01

*One drink is equivalent to 1 $\frac{1}{2}$ oz. 85-proof liquor, 6 oz. wine, or 12 oz. beer.

	A	B	C	D	0
11. A 160-pound person—2 drinks	.01	.02	.03	.04	.05
12. A 200 pound person—3 drinks	.01	.02	.03	.04	.05
13. A 180 pound person—4 drinks	.06	.07	.08	.09	.10
14. A 100 pound person—2 drinks	.01	.02	.03	.04	.05
15. A 240 pound person—3 drinks	.04	.05	.06	.07	.08

GO ON TO THE NEXT PAGE.

Questions *16* to *20* are based on the weekly train schedule given below for the Dumont Line.

WEEKDAY TRAIN LINE SCHEDULE—DUMONT LINE

	Eastbound			**Magic Mall**		**Westbound**		
Train #	Harvard Square Leave	Pleasure Plaza Leave	Harding Street Leave	Arrive	Leave	Harding Street Leave	Pleasure Plaza Leave	Harvard Square Leave
69	7:48	7:51	7:56	8:00	8:06	8:10	8:15	8:18
70	7:54	7:57	8:02	8:06	8:12	8:16	8:21	8:24
71	8:00	8:03	8:08	8:12	8:18	8:22	8:27	8:30
72	8:04	8:07	8:13	8:17	8:22	8:26	8:31	8:34
73	8:08	8:11	8:17	8:21	8:26	8:30	8:35	8:38
74	8:12	8:15	8:20	8:24	8:30	8:34	8:39	8:42
75	8:16	8:19	8:24	8:28	8:34	8:38	8:43	8:46
69	8:20	8:23	8:28	8:32	8:38	8:42	8:47	8:50
70	8:26	8:29	8:34	8:38	8:44	8:48	8:53	8:56

16. Train #73 is scheduled to arrive at Magic Mall at

    (A) 8:26
    (B) 8:21
    (C) 8:22
    (D) 8:17
    (E) 8:24

17. Train #75 is scheduled to leave Harvard Square at

    (A) 8:20
    (B) 8:12
    (C) 8:15
    (D) 8:19
    (E) 8:16

18. Train #70 is scheduled to leave Pleasure Plaza on its second westbound trip to Harvard Square at

    (A) 8:48
    (B) 8:21
    (C) 8:53
    (D) 8:24
    (E) 8:56

19. Going toward Harvard Square, Train #71 is scheduled to leave Pleasure Plaza at

    (A) 8:27
    (B) 8:03
    (C) 8:22
    (D) 8:08
    (E) 8:18

20. Passengers boarding at Harding Street and wishing to get to Harvard Square by 8:42 would have to board a train which is scheduled to leave Magic Mall no later than

    (A) 8:34
    (B) 8:24
    (C) 8:39
    (D) 8:30
    (E) 8:28

Questions *21* to *30* are based on the mileage between the two cities.

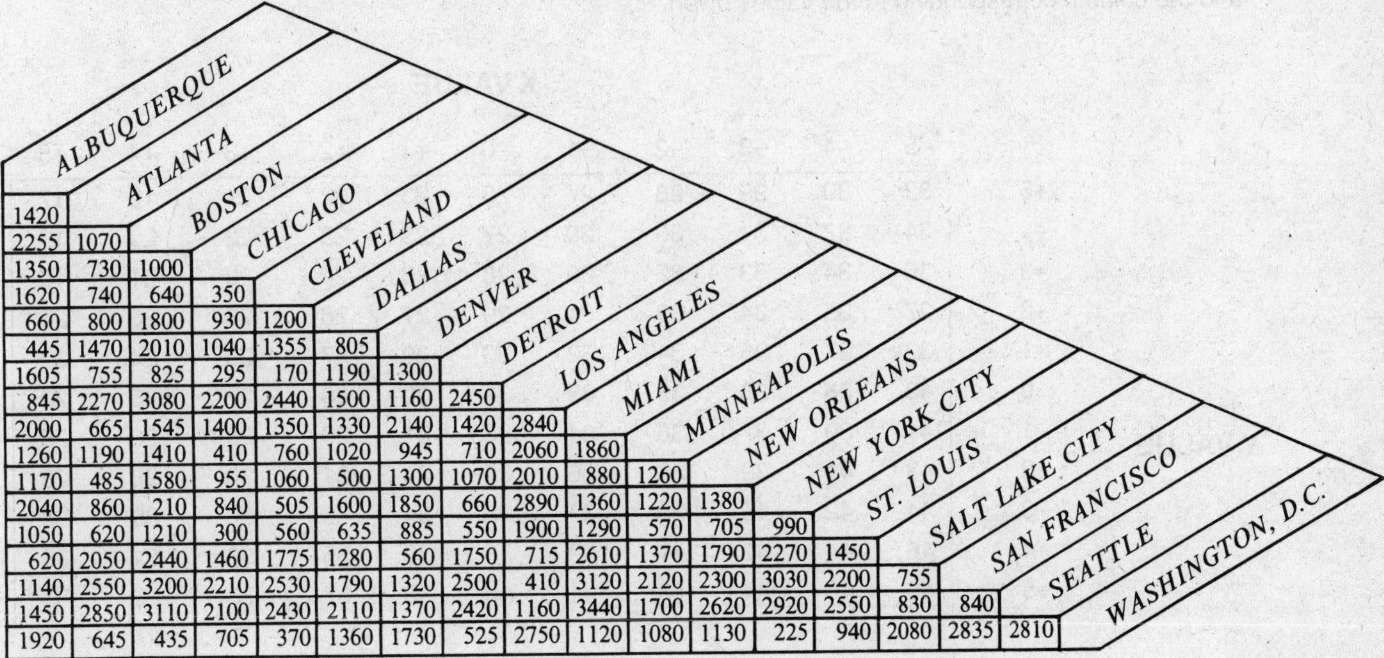

	Albuquerque	Atlanta	Boston	Chicago	Cleveland	Dallas	Denver	Detroit	Los Angeles	Miami	Minneapolis	New Orleans	New York City	St. Louis	Salt Lake City	San Francisco	Seattle
Atlanta	1420																
Boston	2255	1070															
Chicago	1350	730	1000														
Cleveland	1620	740	640	350													
Dallas	660	800	1800	930	1200												
Denver	445	1470	2010	1040	1355	805											
Detroit	1605	755	825	295	170	1190	1300										
Los Angeles	845	2270	3080	2200	2440	1500	1160	2450									
Miami	2000	665	1545	1400	1350	1330	2140	1420	2840								
Minneapolis	1260	1190	1410	410	760	1020	945	710	2060	1860							
New Orleans	1170	485	1580	955	1060	500	1300	1070	2010	880	1260						
New York City	2040	860	210	840	505	1600	1850	660	2890	1360	1220	1380					
St. Louis	1050	620	1210	300	560	635	885	550	1900	1290	570	705	990				
Salt Lake City	620	2050	2440	1460	1775	1280	560	1750	715	2610	1370	1790	2270	1450			
San Francisco	1140	2550	3200	2210	2530	1790	1320	2500	410	3120	2120	2300	3030	2200	755		
Seattle	1450	2850	3110	2100	2430	2110	1370	2420	1160	3440	1700	2620	2920	2550	830	840	
Washington, D.C.	1920	645	435	705	370	1360	1730	525	2750	1120	1080	1130	225	940	2080	2835	2810

	A	B	C	D	E
21. Chicago to Dallas	1040	930	1200	1355	825
22. New Orleans to Miami	1360	1260	570	880	715
23. Albuquerque to Denver	660	845	825	755	445
24. Washington, D.C. to Seattle	2835	2080	2200	2810	2250
25. Atlanta to Salt Lake City	2050	2850	1920	2440	2210
26. San Francisco to Boston	3200	3110	2850	2440	2530
27. Cleveland to Minneapolis	410	1060	1020	760	1350
28. St. Louis to Detroit	660	550	560	885	715
29. Los Angeles to Detroit	2010	2060	2840	2140	2450
30. New York City to Dallas	1300	1850	1600	1060	1280

GO ON TO THE NEXT PAGE.

Questions *31* to *40* are based on the table below. Note that the X values are shown at the top of the table and the Y values are shown on the left of the table. Find the entry that occurs at the intersection of the row and the column corresponding to the values given.

X VALUE

Y VALUE	–5	–4	–3	–2	–1	–0	+1	+2	+3	+4	+5
+5	32	30	29	28	27	25	23	22	21	19	17
+4	34	32	31	30	29	27	25	23	22	20	18
+3	36	34	33	32	30	28	26	24	23	21	19
+2	37	35	34	33	31	29	27	26	25	23	21
+1	39	37	35	34	32	30	29	27	26	24	22
0	**40**	**38**	**36**	**35**	**33**	**31**	**30**	**28**	**27**	**25**	**23**
–1	41	39	37	36	34	32	31	29	28	26	25
–2	43	41	39	38	36	34	33	31	30	28	26
–3	44	42	40	39	37	36	34	33	32	30	28
–4	46	44	42	41	39	38	36	35	33	31	30
–5	48	46	44	43	41	40	38	37	35	33	31

	X	**Y**	**A**	**B**	**C**	**D**	**E**
31.	0	–3	34	38	37	35	36
32.	–4	+2	36	35	33	37	34
33.	+2	–2	31	36	33	38	30
34.	–5	–5	46	19	17	44	48
35.	+1	–3	27	33	36	34	26
36.	–3	+4	28	32	29	31	30
37.	+4	+1	26	39	24	36	25
38.	–1	–5	41	43	37	40	39
39.	+3	+1	27	24	28	25	26
40.	+5	0	4	23	6	25	22

STOP! DO NOT GO ON UNTIL TIME IS UP.

PART 13

AVIATION INFORMATION

13

Directions

This part of the test has 20 questions designed to measure your knowledge of aviation. Each of the questions or incomplete statements is followed by five choices. Decide which one of the options best answers the question or completes the statement.

Now look at the two sample questions below.

1. The force necessary to overcome gravitational force to keep the airplane flying is termed

   (A) power
   (B) drag
   (C) lift
   (D) thrust
   (E) weight

To keep the airplane flying, *lift* must overcome the weight or gravitational force. Option (C) is the correct answer.

2. The ailerons are used primarily to

   (A) bank the airplane
   (B) control the direction of yaw
   (C) permit a slower landing speed
   (D) permit a steep angle of descent
   (E) control the pitch attitude

The ailerons, located on the trailing edge of each wing near the outer tip, are used primarily to bank (roll) the airplane around its longitudinal axis. The banking of the wing results in the airplane turning in the direction of the bank. Option (A) is the correct answer.

Your score on this test will be based on the number of questions you answer correctly. You should try to answer every question. You will not lose points or be penalized for guessing. Do not spend too much time on any one question.

When you begin, be sure to start with question number 1 of Part 13 of your test booklet and number 1 of Part 13 on your answer form.

DO NOT TURN THIS PAGE UNTIL TOLD TO DO SO.

PART 13

AVIATION INFORMATION

TIME: 8 Minutes—20 Questions

1. The four aerodynamic forces acting on an airplane are

   (A) drag, gravity, power, and velocity
   (B) drag, friction, power, and velocity
   (C) drag, lift, thrust, and weight
   (D) friction, power, velocity, and weight
   (E) gravity, lift, thrust, and weight

2. An airplane wing is designed to produce lift resulting from relatively

   (A) positive air pressure below and above the wing's surface
   (B) negative air pressure below the wing's surface and positive air pressure above the wing's surface
   (C) positive air pressure below the wing's surface and negative air pressure above the wing's surface
   (D) negative air pressure below and above the wing's surface
   (E) neutral air pressure below and above the wing's surface

3. Operation of modern airplanes is dependent upon the use of instruments. These instrument dials, displayed in the airplane's cockpit, are referred to as "flight instruments" or "engine instruments." Which one of the following is *not* a "flight instrument"?

   (A) airspeed indicator
   (B) altimeter
   (C) attitude indicator
   (D) tachometer
   (E) vertical velocity indicator

4. Which statement is true regarding the forces acting on an aircraft in a steady flight condition (no change in speed or flightpath)?

   (A) Lift equals weight and thrust equals drag.
   (B) Lift equals thrust and weight equals drag.
   (C) Lift equals drag and thrust equals weight.
   (D) Lift is greater than weight and thrust is less than drag.
   (E) Lift is less than weight and thrust is greater than drag.

5. A flashing green air traffic control signal directed to an aircraft on the surface is a signal that the pilot

   (A) is cleared to taxi
   (B) is cleared for takeoff
   (C) should exercise extreme caution
   (D) should taxi clear of the runway in use
   (E) should stop taxiing

6. What is the difference between a steady red and a flashing red light signal from the tower to an aircraft approaching to land?

   (A) Both light signals mean the same except the flashing red light requires a more urgent reaction.
   (B) Both light signals mean the same except the steady red light requires a more urgent reaction.
   (C) A steady red light signals to continue circling and a flashing red light signals that the airport is unsafe for landing.
   (D) A steady red light signals to continue circling and a flashing red light signals to continue, but exercise extreme caution.
   (E) A steady red light signals that the airport is unsafe and a flashing red light signals to use a different runway.

7. The propeller blades are curved on one side and flat on the other side to

   (A) increase its strength
   (B) produce thrust
   (C) provide proper balance
   (D) reduce air friction
   (E) reduce drag

8. When in the down (extended) position, wingflaps provide

   (A) decreased wing camber (curvature)
   (B) less lift and less drag
   (C) less lift but more drag
   (D) greater lift but less drag
   (E) greater lift and more drag

9. What makes an airplane turn?

   (A) centrifugal force
   (B) horizontal component of lift
   (C) rudder and aileron
   (D) rudder, aileron and elevator
   (E) vertical component of lift

10. What is one advantage of an airplane said to be inherently stable?

   (A) The airplane will not spin.
   (B) The airplane will be difficult to stall.
   (C) The airplane will require less fuel.
   (D) The airplane will require less effort to control.
   (E) The airplane will not overbank during steep turns.

11. If the elevator tabs on a plane are lowered, the plane will tend to

   (A) nose up
   (B) nose down
   (C) pitch fore and aft
   (D) go into a slow roll
   (E) wing over

12. The pilot always advances the throttle during a

   (A) nose dive
   (B) landing
   (C) turn
   (D) spin
   (E) climb

13. The pilot of an airplane can best detect the approach of a stall by the

   (A) increase in speed of the engine
   (B) increase in pitch and intensity of the sound of the air moving past the plane
   (C) increase in effectiveness of the rudder
   (D) ineffectiveness of the ailerons and elevator
   (E) decrease in pitch and intensity of the sound of the air moving past the plane

14. It is ordinarily desirable to provide an unusually long flight strip at municipal airports for the take-off of

   (A) military planes in echelon
   (B) heavily loaded ships in still air
   (C) small airplanes in rainy weather
   (D) any airplane across the wind
   (E) airplanes that have high climbing speeds

Questions *15* to *17* are based on the airport diagram shown below.

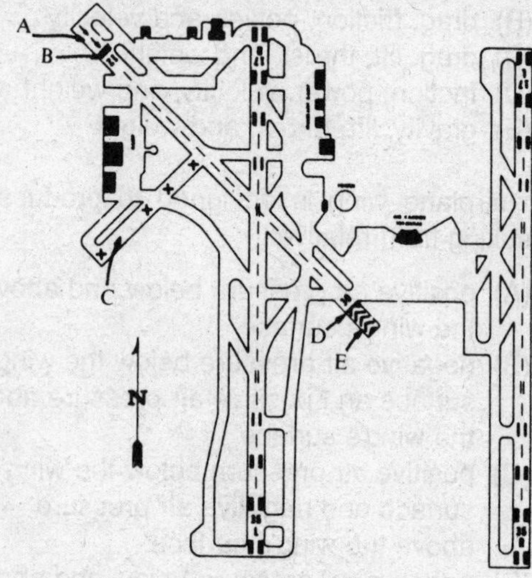

15. According to the above diagram, which of the following is correct?

   (A) Takeoffs and landings are permissible at position C.
   (B) The takeoff and landing portion of Runway 12 begins at position B.
   (C) Runway 30 is equipped at position E with emergency arresting gear to provide a means of stopping military aircraft.
   (D) Takeoffs may be started at position A on Runway 12, and the landing portion of this runway begins at position B.
   (E) Light airplanes only may land in position A on Runway 12.

16. What is the difference between Area A and Area E, as shown above?

    (A) A may be used only for takeoff; E may be used for all operations.
    (B) A may be used only for taxi and takeoff; E may be used for all operations except landing.
    (C) A may be used only for taxi and takeoff; E may be used only for landing.
    (D) A may be used for all operations except heavy aircraft landing; E may be used only as an overrun.
    (E) A may be used for taxi and takeoff; E may be used only as an overrun.

17. Area C on the airport depicted on the previous page is classified as

    (A) an STOL runway
    (B) a parking ramp
    (C) a closed runway
    (D) a multiple heliport
    (E) an active runway

Questions *18* to *20* are based on the figure shown below.

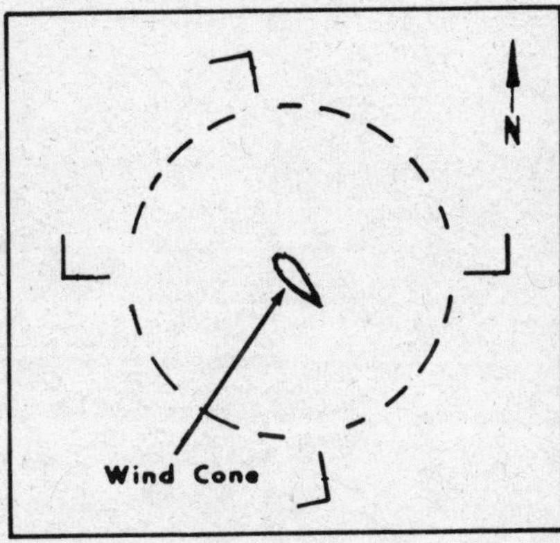

18. The segmented circle shown above indicates that the airport traffic is

    (A) left-hand for Runway 17 and right-hand for Runway 35
    (B) right-hand for Runway 9 and left-hand for Runway 27
    (C) right-hand for Runway 35 and right-hand for Runway 9
    (D) left-hand for Runway 17 and right-hand for Runway 9
    (E) left-hand for Runway 35 and right-hand for Runway 17

19. The segmented circle indicates that a landing on Runway 27 will be with a

    (A) right-quartering headwind
    (B) left-quartering headwind
    (C) right-quartering tailwind
    (D) left-quartering tailwind
    (E) 90° crosswind

20. Which runways and traffic pattern should be used as indicated by the wind cone in the segmented circle?

    (A) right-hand traffic on Runway 35 or left-hand traffic on Runway 27
    (B) left-hand traffic on Runway 35 or right-hand traffic on Runway 27
    (C) right-hand traffic on Runway 17 or left-hand traffic on Runway 9
    (D) left-hand traffic on Runway 17 or right-hand traffic on Runway 9
    (E) left-hand traffic on Runways 9 or 27

STOP! DO NOT GO ON UNTIL TIME IS UP.

PART 14

ROTATED BLOCKS

Directions

This part of the test has 15 questions designed to measure your ability to visualize and manipulate objects in space. In each item, you are shown a picture of a block. The problem is to find a second block which is just like the first.

Look at the two blocks below. Although viewed from different points, the blocks are just alike.

Look at the two blocks below. They are not alike. They can never be turned so that they will be alike.

Now look at the sample item below. Which of the five choices is just like the first block?

1.	A	B	C	D	E
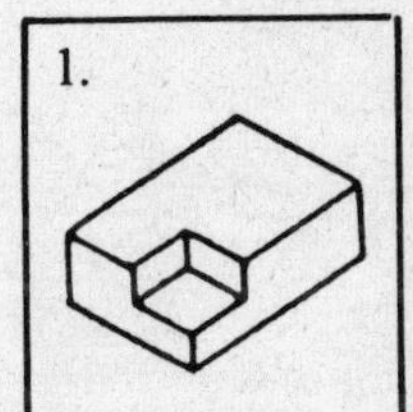	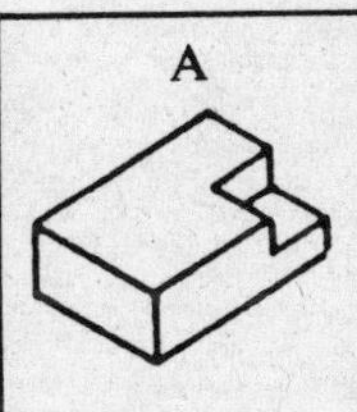		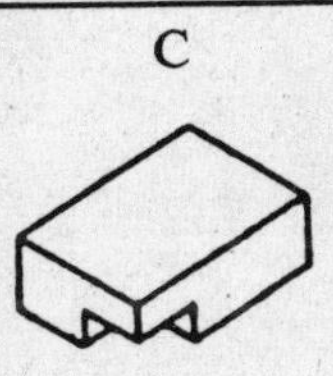		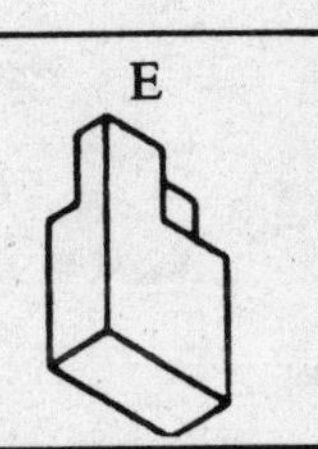

The correct answer is (D). It is the same block as seen from a different side.

2.	A	B	C	D	E
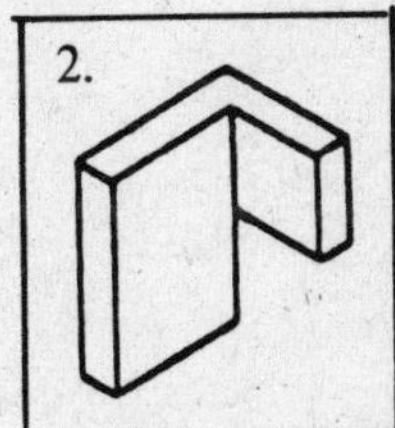	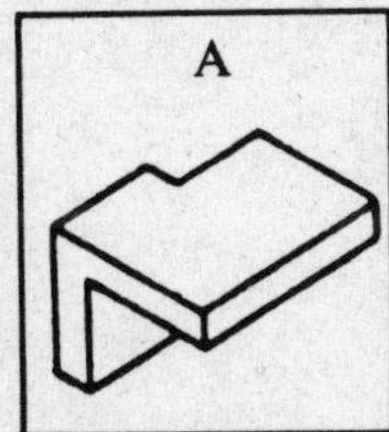				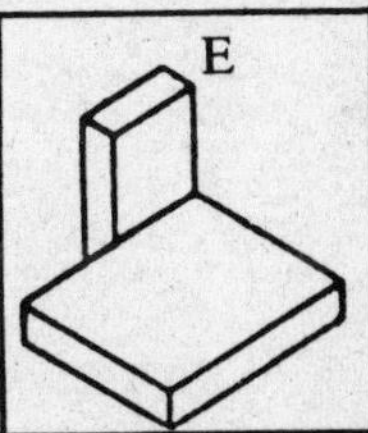

The right answer for 2 is (C).

Your score on this test will be based on the number of questions you answer correctly. You should try to answer every question.

When you begin, be sure to start with question number 1 of Part 14 of your test booklet and number 1 on Part 14 of your answer form.

DO NOT TURN THIS PAGE UNTIL TOLD TO DO SO.

PART 14

ROTATED BLOCKS

TIME: 13 Minutes—15 Questions

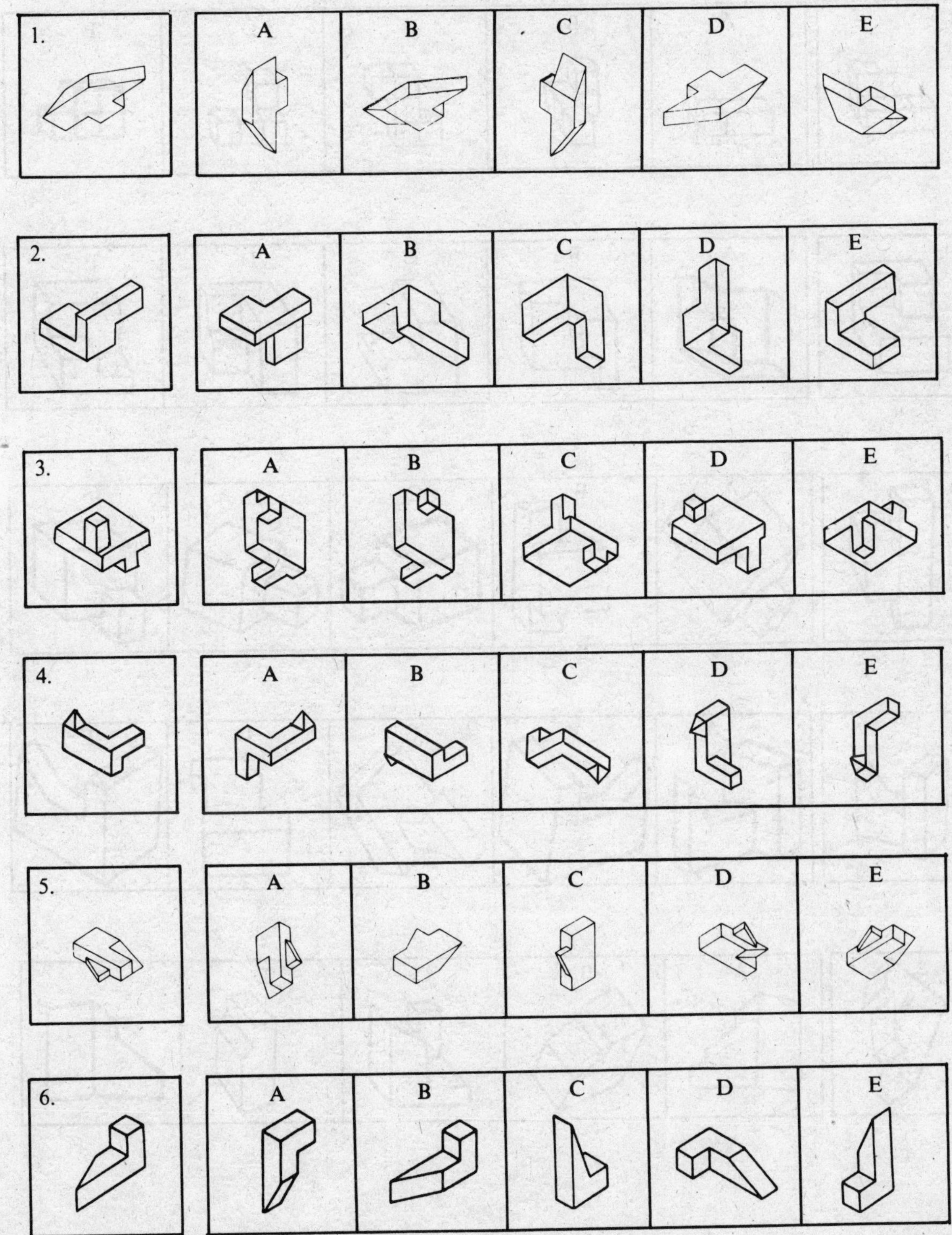

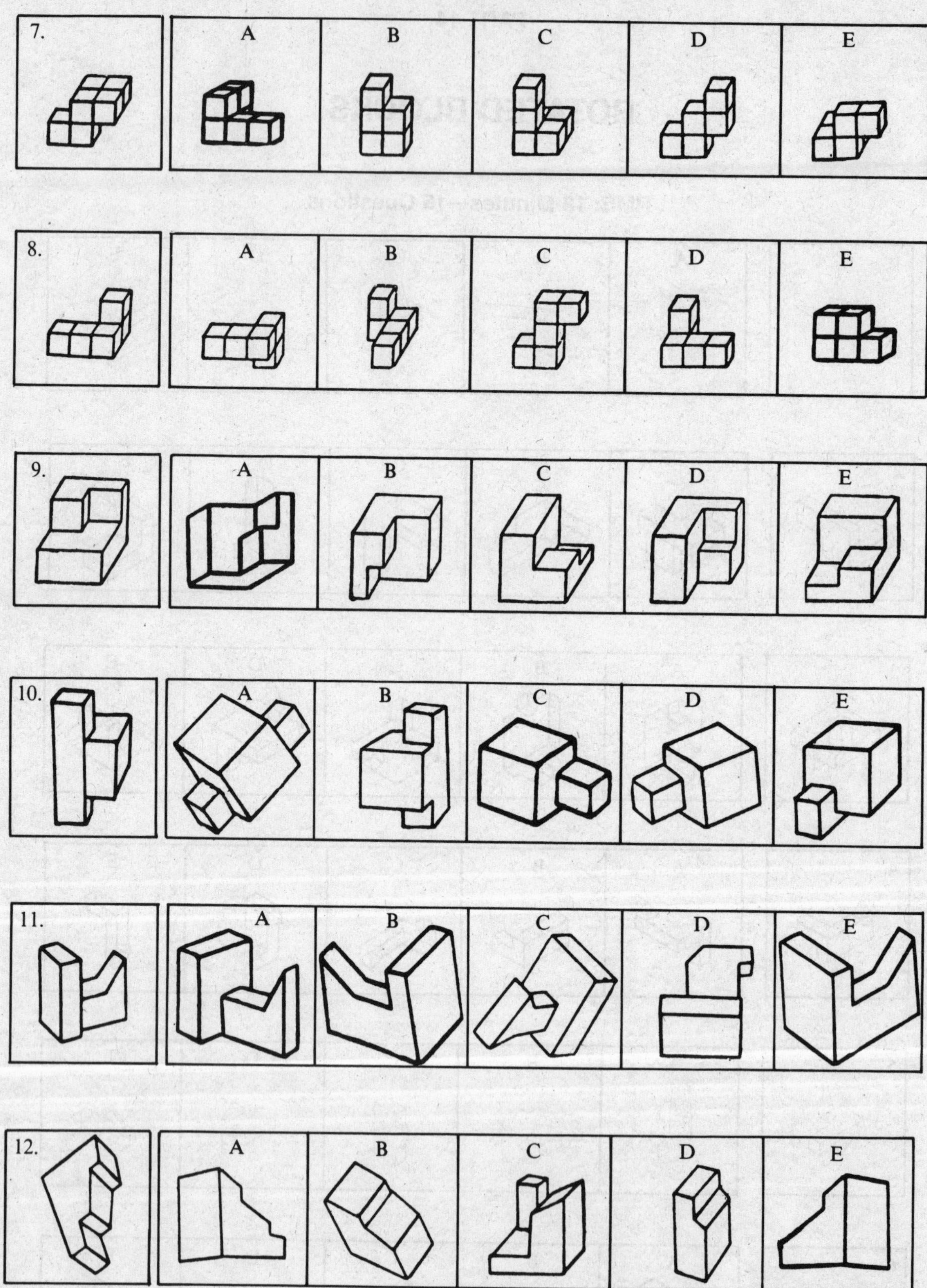
7.
A
B
C
D
E
8.
A
B
C
D
E
9.
A
B
C
D
E
10.
A
B
C
D
E
11.
A
B
C
D
E
12.
A
B
C
D
E

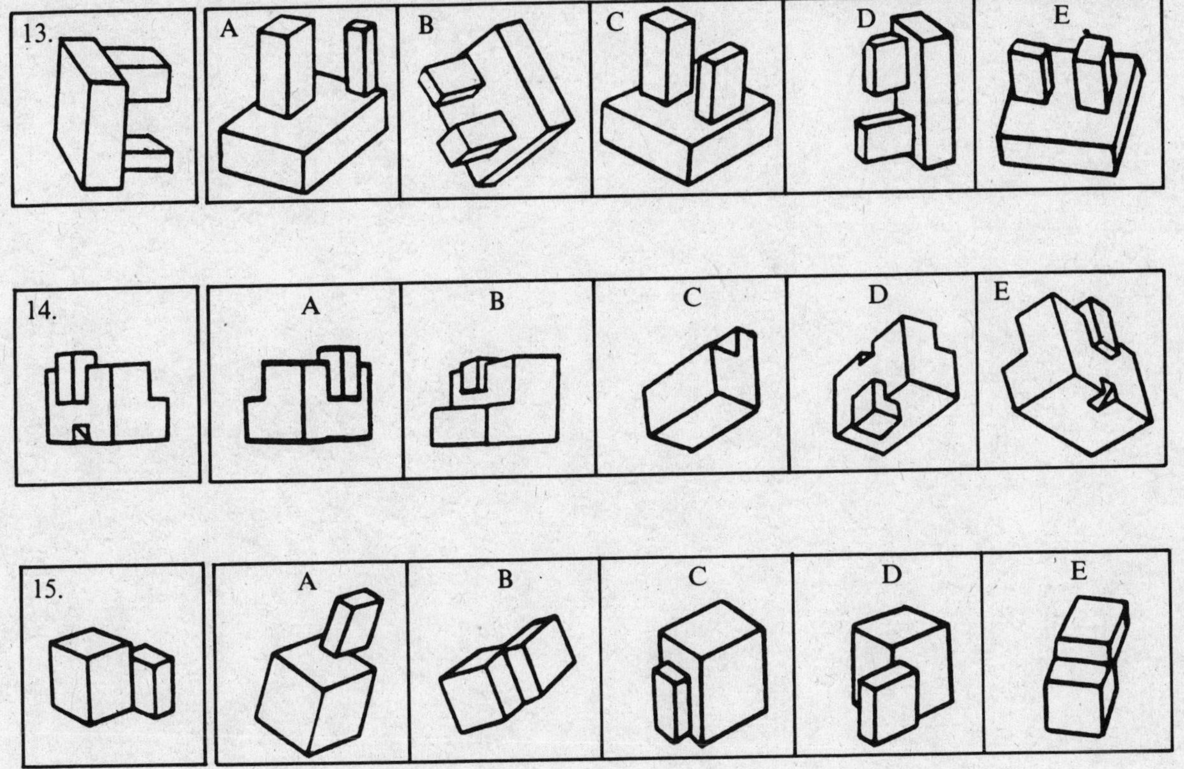

STOP! DO NOT GO UNTIL TIME IS UP.

PART 15

15

GENERAL SCIENCE

Directions

This part of the test has 20 questions designed to measure your scientific knowledge. Each of the questions or incomplete statements is followed by five choices. Decide which one of the choices best answers the question or completes the statement.

Now look at the three sample questions below.

1. An eclipse of the sun throws the shadow of the

   (A) moon on the sun
   (B) earth on the sun
   (C) sun on the earth
   (D) earth on the moon
   (E) moon on the earth

2. Substances which hasten a chemical reaction without themselves undergoing change are called

   (A) buffers
   (B) catalysts
   (C) colloids
   (D) reducers
   (E) polymers

3. Lack of iodine is often related to which of the following diseases?

   (A) beriberi
   (B) scurvy
   (C) rickets
   (D) goiter
   (E) asthma

The correct answers to these three sample questions are: 1. (E); 2. (B); 3. (D).

Your score on this test will be based on the number of questions you answer correctly. You should try to answer every question. You will not lose points or be penalized for guessing. Do not spend too much time on any one question.

When you begin, be sure to start with question number 1 of Part 15 of your test booklet and number 1 of Part 15 on your answer form.

DO NOT TURN THIS PAGE UNTIL TOLD TO DO SO.

PART 15

GENERAL SCIENCE

TIME: 10 Minutes—20 Questions

1. Under natural conditions, large quantities of organic matter decay after each year's plant growth has been completed. As a result of such conditions
   (A) many animals are deprived of adequate food supplies
   (B) soil erosion is accelerated
   (C) soils maintain their fertility
   (D) earthworms are added to the soil
   (E) pollution increases

2. The thin, clear layer that forms the front part of the eyeball is called the
   (A) pupil
   (B) iris
   (C) lens
   (D) retina
   (E) cornea

3. The most likely reason why dinosaurs became extinct was that they
   (A) were killed by erupting volcanoes
   (B) were eaten as adults by the advancing mammalian groups
   (C) failed to adapt to a changing environment
   (D) killed each other in combat
   (E) were destroyed by meteorites

4. Which of the following is a chemical change?
   (A) magnetizing a rod of iron
   (B) burning one pound of coal
   (C) mixing flake graphite with oil
   (D) vaporizing one gram of mercury in a vacuum
   (E) melting ice

5. A person with high blood pressure should
   (A) take frequent naps
   (B) avoid salt
   (C) eat only iodized salt
   (D) exercise vigorously
   (E) avoid proteins

6. The chief nutrient in lean meat is
   (A) starch
   (B) protein
   (C) fat
   (D) carbohydrates
   (E) Vitamin B

7. Spiders can be distinguished from insects by the fact that spiders have
   (A) hard outer coverings
   (B) large abdomens
   (C) four pairs of legs
   (D) biting mouth parts
   (E) jointed appendages

8. An important ore of uranium is called
   (A) hematite
   (B) chalcopyrite
   (C) bauxite
   (D) pitchblende
   (E) feldspar

9. Of the following, the lightest element known on earth is
   (A) hydrogen
   (B) oxygen
   (C) helium
   (D) air
   (E) nitrogen

10. Of the following gases in the air, the most plentiful is
   (A) argon
   (B) oxygen
   (C) nitrogen
   (D) carbon dioxide
   (E) hydrogen

11. The time it takes for light from the sun to reach the earth is approximately

(A) four years
(B) eight minutes
(C) four months
(D) eight years
(E) one week

12. Of the following types of clouds, the ones which occur at the greatest height are called

(A) cirrus
(B) nimbus
(C) cumulus
(D) stratus
(E) altostratus

13. A new drug for treatment of tuberculosis was being tested in a hospital. Patients in Group A actually received doses of the new drug; those in Group B were given only sugar pills. Group B represents

(A) a scientific experiment
(B) a scientific method
(C) an experimental error
(D) an experimental control
(E) a hypothesis

14. After adding salt to water, the freezing point of the water is

(A) variable
(B) inverted
(C) the same
(D) raised
(E) lowered

15. Radium is stored in lead containers because

(A) the lead absorbs the harmful radiation
(B) radium is a heavy substance
(C) lead prevents the disintegration of the radium
(D) lead is cheap
(E) lead is brittle

16. The type of joint that attaches the arm to the shoulder blade is known as a(n)

(A) hinge
(B) pivot
(C) immovable
(D) gliding
(E) ball and socket

17. Limes were eaten by British sailors in order to prevent

(A) anemia
(B) beriberi
(C) night blindness
(D) rickets
(E) scurvy

18. The time that it takes for the earth to rotate 45° is

(A) two hours
(B) four hours
(C) one hour
(D) three hours
(E) five hours

19. Of the following planets, the one which has the shortest revolutionary period around the sun is

(A) Mercury
(B) Jupiter
(C) Earth
(D) Venus
(E) Mars

20. What is the name of the negative particle which circles the nucleus of the atom?

(A) neutron
(B) meson
(C) proton
(D) electron
(E) isotope

STOP! DO NOT GO ON UNTIL TIME IS UP.

PART 16

HIDDEN FIGURES

16

Directions

This part of the test has 15 questions designed to measure your ability to see a simple figure in a complex drawing. At the top of each page are five figures, lettered A, B, C, D, and E. Below these on each page are several numbered drawings. You are to determine which lettered figure is contained in each of the numbered drawings.

The lettered figures are:

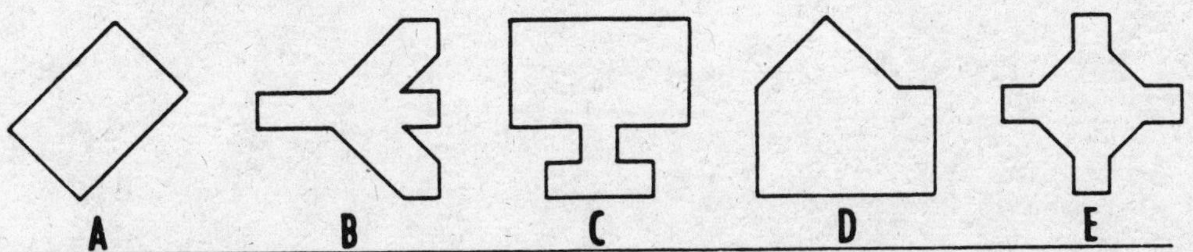

As an example, look at drawing X below. Which one of the five figures is contained in drawing X?

Now look at drawing Y, which is exactly like drawing X except that figure B has been blackened to show where to look for it. Thus, (B) is the answer to sample item X.

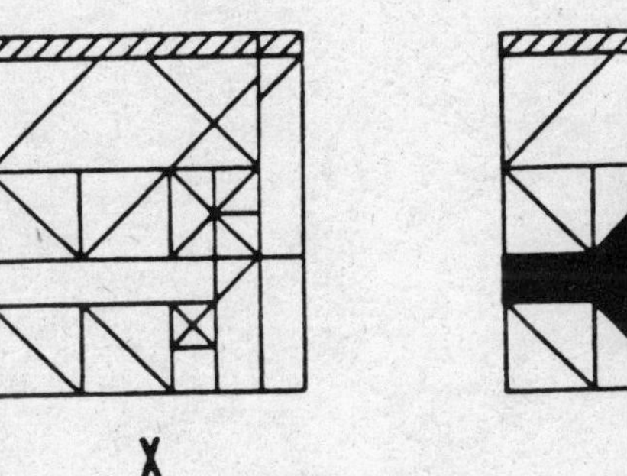

Each numbered drawing contains only *one* of the lettered figures. The correct figure in each drawing will always be of the same size and in the same position as it appears at the top of the page. Therefore, do not rotate the page in order to find it. Look at each numbered drawing and decide which one of the five lettered figures is contained in it.

Your score on this test will be based on the number of questions you answer correctly. You should try to answer every question. You will not lose points or be penalized for guessing. Do not spend too much time on any one question.

When you begin, be sure to start with question number 1 of Part 16 of your test booklet and number 1 of Part 16 of your answer form.

DO NOT TURN THIS PAGE UNTIL TOLD TO DO SO.

PART 16

HIDDEN FIGURES

TIME: 8 Minutes—15 Questions

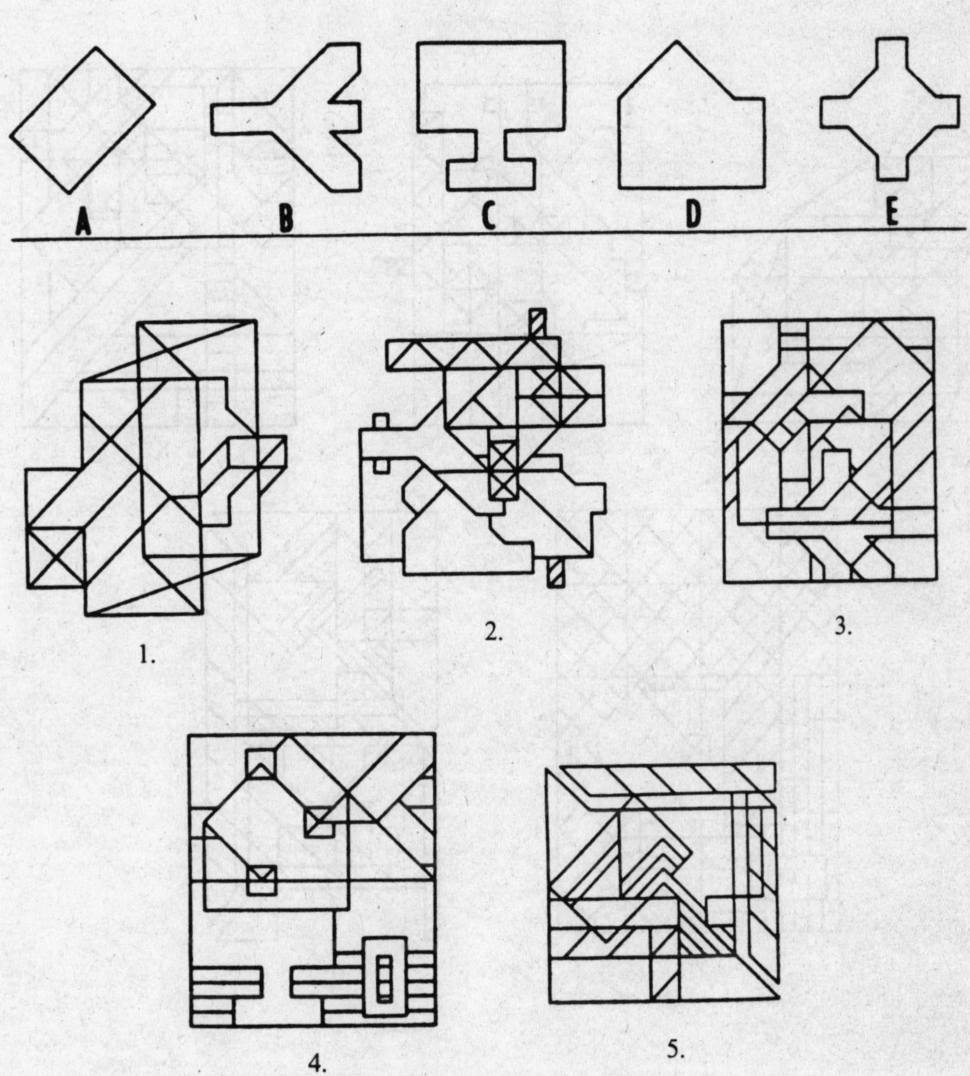

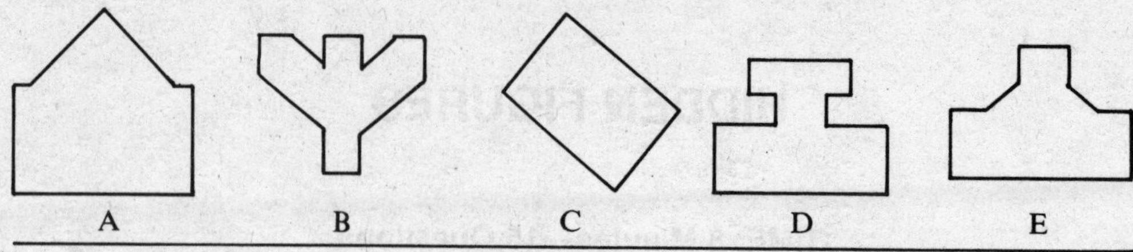
A
B
C
D
E

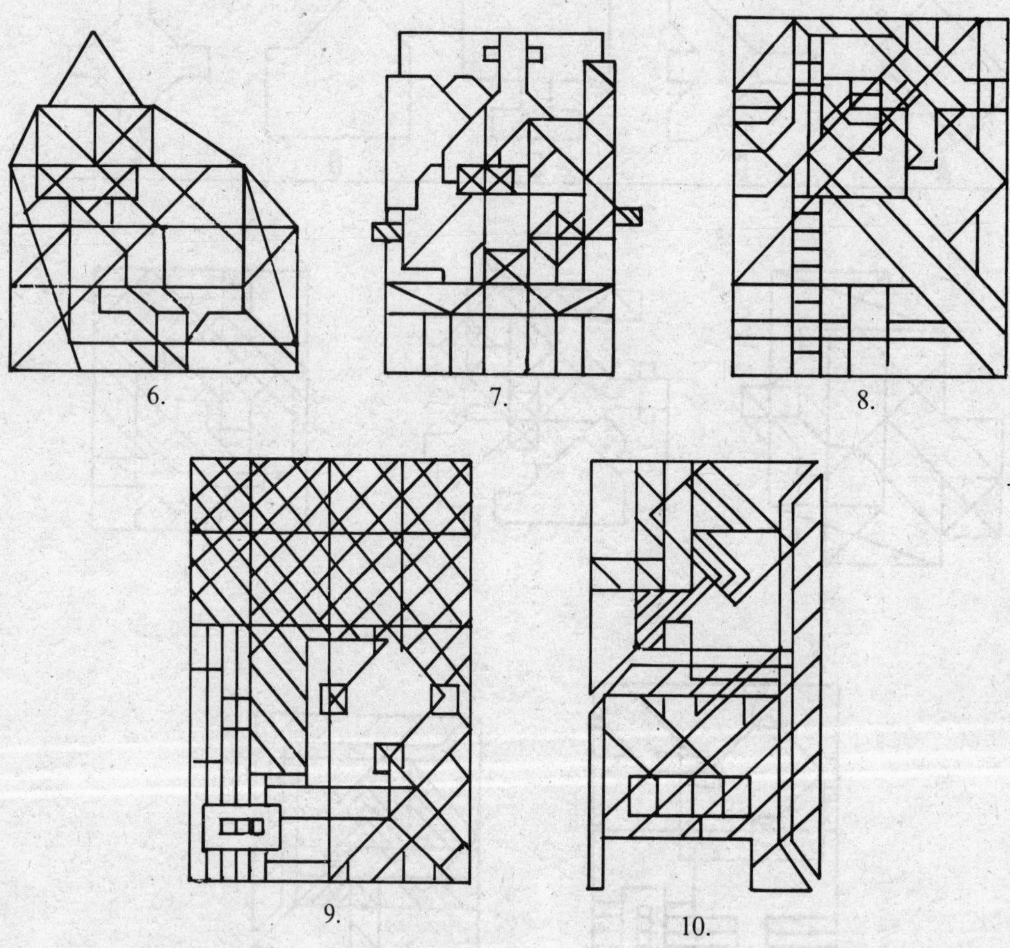
6.
7.
8.
9.
10.

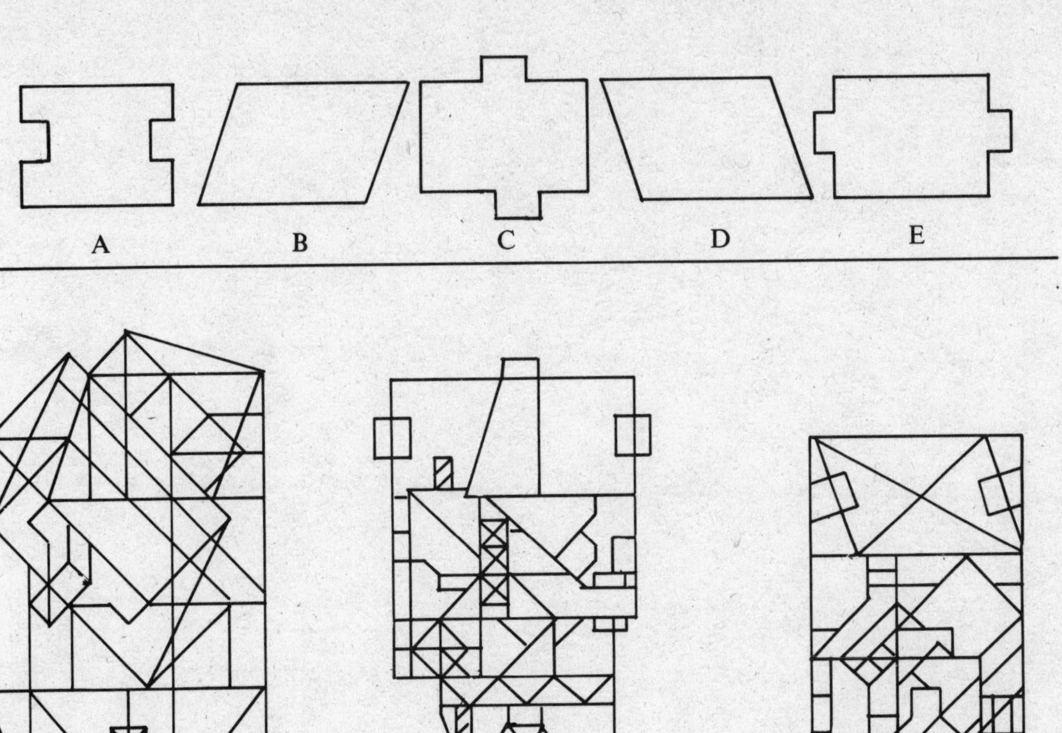

11.

12.

13.

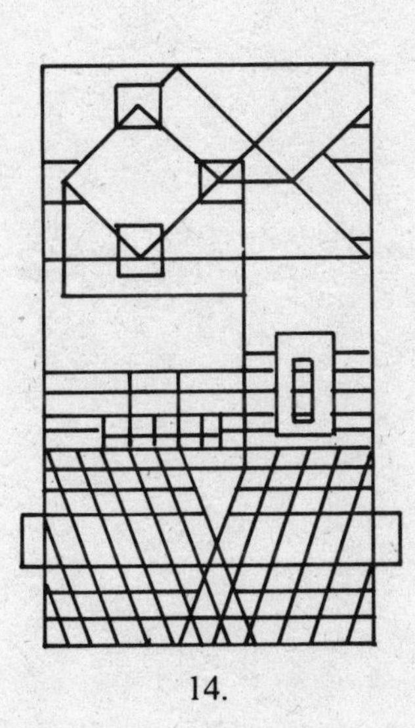

14.

15.

END OF EXAMINATION

SAMPLE AIR FORCE OFFICER QUALIFYING TEST KEY ANSWERS AND RATIONALE

Use these key answers to determine the number of questions you answered correctly on each subtest and to list those questions you answered incorrectly or of which you are unsure how to arrive at the correct answer.

Be certain to review carefully and understand the rationale for arriving at the correct answer for all items you answered incorrectly, as well as those you answered correctly but are unsure of. This is essential in order to acquire the knowledge and expertise necessary to obtain the maximum scores possible on the subtests of the "real" Air Force Officer Qualifying Test.

PART 1—VERBAL ANALOGIES

Key Answers

1. D	5. A	8. E	11. A	14. B	17. E	20. C	23. A
2. D	6. D	9. C	12. E	15. E	18. D	21. A	24. B
3. C	7. D	10. E	13. E	16. C	19. A	22. B	25. D
4. C							

Items Answered Incorrectly: ____; ____; ____; ____; ____; ____; ____; ____.

Items Unsure Of: ____; ____; ____; ____; ____; ____; ____; ____.

Total Number Answered Correctly: ______

Rationale

1–(D) A *chapter* is a numbered division of a *book*; a *story* is a numbered floor of a *building.*

2–(B) *Alpha* is the first letter or the *beginning* of the Greek alphabet; *omega* is the last letter or *end* of the Greek alphabet.

3–(C) *Carrot* is a type of *vegetable; pepper* is a type of *spice.*

4–(C A *micrometer* is a tool used by a *machinist.* A *trowel* is a tool used by a *mason.*

5–(A) *Concave* is hollow and curved like a *cavity; convex* is bulging and curved like a *mound.*

6–(D) *Dozen* or 12 is represented by Roman numeral *XII. Score* or 20 is represented by Roman numeral *XX.*

7–(B) *Gown* is a type of *garment; gasoline* is a type of *fuel.*

8–(E) An *emerald* is a *green* gem; a *ruby* is a *red* gem.

9–(C) *Hyper-* is a prefix meaning *over; hypo-* is a prefix meaning *under.*

10–(E) *Horizontal* is at right angle to the *vertical.* In yarns, *warp* is at right angle to the *woof.*

11–(A) *Immigration* is the act of *arriving* in a new country. *Emigration* is the act of leaving or *departing* one country to settle in another.

12–(E) A *kilometer* is equal to 1000 *meters.* A *millennium* is equal to a period of 1000 *years.*

13–(E) An *octagon* is an eight-sided polygon; a *square* is a four-sided one. A *hexagon* is a six-sided polygon; a *triangle* is a three-sided one.

14–(B) A *priest* is inducted into office by a formal ceremony termed *ordination.* A *president* is inducted into office by a formal ceremony termed *inauguration.*

15–(E) *Perjure* is to willfully make a false *statement* under oath; *trespass* is to wrongfully *enter* the property of another. Both are illegal actions.

16–(C) An *ordinance* is a rule or *regulation; ordinance* is *munition* (weapons and ammunition).

17–(E) *Told* is the past and past participle of *tell; wept* is the past and past participle of *weep.*

18–(D) A *dozen* contains 12 *units;* a *year* consists of 12 *months.*

19–(A) A *lamb* is a young *sheep*; a *colt* is a young *horse.*

20–(C) *Zenith* is the *highest* point; *nadir* is the *lowest* point.

21–(A) *Ignore* and *overlook* have the same or a similar meaning; *agree* and *consent* are synonyms.

22–(B) The outer boundary of a *square* is its *perimeter.* The outer boundary of a *circle* is its *circumference.*

23–(A) *Frequently* and *seldom* have opposite meanings; *always* and *never* are antonyms.

24–(B) A *bus* is a type of *vehicle; baseball* is a type of *game.*

25–(D) *Trickle* means to flow or fall gently; *gush* means to flow plentifully and is much more forceful than a trickle. *Tepid* means moderately warm; *hot* is a much higher temperature than moderately warm.

PART 2—ARITHMETIC REASONING

Key Answers

1. D	5. A	8. A	11. D	14. A	17. B	20. D	23. B
2. E	6. C	9. B	12. E	15. C	18. A	21. B	24. B
3. A	7. D	10. B	13. C	16. E	19. E	22. C	25. D
4. E							

Items Answered Incorrectly: ___; ___; ___; ___; ___; ___; ___; ___.

Items Unsure Of: ___; ___; ___; ___; ___; ___; ___; ___.

Total Number Answered Correctly: ______

Rationale

1–(D) 3 kilometers = 3000 meters; $\frac{3000}{15}$ = 200 meters.

2–(E) 200 feet × 200 feet = 40,000 square feet of floor area; 4000 tons × 2000 = 8,000,000 pounds; $\frac{8,000,000}{40,000}$ = 200 pounds.

3–(A) 12 pounds = 11 pounds, 16 ounces; weight of tool = 9 pounds, 9 ounces. 11 pounds, 16 ounces minus 9 pounds, 9 ounces = 2 pounds, 7 ounces.

4–(E) One million × 12 = 12 million = 12,000,000 (nickels per year); 12,000,000 × .05 = $600,000.00

5–(A) Sample size is 50. Number of defects found in sample = 4. $\frac{4}{50}$ = 8%. If 8% defects were found in the sample, it is probable that the percentage of defective articles in the original shipment is also 8%.

6–(C) There are 200 cigarettes in a carton (20 × 10 = 200). 12 mg × 200 = 2400 mg of tar in 200 cigarettes. 2400 mg = 2.4 grams.

7–(D) 36 tons × 3 man-hours = 108 man-hours to stack 36 tons. $\frac{108}{6}$ = 18 persons needed to complete stacking in 6 hours.

8–(A) Let x = number of envelopes addressed in 1 hour by slower worker. $2x$ = number of envelopes addressed in 1 hour by faster worker. $3x \times 5 = 750$; $15x = 750$; $x = 50$ envelopes per hour for slower worker.

9–(B) 25 × 12 = 300 sq. ft. = area of long wall; 300 × 2 = 600 sq. ft. 15 × 12 = 180 sq. ft. = area of short wall; 180 × 2 = 360 sq. ft. 600 + 360 = 960 sq. ft. = total wall area. 7 × 5 = 35 sq. ft. = area of window; 35 × 2 = 70 sq. ft. = area of windows. 6 × 4 = 24 sq. ft. = area of glass door. 70 + 24 = 94 sq. ft. = total glass area. 960 – 94 = 866 sq. ft. of wall space to be painted.

10–(B) Each stick of margarine = $\frac{1}{4}$ lb. Each stick consists of eight sections or tablespoons. Four sections or tablespoons = $\frac{1}{2}$ of $\frac{1}{4}$ lb. = $\frac{1}{8}$ lb.

11–(D) $100 × .10 = $10.00; $100 – $10 = $90. $90 × .15 = $13.50; $90.00 – 13.50 = $76.50.

12–(E) \$1,100,500 × .07 = \$77,035; \$1,100,500 + \$77,035 = \$1,177,535 = this year's budget. \$1,177,535 × .08 = \$94,203; \$1,177,535 + \$94,203 = \$1,271,738 which is closest to Option (E).

13–(C) Let x = width of rectangle; $4x$ = length of rectangle, $x \times 4x = 324$; $4x^2 = 324$; $x^2 = \frac{324}{4} = 81$; $x = 9$ feet; $4x = 36$ feet.

14–(A) $\frac{1}{2}$ inch on scaled drawing = 3 feet of actual floor dimension. $\frac{75}{3} = 25\frac{1}{2}$ inches = 12.5 inches; $\frac{132}{3} = 44\frac{1}{2}$-inches = 22 inches.

15–(C) $\frac{1}{2} \times \frac{1}{2} \times 1 = \frac{1}{4}$ cu ft; $\frac{1}{4}$ of 62.4 = 15.6 pounds.

16–(E) If 20% are either red or green, 80% are yellow. The chance of blindly picking a yellow marble is 4 out of 5 (80%).

17–(B) 25% + 35% = 60%. 60% were 22 years old or under 22 years of age. 40% were over 22 years old. 560 × .40 = 224.

18–(A) 2 tons + 6 tons = 8 tons carried by 1 passenger and 1 freight plane. $\frac{160 \text{ tons}}{8} = 20$ pairs of passenger and freight planes needed. 20 passenger planes carrying 2 tons each = 40 tons of cargo.

19–(E) The square root of 36 = 6. Each side of the square = 6". 6" × 2 = 12". 12" × 12" = 144 square inches.

20–(D) Let x = the capacity of the tank. $\frac{1}{8}$ of x + 550 = $\frac{1}{2}$ of x.

$$550 = \frac{x}{2} - \frac{x}{8} = \frac{3x}{8}$$

$$x = \frac{8}{3} \times 550 = 1467 \text{ gallons}$$

21–(B) 1200 seconds = 20 minutes ($\frac{1200}{60} = 20$).

20 minutes = $\frac{1}{3}$ hour. $\frac{1}{3}$ of 630 = 210.

22–(C) Interval between 7:00 a.m. and 1:00 p.m is 6 hours or $\frac{1}{4}$ of a day. $\frac{1}{4}$ of 20 minutes = 5 minutes. Subtracting 5 minutes from watch reading of 1:00 p.m. = 12:55 p.m.

23–(B) 132 feet = $\frac{132}{5280} = \frac{1}{40}$ mile

9 seconds = $\frac{9}{3600} = \frac{1}{40}$ hour

$\frac{1}{40}$ mile in $\frac{1}{400}$ hour =

1 mile in $\frac{1}{10}$ hour =

10 miles in 1 hour = 10 mph

24–(B) \$18400

19300

18450

18550

17600

92300

$\frac{92300}{5}$ = 18460 or \$18,460

25–(D) If the radius of the wheel is one meter, its diameter is 2 meters. The circumference is π × diameter = $2 \times \frac{22}{7}$. The distance traveled is $35 \times 2 \times \frac{22}{7} = 70 \times \frac{22}{7} = 220$.

PART 3—READING COMPREHENSION

Key Answers

1. C	5. B	8. A	11. B	14. E	17. D	20. E	23. E
2. D	6. C	9. B	12. E	15. C	18. D	21. A	24. B
3. A	7. B	10. D	13. E	16. C	19. C	22. C	25. B
4. A							

Items Answered Incorrectly: ___; ___; ___; ___; ___; ___; ___; ___.

Items Unsure Of: ___; ___; ___; ___; ___; ___; ___; ___.

Total Number Answered Correctly: ______

Rationale

1–(C) The first sentence of the passage states that organizations must achieve coherence among the component parts to function effectively.

2–(D) The third sentence states that the bacterium that produces the toxin must be treated to temperatures that are just warm enough. The other options are not conditions necessary for the development of botulism toxin.

3–(A) The first sentence states that there is scarcely a language spoken among people that has not some representative in English speech.

4–(A) The first sentence states that the rarely seen black-footed ferret is often confused with the common European polecat. The second sentence indicates that these two mammals resemble each other in some ways.

5–(B) The first two sentences indicate that foreign ministries try to explain the viewpoints of one nation in terms understood by ministries of another in order to overcome the difficulty of one nation trying to understand the viewpoints of another.

6–(C) One ten-millionth is $\frac{1}{10{,}000{,}000}$

7–(B) The second sentence indicates that the metric system is now used in most countries of the world.

8–(A) The last sentence states that half of the programmers employed by business are promoted to their positions from within the organization without regard to education. This implies that a college degree is not needed to do programming work.

9–(B) The second sentence lists the factors which provide for a good first impression. Spacing and cleanliness of the transcript are included. None of the other options is included among the factors which make for a good first impression.

10–(D) Copying figures onto a payroll is a "very difficult seeing" task and the recommended lighting is 150 foot-candles.

11–(B) The second sentence indicates that some evidence will not be allowed in court if an arrest is not considered legal.

12–(E) The second sentence states that personal appearance is a matter of distinctly secondary importance in most positions.

13–(E) The passage states that absenteeism can be controlled, but not eliminated, by mitigating as many of its causes as possible and by increasing job satisfaction. However, remedies for absenteeism are not universally applicable.

14–(E) Although providing postal service is an important government service, it is not an aspect of the fundamental function of government as it is not protection of life and property against anti-social individuals within the country or enemies from without.

15–(C) The first sentence states that unless a sales letter is sent to people selected from a good mailing list, it will be useless.

16–(C) The third sentence states that the techniques of data processing have become highly elaborate and sophisticated with the introduction of computers.

17–(D) Nonrepetitive office work and work that is primarily mental rather than manual are more difficult to measure. The other options are repetitive or manual operations.

18–(D) The passage states that proper business forms indicate a high degree of operational efficiency; improper business forms indicate probable inefficient operations.

19–(C) The last sentence states that the method causing the lowest level of destruction should be employed in combating fires.

20–(E) The last sentence states that when the nation's business is successfully carried on, it renders public service of the highest order. This is accomplished by supplying the material needs of men and women.

21–(A) The passage states that radio enables toll road supervisors to keep in touch with their employees in the field and to receive messages themselves in their radio-equipped cars while traveling on the road.

22–(C) *Conflict* as used in the passage means competition which may be desirable or undesirable in an organization, depending upon whether it is a positive or negative factor in achieving organizational objectives.

23–(E) This is the only violation that was due to deliberate intent or to inexcusable negligence.

24–(B) The fourth sentence states that the most appealing arrangement is when the side margins are even and the bottom margin is slightly wider than the side margins.

25–(B) A misdemeanor is a crime. The other options are all minor offenses or violations.

PART 4—DATA INTERPRETATION

Key Answers

1. B	5. E	8. D	11. A	14. A	17. B	20. B	23. B
2. A	6. B	9. D	12. B	15. C	18. C	21. E	24. D
3. E	7. B	10. D	13. D	16. E	19. A	22. A	25. C
4. A							

Items Answered Incorrectly: ___; ___; ___; ___; ___; ___; ___; ___.

Items Unsure Of: ___; ___; ___; ___; ___; ___; ___; ___.

Total Number Answered Correctly: ______

Rationale

1–(B) A comparison of the number of south-bound vehicles with that of west-bound vehicles each day shows that only on Tuesday did the volume of west-bound traffic exceed the volume of south-bound traffic.

2–(A) Total vehicles recorded on Wednesday = 125 + 75 + 100 + 40 = 340. Percentage of the total vehicles recorded on Wednesday that were south-bound vehicles = $\frac{75}{340}$ = .22 = 22%.

3–(E) 60.0 – 45.5 = 14.5 lbs. difference in weight gain between the group who gained the most and the group who gained the least. As there are 10 rabbits in each group, $\frac{14.5}{10}$ = 1.45 lb. = average difference.

4–(A) The individual rabbit showing the least gain put on only 2.5 lbs. This rabbit was fed Ration A (1st column).

5–(E) The individual rabbit that gained the most put on 8.1 lbs. This rabbit was fed Ration D (4th column).

6–(B) Both Harding and Ford served for 2 years, 5 months. All the other presidents listed served for a longer period.

7–(B) Eisenhower was 62 years old when first sworn into office. He served for 8 years.

8–(D) Roosevelt served 12 years, 1 month

Truman served 7 years , 9 months

Kennedy served 2 years, 10 months

Johnson served 5 years, 2 months

Carter served 4 years

Clinton served 4 years

34 years, 22 months =

35 years, 10 months

9–(D) Adding the figures in the column "Age When First Sworn Into Office," and then dividing by the number of presidents listed will give the average age when first sworn into office.

$\frac{778}{14}$ = 55.6 years

10–(D) 1990 1435; 1980 840. 1435 – 840 = 595; $\frac{595}{840}$ = .71 = 71%.

11–(A) Increase of men (14 – 24) = 1090 – 840 = 250. None of the other options has as great a numerical increase.

12–(B)

	1980	1985	Increase
Men	4815	5305	490
Women	2085	2640	555

555 – 490 = 65. The number of women increased 65 more than that of men.

13–(D) Total # of women in 1990 = 3243

Total # of women in 1985 = 2640

3243 – 2640 = 603 = increase. 3243 + 603 = 3846 = total number of women in labor force in 1995.

14–(A) Combined area of Europe and South America = 3.75 + 7.75 = 11.5. The area of Africa is 11.5 million square miles.

15–(C) Area of Africa = 11.5 million square miles. Area of Australia = 3 million square miles. $\frac{11.5}{3} = 3.8$.

16–(E) For every year from 1988 through 1993, enrollment in social sciences was higher than enrollment in the professions.

17–(C) The number of students enrolled in the humanities was greater than the number of students enrolled in the professions by exactly 1000 in 1988, 1989, and 1993. In 1989 and 1992 the number was less than 1000. In 1991, the number was much more than 1000.

18–(C) Extending the dotted line beyond 1993, note that the enrollment in the professions one year later would be approximately 7000.

19–(A) 20% of $45,000 = $9,000.

20–(B) Food is 30%; income tax is 10%. $\frac{30\%}{10\%} = 3$.

21–(E) 30% of budget is for food.

Recreation, rent, and transportation = 5% + 20% + 5% = 30%.

None of the other options adds up to 30%.

22–(A) In 1989, 60% was spent on salaries and 30% was spent on supplies. In none of the other years was the amount spent on salaries twice that spent on supplies.

23–(B) In 1990, 50% was spent on salaries, 35% was spent on supplies and 15% was spent on equipment. In none of the other years was the amount spent on salaries equal to that spent for both equipment and supplies.

24–(D) In 1989, the percentage for salaries plus the percentage for equipment totaled 70%. It also totaled 70% in 1991. In none of the other years were the totals the same.

25–(C) 70% of $3,000,000,000 = $2,100,000. $2,100,000 divided by 100 = $21,000.

PART 5—WORD KNOWLEDGE

Key Answers

1. C	5. B	8. C	11. C	14. B	17. A	20. D	23. E
2. A	6. D	9. D	12. B	15. E	18. A	21. B	24. B
3. C	7. D	10. C	13. A	16. E	19. A	22. D	25. E
4. E							

Items Answered Incorrectly: ___; ___; ___; ___; ___; ___; ___.

Items Unsure Of: ___; ___; ___; ___; ___; ___; ___.

Total Number Answered Correctly: ______

Rationale

Review those questions you did not answer correctly and those you did answer correctly but are unsure of. Refer to any good abridged dictionary for the meaning of those words that are giving you trouble.

Developing your own list of such words and their meanings will enable you to review these troublesome words periodically. Such practice will aid materially in increasing your vocabulary and raising your scores on word knowledge.

Add to your vocabulary list whenever you come across a word whose meaning is unclear to you.

PART 6—MATH KNOWLEDGE

Key Answers

1. D	5. C	8. D	11. C	14. B	17. B	20. D	23. D
2. C	6. A	9. C	12. B	15. B	18. D	21. E	24. E
3. D	7. D	10. E	13. B	16. E	19. E	22. E	25. C
4. A							

Items Answered Incorrectly: ___; ___; ___; ___; ___; ___; ___; ___.

Items Unsure Of: ___; ___; ___; ___; ___; ___; ___; ___.

Total Number Answered Correctly: ________

Rationale

1–(D) A natural number that has no other factors except 1 and itself is a prime number. 9 is divisible by 1, 3, and 9.

2–(C) Circumference = $\pi \times$ diameter; circumference = $\frac{22}{7} \times 70 = 220$ miles.

3–(D) $5x + 3(x - 1) = 29$

$5x + 3x - 3 = 29$

$8x = 32$

$x = 4$

4–(A) $\frac{2}{7} = 2x^2$; $\frac{2x}{14} = x^2$; $\frac{2}{14} = \frac{x^2}{x}$; $x = \frac{1}{7}$.

5–(C) Squaring an odd integer results in an odd integer. Adding an odd integer to it results in an even integer. Options A, B, and D remain odd.

6–(A) $\frac{x-2}{x^2 - 6x + 8} = \frac{x-2}{(x-2)(x-4)} = \frac{1}{x-4}$

7–(D) To divide powers of the same base, subtract the exponent of the denominator from the exponent of the numerator. 10^x divided by 10^{x-y}.

8–(D) The odd integer power of a negative number is negative; the even integer power of a negative number is positive.

9–(C) $1{,}000{,}000 = 10^6$.

10–(E) $\left(\frac{2}{5}\right)^2 = \frac{2}{5} \times \frac{2}{5} = \frac{4}{25}$

11–(C) $3^n = 9$; $n = 2$; $4^{n+1} = 4^3 = 64$

12–(B) $10^{-2} = \frac{1}{10^2} = \frac{1}{100} = 0.01$

13–(B) $\sqrt{28} - \sqrt{7} = \sqrt{7 \times 4} - \sqrt{7} = 2\sqrt{7} - \sqrt{7} = \sqrt{7}$.

14–(B) $H^2 = 5^2 + 12^2$; $H^2 = 25 + 144$; $H^2 = 169$; $H = \sqrt{169}$; H = 13".

15–(B) A pentagon has 5 sides. (Number of sides – 2) × 180 = sum of angles. 3 × 180 = 540°.

16–(E) $\frac{3x}{5y} = \frac{1}{2}$; $6x = 5y$; $\frac{6x}{y} = 5$; $\frac{x}{y} = \frac{5}{6}$.

17–(B) 1 inch ≅ 2,000 feet; 1 inch ≅ 2,000 × 12 inches ≅ 24,000 inches. No other option, converted into common terms, shows a scale of $\frac{1}{24{,}000}$.

18–(D)

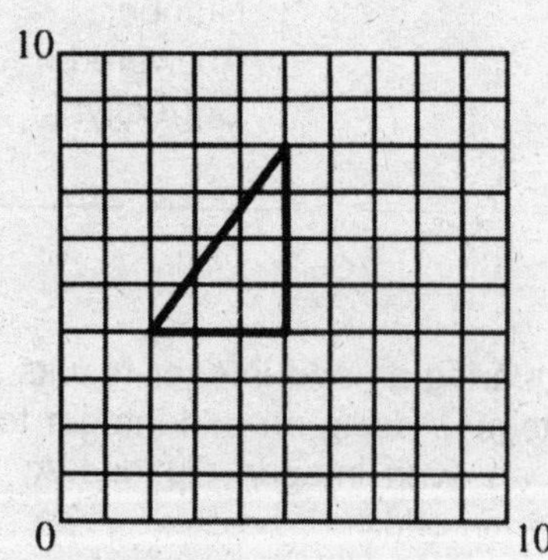

The coordinates form a right triangle with a horizontal leg of 3 and a vertical leg of 4. The distance between the two points is the hypotenuse of the right triangle.
$\text{Hypotenuse}^2 = 3^2 + 4^2 = 25$;
$\text{Hypotenuse} = \sqrt{25} = 5$.

19–(E) The base of the cylinder, πr^2, times the height, h, = volume of the cylinder.$\pi r^2 h$ is not one of the answers listed in the first four options.

20–(C) 5 × 3 = 15 which is divisible by both 3 and 5; 9, 12, 18, and 21 are not divisible by 5.

21–(E) $\frac{4!}{3!} = \frac{4 \times 3 \times 2 \times 1}{3 \times 2 \times 1} = 4$.

22–(E) The cube root of 729 is 9 (9 × 9 × 9). 9 is the square of 3 (3 × 3).

23–(D) The logarithm, 2.5464, consists of two parts. The 2 is called the characteristic; the 5464 is called the mantissa. A character of 2 indicates three digits to the left of the decimal. For example, the logarithm of 100.00 is $10^{2.00}$.

24–(E) The pattern for the arrangement is shown below:

2 4 12 48 ___

× 2 × 3 × 4 × 5

Multiplying 48 by 5, we find the correct answer to be 240.

25–(C) The first and each subsequent odd letter in the series are in regular alphabetical order skipping one letter each time: A C E G . . . The second and each subsequent even letter in the series are in straight alphabetical order: R S T . . . Accordingly, the next two letters in the series are U I.

PART 7—MECHANICAL COMPREHENSION

Key Answers

1. A	4. C	7. D	10. C	13. E	16. B	19. A
2. B	5. B	8. C	11. E	14. E	17. B	20. A
3. E	6. D	9. A	12. D	15. D	18. C	

Items Answered Incorrectly: ___; ___; ___; ___; ___; ___; ___; ___.

Items Unsure Of: ___; ___; ___; ___; ___; ___; ___.

Total Number Answered Correctly: ______

Rationale

1–(A) The teeth of gear R are not engaged with the teeth of gear S. Accordingly, gear S would not be moving.

2–(B) Note that the water outlet for water tank R is near the top of the tank, whereas the water outlet for tank S is at the bottom of the tank. Water wheel R will stop turning as soon as the water level reaches the bottom of the water outlet.

3–(E) Shaft C is at its lowest point. It will be at its highest point when shaft S makes a half-turn and will then return to its lowest point when the turn is completed.

4–(C) Although weight A is four times heavier than weight B, the radius of the outer pulley is not four times greater than the radius of the inner pulley. Accordingly, the system is not in equilibrium and weight A will slide to the left. If weight B is to slide to the right, the radius of the outer pulley must be more than four times larger than the radius of the inner pulley. This can be accomplished by either increasing the radius of the outer pulley (a cumbersome process) or decreasing the radius of the inner pulley.

5–(B) In B, each spring is supporting $3\frac{1}{3}$ pounds ($\frac{1}{3}$ of 10 pounds) and would extend a certain distance. In A, each spring is supporting 10 pounds (the full weight) and would extend three times the distance of that in B.

6–(D) The piston is now in part of the compression stroke, $\frac{1}{4}$ turn will move it to full compression; $\frac{1}{2}$ more turn will move it to the end of the power stroke. Adding $\frac{1}{4} + \frac{1}{2} = \frac{3}{4}$.

7–(D) Gear A has 15 teeth; gear B has 10 teeth. Let x = number of revolutions gear B will make. $15 \times 14 = x \times 10$; $10x = 15 \times 14$; $x = \frac{15 \times 14}{10}$; $x = 21$.

8–(C) The function of A and B in the crankshaft is to counterbalance the weight for smoother piston motion.

9–(A) Study the diagram on page 165 and note that with each complete turn of the cam, the sets-crew will hit the contact point once.

10–(C) The slowest points for lever AB are 3 and 7 where the direction reverses and the velocity momentarily becomes zero. The midpoint 5 represents the maximum speed as it is halfway between these minimum points.

11–(E) The sum of the moments must be zero. Summing around the fulcrum we have: (6 feet × 5 pounds) + (3 feet × 10 pounds) = 6 feet × F. Combining terms, we get: 60 (foot-pounds) = 6 feet × F. Dividing both sides by 6: F = 10 pounds.

12–(D) Let x = theoretical distance moved in the opposite direction. $12 \times 150 = x \times 600$; $600x = 1800$; $x = \frac{1800}{600} = 3$ feet.

13–(E) The centrifugal force acts to pull the balls outward. Since the balls are connected to a yoke around the center bar, the outward motion pulls the balls upward.

14–(E) The water is filling up the tank at the rate of 120 gallons/hour or 2 gallons/minute. The tank is also emptying at the rate of one gallon per minute. The net flow is increasing by one gallon/minute since 2 gallons/minute input – 1 gallon/minute output = 1 gallon/minute increase. NOTE: The easiest way to find the answer is to change all measurements to gallons/minute.

15–(D) One revolution of the rear wheel causes 10 teeth to rotate completely. One revolution of the front sprocket causes 20 teeth to rotate completely thereby making the 10-tooth rear sprocket revolve twice.

16–(B) The distortion of the cam causes the valve to rise when contact is made. The amount of distortion is the length *Y*.

17–(B) If pipe 2 is open while pipe 1 is closed, then the level will drop to the lowest level of 2, leaving the volume below 2 still filled as there is no way for further discharge. All other statements are true.

18–(C) Newton's law of motion states that a body at rest will stay at rest unless acted upon by an outside force. Conversely, a body in motion will stay in motion unless acted on by an outside force. In this picture, both objects are at rest (equilibrium). When an outside force is added to weight 1, the equilibrium changes, moving the weight downward. Since the pulley has practically no friction, the weight strikes the ground.

19–(A) Pulley A has the smallest circumference and therefore turns the fastest.

20–(A) Once every second = 60 times a minute. With 10 projecting rods on the wheel, the wheel must rotate at 6 rpm to make 60 rod contacts per minute.

PART 8—ELECTRICAL MAZE

Key Answers

1. B	4. A	7. B	10. B	13. C	15. E	17. A	19. B
2. C	5. D	8. D	11. A	14. D	16. E	18. A	20. A
3. E	6. C	9. E	12. D				

Items Answered Incorrectly: ___; ___; ___; ___; ___; ___; ___; ___.

Items Unsure Of: ___; ___; ___; ___; ___; ___; ___; ___.

Total Number Answered Correctly: ______

Rationale

1. **(B)**

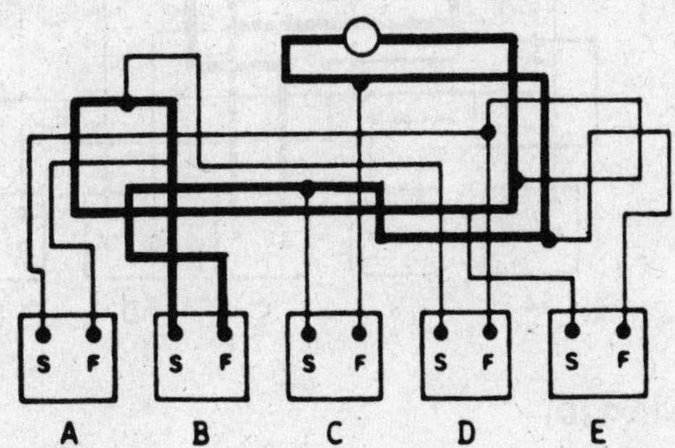

5. **(D)**

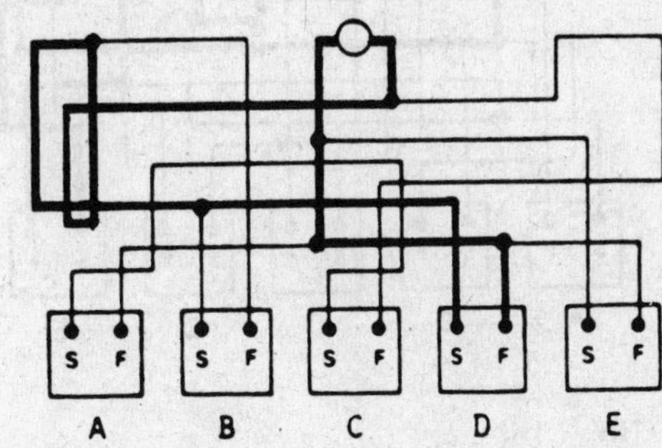

2. **(C)**

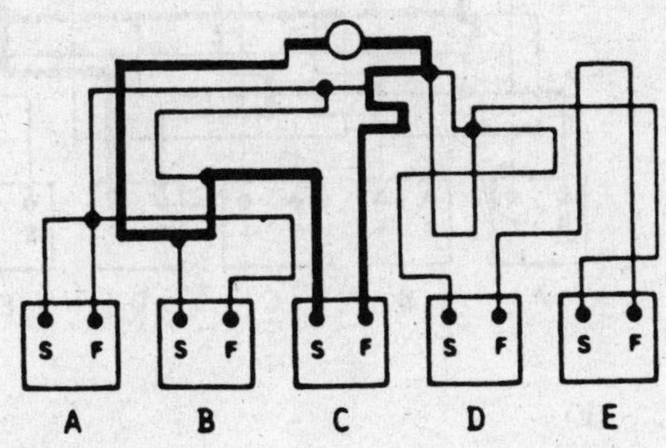

6. **(C)**

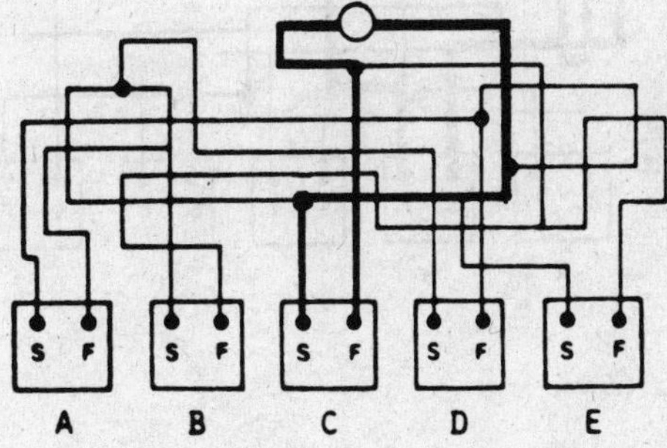

3. **(E)**

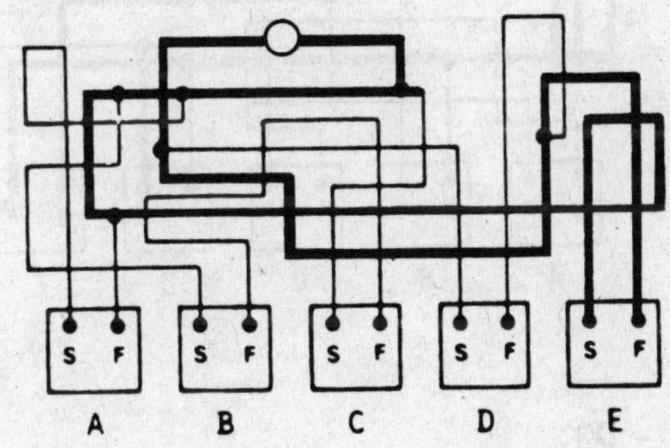

7. **(B)**

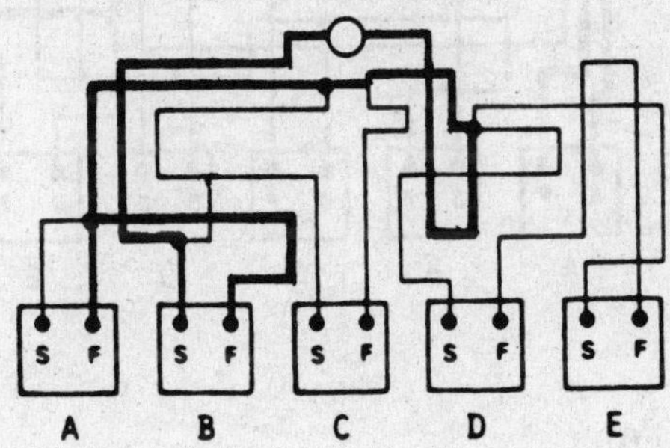

4. **(A)**

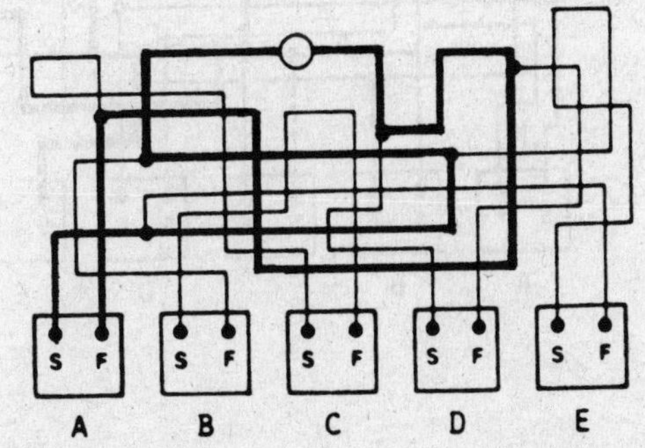

8. **(D)**

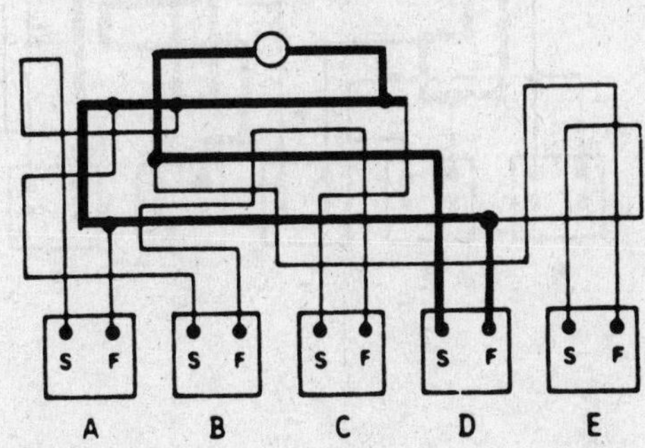

9. **(E)**

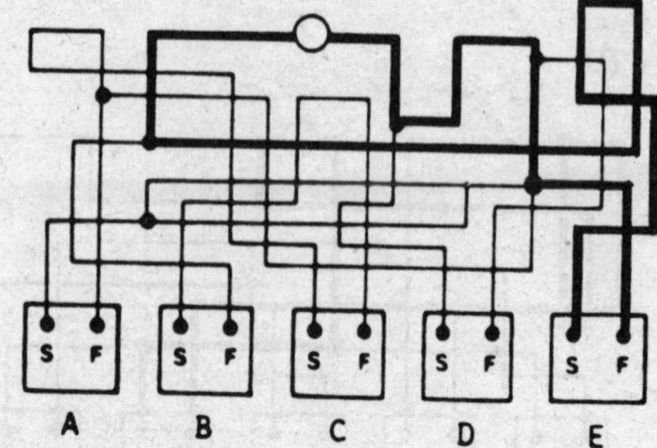

10. **(B)**

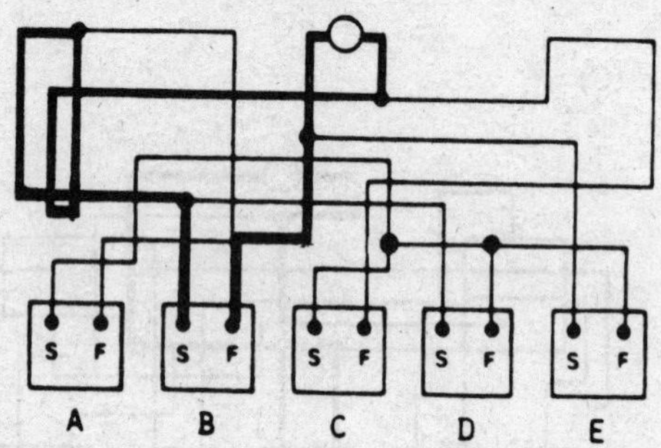

11. **(A)**

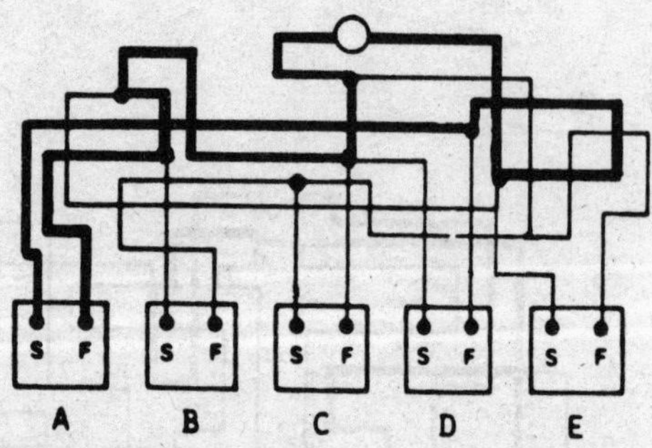

12. **(D)**

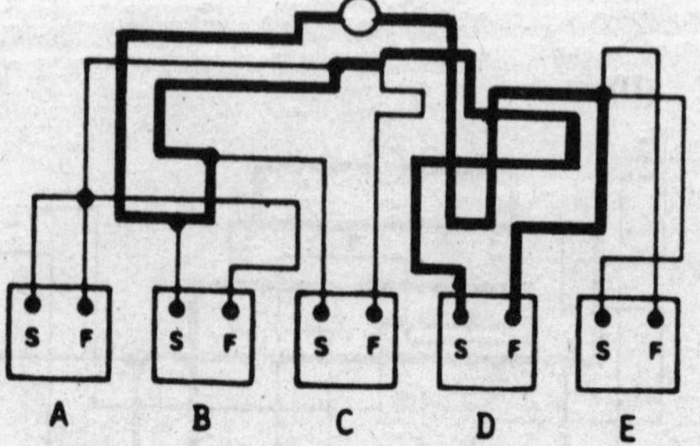

13. **(C)**

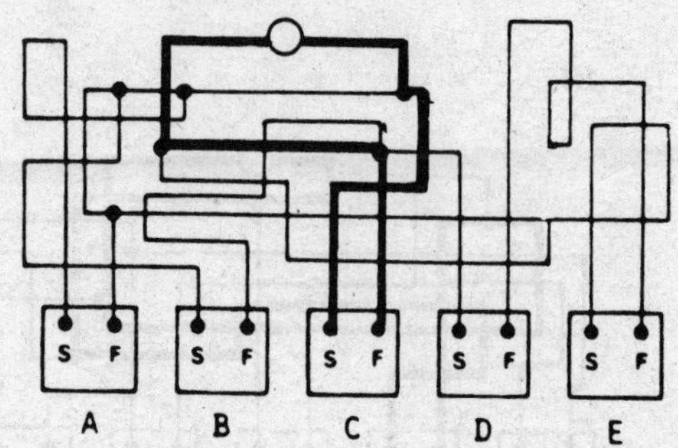

14. **(D)**

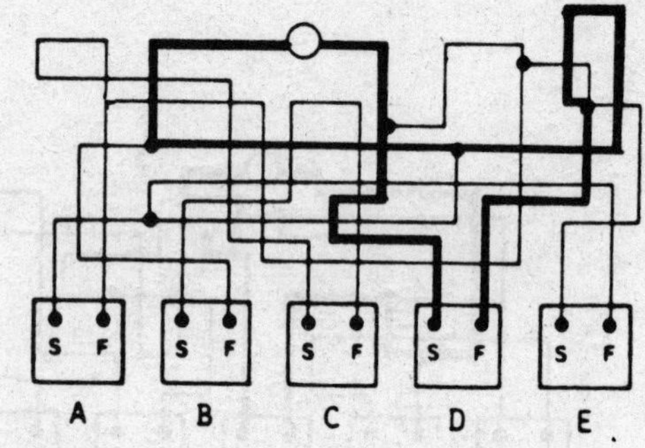

15. **(E)**

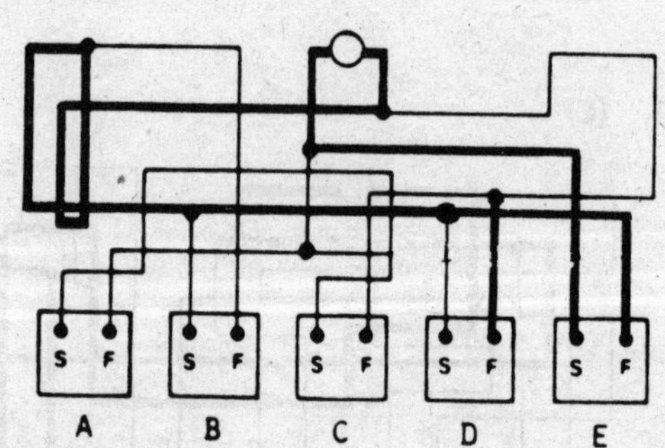

16. **(E)**

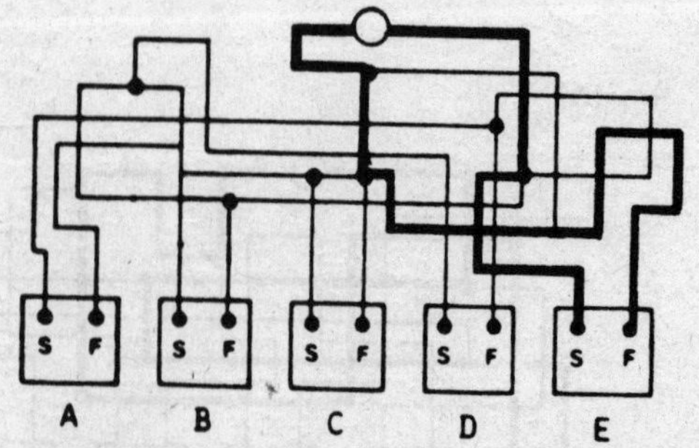

17. **(A)**

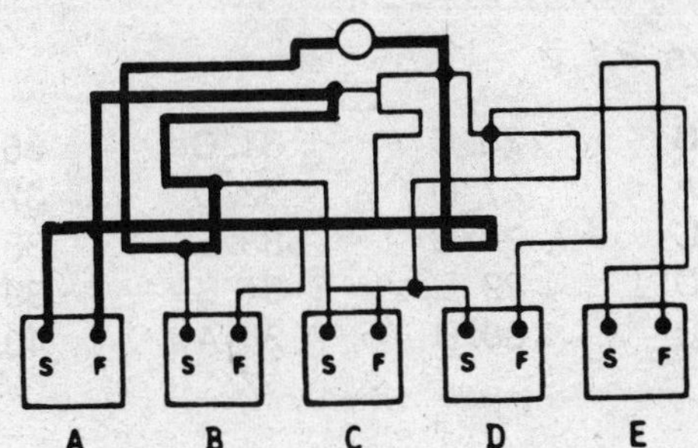

18. **(A)**

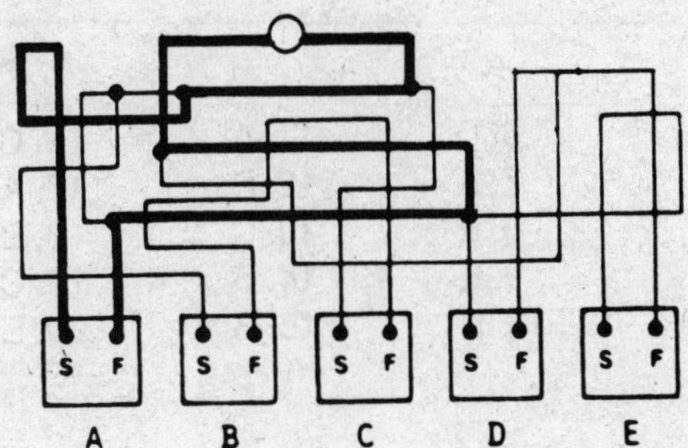

19. **(B)**

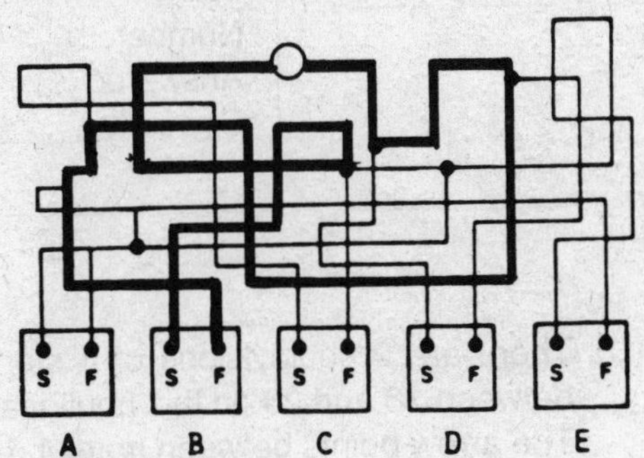

20. **(A)**

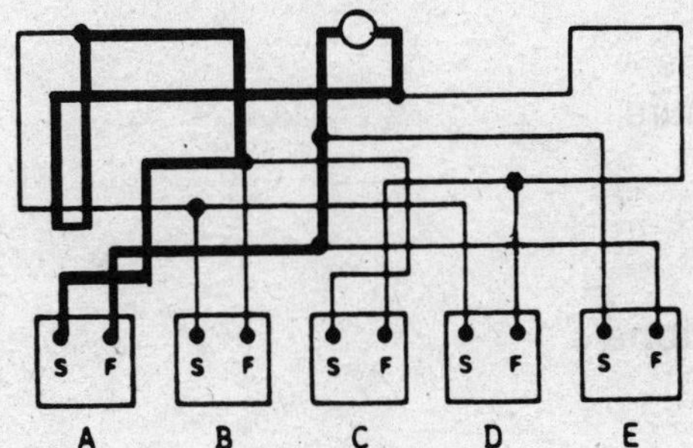

PART 9—SCALE READING

Key Answers

1. A	6. D	11. A	16. C	21. B	26. D	31. C	36. B
2. E	7. A	12. B	17. A	22. A	27. D	32. D	37. D
3. B	8. E	13. C	18. B	23. C	28. C	33. E	38. D
4. C	9. E	14. B	19. C	24. D	29. E	34. B	39. B
5. B	10. D	15. B	20. E	25. D	30. B	35. A	40. A

Items Answered Incorrectly: ___; ___; ___; ___; ___; ___; ___; ___.

Items Unsure Of: ___; ___; ___; ___; ___; ___; ___; ___.

Total Number Answered Correctly: ______

Rationale

1–(A) The scale runs from right to left. Each step is .025. The arrow points between .725 and .750, and just a little below .7375.

2–(E) The scale runs from left to right. There are 6 subdivisions of 2 steps each between 36 and 72. The arrow points just a little to the right of step marker 57 and to the left of subdivision marker 60.

3–(B) The arrow points to the marker midway between 3.25 and 3.50.

4–(C) The scale runs from right to left. There are 4 subdivisions of 4 steps each between 8 and 24. The arrow points midway between marker 18 and marker 19.

5–(B) This is a nonlinear scale—the major scale divisions are not equally spaced. There are 2 subdivisions of 4 steps each between 20 and 24. The arrow points exactly to marker 23.50.

6–(D) There are 2 subdivisions of 4 steps each between 16 and 20 on this nonlinear scale. The arrow points between marker 19.0 and 19.5 at about the midpoint. The 19.25 value is just below the midpoint on this nonlinear scale.

7–(A) There are 5 subdivisions between 1 and 2. The arrow points exactly on marker 1.4.

8–(E) The arrow points midway between marker 3.6 and marker 3.8.

9–(E) The arrow points exactly on marker 7.

10–(D) The arrow points midway between marker 9.8 and 10.0.

11–(A) There are 10 subdivisions between 0 and .1. The arrow points exactly on 0.05.

12–(B) There are 10 subdivisions between .2 and .3. The arrow points midway between marker .24 and marker .25.

13–(C) This is a nonlinear scale that runs from right to left. The arrow points exactly on marker 40.

14–(B) The arrow points directly on marker 2.5 on this nonlinear scale.

15–(B) The arrow points between marker .2 and marker .3, and is just a little closer to .3 on this nonlinear scale.

16–(C) The OHMS scale is a nonlinear scale that runs from right to left. There are 4 subdivisions of 250 ohms each between 1K and 2K. The arrow points exactly on 1250 ohms.

17–(A) There are 5 subdivisions of .02 each between .3 and .4. The arrow points exactly to .34 DC volts.

18–(B) The arrow points exactly to 3 on the AC VOLTS scale.

19–(C) The arrow points just slightly below 37 on the DC MICROAMPERES scale.

20–(E) There are 5 subdivisions of 2 ohms each between marker 0 and marker 10 on this nonlinear OHMS scale. The arrow points between marker 2 and marker 4, and is just a little closer to 4 than to 2.

21–(B) The dial readings from left to right are:

thousands - 6

hundreds - 8

tens - 7 = 6872

units - 2

22–(A) The dial readings from left to right are:

thousands - 7

hundreds - 1

tens - 6 = 7169

units - 9

23–(C) The arrow points midway between the 0 marker and the 1000 marker on the Meters scale.

24–(D) The arrow points between the 2000 marker and the 3000 marker on the Yards scale. Using the extension scale, it is ascertained that the arrow points 400 yards below the 3000 marker.

25–(D) The arrow points between the 1 statute mile marker and the 2 statute mile marker. Using the extension scale, it is ascertained that the arrow points .3 statute miles below the 2 statute mile marker.

26–(D) The arrow points between the 1 nautical mile marker and the 2 nautical mile marker. Using the extension scale, it is ascertained that the arrow points .35 nautical miles below the 2 nautical mile marker.

27–(D) The 10 kilometer marker is positioned between the 0 nautical mile marker and the 10 nautical mile marker, just slightly to the right on the midpoint. Using the extension scale, it is ascertained that the point is 4.5 nautical miles below the 10 nautical mile marker.

28–(C) The midpoint between the 10 nautical mile marker and the 20 nautical mile marker (15 nautical miles) is positioned between the 20 kilometer marker and the 30 kilometer marker. Using the extension scale, it is ascertained that this point is 1 kilometer below the 30 kilometer marker.

29–(E) The midpoint between the 20 nautical mile marker and the 30 nautical mile marker (25 nautical miles) is positioned exactly at the 30 statute mile marker.

30–(B) Ten statute miles is positioned between the 0 nautical mile marker and the 10 nautical mile marker. Using the extension scale, it is ascertained that this point is 1.75 nautical miles below the 10 nautical mile marker.

31–(C) The marker for 24,500 feet is positioned midway between 7400 and 7600 on the meter scale.

32–(D) The midpoint between the 3200 meter marker and the 3400 meter marker is positioned between the 10,500 feet marker and the 11,000 feet marker, but is slightly above the halfway point.

33–(E) The 49°C marker is positioned directly opposite the 120°F marker.

34–(B) The 0°F marker is positioned directly opposite the −18°C marker.

35–(A) The only temperature at which the Fahrenheit and the Celsius or centigrade reading are the same is at −40°.

36–(B) The arrow points to a position only $\frac{1}{4}$ the distance between marker 1.6 and marker 1.8.

37–(D) The arrow points halfway between marker 24 and marker 23.5 on this nonlinear scale. Note that the scale is compressed as the values decrease. Therefore, the arrow points to a value above 23.5 and below 24. Actually, it is approximately 23.75.

38–(D) There are 2 divisions of 4 steps each between 20 and 24 on this nonlinear scale. The arrow points to the marker with a value of 21.5.

39–(B) Each subdivision represents 0.5, however, the subdivisions are of unequal width with each subdivision being approximately $\frac{3}{4}$ as wide as the preceding one. Therefore, the scale is compressed as the values increase. Note that the distance from 0 to arrow point 39 is in the same ratio as the distance from 0 to 0.5 is to the distance from 0 to 1.0. The arrow points to the mid-value point between 0 and 0.5 or 0.25.

40–(A) The arrow points to the midpoint between marker 1.0 and marker 1.5. However, the scale is compressed as the values increase on this nonlinear scale. The value is therefore less than 1.25.

PART 10—INSTRUMENT COMPREHENSION

Key Answers

1. C	5. A	9. B	11. D	13. A	15. A	17. C	19. A
2. D	6. D	10. C	12. D	14. B	16. C	18. B	20. C
3. B	7. B						
4. D	8. D						

Items Answered Incorrectly: ___; ___; ___; ___; ___; ___; ___; ___.

Items Unsure Of: ___; ___; ___; ___; ___; ___; ___; ___.

Total Number Answered Correctly: ___

Rationale

1–(C) Nose up 40°; 90° right bank; heading 270° (west).

2–(D) Nose up 45°; 40° right bank; heading 45° (northeast).

3–(B) Nose down 45°; 45° left bank; heading 45° (northeast).

4–(D) Nose up 45°; 60° left bank; heading 315° (northwest).

5–(A) Nose up 25°; 35° right bank; heading 80°.

6–(D) Nose up 30°; 90° right bank; heading 100°.

7–(B) Nose down 40°; 15° left bank; heading 110°.

8–(D) Nose down 45°; 90° right bank; heading 270° (west).

9–(B) No climb, no dive; 45° left bank; heading 180° (south).

10–(C) Nose up slightly; 30° right bank; heading 250°.

11–(D) Nose up slightly; 80° left bank; heading 250°.

12–(D) Straight and level; heading 135° (southeast).

13–(A) Nose down 30°; 15° left bank; heading 115°.

14–(B) Nose up 20°; heading 135° (southeast).

15–(A) Nose up slightly; 15° right bank; heading 70°.

16–(C) Nose down 30°; 20° left bank; heading 150°.

17–(C) Nose up slightly; heading 45° (northeast).

18–(B) No climb, no dive; 15° left bank; heading 225° (southwest).

19–(A) Nose down slightly; heading 180° (south).

20–(C) Nose down slightly; 15° right bank; heading 90° (east).

PART 11—BLOCK COUNTING

Key Answers

1. D	4. E	7. D	10. A	13. A	15. E	17. E	19. C
2. B	5. C	8. A	11. B	14. B	16. D	18. C	20. B
3. A	6. C	9. E	12. C				

Items Answered Incorrectly: ___; ___; ___; ___; ___; ___; ___; ___.

Items Unsure Of: ___; ___; ___; ___; ___; ___; ___; ___.

Total Number Answered Correctly: ______

Rationale

1–(D) 4 on the side + 2 on the bottom = 6

2–(B) 5 on the side + 1 on the bottom = 6

3–(A) 4 on the side + 1 on the bottom = 5

4–(E) 2 on the top + 3 on the side + 3 on the bottom = 8

5–(C) 3 on the top + 3 on the side = 6

6–(C) 3 on the bottom = 3

7–(D) 1 on top + 1 on the side + 3 on the bottom = 5

8–(A) 3 on top + 1 on the side + 1 on the bottom = 5

9–(E) 3 on top + 3 on the side + 1 on the bottom = 7

10–(A) 1 on top + 1 on the side = 2

11–(B) 3 on the side + 1 on the bottom = 4

12–(C) 5 on the side + 1 on the bottom = 6

13–(A) 1 on top + 1 on the side + 3 on the bottom = 5

14–(B) 3 on top + 1 on the side + 1 on the bottom = 5

15–(E) 3 on top + 3 on the side = 6

16–(D) 3 on the side + 3 on the bottom = 6

17–(E) 3 on the top + 3 on the side + 3 on the bottom = 9

18–(C) 3 on top + 1 on the side + 1 on the bottom = 5

19–(C) 3 on top + 1 on the side = 4

20–(B) 1 on top + 1 on the side = 2

PART 12—TABLE READING

Key Answers

1. C	6. B	11. C	16. B	21. B	26. A	31. E	36. D
2. B	7. E	12. D	17. E	22. D	27. D	32. B	37. C
3. E	8. D	13. B	18. C	23. E	28. B	33. A	38. A
4. C	9. B	14. E	19. A	24. D	29. E	34. E	39. E
5. A	10. A	15. A	20. D	25. A	30. C	35. D	40. B

Items Answered Incorrectly: ___; ___; ___; ___; ___; ___; ___; ___.

Items Unsure Of: ___; ___; ___; ___; ___; ___; ___; ___.

Total Number Answered Correctly: _______

Rationale

1–(C) 32

2–(B) 29

3–(E) 27

4–(C) 35

5–(A) 26

6–(B) 148

7–(E) 131

8–(D) 184

9–(B) 97

10–(A) 224

11–(C) .03

12–(D) .04

13–(B) .07

14–(E) .05

15–(A) .04

16–(B) 8:21

17–(E) 8:16

18–(C) 8:53

19–(A) 8:27

20–(D) 8:30

21–(B) 930

22–(D) 880

23–(E) 445

24–(D) 2810

25–(A) 2050

26–(A) 3200

27–(D) 760

28–(B) 550

29–(E) 2450

30–(C) 1600

31–(E) 36

32–(B) 35

33–(A) 31

34–(E) 48

35–(D) 34

36–(D) 31

37–(C) 24

38–(A) 41

39–(E) 26

40–(B) 23

PART 13—AVIATION INFORMATION

Key Answers

1. C	4. A	7. B	10. D	13. D	15. D	17. C	19. A
2. C	5. A	8. E	11. A	14. B	16. E	18. E	20. B
3. D	6. C	9. B	12. E				

Items Answered Incorrectly: ___; ___; ___; ___; ___; ___; ___; ___.

Items Unsure Of: ___; ___; ___; ___; ___; ___; ___; ___.

Total Number Answered Correctly: ______

Rationale

1–(C) While the airplane is propelled through the air and sufficient lift is developed to sustain it in flight, there are four forces acting on the airplane. These are: thrust or forward force; lift or upward force; drag or rearward acting force; and weight or downward force.

2–(C) The top of the wing is curved while the bottom is relatively flat. The air flowing over the top travels a little farther than the air flowing along the flat bottom. This means that the air on top must go faster. Hence, the pressure decreases, resulting in a lower pressure on top of the wing and a higher pressure below. The higher pressure then pushes (lifts) the wing up toward the lower pressure area.

3–(D) The tachometer is an instrument for indicating speed at which the engine crankshaft is rotating. The other options are all flight instruments.

4–(A) In a steady flight condition, the always present forces that oppose each other are also equal to each other. That is, lift equals weight and thrust equals drag.

5–(A) A flashing green signal directed to an aircraft on the ground signals that the pilot is cleared to taxi.

6–(C) A steady red light from the tower to an aircraft in flight signals to continue circling; a flashing red light signals that the airport is unsafe for landing.

7–(B) The propeller blades, just like a wing, are curved on one side and straight on the other side. As the propeller is rotated by the engine, forces similar to those on the wing "lift" in a forward direction and produce thrust.

8–(E) When in the downward (extended) position, the wingflaps pivot downward from the hinged points. This in effect increases the wing camber and angle of attack, thereby providing greater lift and more drag so that the airplane can descend or climb at a steeper angle or a slower airspeed.

9–(B) The lift acting upward and opposing weight is called the vertical lift component. The lift acting horizontally and opposing inertia or centrifugal force is called the horizontal lift component. The horizontal lift component is the sideward force that forces the airplane from straight flight and causes it to turn.

10–(D) Stability is the inherent ability of a body, after its equilibrium is disturbed, to develop forces or moments that tend to return the body to its original position. The ability of the airplane to return, of its own accord, to its original condition of flight after it has been disturbed by some outside force (such as turbulent air) makes the airplane easier to fly and requires less effort to control.

11–(A) The elevator trim tab is a small auxiliary control surface hinged at the trailing edge of the elevators. The elevator trim tab acts on the elevators which in turn act upon the entire airplane. A downward deflection of the trim tab will force the elevator upward which will force the tail down and the nose up.

12–(E) The thrust required to maintain straight and level flight at a given airspeed is not sufficient to maintain the same airspeed in a climb. Climbing flight takes more power than straight and level flight. Consequently, the engine power control must be advanced to a higher power setting.

13–(D) The feeling of control pressures is very important in recognizing the approach of a stall. As speed is reduced, the "live" resistance to pressures on the controls becomes progressively less. Pressures exerted on the controls tend to become movements of the control surfaces, and the lag between those movements and the response of the airplane becomes greater until in a complete stall all controls can be moved with almost no resistance and with little immediate effect on the airplane.

14–(B) Heavily loaded ships require a longer ground roll and consequently much more space is required to develop the minimum lift necessary for takeoff. Similarly, takeoff in still air precludes a takeoff as nearly into the wind as possible to reduce ground roll. Accordingly, municipal airports have found it desirable to provide an unusually long flight strip to cope with such adverse takeoff factors.

15–(D) A is a no-landing portion of the runway; however, takeoff is permitted. B is the threshold line and marks the start of the usable portion of the runway for landing. Area C is not available for takeoff or landing. E is an emergency over-run only; taxi, takeoff, and landing are not allowed in this area.

16–(E) A, the no-landing portion of the runway, may be used for taxi and takeoff. E may be used only as an emergency overrun; taxi, takeoff, and landing are not allowed in this area.

17–(C) Runway symbol X is a runway marker signifying that the runway is closed.

18–(E) 17-35 runs roughly north-south. 9-27 runs west-east. The traffic pattern indicators (L,⅃) show the direction of the turns when landing on the runways. A left-hand turn is required to land on Runways 9 and 35. A right-hand turn is required to land on Runways 17 and 27.

19–(A) Runway 27 runs due west. When the wind blows through the large end of the wind cone, it causes the small end to stand out and point downward.

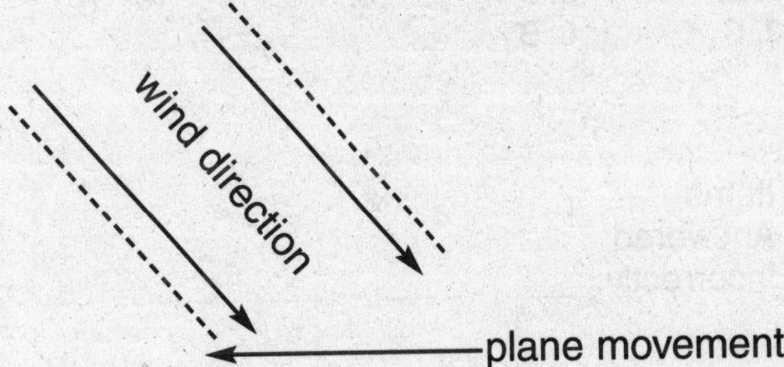

The sketch shows that the landing will be with a right-quartering headwind.

20–(B) Runways 35 and 27 are the two most desirable ones for landing as both would be with a quartering headwind. Runway 35 takes left-hand traffic; Runway 27 takes right-hand traffic.

PART 14—ROTATED BLOCKS

Key Answers

1. D	3. C	5. B	7. E	9. E	11. A	13. C	15. D
2. C	4. D	6. A	8. B	10. B	12. A	14. E	

Items Answered Incorrectly: ___; ___; ___; ___; ___; ___; ___; ___.

Items Unsure Of: ___; ___; ___; ___; ___; ___; ___; ___.

Total Number Answered Correctly: ______

Rationale

Utilization of toy blocks or modeling clay will enable you to visualize better how the views change when the blocks are rotated.

PART 15—GENERAL SCIENCE

Key Answers

1. C	4. B	7. C	9. A	11. B	13. D	15. A	18. D
2. E	5. B	8. D	10. C	12. A	14. E	16. E	19. A
3. C	6. B					17. E	20. D

Items Answered Incorrectly: ___; ___; ___; ___; ___; ___; ___; ___.

Items Unsure Of: ___; ___; ___; ___; ___; ___; ___; ___.

Total Number Answered Correctly: ______

Rationale

1–(C) When organic matter decays, it decomposes into its constituent elements. These elements are returned to the soil, thus increasing its fertility.

2–(E) The cornea, a thin clear layer, forms the front part of the eyeball.

3–(C) The extinction of all sizes and varieties of dinosaurs all over the world cannot be explained by local phenomena nor on a one-by-one basis. The most reasonable assumption is that the dinosaurs failed to adapt and were unable to survive as climatic conditions changed radically.

4–(B) Combustion is a chemical process.

5–(B) Salt contributes to high blood pressure. The critical element in the action of salt upon the blood pressure is sodium. Iodine or the lack of it plays no role in raising blood pressure.

6–(B) Protein is the chief nutrient of lean meat.

7–(C) All spiders have four pairs of legs. True insects have three pairs of legs.

8–(D) Uranium is found in pitchblende and other rare metals. Hematite is a source of iron; chalcopyrite is an ore of copper; bauxite is a source of aluminum; feldspar is a source of silicates.

9–(A) The atomic weight of hydrogen is 1.0080, that of helium is 4.003, and of oxygen is 16.00. Air is a mixture of gases, not an element. The atomic weight of nitrogen is 14.0067.

10–(C) Nitrogen constitutes about four-fifths of the atmosphere by volume. Oxygen is the most plentiful gas on earth, but not in the air.

11–(B) Light travels at the rate of 186,300 miles a second. The sun is 92,900,000 miles from the earth, so its light arrives here in just over 8 minutes.

12–(A) Cirrus clouds occur at 20,000 to 40,000 feet and are made up of ice crystals. Nimbus clouds are gray rain clouds; cumulus clouds are fluffy white clouds; stratus clouds are long, low clouds, generally at altitudes of 2,000 to 7,000 feet; altostratus clouds are at intermediate heights.

13–(D) Group B served as the control group. If the condition of patients in Group A were to improve significantly more than that of patients in Group B, scientists might have reason to believe in the effectiveness of the drug.

14–(E) The freezing point of a solution is generally lower than that of the pure solvent. In extreme cold weather, salt is placed on iced sidewalks to aid in melting the ice.

15–(A) Radiation cannot pass through lead.

16–(E) Ball-and-socket joints permit movement in almost all directions. The shoulder joint is a ball-and-socket joint.

17–(E) Scurvy is a disease caused by a vitamin C deficiency. Limes are rich in vitamin C.

18–(D) The earth rotates 360° in 24 hours; therefore it rotates 45° in three hours.

19–(A) Mercury is closest to the sun, therefore it has the shortest revolutionary period around the sun.

20–(D) An electron is a negative particle. A proton is positively charged; a neutron is neutral and without charge: a meson has both positive and negative charges. An isotope is an atom of the same element but with a different number of neutrons.

PART 16—HIDDEN FIGURES

Key Answers

1. A	3. E	5. C	7. E	9. A	11. B	13. E	15. D
2. A	4. D	6. D	8. B	10. B	12. A	14. C	

Items Answered Incorrectly: ___; ___; ___; ___; ___; ___; ___; ___.

Items Unsure Of: ___; ___; ___; ___; ___; ___; ___; ___.

Total Number Answered Correctly: ______

Rationale

1. (A)

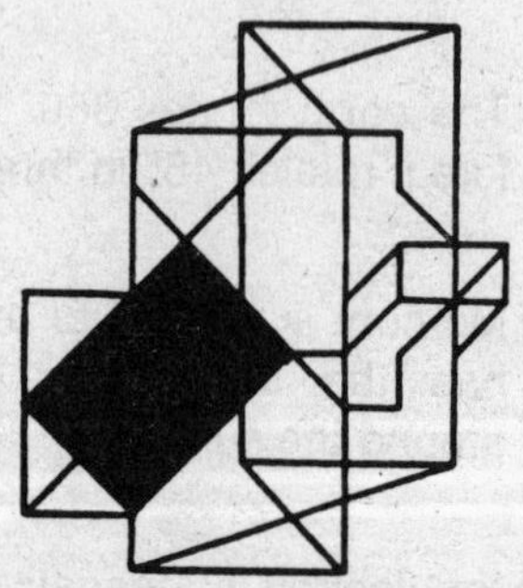

3. (E)

2. (A)

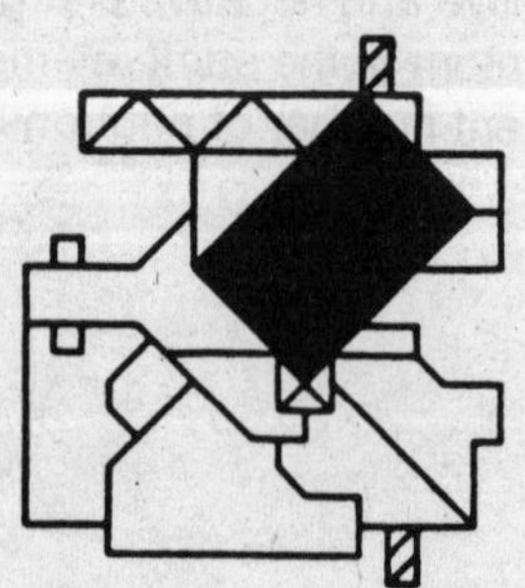

4. (D)

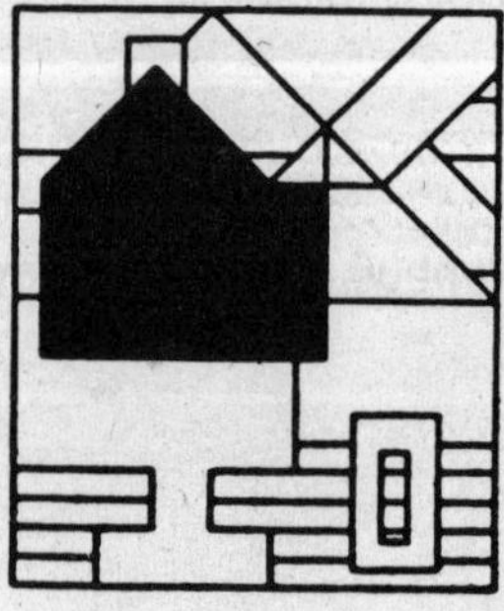

5. **(C)**

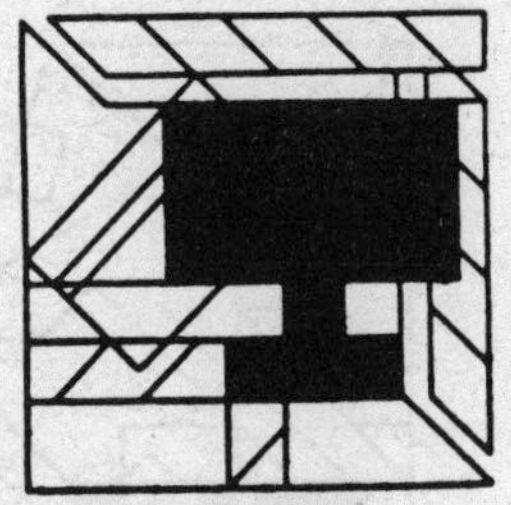

6. **(D)**

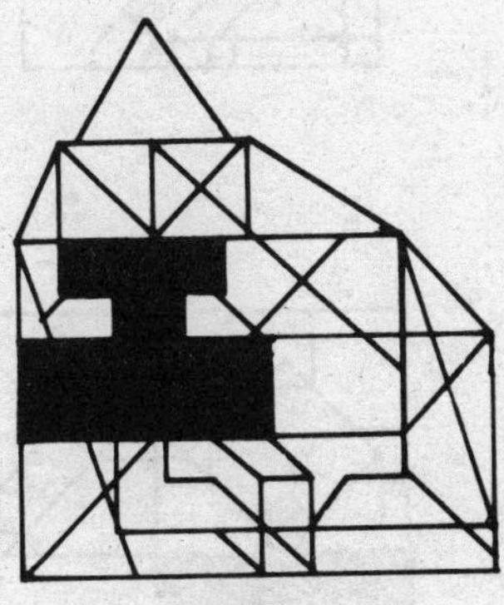

7. **(E)**

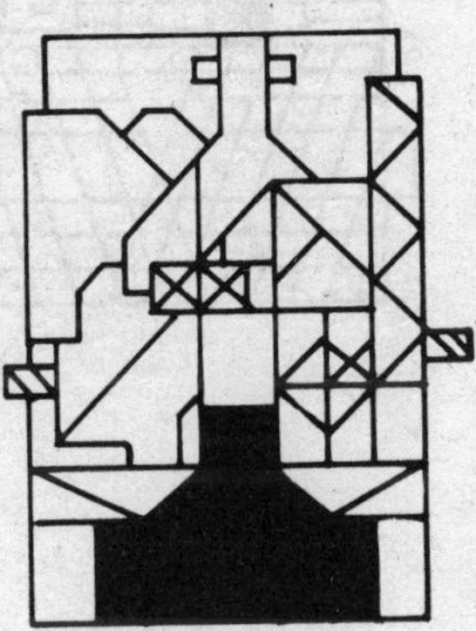

8. **(B)**

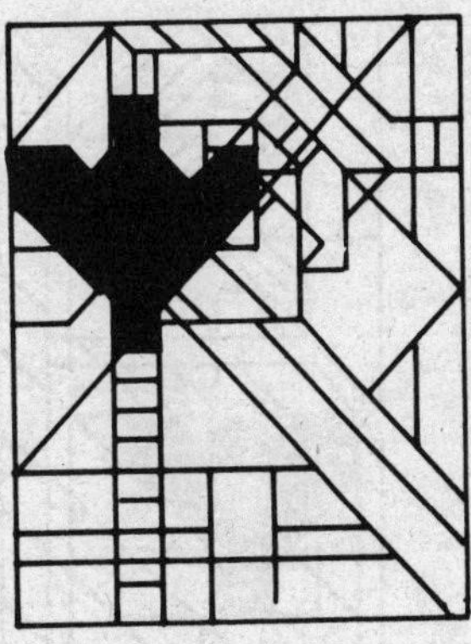

9. **(A)**

10. **(B)**

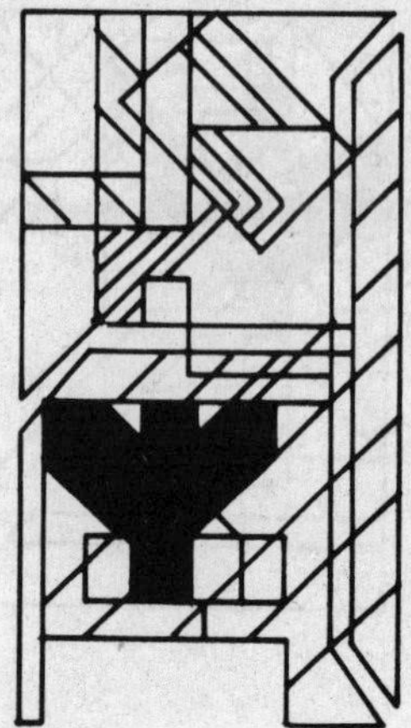

13. **(E)**

11. **(B)**

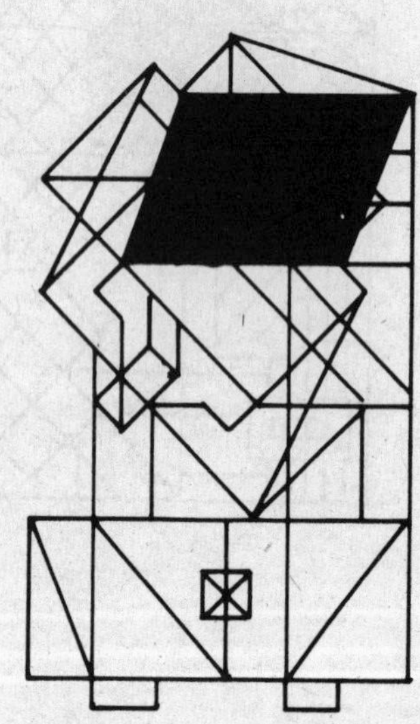

14. **(C)**

12. **(A)**

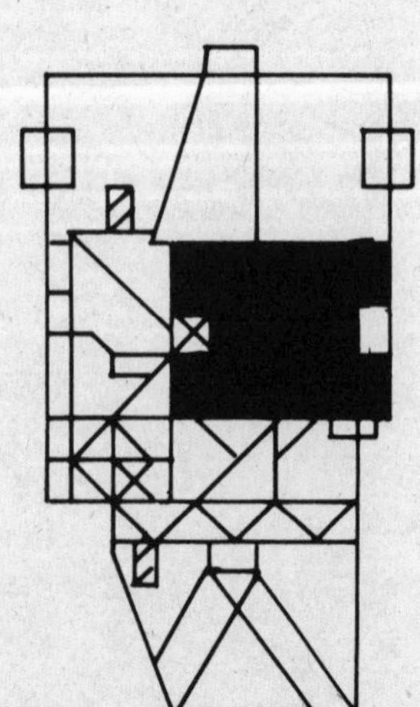

15. **(D)**

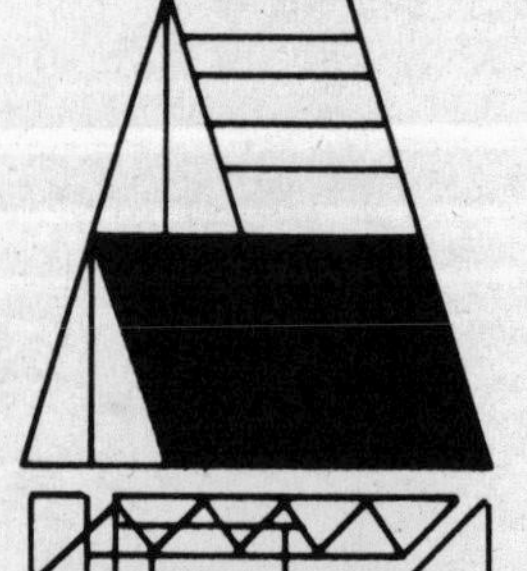

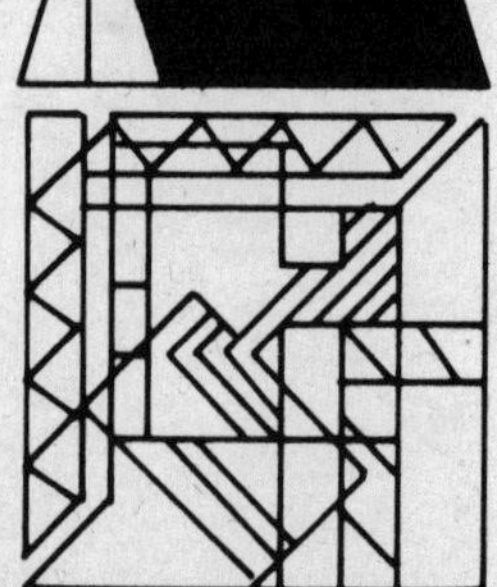

Part 5

Sample Army Alternate Flight Aptitude Selection Test [AFAST]

SAMPLE ARMY ALTERNATE FLIGHT APTITUDE SELECTION TEST [AFAST]

This part contains specimen answer sheets for use in answering the questions on each subtest, a specimen Alternate Flight Aptitude Selection Test, key answers for determining your scores on these subtests, and the rationale or explanation for each key answer.

Remove the specimen answer sheets on the following pages for use in recording your answers to the test questions. The specimen Alternate Flight Aptitude Selection Test is similar in format and content to the actual Alternate Flight Aptitude Selection Test. Take this test under “real” test conditions. Time each subtest carefully.

Use the key answers to obtain your subtest scores and to evaluate your performance on each subtest. Record the number of items you answered correctly, as well as the number of each item you answered incorrectly or wish to review, in the space provided below the key answers for each subtest.

Be certain to review carefully and understand the explanations for the answers to all questions you answered incorrectly and for each of the questions which you answered correctly but are unsure of. This is absolutely essential in order to acquire the knowledge and expertise necessary to obtain the maximum scores possible on the subtests of the real Alternate Flight Aptitude Selection Test.

The introductory material for general orientation, as well as the general directions for taking the test, appears before the actual test questions. It is not included in this specimen test because much of this material was covered previously in this book.

Format of the AFAST

Subtest	Minutes	Questions
1. Background Information Form	10	25
2. Instrument Comprehension	5	15
3. Complex Movements	5	30
4. Helicopter Knowledge	10	20
5. Cyclic Orientation	5	15
6. Mechanical Functions	10	20
7. Self-Description Form	25	75

SCHEMATIC SAMPLE

B. YOUR NAME

[A] [B] [C] [D] [E] [F] [G] [H] [I] [J] [K] [L] [M] [N] [O] [P] [Q] [R] [S] [T] [U] [V] [W] [X] [Y] [Z]

C. EXAMINEE STATUS

Civilian ◯ Officer ◯ ROTC ◯ Enlisted ◯

E. DATE OF BIRTH

DAY MO. YR.

[0] [1] [2] [3] [4] [5] [6] [7] [8] [9]

D. YOUR SOCIAL SECURITY ACCOUNT NUMBER

[0] [1] [2] [3] [4] [5] [6] [7] [8] [9]

LEAVE BLANK

F. Station Code

[0] [1] [2] [3] [4] [5] [6] [7] [8] [9]

A. AFAST IDENTIFICATION BLANK

1. SIGNATURE ____________________

2. Sex Male ◯ Female ◯

3. GRADE or RANK ____________ 4. DATE ____________ (Day) (Month) (Year)

5. RACIAL/ETHNIC GROUP

American Indian ◯ Black ◯ White ◯ Asian American ◯ Spanish Heritage ◯ Other ◯

6. MILITARY ORGANIZATION ____________________

7. INSTALLATION OR PLACE OF TESTING ____________________

T1. BACKGROUND INFORMATION FORM

1. Ⓐ Ⓑ Ⓒ Ⓓ Ⓔ	2. Ⓐ Ⓑ Ⓒ Ⓓ Ⓔ	3. Ⓐ Ⓑ Ⓒ Ⓓ Ⓔ	4. Ⓐ Ⓑ Ⓒ Ⓓ Ⓔ	5. Ⓐ Ⓑ Ⓒ Ⓓ Ⓔ
6. Ⓐ Ⓑ Ⓒ Ⓓ Ⓔ	7. Ⓐ Ⓑ Ⓒ Ⓓ Ⓔ	8. Ⓐ Ⓑ Ⓒ Ⓓ Ⓔ	9. Ⓐ Ⓑ Ⓒ Ⓓ Ⓔ	10. Ⓐ Ⓑ Ⓒ Ⓓ Ⓔ
11. Ⓐ Ⓑ Ⓒ Ⓓ Ⓔ	12. Ⓐ Ⓑ Ⓒ Ⓓ Ⓔ	13. Ⓐ Ⓑ Ⓒ Ⓓ Ⓔ	14. Ⓐ Ⓑ Ⓒ Ⓓ Ⓔ	15. Ⓐ Ⓑ Ⓒ Ⓓ Ⓔ
16. Ⓐ Ⓑ Ⓒ Ⓓ Ⓔ	17. Ⓐ Ⓑ Ⓒ Ⓓ Ⓔ	18. Ⓐ Ⓑ Ⓒ Ⓓ Ⓔ	19. Ⓐ Ⓑ Ⓒ Ⓓ Ⓔ	20. Ⓐ Ⓑ Ⓒ Ⓓ Ⓔ
21. Ⓐ Ⓑ Ⓒ Ⓓ Ⓔ	22. Ⓐ Ⓑ Ⓒ Ⓓ Ⓔ	23. Ⓐ Ⓑ Ⓒ Ⓓ Ⓔ	24. Ⓐ Ⓑ Ⓒ Ⓓ Ⓔ	25. Ⓐ Ⓑ Ⓒ Ⓓ Ⓔ

T2. INSTRUMENT COMPREHENSION

26. Ⓐ Ⓑ Ⓒ Ⓓ Ⓔ	27. Ⓐ Ⓑ Ⓒ Ⓓ Ⓔ	28. Ⓐ Ⓑ Ⓒ Ⓓ Ⓔ	29. Ⓐ Ⓑ Ⓒ Ⓓ Ⓔ	30. Ⓐ Ⓑ Ⓒ Ⓓ Ⓔ
31. Ⓐ Ⓑ Ⓒ Ⓓ Ⓔ	32. Ⓐ Ⓑ Ⓒ Ⓓ Ⓔ	33. Ⓐ Ⓑ Ⓒ Ⓓ Ⓔ	34. Ⓐ Ⓑ Ⓒ Ⓓ Ⓔ	35. Ⓐ Ⓑ Ⓒ Ⓓ Ⓔ
36. Ⓐ Ⓑ Ⓒ Ⓓ Ⓔ	37. Ⓐ Ⓑ Ⓒ Ⓓ Ⓔ	38. Ⓐ Ⓑ Ⓒ Ⓓ Ⓔ	39. Ⓐ Ⓑ Ⓒ Ⓓ Ⓔ	40. Ⓐ Ⓑ Ⓒ Ⓓ Ⓔ

T3. COMPLEX MOVEMENTS

PRACTICE QUESTIONS

1. Ⓐ Ⓑ Ⓒ Ⓓ Ⓔ	2. Ⓐ Ⓑ Ⓒ Ⓓ Ⓔ	3. Ⓐ Ⓑ Ⓒ Ⓓ Ⓔ	4. Ⓐ Ⓑ Ⓒ Ⓓ Ⓔ	5. Ⓐ Ⓑ Ⓒ Ⓓ Ⓔ

41. Ⓐ Ⓑ Ⓒ Ⓓ Ⓔ	42. Ⓐ Ⓑ Ⓒ Ⓓ Ⓔ	43. Ⓐ Ⓑ Ⓒ Ⓓ Ⓔ	44. Ⓐ Ⓑ Ⓒ Ⓓ Ⓔ	45. Ⓐ Ⓑ Ⓒ Ⓓ Ⓔ
46. Ⓐ Ⓑ Ⓒ Ⓓ Ⓔ	47. Ⓐ Ⓑ Ⓒ Ⓓ Ⓔ	48. Ⓐ Ⓑ Ⓒ Ⓓ Ⓔ	49. Ⓐ Ⓑ Ⓒ Ⓓ Ⓔ	50. Ⓐ Ⓑ Ⓒ Ⓓ Ⓔ
51. Ⓐ Ⓑ Ⓒ Ⓓ Ⓔ	52. Ⓐ Ⓑ Ⓒ Ⓓ Ⓔ	53. Ⓐ Ⓑ Ⓒ Ⓓ Ⓔ	54. Ⓐ Ⓑ Ⓒ Ⓓ Ⓔ	55. Ⓐ Ⓑ Ⓒ Ⓓ Ⓔ
56. Ⓐ Ⓑ Ⓒ Ⓓ Ⓔ	57. Ⓐ Ⓑ Ⓒ Ⓓ Ⓔ	58. Ⓐ Ⓑ Ⓒ Ⓓ Ⓔ	59. Ⓐ Ⓑ Ⓒ Ⓓ Ⓔ	60. Ⓐ Ⓑ Ⓒ Ⓓ Ⓔ
61. Ⓐ Ⓑ Ⓒ Ⓓ Ⓔ	62. Ⓐ Ⓑ Ⓒ Ⓓ Ⓔ	63. Ⓐ Ⓑ Ⓒ Ⓓ Ⓔ	64. Ⓐ Ⓑ Ⓒ Ⓓ Ⓔ	65. Ⓐ Ⓑ Ⓒ Ⓓ Ⓔ
66. Ⓐ Ⓑ Ⓒ Ⓓ Ⓔ	67. Ⓐ Ⓑ Ⓒ Ⓓ Ⓔ	68. Ⓐ Ⓑ Ⓒ Ⓓ Ⓔ	69. Ⓐ Ⓑ Ⓒ Ⓓ Ⓔ	70. Ⓐ Ⓑ Ⓒ Ⓓ Ⓔ

SCHEMATIC SAMPLE

T4. HELICOPTER KNOWLEDGE

71. Ⓐ Ⓑ Ⓒ Ⓓ Ⓔ 72. Ⓐ Ⓑ Ⓒ Ⓓ Ⓔ 73. Ⓐ Ⓑ Ⓒ Ⓓ Ⓔ 74. Ⓐ Ⓑ Ⓒ Ⓓ Ⓔ 75. Ⓐ Ⓑ Ⓒ Ⓓ Ⓔ
76. Ⓐ Ⓑ Ⓒ Ⓓ Ⓔ 77. Ⓐ Ⓑ Ⓒ Ⓓ Ⓔ 78. Ⓐ Ⓑ Ⓒ Ⓓ Ⓔ 79. Ⓐ Ⓑ Ⓒ Ⓓ Ⓔ 80. Ⓐ Ⓑ Ⓒ Ⓓ Ⓔ
81. Ⓐ Ⓑ Ⓒ Ⓓ Ⓔ 82. Ⓐ Ⓑ Ⓒ Ⓓ Ⓔ 83. Ⓐ Ⓑ Ⓒ Ⓓ Ⓔ 84. Ⓐ Ⓑ Ⓒ Ⓓ Ⓔ 85. Ⓐ Ⓑ Ⓒ Ⓓ Ⓔ
86. Ⓐ Ⓑ Ⓒ Ⓓ Ⓔ 87. Ⓐ Ⓑ Ⓒ Ⓓ Ⓔ 88. Ⓐ Ⓑ Ⓒ Ⓓ Ⓔ 89. Ⓐ Ⓑ Ⓒ Ⓓ Ⓔ 90. Ⓐ Ⓑ Ⓒ Ⓓ Ⓔ

T5. CYCLIC ORIENTATION

91. 92. 93. 94. 95. 96. 97. 98.
99. 100. 101. 102. 103. 104. 105.

T6. MECHANICAL FUNCTIONS

106. Ⓐ Ⓑ 107. Ⓐ Ⓑ 108. Ⓐ Ⓑ 109. Ⓐ Ⓑ 110. Ⓐ Ⓑ 111. Ⓐ Ⓑ 112. Ⓐ Ⓑ 113. Ⓐ Ⓑ 114. Ⓐ Ⓑ 115. Ⓐ Ⓑ
116. Ⓐ Ⓑ 117. Ⓐ Ⓑ 118. Ⓐ Ⓑ 119. Ⓐ Ⓑ 120. Ⓐ Ⓑ 121. Ⓐ Ⓑ 122. Ⓐ Ⓑ 123. Ⓐ Ⓑ 124. Ⓐ Ⓑ 125. Ⓐ Ⓑ

T7. SELF-DESCRIPTION FORM

SECTION A

126. Ⓐ Ⓑ Ⓒ Ⓓ Ⓔ 127. Ⓐ Ⓑ Ⓒ Ⓓ Ⓔ 128. Ⓐ Ⓑ Ⓒ Ⓓ Ⓔ 129. Ⓐ Ⓑ Ⓒ Ⓓ Ⓔ 130. Ⓐ Ⓑ Ⓒ Ⓓ Ⓔ
131. Ⓐ Ⓑ Ⓒ Ⓓ Ⓔ 132. Ⓐ Ⓑ Ⓒ Ⓓ Ⓔ 133. Ⓐ Ⓑ Ⓒ Ⓓ Ⓔ 134. Ⓐ Ⓑ Ⓒ Ⓓ Ⓔ 135. Ⓐ Ⓑ Ⓒ Ⓓ Ⓔ
136. Ⓐ Ⓑ Ⓒ Ⓓ Ⓔ 137. Ⓐ Ⓑ Ⓒ Ⓓ Ⓔ 138. Ⓐ Ⓑ Ⓒ Ⓓ Ⓔ 139. Ⓐ Ⓑ Ⓒ Ⓓ Ⓔ 140. Ⓐ Ⓑ Ⓒ Ⓓ Ⓔ
141. Ⓐ Ⓑ Ⓒ Ⓓ Ⓔ 142. Ⓐ Ⓑ Ⓒ Ⓓ Ⓔ 143. Ⓐ Ⓑ Ⓒ Ⓓ Ⓔ 144. Ⓐ Ⓑ Ⓒ Ⓓ Ⓔ 145. Ⓐ Ⓑ Ⓒ Ⓓ Ⓔ

SECTION B

146. Ⓨ Ⓝ 147. Ⓨ Ⓝ 148. Ⓨ Ⓝ 149. Ⓨ Ⓝ 150. Ⓨ Ⓝ 151. Ⓨ Ⓝ 152. Ⓨ Ⓝ 153. Ⓨ Ⓝ 154. Ⓨ Ⓝ 155. Ⓨ Ⓝ
156. Ⓨ Ⓝ 157. Ⓨ Ⓝ 158. Ⓨ Ⓝ 159. Ⓨ Ⓝ 160. Ⓨ Ⓝ 161. Ⓨ Ⓝ 162. Ⓨ Ⓝ 163. Ⓨ Ⓝ 164. Ⓨ Ⓝ 165. Ⓨ Ⓝ

SECTION C

166. Ⓛ Ⓓ 167. Ⓛ Ⓓ 168. Ⓛ Ⓓ 169. Ⓛ Ⓓ 170. Ⓛ Ⓓ 171. Ⓛ Ⓓ 172. Ⓛ Ⓓ 173. Ⓛ Ⓓ 174. Ⓛ Ⓓ 175. Ⓛ Ⓓ
176. Ⓛ Ⓓ 177. Ⓛ Ⓓ 178. Ⓛ Ⓓ 179. Ⓛ Ⓓ 180. Ⓛ Ⓓ 181. Ⓛ Ⓓ 182. Ⓛ Ⓓ 183. Ⓛ Ⓓ 184. Ⓛ Ⓓ 185. Ⓛ Ⓓ

SECTION D

186. Ⓐ Ⓑ 187. Ⓐ Ⓑ 188. Ⓐ Ⓑ 189. Ⓐ Ⓑ 190. Ⓐ Ⓑ 191. Ⓐ Ⓑ 192. Ⓐ Ⓑ 193. Ⓐ Ⓑ 194. Ⓐ Ⓑ

SECTION E

195. Ⓐ Ⓑ Ⓒ Ⓓ 196. Ⓐ Ⓑ Ⓒ Ⓓ 197. Ⓐ Ⓑ Ⓒ Ⓓ 198. Ⓐ Ⓑ Ⓒ Ⓓ 199. Ⓐ Ⓑ Ⓒ Ⓓ
200. Ⓐ Ⓑ Ⓒ Ⓓ

SUBTEST 1 BACKGROUND INFORMATION FORM

1

a. Description—This subtest has 25 questions about your background. (Time: 10 minutes)

b. Instructions—Answer each question as accurately as you can, to the best of your ability and recollection. Skip those questions that do not pertain. The 25 questions on this subtest are all five-option items.

Sample Item:

1. What type of high school program did you take?

(A) Academic
(B) General
(C) Technical
(D) Vocational
(E) High school equivalency

If you took the academic program and graduated, select option (A). ● Ⓑ Ⓒ Ⓓ Ⓔ

If you took the general program and graduated, select option (B). Ⓐ ● Ⓒ Ⓓ Ⓔ

If you took the technical program and graduated, select option (C). Ⓐ Ⓑ ● Ⓓ Ⓔ

If you took the vocational program and graduated, select option (D). Ⓐ Ⓑ Ⓒ ● Ⓔ

If you did not graduate from high school but earned the high school equivalency diploma, select option (E). Ⓐ Ⓑ Ⓒ Ⓓ ●

When you begin, be sure to start with question number 1 on your test booklet and number 1 on your answer form.

DO NOT TURN THIS PAGE UNTIL TOLD TO DO SO.

SUBTEST 1

BACKGROUND INFORMATION

TIME: 10 minutes—25 Questions

The questions in this subtest are biographical and pertain to your general background. Answer each question to the best of your ability and recollection. Skip those questions that do not pertain to you.

1. What is your age?

   (A) Under 20 years
   (B) 20 to 23 years
   (C) 24 to 27 years
   (D) 28 to 31 years
   (E) 32 years or more

2. Where did you live most of the time before you were 20 years of age?

   (A) The Northeast region of the United States
   (B) The Southern region of the United States
   (C) The Central region of the United States
   (D) The Western region of the United States
   (E) Outside the continental United States

3. If foreign born, when did you come to the United States to stay?

   (A) 0–5 years ago
   (B) 6–10 years ago
   (C) 11–15 years ago
   (D) 16–20 years ago
   (E) 21 or more years ago

4. If foreign born, in which geographical area were you born?

   (A) Asia
   (B) Africa
   (C) the Americas
   (D) Europe
   (E) Australia

5. What is your parents' citizenship status?

   (A) Both are native-born American citizens.
   (B) One is native-born; the other is naturalized.
   (C) Both are naturalized American citizens.
   (D) One is a naturalized citizen; the other is a permanent resident.
   (E) Both are legally admitted permanent residents.

6. How many years of schooling did your father complete?

   (A) College graduation
   (B) Some college training
   (C) High school graduation
   (D) Some high school training
   (E) Elementary school training

7. If your father served in the U.S. Armed Forces, did he serve in the

   (A) Navy
   (B) Marines
   (C) Coast Guard
   (D) Army
   (E) Air Force

8. How many years of schooling did your mother complete?

   (A) College graduation
   (B) Some college training
   (C) High school graduation
   (D) Some high school training
   (E) Elementary school training

9. If your mother served in the U.S. Armed Forces, did she serve in the

   (A) Navy
   (B) Marines
   (C) Coast Guard
   (D) Army
   (E) Air Force

10. How many sisters and brothers do you have in your family?

    (A) 0
    (B) 1
    (C) 2
    (D) 3
    (E) 4 or more

11. How were you raised?

    (A) In a two-parent household
    (B) In a single-parent household
    (C) By relatives
    (D) By foster parents
    (E) In an institution

12. Which one of the following best characterizes the behavior of your parents toward you?

    (A) They always were very strict with you.
    (B) They usually were very strict with you.
    (C) They often were very strict with you.
    (D) They seldom were very strict with you.
    (E) They never were very strict with you.

13. In what type of community did you live most of the time before you were 20 years old?

    (A) Large city (population of more than 250,000)
    (B) Small city (population of less than 250,000)
    (C) Suburb of the city
    (D) Town or village
    (E) Rural community

14. Which of the following types of high schools did you attend?

    (A) Public, academic
    (B) Public, vocational
    (C) Private, parochial
    (D) Private, non-parochial
    (E) Military

15. How old were you when you were graduated from high school?

    (A) 16 years or less
    (B) 17
    (C) 18
    (D) 19
    (E) 20 or more years

16. How many years of college work have you completed?

    (A) less than one year
    (B) 1 year
    (C) 2 years
    (D) 3 years
    (E) 4 or more years

17. If you were employed on school days during the last four years of your schooling, how many hours did you work per week?

    (A) 5 or less
    (B) 6–10
    (C) 11–15
    (D) 16 or more
    (E) Did not work on school days

18. How did you usually travel to and from school during the last four years of your schooling?

    (A) Walking
    (B) Bus
    (C) Private car
    (D) Taxi
    (E) Train or subway

19. How many hours a week did you devote to volunteer work in the community during the last four years of your schooling?

    (A) 5 or less
    (B) 6–10
    (C) 11–15
    (D) 16 or more
    (E) Did no volunteer work

20. If you were a volunteer, which of the following best describes the nature of the volunteer work?

    (A) Religious
    (B) Educational
    (C) Civil or political
    (D) Charitable
    (E) Health-care-related

21. If you took the Armed Services Vocational Aptitude Battery (ASVAB), in which of the following categories did your score fall?

    (A) Category I 93rd–100th percentile range
    (B) Category II 65th–92nd percentile range
    (C) Category III 31st–64th percentile range
    (D) Category IV 10th–30th percentile range
    (E) Category V 9th percentile and below

22. If a college graduate, how old were you when you were graduated from college?

    (A) 20 years or less
    (B) 21 years
    (C) 22 years
    (D) 23 years
    (E) 24 years or more

23. What was your standing in your college graduating class?

    (A) Honor graduate
    (B) Top third but not an honor graduate
    (C) Middle third
    (D) Bottom third
    (E) Not a college graduate

24. What is your present marital status?

    (A) Married
    (B) Divorced
    (C) Separated
    (D) Widowed
    (E) Never married

25. What is your current or most recent employment?

    (A) Employee of private company, business, or individual for wages, salary, or commission
    (B) Government employee
    (C) Self-employed in own business, professional practice, or farm
    (D) Working without pay in family business or farm
    (E) Never employed

DO NOT GO ON UNTIL TOLD TO DO SO.
STOP! IF YOU FINISH BEFORE THE TIME IS UP, YOU MAY CHECK OVER YOUR WORK ON THIS PART ONLY.

2

SUBTEST 2

INSTRUMENT COMPREHENSION

a. Description—In this subtest, you will have to determine the position of an airplane in flight by looking at two dials, one showing the artificial horizon, the other showing the compass heading. From these you will determine the amount of climb or dive, the degree of bank to left or right, and the heading. Five airplane silhouettes are shown from which you will choose the one that *most nearly represents the position indicated on the dials.* There are 15 questions. (Time: 5 minutes)

b. Instructions—Below are shown two sets of dials, labeled ARTIFICIAL HORIZON and COMPASS. The *heavy black line* on the ARTIFICIAL HORIZON represents the horizon line. If the airplane is *above* the horizon, it is climbing. If it is *below* the horizon, it is diving. The greater amount of climb or dive, the farther up or down the horizon line is seen. The ARTIFICIAL HORIZON dial also has a black arrowhead showing the degree of bank to left or right. If the airplane has *no* bank, the arrowhead points to *zero.* If it is banked to the *left*, the arrowhead points to the *right* of zero. If the airplane is banked to the *right*, the arrowhead points to the *left* of zero.

Examples of the Artificial Horizon

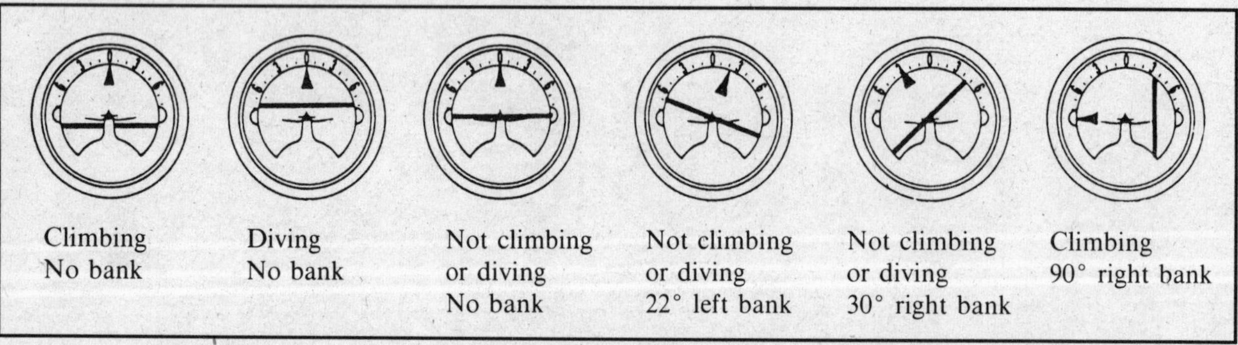

The COMPASS dial shows the direction the airplane is headed at the moment.

Examples of the Compass Dial

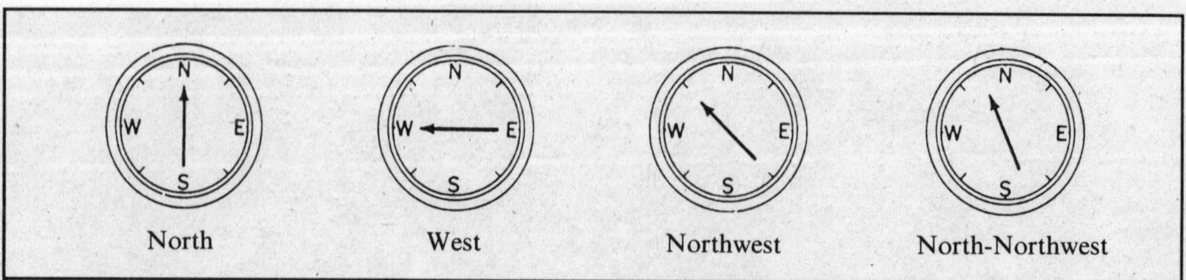

Now look at sample item X and decide which airplane is in the position indicated by the dials. You are always looking north at the same altitude as each of the planes. East is always to your right as you look at the page.

X

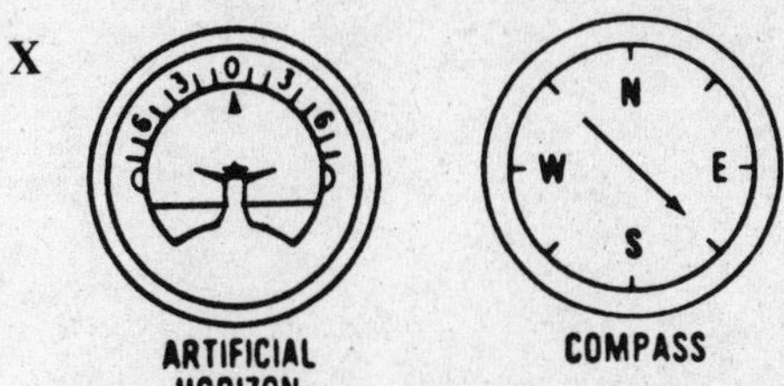

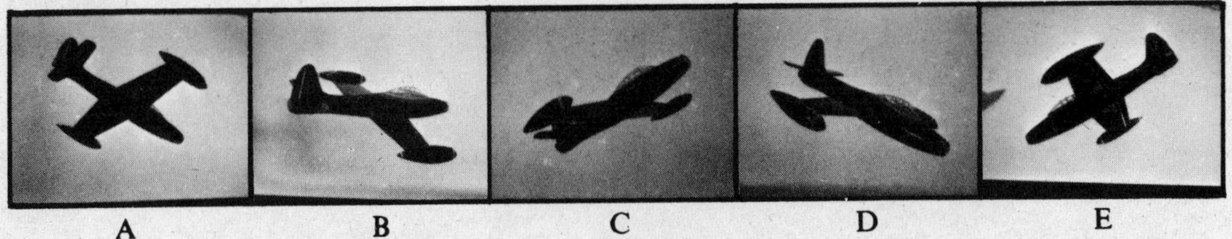

In sample item X, the dial labeled ARTIFICIAL HORIZON shows that the airplane is climbing but is not banked. The COMPASS shows that it is headed southeast. The only one of the five airplane silhouettes that meets these specifications is in the box lettered C, so the answer to sample item X is C.

When you begin, be sure to start with question number 26 on Subtest 2 in your test booklet and number 26 on your answer form. Do not spend too much time on any one question.

DO NOT GO ON UNTIL TOLD TO DO SO.

SUBTEST 2

INSTRUMENT COMPREHENSION

TIME: 5 Minutes—15 Questions

26.

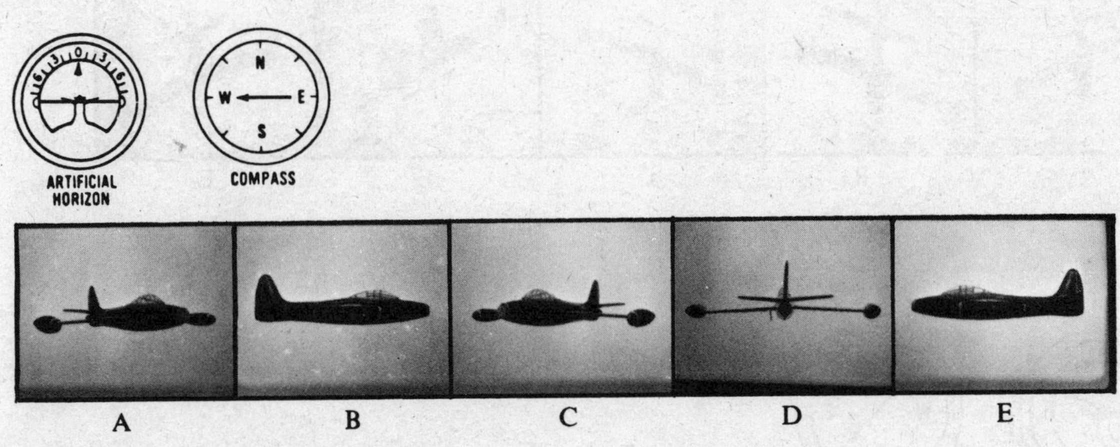

27.

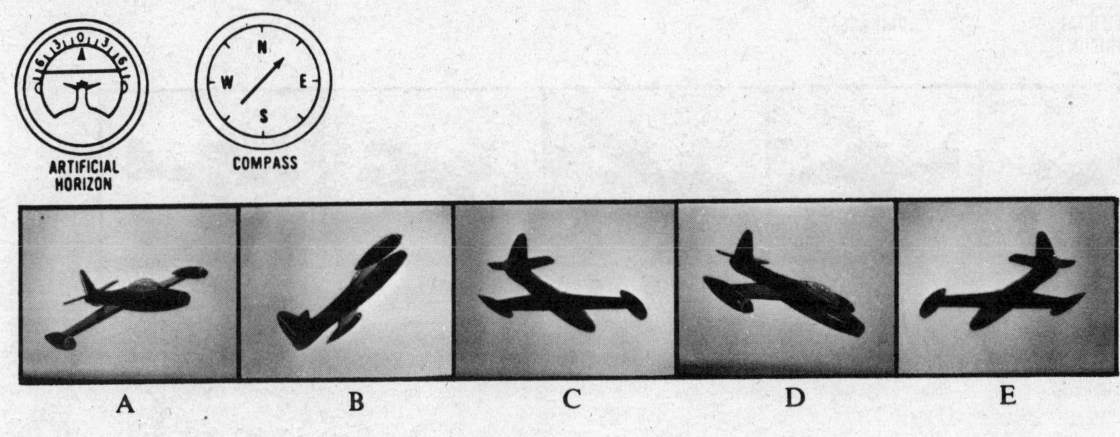

28.

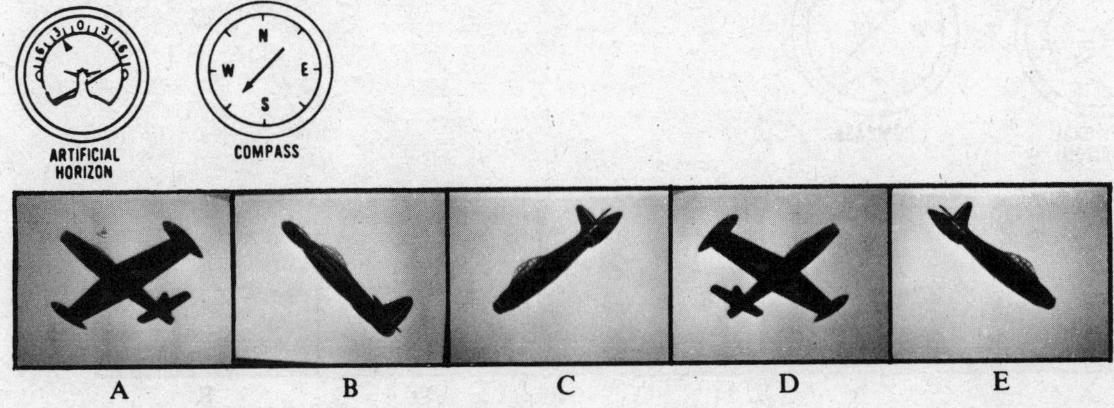

GO ON TO THE NEXT PAGE.

29.

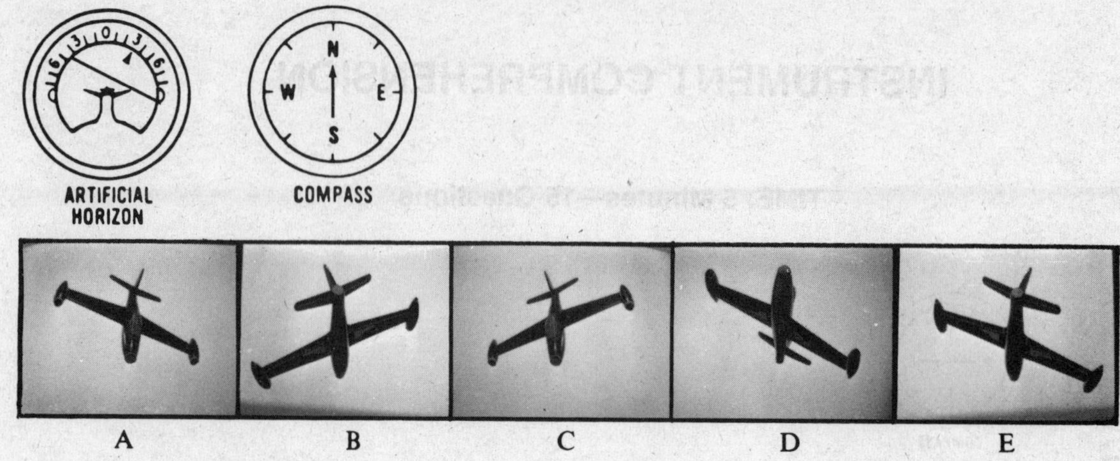
ARTIFICIAL HORIZON
COMPASS
N
E
S
W
A
B
C
D
E

30.

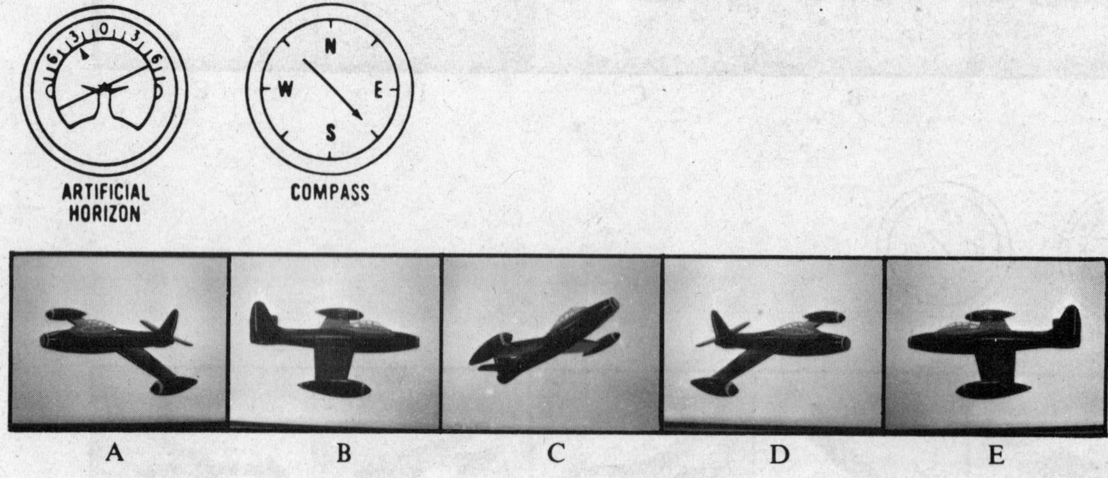
ARTIFICIAL HORIZON
COMPASS
N
E
S
W
A
B
C
D
E

31.

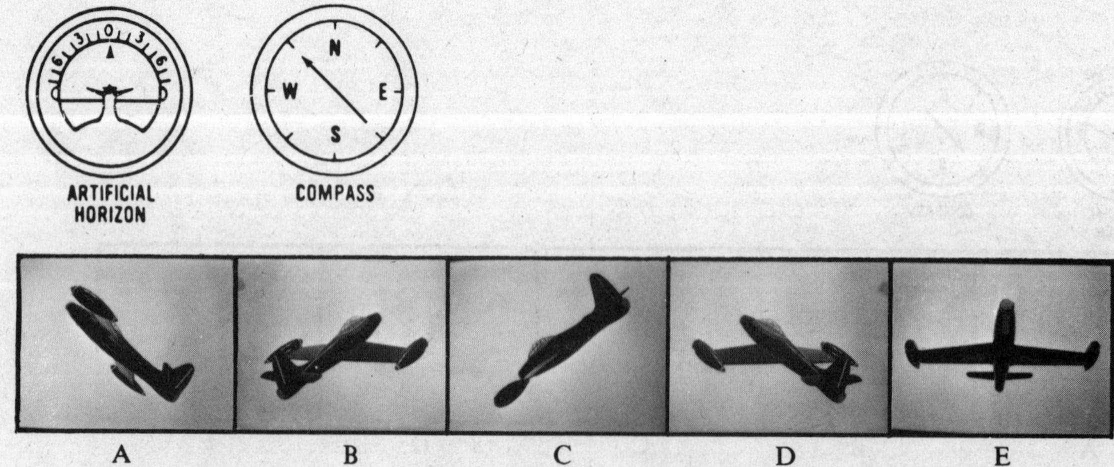
ARTIFICIAL HORIZON
COMPASS
N
E
S
W
A
B
C
D
E

32.

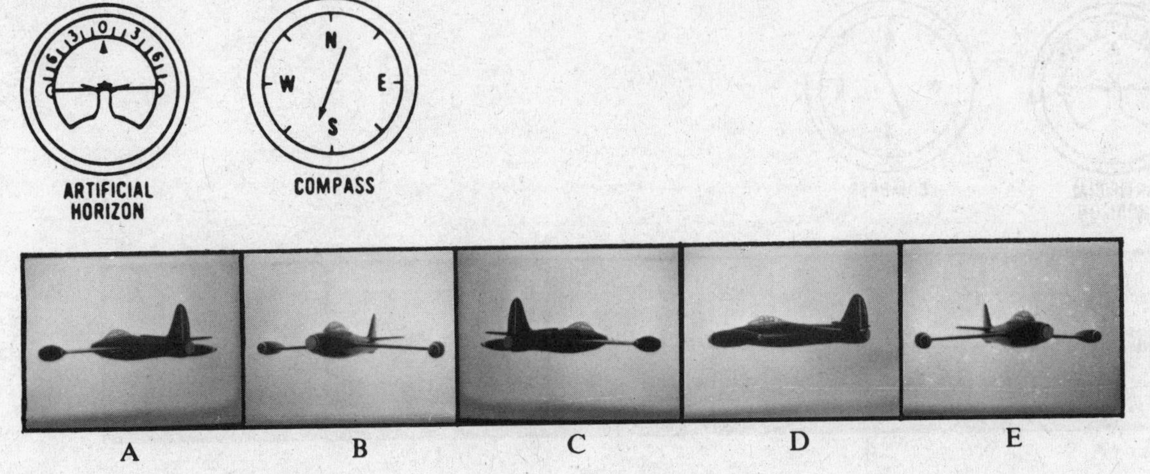

33.

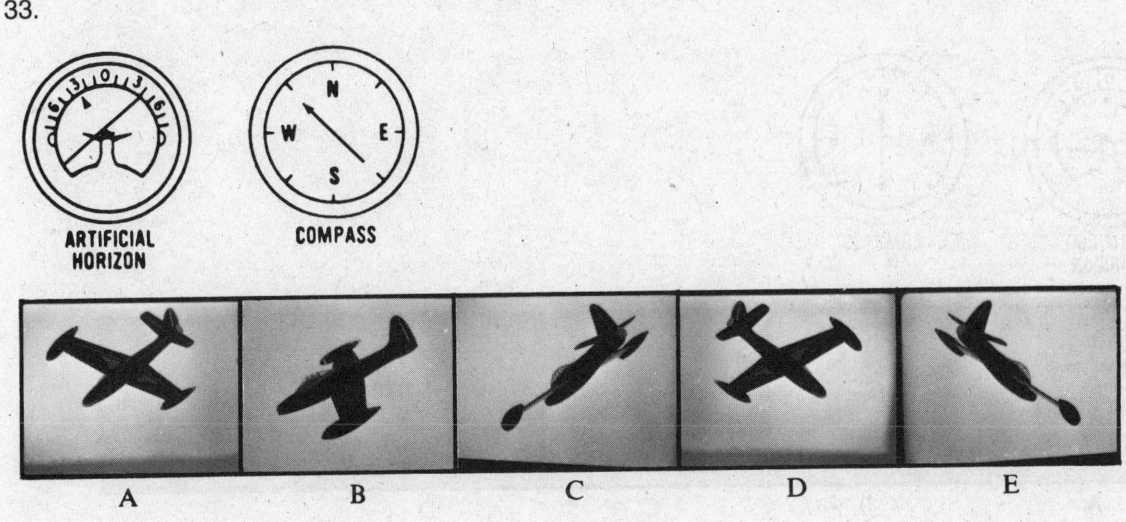

34.

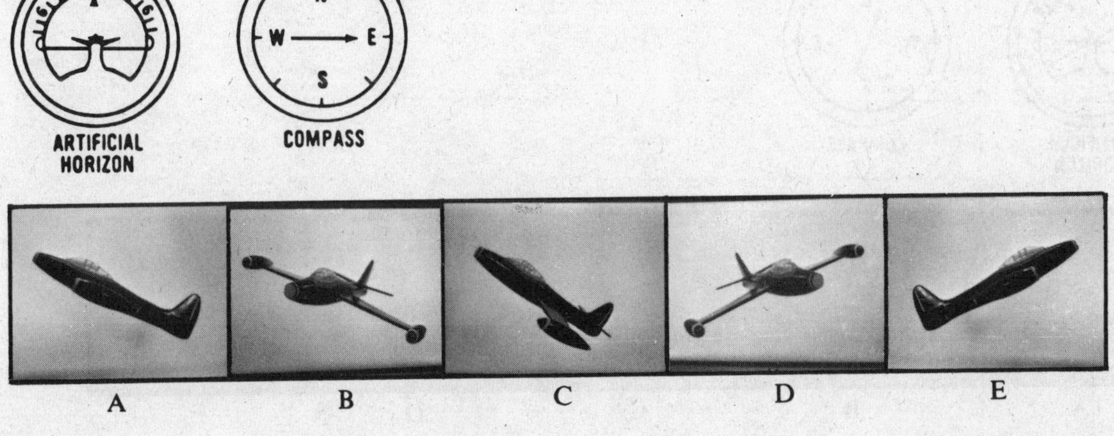

GO ON TO THE NEXT PAGE.

35.

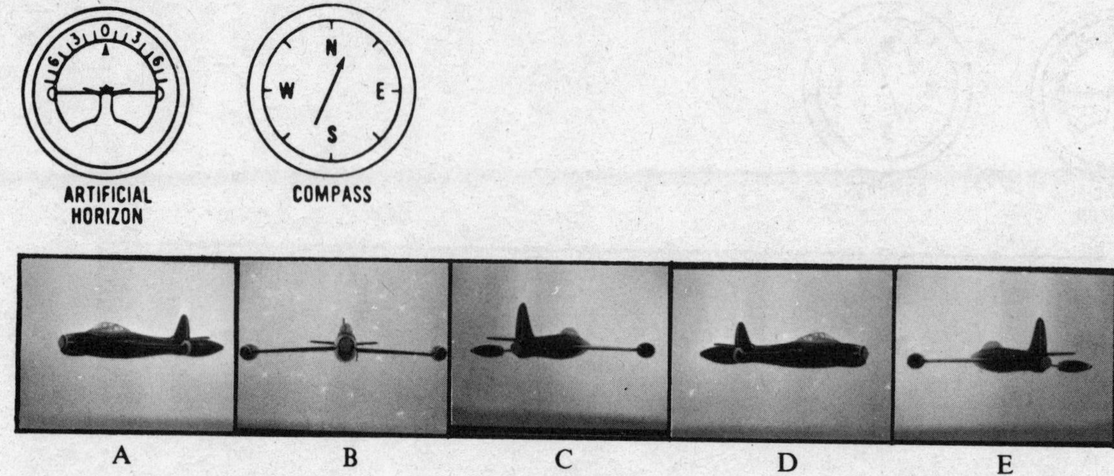
ARTIFICIAL HORIZON
COMPASS
N
W
E
S
A
B
C
D
E

36.

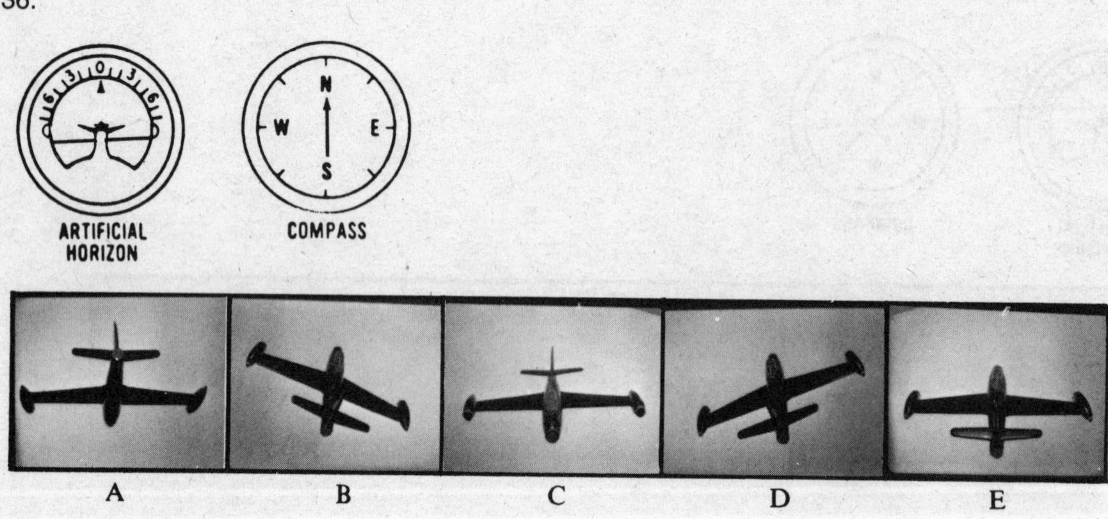
ARTIFICIAL HORIZON
COMPASS
N
W
E
S
A
B
C
D
E

37.

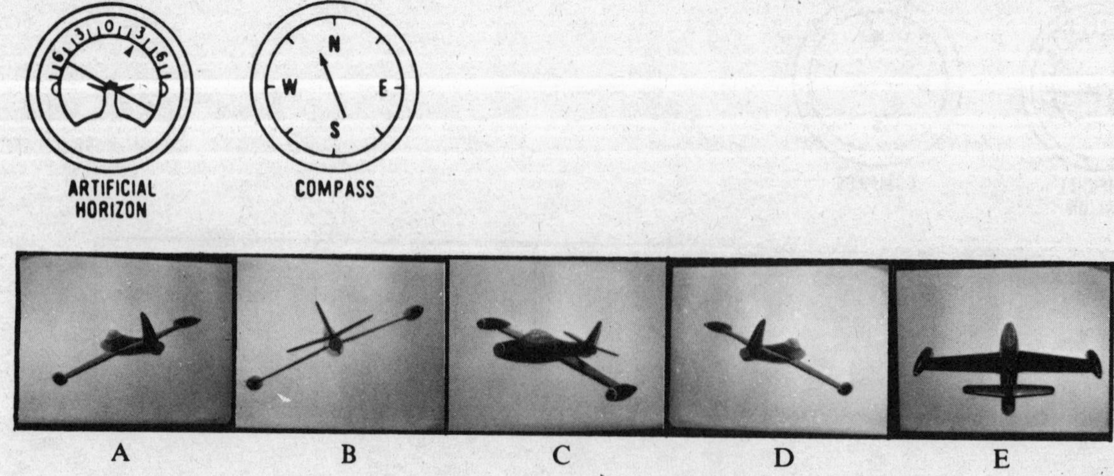
ARTIFICIAL HORIZON
COMPASS
N
W
E
S
A
B
C
D
E

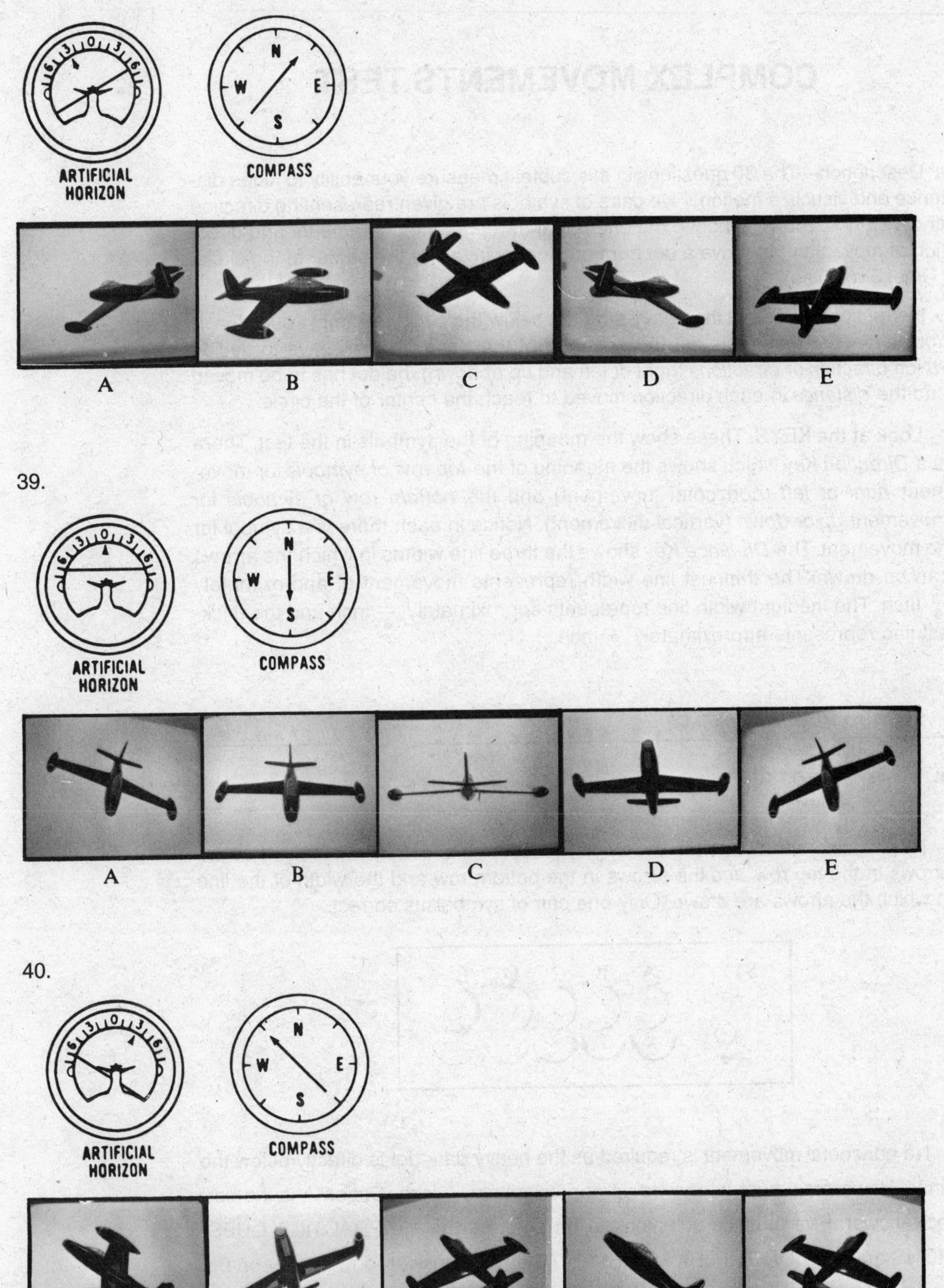

STOP! DO NOT TURN THIS PAGE UNTIL TOLD TO DO SO.

3

SUBTEST 3

COMPLEX MOVEMENTS TEST

a. Description—The 30 questions in this subtest measure your ability to judge distance and visualize motion. Five pairs of symbols are given representing direction and distance. You will choose the one pair that represents the amount and direction of movement, to move a dot from outside a circle into the center of the circle. (Time: 5 minutes)

b. Instructions—Look at the heavy dark dot below the circle in sample question 1. Your task is to move this dot to the center of the circle. You will have to decide which *direction* or *directions* (right or left and up or down) the dot has to be moved and the *distance* in each direction moved to reach the center of the circle.

Look at the KEYS. These show the meaning of the symbols in the test. There is a *Direction Key* which shows the meaning of the *top row of symbols* for movement *right* or *left* (horizontal movement) and the *bottom row of symbols* for movement *up* or *down* (vertical movement). Notice in each there is a symbol for no movement. The *Distance Key* shows the three line widths in which the arrows can be drawn. The thinnest line width represents movement of approximately $\frac{1}{8}$ inch. The medium width line represents approximately $\frac{2}{8}$ inch and the thickest line represents approximately $\frac{3}{8}$ inch.

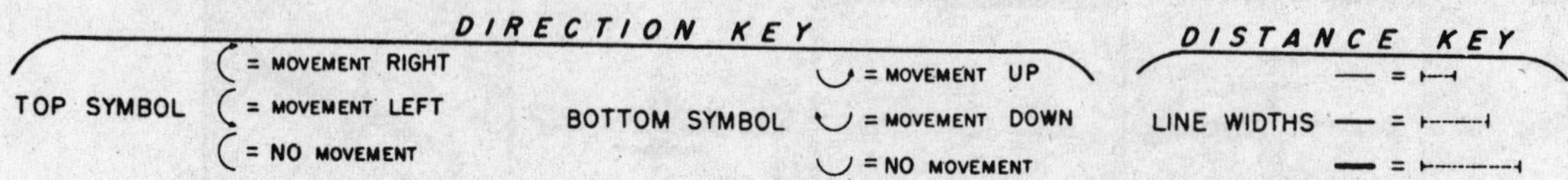

Now decide which answer in sample question 1 is correct by looking at the arrows in the top row *and* the arrows in the bottom row and the width of the line in which the arrows are drawn. Only one pair of symbols is correct.

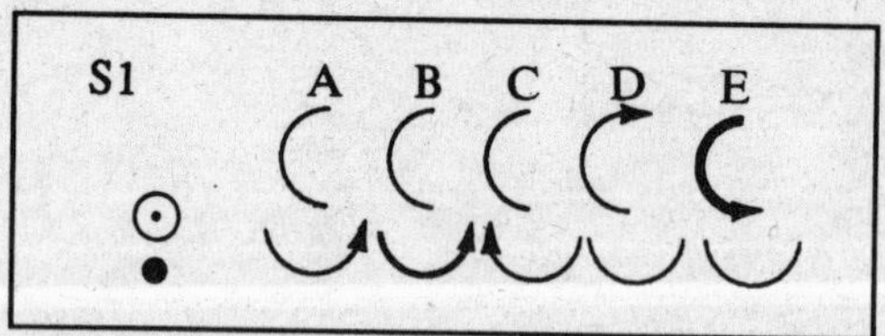

No horizontal movement is required as the heavy dark dot is directly below the circle. However, it must be moved up approximately $\frac{1}{8}$ inch. Option A is the correct answer. Five practice questions to be answered in the PRACTICE QUESTIONS area of T3. COMPLEX MOVEMENTS of your answer form appear on the next page.

Look at the T3. COMPLEX MOVEMENTS section of your answer sheet labeled PRACTICE QUESTIONS. Notice that there are five answer spaces marked P1, P2, P3, P4, and P5. Now do practice questions P1 through P5 by yourself using the DIRECTION KEY and the DISTANCE KEY. Find the correct answer to the practice question, then mark the space on your answer form that has the same letter as the answer you picked. Do this now.

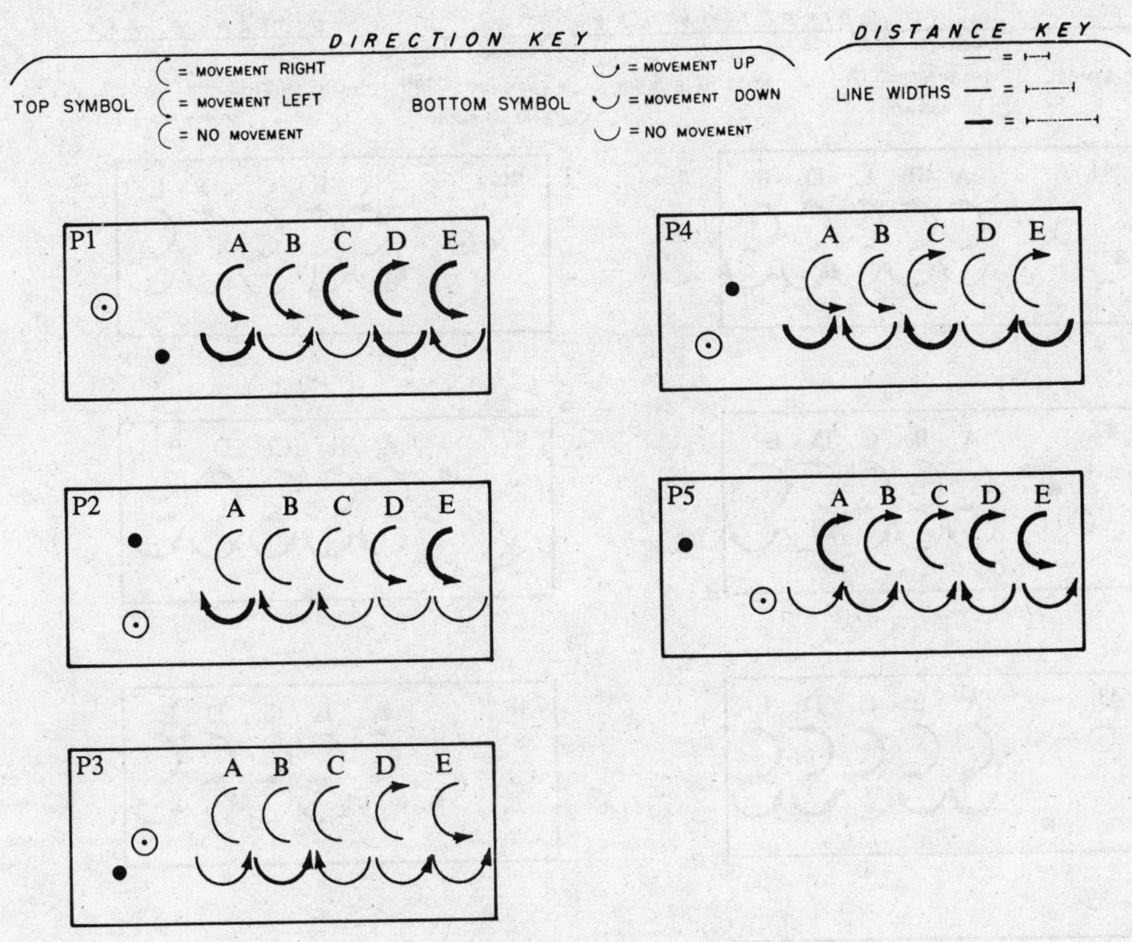

You should have marked the practice questions as follows:

P1 (B) (2 left, 2 up)
P2 (A) (no horizontal movement, 3 down)
P3 (D) (1 right, 1 up)
P4 (B) (1 left, 2 down)
P5 (D) (3 right, 2 down)

If you made any mistakes, erase your mark carefully and blacken the correct answer space. Do this now.

Be sure to start with question number 41 of Subtest 3 of your test booklet and number 41 on your answer form. Do not spend too much time on any one question.

DO NOT TURN THIS PAGE UNTIL TOLD TO DO SO.

SUBTEST 3

COMPLEX MOVEMENTS

TIME: 5 minutes—30 Questions

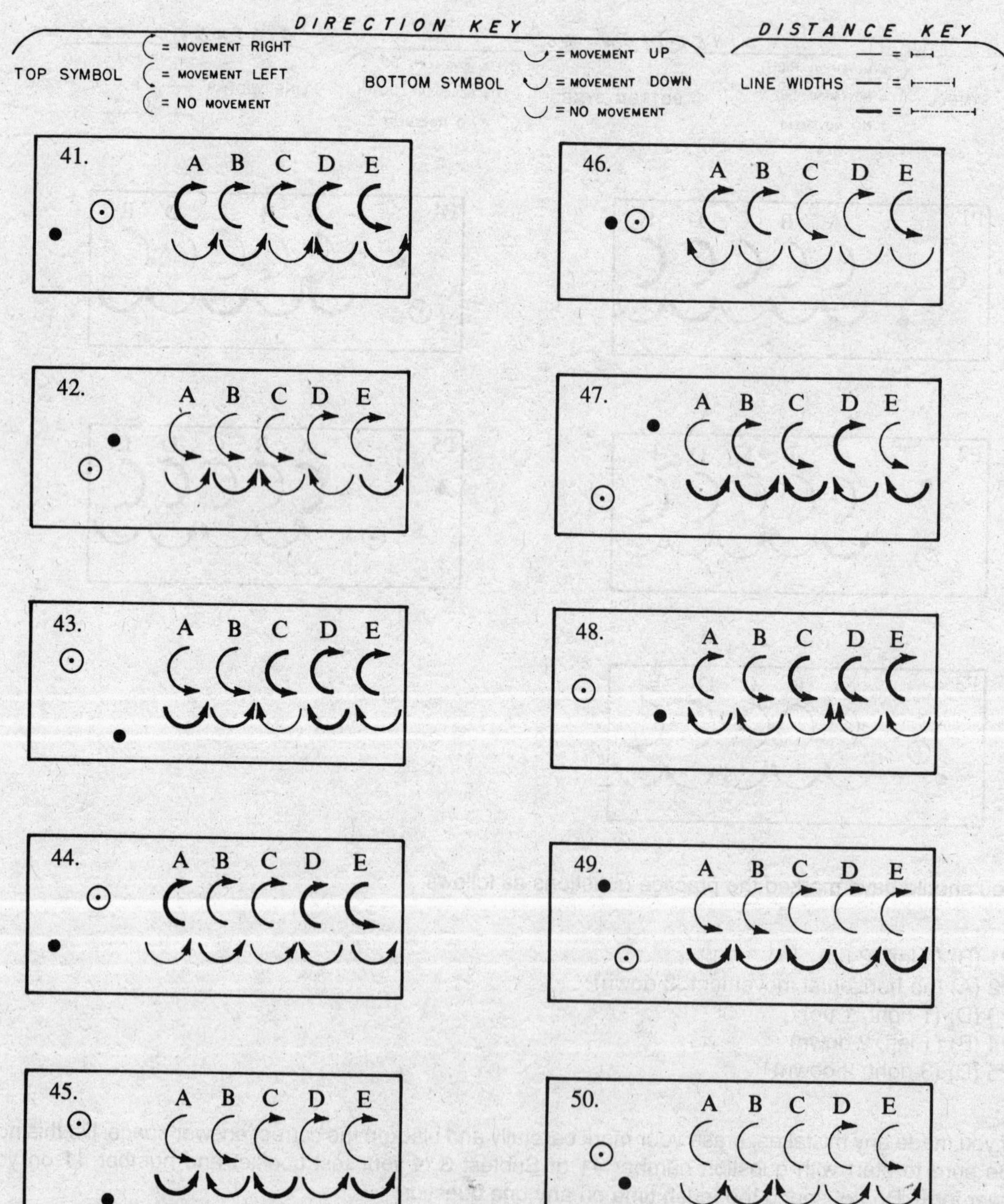

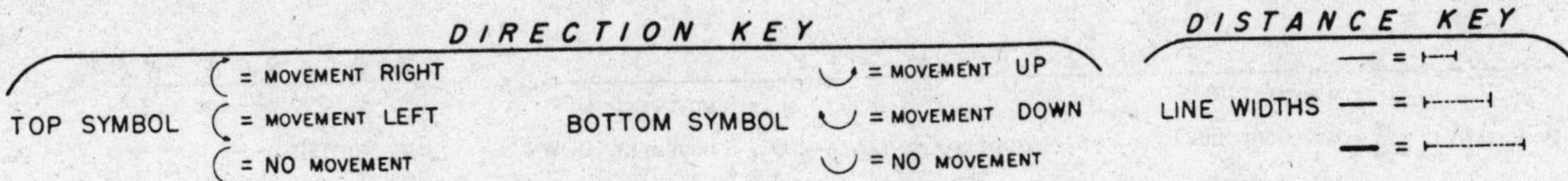

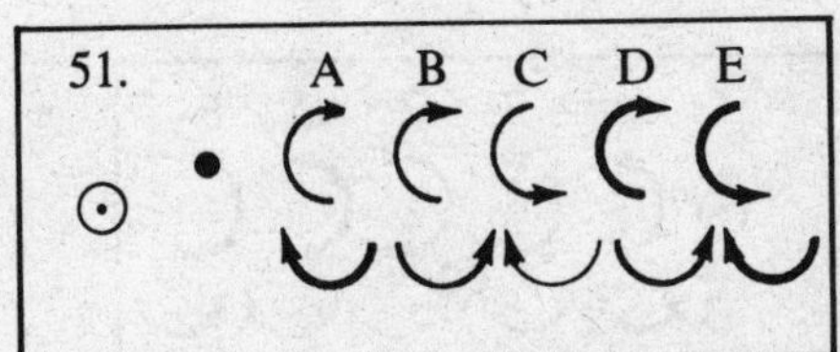

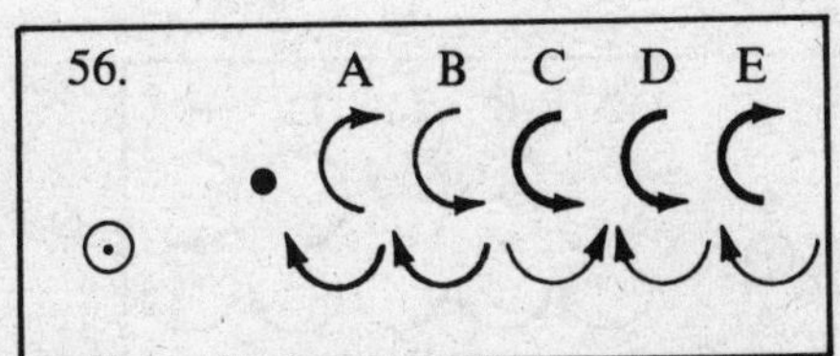

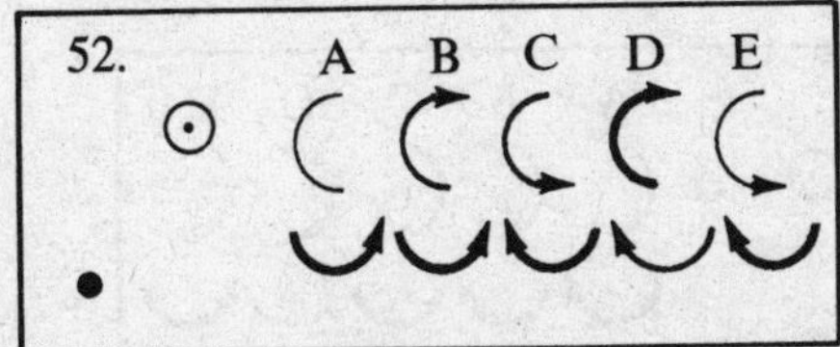

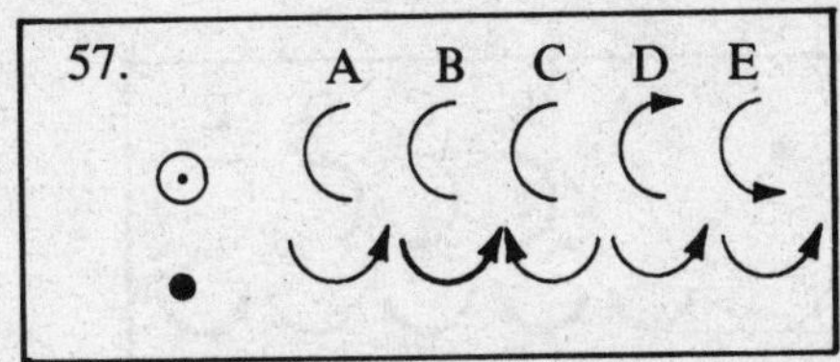

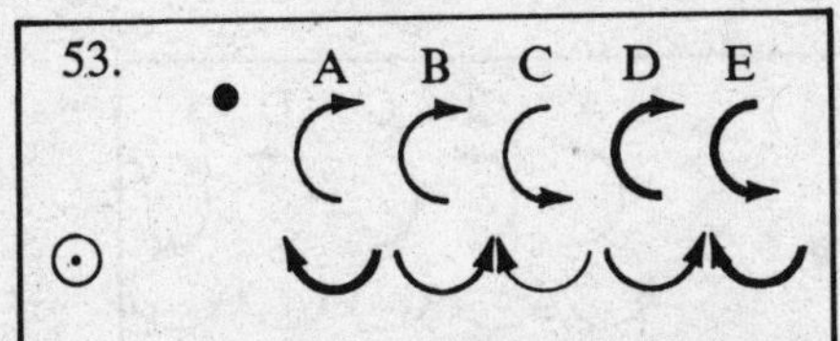

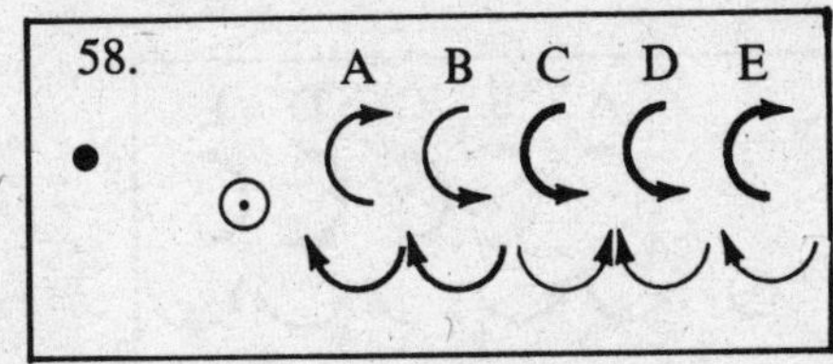

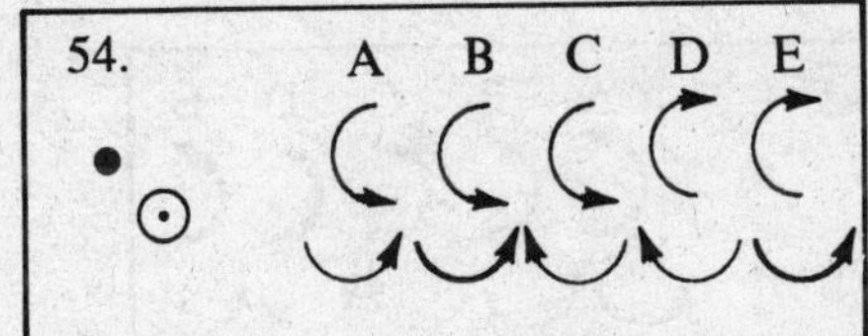

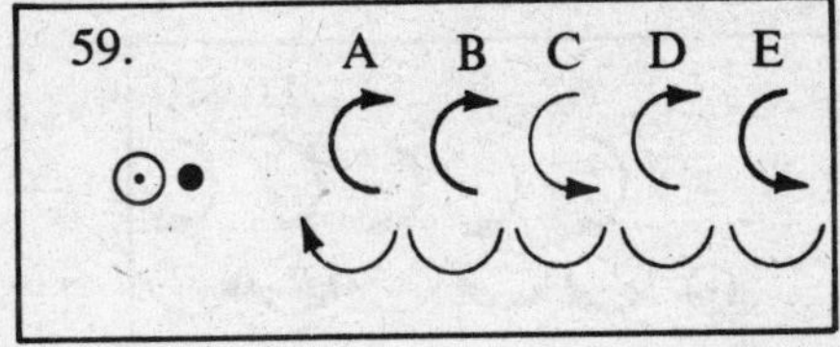

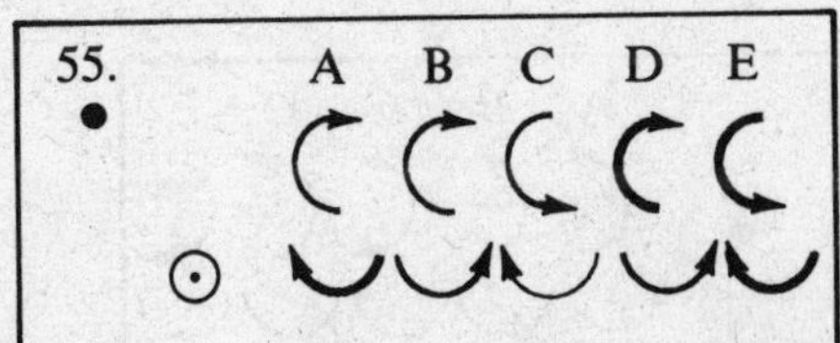

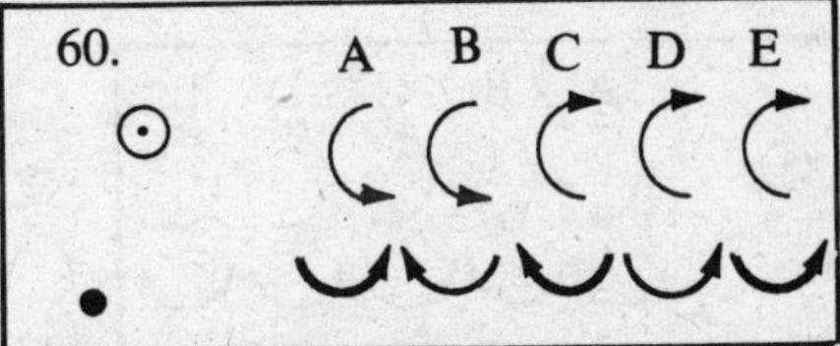

GO ON TO THE NEXT PAGE.

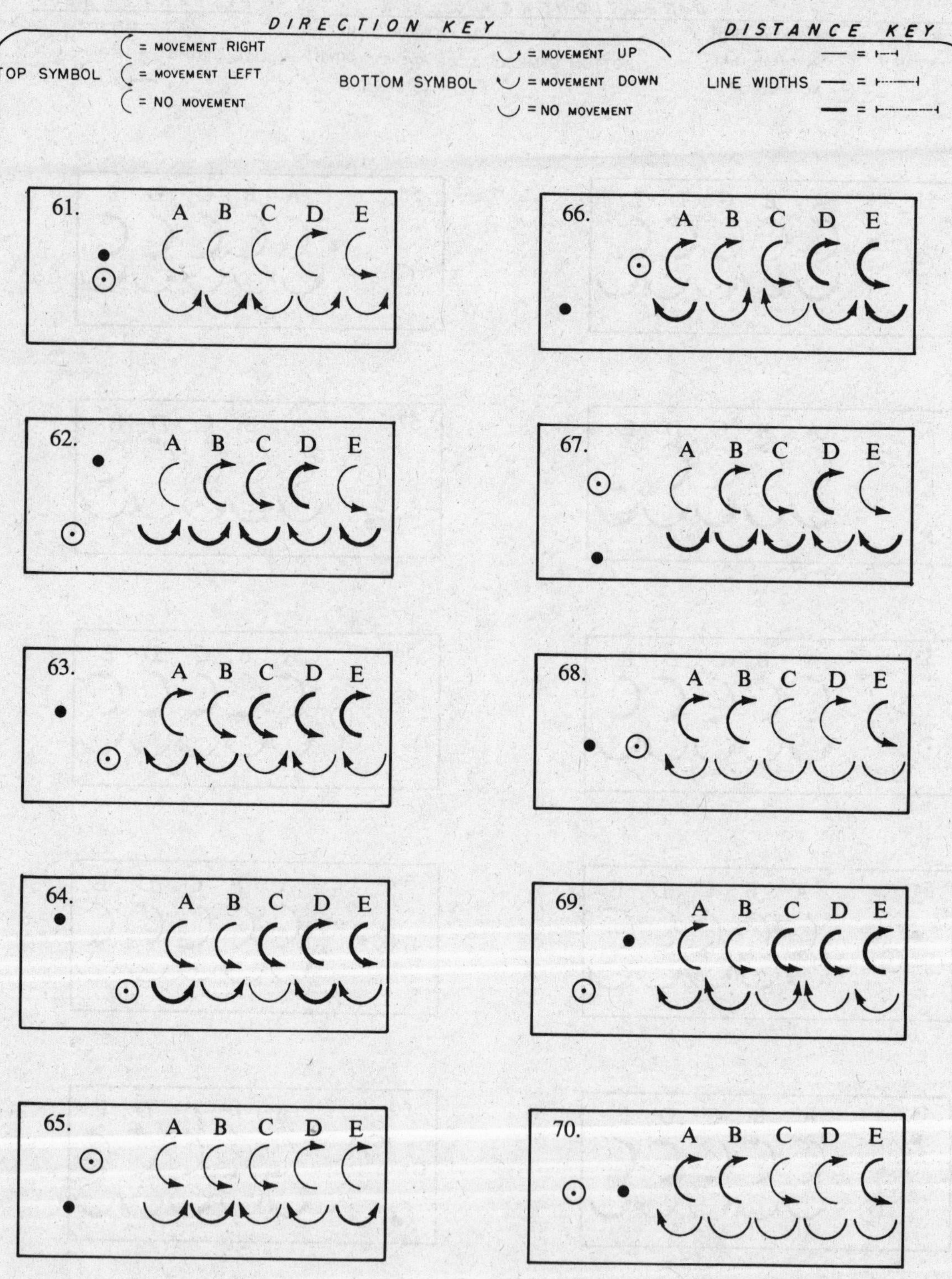

DO NOT GO ON UNTIL TOLD TO DO SO.
STOP! IF YOU FINISH BEFORE THE TIME IS UP, YOU MAY CHECK OVER YOUR WORK ON THIS PART ONLY.

SUBTEST 4

HELICOPTER KNOWLEDGE

4

a. Description—This subtest deals with your general understanding of the principles of helicopter flight. It contains 20 incomplete statements, each of which is followed by 5 choices. You will decide which one of the 5 choices *best* completes the statement. (Time: 10 minutes)

b. Instructions—The incomplete statement is followed by several choices. Decide which one of the choices *best* completes the statement. Then mark the space on your answer form which has the same number and letter as your choice.

The questions are intended to be general in nature and should apply to most helicopters having these characteristics.

Unless otherwise indicated, these questions are based on a helicopter that has the following characteristics:

1—An unsupercharged reciprocating engine
2—A single main rotor rotating in a counterclockwise direction (looking downward on the rotor)
3—An antitorque (tail) rotor
4—kid-type landing gear

Now look at the sample question that follows.

1. You are in a helicopter in straight and level flight with a constant power setting. When the nose of the helicopter is pulled up, the altitude will:

   (A) remain the same
   (B) initially increase
   (C) initially decrease
   (D) initially decrease and then remain the same
   (E) none of the above

When the nose of the helicopter is pulled up, the altitude will initially increase. Option B is the correct answer.

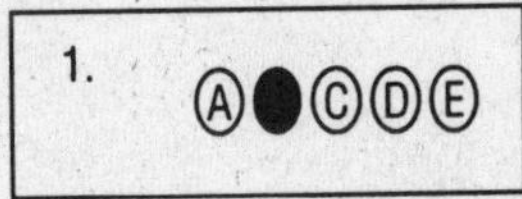

When you begin, be sure to start with question number 71 of Subtest 4 of your test booklet and number 71 on your answer form.

DO NOT TURN THIS PAGE UNTIL TOLD TO DO SO.

SUBTEST 4

HELICOPTER KNOWLEDGE

TIME: 10 minutes—20 Questions

71. A lighted heliport may be identified by
    (A) a flashing yellow light
    (B) a blue lighted square landing area
    (C) white and red lights
    (D) a green, yellow, and white rotating beacon
    (E) blue and red alternating flashes

72. The primary purpose of the tail rotor system is to
    (A) assist in making a coordinated turn
    (B) maintain heading during forward flight
    (C) counteract the torque effect of the main rotor
    (D) provide additional thrust and lift
    (E) increase maximum speed

73. During a hover, a helicopter tends to drift in the direction of tail rotor thrust. This movement is called
    (A) flapping
    (B) gyroscopic precession
    (C) transverse flow effect
    (D) translating tendency
    (E) Coriolis force

74. The upward bending of the rotor blades resulting from the combined forces of lift and centrifugal force is known as
    (A) translational lift
    (B) blade flapping
    (C) Coriolis effect
    (D) dissymmetry of lift
    (E) coning

75. In a helicopter, the center of gravity (CG) range is usually located
    (A) in front of the main rotor mast
    (B) in the rear of the main rotor mast
    (C) directly above the main fuel tank
    (D) directly below the main fuel tank
    (E) a short distance fore and aft of the main rotor mast

76. The lift differential that exists between the advancing main rotor blade and the retreating main rotor blade is known as
    (A) Coriolis effect
    (B) dissymmetry of lift
    (C) translating tendency
    (D) translational lift
    (E) lift vector

77. Ground resonance is most likely to develop when
    (A) there is a sudden change in blade velocity in the plane of rotation
    (B) a series of shocks causes the rotor system to become unbalanced
    (C) there is a combination of a decrease in the angle of attack on the advancing blade and an increase in the angle of attack on the retreating blade
    (D) initial ground contact is made with a combination of high gross weight and low RPM
    (E) there is a defective clutch or missing or bent fan blades in the helicopter engine

78. The proper action to initiate a quick stop is to
    (A) increase the RPM
    (B) decrease the RPM
    (C) raise the collective pitch
    (D) lower collective pitch and apply forward cyclic
    (E) lower collective pitch and apply aft cyclic

GO ON TO THE NEXT PAGE.

79. Takeoff from a slope in a helicopter with skid-type landing gear is normally accomplished by
    (A) simultaneously applying collective pitch and downslope cyclic control
    (B) bringing the helicopter to a level attitude before completely leaving the ground
    (C) making a downslope running takeoff if the surface is smooth
    (D) rapidly increasing collective pitch and upslope cyclic controls to avoid sliding downslope
    (E) turning the tail upslope, when moving away from the slope, to reduce the danger of the tail rotor striking the surface

80. The proper procedure for a slope landing in a helicopter with skid-type landing gear is
    (A) use maximum RPM and maximum manifold pressure
    (B) when parallel to the slope, slowly lower the downslope skid to the ground prior to lowering the upslope skid
    (C) if the slope is 10° or less, the landing should be made perpendicular to the slope
    (D) when parallel to the slope, slowly lower the upslope skid to the ground prior to lowering the downslope skid
    (E) if the slope is 10° or less, the landing should be downslope or downhill

81. Density altitude refers to a theoretical air density which exists under standard conditions at a given altitude. Standard conditions at sea level are
    (A) 29.92 in. of Hg (inches of mercury) and 15°C
    (B) 29.92 in. of Hg (inches of mercury) and 20°C
    (C) 29.92 in. of Hg (inches of mercury) and 30°C
    (D) 14.96 in. of Hg (inches of mercury) and 15°C
    (E) 14.96 in. of Hg (inches of mercury) and 30°C

82. A helicopter pilot should consider using a running takeoff
    (A) if the helicopter cannot be lifted vertically
    (B) when a normal climb speed is assured between 10 and 20 feet
    (C) when power is insufficient to hover at a very low altitude
    (D) when the additional airspeed can be quickly converted to altitude
    (E) when gross weight or density altitude prevents a sustained hover at normal hovering altitude

83. Foot pedals in the helicopter cockpit enable the pilot to
    (A) control torque effect
    (B) regulate flight speed
    (C) regulate rate of climb
    (D) regulate rate of descent
    (E) stabilize rotor RPM

84. If the helicopter is moving forward, the advancing blade will be in the
    (A) forward half of the rotor disc
    (B) left half of the rotor disc
    (C) rear half of the rotor disc
    (D) right half of the rotor disc

85. The method of control by which the pitch of all main rotor blades is varied equally and simultaneously is the
    (A) auxiliary rotor control
    (B) collective pitch control
    (C) cyclic pitch control
    (D) tail rotor control
    (E) throttle control

86. The combination of factors that will reduce helicopter performance the most is
    (A) low altitude, low temperature, and low humidity
    (B) low altitude, high temperature, and low humidity
    (C) low altitude, low temperature, and high humidity
    (D) high altitude, low temperature, and low humidity
    (E) high altitude, high temperature, and high humidity

87. The most favorable conditions for helicopter performance are the combination of

    (A) low-density altitude, light gross weight, and moderate to strong winds
    (B) high-density altitude, heavy gross weight, and calm or no wind
    (C) low-density altitude, light gross weight, and calm or no wind
    (D) high-density altitude, light gross weight, and moderate to strong winds
    (E) low-density altitude, heavy gross weight, and moderate to strong winds

88. Refer to the figure below. The acute angle A is the angle of

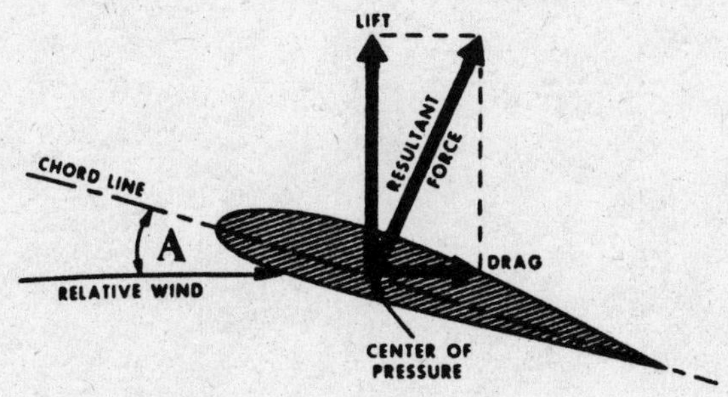

    (A) dihedral
    (B) attack
    (C) camber
    (D) incidence
    (E) pitch

89. During surface taxiing, the helicopter pilot should use the pedals to maintain heading and the cyclic to maintain

    (A) ground track
    (B) proper RPM
    (C) starting
    (D) stopping
    (E) all of the above

90. The thinner air of higher altitudes causes the airspeed indicator to read "too low." An indicated airspeed of 80 mph at 5,000 feet is actually a true airspeed of approximately

    (A) 72 mph
    (B) 88 mph
    (C) 96 mph
    (D) 104 mph
    (E) 112 mph

DO NOT GO ON UNTIL TOLD TO DO SO.
STOP! IF YOU FINISH BEFORE THE TIME IS UP, YOU MAY CHECK OVER YOUR WORK ON THIS PART ONLY.

SUBTEST 5

CYCLIC ORIENTATION

5

a. Description—This is a test of your ability to recognize simple changes in helicopter position and to indicate the corresponding cyclic (stick) movement. You will look at a series of three sequential pictures that represents the pilot's view out of a helicopter windshield. The three pictures change from top to bottom showing a view from an aircraft in a climb, dive, bank to the left or right, or a combination of these maneuvers. You will determine which position the cyclic would be in to perform the maneuver indicated by the pictures. This test contains 15 questions of this type. (Time: 5 minutes)

b. Instructions—You are the pilot of a helicopter with a constant power setting going through a maneuver as shown in the pictures on the next page. The helicopter can be climbing, diving, banking (turning) to the right or left, or in a climbing or diving bank. Look at the pictures from *top* to *bottom* and decide what maneuver it is doing. Next, your task is to decide which position the cyclic (stick) would be in to perform the maneuver.

For items in this test, the cyclic is moved as follows:

For banks: To bank left, move the cyclic stick to left. To bank right, move the cyclic to right.
For climbs and dives: To dive, push the cyclic forward. To climb, pull the cyclic back.

EXAMPLE OF CYCLIC MOVEMENT

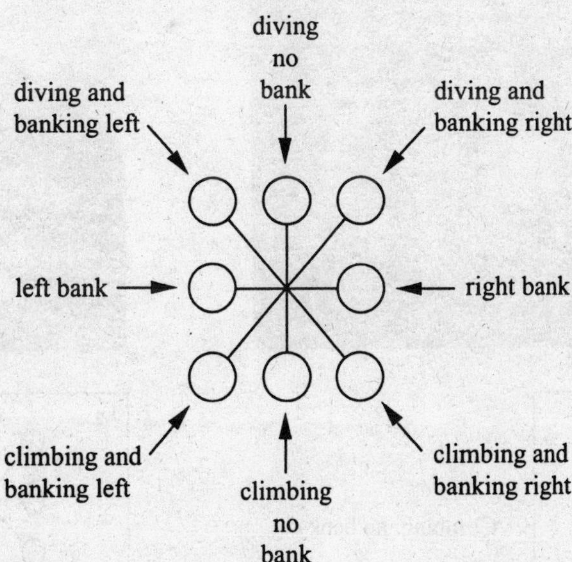

GO ON TO THE NEXT PAGE.

Now look at the set of pictures below in sample item 1 and decide the cyclic position for the maneuver shown.

1.

Now look at the set of pictures below in sample item 2 and decide the cyclic position for the maneuver shown.

2.

1.

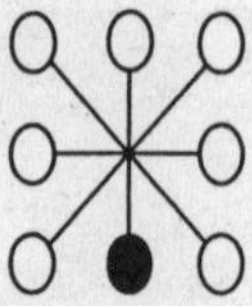

Climbing; no bank

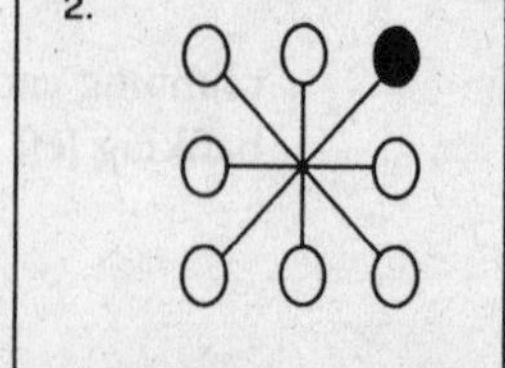

Diving and banking right

When you begin, be sure to start with question number 91 on Subtest 5 in your test booklet and number 91 on your answer form. Do not spend too much time on any one question.

DO NOT GO ON UNTIL TOLD TO DO SO.

SUBTEST 5

CYCLIC ORIENTATION

TIME: 5 minute—15 Questions

Each of the following questions consists of a series of three sequential pictures that represents the pilot's view out of a helicopter windshield. The three pictures change from top to bottom showing a view from an aircraft in a climb, dive, bank to the left or right or a combination of these maneuvers. Determine which position the cyclic would be in to perform the maneuver indicated by the pictures and blacken the appropriate cyclic circle on your answer sheet.

91.

92.

GO ON TO THE NEXT PAGE.

93.

94.

95.

96.

GO ON TO THE NEXT PAGE.

97.

98.

99.

100.

GO ON TO THE NEXT PAGE.

101.

102.

103.

104.

GO ON TO THE NEXT PAGE.

105.

DO NOT GO ON UNTIL TOLD TO DO SO.
STOP! IF YOU FINISH BEFORE THE TIME IS UP, YOU MAY CHECK OVER YOUR WORK ON THIS PART ONLY.

6

SUBTEST 6

MECHANICAL FUNCTIONS TEST

a. Description—This subtest determines your understanding of general mechanical principles. In this part, pictures are shown, and questions are asked on the mechanical principles illustrated. There are 20 questions in this test. (Time: 10 minutes)

b. Instructions—Looking at the picture, decide which mechanical principle is illustrated. Pick the best answer. There is only *one* right answer.

Now look at the sample question below.

1. At which point should one pull down to raise the weight more easily: At Point A or at Point B?

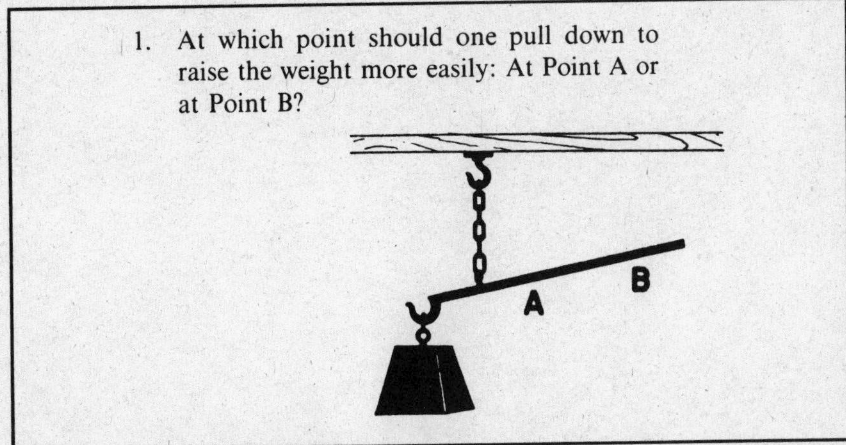

Pulling down at B gives a longer lever arm which results in raising the weight more easily. Option B is the correct answer.

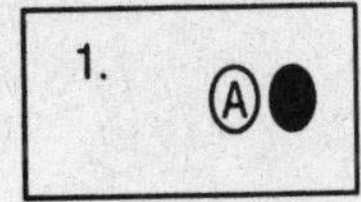

When you begin, be sure to start with question number 106 of Subtest 6 of your test booklet and number 106 on your answer form.

DO NOT TURN THIS PAGE UNTIL TOLD TO DO SO.

SUBTEST 6

MECHANICAL FUNCTIONS

TIME: 10 minutes—20 Questions

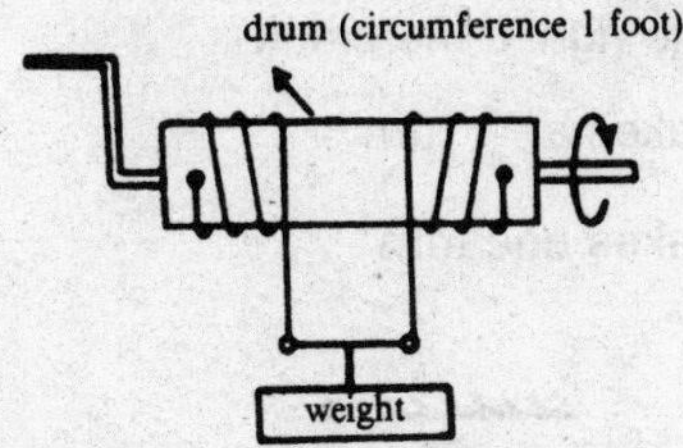

106. In the figure shown above, one complete revolution of the windlass drum will move the weight up

(A) 6 inches
(B) 12 inches

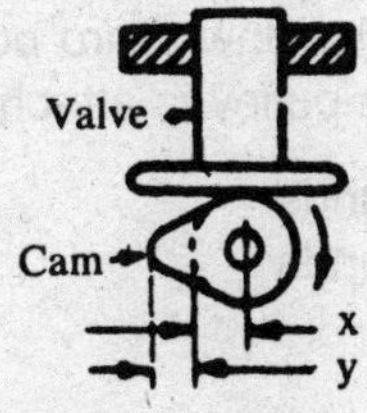

107. The figure above shows a cam and a valve. For each cam revolution, the vertical valve rise equals distance

(A) Y
(B) X

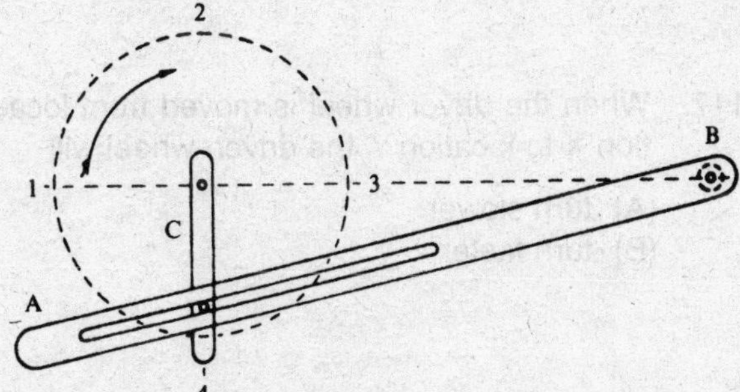

108. In the diagram above, crank arm C revolves at a constant speed of 400 RPM and drives the lever AB. When lever AB is moving the fastest, arm C will be in positions

(A) 1 and 3
(B) 2 and 4

109. What is the function of A and B in the crankshaft shown in the drawing above?

(A) They strengthen the crankshaft by increasing its weight.
(B) They are necessary to maintain the proper balance of the crankshaft.

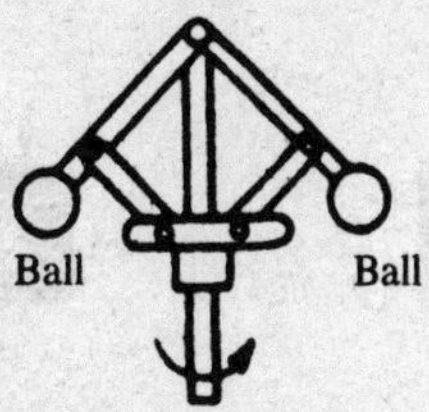

110. The figure above shows a governor on a rotating shaft. As the shaft speeds up, the governor balls will

(A) move down
(B) move upward

111. The figure above shows a brass and an iron strip continuously riveted together. High temperatures would probably

(A) have no effect at all
(B) bend the strips

GO ON TO THE NEXT PAGE.

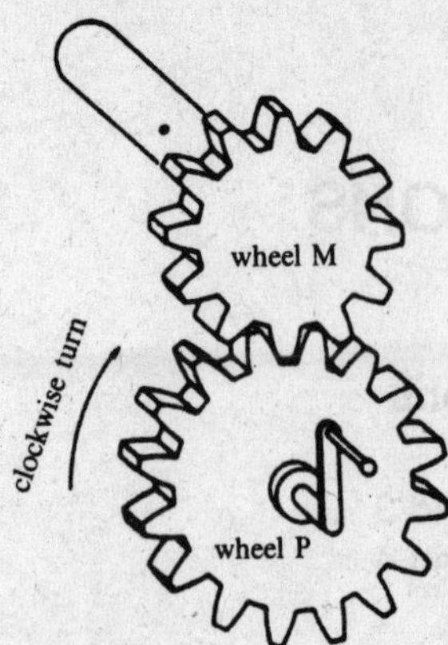

112. Study the gear wheels in the figure above, then determine which of the following statements is true.
   (A) It will take less time for a tooth of wheel P to make a full turn than it will take a tooth of wheel M.
   (B) It will take more time for a tooth of wheel P to make a full turn than it will for a tooth of wheel M.

A

B

113. Which hydraulic press requires the least force to lift the weight?
   (A) A
   (B) B

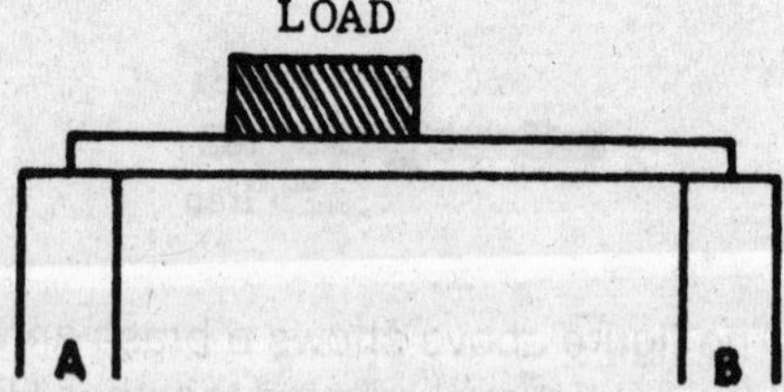

114. In the figure above, which upright supports the greater part of the load?
   (A) upright A
   (B) upright B

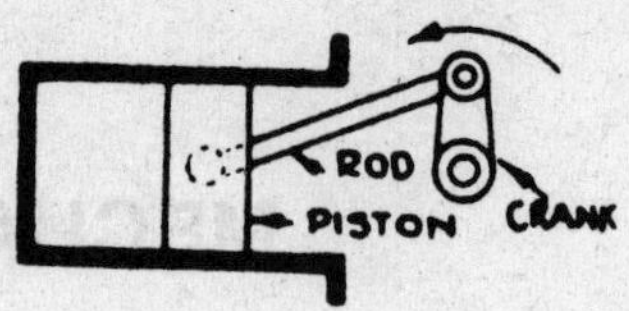

115. The figure above shows a crank and piston. The piston moves from mid-position to the extreme right if the crank
   (A) makes a $\frac{3}{4}$ turn
   (B) makes one turn

116. When the 100-pound weight is being slowly hoisted up by the pulley, as shown in the figure below, the downward pull on the ceiling to which the pulley is attached is
   (A) 100 pounds
   (B) 150 pounds

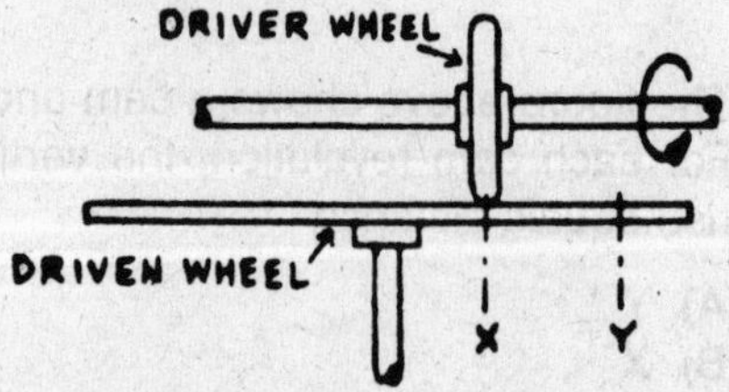

117. When the driver wheel is moved from location X to location Y, the driven wheel will
   (A) turn slower
   (B) turn faster

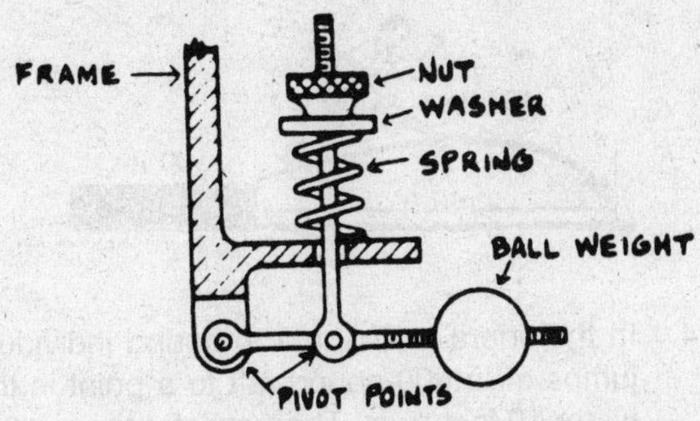

118. If the ball and spring mechanism are balanced in the position shown above, the ball will move upward if

(A) the nut is loosened
(B) the nut is tightened

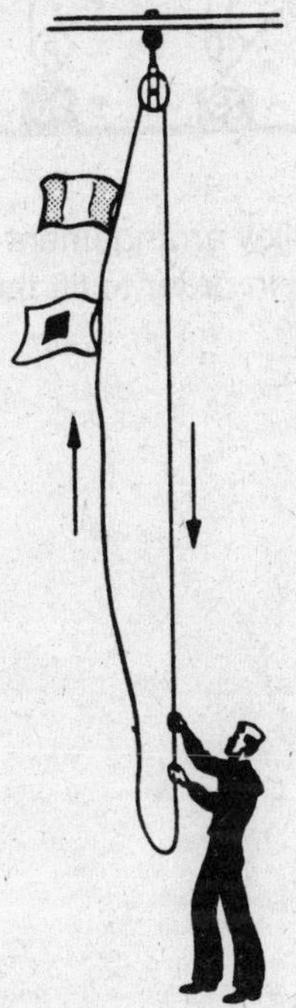

119. Neglecting friction, what is the mechanical advantage in using the single fixed pulley shown above?

(A) 1
(B) 2

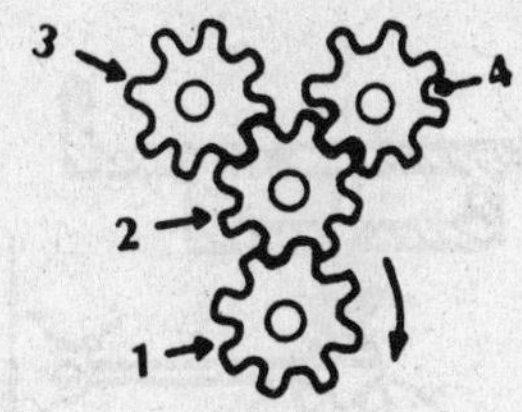

120. Four gears are shown in the figure above. If gear 1 turns as shown, then the gears turning in the same direction are

(A) 2 and 3
(B) 3 and 4

121. If both cyclists pedal at the same rate on the same surface, the cyclist in front will

(A) travel at the same speed as the cyclist behind
(B) move faster than the cyclist behind

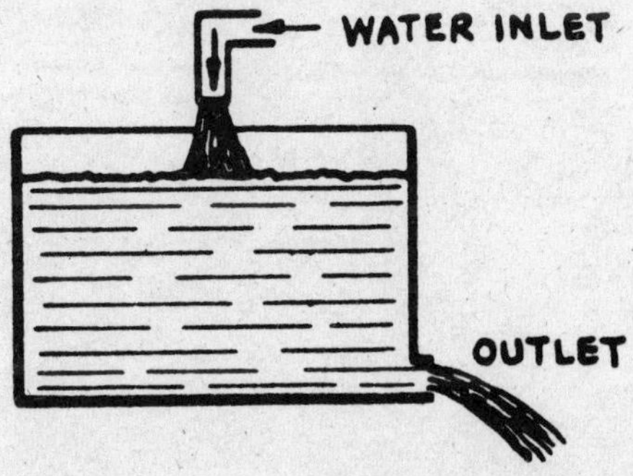

122. If water is flowing into the tank at the rate of 120 gallons per hour and flowing out of the tank at a constant rate of one gallon per minute, the water level in the tank will

(A) rise 1 gallon per minute
(B) rise 2 gallons per minute

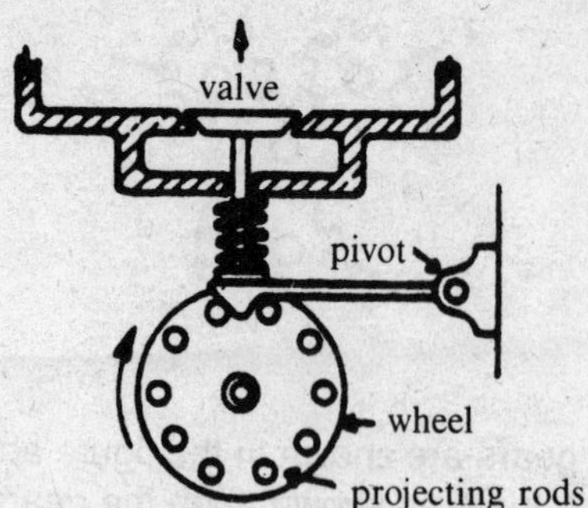

123. In order to open the valve in the figure above once every second, the wheel must rotate at

(A) 6 rpm
(B) 10 rpm

124. In the figure above, a 150-pound individual jumps off a 500-pound raft to a point in the water 10 feet away. Theoretically, the raft will move

(A) 1 foot in the opposite direction
(B) 3 feet in the opposite direction

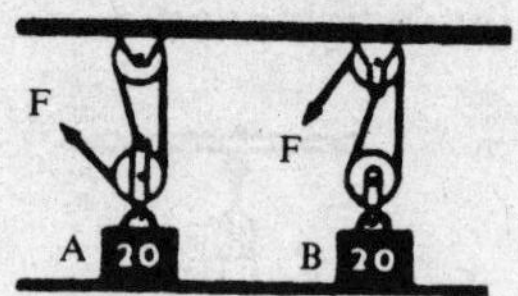

125. Which pulley arrangement requires the least force at F in order to lift the weight?

(A) A
(B) B

DO NOT GO ON UNTIL TOLD TO DO SO.
STOP! IF YOU FINISH BEFORE THE TIME IS UP, YOU MAY CHECK OVER YOUR WORK ON THIS PART ONLY.

SUBTEST 7

7

SELF-DESCRIPTION

a. Description—This subtest has 75 questions dealing with your interests, likes, and dislikes. (Time: 25 minutes)

b. Instructions—On this subtest you will read the question, then pick the one answer that applies best to you. Be forthright in responding to these questions. Answer them as accurately as you can, to the best of your ability and recollection.

Now look at the sample question below.

1. From each pair, select the one activity you would prefer

   (A) Keep a set of office files in order
   (B) Keep a piece of machinery in order

If you would prefer to keep a set of office files rather than a piece of machinery in order, select option A and mark it in the appropriate space.

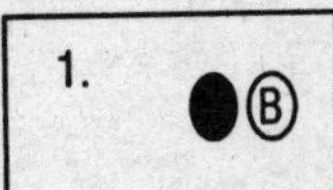

If you would prefer to keep a piece of machinery rather than a set of office files in order, select option B and mark it in the appropriate space.

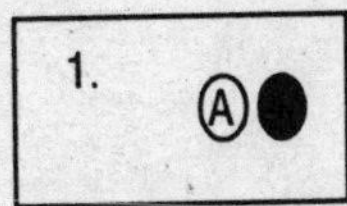

The 75 questions on this subtest are divided into five sections, as follows:

Section A Questions 126–145 5-option items
Section B Questions 146–165 2-option items
Section C Questions 166–185 2-option items
Section D Questions 186–194 2-option items
Section E Questions 195–200 4-option items

When you begin, be sure to start with question number 126 in Section A of your test booklet and number 126 in Section A on your answer form.

DO NOT GO ON UNTIL TOLD TO DO SO.

SUBTEST 7

SELF-DESCRIPTION FORM

TIME: 25 minutes—75 Questions

Section A: Questions 126–145

The questions in this section consist of sets of five descriptive words from which you are to select the option that *most* accurately describes you or the option that *least* describes you.

126. Which of the following *most* accurately describes you?

(A) Adventurous
(B) Energetic
(C) Impetuous
(D) Impulsive
(E) Restless

127. Which one of the following *least* describes you?

(A) Adventurous
(B) Energetic
(C) Impetuous
(D) Impulsive
(E) Restless

128. Which one of the following *most* accurately describes you?

(A) Ambitious
(B) Emotional
(C) Logical
(D) Resourceful
(E) Sentimental

129. Which one of the following *least* describes you?

(A) Ambitious
(B) Emotional
(C) Logical
(D) Resourceful
(E) Sentimental

130. Which one of the following *most* accurately describes you?

(A) Cautious
(B) Deliberate
(C) Impatient
(D) Impulsive
(E) Patient

131. Which one of the following *least* describes you?

(A) Cautious
(B) Deliberate
(C) Impatient
(D) Impulsive
(E) Patient

132. Which one of the following *most* accurately describes you?

(A) Competent
(B) Gifted
(C) Intelligent
(D) Quick-witted
(E) Skillful

133. Which one of the following *least* describes you?

(A) Competent
(B) Gifted
(C) Intelligent
(D) Quick-witted
(E) Skillful

134. Which one of the following *most* accurately describes you?

(A) Compromising
(B) Dependable
(C) Independent
(D) Sincere
(E) Studious

135. Which one of the following *least* describes you?

(A) Compromising
(B) Dependable
(C) Independent
(D) Sincere
(E) Studious

136. Which one of the following *most* accurately describes you?

(A) Condescending
(B) Friendly
(C) Pleasant
(D) Polite
(E) Reserved

137. Which one of the following *least* describes you?

(A) Condescending
(B) Friendly
(C) Pleasant
(D) Polite
(E) Reserved

138. Which one of the following *most* accurately describes you?

(A) Courteous
(B) Curious
(C) Patronizing
(D) Studious
(E) Thoughtful

139. Which one of the following *least* describes you?

(A) Courteous
(B) Curious
(C) Patronizing
(D) Studious
(E) Thoughtful

140. Which one of the following *most* accurately describes you?

(A) Discreet
(B) Jealous
(C) Loyal
(D) Open-minded
(E) Suspicious

141. Which one of the following *least* describes you?

(A) Discreet
(B) Jealous
(C) Loyal
(D) Open-minded
(E) Suspicious

142. Which one of the following *most* accurately describes you?

(A) Economical
(B) Extravagant
(C) Lavish
(D) Sensible
(E) Thrifty

143. Which one of the following *least* describes you?

(A) Economical
(B) Extravagant
(C) Lavish
(D) Sensible
(E) Thrifty

144. Which one of the following *most* accurately describes you?

(A) Generous
(B) Intolerant
(C) Judgmental
(D) Opportunistic
(E) Sensitive

145. Which one of the following *least* describes you?

(A) Generous
(B) Intolerant
(C) Judgmental
(D) Opportunistic
(E) Sensitive

Section B: Questions 146–165

The items in this section consist of questions that are to be answered by either a "Yes" or a "No."

146. Did you generally start each new school year with a great deal of enthusiasm?

(Y) Yes
(N) No

147. Do you trust people readily?

(Y) Yes
(N) No

148. Do you generally have a strong opinion on most matters?

(Y) Yes
(N) No

149. Do you tend to speak rapidly?

(Y) Yes
(N) No

150. Do you like sports?

(Y) Yes
(N) No

151. Are you often in low spirits?

(Y) Yes
(N) No

152. Do you find off-color language offensive?

(Y) Yes
(N) No

153. Do you often find yourself finishing sentences for other people?

(Y) Yes
(N) No

154. Do you like to visit museums?

(Y) Yes
(N) No

155. Are you frequently in a hurry?

(Y) Yes
(N) No

156. Do you get much time to keep up with the things you like to do?

(Y) Yes
(N) No

157. When under pressure, do you tend to lose your temper?

(Y) Yes
(N) No

158. Did you enjoy going to school dances?

(Y) Yes
(N) No

159. Do you become upset when you think something is taking too long?

(Y) Yes
(N) No

160. Do you have trouble going to sleep at night?

(Y) Yes
(N) No

161. Do you wish you could do over some of the things you have done?

(Y) Yes
(N) No

162. Did you ever build a model airplane?

(Y) Yes
(N) No

163. Did you ever build a model airplane that would fly?

(Y) Yes
(N) No

164. Did you ever fly in a helicopter?

(Y) Yes
(N) No

165. Did you ever fly in a glider or pilot a hang glider?

(Y) Yes
(N) No

SECTION C: Questions 166–185

The items in this section consist of a listing of many occupations. Some may appeal to you; others may not. For each of the listed occupations you would like for a life career, answer by selecting "Like." For each of the listed occupations you would *not* like for a life career, answer by selecting "Dislike."

166. Artist

(L) Like
(D) Dislike

189.

(A) New and different experiences excite me.
(B) New and different experiences frighten me.

190.

(A) I prefer to work with competent coworkers.
(B) I prefer to work with congenial coworkers.

191.

(A) I enjoy engaging actively in athletic sports.
(B) I enjoy watching athletic events.

192.

(A) One of my most important career goals is security.
(B) One of my most important career goals is high income.

193.

(A) I rarely worry about what other people think of me.
(B) It bothers me that people have wrong ideas about me.

194.

(A) I prefer having a few close friends.
(B) I prefer having many friends.

SECTION E: Questions 195–200

Each question in this section consists of a statement that may be considered to be somewhat controversial. Select one of the following options that best describes the extent to which you agree or disagree with each statement:

(A) Strongly agree
(B) Tend to agree
(C) Tend to disagree
(D) Strongly disagree.

195. Generally speaking, people get the recognition they deserve.

(A) Strongly agree
(B) Tend to agree
(C) Tend to disagree
(D) Strongly disagree

196. There is too much power concentrated in the hands of labor union officials.

(A) Strongly agree
(B) Tend to agree
(C) Tend to disagree
(D) Strongly disagree

197. Acid rain is one of the most serious environmental problems facing us today.

(A) Strongly agree
(B) Tend to agree
(C) Tend to disagree
(D) Strongly disagree

198. Success at work depends on hard work; luck has very little to do with it.

(A) Strongly agree
(B) Tend to agree
(C) Tend to disagree
(D) Strongly disagree

199. Most people use politeness to cover up what is actually ruthless competition.

(A) Strongly agree
(B) Tend to agree
(C) Tend to disagree
(D) Strongly disagree

200. Breaking the law is hardly ever justified.

(A) Strongly agree
(B) Tend to agree
(C) Tend to disagree
(D) Strongly disagree

STOP! IF YOU FINISH BEFORE THE TIME IS UP, YOU MAY CHECK OVER YOUR WORK ON THIS PART ONLY.

SAMPLE ARMY ALTERNATE FLIGHT APTITUDE SELECTION TEST KEY ANSWERS AND RATIONALE

SUBTEST 1—BACKGROUND INFORMATION FORM

There are no "correct" answers to these questions.

SUBTEST 2—INSTRUMENT COMPREHENSION

Key Answers

26. E	28. A	30. D	32. B	34. E	36. E	38. D	40. C
27. C	29. B	31. D	33. A	35. C	37. A	39. B	

Items Answered Incorrectly: ___; ___; ___; ___; ___; ___; ___; ___.

Items Unsure Of: ___; ___; ___; ___; ___; ___; ___; ___.

Total Number Answered Correctly: ___

Rationale

26–(E) Not climbing or diving; no bank; heading 270° (west)

27–(C) Diving; no bank; heading 45° (northeast)

28–(A) Climbing; 30° right bank; heading 225° (southwest)

29–(B) Diving; 30° left bank; heading 360° (north)

30–(D) Not climbing or diving; 30° right bank; heading 135° (southeast)

31–(D) Climbing; no bank; heading 315° (northwest)

32–(B) Not climbing or diving; no bank; heading $202\frac{1}{2}$° (south-southwest)

33–(A) Diving; 30° right bank; heading 315° (northwest)

34–(E) Climbing; no bank; heading 90° (east)

35–(C) Not climbing or diving; no bank; heading $22\frac{1}{2}$° (north-northeast)

36–(E) Climbing; no bank; heading 360° (north)

37–(A) Not climbing or diving; 30° left bank; heading $337\frac{1}{2}$° (north-northwest)

38–(D) Not climbing or diving; 30° right bank; heading 45° (northeast)

39–(B) Diving; no bank; heading 180° (south)

40–(C) Climbing; 30° left bank; heading 315° (northwest)

SUBTEST 3—COMPLEX MOVEMENTS

Key Answers

41. C	45. A	49. C	53. E	57. B	61. C	65. E	69. B
42. C	46. D	50. E	54. D	58. E	62. E	66. D	70. E
43. A	47. C	51. C	55. A	59. C	63. A	67. A	
44. B	48. C	52. B	56. D	60. E	64. D	68. B	

Items Answered Incorrectly: ___; ___; ___; ___; ___; ___; ___; ___.

Items Unsure Of: ___; ___; ___; ___; ___; ___; ___; ___.

Total Number Answered Correctly: ___

Rationale

41–(C) (2 right, 1 up)

42–(C) (1 left, 1 down)

43–(A) (2 left, 3 up)

44–(B) (2 right, 2 up)

45–(A) (1 left, 3 up)

46–(D) (1 right, no vertical movement)

47–(C) (2 left, 3 down)

48–(C) (3 left, 1 up)

49–(C) (1 right, 3 down)

50–(E) (1 left, 1 up)

51–(C) (2 left, 1 down)

52–(B) (2 right, 3 up)

53–(E) (3 left, 3 down)

54–(D) (1 right, 1 down)

55–(A) (2 right, 3 down)

56–(D) (3 left, 1 down)

57–(B) (no horizontal movement, 2 up)

58–(E) (3 right, 1 down)

59–(C) (1 left, no vertical movement)

60–(E) (1 right, 3 up)

61–(C) (no horizontal movement, 1 down)

62–(E) (1 left, 3 down)

63–(A) (2 right, 2 down)

64–(D) (3 right, 3 down)

65–(E) (1 right, 2 up)

66–(D) (3 right, 2 up)

67–(A) (no horizontal movement, 3 up)

68–(B) (2 right, no vertical movement)

69–(B) (2 left, 2 down)

70–(E) (2 left, no vertical movement)

SUBTEST 4—HELICOPTER KNOWLEDGE

Key Answers

71. D	74. E	77. B	80. D	83. A	85. B	87. A	89. A
72. C	75. E	78. E	81. A	84. D	86. E	88. B	90. B
73. D	76. B	79. B	82. E				

Items Answered Incorrectly: ___; ___; ___; ___; ___; ___; ___; ___.

Items Unsure Of: ___; ___; ___; ___; ___; ___; ___; ___.

Total Number Answered Correctly: ______

Rationale

71–(D) The color combination of green, yellow, and white flashed by beacons indicates a lighted heliport.

72–(C) The auxiliary or tail rotor is the anti-torque rotor that produces thrust in the direction opposite to the torque reaction developed by the main rotor.

73–(D) The entire helicopter has a tendency to move in the direction of tail rotor thrust when hovering. This movement is generally referred to as translating tendency or drift.

74–(E) The upward bending of the rotor blades caused by the combined forces of lift and centrifugal force is called coning.

75–(E) The exact location and length of the CG range is specified for each helicopter, but it usually extends a short distance fore and aft of the main rotor mast.

76–(B) Dissymmetry of lift is created by horizontal flight or by wind during hovering flight. It is the difference in lift (unequal lift) across the rotor disc resulting from the difference in the velocity of air over the advancing blade half of the disc area and retreating blade half of the disc area.

77–(B) Ground resonance may develop when a series of shocks causes the rotor head to become unbalanced. When one landing gear of the helicopter strikes the surface first, a shock is transmitted through the fuselage to the rotor. When one of the other landing gears strikes, the unbalance can be aggravated and become even greater. This establishes a resonance which sets up a pendulum-like oscillation of the fuselage—a severe wobbling or shaking.

78–(E) Rapid deceleration or quick stop is initiated by applying aft cyclic to reduce forward speed and lowering the collective pitch to counteract climbing.

79–(B) For slope takeoff, first obtain takeoff RPM and move cyclic stick so that the rotor rotation is parallel to the true horizon rather than the slope. Apply up-collective pitch and apply pedal to maintain heading. As the downslope skid rises and the helicopter approaches a level altitude, move the cyclic stick back to the neutral position and take the helicopter straight up to a hover before moving away from the slope. The tail should not be turned upslope because of the danger of the tail rotor striking the surface.

80–(D) Helicopter should be landed on a crosss-lope rather than on either an upslope or downslope. As the upslope skid touches the ground, the pilot should apply the cyclic stick in the direction of the slope. This will hold the skid against the slope while the downslope skid continues to be let down with the collective pitch.

81–(A) Standard conditions at sea level are: Atmospheric pressure—29.92 in. of Hg (inches of mercury).

Temperature—59°F.(15°C.)

82–(E) A running takeoff is used when conditions of load and/or density altitude prevent a sustained hover at normal hovering altitude. It is often referred to as a high-altitude takeoff. A running takeoff may be accomplished safely only if surface area of sufficient length and smoothness is available, and if no barriers exist in the flight-path to interfere with a shallow climb.

83–(A) Foot pedals in the cockpit permit the pilot to increase or decrease tail-rotor thrust, as needed, to neutralize torque effect.

84–(D) With a single main rotor rotating in a counterclockwise direction, the advancing blade will be in the right half of the rotor disc during forward flight.

85–(B) The collective pitch control lever changes the pitch angle of the main rotor blades simultaneously and equally.

86–(E) High altitude, high temperature, and high moisture content contribute to a high density altitude condition which lessens helicopter performance.

87–(A) The most favorable conditions for helicopter performance are the combination of a low-density altitude, light gross weight, and moderate to strong winds. The most adverse conditions are the combination of a high-density altitude, heavy gross weight, and calm or no wind. Any other combination of density altitude, gross weight, and wind conditions fall somewhere between the most adverse conditions and the most favorable conditions.

88–(B) The acute angle between the chord line of an airfoil and the relative wind is called the angle of attack.

89–(A) The collective pitch controls starting, stopping, and rate of speed. Pedals are used to maintain heading and the cyclic is used to maintain ground track.

90–(B) True airspeed may be roughly computed by adding to the indicated airspeed, two percent of the indicated airspeed for each 1,000 feet of altitude above sea level.

SUBTEST 5—CYCLIC ORIENTATION

Items Answered Incorrectly: ___; ___; ___; ___; ___; ___; ___; ___.

Items Unsure Of: ___; ___; ___; ___; ___; ___; ___; ___.

Total Number Answered Correctly: ___

Key Answers and Rationale

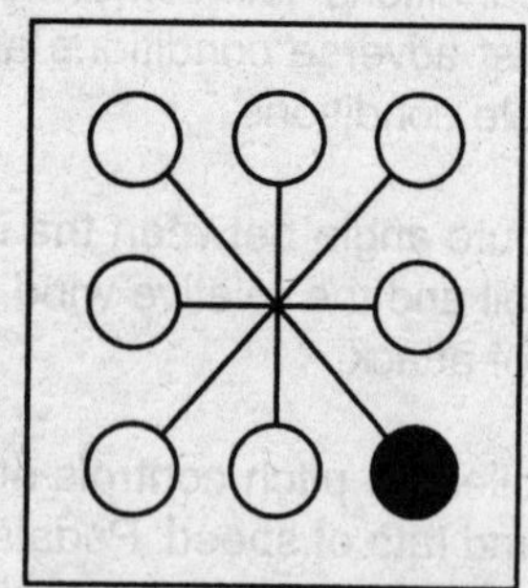

91. Climbing and banking right

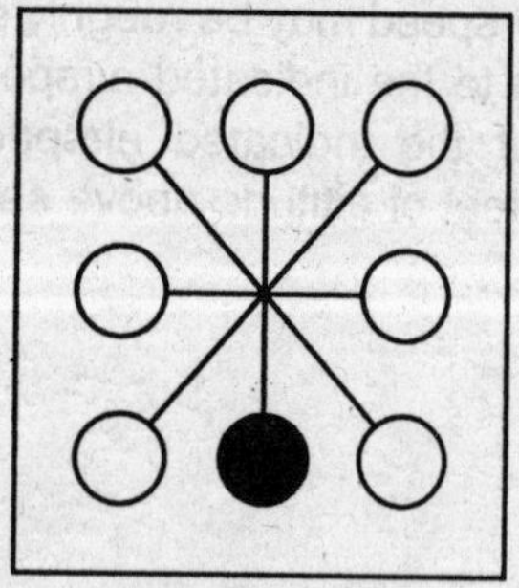

92. Climbing; no bank

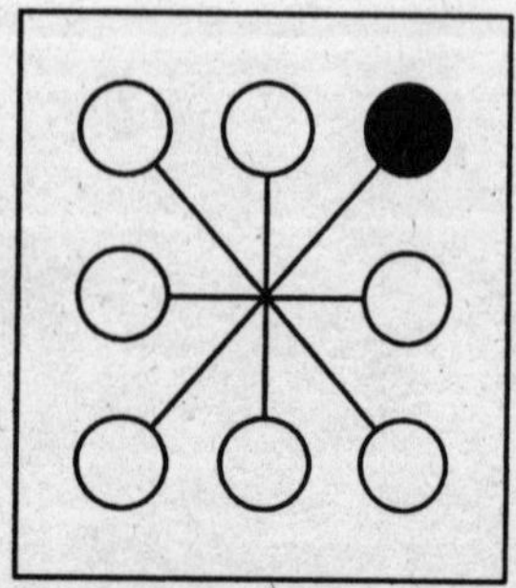

93. Diving and banking right

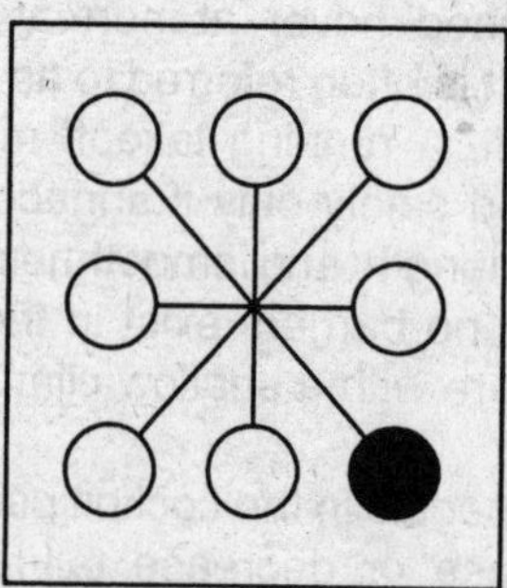

94. Climbing and banking right

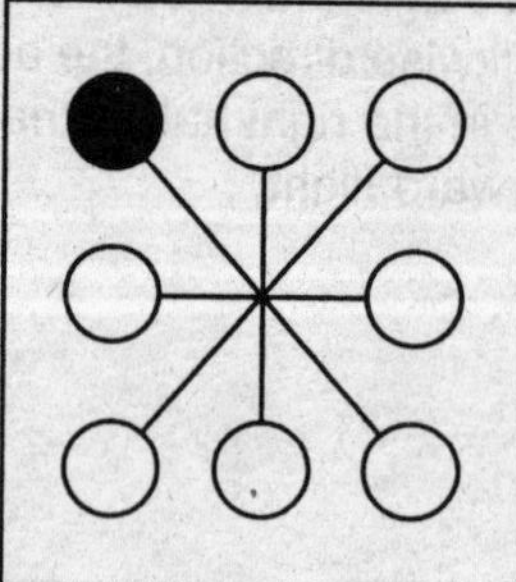

95. Diving and banking left

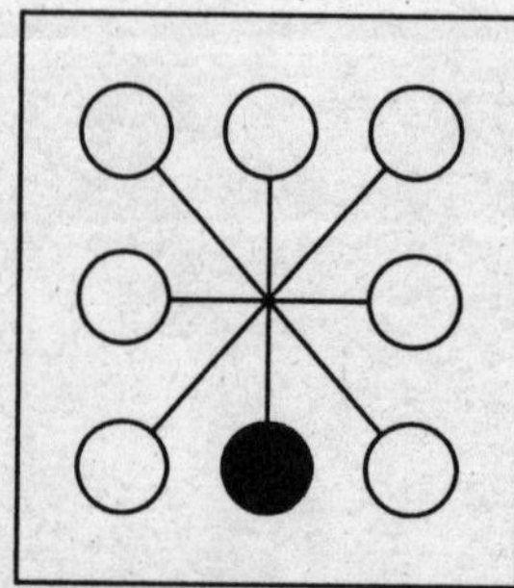

96. Climbing; no bank

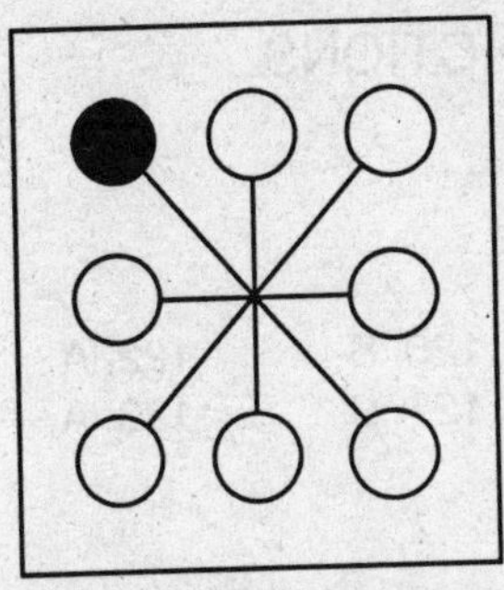
97. Diving and banking left

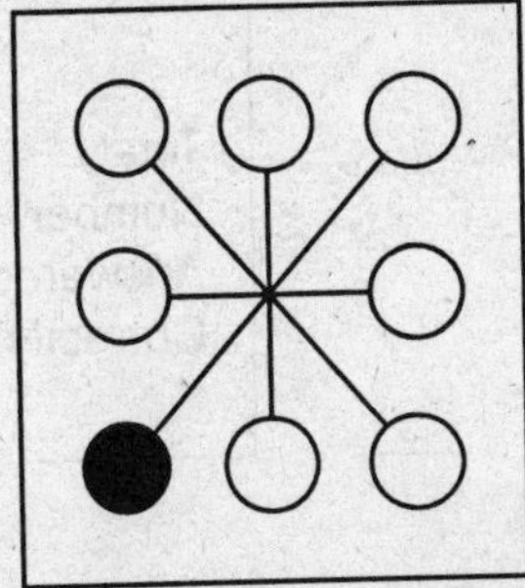
98. Climbing and banking left

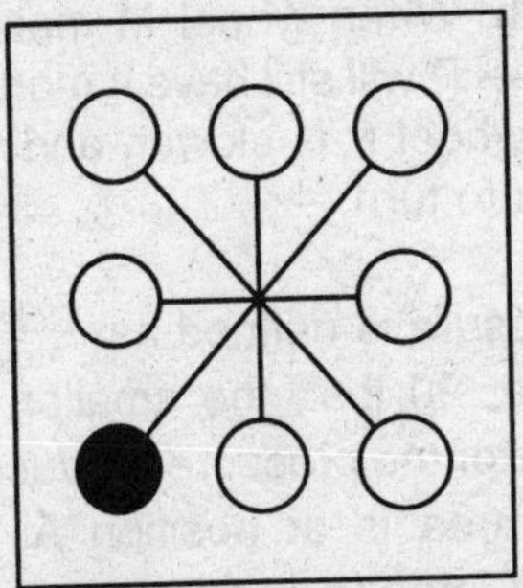
99. Climbing and banking left

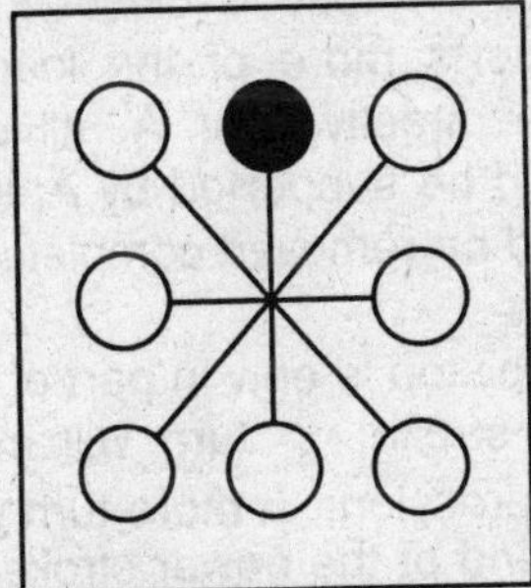
100. Diving; no bank

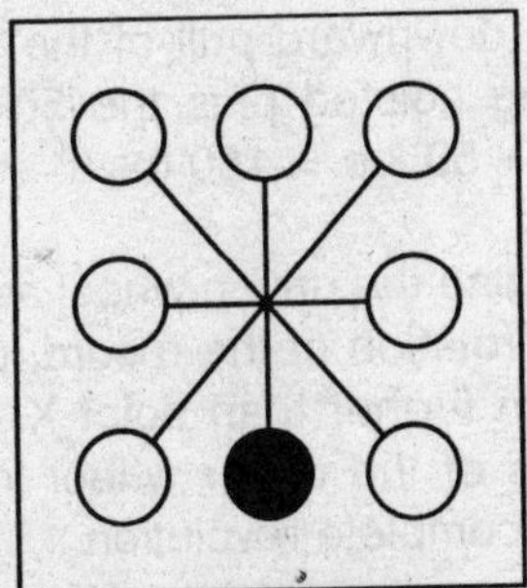
101. Climbing; no bank

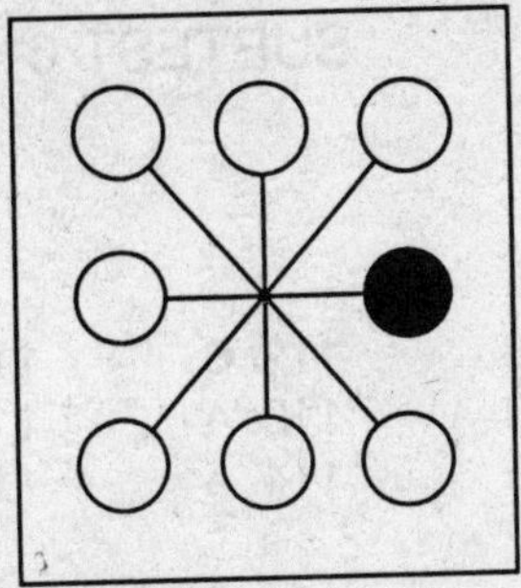
102. Right bank

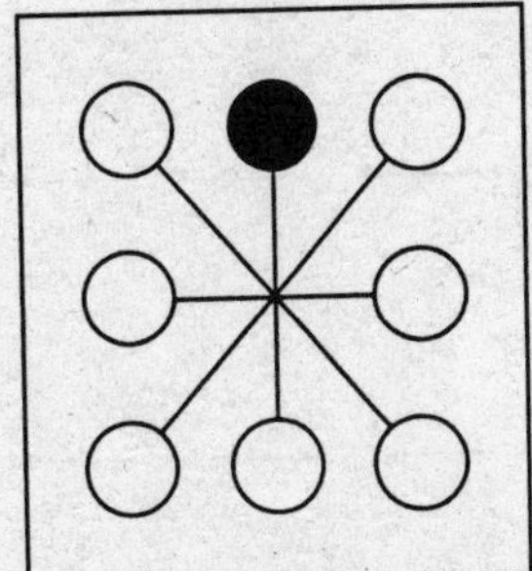
103. Diving; no bank

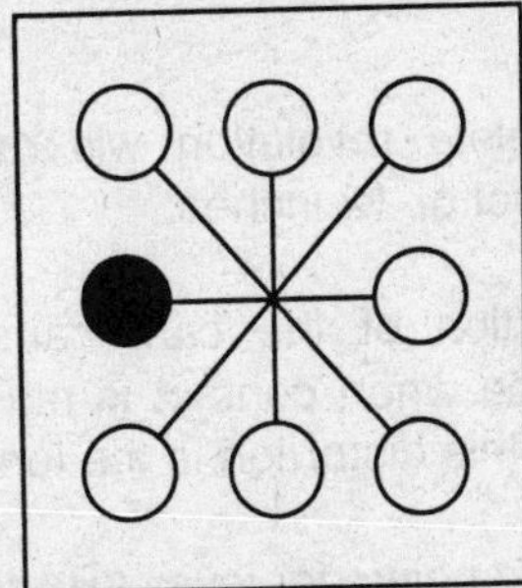
104. Left bank

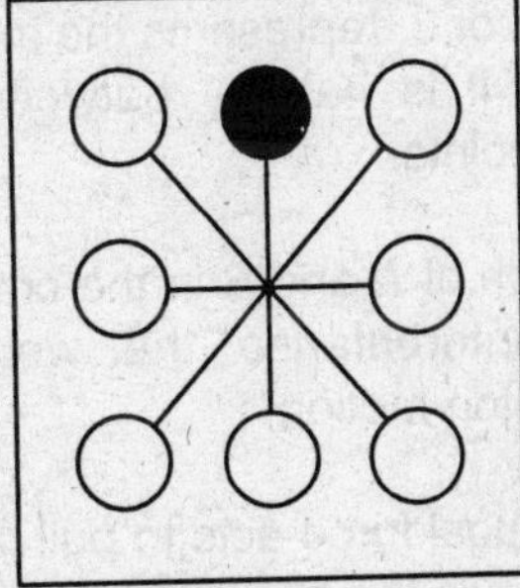
105. Diving; no bank

SUBTEST 6—MECHANICAL FUNCTIONS

Key Answers

106. B	109. B	112. B	115. A	118. B	120. B	122. A	124. B
107. A	110. B	113. A	116. B	119. A	121. B	123. A	125. A
108. A	111. B	114. A	117. A				

Items Answered Incorrectly: ___; ___; ___; ___; ___; ___; ___; ___.

Items Unsure Of: ___; ___; ___; ___; ___; ___; ___; ___.

Total Number Answered Correctly: ______

Rationale

106–(B) One complete revolution will raise the weight 1 foot or 12 inches.

107–(A) The distortion of the cam causes the valve to rise when contact is made. The amount of this distortion is the length Y.

108–(A) The slowest points for lever AB are 2 and 4, where the direction reverses and the velocity momentarily becomes zero. The midpoint, 1 or 3, represents the maximum speed, as it is halfway between these minimum points.

109–(B) The function of A and B in the crankshaft is to counterbalance the weight for smooth piston motion.

110–(B) The centrifugal force acts to pull the balls outward. Since the two balls are connected to a yolk around the center bar, this outward motion pulls the balls upward.

111–(B) The figure shown is a bimetallic strip that works like the wire in a thermostat. High temperatures will cause the metals to heat unevenly. The rivets will keep the strips together, so the only thing that they can do is bend.

112–(B) Wheel P has 16 teeth; wheel M has 12 teeth. When wheel M makes a full turn, wheel P will still have 4 more teeth to turn. So wheel P is slower, and will take more time to turn.

113–(A) Pressure is defined as $\frac{\text{Force}}{\text{Area}}$. For a given force, 20 lbs., the smaller the area, the greater the pressure produced. The smallest area is at position A, requiring the least force to lift the weight.

114–(A) Since the load is closer to upright A, it supports more of the load. If the load were directly over A, all of the weight would be supported by A; then upright B could be removed completely.

115–(A) The piston is now in part of the compression stroke; $\frac{1}{4}$ turn will move it to full compression; $\frac{1}{2}$ more turn will move it to the end of the power stroke. Adding $\frac{1}{4} + \frac{1}{2} = \frac{3}{4}$ turn.

116–(B) The downward pull of the 100-lb. weight being hoisted plus the 50-lb. effort. 100 lbs. + 50 lbs. = 150 lbs.

117–(A) Imagine the driven wheel as a record. For one rotation of the record, point Y travels much further than point X. It takes more turns of the driver wheel to turn point Y one complete revolution.

118–(B) The ball will move up if the arm holding it is pulled up. This will happen when the nut is tightened.

119–(A) A single fixed pulley is actually a first-class lever with equal arms. The mechanical advantage, neglecting friction, is 1.

120–(B) Gear 1 turns clockwise; gear 2 turns counterclockwise; gears 3 and 4 turn clockwise.

121–(B) The formula for circumference of a wheel is $C = 2\pi r$. The wheel radius of the bike in front is larger. One revolution of the larger wheel will cover a greater linear distance along the road in a given period of time.

122–(A) The water is filling up in the tank at a rate of 120 gallons per hour, or 2 gallons per minute ($\frac{120}{60} = 2$). The tank is also emptying at a rate of 1 gallon per minute. The net flow is increasing by 1 gallon per minute, since 2 gal./min, input − 1 gal./min, output = 1 gal./min, increase. *Note:* The easiest way to find the answer is to change all measurements to gallons per minute.

123–(A) Once every second = 60 times a minute. With 10 projection rods on the wheel, the wheel must rotate at 6 rpm to make 60 rod contacts per minute.

124–(B) The raft will move in the opposite direction. Let x = theoretical distance moved.

$10 \times 150 = x \times 500$; $500x = 1500$; $x = \frac{1500}{500}$ = 3 feet.

125–(A) The mechanical advantage is calculated by the number of strands supporting the weight. A has 3 strands, B has 2.

SUBTEST 7—SELF-DESCRIPTION FORM

There are no “correct” answers to these questions.

Part 6

SPECIMEN NAVY AND MARINE CORPS AVIATION SELECTION TEST BATTERY

SPECIMEN NAVY AND MARINE CORPS AVIATION SELECTION TEST BATTERY

This part contains specimen answer sheets for use in answering the questions on each test, a specimen Navy and Marine Corps Aviation Selection Test Battery, key answers for determining your scores on these tests, and the rationale or explanation for each key answer.

Remove the specimen answer sheets on the following pages for use in recording your answers to the test questions. The specimen Navy and Marine Corps Aviation Selection Test Battery is similar in format and content to the actual Navy and Marine Corps Aviation Selection Test Battery. Take these tests under "real" test conditions. Time each test carefully.

Use the key answers to obtain your test scores and to evaluate your performance on each test. Record the number of items you answered correctly, as well as the number of each question you answered incorrectly or wish to review, in the space provided below the key answers for each test.

Be certain to review carefully and understand the explanations for the answers to all questions you answered incorrectly and for each of the questions which you answered correctly but are unsure of. This is absolutely essential in order to acquire the knowledge and expertise necessary to obtain the maximum score possible on the tests of the real Navy and Marine Corps Aviation Selection Test Battery.

The introductory material for general orientation, as well as the general directions for taking the test battery, appears before the actual test questions in the test booklets. Most of this material was covered previously in this book.

Format of the Test Battery

Test	Minutes	Questions
1. Math/Verbal Test	35	37
2. Mechanical Comprehension Test	15	30
3. Spatial Apperception Test	10	35
4. Biographical Information	20	76
5. Aviation/Nautical Information	15	30

SIDE 1

ANSWER SHEET for NAVY and MARINE CORPS AVIATION SELECTION TEST BATTERY

SCHEMATIC SAMPLE

STATUS

- ○ Civilian
- ○ Officer, Navy
- ○ Officer, Marine Corps
- ○ Officer, Coast Guard
- ○ Enlisted, Navy
- ○ Enlisted, Marine Corps
- ○ Enlisted, Coast Guard
- ○ Officer Candidate–ROTC
- ○ Naval Academy
- ○ Other

NAME ______________________________
Last First MI.

TEST DATE ____/____/____
Month Day Year

INSTALLATION OR PLACE OF TESTING ______________________________

EDUCATION LEVEL	RACE/ETHNIC GROUP	SEX	SOCIAL SECURITY NUMBER	DATE OF BIRTH (MO. / DAY / YR.)
○ High School Graduate	○ American Indian	○ Male	⓪–⑨ (9 columns)	MO. ⓪–① / ⓪–⑨; DAY ⓪–③; YR. ⓪–⑨ / ⓪–⑨
○ College Freshman	○ Hispanic	○ Female		
○ College Sophomore	○ Asian			
○ College Junior	○ Black			
○ College Senior	○ White			
○ College Graduate	○ Other			
○ Graduate Student				
○ Other				

MATH/VERBAL TEST

1. Ⓐ Ⓑ Ⓒ Ⓓ	6. Ⓐ Ⓑ Ⓒ Ⓓ	11. Ⓐ Ⓑ Ⓒ Ⓓ	16. Ⓐ Ⓑ Ⓒ Ⓓ	21. Ⓐ Ⓑ Ⓒ Ⓓ	26. Ⓐ Ⓑ Ⓒ Ⓓ	31. Ⓐ Ⓑ Ⓒ Ⓓ
2. Ⓐ Ⓑ Ⓒ Ⓓ	7. Ⓐ Ⓑ Ⓒ Ⓓ	12. Ⓐ Ⓑ Ⓒ Ⓓ	17. Ⓐ Ⓑ Ⓒ Ⓓ	22. Ⓐ Ⓑ Ⓒ Ⓓ	27. Ⓐ Ⓑ Ⓒ Ⓓ	32. Ⓐ Ⓑ Ⓒ Ⓓ
3. Ⓐ Ⓑ Ⓒ Ⓓ	8. Ⓐ Ⓑ Ⓒ Ⓓ	13. Ⓐ Ⓑ Ⓒ Ⓓ	18. Ⓐ Ⓑ Ⓒ Ⓓ	23. Ⓐ Ⓑ Ⓒ Ⓓ	28. Ⓐ Ⓑ Ⓒ Ⓓ	33. Ⓐ Ⓑ Ⓒ Ⓓ
4. Ⓐ Ⓑ Ⓒ Ⓓ	9. Ⓐ Ⓑ Ⓒ Ⓓ	14. Ⓐ Ⓑ Ⓒ Ⓓ	19. Ⓐ Ⓑ Ⓒ Ⓓ	22. Ⓐ Ⓑ Ⓒ Ⓓ	29. Ⓐ Ⓑ Ⓒ Ⓓ	34. Ⓐ Ⓑ Ⓒ Ⓓ
5. Ⓐ Ⓑ Ⓒ Ⓓ	10. Ⓐ Ⓑ Ⓒ Ⓓ	15. Ⓐ Ⓑ Ⓒ Ⓓ	20. Ⓐ Ⓑ Ⓒ Ⓓ	25. Ⓐ Ⓑ Ⓒ Ⓓ	30. Ⓐ Ⓑ Ⓒ Ⓓ	35. Ⓐ Ⓑ Ⓒ Ⓓ
						36. Ⓐ Ⓑ Ⓒ Ⓓ
						37. Ⓐ Ⓑ Ⓒ Ⓓ

MECHANICAL COMPREHENSION TEST

1. Ⓐ Ⓑ Ⓒ	6. Ⓐ Ⓑ Ⓒ	11. Ⓐ Ⓑ Ⓒ	16. Ⓐ Ⓑ Ⓒ	21. Ⓐ Ⓑ Ⓒ	26. Ⓐ Ⓑ Ⓒ
2. Ⓐ Ⓑ Ⓒ	7. Ⓐ Ⓑ Ⓒ	12. Ⓐ Ⓑ Ⓒ	17. Ⓐ Ⓑ Ⓒ	22. Ⓐ Ⓑ Ⓒ	27. Ⓐ Ⓑ Ⓒ
3. Ⓐ Ⓑ Ⓒ	8. Ⓐ Ⓑ Ⓒ	13. Ⓐ Ⓑ Ⓒ	18. Ⓐ Ⓑ Ⓒ	23. Ⓐ Ⓑ Ⓒ	28. Ⓐ Ⓑ Ⓒ
4. Ⓐ Ⓑ Ⓒ	9. Ⓐ Ⓑ Ⓒ	14. Ⓐ Ⓑ Ⓒ	19. Ⓐ Ⓑ Ⓒ	24. Ⓐ Ⓑ Ⓒ	29. Ⓐ Ⓑ Ⓒ
5. Ⓐ Ⓑ Ⓒ	10. Ⓐ Ⓑ Ⓒ	15. Ⓐ Ⓑ Ⓒ	20. Ⓐ Ⓑ Ⓒ	25. Ⓐ Ⓑ Ⓒ	30. Ⓐ Ⓑ Ⓒ

ANSWER SHEET
for
NAVY and MARINE CORPS
AVIATION SELECTION TEST BATTERY

SIDE 2

SCHEMATIC SAMPLE

SPATIAL APPERCEPTION TEST

1. ⒶⒷⒸⒹⒺ	6. ⒶⒷⒸⒹⒺ	11. ⒶⒷⒸⒹⒺ	16. ⒶⒷⒸⒹⒺ	21. ⒶⒷⒸⒹⒺ	26. ⒶⒷⒸⒹⒺ	31. ⒶⒷⒸⒹⒺ
2. ⒶⒷⒸⒹⒺ	7. ⒶⒷⒸⒹⒺ	12. ⒶⒷⒸⒹⒺ	17. ⒶⒷⒸⒹⒺ	22. ⒶⒷⒸⒹⒺ	27. ⒶⒷⒸⒹⒺ	32. ⒶⒷⒸⒹⒺ
3. ⒶⒷⒸⒹⒺ	8. ⒶⒷⒸⒹⒺ	13. ⒶⒷⒸⒹⒺ	18. ⒶⒷⒸⒹⒺ	23. ⒶⒷⒸⒹⒺ	28. ⒶⒷⒸⒹⒺ	33. ⒶⒷⒸⒹⒺ
4. ⒶⒷⒸⒹⒺ	9. ⒶⒷⒸⒹⒺ	14. ⒶⒷⒸⒹⒺ	19. ⒶⒷⒸⒹⒺ	24. ⒶⒷⒸⒹⒺ	29. ⒶⒷⒸⒹⒺ	34. ⒶⒷⒸⒹⒺ
5. ⒶⒷⒸⒹⒺ	10. ⒶⒷⒸⒹⒺ	15. ⒶⒷⒸⒹⒺ	20. ⒶⒷⒸⒹⒺ	25. ⒶⒷⒸⒹⒺ	30. ⒶⒷⒸⒹⒺ	35. ⒶⒷⒸⒹⒺ

BIOGRAPHICAL INVENTORY

1. ⒶⒷⒸⒹⒺ	12. ⒶⒷⒸⒹⒺ	23. ⒶⒷⒸⒹⒺ	34. ⒶⒷⒸⒹⒺ	45. ⒶⒷⒸⒹⒺ	56. ⒶⒷⒸⒹⒺ	67. ⒶⒷⒸⒹⒺ
2. ⒶⒷⒸⒹⒺ	13. ⒶⒷⒸⒹⒺ	24. ⒶⒷⒸⒹⒺ	35. ⒶⒷⒸⒹⒺ	46. ⒶⒷⒸⒹⒺ	57. ⒶⒷⒸⒹⒺ	68. ⒶⒷⒸⒹⒺ
3. ⒶⒷⒸⒹⒺ	14. ⒶⒷⒸⒹⒺ	25. ⒶⒷⒸⒹⒺ	36. ⒶⒷⒸⒹⒺ	47. ⒶⒷⒸⒹⒺ	58. ⒶⒷⒸⒹⒺ	69. ⒶⒷⒸⒹⒺ
4. ⒶⒷⒸⒹⒺ	15. ⒶⒷⒸⒹⒺ	26. ⒶⒷⒸⒹⒺ	37. ⒶⒷⒸⒹⒺ	48. ⒶⒷⒸⒹⒺ	59. ⒶⒷⒸⒹⒺ	70. ⒶⒷⒸⒹⒺ
5. ⒶⒷⒸⒹⒺ	16. ⒶⒷⒸⒹⒺ	27. ⒶⒷⒸⒹⒺ	38. ⒶⒷⒸⒹⒺ	49. ⒶⒷⒸⒹⒺ	60. ⒶⒷⒸⒹⒺ	71. ⒶⒷⒸⒹⒺ
6. ⒶⒷⒸⒹⒺ	17. ⒶⒷⒸⒹⒺ	28. ⒶⒷⒸⒹⒺ	39. ⒶⒷⒸⒹⒺ	50. ⒶⒷⒸⒹⒺ	61. ⒶⒷⒸⒹⒺ	72. ⒶⒷⒸⒹⒺ
7. ⒶⒷⒸⒹⒺ	18. ⒶⒷⒸⒹⒺ	29. ⒶⒷⒸⒹⒺ	40. ⒶⒷⒸⒹⒺ	51. ⒶⒷⒸⒹⒺ	62. ⒶⒷⒸⒹⒺ	73. ⒶⒷⒸⒹⒺ
8. ⒶⒷⒸⒹⒺ	19. ⒶⒷⒸⒹⒺ	30. ⒶⒷⒸⒹⒺ	41. ⒶⒷⒸⒹⒺ	52. ⒶⒷⒸⒹⒺ	63. ⒶⒷⒸⒹⒺ	74. ⒶⒷⒸⒹⒺ
9. ⒶⒷⒸⒹⒺ	20. ⒶⒷⒸⒹⒺ	31. ⒶⒷⒸⒹⒺ	42. ⒶⒷⒸⒹⒺ	53. ⒶⒷⒸⒹⒺ	64. ⒶⒷⒸⒹⒺ	75. ⒶⒷⒸⒹⒺ
10. ⒶⒷⒸⒹⒺ	21. ⒶⒷⒸⒹⒺ	32. ⒶⒷⒸⒹⒺ	43. ⒶⒷⒸⒹⒺ	54. ⒶⒷⒸⒹⒺ	65. ⒶⒷⒸⒹⒺ	76. ⒶⒷⒸⒹⒺ
11. ⒶⒷⒸⒹⒺ	22. ⒶⒷⒸⒹⒺ	33. ⒶⒷⒸⒹⒺ	44. ⒶⒷⒸⒹⒺ	55. ⒶⒷⒸⒹⒺ	66. ⒶⒷⒸⒹⒺ	

AVIATION/NAUTICAL INFORMATION

1. ⒶⒷⒸⒹⒺ	6. ⒶⒷⒸⒹⒺ	11. ⒶⒷⒸⒹⒺ	16. ⒶⒷⒸⒹⒺ	21. ⒶⒷⒸⒹⒺ	26. ⒶⒷⒸⒹⒺ
2. ⒶⒷⒸⒹⒺ	7. ⒶⒷⒸⒹⒺ	12. ⒶⒷⒸⒹⒺ	17. ⒶⒷⒸⒹⒺ	22. ⒶⒷⒸⒹⒺ	27. ⒶⒷⒸⒹⒺ
3. ⒶⒷⒸⒹⒺ	8. ⒶⒷⒸⒹⒺ	13. ⒶⒷⒸⒹⒺ	18. ⒶⒷⒸⒹⒺ	23. ⒶⒷⒸⒹⒺ	28. ⒶⒷⒸⒹⒺ
4. ⒶⒷⒸⒹⒺ	9. ⒶⒷⒸⒹⒺ	14. ⒶⒷⒸⒹⒺ	19. ⒶⒷⒸⒹⒺ	24. ⒶⒷⒸⒹⒺ	29. ⒶⒷⒸⒹⒺ
5. ⒶⒷⒸⒹⒺ	10. ⒶⒷⒸⒹⒺ	15. ⒶⒷⒸⒹⒺ	20. ⒶⒷⒸⒹⒺ	25. ⒶⒷⒸⒹⒺ	30. ⒶⒷⒸⒹⒺ

TEST 1

MATH/VERBAL TEST (MVT)

TIME: 35 Minutes—37 Questions

Each of the following five questions numbered *1* to *5* consists of an arithmetic problem followed by four possible answers. Decide which one of the four options is the correct answer.

1. Two trains running on the same track travel at the rates of 30 and 35 mph, respectively. If the slower train starts out an hour earlier, how long will it take the faster train to catch up with it?

   (A) 4 hours
   (B) 5 hours
   (C) 6 hours
   (D) 7 hours

2. A naval detachment has enough rations to feed 16 persons for 10 days. If 4 more persons join the detachment, for how many fewer days will the rations last?

   (A) 1
   (B) 2
   (C) 3
   (D) 4

3. A field can be plowed by 9 machines in 5 hours. If 3 machines are broken and cannot be used, how many hours will it take to plow the field?

   (A) $7\frac{1}{2}$ hours
   (B) $8\frac{1}{2}$ hours
   (C) $9\frac{1}{2}$ hours
   (D) $10\frac{1}{2}$ hours

4. What is the square root of 9 raised to the fourth power?

   (A) 12
   (B) 27
   (C) 49
   (D) 81

5. If $2^{n-2} = 32$, then *n* equals

   (A) 5
   (B) 7
   (C) 8
   (D) 12

Questions *6* to *10* consist of sentences in which one word is omitted. For each question, select the lettered option which best completes the thought expressed in the sentence.

6. The voters showed their ____ by staying away from the polls.

   (A) affluence
   (B) apathy
   (C) interest
   (D) registration

7. Through his ____, he managed to cheat his partners out of their profits.

   (A) ineffectiveness
   (B) ineptness
   (C) machinations
   (D) transactions

8. No elected official who remains ____ can be a viable candidate for reelection; compromise is the lifeblood of politics.

   (A) arrogant
   (B) irreconcilable
   (C) opinionated
   (D) suspicious

9. Alchemists expended much of their energies attempting to ____ base elements into gold.

   (A) commute
   (B) transfer
   (C) translate
   (D) transmute

10. The new regulations turned out to be ____, not permissive.

    (A) impermissive
    (B) liberal
    (C) stringent
    (D) unrestrictive

Each of the following five questions numbered *11* to *15* consists of an arithmetic problem followed by four possible answers. Decide which one of the four options is the correct answer.

11. Jane received grades of 90, 88, and 75 on three tests. What grade must she receive on the next test so that her average for these four tests is 86?

    (A) 88
    (B) 89
    (C) 90
    (D) 91

12. A family drove from New York to San Francisco, a distance of 3000 miles. They drove $\frac{1}{10}$ of the distance the first day and $\frac{1}{9}$ of the remaining distance the second day. How many miles were left to be driven?

    (A) 2200 miles
    (B) 2300 miles
    (C) 2400 miles
    (D) 2500 miles

13. In a 3-hour examination of 320 questions, there are 40 mathematics problems. If twice as much time should be allowed for each mathematics problem as for each of the other questions, how many minutes should be spent on the mathematics problems?

    (A) 40 minutes
    (B) 45 minutes
    (C) 50 minutes
    (D) 55 minutes

14. 100,000 may be represented as

    (A) 10^4
    (B) 10^5
    (C) 10^6
    (D) 10^7

15. If $a = 3b$ and $6b = 12c$, then $a =$

    (A) $6c$
    (B) $9c$
    (C) $12c$
    (D) $15c$

Questions *16* to *20* consist of quotations which contain one word that is incorrectly used because it is not in keeping with the meaning that each quotation is evidently intended to convey. Determine which word is incorrectly used. Then select from the lettered options the word which, when substituted for the incorrectly used word, would *best* help to convey the intended meaning of the quotation.

16. "It is difficult to determine whether the large or small organization would receive the greater benefit from scientific work measurement, for while the large organization undoubtedly receives greater returns in terms of money savings, the effect of proportionate savings on a small organization is probably even more uncertain."

    (A) beneficial
    (B) certainly
    (C) realistic
    (D) unimportant

17. "The law of almost all states permits certain classes of persons to vote despite their absence from home at election time; sometimes this privilege is given only to members of the Armed Forces of the United States, though generally it is extended to all voters whose occupations make absence preventable."

    (A) avoidable
    (B) necessary
    (C) prohibition
    (D) sanction

GO ON TO THE NEXT PAGE.

18. "The criticism that supervisors are discriminatory in their treatment of subordinates is to some extent untrue, for the subjective nature of many supervisory decisions makes it probable that many employees who have not progressed will ascribe their lack of progress to supervisory favoritism."

    (A) apathetic
    (B) deny
    (C) success
    (D) unavoidable

19. "Only when it is deliberate and when it is clearly understood what impressions the ease of communications will probably create in the minds of employees and lower management should top management refrain from commenting on a subject that is of general concern."

    (A) absence
    (B) advantage
    (C) doubt
    (D) obvious

20. "Determining the value of employees in an organization is fundamental not only as a guide to evaluating personnel policies on promotions, demotions, and transfers, but also as a means of keeping the workforce on its toes and of checking the originality of selection methods."

    (A) administration
    (B) effectiveness
    (C) increasing
    (D) initiative

Each of the following five questions numbered *21* to *25* consists of an arithmetic problem followed by four possible answers. Decide which one of the four options is the correct answer.

21. A tank which holds 450 gallons of water can be filled by one pipe in 15 minutes and emptied by another in 30 minutes. How long would it take to fill the tank if both pipes are open?

    (A) 30 minutes
    (B) 31 minutes
    (C) 32 minutes
    (D) 33 minutes

22. A class of 204 recruits consists of three racial and ethnic groups. If $\frac{1}{3}$ are black and $\frac{1}{4}$ are Hispanic, and the remaining recruits are white, how many of the recruits in the class are white?

    (A) 94
    (B) 85
    (C) 75
    (D) 68

23. If a driver completes a trip of 120 miles at the rate of 30 mph, at what rate would the driver have to travel on the return trip in order to average 40 mph for the round trip?

    (A) 50 mph
    (B) 55 mph
    (C) 60 mph
    (D) 65 mph

24. If x is less than 0 and y is less than 0, then

    (A) x is greater than y
    (B) y is greater than x
    (C) xy is less than 0
    (D) xy is greater than 0

25. Angle E is 30° larger than its complement. The number of degrees in angle E is

    (A) 30°
    (B) 45°
    (C) 60°
    (D) 90°

Questions *26* to *30* are based on different reading passages. Answer each question on the basis of the information contained in the quotation.

26. "Genuine coins have an even and distinct corrugated outer edge; the corrugated outer edges on counterfeit coins are usually uneven, crooked, or missing."

    According to this quotation,

    (A) counterfeit coins can rarely be distinguished from genuine coins
    (B) counterfeit coins never lose their corrugated outer edge
    (C) genuine coins never lose their uneven, corrugated outer edge
    (D) the quality of the outer edge may show that a coin is counterfeit

27. "In most states, no crime is considered to occur unless there is a written law forbidding the act, and even though an act may not be exactly in harmony with public policy, such act is not a crime unless it is expressly forbidden by legislative enactment."

The one of the following statements which is most nearly in keeping with the meaning of the above quotation is:

(A) A crime is committed only with reference to a particular law.
(B) All acts not in harmony with public policy should be expressly forbidden by law.
(C) Legislative enactments frequently forbid actions which are exactly in harmony with public policy.
(D) Nothing contrary to public policy can be done without legislative authority.

28. "Only one measure, but a quite obvious measure, of the merits of the personnel policies of an organization and of the adequacy and fairness of the wages and other conditions of employment prevailing in it is the rate at which replacements must be made in order to maintain the work force."

This statement means most nearly that

(A) maximum effectiveness in personnel management has been achieved when there is no employee turnover
(B) organization policies should be based on both social and economic considerations
(C) rate of employee turnover is one indicator of the effectiveness of personnel management
(D) wages and working conditions are of prime importance to both union leaders and managers

29. "Education should not stop when the individual has been prepared to make a livelihood and to live in modern society; living would be mere existence were there no appreciation and enjoyment of the riches of art, literature and science."

This quotation best supports the statement that true education

(A) deals chiefly with art, literature, and science
(B) disregards practical goals
(C) prepares an individual for a full enjoyment of life
(D) teaches a person to focus on the routine problems of life

30. "Just as the procedure of a collection department must be clear-cut and definite, the steps being taken with the sureness of a skilled chess player, so the various paragraphs of a collection letter must show clear organization, giving evidence of a mind that, from the beginning, has had a specific end in view."

The quotation means most nearly that a collection letter should always

(A) be carefully planned
(B) be courteous but brief
(C) be divided into several long paragraphs
(D) show a spirit of sportsmanship

Each of the following five questions numbered *31* to *35* consists of an arithmetic problem followed by four possible answers. Decide which one of the four options is the correct answer.

31. Two ships are 1800 miles apart and sailing toward each other. One sails at the rate of 95 miles per day and the other at the rate of 75 miles per day. How far apart will they be at the end of 8 days?

(A) 364 miles
(B) 380 miles
(C) 440 miles
(D) 500 miles

32. Successive discounts of 20% and 15% are equivalent to a single discount of

(A) 32%
(B) 33%
(C) 34%
(D) 35%

33. A bridge crosses a river that is 1520 feet wide. One bank of the river holds $\frac{1}{5}$ of the bridge while the other holds $\frac{1}{6}$ of it. How long is the bridge?

(A) 2200 feet
(B) 2300 feet
(C) 2400 feet
(D) 2500 feet

34. What is the perimeter of a right triangle whose legs are 6 and 8 feet?

    (A) 10 feet
    (B) 14 feet
    (C) 20 feet
    (D) 24 feet

35. The fourth root of 16 is

    (A) 2
    (B) 3
    (C) 4
    (D) 8

Questions *36* and *37* are based on reading passages. Answer each question on the basis of the information contained in the quotation.

36. "The prevention of accidents makes it necessary not only that safety devices be used to guard exposed machinery but also that mechanics be instructed in safety rules which they must follow for their own protection and that the lighting in the plant be adequate."

    The quotation best supports the statement that industrial accidents

    (A) are always avoidable
    (B) cannot be entirely overcome
    (C) may be due to ignorance
    (D) usually result from inadequate machinery

37. "Although manufacturers exercise, through advertising, a high degree of control over consumers' desires, the manufacturer assumes enormous risks in attempting to predict what consumers will want and in producing goods in quantity and distributing them in advance of final selection by the consumers."

    The quotation best supports the statement that manufacturers

    (A) can predict with great accuracy the success of any product they put on the market
    (B) must depend upon the final consumers for the success of their undertakings
    (C) must distribute goods directly to the consumers
    (D) must eliminate the risk of overproduction by advertising

END OF MATH/VERBAL TEST

MECHANICAL COMPREHENSION TEST (MCT)

TIME: 15 Minutes—30 Questions

This test has 30 questions designed to measure your ability to learn and reason with mechanical terms. Each diagram is followed with a question or an incomplete statement. Study the diagram carefully and select the choice that best answers the question or completes the statement. Then mark the space on your answer form that has the same number and letter as your choice.

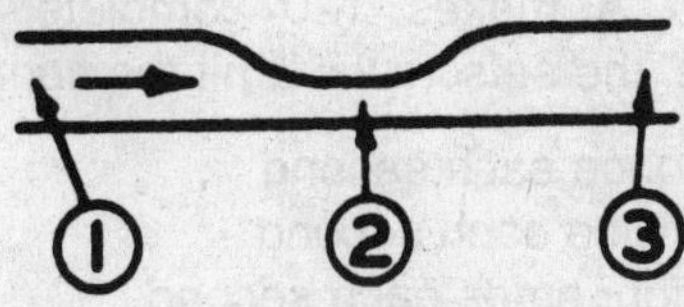

1. The figure above represents a pipe through which water is flowing in the direction of the arrow. There is a constriction in the pipe at the point indicated by the number 2. Water is being pumped into the pipe at a constant rate of 350 gallons per minute. Of the following, the most accurate statement is that

   (A) the velocity of the water at point 2 is the same as the velocity of the water at point 3
   (B) a greater volume of water is flowing past point 1 in a minute than is flowing past point 2
   (C) the volume of water flowing past point 2 in a minute is the same as the volume of water flowing past point 1 in a minute

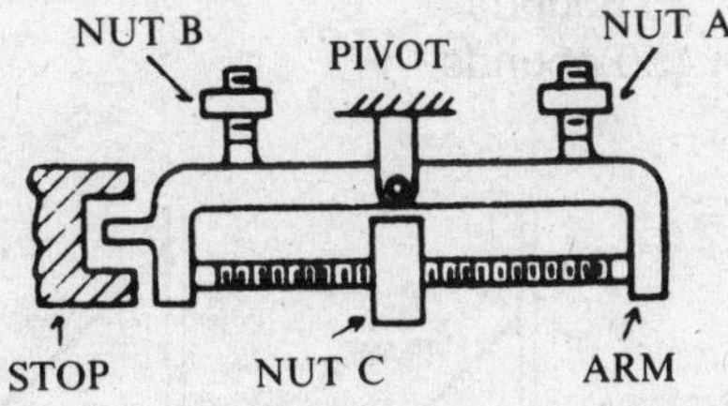

2. The arm in the figure above is exactly balanced as shown. If nut A is removed entirely, then, in order to rebalance the arm, it will be necessary to turn

   (A) nut C toward the right
   (B) nut C toward the left
   (C) nut B up

3. The reading of the voltmeter should be

   (A) 600
   (B) 120
   (C) 0

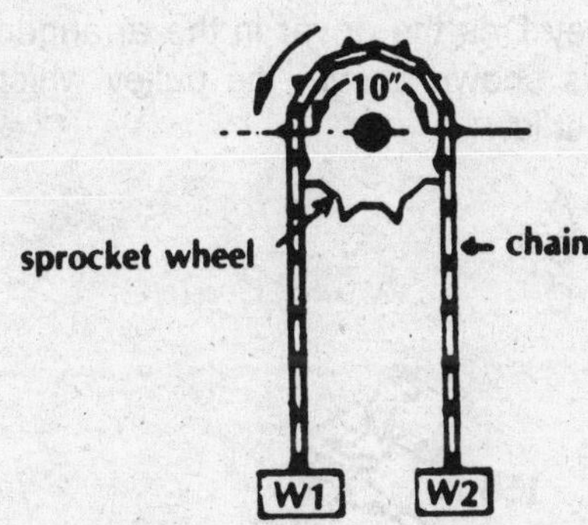

4. In the figure shown above, one complete revolution of the sprocket wheel will bring weight W2 higher than weight W1 by

   (A) 24 inches
   (B) 36 inches
   (C) 48 inches

GO ON TO THE NEXT PAGE.

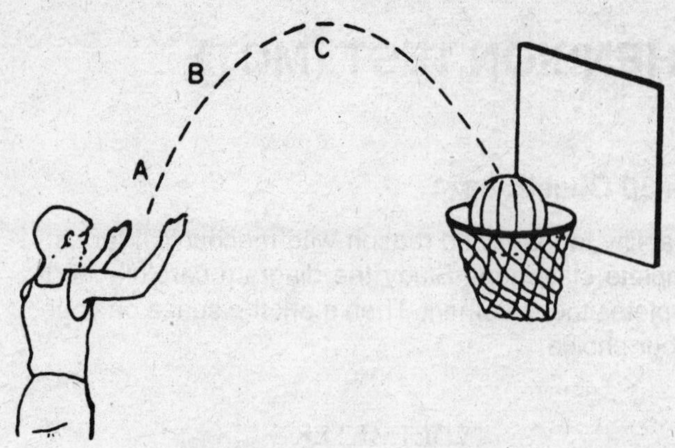

5. At which point was the basketball moving slowest?

   (A) A
   (B) B
   (C) C

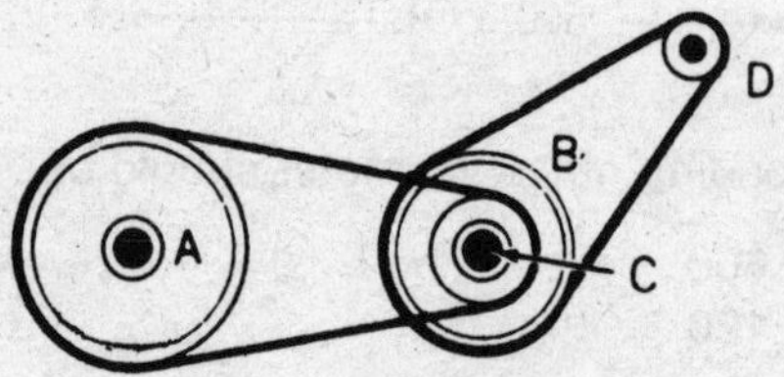

6. If pulley D is the driver in the arrangement of pulleys shown above, the pulley which turns slowest is

   (A) A
   (B) B
   (C) C

7. A 150-pound person jumps off a 600-pound raft to a point in the water 10 feet away. Theoretically, the raft would move in the opposite direction a distance of

   (A) $2\frac{1}{2}$ feet
   (B) 3 feet
   (C) $3\frac{1}{2}$ feet

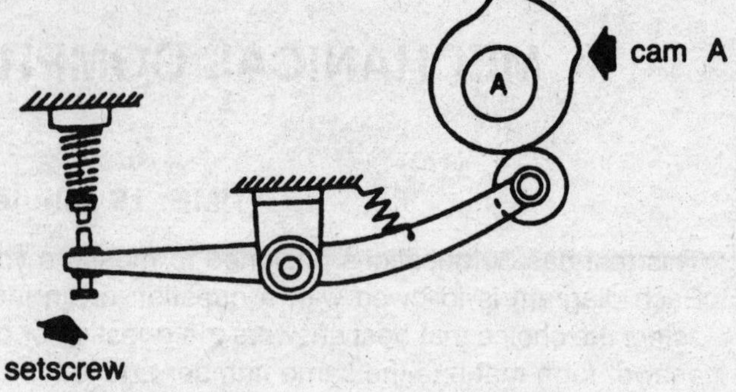

8. If cam A makes 120 complete turns per minute, the setscrew will hit the contact point

   (A) once each second
   (B) twice each second
   (C) four times each second

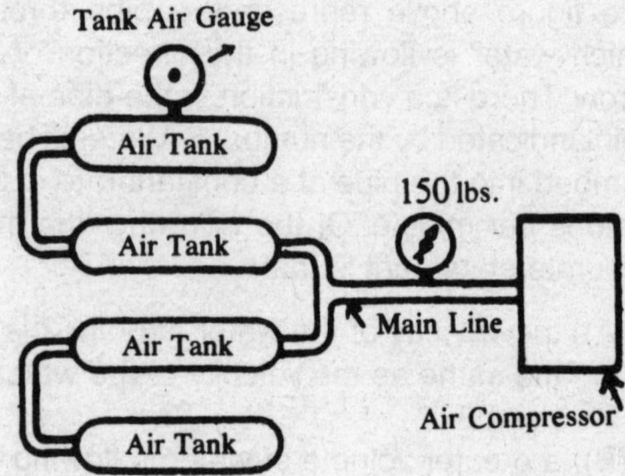

9. As shown in the figure above, four air reservoirs have been filled with air by the air compressor. If the main gauge reads 150 pounds, then the tank air gauge will read

   (A) 50 pounds
   (B) 75 pounds
   (C) 150 pounds

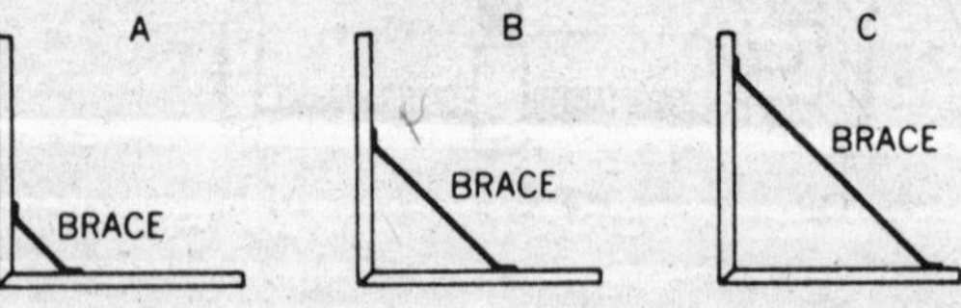

10. Which of the angles is braced most securely?

   (A) A
   (B) B
   (C) C

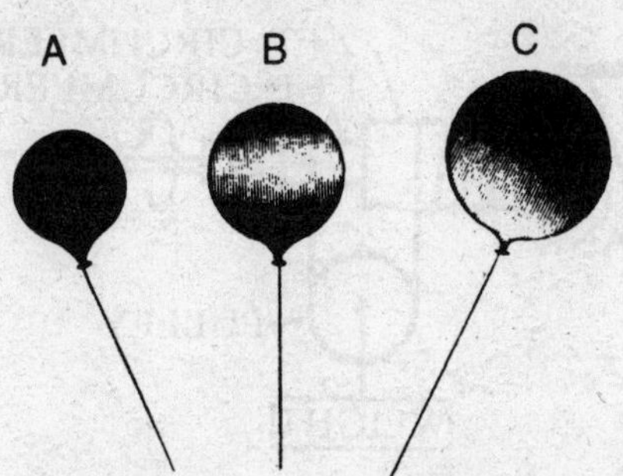

11. The amount of gas in the balloons is equal. The atmospheric pressure outside the balloons is lowest on which balloon?

    (A) A
    (B) B
    (C) C

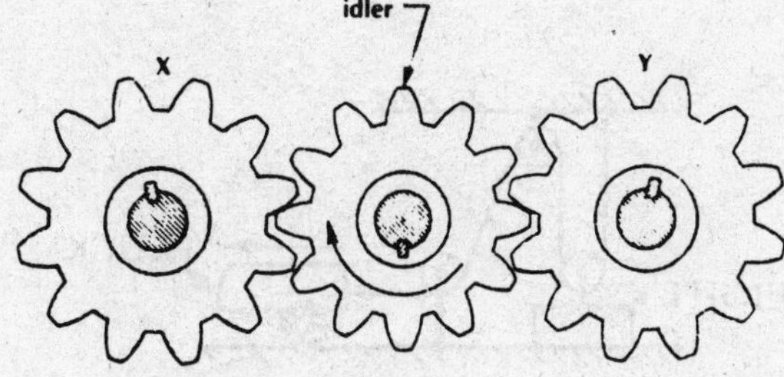

12. In the figure shown above, X is the driver gear and Y is the driven gear. If the idler gear is rotating clockwise,

    (A) gear X and gear Y are rotating clockwise
    (B) gear X and gear Y are rotating counterclockwise
    (C) gear X is rotating clockwise while gear Y is rotating counterclockwise.

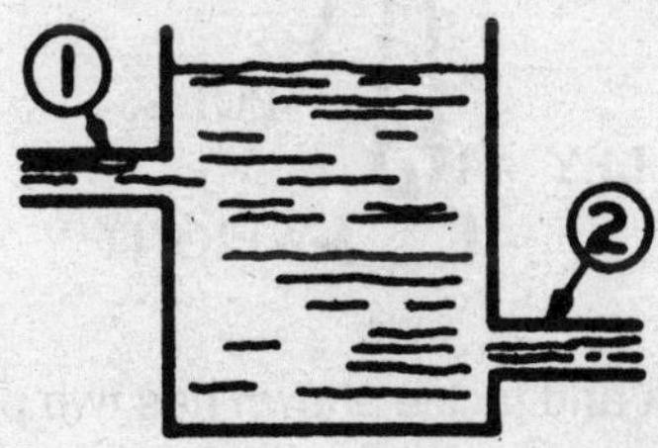

13. The figure shown above represents a water tank containing water. The number 1 indicates an intake pipe and 2 indicates a discharge pipe. Of the following, the correct statement is that

    (A) the tank will eventually overflow if water flows through the intake pipe at a slower rate than it flows out through the discharge pipe
    (B) the tank will empty completely if the intake pipe is closed and the discharge pipe is allowed to remain open
    (C) the water in the tank will remain at a constant level if the rate of intake is equal to the rate of discharge

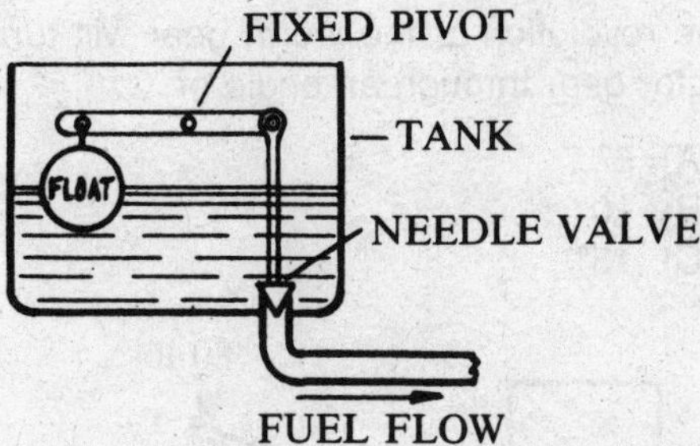

14. If the float in the tank develops a bad leak, then

    (A) the flow of fuel will stop
    (B) the float will stay in the position shown
    (C) the needle value will remain in the open position

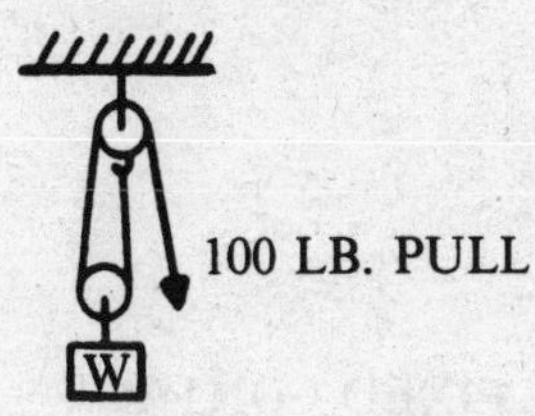

15. The maximum weight "W" that can be lifted as shown with a pull of 100 pounds is

    (A) 100 pounds
    (B) 200 pounds
    (C) 300 pounds

GO ON TO THE NEXT PAGE.

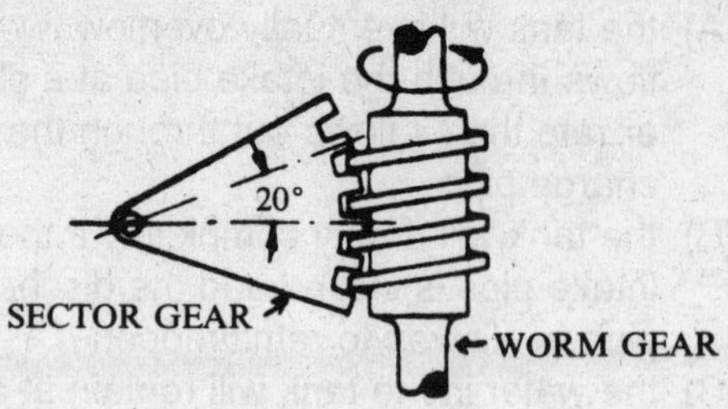

16. One revolution of the worm gear will turn the sector gear through an angle of

(A) 5°
(B) 10°
(C) 15°

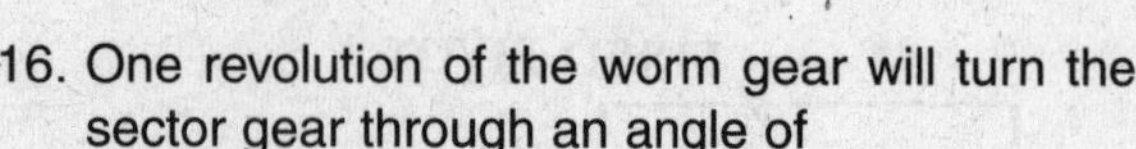

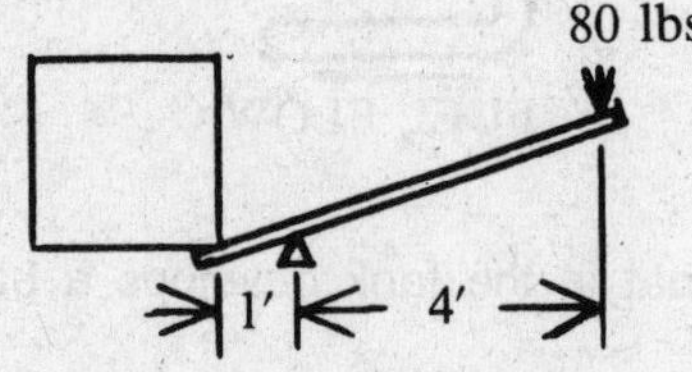

17. A pry bar is used to move a concrete block. A force of 80 lbs. applied as shown will produce a tipping force on the edge of the block of

(A) 80 lbs.
(B) 240 lbs.
(C) 320 lbs.

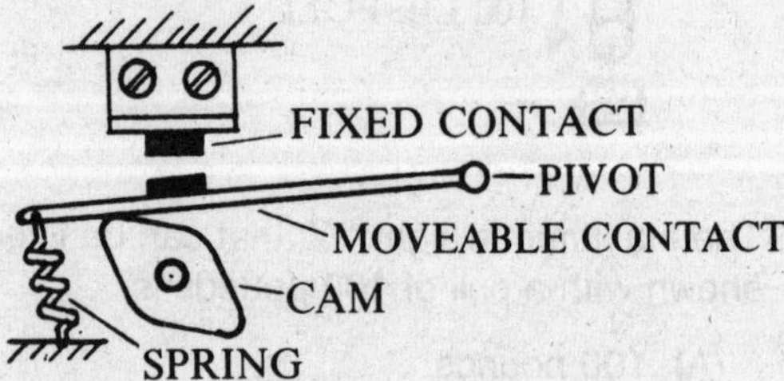

18. If the contacts come together once every second, the cam is rotating at

(A) 30 rpm
(B) 45 rpm
(C) 60 rpm

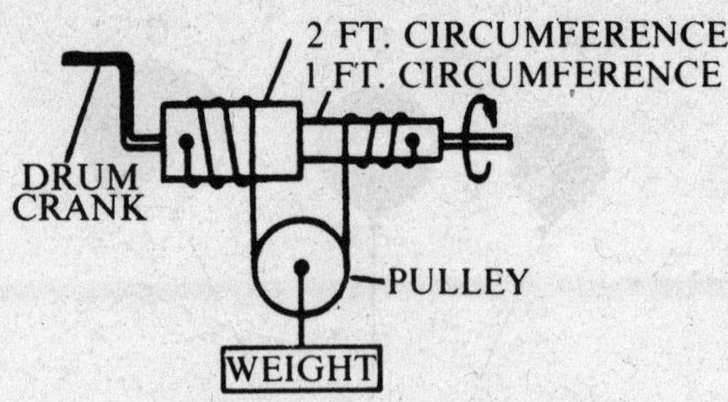

19. One complete turn of the drum crank will move the weight vertically upward a distance of

(A) 3 feet
(B) $2\frac{1}{2}$ feet
(C) $1\frac{1}{2}$ feet

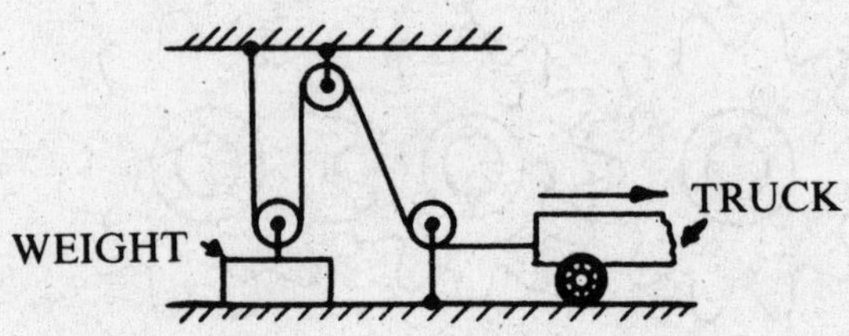

20. The weight is to be raised by means of the rope attached to the truck. If the truck moves forward 30 feet, then the weight will rise

(A) 20 feet
(B) 15 feet
(C) 10 feet

21. The block and tackle shown has two pulleys of equal diameter. While the weight is being raised, pulley #2 will rotate at

(A) twice the speed of pulley #1
(B) the same speed as pulley #1
(C) one-half the speed of pulley #1

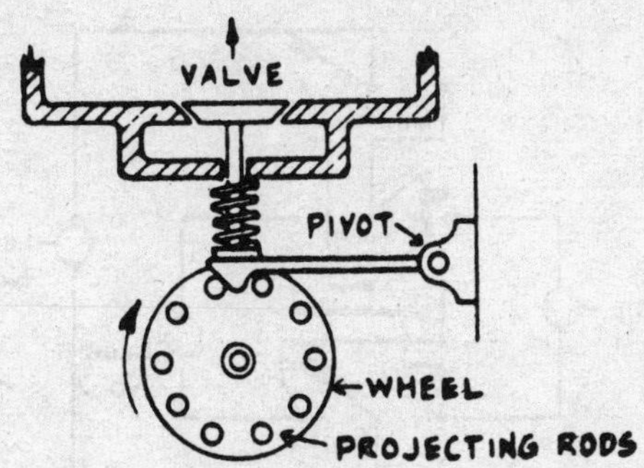

22. In order to open the valve twice every second, the wheel must rotate at

(A) 6 rpm
(B) 9 rpm
(C) 12 rpm

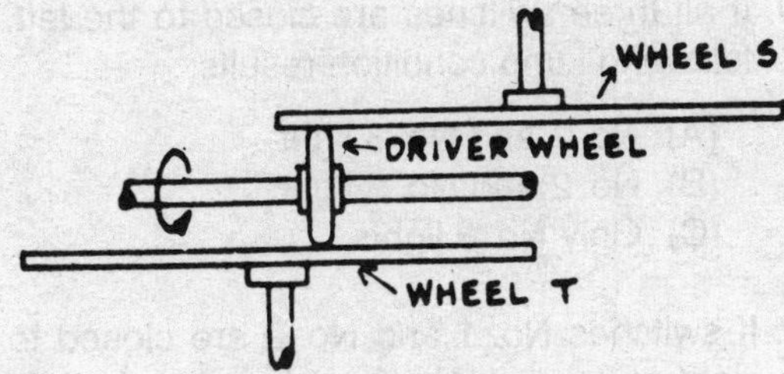

23. With the wheels in the position shown

(A) wheel S will rotate at a faster speed than wheel T
(B) wheels S and T will rotate at the same speed
(C) wheel S will rotate at a slower speed than wheel T

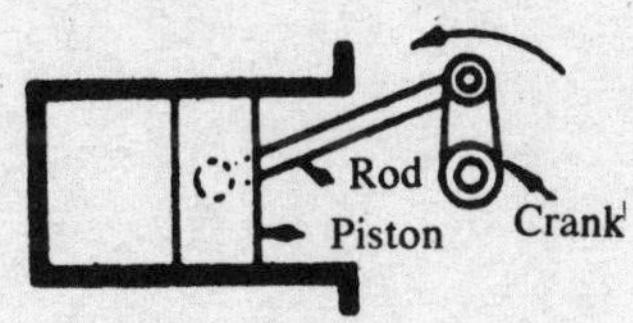

24. The figure above shows a crank and piston. The piston moves from mid-position to the extreme left and then back to the mid position if the crank

(A) makes a $\frac{1}{4}$ turn

(B) makes a $\frac{1}{2}$ turn

(C) makes a $\frac{3}{4}$ turn

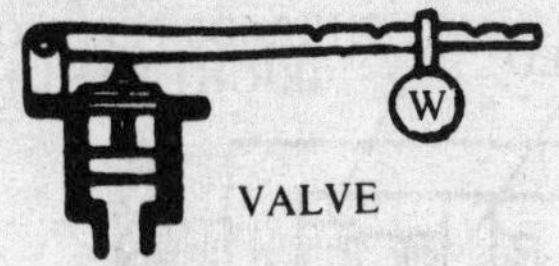

25. The figure above shows a lever-type safety valve. It will blow off at a higher pressure if weight W is

(A) decreased
(B) moved to the left
(C) moved to the right

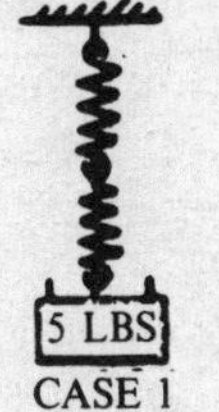

26. In the figure above, all four springs are identical. In Case 1 with the springs end to end, the stretch of each spring due to the 5-pound weight is

(A) $\frac{1}{2}$ as much as in Case 2

(B) the same as in Case 2

(C) twice as much as in Case 2

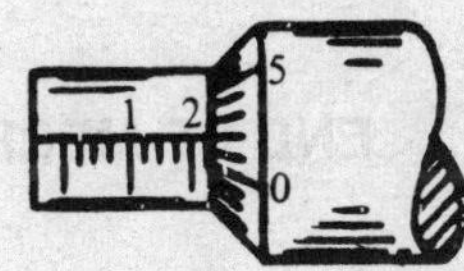

27. In the figure above, the micrometer reads

(A) .2270
(B) .2250
(C) .2120

GO ON TO THE NEXT PAGE.

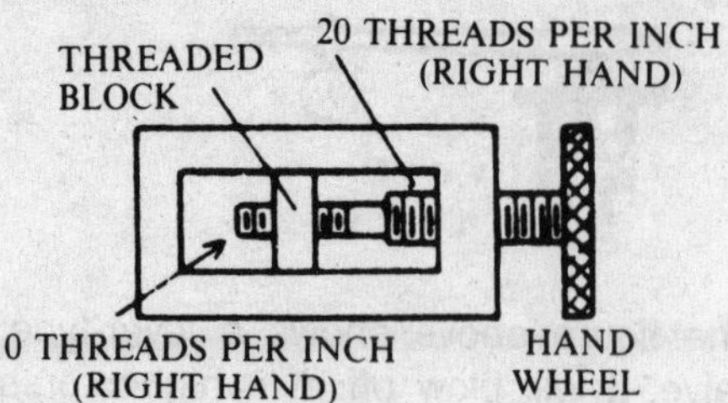

28. In the figure above, the threaded block can slide in the slot, but cannot revolve. If the hand wheel is turned 20 revolutions clockwise, the threaded block will move

    (A) one inch to the left

    (B) $\frac{1}{2}$ inch to the left

    (C) one inch to the right

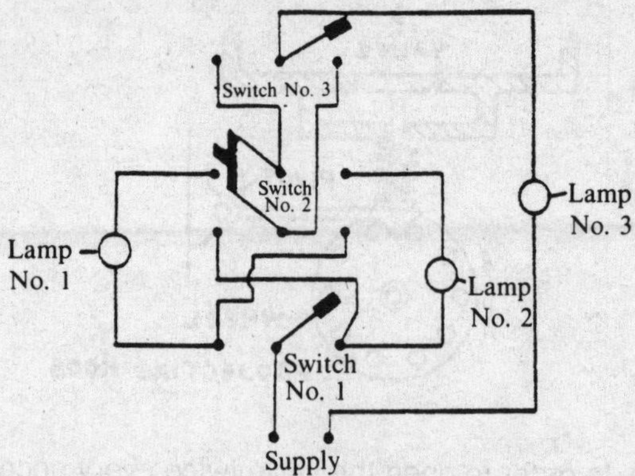

Answer questions 29 and 30 on the basis of the wiring diagram with three switches and three lamps shown above. (Symbol —⌒— indicates that wires cross but are not connected.)

29. If all three switches are closed to the left, the following lamp condition results:

    (A) No. 1 and No. 3 light
    (B) No. 2 and No. 3 light
    (C) Only No. 3 lights

30. If switches No. 1 and No. 2 are closed to the right and switch No. 3 is closed to the left, the following lamp condition results:

    (A) No. 1 and No. 3 light
    (B) No. 2 and No. 3 light
    (C) Only No. 3 lights

END OF MECHANICAL COMPREHENSION TEST

TEST 3

SPATIAL APPERCEPTION TEST

TIME: 10 Minutes—35 Questions

You will have five minutes to read these instructions. It is suggested that you *read them carefully.*

The two pictures below show an aerial view and a picture of a plane from which the view might have been seen. Note that the view is out at sea and that the horizon appears to be tilted. Note also that the plane is shown flying out to sea and that it is banked. You can determine the position of a plane by the view that the pilot has when he or she looks directly ahead through the windshield of the cockpit.

Each problem in this test consists of six pictures: an aerial view at the upper left and five pictured options below labeled A, B, C, D, and E. Each pictured option shows a plane in flight. The picture at the upper left shows the view that the pilot would have looking straight ahead from the cockpit of one of the five pictured planes. Determine which of the five lettered sketches most nearly represents the position or attitude of the plane and the direction of flight from which the view would have been seen.

Try the two sample problems on the following pages.

GO ON TO THE NEXT PAGE.

1.

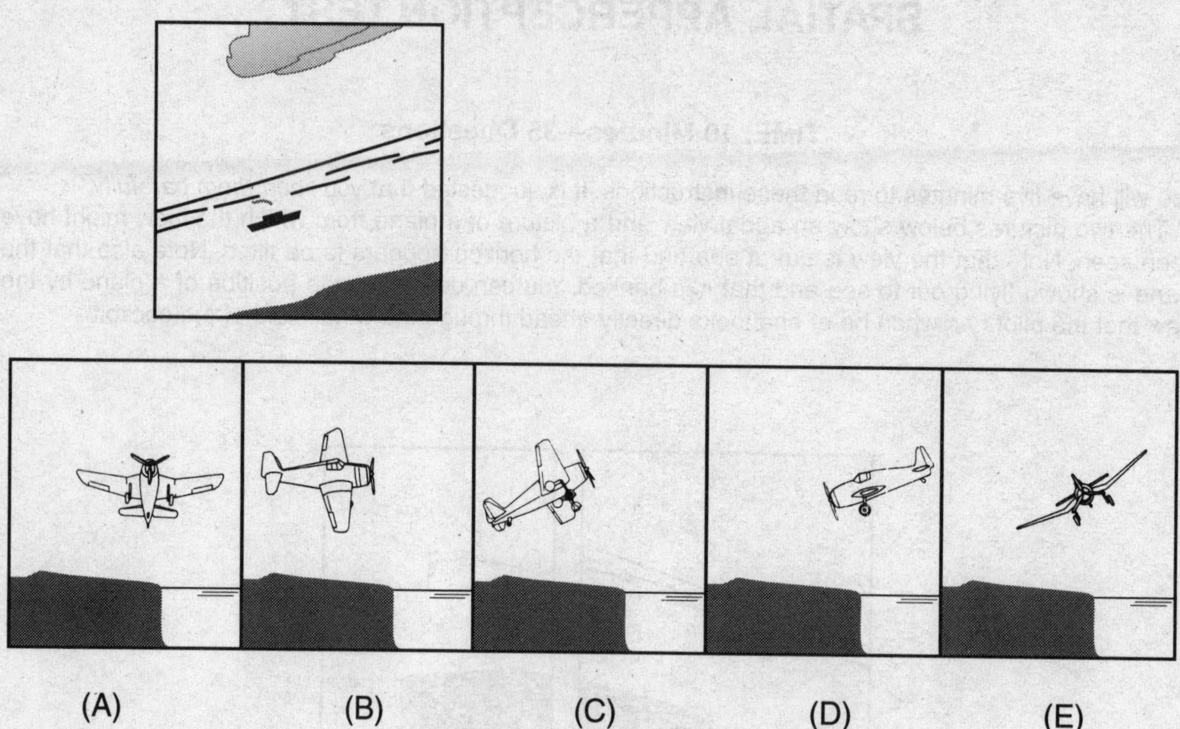

The answer to sample problem 1 is B, because the B option shows the plane in the position from which the pilot would have seen through the windshield of the cockpit the view shown in the upper left aerial view. The plane is shown on a level flight, banking right, and flying out to sea.

2.

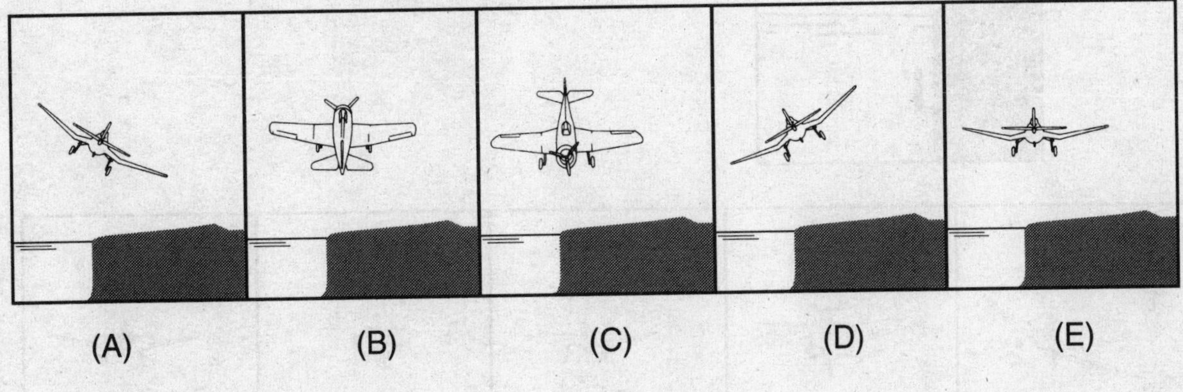

The answer to sample problem 2 is D. The plane is shown on a level flight, banking left, and flying up the coastline.

You will have 10 minutes to answer the 35 questions on the test.

DO NOT TURN THIS PAGE UNTIL TOLD TO DO SO.

SPATIAL APPERCEPTION TEST

TIME: 10 Minutes—35 Questions

1.

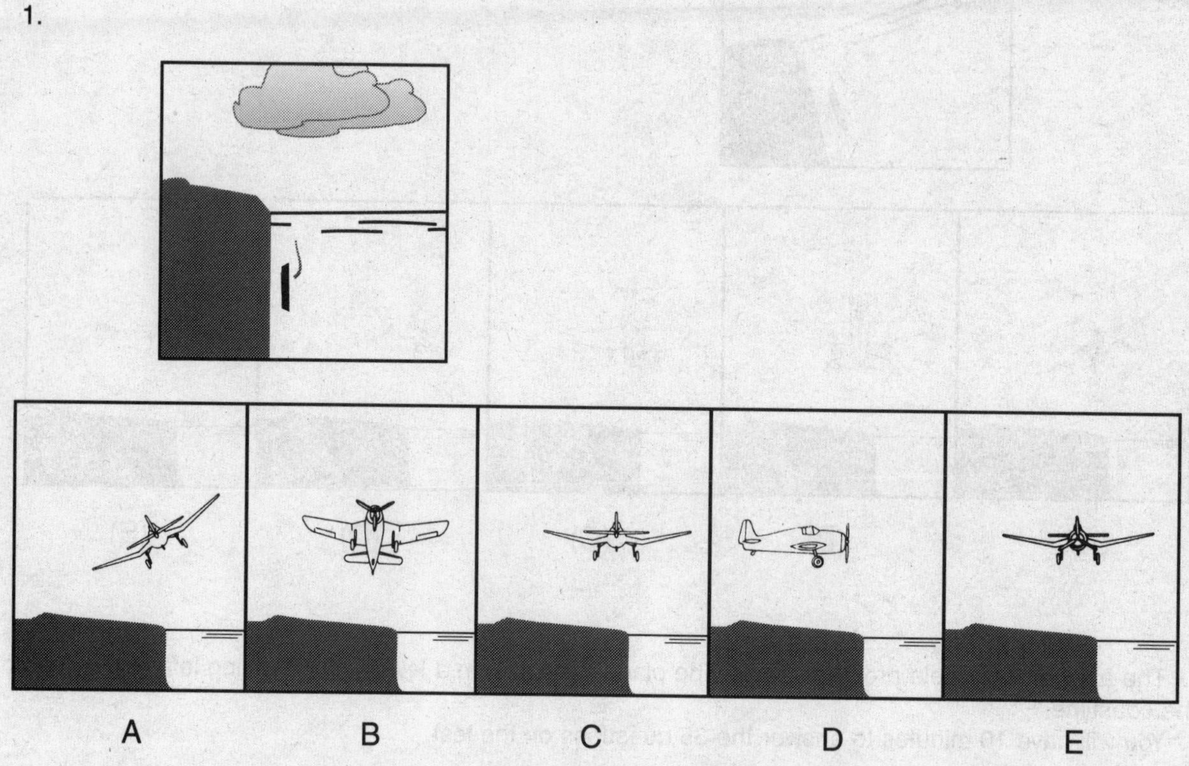

2.

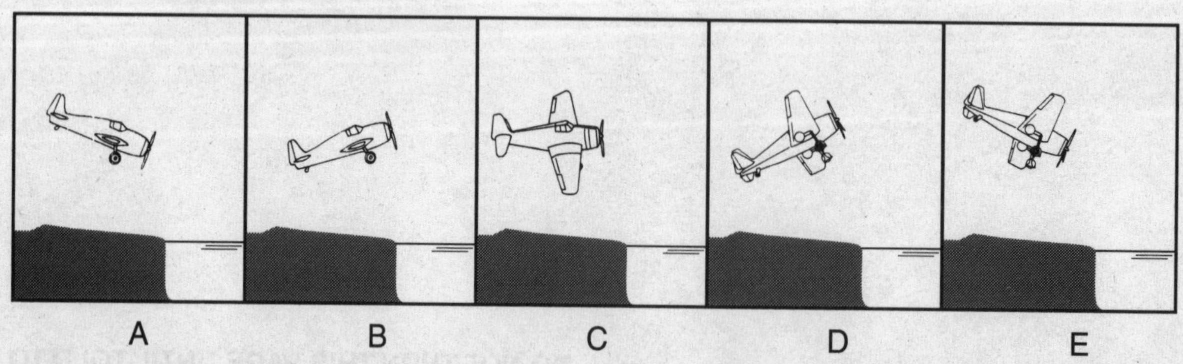

3.

4.

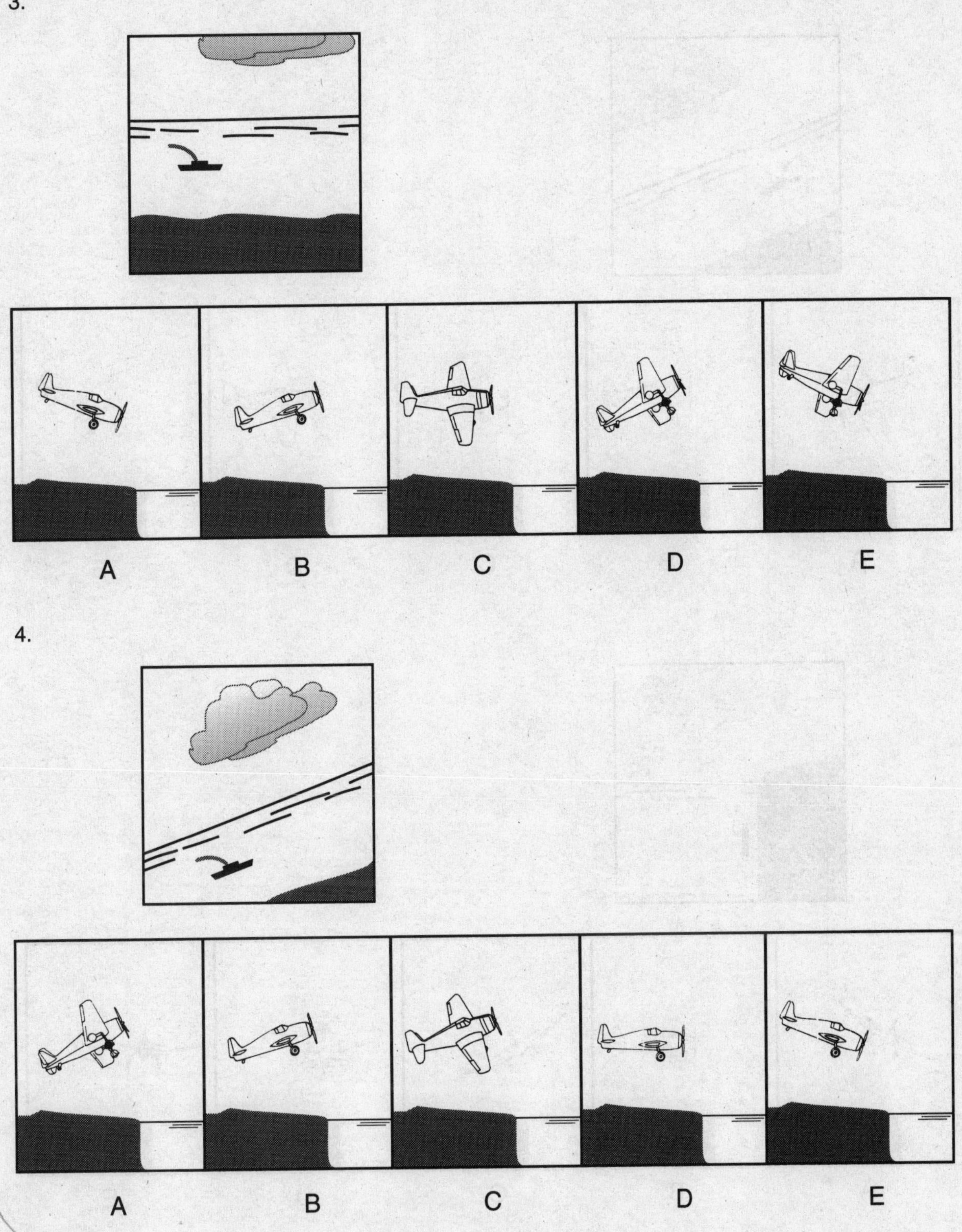

GO ON TO THE NEXT PAGE.

5.

A B C D E

6.

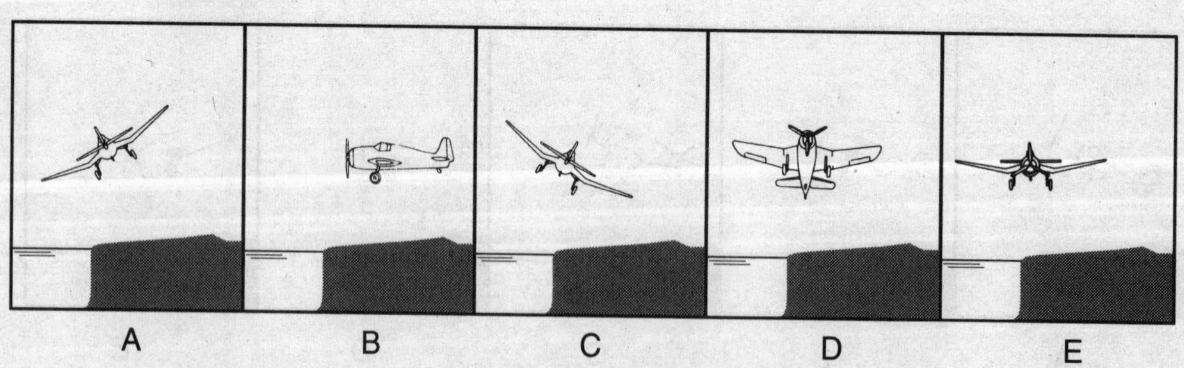

7.

A B C D E

8.

A B C D E

GO ON TO THE NEXT PAGE.

9.

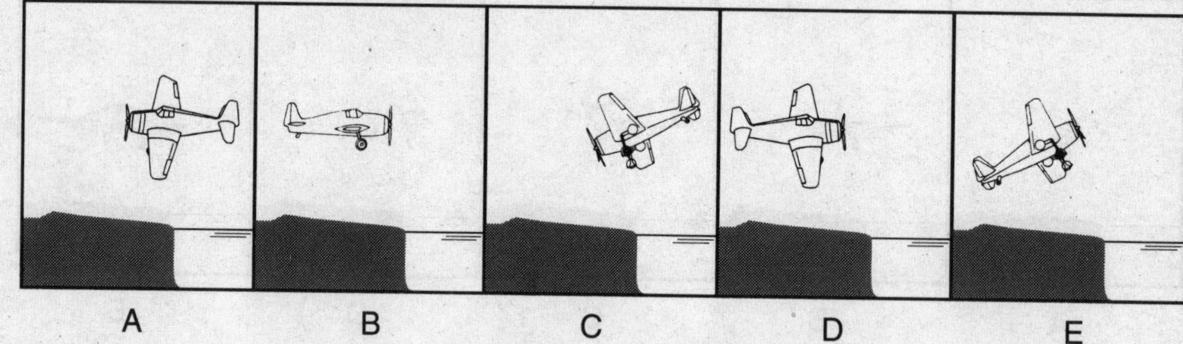

A B C D E

10.

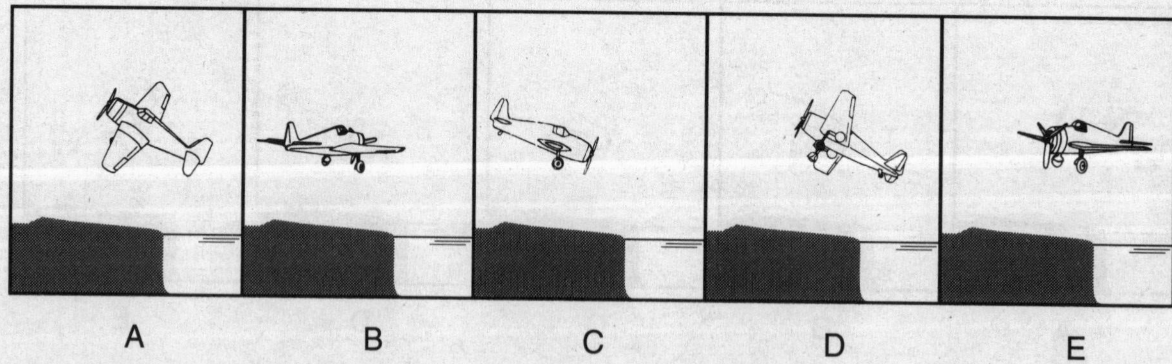

A B C D E

11.

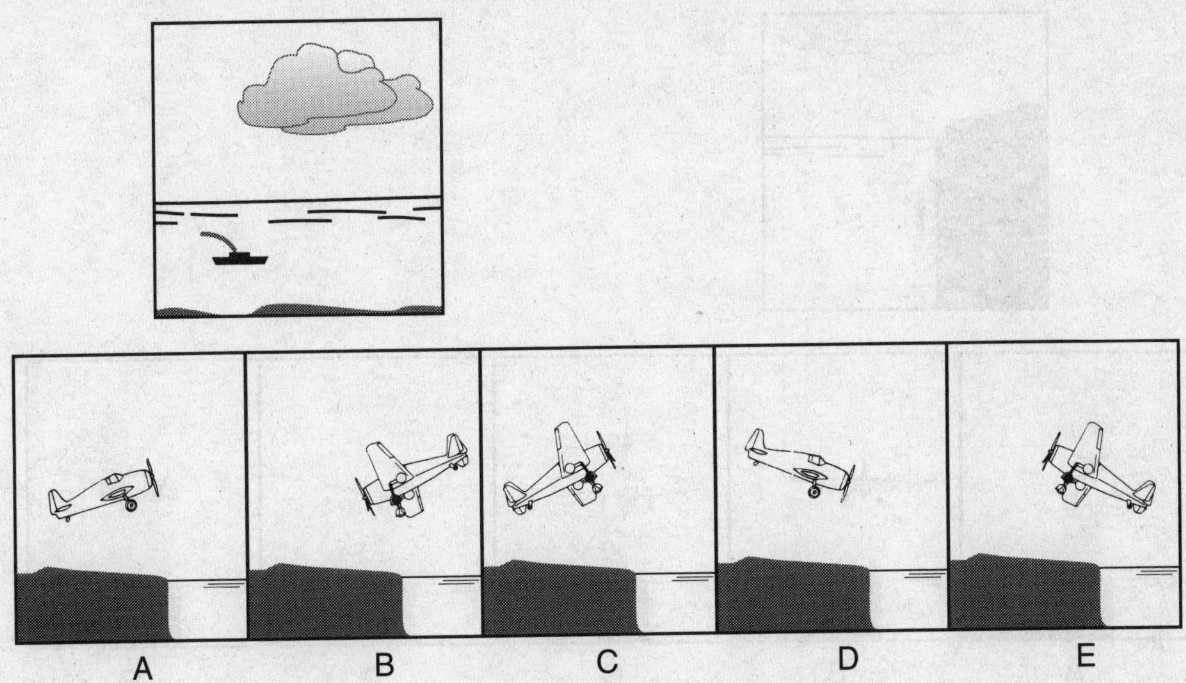

12.

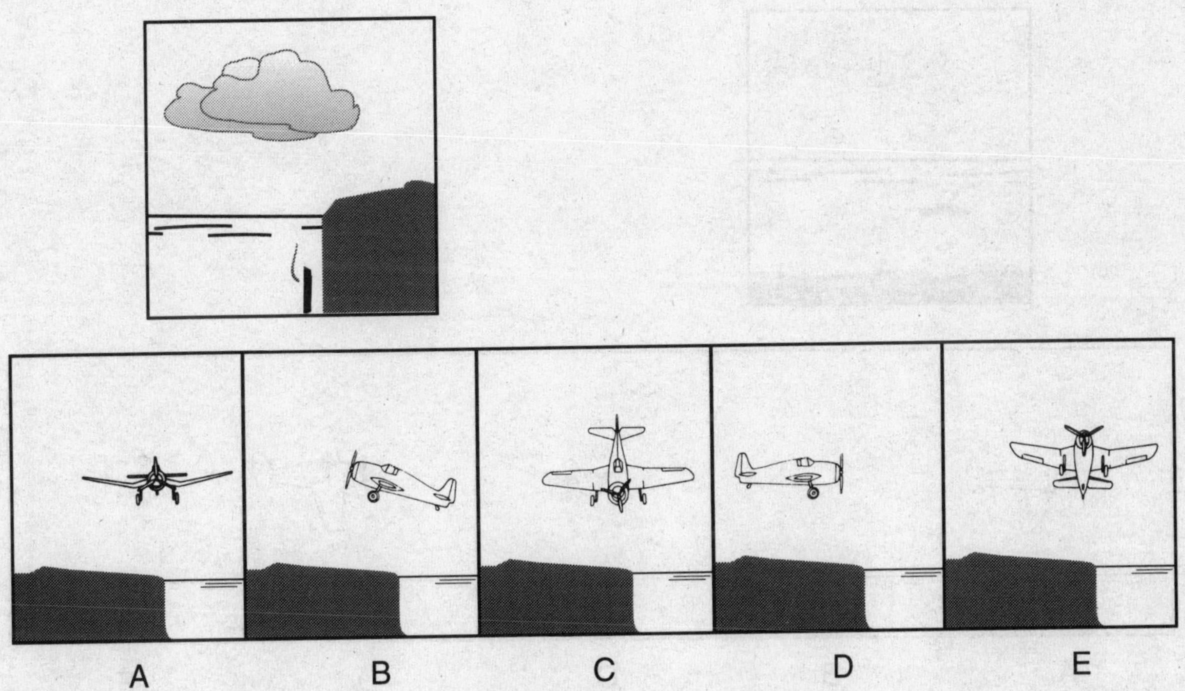

GO ON TO THE NEXT PAGE.

13.

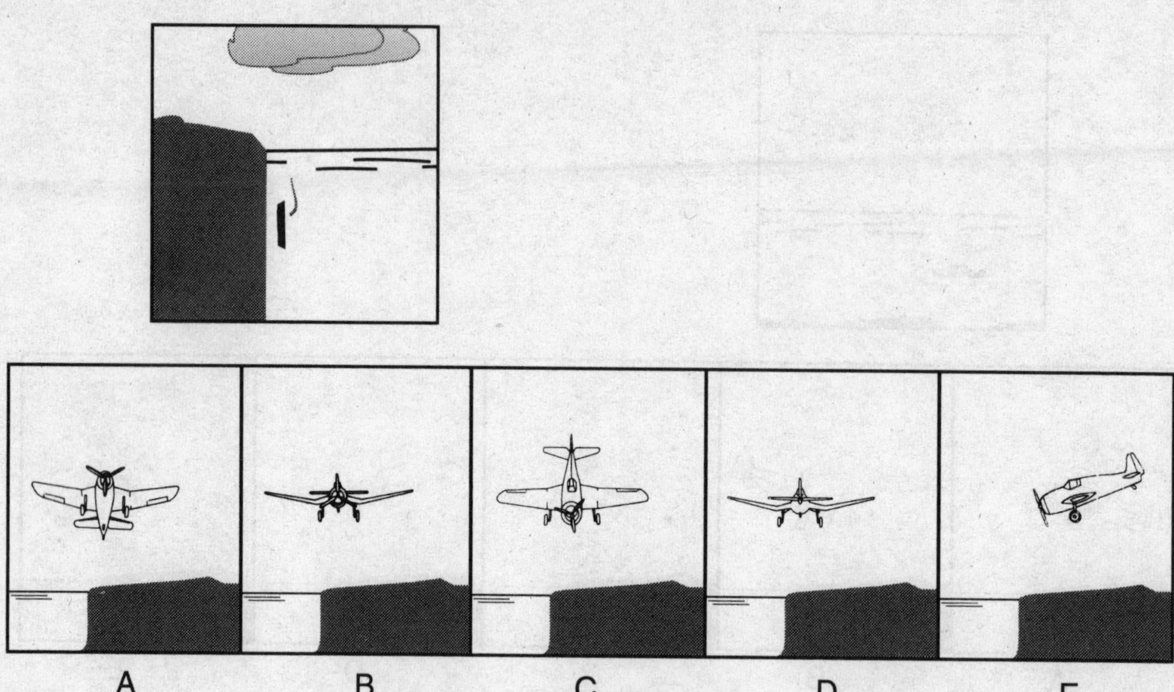

14.

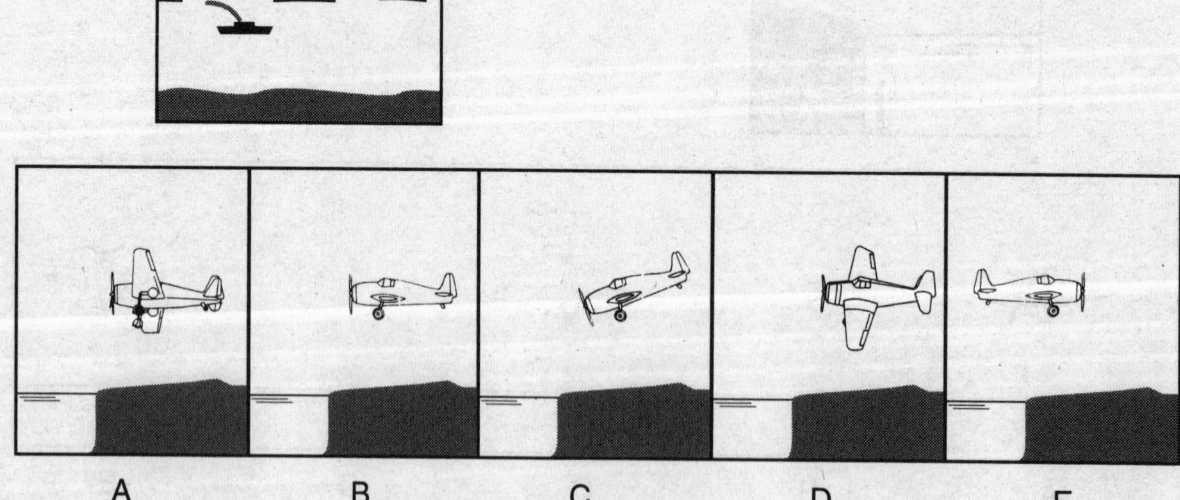

15.

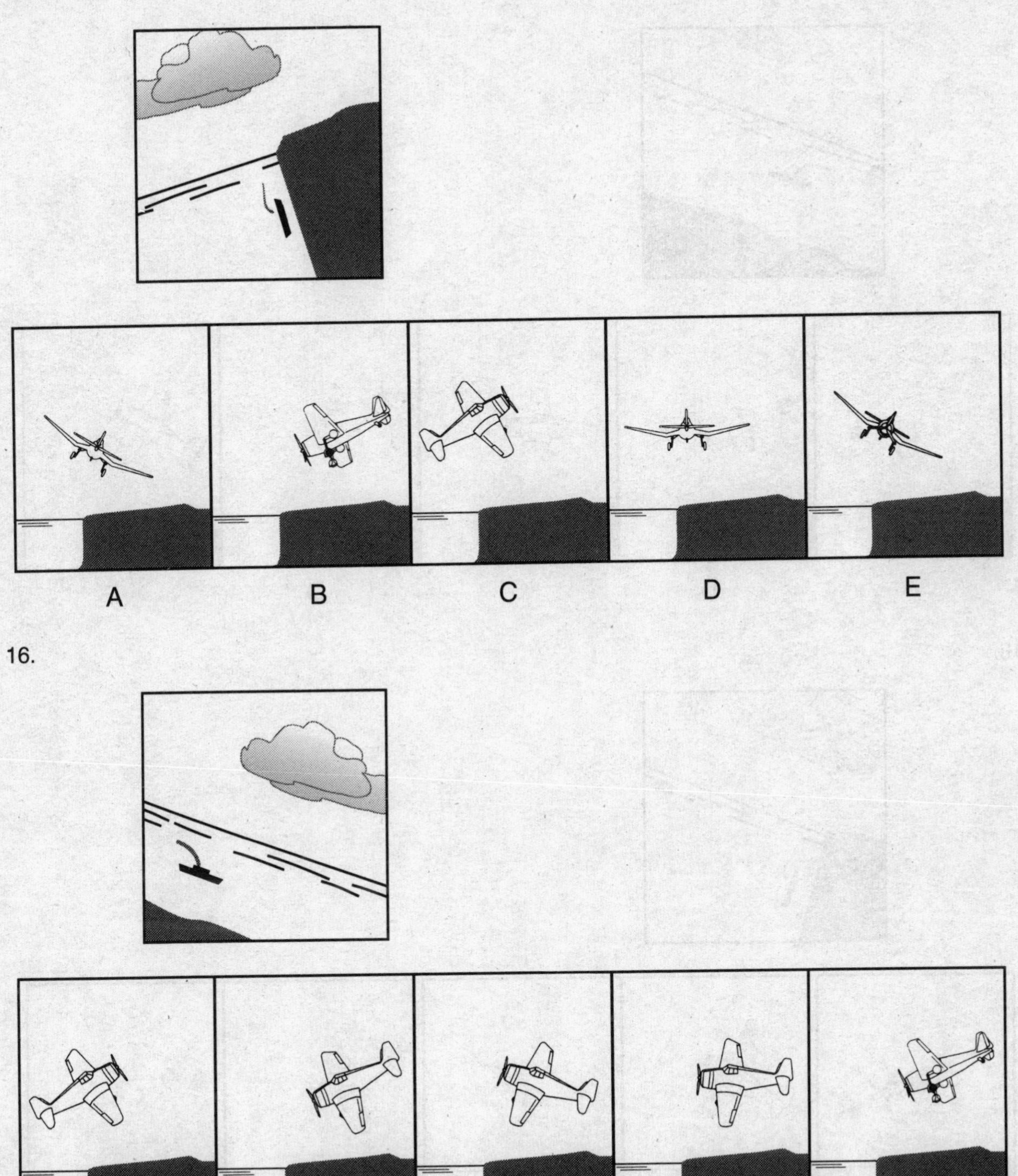

GO ON TO THE NEXT PAGE.

17.

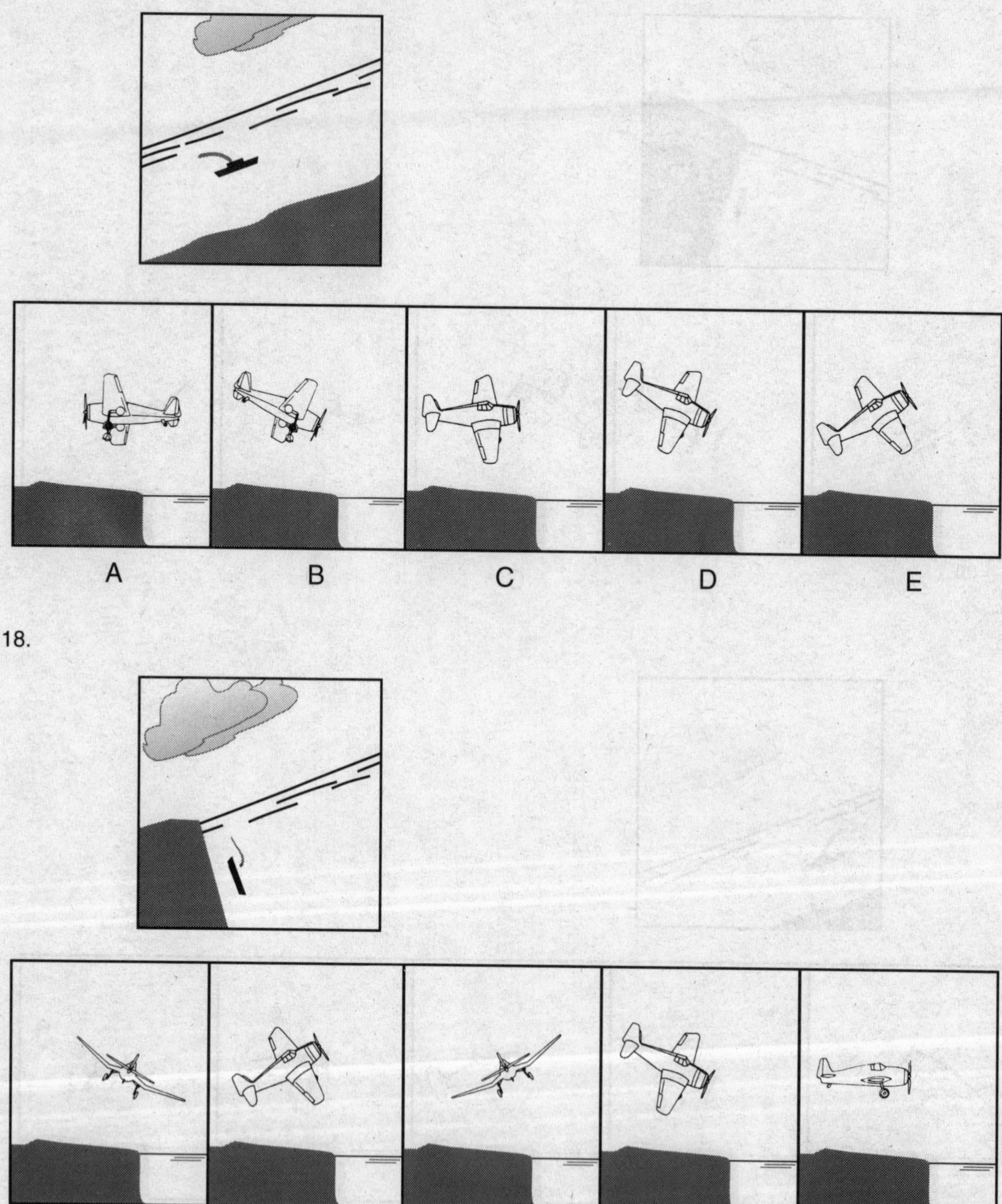

18.

19.

A B C D E

20.

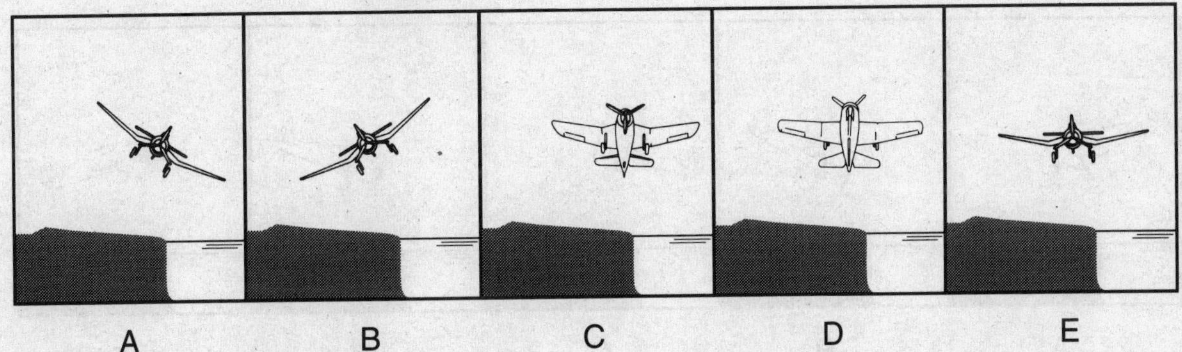

GO ON TO THE NEXT PAGE.

21.

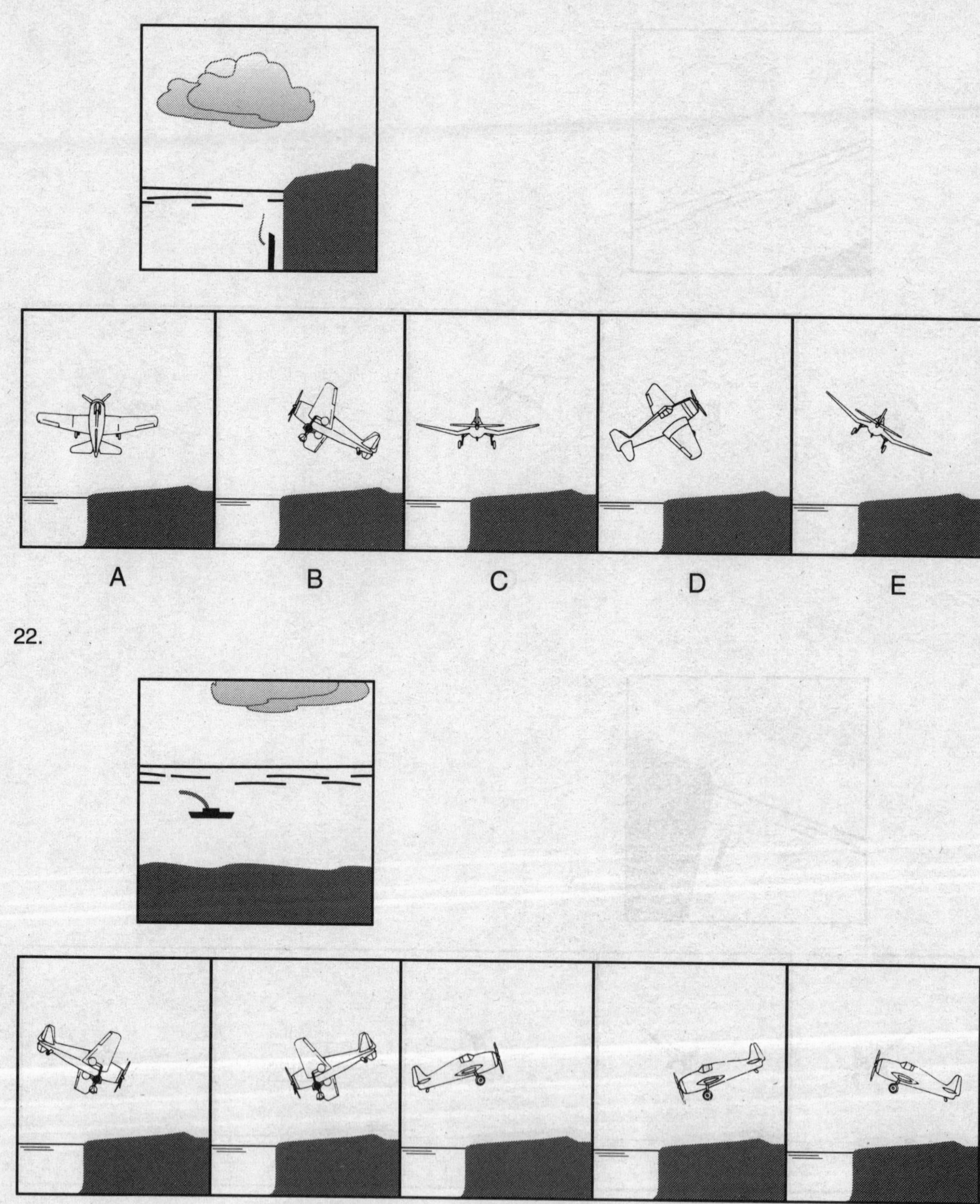

23.

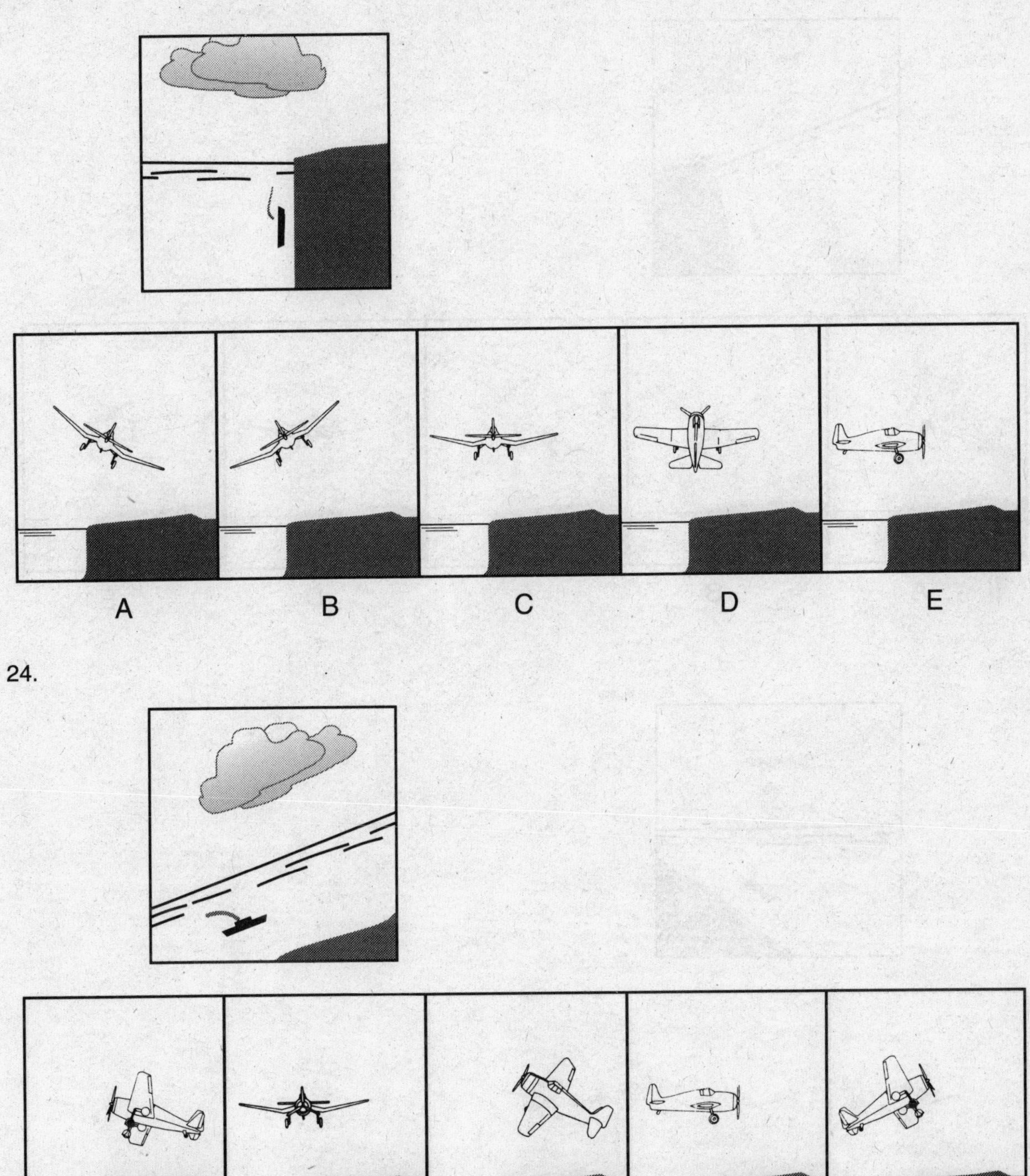

24.

A B C D E

GO ON TO THE NEXT PAGE.

25.

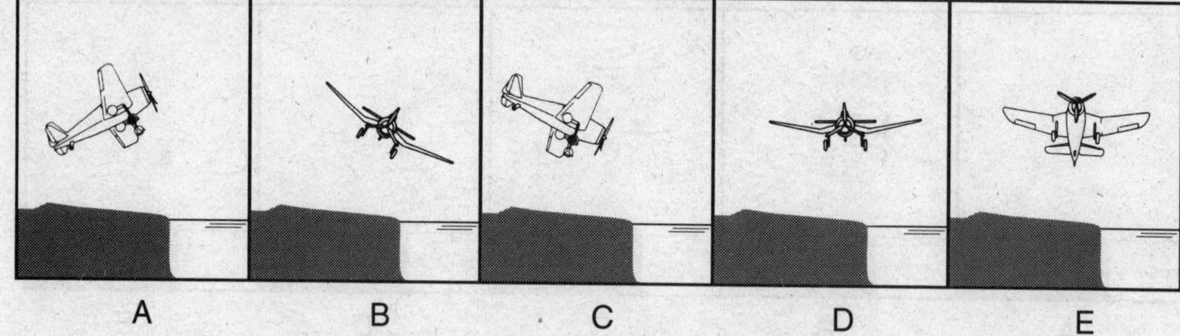

A B C D E

26.

A B C D E

27.

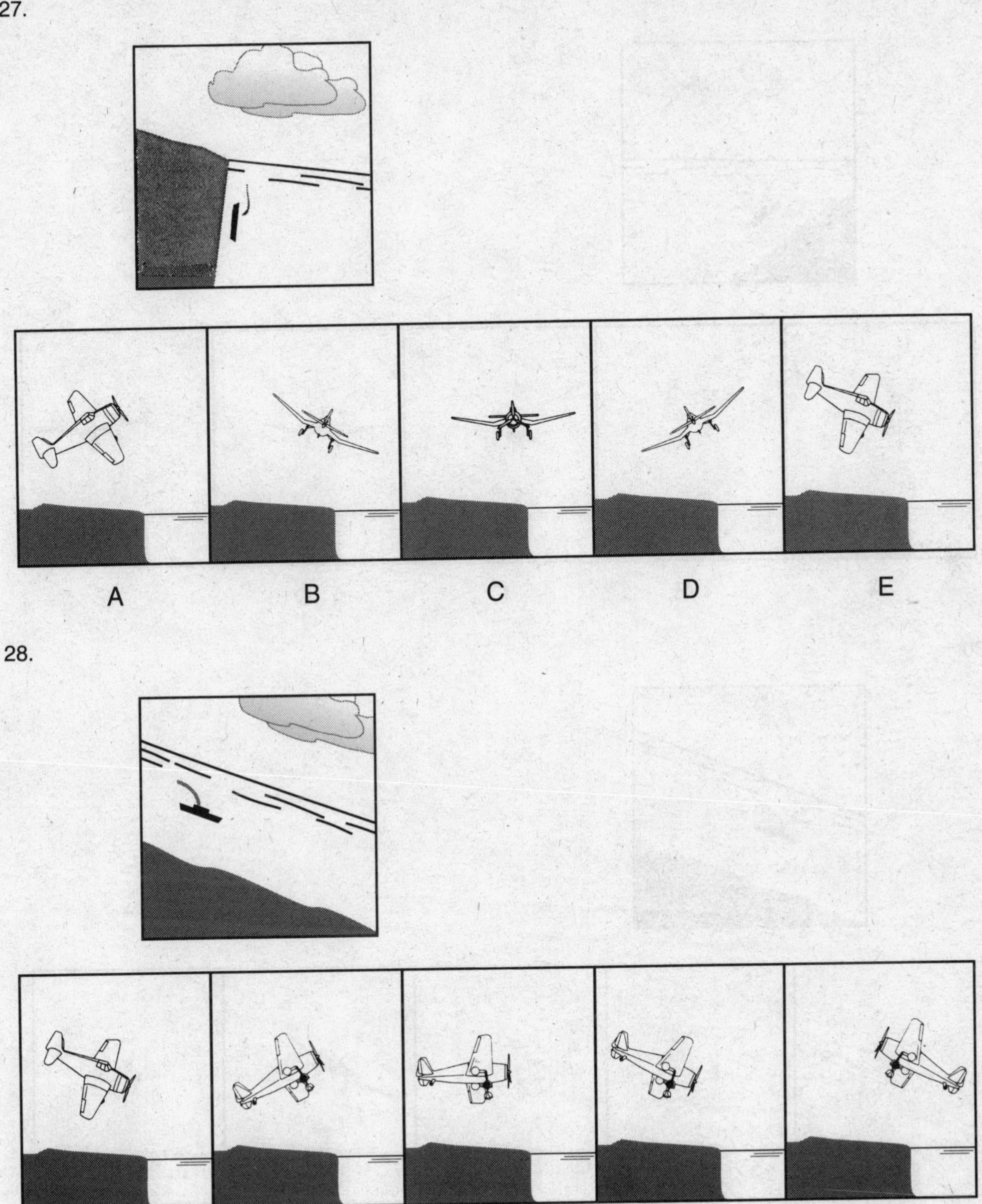

GO ON TO THE NEXT PAGE.

29.

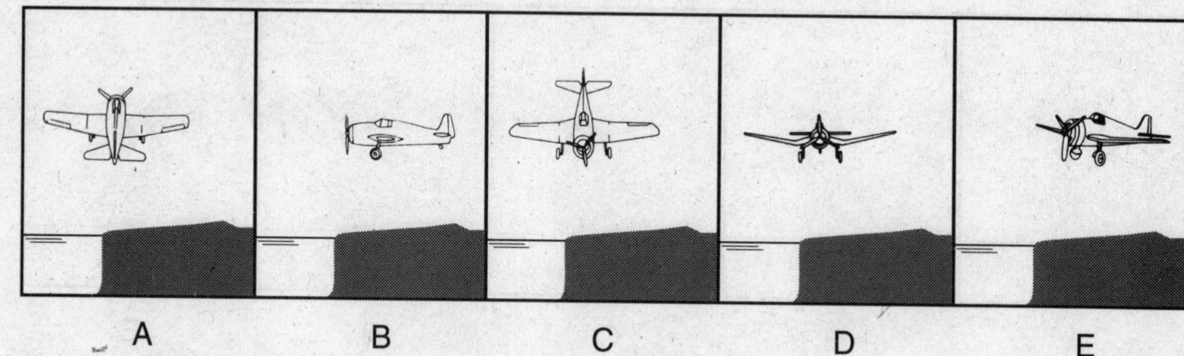

A B C D E

30.

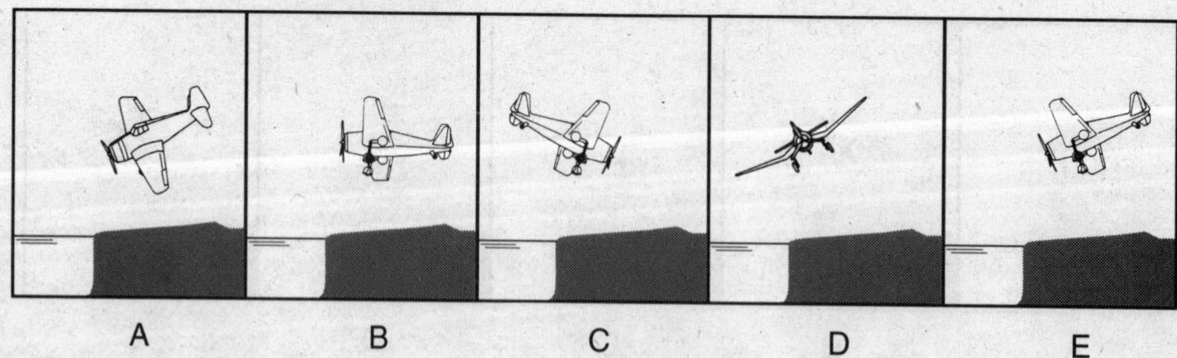

A B C D E

31.

32.

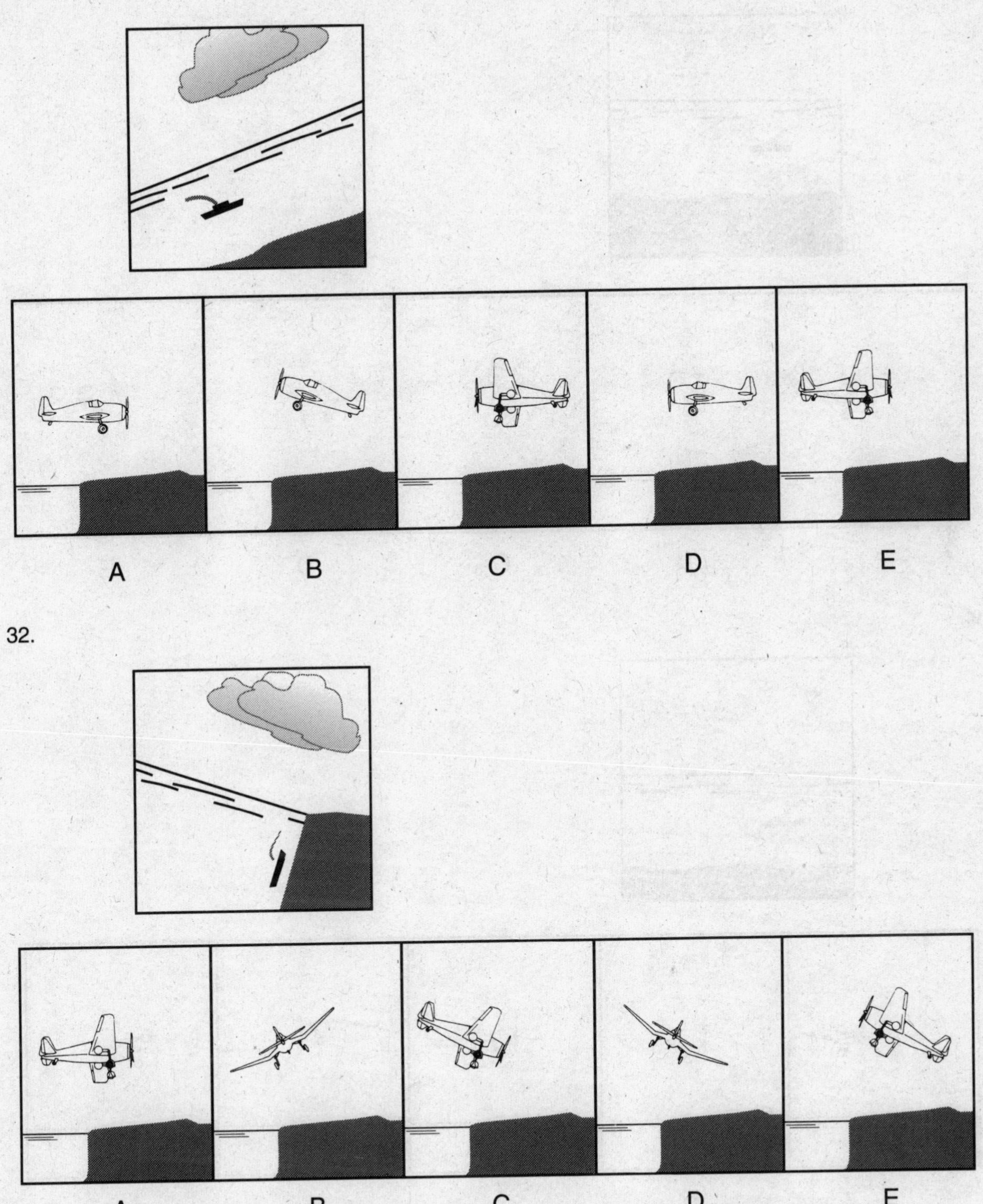

GO ON TO THE NEXT PAGE.

33.

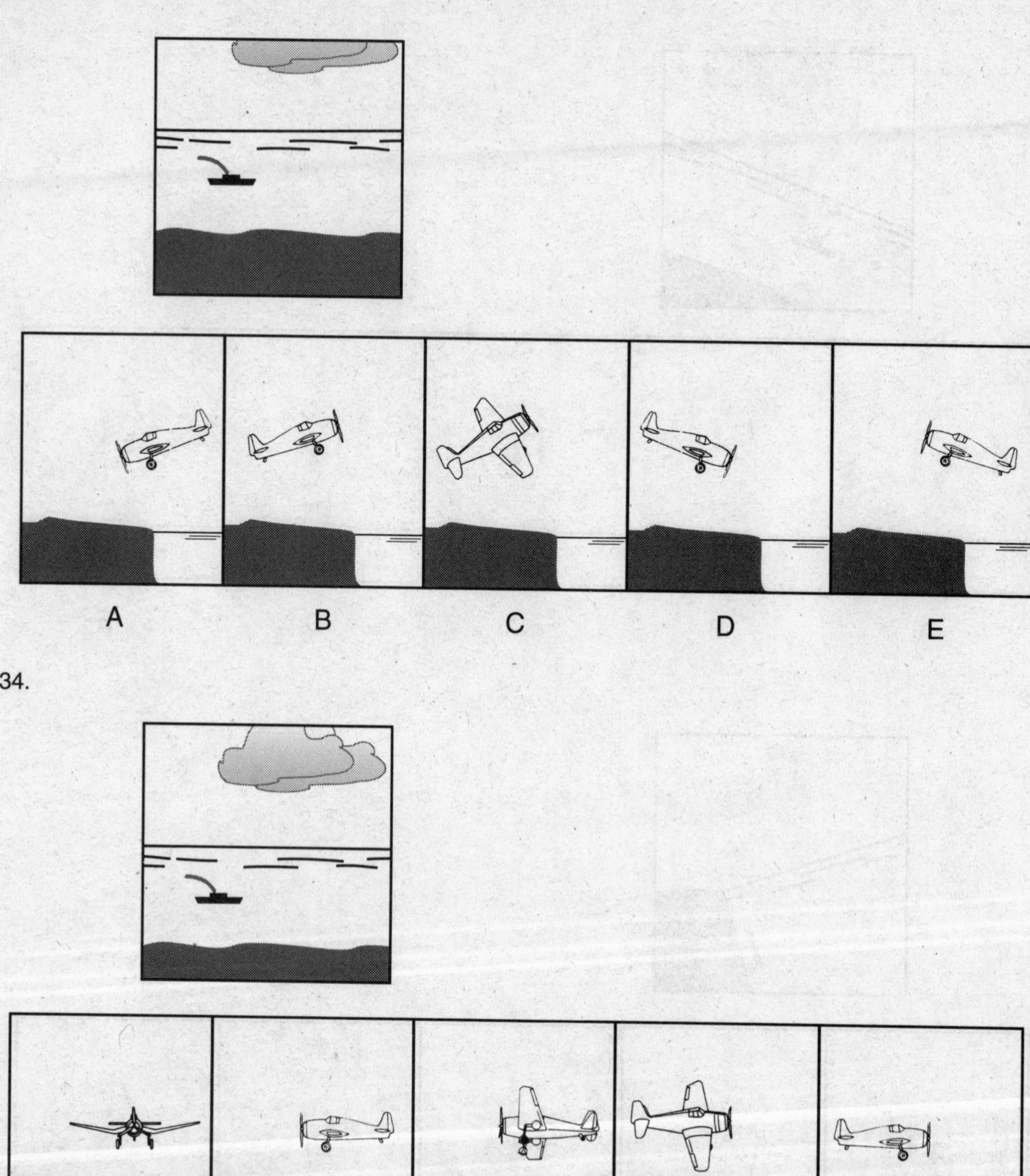

A B C D E

34.

A B C D E

35.

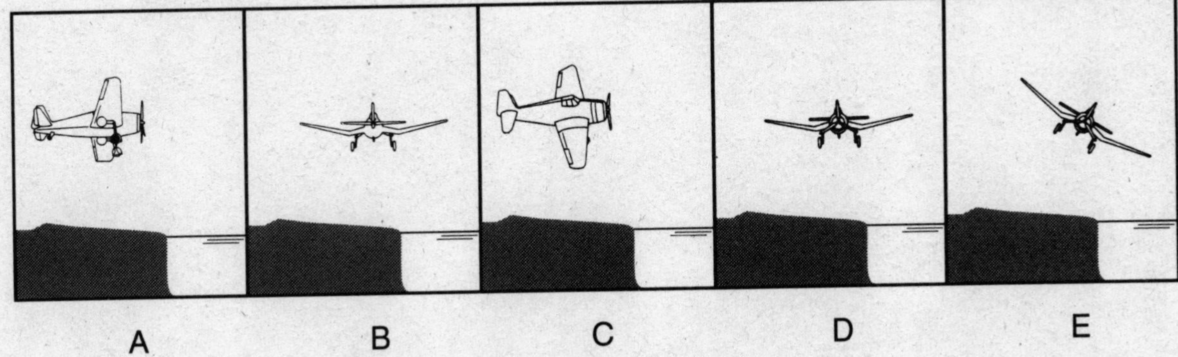

A B C D E

END OF SPATIAL APPERCEPTION TEST

TEST 4

BIOGRAPHICAL INVENTORY (BI)

TIME: 20 Minutes—76 Questions

Questions *1* to *76* are biographical inventory items used to obtain general background information, as well as information regarding personal characteristics and interests. These questions should be answered truthfully and to the best of your ability and recollection.

1. What is your age?

   (A) Under 20 years
   (B) 20 to 23 years
   (C) 24 to 27 years
   (D) 28 to 31 years
   (E) 32 years or more

2. If foreign born, when did you come to the United States to stay?

   (A) 0–5 years ago
   (B) 6–10 years ago
   (C) 11–15 years ago
   (D) 16–20 years ago
   (E) 21 or more years ago

3. If foreign born, in which geographical area were you born?

   (A) Asia
   (B) Africa
   (C) the Americas
   (D) Europe
   (E) Australia

4. What is your parents' citizenship status?

   (A) Both are native-born American citizens.
   (B) One is native-born; the other is naturalized.
   (C) Both are naturalized American citizens.
   (D) One is a naturalized citizen; the other is a permanent resident.
   (E) Both are legally admitted permanent residents.

5. How many years of schooling did your father complete?

   (A) College graduation
   (B) Some college training
   (C) High school graduation
   (D) Some high school training
   (E) Elementary school training

6. How many years of schooling did your mother complete?

   (A) College graduation
   (B) Some college training
   (C) High school graduation
   (D) Some high school training
   (E) Elementary school training

7. How many sisters and brothers do you have in your family?

   (A) 0
   (B) 1
   (C) 2
   (D) 3
   (E) 4 or more

8. Were you raised

   (A) in a two-parent household
   (B) in a single-parent household
   (C) by relatives
   (D) by foster parents
   (E) in an institution

9. Which one of the following best characterizes the behavior of your parents towards you?

   (A) They were always very strict with you.
   (B) They were usually very strict with you.
   (C) They were often very strict with you.
   (D) They were seldom very strict with you.
   (E) They were never very strict with you.

10. Where did you live most of the time before you were 20 years of age?

    (A) The Northeast region of the United States
    (B) The Southern region of the United States
    (C) The Central region of the United States
    (D) The Western region of the United States
    (E) Outside the continental United States

11. In what type of community did you live most of the time before you were 20 years old?

    (A) Large city (population of more than 250,000)
    (B) Small city (population of less than 250,000)
    (C) Suburb of the city
    (D) Town or village
    (E) Rural community

12. How many rooms did your household generally have? (Do not count bathrooms, porches, balconies, foyers, halls, or half-rooms.)

    (A) 1 room
    (B) 2 rooms
    (C) 3 rooms
    (D) 4 rooms
    (E) 5 or more rooms

13. How many apartments or living quarters were generally in the building your family lived in during this time?

    (A) 1
    (B) 2–4
    (C) 5–9
    (D) 10–19
    (E) 20 or more

Questions *14* to *27* pertain to the time you were in high school.

14. Which of the following types of high schools did you attend?

    (A) Public, academic
    (B) Public, vocational
    (C) Private, parochial
    (D) Private, non-parochial
    (E) Military

15. If you were employed on school days while in high school, how many hours did you work per week?

    (A) 5 or less
    (B) 6–10
    (C) 11–15
    (D) 16 or more
    (E) Did not work on school days

16. How did you usually travel to and from high school each day?

    (A) Walking
    (B) Bus
    (C) Private car
    (D) Taxi
    (E) Train or subway

17. In high school, how many hours a week did you devote to volunteer work in the community?

    (A) 5 or less
    (B) 6–10
    (C) 11–15
    (D) 16 or more
    (E) Did no volunteer work

18. If you were a volunteer, what type of work was it predominantly?

    (A) Religious
    (B) Educational
    (C) Civic or political
    (D) Charitable
    (E) Health-care-related

19. In which of the following capacities, if any, did you serve as class officer in high school?

    (A) President
    (B) Vice President
    (C) Secretary
    (D) Treasurer
    (E) Did not serve as class officer

20. In which of the following capacities, if any, did you serve on the student council in high school?

    (A) President
    (B) Vice President
    (C) Secretary
    (D) Treasurer
    (E) Did not serve in any of the above

21. In which of the following athletic activities, if any, did you earn a varsity letter or receive a special recognition award?

    (A) Basketball
    (B) Baseball/softball
    (C) Football
    (D) Hockey/Lacrosse
    (E) None of the above

22. In which of the following athletic activities, if any, did you earn a varsity letter or receive a special recognition award?

    (A) Boxing
    (B) Wrestling
    (C) Track
    (D) Soccer
    (E) None of the above

23. In which of the following athletic activities, if any, did you earn a varsity letter or receive a special recognition award?

    (A) Cross-country
    (B) Fencing
    (C) Gymnastics
    (D) Rifle
    (E) None of the above

24. How old were you when you were graduated from high school?

    (A) 16 years or less
    (B) 17 years
    (C) 18 years
    (D) 19 years
    (E) 20 or more years

25. What was your high school grade-point average (GPA) on the 4-point scale?

    (A) less than 2.00
    (B) 2.00–2.49
    (C) 2.50–2.99
    (D) 3.00–3.49
    (E) 3.50–4.00

26. What was your standing in your high school graduating class?

    (A) Honor graduate
    (B) Top quarter but not an honor student
    (C) Second quarter
    (D) Third quarter
    (E) Bottom quarter

27. If you took the Armed Services Vocational Aptitude Battery (ASVAB), in which of the following categories did your score fall?

    (A) Category I 93rd–100th percentile range
    (B) Category II 65th–92nd percentile range
    (C) Category III 31st–64th percentile range
    (D) Category IV 10th–30th percentile range
    (E) Category V 9th percentile range and below

Questions 28 to 42 pertain to the time you were in college.

28. How old were you when you entered college?

    (A) 16 years or less
    (B) 17 years
    (C) 18 years
    (D) 19 years
    (E) 20 years or more

29. The undergraduate school you attended was a

    (A) public college or university (4-year course
    (B) private, non-parochial college or university (4-year course)
    (C) private, parochial college or university (4-year course)
    (D) community college (2-year course)
    (E) junior college (2-year course)

30. Where did you live while attending college?

    (A) At home
    (B) Fraternity or sorority
    (C) School dormitory
    (D) Rented room or apartment
    (E) With relatives or friends

31. How did you generally travel to and from college each day?

    (A) Walking
    (B) Bus
    (C) Private car
    (D) Taxi
    (E) Train or subway

GO ON TO THE NEXT PAGE.

32. If you were employed on school days while in college, how many hours did you work per week?

(A) 5 or less
(B) 6–10
(C) 11–15
(D) 16 or more
(E) Did not work on school days

33. In college, how many hours a week did you devote to volunteer work to the community?

(A) 5 or less
(B) 6–10
(C) 11–15
(D) 16 or more
(E) Did no volunteer work

34. If you were a volunteer, which of the following best describes the nature of the volunteer work?

(A) Religious
(B) Educational
(C) Civic or political
(D) Charitable
(E) Health-care-related

35. What was your major or area of concentration?

(A) Science, engineering, or mathematics
(B) Social science or humanities
(C) Accounting, business administration, or management
(D) Art, fine arts, or mass communication
(E) None of the above

36. What was your main extracurricular activity?

(A) Athletics
(B) Dramatics or debating
(C) Orchestra or glee club
(D) School newspaper
(E) Other school or community activity

37. While in college, how did you generally spend your summers?

(A) Went to summer school
(B) Worked to earn income
(C) Engaged in volunteer work
(D) Traveled
(E) Relaxed at home

Skip the next two items if you did not make any of the college varsity teams in the athletic activities listed.

38. In which of the following athletic activities did you make the college varsity team?

(A) Basketball
(B) Baseball
(C) Hockey/Lacrosse
(D) Boxing
(E) Wrestling

39. In which of the following athletic activities did you make the college varsity team?

(A) Track
(B) Soccer
(C) Cross-country
(D) Fencing
(E) Gymnastics

40. What was your undergraduate cumulative grade-point average on a 4-point scale?

(A) Less than 2.1
(B) 2.1–2.5
(C) 2.6–3.0
(D) 3.1–3.5
(E) 3.6–4.0

41. What was your standing in your college graduating class?

(A) Honor graduate
(B) Top quarter but not an honor graduate
(C) Second quarter
(D) Third quarter
(E) Bottom quarter

42. How old were you when you completed your undergraduate work?

(A) 20 years or less
(B) 21 years
(C) 22 years
(D) 23 years
(E) 24 years or more

43. Which of the following best describes your current or most recent employment?

    (A) Employee of private company, business, or individual for wages, salary, or commissions
    (B) Federal government employee
    (C) State or municipal employee
    (D) Self-employed in own business, professional practice, or farm
    (E) Working without pay in family business or farm

44. Within the last two years, how often have you been fired from any job for any reason?

    (A) Never
    (B) Once
    (C) Twice
    (D) Three times
    (E) Four or more times

45. Within the last two years, how often have you quit a job after being notified that you would be fired?

    (A) Never
    (B) Once
    (C) Twice
    (D) Three times
    (E) Four or more times

46. How much time have you lost at school or at work due to illness or injury during the past two years?

    (A) None
    (B) 1 to 15 days
    (C) 16 to 30 days
    (D) 1 to 2 months
    (E) More than 2 months

47. How often have you been hospitalized for an illness or injury during the past two years?

    (A) Never
    (B) Once
    (C) Twice
    (D) Three times
    (E) Four or more times

48. What is your present marital status?

    (A) Married
    (B) Divorced
    (C) Separated
    (D) Widowed
    (E) Never married

49. How many children do you have?

    (A) None
    (B) One
    (C) Two
    (D) Three
    (E) Four or more

50. In the last year, how often did you attend religious services in a church, synagogue, or temple?

    (A) Once a week (or more frequently)
    (B) Once every two weeks
    (C) Once every month
    (D) Several times a year
    (E) Did not attend

51. In the last year, how often did you go to concerts?

    (A) Once
    (B) Twice
    (C) Three times
    (D) Four or more times
    (E) Did not go to any concerts

52. In the last year, how often did you go to the theatre?

    (A) Once
    (B) Twice
    (C) Three times
    (D) Four times
    (E) Did not go to the theatre

53. How many books (other than textbooks) have you read during the past year?

    (A) 0
    (B) 1
    (C) 2
    (D) 3
    (E) 4 or more

54. How many magazines (weekly, semimonthly, and monthly) do you read regularly?

    (A) 0
    (B) 1
    (C) 2
    (D) 3
    (E) 4 or more

GO ON TO THE NEXT PAGE.

55. How much time do you spend each day watching television?

(A) Less than 1 hour
(B) 1 to but not including 2 hours
(C) 2 to 3 hours
(D) More than 3 hours
(E) Do not watch television

56. How many foreign languages do you speak fluently?

(A) 0
(B) 1
(C) 2
(D) 3
(E) 4 or more

57. How many foreign languages do you read proficiently?

(A) 0
(B) 1
(C) 2
(D) 3
(E) 4 or more

58. In the last year, how often did you visit museums?

(A) Once
(B) Twice
(C) Three times
(D) Four or more times
(E) Did not visit any museums

59. Which of the following best describes your ability as a bridge player?

(A) Excellent
(B) Good
(C) Fair
(D) Poor
(E) Do not play bridge

60. Which of the following best describes your ability as a chess player?

(A) Excellent
(B) Good
(C) Fair
(D) Poor
(E) Do not play chess

61. Which of the following best describes your ability as a poker player?

(A) Excellent
(B) Good
(C) Fair
(D) Poor
(E) Do not play poker

62. Which of the following best describes your ability to play a musical instrument?

(A) Excellent
(B) Good
(C) Fair
(D) Poor
(E) Do not play a musical instrument

63. Which of the following describes your ability as a bicyclist?

(A) Excellent
(B) Good
(C) Fair
(D) Poor
(E) Do not ride a bicycle

64. Which of the following best describes your ability as a swimmer?

(A) Excellent
(B) Good
(C) Fair
(D) Poor
(E) Do not swim

65. Which of the following best describes your ability as a skier?

(A) Excellent
(B) Good
(C) Fair
(D) Poor
(E) Do not ski

66. Which of the following best describes your ability as a bowler?

(A) Excellent
(B) Good
(C) Fair
(D) Poor
(E) Do not bowl

67. In the last year, how often did you go hiking?
    (A) Once
    (B) Twice
    (C) Three times
    (D) Four or more times
    (E) Did not hike

68. How often do you jog each week?
    (A) Once
    (B) Twice
    (C) Three times
    (D) Four or more times
    (E) Do not jog

69. How many miles do you jog each time?
    (A) 1 mile
    (B) 2 miles
    (C) 3 miles
    (D) 4 or more miles
    (E) Do not jog

70. For how many years have you been licensed to operate a motor vehicle?
    (A) Less than 1 year
    (B) 1–3 years
    (C) 4–6 years
    (D) 7 or more years
    (E) Not licensed

Skip the next three items if you are not licensed to operate a motor vehicle.

71. How many miles have you driven in the last year?
    (A) Less than 2,500
    (B) 2,500–4,999 miles
    (C) 5,000–7,499 miles
    (D) 7,500–9,999 miles
    (E) 10,000 miles or more

72. In the last year, how many parking tickets have you received?
    (A) 0
    (B) 1–3
    (C) 4–6
    (D) 7–9
    (E) 10 or more

73. In the last year, how many tickets have you received for a moving violation?
    (A) 0
    (B) 1
    (C) 2
    (D) 3
    (E) 4 or more

74. If currently on active duty with the U.S. Armed Forces, in which service are you?
    (A) Navy
    (B) Marine Corps
    (C) Coast Guard
    (D) Air Force
    (E) Army

75. If currently on active duty with the U.S. Armed Forces, what is your rank or grade?
    (A) Commissioned officer
    (B) Warrant officer
    (C) Noncommissioned officer, E-7–E-9 (Top three grades)
    (D) Noncommissioned officer, E-4–E-6
    (E) Private, private first class, seaman, seaman apprentice, airman, airman first class, lance corporal, fireman, fireman apprentice, E-1–E-3

76. Which of the following most influenced you to seek a military career as a commissioned officer?
    (A) Guidance counselor or other school personnel
    (B) Parents, other relatives or friends
    (C) Recruiting officers or recruiting representatives
    (D) Self-interest
    (E) Other

END OF BIOGRAPHICAL INVENTORY

TEST 5

AVIATION/NAUTICAL INFORMATION (ANT)

TIME: 15 Minutes—30 Questions

Questions *1* to *15* pertain to aviation information.

1. The wing shape shown below is best described as a

   (A) delta wing
   (B) elliptical wing
   (C) rectangular wing
   (D) rotary wing
   (E) sweptback wing

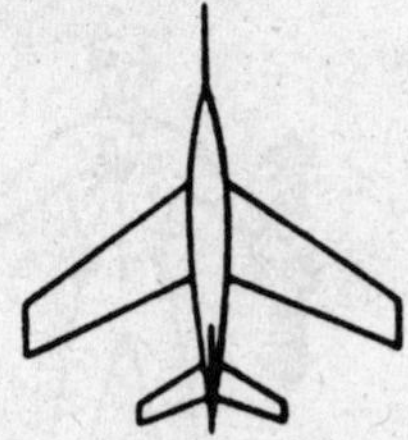

2. The wing span is the distance from

   (A) leading edge to trailing edge
   (B) top to bottom of airfoil
   (C) wing root to wing tip
   (D) wing tip to center of the fuselage
   (E) wing tip to wing tip

3. The pilot banks the airplane by using the

   (A) ailerons
   (B) brakes
   (C) elevators
   (D) flaps
   (E) rudder

4. The airplane is controlled around its vertical axis by means of the

   (A) ailerons
   (B) elevators
   (C) pilot
   (D) rudder
   (E) wing flaps

5. There are several forces acting on an aircraft in straight-and-level flight. The backward or retarding force produced by air resistance is termed

   (A) drag
   (B) gravity
   (C) lift
   (D) thrust
   (E) weight

6. The angle between the chord line of the airfoil and the direction of the relative wind is termed

   (A) angle of attack
   (B) angle of bank
   (C) angle of deflection
   (D) angle of incidence
   (E) pitch angle

7. In a steady flight condition,

   (A) lift equals drag; weight equals thrust
   (B) lift equals gravity; weight equals drag
   (C) lift equals thrust; weight equals drag
   (D) lift equals weight; gravity equals drag
   (E) lift equals weight; thrust equals drag

8. If a hard-surfaced runway is numbered 22, the opposite direction of the same runway would be numbered

   (A) 4
   (B) 12
   (C) 22
   (D) 26
   (E) 40

GO ON TO THE NEXT PAGE.

9. In the illustration shown at the top of this page, the runway is aligned in a
   (A) North-South direction
   (B) East-West direction
   (C) NE-SW direction
   (D) NW-SE direction
   (E) NNE-SSW direction

10. The hand signal that directs an airplane to make an emergency stop is
    (A) A
    (B) B
    (C) C
    (D) D
    (E) E

11. What was the name of the space vehicle that carried the American astronauts who first landed on the moon?
    (A) Apollo 11
    (B) Aurora 7
    (C) Gemini 11
    (D) Faith 7
    (E) Skylab 1

12. If an astronaut weighed 60 kilograms on earth, his or her weight on the moon would be
    (A) more than 60 kilograms
    (B) less than 60 kilograms
    (C) the same
    (D) more or less, depending on location on lunar surface
    (E) more or less, depending on the earth's season

13. Which one of the following engines can operate outside the earth's atmosphere?

    (A) four-stroke diesel engine
    (B) four-stroke gasoline engine
    (C) jet engine
    (D) rocket engine
    (E) steam turbine

14. Which one of the following is an important performance deficiency of an overloaded airplane?

    (A) higher landing speed
    (B) higher maximum altitude
    (C) increased rate and angle of climb
    (D) increased cruising speed
    (E) shorter takeoff run

15. During takeoff, a headwind will

    (A) increase both the takeoff run and the angle of climb
    (B) increase the takeoff run and decrease the angle of climb
    (C) shorten the takeoff run and increase the angle of climb
    (D) shorten the takeoff run and decrease the angle of climb
    (E) have the same effect on airplane performance as a tailwind

Questions *16* to *30* pertain to nautical information.

16. The outer walls of a ship are called the

    (A) bulkhead
    (B) frame
    (C) hull
    (D) keel
    (E) trim

17. A ship's windlass is designed primarily for

    (A) cargo handling
    (B) fueling at sea
    (C) handling anchor chain
    (D) propulsion
    (E) steering

18. A nautical mile is approximately

    (A) 5280 feet
    (B) 6076 feet
    (C) 7076 feet
    (D) 7400 feet
    (E) 8000 feet

19. The coordinates, latitude and longitude, are generally used by the navigator to express

    (A) direction
    (B) distance
    (C) position
    (D) speed
    (E) time

20. Using the 24-hour basis in navigation, 9:05 p.m. would be written as

    (A) 9.05
    (B) 905
    (C) 0905
    (D) 21.05
    (E) 2105

21. At sea, the time zones are generally bands of longitude

    (A) $7\frac{1}{2}°$ in width
    (B) 15° in width
    (C) 24° in width
    (D) 30° in width
    (E) 45° in width

22. A ship is at a latitude of 25°N and a longitude of 90°W. It is sailing in the

    (A) Adriatic Sea
    (B) Black Sea
    (C) Gulf of Mexico
    (D) Hudson Bay
    (E) Red Sea

23. A line drawn from a fix in the direction in which a ship is moving is called a

    (A) course line
    (B) date line
    (C) line of position
    (D) line of sights
    (E) parallel line

24. In marine navigation, soundings are used to measure

    (A) depth of water
    (B) direction
    (C) Greenwich time
    (D) position of stars
    (E) standard time

GO ON TO THE NEXT PAGE.

25. As the weight of the load carried by a ship increases,

    (A) both the freeboard and draft decrease
    (B) both the freeboard and draft increase
    (C) freeboard increases and draft decreases
    (D) freeboard decreases and draft increases
    (E) none of the above

26. Which of the following is *not* considered to be an "aid to navigation"?

    (A) buoys
    (B) fog signals
    (C) lightships
    (D) Loran
    (E) mountain peaks

27. Fog is generally formed when

    (A) cold air moves over cold water
    (B) cold air moves over hot water
    (C) colder air moves over warmer water
    (D) warm air moves over warm water
    (E) warmer air moves over colder water

28. The navigation light associated with "starboard" is colored

    (A) green
    (B) red
    (C) white
    (D) yellow
    (E) none of the above

29. An unlighted buoy, used to mark the right side of a channel when facing inland, is called a

    (A) bell buoy
    (B) can buoy
    (C) gong buoy
    (D) nun buoy
    (E) spar

30. Ships or boats are steered by one or more rudders at the stern. The faster the vessel is moving,

    (A) the greater the pressure against the rudder and the quicker the turning effect
    (B) the greater the pressure against the rudder and the slower the turning effect
    (C) the less the pressure against the rudder and the quicker the turning effect
    (D) the less the pressure against the rudder and the slower the turning effect
    (E) none of the above

END OF AVIATION/NAUTICAL INFORMATION

END OF TEST BATTERY

SPECIMEN NAVY AND MARINE CORPS AVIATION SELECTION TEST BATTERY KEY ANSWERS AND RATIONALE

Use these key answers to determine the number of questions you answered correctly on each test and to list those questions you answered incorrectly or of which you are unsure how to arrive at the correct answer.

Be certain to review carefully and understand the rationale for arriving at the correct answer for all items you answered incorrectly, as well as those you answered correctly but are unsure of. This is essential in order to acquire the knowledge and expertise necessary to obtain the maximum score possible on the "real" Navy and Marine Corps Aviation Selection Test Battery.

TEST 1—MATH/VERBAL TEST

Key Answers

1. C	6. B	11. D	16. A	21. A	26. D	31. C	36. C
2. B	7. C	12. C	17. B	22. B	27. A	32. A	37. B
3. A	8. B	13. A	18. D	23. C	28. C	33. C	
4. D	9. D	14. B	19. A	24. D	29. C	34. D	
5. B	10. C	15. A	20. B	25. C	30. A	35. A	

Items Answered Incorrectly: ____; ____; ____; ____; ____; ____; ____; ____.

Items Unsure Of: ____; ____; ____; ____; ____; ____; ____; ____.

Total Number Answered Correctly: ________

Rationale

1–(C) Slower train is 30 miles ahead in one hour. Difference in rate is 5 mph. $\frac{30}{5} = 6$ hours.

2–(B) Let x = number ration days for 20 persons.

$16 \times 10 = 20 \times x$; $20x = 160$; $x = \frac{180}{20} = 8$ ration days for 20 persons.

10 days – 8 days = 2 days fewer.

3–(A) Let x = number of hours to plow with 6 machines.

$9 \times 5 = 6 \times x$; $6x = 45$; $x = \frac{45}{8} = 7\frac{1}{2}$ hours.

4–(D) $\sqrt{9} = 3$; $3^4 = 3 \times 3 \times 3 \times 3 = 81$.

5–(B) $2^{n-2} = 32$; $2^5 = 32$; $n - 2 = 5$; $n = 7$.

6–(B) Voters would stay away from the polls to show their apathy or lack of interest.

7–(C) Cheating partners necessitates scheming with evil intent. Option (C) is the only correct answer.

8–(B) If compromise is the lifeblood of politics, no elected official can refuse to compromise and still expect to be reelected. Option (B) is the correct answer.

9–(D) To change base elements into gold is to transform or transmute a substance into another substance.

10–(C) If the new regulations were not permissive, they would be strict or stringent.

11–(D) $86 \times 4 = 344$; $90 + 88 + 75 = 253$; $344 - 253 = 91$.

12–(C) $\frac{1}{10}$ of $3000 = 300$; $3000 - 300 = 2700$; $\frac{1}{9}$ of $2700 = 300$; $2700 - 300 = 2400$ miles still to be driven.

13–(A) Let x = minutes to be spent on each math problem, $x \times 40 + \frac{x}{2} \times 280 = 180$; $40x + 140x = 180$; $180x = 180$; $x = 1$; $40x = 40$ minutes to be spent on the 40 math problems.

14–(B) $10 \times 10 \times 10 \times 10 \times 10 = 100{,}000$ or 10 raised to the 5th power.

15–(A) $a = 3b$; $2a = 6b = 12c$; $2a = 12c$; $a = 6c$.

16–(A) The word *uncertain* is not consistent with the rest of the sentence. Changing *uncertain* to *beneficial* conveys the meaning of the quotation as intended.

17–(B) The word *preventable* is not consistent with the rest of the sentence. Changing *preventable* to *necessary* conveys the meaning intended.

18–(D) The word *untrue* is not consistent with the rest of the sentence. Changing untrue to *unavoidable* conveys the meaning intended in the quotation.

19–(A) The word *ease* is not consistent with the rest of the sentence. Substituting *absence* for *ease* conveys the meaning intended in the quotation.

20–(B) The word *originality* is inconsistent and inappropriate. Substituting *effectiveness* for *originality* conveys the meaning intended in the quotation.

21–(A) $\frac{450}{15} = 30$ gallons/minute, filling rate. $\frac{450}{30} =$ 15 gallons/minute, emptying rate.

$30 - 15 = 15$ gallons added per minute with both pipes open.

$\frac{450}{15} = 30$ minutes.

22–(B) $\frac{1}{3} \times 204 = 68$ blacks

$\frac{1}{4} \times 204 = 51$ Hispanics

$68 + 51 = 119$

$204 - 119 = 85$ whites

23–(C) 30 mph for 4 hours = 120 miles; round trip = 240 miles; 240 miles at 40 mph would take 6 hours; if first 120 miles took 4 hours, return 120 miles must be covered in 2 hours or at 60 mph.

24–(D) When two negative numbers are multiplied, the product is positive.

25–(C) Let x = number of degrees in angle E; $x + x - 30 = 90$; $2x = 90 + 30$; $2x = 120$; $x = 60°$.

26–(D) There is nothing in the quotation to support options (A), (B), or (C). Option (D) summarizes the data given in the passage.

27–(A) There is nothing in the quotation to support options (B), (C), or (D). Option (A) is supported by "... no crime is considered to occur unless there is a written law forbidding the act ..." at the beginning of the sentence.

28–(C) There is nothing in the passage to support options (A), (B), or (D). Option (C) is supported by "Only one measure . . . is the rate at which replacements must be made in order to maintain the work force."

29–(C) There is nothing in the sentence to support options (A), (B), or (D). Option (C) summarizes the ideas expressed in the quotation.

30–(A) There is nothing in the quotation to support options (B), (C), or (D). Option (A) is clearly implied from the ideas expressed in the passage.

31–(C) $95 \times 8 = 760$; $75 \times 8 = 600$; $760 + 600 = 1360$; $1800 - 1360 = 440$ miles.

32–(A) $100 \times .20 = 20$; $100 - 20 = 80$; $80 \times .15 = 12$; $80 - 12 = 68$; $100 - 68 = 32$.

33–(C) $\frac{1}{5}x + \frac{1}{6}x + 1520 = x$

$6x + 5x + 45600 = 30x$

$45600 = 19x$

$2400 = x$

34–(D) The hypotenuse of the right angle = 10 (Pythagorean theorem). 6' + 8' + 10' = 24'.

35–(A) $2 \times 2 \times 2 \times 2 = 16$.

36–(C) There is nothing in the quotation to support options (A), (B), or (D). Option (C) is clearly implied from the information given in the passage.

37–(B) There is nothing in the quotation to support options (A), (C), or (D). Option (B) is supported by ". . . the manufacturer assumes enormous risks in attempting to predict what consumers will want and in providing goods in quantity and distributing them in advance of final selection by the consumers."

TEST 2—MECHANICAL COMPREHENSION TEST

Key Answers

1. C	5. C	9. C	13. C	17. C	21. A	25. C	29. A
2. A	6. A	10. C	14. C	18. A	22. C	26. C	30. B
3. A	7. A	11. C	15. B	19. C	23. C	27. A	
4. C	8. B	12. B	16. B	20. B	24. B	28. C	

Items Answered Incorrectly: ___; ___; ___; ___; ___; ___; ___; ___.

Items Unsure Of: ___; ___; ___; ___; ___; ___; ___; ___.

Total Number Answered Correctly: ______

Rationale

1–(C) The volume of water flowing at points 1, 2, and 3 must be the same because of the conservation of mass: mass in = mass out. Also, since no water is added or removed after point 1, there cannot be any change of volume.

2–(A) If nut A were removed, it would be necessary to move nut C to the right to counterbalance the loss of the weight of nut A.

3–(A) No electricity flows through a burned out bulb. However, the voltmeter acts as a bypass around the burned out bulb and is therefore connected in series. It measures all of the voltage in the circuit. The voltage is 600 volts.

4–(C) The circumference of the wheel is 24". One complete revolution will raise W2 24" and lower W1 24", a difference of 48".

5–(C) The vertical component of the momentum of the ball is zero only at position C.

6–(A) Pulley A has the largest circumference. In the arrangement shown, pulley A turns slowest.

7–(A) Let x = theoretical distance moved in the opposite direction. $10 \times 150 = x \times 600$; $600x = 1500$; $x = \frac{1500}{600} = 2\frac{1}{2}$ feet.

8–(B) Note that with each complete turn of the cam, the setscrew will hit the contact point once.

9–(C) The pressure is uniform in the system given. If the main line air gauge reads 150 pounds, the tank air gauge will also read 150 pounds.

10–(C) As brace C has the greatest area support, it is the most secure.

11–(C) The greater the pressure outside the balloon, the less expansion within the balloon; the less pressure, the greater the expansion.

12–(B) When two external gears mesh, they rotate in opposite directions. To avoid this, an idler gear is put between the driver gear and the driven gear.

13–(C) The tank would overflow only if water flows through the intake pipe at a faster, not slower, rate. The water in the tank would remain at a constant level if rate of intake is equal to rate of discharge. The tank cannot empty completely, as the discharge pipe is not located at the tank's bottom.

14–(C) If the float in the tank develops a bad leak, it will fill with water and submerge. This will elevate the needle valve causing it to remain in an open position.

15–(B) The number of parts of the rope going to and from the movable block indicates a mechanical advantage of 2. Accordingly, a 100-lb. pull can lift theoretically a 200-lb. weight.

16–(B) Note that 2 revolutions of the worm gear will turn the sector gear 20°. Accordingly, one revolution of the worm gear will turn the sector gear through an angle of 10°.

17–(C) Let x = tipping force produced on the edge of the block.

$80 \times 4 = 1 \times x$; $x = 320$ lbs.

18–(A) Note that with each complete turn of the cam, the contacts come together twice. If the contacts come together 60 times a minute, the cam must be rotating at 30 rpm.

19–(C) One complete turn of the drum crank will raise the rope 2' on the 2' portion of the drum and 1' on the 1' portion of the drum. The net result is vertical movement upward a distance of $1\frac{1}{2}$'.

20–(B) The TMA of the pulley system is 2.

$$TMA = \frac{d_E}{d_R};\ 2 = \frac{30}{d_R}$$

$$2d_R = 30;\ d_R = \frac{30}{2} = 15 \text{ feet}$$

21–(A) Pulley #2 is a fixed pulley; pulley #1 is a movable one. Both are of equal diameter. If the rope is pulled a distance equal to the circumference of pulley #2 (one full turn), pulley #1 would move up only half that distance making only a half turn.

22–(C) Twice per second = 120 times a minute. With 10 projection rods on the wheel, the wheel must rotate at 12 rpm (120/10 = 12) to make 120 rod contacts per minute.

23–(C) Both wheels S and T have the same diameter. However, the driver wheel makes contact with wheel T close to its center and makes contact with wheel S near its very edge. Accordingly, wheel T will rotate at a much faster speed than wheel S.

24–(B) A $\frac{1}{4}$ turn is needed to get to the extreme left position and another $\frac{1}{4}$ turn is required to return to the mid position. $\frac{1}{4} + \frac{1}{4} = \frac{1}{2}$

25–(C) By increasing the length of the level arm, the effort is increased enabling the valve to blow off at a higher pressure.

26–(C) In case 2, each spring is supporting $2\frac{1}{2}$ pounds ($\frac{1}{2}$ of 5 pounds) and would extend a certain distance. In case 1, each spring is supporting 5 pounds (the full weight) and would extend twice the distance of that for case 2.

27–(A) The reading is obtained as follows:

.2 (on the sleeve scale)
.025 (on the sleeve scale)
.002 (on the thimble scale)
.227

28–(C) The hand wheel tightens to the left when rotated clockwise since it has a right-handed thread. If the hand wheel is turned 20 revolutions, it moves one inch to the left pulling the threaded block one inch in the opposite direction (to the right).

29–(A) If all three switches are closed to the left, the closed circuit would not include Lamp No. 2.

30–(B) If switches No. 1 and No. 2 are closed to the right and switch No. 3 is closed to the left, the closed circuit would not include Lamp No. 1.

TEST 3—SPATIAL APPERCEPTION TEST

Key Answers

1. C	6. E	11. A	16. C	20. B	24. A	28. D	32. B
2. A	7. E	12. E	17. D	21. A	25. B	29. E	33. D
3. B	8. B	13. C	18. A	22. D	26. C	30. E	34. E
4. C	9. D	14. B	19. E	23. C	27. D	31. C	35. A
5. D	10. B	15. A					

Items Answered Incorrectly: ___; ___; ___; ___; ___; ___; ___; ___.

Items Unsure Of: ___; ___; ___; ___; ___; ___; ___; ___.

Total Number Answered Correctly: ______

Rationale

1–(C)

Straight-and-level; flying up the coastline

2–(A)

Diving; no bank; flying out to sea

3–(B)

Climbing; no bank; flying out to sea

4–(C)

Climbing and banking right; flying out to sea

5–(D)

Level flight; left bank; flying out to sea

6–(E)

Straight-and-level; flying down the coastline

7–(E)

Straight-and-level; heading 45° left of coastline

8–(B)

Diving; banking left; flying out to sea

9–(D)

Level flight; right bank; flying out to sea

10–(B)

Straight-and-level; heading 45° right of coastline

11–(A)

Climbing; no bank; flying out to sea

12–(E)

Climbing; no bank; flying down the coastline

13–(C)

Diving; no bank; flying down the coastline

14–(B)

Straight-and-level; flying out to sea

15–(A)

Level flight; right bank; flying up the coastline

16–(C)

Climbing and banking left; flying out to sea

17–(D)

Diving and banking right; flying out to sea

18–(A)

Level flight; right bank; flying up the coastline

19–(E)

Climbing and banking left; flying out to sea

20–(B)

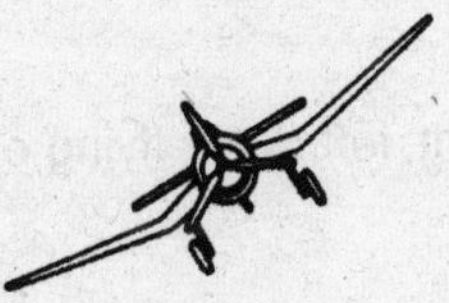

Level flight; right bank; flying down the coastline

21–(A)

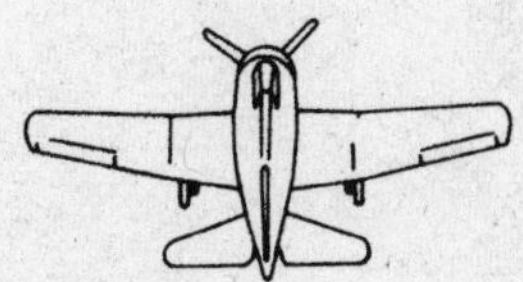

Climbing; no bank; flying up the coastline

22–(D)

Diving; no bank; flying out to sea

23–(C)

Straight-and-level; flying up the coastline

24–(A)

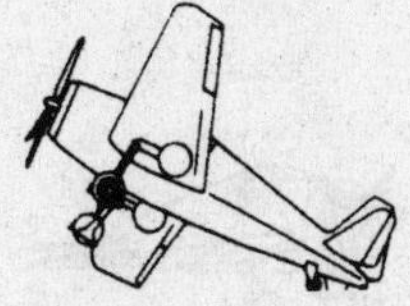

Climbing and banking right; flying out to sea

25–(B)

Level flight; left bank; flying down the coastline

26–(C)

Straight-and-level; heading 45° left of coastline

27–(D)

Level flight; left bank; flying up the coastline

28–(D)

Diving and banking left; flying out to sea

29–(E)

Straight-and-level; heading 45° right of coastline

30–(E)

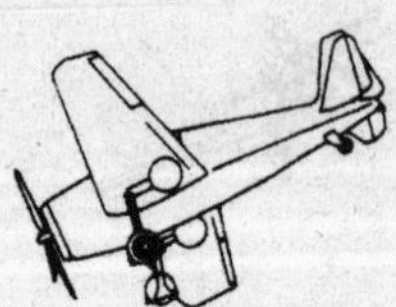

Diving and banking right; flying out to sea

31–(C)

Level flight; right bank; flying out to sea

32–(B)

Level flight; left bank; flying up the coastline

33–(D)

Diving; no bank; flying out to sea

34–(E)

Straight-and-level; flying out to sea

35–(A)

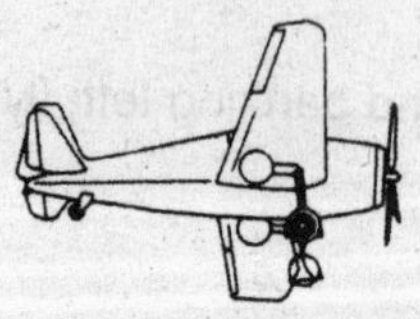

Level flight; left bank; flying out to sea

TEST 4—BIOGRAPHICAL INVENTORY

Key answers and rationale are *not* being furnished for questions *1* to *76* of this test as there are no "c rect" answers to these questions. Biographical inventory items are used to obtain general background info mation and information regarding personal characteristics and interests.

TEST 5—AVIATION/NAUTICAL INFORMATION

Key Answers

1. E	5. A	9. A	13. D	17. C	21. B	25. D	29. D
2. E	6. A	10. C	14. A	18. B	22. C	26. E	30. A
3. A	7. E	11. A	15. C	19. C	23. A	27. E	
4. D	8. A	12. B	16. C	20. E	24. A	28. A	

Items Answered Incorrectly: ____; ____; ____; ____; ____; ____; ____; ____.

Items Unsure Of: ____; ____; ____; ____; ____; ____; ____; ____.

Total Number Answered Correctly: ______

Rationale

1–(E) Note the sweptback wings.

2–(E) The maximum distance from wing tip to wing tip is called the wing span.

3–(A) Ailerons are used to bank the airplane.

4–(D) The rudder is used by the pilot to control the direction of yaw about the airplane's vertical axis.

5–(A) Drag is the resistance created by air particles striking and flowing around the airplane when it is moving through the air.

6–(A) The angle at which the wing meets the relative wind is called the angle of attack.

7–(E) In a steady flight condition, the forces that oppose each other are also equal to each other. Lift equals weight; thrust equals drag.

8–(A) Hard-surfaced runways are numbered by their magnetic headings. Runway 22 means a magnetic heading of 220° when taking off or landing. The opposite direction of the same runway would have a magnetic heading of approximately 40° and would be numbered 4.

9–(A) Runway 36 means a magnetic heading of 360°. The opposite direction of the same runway would have a magnetic heading of 180° and would be numbered 18. Accordingly, the runway is aligned in a North-South direction.

shown are:

ocks

...pace vehicle Apollo 11 carried Neil A. ...nstrong, Edwin E. Aldrin, Jr., and ...ichael Collins, who landed on the moon in 1969.

12–(B) The force of gravity on the surface of the moon is $\frac{1}{6}$ the force of gravity on the surface of the earth. Although the mass remains the same, the weight would be about 10 kilograms on the moon.

13–(D) Because the rocket carries its own oxidizer, it is able to travel into outer space where there is no oxygen.

14–(A) A higher landing speed is an important performance deficiency of an overloaded airplane. The other options are not deficiencies but desirable performance characteristics.

15–(C) During takeoff, a headwind will shorten the takeoff run and increase the angle of climb. A tailwind during takeoff will increase the takeoff run and decrease the angle of climb.

16–(C) The outer walls of a ship form the hull, the main body of the ship below the main outside deck.

17–(C) A ship's windlass is designed primarily for handling anchor chain.

18–(B) A nautical mile is equal to 1852 meters, just a little more than 6076 feet.

19–(C) Position is generally expressed in terms of the coordinates latitude and longitude.

20–(E) The 24-hour clock uses four digits. Hours and minutes less than 10 are preceded by a zero. 9:05 p.m. would be written as 2105.

21–(B) They are generally 15° in width. $\frac{360}{15} = 24$ time zones.

22–(C) The coordinates given indicate a position in the Gulf of Mexico.

23–(A) A line drawn from the fix in the direction in which a ship is moving is called a course line, showing direction or course.

24–(A) Soundings are used to measure depth of water by using a lead line or other means.

25–(D) Increasing the weight of the load raises the waterline, decreasing the freeboard and increasing the draft.

26–(E) Objects not established for the sole purpose of assisting a navigator in fixing a position are not considered to be an "aid to navigation."

27–(E) Fog generally forms at night when warmer air moves over colder water.

28–(A) Red is for port; green is starboard; white indicates in which direction a vessel is going; yellow is for special circumstances.

29–(D) The nun buoy is a conical-shaped buoy used to mark the right-hand side of a channel.

30–(A) The heading of the ship causes water to push against the side of the rudder, creating a force that swings the stem of the ship to the opposite side. The faster the vessel is moving, the greater the pressure against the rudder the quicker the turning effect.